Collins easy learning

Complete Italian

Grammar + Verbs + Vocabulary

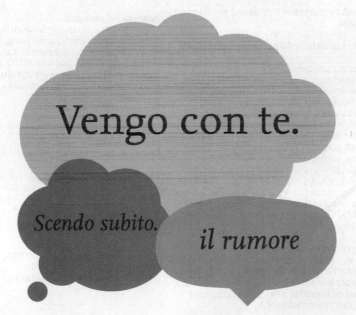

Vengo con te.

Scendo subito.

il rumore

Published by Collins
An imprint of HarperCollins Publishers
Westerhill Road
Bishopbriggs
Glasgow G64 2QT

Second edition 2016

ISBN 978-0-00-814175-2

10 9 8 7 6 5 4 3

www.collinsdictionary.com
www.collins.co.uk/languagesupport

Typeset by Davidson Publishing Solutions,
Glasgow

Printed in Italy by GRAFICA VENETA S.p.A.

If you would like to comment on any aspect
of this book, please contact us at the given
address or online.
E-mail: dictionaries@harpercollins.co.uk
f www.facebook.com/collinsdictionary
@collinsdict

Acknowledgements
We would like to thank those authors and
publishers who kindly gave permission for
copyright material to be used in the Collins
Corpus. We would also like to thank Times
Newspapers Ltd for providing valuable data.

MANAGING EDITOR
Maree Airlee

CONTRIBUTORS
Francesca Logi
Janice McNeillie

FOR THE PUBLISHER
Craig Balfour
Gerry Breslin
Hannah Dove
Chloe Osborne

BASED ON:
Collins Easy Learning Italian Grammar
Collins Easy Learning Italian Verbs
Collins Easy Learning Italian Vocabulary

Contents

Foreword for language teachers

The *Easy Learning Complete Italian* is designed to be used with both young and adult learners, as a group reference book to complement your course book during classes, or as a recommended text for self-study and homework/coursework.

The text specifically targets learners from beginners to intermediate or GCSE level, and therefore its structural content and vocabulary have been matched to the relevant specifications up to and including Higher GCSE.

The approach aims to develop knowledge and understanding of grammar and your learners' ability to apply it by:

- defining parts of speech at the start of each major section with examples in English to clarify concepts
- minimizing the use of grammar terminology and providing clear explanations of terms both within the text and in the **Glossary**
- illustrating all points with examples (and their translations) based on topics and contexts which are relevant to beginner and intermediate course content

The text helps you develop positive attitudes to grammar learning in your classes by:

- giving clear, easy-to-follow explanations
- prioritizing content according to relevant specifications for the levels
- sequencing points to reflect course content, e.g. verb tenses
- highlighting useful **Tips** to deal with common difficulties
- summarizing **Key points** at the end of sections to consolidate learning

In addition to fostering success and building a thorough foundation in Italian grammar, the optional **Grammar Extra** sections will encourage and challenge your learners to further their studies to higher and advanced levels.

The blue pages in the middle section of the book contain **Verb Tables** and a **Verb Index** which students can use as a reference in their work.

Finally the **Vocabulary** section in the last part of the book provides thematic vocabulary lists which can either be used for self-study or as an additional teaching resource.

Introduction for students

Whether you are starting to learn Italian for the very first time, brushing up on topics you have studied in class, or revising for your GCSE exams, the *Easy Learning Complete Italian* is here to help. This easy-to-use guide takes you through all the basics you will need to speak and understand modern everyday Italian.

Learners sometimes struggle with the technical terms they come across when they start to explore the grammar of a new language. The *Easy Learning Complete Italian* explains how to get to grips with all the parts of speech you will need to know, using simple language and cutting out jargon.

The text is divided into sections, each dealing with a particular area of grammar. Each section can be studied individually, as numerous cross-references in the text point you to relevant points in other sections of the book for further information.

Every major section begins with an explanation of the area of grammar covered on the following pages. For quick reference, these definitions are also collected together on pages x-xiv in a glossary of essential grammatical terms.

What is a verb?
A **verb** is a word which describes what somebody or something does, what they are, or what happens to them, for example, *play, be, disappear*.

Each grammar point in the text is followed by simple examples of real Italian, with English translations, to help you understand the rules. Underlining has been used in examples throughout the text to highlight the grammatical point being explained.

➤ To say *the one* in Italian use **quello** to refer to masculine nouns or **quella** to refer to feminine nouns. The relative pronoun is **che**.

    È quello che non funziona.   That's the one which isn't working.

This book marks which vowel is stressed in some Italian words by putting those vowels into italic.

      il m*a*nager   the manager

⇨ *For more information on **Stress**, see page 196.*

Tips and **Information** notes throughout the text are useful reminders of the things that often trip learners up when learning Italian.

Key points sum up all the important facts about a particular area of grammar, to save you time when you are revising and help you focus on the main grammatical points.

If you think you would like to continue with your Italian studies to a higher level, look at the **Grammar Extra** sections. These are intended for advanced students who are interested in knowing a little more about the structures they will come across beyond GCSE.

The blue pages in the middle of the book contain **Verb Tables**, where 120 important Italian verbs (both regular and irregular) are declined in full. Examples show you how to use these verbs in your own work. You can look up any common verbs in the **Verb Index** on pages 454-59 to find either the conjugation of the verb itself, or a cross-reference to a model verb, which will show you the patterns that verb follows.

Finally the **Vocabulary** section at the end of the book is divided into 50 topics, followed by a list of supplementary vocabulary.

Glossary of Grammar Terms

ABSTRACT NOUN a word used to refer to a quality, idea, feeling or experience, rather than a physical object, for example, *size, reason, happiness*. Compare with **concrete noun**.

ACTIVE a form of the verb that is used when the subject of the sentence does the action, for example, *A dog bit him* (subject: *a dog*; active verb: *bit*).Compare with **passive**.

ADJECTIVE a 'describing' word that tells you something about a person or thing, for example, a *blue* shirt, a *big* car, a *good* idea.

ADVERB a word used with verbs to give information on where, when or how an action takes place, for example, *here, today, quickly*. An adverb can also add information to adjectives and other adverbs, for example, *extremely* quick, *very* quickly.

AGREEMENT the matching of words or word endings to the person or thing they refer to. For example, the verb *to be* has different forms for *I, you* and *he*: I *am*, you *are*, he *is*. In Italian you use verbs in the form appropriate to the person doing the action, and articles and adjectives have masculine, feminine and plural forms to match (or *agree* with) the noun they go with.

APOSTROPHE s an ending ('s) added to a noun to show ownership, for example, *Peter's car, the company's headquarters*.

ARTICLE a word such as *the, a,* and *an* which goes with nouns: *the sun, a happy boy, an orange*. See also **definite article**, **indefinite article**.

AUXILIARY VERB a verb such as *be, have* and *do* that is used with a main verb to form tenses, negatives and questions.

BASE FORM the form of the verb that has no ending added to it, for example, *walk, have, be, go*. Compare with **infinitive**.

CARDINAL NUMBER a number used in counting, for example, *one, seven, ninety*. Compare with **ordinal number**.

CLAUSE a group of words containing a verb.

COMPARATIVE an adjective or adverb with –*er* on the end of it or *more* or *less* in front of it that is used to compare things or people, for example, *faster, more important, less interesting*.

COMPOUND NOUN a word for a living being, thing or idea which is made up of two or more words, for example, *prime minister, mobile phone, home truth*.

CONCRETE NOUN a word that refers to a physical object rather than a quality or idea, for example, *ball, school, apples*. Compare with **abstract noun**.

CONDITIONAL a verb form used to talk about things that would happen or would be true under certain conditions, for example, *I would help you if I could*. It is also used in requests and offers, for example, *Could you lend me some money?; I could give you a lift*.

CONJUGATE (to) to give a verb different endings depending on whether its subject is *I, you, he* and so on, and depending on whether you are referring to the present, past or future, for example, *I have, she has, they listened*.

CONJUGATION a group of verbs that has a particular pattern of endings.

CONJUNCTION a word such as *and, but* or *because* that links two words or phrases, or two parts of a sentence, for example, *Diane and I have been friends for years*.

CONSONANT a sound made by letters such as b, g, m, s and t. In English y is sometimes a consonant, as in *year*, and sometimes a vowel, as in *any*. In Italian **i** sometimes has a vowel sound (ee) and sometimes the consonant sound of *y* in *year*, for example, **italiano** (eetalyano). Compare with **vowel**.

CONTINUOUS TENSE a verb form made up of *to be* and the *–ing* form, for example, *I'm thinking; They were quarrelling*. Italian continuous tenses are made with **stare** and the gerund.

DEFINITE ARTICLE the word *the*. Compare with **indefinite article**.

DEMONSTRATIVE ADJECTIVE a word used to point out a particular thing or person. There are four demonstrative adjectives in English: *this, these, that* and *those*.

DEMONSTRATIVE PRONOUN a word used instead of a noun to point out people or things, for example, *That's my brother*. In English the demonstrative pronouns are *this, that, these* and *those*.

DIRECT OBJECT a noun or pronoun used to show who or what is affected by the verb. For example, in the sentence *He sent flowers*, the subject of the verb is *He* (the person who did the sending) and the direct object of the verb is *flowers* (what he sent). Compare with **indirect object**.

DIRECT OBJECT PRONOUN a word such as *me, him, us* and *them* used instead of a noun to show who or what is affected by the action of the verb, for example *His friends helped him*. Compare **indirect object pronoun**.

ENDING something added to the end of a word. In English nouns have plural endings, for example boy → boys, child → children and verbs have the endings *–s, –ed* and *–ing*, for example *walk → walks, walked, walking*. In Italian there are plural endings for nouns, verb endings, and masculine, feminine and plural endings for adjectives and pronouns.

EXCLAMATION a sound, word or sentence that is spoken suddenly by somebody who is surprised, excited or angry, for example *Oh!; Look who's coming!; How dare you!*

FEMININE a noun, pronoun, article or form of adjective used to refer to a living being, thing or idea that is not classed as masculine. For example, **una** (feminine indefinite article) **bella** (adjective with a feminine ending) **casa** (feminine noun).

FUTURE a tense used to talk about something that will happen, or be true in the future, for example *He'll be here soon; I'll give you a call; It will be sunny tomorrow*.

GENDER whether a noun, pronoun or adjective is masculine or feminine.

GERUND in English, a verb form ending in *–ing*, for example, *eating, sleeping*. In Italian the gerund ends in **–ando** or **–endo**.

IMPERATIVE a form of the verb used to give orders and instructions, for example, *Sit down!;Don't go!;Let's start!*

IMPERFECT a tense used to say what was happening, what used to happen and what things were like in the past, for example; *It was sunny at the weekend; They weren't listening; They used to live in Spain*.

IMPERSONAL VERB a verb with the subject *it*, where 'it' does not refer to any specific thing; for example, *It's going to rain; It's nine o'clock*.

INDEFINITE ADJECTIVE one of a small group of adjectives used to give an idea of amounts and numbers, for example, *several, all, every*.

INDEFINITE ARTICLE the word *a* or *an*. Compare with **definite article**.

INDEFINITE PRONOUN a word like *everything, nobody and something* which is used to refer to people or things in a non-specific way.

INDIRECT OBJECT a noun or pronoun used to show who benefits or suffers from an action. For example, in the sentence *He sent Claire flowers*, the <u>direct</u> object (what was sent) is *flowers* and the <u>indirect</u> object is *Claire* (the person the flowers were sent to). An indirect object often has *to* in front of it: *He told lies to everyone; He told everyone lies*. In both these sentences the direct object is *lies* and the indirect object is *everyone*. Compare with **direct object**.

INDIRECT OBJECT PRONOUN a pronoun such as *to me* (or *me*), *to you* (or *you*) and *to her* (or *her*). In the sentence *He gave the chocolates <u>to me</u> and the flowers <u>to her</u>*, the direct objects are *the chocolates* and *the flowers* (what he gave), and the <u>indirect object pronouns</u> are *to me* and *to her* (who he gave them to). In the sentence *He gave me the chocolates and her the flowers*, the indirect object pronouns are *me* and *her*. Compare with **direct object pronoun**.

INDIRECT QUESTION a more roundabout way of asking a question, for example, instead of *Where are you going?* you can say *Tell me where you are going*, or *I'd like to know where you are going*.

INDIRECT SPEECH the words you use to report what someone has said when you aren't using their actual words, for example, *He said that he was going out*. Also called **reported speech**.

INFINITIVE the base form of the verb, for example, *walk, see, hear*. It is used after other verbs such as *should, must and can*. The infinitive is often used with *to*: *to speak, to eat, to live*. Compare with **base form**.

INTERROGATIVE ADJECTIVE a question word such as *which, what* or *how much* that is used when asking about a noun, for example, *Which colour?; What size?; How much sugar?*

INTERROGATIVE PRONOUN one of the following: *who, which, whose, whom* and *what*. These words are used without a noun, when asking questions, for example, *What do you want?*

INTRANSITIVE VERB a verb used without a direct object, for example, *The shop is closing; Nothing grows here*. Compare with **transitive verb**.

INVARIABLE the term used to describe an adjective which does not change its form for the feminine or the plural, or a noun which does not change its ending in the plural.

IRREGULAR VERB In Italian, a verb whose forms do not follow one of the three main patterns. Compare with **regular verb**.

MASCULINE a noun, pronoun, article or form of adjective used to refer to a living being, thing or idea that is not classed as feminine. For example, **il** (masculine definite article) **primo** (adjective with a masculine ending) **treno** (masculine noun).

NEGATIVE a question or statement which contains a word such as *not, never* or *nothing*: *Isn't he here?; I <u>never</u> eat meat; She's doing <u>nothing</u> about it*. Compare with **positive**.

NOUN a naming word for a living being, thing or idea, for example, *woman, Andrew, desk, happiness*.

NUMBER in grammar a verb agrees in number with its subject by being singular with a singular subject and plural with a plural subject, for example, *I <u>am</u> a teacher; they <u>are</u> teachers*.

OBJECT a noun or pronoun that, in English, usually comes after the verb and shows who or what is affected by it, for example, *I (subject) want (verb) a new car (object), They (subject) phoned (verb) him (object)*.

OBJECT PRONOUN one of the following: *me, you, him, her, it, us, them*. They are used instead of nouns after prepositions, for example, *for me, with us* and as the object of verbs, for example, *The company sacked <u>him</u>; You'll enjoy <u>it</u>.* Compare **subject pronoun**.

ORDINAL NUMBER an adjective used to show where something comes in numerical order, for example, *first, seventh, ninetieth*. Compare with **cardinal number**.

PART OF SPEECH a word with a particular grammatical function, for example, *noun, adjective, verb, preposition, pronoun*.

PASSIVE a verb form that is used when the subject of the verb is the person or thing the action is done to, for example, *Shaun was bitten by a dog. Shaun* is the subject of the sentence, but he did not do the action. Compare with **active**.

PAST PARTICIPLE a verb form usually ending –*ed*, for example *lived, worked*. Some past participles are irregular, for example, *gone, sat, broken*. Past participles are used to make the perfect, pluperfect and passive, for example *They've <u>gone</u>; They hadn't <u>noticed</u> me; Nobody was <u>hurt</u>.* Past participles are also used as adjectives, for example, *a <u>boiled</u> egg*.

PAST PERFECT see **pluperfect**.

PERFECT a tense used in English to talk about what has or hasn't happened, for example *We've won, I haven't touched it*. Compare **simple past**.

PERSON in grammar one of the following: the first person (*I, we*), the second person (*you*) or the third person (*he, she, it, they*).

PERSONAL PRONOUN a word such as *I, you, he, she, us, them*, which make it clear who you are talking about or talking to.

PLUPERFECT a tense used to talk about what had happened or had been true at a point in the past, for example, *I'd forgotten to send her a card.* Also called **past perfect**.

PLURAL the form of a word which is used to refer to more than one person or thing. In Italian, nouns, adjectives, articles, pronouns and verbs can be plural.

POSITIVE a positive sentence does not contain a negative word such as *not*. Compare with **negative**.

POSSESSIVE ADJECTIVE a word such as *my, your, his* that is used with a noun to show who it belongs to.

POSSESSIVE PRONOUN a word such as *mine, yours, his* that is used instead of a possessive adjective followed by a noun. For example, instead of *My bag is the blue one*, you can say *<u>Mine</u>'s the blue one.*

PREPOSITION a word such as *at, for, with, into* or *from*, or a phrase such as *in front of* or *near to*. Prepositions are usually followed by a noun or a pronoun and show how people and things relate to the rest of the sentence, for example, *She's <u>at</u> home; It's <u>for</u> you; You'll get <u>into</u> trouble; It's <u>in front of</u> you.*

PRESENT a verb form used to talk about what is true at the moment, what generally happens and what is happening now; for example, *I'm a student; I travel to college by train; The phone's ringing.*

PRESENT PARTICIPLE a verb form ending in –*ing*, for example, *eating, sleeping*. Compare with **gerund**.

PRONOUN a word you use instead of a noun, when you do not need or want to name someone or something directly, for example, *it, you, somebody*.

PROPER NOUN the name of a person, place or organization. Proper nouns are always written with a capital letter, for example, Kate, New York, the Forestry Commission.

QUESTION WORD a word such as *why, where, who, which* or *how* that is used to ask a question.

REFLEXIVE PRONOUN a word ending in –self or –selves, such as *myself* and *ourselves*, that is used as the object of a verb, for example *I surprised myself; We're going to treat ourselves*.

REFLEXIVE VERB a verb where the subject and object are the same, and which uses reflexive pronouns such as *myself, yourself* and *themselves*, for example *I've hurt myself; Look after yourself!; They're enjoying themselves*.

REGULAR VERB in Italian, a verb whose forms follow one of the three main patterns. Compare with **irregular verb**.

RELATIVE PRONOUN one of the following: *who, which, that* and *whom*. They are used to specify exactly who or what is being talked about, for example, *The man who has just come in* is Anna's boyfriend; *The vase that you broke* cost a lot of money.

REPORTED SPEECH see **indirect speech**.

SENTENCE a group of words which usually has a subject and a verb. In writing, a sentence begins with a capital and ends with a full stop, question mark or exclamation mark.

SIMPLE TENSE a verb form made up of one word, for example, *She lives here; They arrived late*. Compare with **continuous tense** and **perfect tense**.

SIMPLE PAST a tense used in English to say when exactly something happened, for example, *We met last summer; I ate it last night; It rained a lot yesterday*. In Italian the perfect tense is used in this kind of sentence.

SINGULAR the form of a word used to refer to one person or thing. Compare with **plural**.

STEM what is left of an Italian verb when you take away the **–are**, **–ere** or **–ire** ending of the infinitive.

STRESSED PRONOUN an object pronoun used in Italian after prepositions and when you want to stress the word for *me, him, them* and so on. Compare **unstressed pronoun**.

SUBJECT a noun or pronoun that refers to the person or thing doing the action or being in the state described by the verb, for example *Pat likes climbing; The bus is late*. Compare with **object**.

SUBJECT PRONOUN a word such as *I, he, she* and *they* used for the person or thing carrying out the action described by the verb. Pronouns replace nouns when it is clear who is being talked about, for example, *My brother's not here at the moment. He'll be back in an hour*. Compare with **object pronoun**.

SUBJUNCTIVE a verb form often used in Italian to express wishes, thoughts and suppositions. In English the subjunctive is only used occasionally, for example, *If I were you...; So be it; He asked that they be removed*.

SUPERLATIVE an adjective or adverb with –est on the end of it or *most* or *least* in front of it that is used to compare things or people, for example, *fastest, most important, least interesting*.

SYLLABLE a unit containing a vowel sound. A word can have one or more syllables, for example, *I, o-pen, ca-the-dral*.

TENSE a particular form of the verb. It shows whether you are referring to the present, past or future.

TRANSITIVE VERB a verb used with a direct object, for example, *Close the door!; They grow wheat*. Compare with **intransitive verb**.

UNSTRESSED PRONOUN an object pronoun used in Italian when you don't want to put any special emphasis on the word for *me, him, them* and so on. Compare **stressed pronoun**.

VERB a word that describes what somebody or something does, what they are, or what happens to them, for example, *play, be, disappear*.

VOWEL one of the sounds made by the letters *a, e, i, o, u*, and sometimes *y*. Compare with **consonant**.

Nouns

> **What is a noun?**
> A **noun** is a naming word for a living being, a thing, or an idea, for example, *woman, Andrew, desk, happiness.*

Using nouns

1 The basics

➤ In Italian, all nouns, whether referring to living beings or to things and ideas, are either <u>masculine</u> or <u>feminine</u>. This is their <u>gender.</u>

Masculine		Feminine	
olio	oil	**acqua**	water
uomo	man	**donna**	woman
delfino	dolphin	**tigre**	tiger
concetto	concept	**idea**	idea
armadio	wardrobe	**sedia**	chair

➤ The letter a noun ends with is often a reliable guide to its gender. For instance, words ending in **–o** will nearly always be masculine.

➤ When you use an Italian noun you need to know if it is masculine or feminine so that you can make other words that go with it masculine or feminine too:

- how you translate the words for '*the*' or '*a*' depends on the noun's gender. For instance, with masculine nouns you use **il** and **un**, and with feminine nouns you use **la** and **una**.

Masculine		Feminine	
<u>il</u> **giorno**	the day	<u>la</u> **notte**	the night
<u>un</u> **gelato**	an ice cream	<u>una</u> **mela**	an apple

- adjectives describing a noun are masculine or feminine in form.

Masculine	Feminine
un *abito* car<u>o</u> – an expensive suit	una *macchina* car<u>a</u> – an expensive car
l'Antic<u>o</u> Testamento – the Old Testament	l'antic<u>a</u> Roma - ancient Rome

- words that replace nouns – called <u>pronouns</u> – must also be masculine or feminine. The translation for *Do you want it?* is "**Lo vuoi?**" if you're offering **un gelato** (*an ice cream*), and "**La vuoi?**" if you're referring to **una mela** (*an apple*).

⇨ *For more information on* **Articles**, **Adjectives** *or* **Pronouns**, *see pages* 10, 20 *and* 40.

Nouns

➤ Just like English nouns, Italian nouns can be <u>singular</u> or <u>plural</u>. Most English nouns add –s in the plural, for example *days*, *apples*. Most Italian nouns change their final letter from one vowel to another:

Singular		Plural	
giorn<u>o</u>	day	giorn<u>i</u>	days
mel<u>a</u>	apple	mel<u>e</u>	apples
rivoluzion<u>e</u>	revolution	rivoluzion<u>i</u>	revolutions

Tip

When in doubt, you can find out a noun's gender by looking it up in a dictionary. When you come across a new word it's a good idea to memorize the article that goes with it, to help you remember its gender.

Key points

✔ All nouns in Italian are either masculine or feminine.

✔ This affects the words you use with them.

✔ In most cases it is possible to work out a noun's gender from its ending.

---

2 How to recognize what gender a noun is

➤ There are some simple rules that will enable you to work out the gender of a very large number of Italian nouns from their last letter in the singular:

- nearly all words ending in –o are <u>masculine</u>.
- nearly all words ending in –a are <u>feminine</u>.
- nearly all words ending in –à, –sione and –zione are <u>feminine</u>.
- nearly all words ending with a consonant are <u>masculine</u>.

[i] Note that words ending in –e are masculine in some cases and feminine in others.

➤ The following are typical masculine nouns ending in –o:

il treno	the train
il supermercato	the supermarket
l'aeroporto	the airport
il toro	the bull
un topo	a mouse
un gatto	a (tom) cat
un italiano	an Italian (man)

For further explanation of grammatical terms, please see pages viii–xii.

Nouns

📘 Note that a few very common nouns ending in **–o** are feminine.

la mano	the hand
una foto	a photo
la radio	the radio
una moto	a motorbike

➤ The following are typical feminine nouns ending in **–a**:

la casa	the house
la macchina	the car
una donna	a woman
una regola	a rule
una gatta	a (she) cat
un'italiana	an Italian (woman)

📘 Note that some very common words ending in **–a** are masculine.

il problema	the problem
il programma	the programme
il sistema	the system
il clima	the climate

● Most words for professions and jobs ending in **–ta** are masculine or feminine, according to whether a male or female is meant.

<u>**un**</u> **giornalista**	a (male) journalist
<u>**una**</u> **giornalista**	a (female) journalist
<u>**un**</u> **dentista**	a (male) dentist
<u>**una**</u> **dentista**	a (female) dentist

➤ The following are typical feminine nouns ending in **–à**, **–sione**, and **–zione**:

Ending	Example	Meaning
–à	una difficoltà	a difficulty
	la realtà	the reality
–sione	la versione	the version
	un'occasione	an opportunity
–zione	una lezione	a lesson
	una conversazione	a conversation

➤ Nouns ending in a <u>consonant</u> are nearly always masculine.

un film	a film
un bar	a bar
un computer	a computer
BUT	
una jeep	a jeep

Nouns

➤ Nouns ending in –e can be masculine in some cases and feminine in others.

un mese	a month
il mare	the sea
la gente	the people
la mente	the mind
il mese di giugno	the month of June
una mente logica	a logical mind

[i] Note that the names of languages are always masculine, whether they end in –e or in –o.

Il giapponese è molto difficile.	Japanese is very difficult.
L'italiano è bellissimo.	Italian is beautiful.

Grammar Extra!

Some words have different meanings depending on whether they are masculine or feminine.

Masculine	Meaning	Feminine	Meaning
il fine	the objective	la fine	the end
un posto	a place	la posta	the mail
un modo	a way	la moda	the fashion
il capitale	capital (money)	una capitale	a capital city
un bel posto	a nice place	posta prioritaria	first class

---

3 Nouns for males and females

➤ In Italian, just as in English, there are sometimes very different words for male and female people and animals.

un uomo	a man
una donna	a woman
un fratello	a brother
una sorella	a sister
un toro	a bull
una mucca	a cow

For further explanation of grammatical terms, please see pages viii–xii.

Nouns

➤ In most cases, though, a noun referring to a male can be made to refer to a female by changing the ending:

- Many Italian nouns ending in –o can be made feminine by changing the ending to –a.

un cuoco	a (male) cook
una cuoca	a (female) cook
un ragazzo	a boy
una ragazza	a girl
un fotografo	a (male) photographer
una fotografa	a (female) photographer
un italiano	an Italian (man)
un'italiana	an Italian (woman)
un gatto	a (tom) cat
una gatta	a (she) cat

- If a noun describing a male ends in –tore, the feminine form ends in –trice.

un attore	a (male) actor
un'attrice	a (female) actor
un pittore	a (male) painter
una pittrice	a (female) painter
uno scrittore	a (male) writer
una scrittrice	a (female) writer

- Certain nouns describing males ending in –e have feminine forms ending in –essa.

il professore	the (male) teacher
la professoressa	the (female) teacher
uno studente	a (male) student
una studentessa	a (female) student
un leone	a lion
una leonessa	a lioness

➤ Many nouns ending in –a can refer either to males or to females, so there is no change of ending for the feminine.

un turista	a (male) tourist
una turista	a (female) tourist
un collega	a (male) colleague
una collega	a (female) colleague
il mio dentista	my dentist (if it's a man)
la mia dentista	my dentist (if it's a woman)

Nouns

➤ Many nouns ending in **-e** can refer either to males or to females, so there is no change of ending for the feminine.

un nipote	a grandson
una nipote	a granddaughter
un cantante	a (male) singer
una cantante	a (female) singer

Grammar Extra!

A few nouns that are feminine refer both to men and women.

una guida	a guide (male or female)
una persona	a person (male or female)
una spia	a spy (male or female)
una star	a star (male or female)
Sean Connery è ancora una star.	Sean Connery's still a star.

Key points

✔ Most nouns referring to males can be made to refer to females by changing the ending.

✔ Some nouns are the same whether they refer to males or to females, but the words used with them change.

✔ In a few cases the nouns used for male and female are completely different.

For further explanation of grammatical terms, please see pages viii–xii.

Making nouns plural

➤ There are two main ways of making nouns plural in Italian. In most cases you change the ending, but in a few cases the same form as the singular is used. There are also some plurals which are irregular.

1 Nouns which you make plural by changing the ending

➤ In English you usually make nouns plural by adding –s. In Italian you usually do it by changing the ending from one vowel to another:

● Change the –o, –a or –e ending of masculine nouns to –i. Nearly all masculine plurals end in –i.

–o	un anno	one year
	due anni	two years
	un ragazzo	one boy
	due ragazzi	two boys
–a	un ciclista	a (male) cyclist
	due ciclisti	two cyclists
	un problema	a problem
	molti problemi	lots of problems
–e	un mese	one month
	due mesi	two months
	un francese	a Frenchman
	due francesi	two Frenchmen

● Change the –a ending of feminine nouns to –e.

una settimana	one week
due settimane	two weeks
una ragazza	one girl
due ragazze	two girls

● Change the –e ending of feminine nouns to –i.

un'inglese	an Englishwoman
due inglesi	two Englishwomen
la vite	the vine
le viti	the vines

2 Nouns you do not change in the plural

● You do not change feminine nouns ending in –à. You show that they are plural by using the plural word for *the*, adjectives in the plural, and so on.

la città	the city
le città	the cities
grandi città	great cities

la loro università	their university
le loro università	their universities

⇨ For more information on **Articles** and **Adjectives**, see pages 10 and 20.

● You do not change words ending in a consonant, which are often words borrowed from English and other languages.

il film	the film
i film	the films
il manager	the manager
i manager	the managers
il computer	the computer
i computer	the computers
la jeep	the jeep
le jeep	the jeeps

3 Nouns with irregular plurals

➤ A small number of common masculine nouns take the ending **–a** in the plural.

il dit<u>o</u>	the finger
le dit<u>a</u>	the fingers
un uov<u>o</u>	an egg
le uov<u>a</u>	the eggs
il lenzuol<u>o</u>	the sheet
le lenzuol<u>a</u>	the sheets

ℹ️ Note that the plural of **uomo** (meaning *man*) is **uomini**. The plural of **la mano** (meaning *hand*) is **le mani**.

➤ All nouns ending in **–ca** and **–ga** add an **h** before the plural ending.

Singular		Plural	
amica	(female) friend	amiche	(female) friends
buca	hole	buche	holes
riga	line	righe	lines
vanga	spade	vanghe	spades

➤ Some nouns ending in **–co** and **–go** also add an **h** before the plural ending.

Singular		Plural	
gioco	game	giochi	games
fuoco	fire	fuochi	fires
luogo	place	luoghi	places
borgo	district	borghi	districts

For further explanation of grammatical terms, please see pages viii–xii.

i Note that there are many exceptions: the plurals of **amico** (meaning *friend*) and **psicologo** (meaning *psychologist*) are **amici** and **psicologi**.

⇨ *For more information on **Italian spelling rules**, see page 191.*

4 | Plural or singular?

➤ Bear in mind that some words are <u>plural</u> in Italian but <u>singular</u> in English.

<u>i</u> miei capell<u>i</u>	my hair
<u>gli</u> affar<u>i</u>	business
<u>le</u> notiz<u>ie</u>	the news
consigl<u>i</u>	advice
<u>i</u> mobil<u>i</u>	the furniture
sciocchezz<u>e</u>	nonsense

i Note that you use the singular of some of these words to refer to *a piece of* something.

un mobile	a piece of furniture
un consiglio	a piece of advice
una notizia	a piece of news

Tip

An important word that is <u>singular</u> in Italian but <u>plural</u> in English is **la gente** (meaning *people*). Remember to use a singular verb with **la gente**.

È gente molto simpatica.   They're very nice people.

Grammar Extra!

When nouns are made by combining two words, such as **pescespada** (meaning *swordfish*), or **capolavoro** (meaning *masterpiece*), the plural is often not formed according to the usual rules. You can check by looking in a dictionary.

Key points

✔ You can make most Italian nouns plural by changing their ending from one vowel to another.

✔ Some nouns are the same in the plural as in the singular.

✔ Some nouns which are singular in English are plural in Italian.

Articles

> **What is an article?**
> In English, an **article** is one of the words *the*, *a* and *an* which go with nouns: <u>the</u> sun, <u>a</u> happy boy, <u>an</u> orange.

Two types of article

➤ There are two types of article: the <u>definite</u> article and the <u>indefinite</u> article.

- ● The <u>definite</u> article is *the*. You use it to refer to a specified thing or person.

    I'm going to <u>the</u> supermarket.

    That's <u>the</u> woman I was talking to.

- ● The <u>indefinite</u> article is *a* or *an*. You use it if you are not referring to any particular thing or person.

    Is there <u>a</u> supermarket near here?

    She was talking to <u>a</u> little girl.

The definite article

1 The basics

➤ There are three questions you need to ask yourself to decide which definite article to use in Italian:

- Is the noun masculine or feminine? (This is known as its gender).

- Is it singular or plural?

      the child   **il bambino** (SINGULAR)
      the children   **i bambini**   (PLURAL)

- Does the following word begin with a vowel (*a, e, i, o, u*) or with another letter?

⇨ *For more information on* **Nouns**, *see page 1.*

2 Which definite article do you use?

➤ The definite article to use for masculine singular nouns is:

- **il** with most nouns starting with a consonant.

      il ragazzo   the boy
      il telefonino   the mobile phone

- **lo** with nouns starting with z, or s + another consonant, gn, pn, ps, x or y.

      lo zio   the uncle
      lo studente   the student
      lo pneumatico   the tyre
      lo psichiatra   the psychiatrist
      lo yogurt   the yoghurt

- **l'** with all nouns starting with a vowel.

      l'ospedale   the hospital
      l'albergo   the hotel

➤ The definite article to use for masculine plural nouns is:

- **i** with most nouns starting with a consonant.

      i fratelli   the brothers
      i tablet   the tablets

- **gli** with nouns starting with z, s + another consonant, gn, pn, ps, x or y.

      gli studenti   the students
      gli zii   the uncles
      gli gnocchi   the gnocchi
      gli pneumatici   the tyres
      gli yogurt   the yoghurts

- **gli** with all nouns starting with a <u>vowel</u>.

gli amici	the friends
gli orari	the timetables

➤ The definite article to use for <u>feminine singular nouns</u> is:

- **la** with all nouns starting with a <u>consonant</u>.

la ragazza	the girl
la macchina	the car

- **l'** with all nouns starting with a <u>vowel</u>.

l'amica	the (girl)friend
l'arancia	the orange

➤ The definite article to use for <u>feminine plural nouns</u> is:

- **le** with all nouns, whether they start with a <u>consonant</u> or a <u>vowel</u>.

le ragazze	the girls
le amiche	the (girl)friends

Tip

When you're learning vocabulary, remember to learn the article that goes with each noun.

ℹ️ Note that the article you choose depends on the first or first two letters of the following word, which can be an adjective or a noun.

l'amico	the friend
BUT	
il migliore amico	the best friend
lo studente	the student
BUT	
il migliore studente	the best student
gli studenti	the students
BUT	
i migliori studenti	the best students

⇨ *For more information on **Adjectives**, see page 20.*

3 Combining the definite article with other words

➤ In Italian, when you say *at the cinema*, *in the cinema*, and so on, the word for *at* and *in* combines with the article. How this works for **a** (meaning *at* or *to*) is shown below:

a + il = **al**	al cinema	at *or* to the cinema
a + l' = **all'**	all'albergo	at *or* to the hotel
a + lo = **allo**	allo stadio	at *or* to the stadium
a + la = **alla**	alla stazione	at *or* to the station
a + i = **ai**	ai concerti	at *or* to the concerts
a + gli = **agli**	agli aeroporti	at *or* to the airports
a + le = **alle**	alle partite	at *or* to the matches

➤ The other words which combine in the same way are: **da**, **di**, **in** and **su**:

● **da** (meaning *from*)

da + il = **dal**	dal cinema	from the cinema
da + l' = **dall'**	dall'albergo	from the hotel
da + lo = **dallo**	dallo stadio	from the stadium
da + la = **dalla**	dalla stazione	from the station
da + i = **dai**	dai concerti	from the concerts
da + gli = **dagli**	dagli aeroporti	from the airports
da + le = **dalle**	dalle partite	from the matches

● **di** (meaning *of*)

di + il = **del**	del cinema	of the cinema
di + l' = **dell'**	dell'albergo	of the hotel
di + lo = **dello**	dello stadio	of the stadium
di + la = **della**	della stazione	of the station
di + i = **dei**	dei concerti	of the concerts
di + gli = **degli**	degli aeroporti	of the airports
di + le = **delle**	delle partite	of the matches

● **in** (meaning *in*)

in + il = **nel**	nel cinema	in the cinema
in + l' = **nell'**	nell'albergo	in the hotel
in + lo = **nello**	nello stadio	in the stadium
in + la = **nella**	nella stazione	in the station
in + i = **nei**	nei concerti	in the concerts
in + gli = **negli**	negli aeroporti	in the airports
in + le = **nelle**	nelle partite	in the matches

- **su** (meaning *on*)

su + il = **sul**	sul pavimento	on the floor
su + l' = **sull'**	sull'orlo	on the edge
su + lo = **sullo**	sullo scoglio	on the rock
su + la = **sulla**	sulla spiaggia	on the beach
su + i = **sui**	sui monti	on the mountains
su + gli = **sugli**	sugli scaffali	on the bookshelves
su + le = **sulle**	sulle strade	on the roads

➤ In English, you can use *some* with singular and plural nouns: *some sugar*, *some students*. One way of expressing the idea of *some* in Italian is to use the word **di** together with the definite article.

del burro	some butter
dell'olio	some oil
della carta	some paper
dei fiammiferi	some matches
delle uova	some eggs
Hanno rotto **dei** bicchieri.	They broke some glasses.
Ci vuole **del** sale.	It needs some salt.
Aggiungi **della** farina.	Add some flour.

4 │ When do you use the definite article?

➤ Italian uses the definite article much more than English does. As a rule of thumb, Italian sentences rarely start with a noun that has no article.

I bambini soffrono.	Children are suffering.
Mi piacciono **gli** animali.	I like animals.
Le cose vanno meglio.	Things are going better.
Il nuoto è il mio sport preferito.	Swimming is my favourite sport.
Non mi piace **il** riso.	I don't like rice.
Lo zucchero non fa bene.	Sugar isn't good for you.
La povertà è un grande problema.	Poverty is a big problem.
L'Australia è molto grande.	Australia is very big.
La Calabria è bella.	Calabria is beautiful.

ℹ️ Note that if the name of a country comes after the Italian word **in**, which means *to* or *in*, the article is **not** used.

Vado in Francia a giugno.	I'm going to France in June.
Lavorano in Germania.	They work in Germany.

> **Tip**
>
> When you translate an English sentence which starts with a noun, don't forget to use the definite article in Italian.
>
> | | |
> |---|---|
> | **Le macchine costano caro.** | Cars cost a lot. |
> | **La frutta fa bene.** | Fruit is good for you. |

➤ In the following cases, the article is used rather differently in Italian from in English:

- When you're talking about <u>parts of the body and bodily actions</u>, use the definite article. The English adjectives *my*, *your*, *his* and so on are not translated.

Dammi <u>la</u> mano.	Give me your hand.
Mi fa male <u>il</u> piede.	My foot is hurting.
Soffiati <u>il</u> naso!	Blow your nose!

- Use the definite article when talking about <u>clothes</u>.

Si è tolto <u>il</u> cappotto.	He took off his coat.
Mettiti <u>le</u> scarpe.	Put your shoes on.

- Use the definite article with the <u>time</u>, <u>dates</u> and <u>years</u>.

<u>all'</u>una	at one o'clock
<u>alle</u> due	at two o'clock
Era <u>l'</u>una.	It was one o'clock.
Sono <u>le</u> due.	It's two o'clock.
Sono nata <u>il</u> primo maggio 2001.	I was born on May 1 2001.
Verranno <u>nel</u> 2017.	They're coming in 2017.

- Use the definite article with words such as *my*, *your*, and *his*.

<u>la</u> mia casa	my house
<u>le</u> sue figlie	her daughters
<u>i</u> vostri amici	your friends

⇨ *For more information on **Possessive adjectives**, see page 34.*

- When you talk about how much something costs <u>per pound</u>, <u>per kilo</u>, and so on; about <u>rates</u>, <u>speeds</u>, and about <u>how often</u> something happens, use the word **a** and the definite article.

Costano 3 euro <u>al</u> chilo.	They cost 3 euro a kilo.
70 km <u>all'</u>ora	70 km an hour
50.000 dollari <u>al</u> mese	50,000 dollars per month
due volte <u>alla</u> settimana	twice a week

- You use the definite article when you are referring to people by using their titles, but NOT when you are speaking to them directly.

La signora Rossi è qui.	Mrs. Rossi is here.
Il dottor Gentile	Doctor Gentile
BUT	
Scusi, signora Rossi.	Excuse me, Mrs. Rossi.

Key points

✔ Definite articles are used much more in Italian than in English.

✔ Italian sentences rarely start with a noun that has no article.

✔ Sometimes the definite article is used very differently from English. For instance, you use it with parts of the body and the time.

The indefinite article

1 The basics

➤ In English the indefinite article is either *a* – *a boy* - or *an* - *an apple*.

➤ In Italian there are four indefinite articles: **un**, **uno**, **una** and **un'**.

➤ Which one you need to choose depends on the gender of the noun it goes with, and the letter the noun starts with.

⇨ *For more information on* **Nouns**, *see page 1.*

2 Which indefinite article do you use?

➤ The indefinite article to use for <u>masculine nouns</u> is:

- **un** with nouns starting with <u>most consonants</u> and <u>all vowels</u>.

un telefonino	a mobile phone
un uomo	a man

- **uno** with nouns starting with <u>s + another consonant, z, gn, pn, ps, x and y</u>.

uno studente	a student
uno zio	an uncle
uno psichiatra	a psychiatrist

➤ The indefinite article to use for <u>feminine nouns</u> is:

- **una** with nouns starting with a <u>consonant</u>.

una ragazza	a girl
una mela	an apple

- **un'** with nouns starting with a <u>vowel</u>.

un'ora	an hour
un'amica	a (girl)friend

> ⓘ Note that the article you choose depends on the first or first two letters of the following word, which can be an adjective or a noun.

<u>un</u> albergo	a hotel
BUT	
<u>uno</u> splendido albergo	a magnificent hotel
<u>uno</u> scultore	a sculptor
BUT	
<u>un</u> bravo scultore	a good sculptor

3 Using the indefinite article

➤ You generally use the indefinite article in Italian when *a* or *an* are used in English.

Era con un'amica.	She was with a friend.
Vuoi un gelato?	Do you want an ice cream?

➤ There are some cases where the article is used in English, but **not** in Italian:

● with the words **cento** and **mille**

cento volte	a hundred times
mille sterline	a thousand pounds

● when you translate *a few* or *a lot*

qualche parola	a few words
molti soldi	a lot of money

● in exclamations with **che**

Che sorpresa!	What a surprise!
Che peccato!	What a pity!

ℹ Note that to say what someone's job is you either leave out the article:

È medico.	He's a doctor.
Sono professori.	They're teachers.

Or you use the verb **fare** with the <u>definite</u> article:

Faccio l'ingegnere.	I'm an engineer.
Fa l'avvocato.	She's a lawyer.

4 Plural nouns used without the article

➤ There are some cases where you use plural nouns without any article:

● in negative sentences

Non ha amici.	He hasn't got any friends.
Non ci sono posti liberi.	There aren't any empty seats.

● in questions where *any* is used in English

Hai fratelli?	Have you got any brothers or sisters?
Ci sono problemi?	Are there any problems?

⇨ For more information on **Negatives** and **Questions**, see pages 149 and 152.

- in lists

Ci vogliono patate, cipolle e carote.	You need potatoes, onions and carrots.
Vendono giornali, riviste e cartoline.	They sell newspapers, magazines and postcards.

- when you are not giving details

Abbiamo visitato castelli e musei.	We visited castles and museums.
Ci sono cose da vedere.	There are things to see.
Hanno problemi.	They've got problems.

Key points

✔ You generally use the indefinite article in a very similar way to English.

✔ You do not use it with the numbers **cento** and **mille**, and in exclamations with **che**.

✔ The indefinite article is not used when saying what someone's job is.

Adjectives

> **What is an adjective?**
> An **adjective** is a 'describing' word that tells you more about a person or thing, for example, *blue*, *big*, *good*.

Using adjectives

➤ You use adjectives like *nice*, *expensive* and *good* to say something about nouns (living beings, things or ideas). You can also use them with words such as *you*, *he* and *they*. You can use them immediately in front of a noun, or after verbs like *be*, *look* and *feel*.

  a <u>nice</u> girl
  an <u>expensive</u> coat
  a <u>good</u> idea
  He's <u>nice</u>.
  They look <u>expensive</u>.

⇨ *For more information on **Nouns**, see page 1.*

➤ In English, adjectives don't change according to the noun they go with.

  a nice boy
  nice girls

➤ In Italian you have to ask:

  ● Is the noun masculine or feminine?

  ● Is it singular or plural?

➤ You then choose the adjective ending accordingly. This is called making the adjective agree.

un ragazzo <u>alto</u>	a tall boy
una ragazza <u>alta</u>	a tall girl
ragazzi <u>alti</u>	tall boys
ragazze <u>alte</u>	tall girls

➤ In English you put adjectives <u>IN FRONT OF</u> the noun you're describing, but in Italian you usually put them <u>AFTER</u> it.

  una casa <u>bianca</u>   a <u>white</u> house

⇨ *For more information on **Word order with adjectives**, see page 24.*

For further explanation of grammatical terms, please see pages viii–xii.

How to make adjectives agree

1 The basics

➤ When you look up an adjective in a dictionary you find the <u>masculine</u> <u>singular</u> form.

➤ If you want to use an adjective to describe a feminine noun you <u>often</u> have to change the ending.

➤ If you want to use an adjective to describe a plural noun you <u>nearly always</u> have to change the ending.

2 How to make adjectives feminine

➤ If the masculine adjective ends in **–o**, change **–o** to **–a**.

un ragazzo <u>simpatico</u>	a nice boy
una ragazza <u>simpatica</u>	a nice girl
un film <u>italiano</u>	an Italian film
una squadra <u>italiana</u>	an Italian team

➤ You don't change the ending for the feminine:

- if the masculine adjective ends in **–e**

un libro <u>inglese</u>	an English book
una famiglia <u>inglese</u>	an English family
un treno <u>veloce</u>	a fast train
una macchina <u>veloce</u>	a fast car

📝 Note that adjectives such as **italiano**, **inglese**, **francese** do not start with a capital letter in Italian.

- in the case of some colours

un calzino <u>rosa</u>	a pink sock
una maglietta <u>rosa</u>	a pink T-shirt
un tappeto <u>blu</u>	a blue rug
una macchina <u>blu</u>	a blue car
un vestito <u>beige</u>	a beige suit
una gonna <u>beige</u>	a beige skirt

📝 Note that these adjectives don't change in the plural either.

- if the adjective ends with a consonant

un gruppo <u>pop</u>	a pop group
la musica <u>pop</u>	pop music
un tipo <u>snob</u>	a posh guy
una persona <u>snob</u>	a posh person

📝 Note that these adjectives don't change in the plural either.

> ### Tip
>
> If you are female, make sure you always use a feminine adjective when talking about yourself:
>
> | | |
> |---|---|
> | **Sono stanca.** | I'm tired. |
> | **Sono pronta.** | I'm ready. |

3 | How to make adjectives plural

➤ If the masculine singular adjective ends in **–o**, change **–o** to **–i**.

un fiore <u>rosso</u>	a red flower
dei fiori <u>rossi</u>	red flowers
un computer <u>nuovo</u>	a new computer
dei computer <u>nuovi</u>	new computers

➤ If the feminine singular adjective ends in **–a**, change **–a** to **–e**.

una strada <u>pericolosa</u>	a dangerous road
delle strade <u>pericolose</u>	dangerous roads
una gonna <u>nera</u>	a black skirt
delle gonne <u>nere</u>	black skirts

➤ If the adjective ends in **–e**, change **–e** to **–i** for both masculine and feminine plural.

un esercizio <u>difficile</u>	a difficult exercise
degli esercizi <u>difficili</u>	difficult exercises
un sito <u>interessante</u>	an interesting site
dei siti <u>interessanti</u>	interesting sites
una storia <u>triste</u>	a sad story
delle storie <u>tristi</u>	sad stories
una valigia <u>pesante</u>	a heavy case
delle valigie <u>pesanti</u>	heavy cases

➤ Some adjectives do not change in the plural.

un paio di guanti <u>rosa</u>	a pair of pink gloves
delle tende <u>blu</u>	blue curtains
dei gruppi <u>pop</u>	pop groups

➤ Adjectives that do not change for the feminine or plural are called <u>invariable</u>, which is abbreviated to *inv* in some dictionaries.

> **Tip**
>
> Remember that **spaghetti**, **ravioli**, **lasagne** and so on are plural nouns in Italian, so you must use plural adjectives with them.
>
> | | |
> |---|---|
> | **Sono buoni gli spaghetti?** | Is the spaghetti nice? |
> | **Le lasagne sono finite.** | The lasagne is all gone. |

[i] Note that when you're describing a couple consisting of a man and a woman or a group of people, use a masculine plural adjective unless the group consists entirely of females.

Paolo e Loredana sono pronti.	Paolo and Loredana are ready.
I bambini sono stanchi.	The children are tired.
Le ragazze sono stanche.	The girls are tired.

4 | Irregular adjectives

➤ There are three very common adjectives which are different from other adjectives – **bello**, **buono** and **grande**.

➤ When the adjective **bello** (meaning *beautiful*) is used in front of a masculine noun it has different forms depending on which letter follows it, just like the definite article.

bello	Masculine Singular	Feminine Singular	Masculine Plural	Feminine Plural
used before a noun	bel	bella	bei	belle
used after a verb or a noun	bello	bella	belli	belle

bel tempo	beautiful weather
bei nomi	beautiful names
Il tempo era bello.	The weather was beautiful.
I fiori sono belli.	The flowers are beautiful.

➤ **bell'** is used before vowels in the masculine and feminine singular forms.

un bell'albero	a beautiful tree

➤ **bello** is used in front of **z** and **s** + another consonant in the masculine singular form.

un bello strumento	a beautiful instrument

➤ **begli** is used in front of vowels, **z** and **s** + another consonant in the masculine plural form.

begli alberi	beautiful trees
begli strumenti	beautiful instruments

➤ The adjective **buono** (meaning *good*) is usually shortened to **buon** when it comes before a masculine singular noun.

Buon viaggio!	Have a good journey!
un buon uomo	a good man

➤ The shortened form of **buono** is <u>not</u> used in front of nouns that start with **z** or **s** + another consonant.

un buono studente	a good student

➤ The adjective **grande** (meaning *big*, *large* or *great*) is often shortened to **gran** when it comes before a singular noun starting with a consonant.

la Gran Bretagna	Great Britain
un gran numero di macchine	a large number of cars

Key points

✔ In Italian adjectives agree with the person or thing they are describing.

✔ Adjectives ending in **–o** in the masculine have different endings in the feminine and plural forms.

✔ Some adjectives don't have a different feminine or plural form.

---

5 Where do you put the adjective?

➤ You put most adjectives <u>AFTER</u> the noun.

un gesto <u>spontaneo</u>	a spontaneous gesture
una partita <u>importante</u>	an important match
capelli <u>biondi</u>	blonde hair

📖 Note that if you have two adjectives you link them with **e** (meaning *and*).

ragazze <u>antipatiche</u> e <u>maleducate</u>	nasty rude girls

➤ The meaning of some adjectives changes depending on whether they come after or before the noun.

gente povera	poor people BUT
Povera Anna!	Poor (meaning *unfortunate*) Anna!
un uomo grande	a big man BUT
una grande sorpresa	a great surprise
una macchina nuova	a new car BUT
la sua nuova ragazza	his new (meaning *latest*) girlfriend

---

una casa vecchia	an old house BUT
un mio vecchio amico	an old (meaning *long-standing*) friend of mine
una borsa cara	an expensive handbag BUT
un caro amico	a dear friend

ℹ Note that if you add **molto** (meaning *very*) to an adjective, the adjective always goes after the noun.

una bella casa	a nice house
una casa molto bella	a very nice house

➤ Some types of adjectives always go in front of the noun:

- adjectives that are used to point things out, such as **questo** (meaning *this*) and **quello** (meaning *that*)

Questo telefonino è di mio fratello.	This mobile phone is my brother's.
Quello studente è un mio amico.	That student is a friend of mine.

⇨ *For more information on **Demonstrative adjectives**, see page 30.*

- possessive adjectives such as **mio** (meaning *my*), **tuo** (meaning *your*) and **suo** (meaning *his* or *her*)

mio padre	my father
tuo fratello	your brother
suo marito	her husband

- **ogni** (meaning *each*, *every*), **qualche** (meaning *some*) and **nessuno** (meaning *no*)

ogni giorno	every day
qualche volta	sometimes
Non c'è **nessun** bisogno di andare.	There's no need to go.

⇨ *For more information on **Indefinite adjectives**, see page 37.*

- question words

Quali programmi hai?	What plans have you got?
Quanto pane hai comprato?	How much bread did you buy?

⇨ *For more information on **Questions**, see page 152.*

Key points

✔ Most Italian adjectives go after the noun.

✔ The meaning of some adjectives changes depending on whether they come before or after the noun.

Comparing people or things

1 Comparative adjectives

> **What is a comparative adjective?**
> In English a **comparative adjective** is one with –er on the end, or more or less in front of it, for example faster, more important, less interesting. These adjectives are used when you are comparing people or things.

2 How to make a comparative adjective in Italian

➤ To say that something is faster, bigger, more important and so on use **più** in front of the adjective.

una macchina **più** grande	a bigger car
un film **più** interessante	a more interesting film
Queste scarpe sono **più** comode.	These shoes are more comfortable.

➤ To say that something is less expensive, less interesting and so on use **meno** in front of the adjective.

un computer **meno** caro	a less expensive computer
un viaggio **meno** faticoso	a less tiring journey

3 How to compare one person or thing with another

➤ Put either **più** or **meno** in front of the adjective and use **di** to translate than.

Sono **più** alto **di** te.	I'm taller than you.
Milano è **più** grande **di** Genova.	Milan is bigger than Genoa.
Carlo è **più** ambizioso **di** Luca.	Carlo is more ambitious than Luca.
Quello verde è **meno** caro **del** nero.	The green one is less expensive than the black one.
La mia borsa è **meno** pesante **della** tua.	My bag is less heavy than yours.

(i) Note that **di** combines with the article to make one word: **di** + **il** = **del**, **di** + **la** = **della**, and so on.

⇨ For more information on **di**, see **Prepositions** page 174.

4 | Superlative adjectives

What is a superlative adjective?
In English a **superlative adjective** is one with *–est* on the end, or *most* or *least* in front of it, for example *fastest, most important, least interesting*. The definite article is used with superlative adjectives: *the fastest, the most important, the least interesting*.

5 | How to make a superlative adjective in Italian

➤ Making a superlative adjective is very easy: you simply put a <u>definite article</u> in front of the comparative adjective.

il più alto	the tallest
il meno interessante	the least interesting

➤ The definite article <u>must</u> agree with the person or thing you're describing.

Matteo è <u>il</u> più alto.	Matteo is the tallest.
Lidia è <u>la</u> più alta.	Lidia is the tallest.
Queste scarpe sono <u>le</u> più comode.	These shoes are the most comfortable.
Gianni è <u>il</u> meno ambizioso.	Gianni is the least ambitious.

➤ If there is a definite article in front of the noun, <u>do not</u> put a second definite article in front of **più** or **meno**.

il ragazzo più alto	the tallest boy
la banca più vicina	the nearest bank
lo studente più intelligente	the most intelligent student
i voli più economici	the cheapest flights
i suoi film meno interessanti	his least interesting films

➡ *For more information on the **Definite article**, see page 11.*

Tip

In phrases like *the most famous in the world*, and *the biggest in Italy*, use **di** to translate *in*.

lo stadio più grande d'Italia	the biggest stadium in Italy
il ristorante più caro della città	the most expensive restaurant in the town

6 Irregular comparatives and superlatives

➤ In English the comparatives of *good* and *bad* are irregular: *better, best, worse* and *worst*. In Italian there are regular forms of **buono** and **cattivo**.

Questo è più buono.	This one's better.
I rossi sono i più buoni.	The red ones are the best.
Quello è ancora più cattivo.	That one's even worse.

➤ There are also irregular forms of **buono** and **cattivo**, as there are of **grande**, **piccolo**, **alto** and **basso**:

Adjective	Meaning	Comparative	Meaning	Superlative	Meaning
buono	good	migliore	better	il migliore	the best
cattivo	bad	peggiore	worse	il peggiore	the worst
grande	big	maggiore	bigger/ older	il maggiore	the biggest/ oldest
piccolo	small	minore	smaller/ younger	il minore	the smallest/ youngest
alto	high	superiore	higher	il superiore	the highest
basso	low	inferiore	lower	l'inferiore	the lowest

i Note that these irregular comparatives and superlatives are adjectives ending in **–e**, so their plural ending is **–i**.

il modo **migliore**	the best way
il mio fratello **minore**	my younger brother
le mie sorelle **maggiori**	my older sisters
il labbro **inferiore**	the lower lip
Il libro è **migliore** del film.	The book is better than the film.
Giorgia è **la peggiore** della classe.	Giorgia is the worst in the class.

7 as ... as ...

➤ Sometimes you want to say that people or things are similar or the same:

I'm <u>as</u> tall <u>as</u> you.

➤ In Italian you use **come**, or **quanto** to make this kind of comparison.

Pietro è alto **come** Michele.	Pietro is as tall as Michele.
La mia macchina è grande **come** la tua.	My car is as big as yours.
Sono stanca **quanto** te.	I'm just as tired as you are.

➤ You can make these sentences negative by adding **non**.

Pietro <u>non</u> è alto come Michele.	Pietro is not as tall as Michele.
<u>Non</u> sono stanca quanto te.	I'm not as tired as you are.

Grammar Extra!

In English you emphasize adjectives by adding words like *very*, *really* or *terribly*. You do the same in Italian, using **molto**, **veramente** and **terribilmente**.

Lui è molto ricco.	He's very rich.
I fiori sono veramente belli.	The flowers are really lovely.
Sono terribilmente stanca.	I'm terribly tired.

➤ Another way of adding emphasis to Italian adjectives is to replace the **–o** or **–e** ending with **–issimo**.

bello	beautiful
bellissimo	very beautiful
elegante	smart
elegantissimo	very smart

🔃 Note that these **-issimo** adjectives change their endings for the feminine and the plural.

Il tempo era bellissimo.	The weather was really beautiful.
Anna è sempre elegantissima.	Anna is always terribly smart.
Sono educatissimi.	They're extremely polite.

Key points

✔ You make comparative adjectives in Italian by using **più** and **meno**, and translate *than* by **di**.

✔ You add the definite article to the comparative adjective to make a superlative adjective.

Demonstrative adjectives

> **What is a demonstrative adjective?**
> A **demonstrative adjective** is used to point out a particular thing or person.
> There are four demonstrative adjectives in English: *this, these, that* and *those*.

1 Using demonstrative adjectives

➤ As in English, Italian demonstrative adjectives go <u>BEFORE</u> the noun. Like other adjectives in Italian, they have to change for the feminine and plural forms.

➤ To say *this*, use **questo**, which has four forms, like any other adjective ending in –**o**.

	Masculine	Feminine	Meaning
Singular	questo	questa	this
Plural	questi	queste	these

Questa gonna è troppo stretta.	This skirt is too tight.
Questi pantaloni mi piacciono.	I like these trousers.
Queste scarpe sono comode.	These shoes are comfortable.

➤ To say *that*, use **quello**, which has several different forms, like the definite article:

- use **quel** with a masculine noun starting with a consonant
  quel ragazzo   that boy
- use **quello** with a masculine noun starting with **z** or **s** + another consonant
  quello zaino   that rucksack
  quello studente   that student
- use **quell'** with nouns starting with a vowel
  quell'albero   that tree
  quell'amica   that friend
- use **quella** with a feminine noun starting with a consonant
  quella ragazza   that girl
- use **quei** with a masculine plural noun starting with a consonant
  quei cani   those dogs
- use **quegli** with a masculine plural noun starting with a vowel, with **z** or with **s** + another consonant
  quegli uomini ← *irreg*   those men
  quegli studenti   those students

- use **quelle** before all <u>feminine plural nouns</u>

  quelle macchine those cars

Tip

When you want to say *this one*, don't translate *one*. Use **questo** if what you're referring to is masculine, and **questa** if it's feminine. The same goes when you want to say *that one*: use **quello**, or **quella**.

Quale casa? – Questa. Which house? – This one.

Quale zaino? – Quello. Which rucksack? – That one.

Key points

✔ Use **questo** or **questa** for *this*, and **questi** or **queste** for *these*.

✔ Use **quello** for *that*: **quello** behaves like the definite article, **il**.

Interrogative adjectives

> **What is an interrogative adjective?**
> An **interrogative adjective** is a question word such as *which, what* or *how much* that is used when asking about a noun, for example: *Which colour?; What size?; How much sugar?*

➤ In Italian the interrogative adjectives are **che**, **quale** and **quanto**.

➤ **che** and **quale** are used to ask *which* or *what*:

- Use **che** or **quale** with <u>singular nouns</u>.

<u>Che</u> giorno è oggi?	What day is it today?
A <u>che</u> ora ti alzi?	What time do you get up at?
<u>Quale</u> tipo vuoi?	What kind do you want?
Per <u>quale</u> squadra tifi?	Which team do you support?

- Use **che** or **quali** with <u>plural nouns</u>.

<u>Che</u> gusti preferisci?	Which flavours do you like best?
<u>Quali</u> programmi hai?	What plans have you got?

- Use **quanto** with <u>masculine nouns</u> and **quanta** with <u>feminine nouns</u> to ask *how much*.

<u>Quanto</u> pane hai comprato?	How much bread did you buy?
<u>Quanta</u> minestra vuoi?	How much soup do you want?

- Use **quanti** with <u>masculine nouns</u> and **quante** with <u>feminine nouns</u> to ask *how many*.

<u>Quanti</u> bicchieri ci sono?	How many glasses are there?
<u>Quante</u> uova vuoi?	How many eggs do you want?

⟹ *For more information on* **Questions**, *see page 152.*

Key points

✔ Use **che** with any noun to mean *which* or *what*.

✔ **quale** has the plural form **quali**.

✔ **quanto** has feminine and plural forms.

Adjectives used in exclamations

➤ In Italian **che...!** is often used with a noun where we would say *What a ...!* in English.

Che peccato!	What a pity!
Che disordine!	What a mess!
Che bella giornata!	What a lovely day!
Che brutto tempo!	What awful weather!

➤ **che** can also be used with an adjective when you're commenting on somebody or something.

Che carino!	Isn't he sweet!
Che brutti!	They're horrible!

➤ You can also use an Italian adjective by itself when you are commenting on someone's behaviour.

Furbo!	Cunning devil!
Brava!	Good girl!
Bravi!	Well done!

➤ As in English, you can use an Italian adjective alone when you are commenting on something you see or taste.

Bello!	Lovely!
Buono!	Nice!

> ## Tip
> Remember to make the adjective agree with the person or thing you're commenting on.

➤ You can use **quanto**, **quanta**, **quanti** and **quante** when you are exclaiming about a large amount or number.

Quanto tempo sprecato!	What a waste of time!
Quanta gente!	What a lot of people!
Quanti soldi!	What a lot of money!
Quante storie!	What a fuss!

Possessive adjectives

> **What is a possessive adjective?**
> In English a **possessive adjective** is a word such as *my, your, his* that is used with a noun to show who it belongs to.

How to use possessive adjectives

1 The basics

➤ Unlike English you usually put the <u>definite</u> article (**il**, **la**, **i**, **le**) in front of the possessive adjective.

➤ As with all adjectives ending in –**o**, change the ending to:

- –**a** for the feminine singular
- –**i** for the masculine plural
- –**e** for the feminine plural

il mio indirizzo	my address
la mia scuola	my school
i miei amici	my friends
le mie speranze	my hopes

➪ *For more information on the **Definite article**, see page 11.* *see page 11*

➤ You can also use the <u>indefinite article</u> in front of the possessive adjective in examples like:

una mia amica	a friend of mine
un suo studente	one of her students

➤ You usually put possessive adjectives in front of the noun they describe.

➤ The following table shows all the possessive adjectives:

Singular		Plural		Meaning
Masculine	**Feminine**	**Masculine**	**Feminine**	
il mio	la mia	i miei	le mie	my
il tuo	la tua	i tuoi	le tue	your (belonging to someone you call **tu**)
il suo	la sua	i suoi	le sue	his; her; its; your (belonging to someone you call **Lei**)
il nostro	la nostra	i nostri	le nostre	our
il vostro	la vostra	i vostri	le vostre	your (belonging to people you call **voi**)
il loro	la loro	i loro	le loro	their

➪ *For more information on **Ways of saying 'you' in Italian**, see page 42.* *see page 42*

For further explanation of grammatical terms, please see pages viii–xii.

Dove sono <u>le mie</u> chiavi?	Where are my keys?
Luca ha perso <u>il suo</u> portafoglio.	Luca has lost his wallet.
Ecco <u>i nostri</u> passaporti.	Here are our passports.
Qual è <u>la vostra</u> camera?	Which is your room?
<u>Il tuo</u> amico ti aspetta.	Your friend is waiting for you.

Tip

Possessive adjectives agree with the noun they go with, <u>NOT</u> with the person who is the owner.

Anna ha perso <u>il suo</u> Smartphone.	Anna has lost her smartphone.
Marco ha trovato <u>la sua</u> agenda.	Marco's found his diary.
Le ragazze hanno <u>i loro</u> biglietti.	The girls have got their tickets.

i Note that possessive adjectives aren't normally used with parts of the body. You usually use **il**, **la**, and so on (the <u>definite article</u>) instead.

Mi sono fatto male al<u>la</u> gamba.	I've hurt my leg.
Si sta lavando <u>i</u> capelli.	She's washing her hair.

⇨ *For more information on the **Definite article**, see page 11.*

Key points

✔ Italian possessive adjectives agree with the nouns they describe.

✔ Italian possessive adjectives are usually preceded by an article.

✔ Possessive adjectives are not usually used with parts of the body.

2 How to use possessive adjectives when talking about relatives

➤ To say *my mother*, *your father*, *her husband*, *his wife* and so on, use the possessive adjective <u>without</u> the definite article.

mia madre	my mother
tuo padre	your father
suo marito	her husband
sua moglie	his wife
mia sorella	my sister
tuo fratello	your brother

➤ This applies to all family members in the <u>singular</u>, except for the words **mamma** (meaning *mum*) and **babbo** and **papà** (both meaning *dad*).

la mia mamma	my mum
Maria e il suo babbo	Maria and her dad

[*i*] Note that if you describe a family member with an adjective, for example *my <u>dear</u> wife*, *her <u>younger</u> sister*, you DO use the definite article with the possessive.

<u>il mio caro</u> marito	my dear husband
<u>il suo</u> fratello <u>maggiore</u>	his older brother

➤ You DO use the definite article with the possessive adjective when you're referring to family members in the <u>plural</u>.

Sandro e i suoi fratelli	Sandro and his brothers
Laura e le sue cognate	Laura and her sisters-in-law

Key points

✔ Use the possessive adjective without the definite article when talking about family members in the singular.

✔ Use the possessive adjective with the definite article when talking about family members in the plural.

Indefinite adjectives

> **What is an indefinite adjective?**
> An **indefinite adjective** is one of a small group of adjectives used to give an idea
> of amounts and numbers, for example, *several*, *all*, *every*.

➤ The indefinite adjectives **ogni** (meaning *each*), **qualche** (meaning *some*) and
qualsiasi (meaning *any*) are <u>invariable</u>, that is they do not change their form for
the feminine or plural.

ogni giorno	every day
ogni volta	every time
fra qualche mese	in a few months
qualche volta	sometimes
in qualsiasi momento	at any time
qualsiasi cosa	anything

➤ The following indefinite adjectives end in **–o**, and change their endings in the
normal way.

altro	other
tutto	all
molto	much
parecchio	a lot of
poco	a little
tanto	so much
troppo	too much

➤ Put the indefinite or definite article <u>IN FRONT OF</u> **altro**.

<u>un</u> altro giorno	another day
<u>un'</u>altra volta	another time
<u>gli</u> altri studenti	the other students

➤ Put the definite article <u>AFTER</u> **tutto**, even when there is no article in English.

tutta <u>la</u> giornata	all day
tutte <u>le</u> ragazze	all the girls

➤ Use **molto** (masculine) and **molta** (feminine) to talk about large amounts.

Non abbiamo <u>molto</u> tempo.	We haven't much time.
C'è <u>molta</u> roba.	There's a lot of stuff.

➤ Use **molti** (masculine plural) and **molte** (feminine plural) to talk about large
numbers.

Abbiamo <u>molti</u> problemi.	We've got a lot of problems.
L'ho fatto <u>molte</u> volte.	I've done it many times.

➤ You can also use **parecchio** and **parecchia** to talk about quite large amounts, and **parecchi** and **parecchie** to talk about quite large numbers.

Non lo vedo da <u>parecchio</u> **tempo.**	I haven't seen him for quite some time.
C'era <u>parecchia</u> **neve in montagna.**	There was quite a lot of snow on the hills.
Ho avuto <u>parecchi</u> **guai.**	I had quite a few problems.
Ha <u>parecchie</u> **amiche inglesi.**	She has several English friends.

☑ Note that the masculine singular ending of **parecchio** changes to a single **–i** in the plural.

➤ Use **poco** and **poca** to talk about small amounts and **pochi** and **poche** to talk about small numbers.

C'è <u>poco</u> **tempo.**	There's not much time.
Ha <u>pochi</u> **amici.**	He has few friends.

☑ Note that the singular endings **–co** and **–ca** change to **–chi** and **–che** in the plural.

⇨ *For more information on **Spelling**, see page* 191.

➤ Use **troppo** and **troppa** to say *too much*, and **troppi** and **troppe** to say *too many*.

Questa minestra è <u>troppa</u> **per me.**	This is too much soup for me.
Ho <u>troppe</u> **cose da fare.**	I've got too many things to do.

➤ Use **tanto** and **tanta** to talk about very large amounts, and **tanti** and **tante** to talk about very large numbers.

Ho mangiato <u>tanta</u> **pasta!**	I ate so much pasta!
Abbiamo avuto <u>tanti</u> **problemi.**	We've had a whole lot of problems.

Grammar Extra!

ciascuno (meaning *each*) and **nessuno** (meaning *no*) have no plural and behave like the indefinite article **uno**.

Before a masculine noun starting with a vowel, or most consonants, use **ciascun** and **nessun**.

<u>ciascun</u> **candidato**	each candidate
<u>ciascun</u> **amico**	each friend
<u>nessun</u> **irlandese**	no Irishman
Non ha fatto <u>nessun</u> **commento.**	He made no comment.

Before a masculine noun starting with **z** or **s** + another consonant use **ciascuno** and **nessuno**.

<u>ciascuno</u> **studente**	each student
<u>nessuno</u> **spagnolo**	no Spanish person

For further explanation of grammatical terms, please see pages viii–xii.

Before a feminine noun starting with a consonant use **ciascuna** and **nessuna**.

<u>ciascuna</u> ragazza	each girl
<u>nessuna</u> ragione	no reason

Before a feminine noun beginning with a vowel use **ciascun'** and **nessun'**.

<u>ciascun'</u>amica	each friend (*female*)
<u>nessun'</u>alternativa	no alternative

Key points

✔ **ogni**, **qualche** and **qualsiasi** always have the same form.

✔ **altro**, **tutto**, **molto**, **poco**, **parecchio**, **troppo** and **tanto** change their endings in the feminine and plural.

Pronouns

What is a pronoun?

A **pronoun** is a word you use instead of a noun, when you do not need or want to name someone or something directly, for example, *it, you, somebody, who, that*.

➤ There are many different kinds of pronoun, and all the words underlined in the sentences below are classified as pronouns. As you will see, they are extremely important and versatile words in everyday use.

<u>I</u> liked the black trousers but I couldn't afford <u>them</u>.	(*subject pronoun; direct object pronoun*)
<u>I</u>'m not going to eat it.	(*subject pronoun*)
You know Jack? I saw <u>him</u> at the weekend.	(*direct object pronoun*)
I emailed <u>her</u> my latest ideas.	(*indirect object pronoun*)
It's <u>mine</u>.	(*possessive pronoun*)
<u>Someone</u> came to see you yesterday.	(*indefinite pronoun*)
There's <u>nothing</u> I can do about it.	(*indefinite pronoun*)
<u>This</u> is the book I meant.	(*demonstrative pronoun*)
<u>That</u>'s Ian.	(*demonstrative pronoun*)
<u>Who</u>'s he?	(*interrogative pronoun*)
<u>What</u> are those lights over there?	(*interrogative pronoun*)

➤ **Personal pronouns** are words such as *I, you, he, she, us, them*, and so forth, which make it clear who you are talking about or talking to. Personal pronouns replace nouns when it's clear who or what is being referred to, for example, *My brother's not here at the moment. He'll be back in an hour.*

➤ There are two types of personal pronoun:

- <u>subject pronouns</u> for the person or thing performing the action expressed by the verb.

   <u>I</u> like you a lot.
   <u>They</u> always go there on Sundays.

- <u>object pronouns</u> for the person or thing most directly affected by the action.

   I'll help <u>you</u>.
   They sent it to <u>me</u> yesterday.
   He gave <u>us</u> a very warm welcome.

Subject pronouns

➤ Here are the Italian subject pronouns:

Singular	Meaning	Plural	Meaning
io	I	noi	we
tu	you (familiar singular)	voi	you
lui	he	loro	they
lei	she; you (polite singular)		

Tip

You also use **lei** as a polite word for *you*. You will sometimes see it with a capital letter when used in this way.

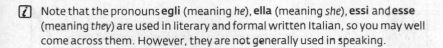

Note that the pronouns **egli** (meaning *he*), **ella** (meaning *she*), **essi** and **esse** (meaning *they*) are used in literary and formal written Italian, so you may well come across them. However, they are not generally used in speaking.

1 When to use subject pronouns in Italian

➤ In English we nearly always put a subject pronoun in front of a verb: *I know Paul*; *they're nice*. Without the pronouns it would not be clear who or what is the subject of the verb.

➤ In Italian the verb ending usually makes it clear who the subject is, so generally no pronoun is necessary.

Conosco Paul.	I know Paul.
Conosci Paul?	Do you know Paul?
Conosciamo Paul.	We know Paul.
Cosa sono? – Sono noci.	What are they? – They're walnuts.

⇨ *For more information on **Verbs**, see page 66.*

➤ You do <u>not</u> use a subject pronoun in Italian to translate *it* at the beginning of a sentence.

Fa caldo.	It's hot.
Sono le tre.	It's three o'clock.
Che cos'è? – È una sorpresa.	What is it? – It's a surprise.

➤ When you do use subject pronouns, it is for one of the following special reasons:

● for emphasis

Tu cosa dici?	What do you think?
Pago io.	I'll pay.
Ci pensiamo noi.	We'll see to it.

[*i*] The subject pronoun can come after the verb:

- for contrast or clarity

Io ci vado, **tu** fai come vuoi.	I'm going, you do what you like.
Aprilo **tu**, **io** non ci riesco.	You open it, I can't.

- after **anche** (meaning *too*) and **neanche** (meaning *neither*)

Vengo anch'**io**.	I'm coming too.
Prendi un gelato anche **tu**?	Are you going to have an ice cream too?
Non so perché. – Neanch'**io**.	I don't know why. – Neither do I.

- when there is no verb in Italian

Chi è il più bravo? – **Lui**.	Who's the best? – He is.
Viene lui, ma **lei** no.	He's coming, but she isn't.

Tip

To say *it's me*, for instance when knocking on someone's door, and to say who someone is, you use the subject pronoun.

Chi è? – Sono **io**.	Who's that? – It's me.
Guarda! È **lui**.	Look, it's him!

---

2 How to say *you* in Italian

➤ In English we have one way of saying *you*. In Italian, the word you choose depends on:

- whether you're talking to one person or more than one
- how well you know the person concerned.

➤ Use **tu** when you are speaking to a person you know well, or to a child. If you are a student you can call another student **tu**. If you have Italian relations, of course you call them **tu**.

➤ Use **Lei** when speaking to strangers, or anyone you're not on familiar terms with. As you get to know someone better they may suggest that you call each other **tu** instead of **Lei**.

➤ Use **voi** when you are speaking to more than one person, whether you know them well or not.

➤ **tu**, **Lei** and **voi** are subject pronouns. There are also different forms for *you* when it is not a subject. These are explained in the section of this chapter on object pronouns.

For further explanation of grammatical terms, please see pages viii–xii.

ℹ Note that **Lei**, the polite word for *you*, also means *she*. This is rarely confusing, as the context makes it clear – if someone speaks directly to you using **Lei**, the meaning is obviously *you*.

Key points

✔ You don't generally need to use a subject pronoun in Italian. The verb ending makes it clear who is being referred to.

✔ You use subject pronouns in Italian only for emphasis or for contrast.

✔ There are two different ways of saying *you* when talking to one person: **tu** for people you know well; **Lei** for people you don't know.

✔ You use **voi** if you are speaking to more than one person.

Object pronouns

1 What are object pronouns?

➤ Object pronouns are words such as *me, him, us* and *them* used instead of a noun to show who is affected by the action of the verb.

> Do you like Claire? – Yes I like her a lot.
> I've lost my purse, have you seen it?
> He gave us a fantastic send-off.
> Why don't you send them a note?

➤ In English we use object pronouns in two different ways:

● when the person or thing is directly affected by the action:
> I saw them yesterday.
> They admire him immensely.

➤ In the above examples, *them* and *him* are called direct objects.

● when the person or thing is indirectly affected by the action. In English you often use *to* with the pronoun in such cases.
> I sent it to them yesterday.
> They awarded him a medal.

➤ In the above examples, *them* and *him* are called indirect objects.

➤ For both direct and indirect objects there is one form you use on most occasions. This is called the unstressed form.

2 Unstressed direct object pronouns

➤ Here are the Italian unstressed object pronouns:

mi	me
ti	you (familiar singular)
lo	him, it
la	her, you (polite singular), it
ci	us
vi	you (plural)
li	them (masculine)
le	them (feminine)

➤ Unlike English, you usually put them before the verb.

Ti amo.	I love you.
Lo invito alla festa.	I'm inviting him to the party.
Non lo mangio.	I'm not going to eat it.

For further explanation of grammatical terms, please see pages viii–xii.

<u>La</u> guardava.	He was looking at her.
<u>Vi</u> cercavo.	I was looking for you.
<u>Li</u> conosciamo.	We know them.

⇨ *For more information on* **Where to place pronouns**, *see page 49.*

> ## Tip
>
> Remember that you use **ti** only when speaking to someone you know well.

3 Lo, la, li and le

➤ You need to pay particular attention to how **lo**, **la**, **li** and **le** are used in Italian.

➤ To translate *it* you need to choose between **lo** or **la**. Use **lo** if the noun referred to is masculine, and **la** if it's feminine.

Ho <u>un</u> panino, <u>lo</u> vuoi?	I've got a roll, do you want it?
Ho <u>una</u> mela, <u>la</u> vuoi?	I've got an apple, do you want it?

➤ To translate *them* you choose between **li** or **le**. Use **li** if the noun referred to is masculine, and **le** if it's feminine.

Sto cercando <u>i biglietti</u>. **<u>Li</u> hai visti?**	I'm looking for the tickets, have you seen them?
Dove sono <u>le caramelle</u>? **<u>Le</u> hai mangiate?**	Where are the sweets? Have you eaten them?

➤ When **lo** and **la** are followed by **ho**, **hai**, **ha**, **abbiamo**, **avete** and **hanno**, they drop the vowel and are spelled **l'**.

Non <u>l'</u>ho visto ieri.	I didn't see it yesterday.
<u>L'</u>abbiamo portato con noi.	We took it with us.
<u>L'</u>hanno cercato tutta la giornata.	They looked for it all day.

Grammar Extra!

When you are talking about the past and using the pronouns **lo**, **la**, **li** and **le** you must make the past participle agree with the noun being referred to. Past participles are just like adjectives ending in **−o**. You change the **−o** to **−a** for the feminine singular, to **−i** for the masculine plural, and to **−e** for the feminine plural.

Il suo **ultimo** film? L'ho vist<u>o</u>.	His new film? I've seen it.
Silvia? L'ho incontrat<u>a</u> ieri.	Silvia? I met her yesterday.
I biglietti? Li ho già pres<u>i</u>.	The tickets? I've already got them.
Queste scarpe? Le ho comprat<u>e</u> anni fa.	These shoes? I bought them years ago.

⇨ *For more information on the* **Perfect tense**, *see page 108.*

> **Key points**
> ✔ You generally use the unstressed direct object pronoun.
> ✔ Unstressed direct object pronouns usually come before the verb.
> ✔ You need to pay special attention when translating *it* and *them*.

4 Unstressed indirect object pronouns

➤ In English some verbs have to be followed by an indirect object pronoun – *explain to him, write to him* – but other similar verbs do not: you say *tell him, phone him*.

➤ In Italian you have to use indirect object pronouns with verbs such as **dire** (meaning *to tell*) and **telefonare** (meaning *to phone*).

➤ As with direct object pronouns, there are <u>unstressed</u> and <u>stressed</u> indirect object pronouns.

➤ You will generally need to use <u>unstressed</u> pronouns rather than stressed ones.

➤ Here are the unstressed indirect pronouns.

mi	to me, me
ti	to you, you (familiar singular)
gli	to him, him
le	to her, her; to you, you (polite singular)
ci	to us, us
vi	to you, you (plural)
gli, loro	to them, them

➤ Unlike English, you usually put these pronouns <u>before</u> the verb.

➤ Just as in English, when you are telling somebody something, giving somebody something and so on, you use an indirect pronoun for the person concerned.

> **Le** ho detto la verità.   I told her the truth.
> **Gli** ho dato la cartina.   I gave him the map.

➤ Indirect pronouns are also generally used with verbs to do with communicating with people.

> **Gli** chiederò il permesso.   I'll ask him for permission.
>   (*literally, I'll ask to him*)
> **Gli** ho telefonato.   I phoned him. (*literally, I phoned to him*)
> **Le** scriverò.   I'll write to her.
> **Se li vedi chiedigli** di venire.   If you see them ask them to come.
>   (*literally, ...ask to them...*)

➤ You use indirect object pronouns when you are using verbs such as **piacere**, **importare**, and **interessare** to talk about what people like, care about or are interested in.

<u>Gli</u> piace l'Italia.	He likes Italy.
<u>Le</u> piacciono i gatti.	She likes cats.
Non <u>gli</u> importa il prezzo, sono ricchi.	They don't care about the price, they're rich.
Se <u>gli</u> interessa può venire con me.	If he's interested he can come with me.

Tip

It is worth checking in your dictionary to see if a verb needs a direct or an indirect object. If you look up the verb *to give*, for example, and find the example *to give somebody something*, the **a** in the translation (**dare qualcosa a qualcuno**) shows you that you use an indirect pronoun for the person you give something to.

Gli ho dato il mio numero di telefono.	I gave him my phone number.

Key points

✔ You generally use the unstressed indirect object pronoun.

✔ Unstressed indirect object pronouns are used with many verbs in Italian which do not use them in English such as **chiedere** (meaning *to ask*) and **interessare** (meaning *to interest*).

✔ Unstressed indirect object pronouns usually come before the verb.

---

5 Stressed object pronouns

➤ You use stressed pronouns for special emphasis. They generally go <u>after</u> the verb.

Cercavo proprio <u>voi</u>.	You're just the people I was looking for.
Invitano <u>me</u> e mio fratello.	They're inviting me and my brother.

➤ They are exactly the same as the <u>subject</u> pronouns, except that **me** is used instead of **io** and **te** is used instead of **tu**.

➤ You use the same words for stressed <u>direct</u> and <u>indirect</u> objects. When you use them as indirect objects you put the word **a** (meaning *to*) before them.

DIRECT	
me	me
te	you (*familiar form*)
lui	him
lei/Lei	her, you (*polite singular*)

noi	us
voi	you (*plural*)
loro	them
INDIRECT	
a me	(to) me
a te	(to) you (familiar form)
a lui	(to) him
a lei	(to) her, you (polite singular)
a noi	(to) us
a voi	(to) you (plural)
a loro	(to) them

➤ You use stressed pronouns:

- when you want to emphasize that you mean a particular person and not somebody else, and for contrast:

Amo solo <u>te</u>.	I love only you.
Invito <u>lui</u> alla festa, ma <u>lei</u> no.	I'm inviting him to the party but not her.
Non guardava <u>me</u>, guardava <u>lei</u>.	He wasn't looking at me, he was looking at her.
Ho scritto <u>a lei</u>, <u>a lui</u> no.	I wrote to her, but not to him.
Questo piace <u>a me</u>, ma Luca preferisce l'altro.	I like this one but Luca prefers the other one.

- after a preposition

Vengo con <u>te</u>.	I'll come with you.
Sono arrivati dopo di <u>noi</u>.	They arrived after us.

➡ *For more information about **Prepositions**, see page 172.*

- after **di** when you're comparing one person with another

Sei più alto di <u>me</u>.	You're taller than me.
Sono più ricchi di <u>lui</u>.	They're richer than him.

Key points

✔ Stressed object pronouns are nearly all the same as subject pronouns.

✔ You use them for emphasis, after prepositions and in comparisons.

✔ You generally put stressed object pronouns after the verb.

✔ You use the same words for direct and indirect objects, but add **a** before them for indirect objects.

For further explanation of grammatical terms, please see pages viii–xii.

6 | Before or after the verb?

➤ Unstressed pronouns generally come <u>before</u> the verb.

Mi aiuti?	Could you help me?
Ti piace?	Do you like it?
Ci hanno visto.	They saw us.
Vi ha salutato?	Did he say hello to you?

➤ In some cases, <u>unstressed</u> pronouns come <u>after</u> the verb:

● when you are using the imperative to tell someone to do something. The pronoun is joined onto the verb.

Aiutami!	Help me!
Lasciala stare.	Leave her alone.
Daglielo.	Give it to him (or her).
Arrivano. Non dirgli niente!	They're coming. Don't tell them anything!

[i] Note that if the verb consists of just one syllable you double the consonant the pronoun starts with, except in the case of **gli**.

Fallo subito!	Do it right away!
Dille la verità!	Tell her the truth!
Dimmi dov'è.	Tell me where it is.
Dacci una mano.	Give us a hand.
Dagli una mano.	Give him a hand.

● when you are using a pronoun with the infinitive (the form of the verb ending in **–re** in Italian). The pronoun is joined onto the verb.

Potresti venire a prendermi?	Could you come and get me?
Non posso aiutarvi.	I can't help you.
Devo farlo?	Do I have to do it?
Dovresti scriverle.	You ought to write to her.
Luigi? Non voglio parlargli.	Luigi? I don't want to talk to him.

[i] Note that the final **e** of the infinitive is dropped: **prendere + mi** becomes **prendermi**, **fare + ti** becomes **farti** and so on.

➤ Stressed pronouns often come after the verb.

Amo solo te.	I love only you.
Invito lui alla festa, ma lei no.	I'm inviting him to the party but not her.

7 Using two pronouns together

➤ In English you sometimes use two pronouns together, one referring to the indirect object and the other to the direct object, for example, *I gave him it*.

➤ You often do the same kind of thing in Italian, and must always put the indirect object first.

➤ When you use two pronouns together like this, some of them change:

> **mi** becomes **me**
> **ti** becomes **te**
> **ci** becomes **ce**
> **vi** becomes **ve**

Me li dai?	Will you give me it?
È mia, non te la do.	It's mine, I'm not going to give it to you.
Ce l'hanno promesso.	They promised it to us.
Ve lo mando domani.	I'll send it to you tomorrow.

➤ When you want to use **gli** (meaning *to him* or *to them*) and **le** (meaning *to her*) with **lo**, **la**, **li** or **le**, you add an **−e** to **gli** and join it to **lo**, **la**, and so forth.

> gli/le + lo → glielo
> gli/le + la → gliela
> gli/le + li → glieli
> gli/le + le → gliele

Glieli hai promessi.	You promised them to her.
Gliele ha spedite.	He sent them to them.
Carlo? Glielo dirò domani.	Carlo? I'll tell him tomorrow.

➤ When you use two pronouns together to give an order or when using the infinitive (**−re** form of the verb), they join together and are added on to the verb.

Mi piacciono, ma non vuole comprarmeli.	I like them but he won't buy me them.
Ecco la lettera di Rita, puoi dargliela?	Here's Rita's letter, can you give it to her?
Le chiavi? Dagliele.	The keys? Give them to her.
Non abbiamo i biglietti – può mandarceli?	We haven't got the tickets – can you send us them?

[*i*] Note that the final **e** of the infinitive is dropped: **prendere** + **mi** + **li** becomes **prendermeli**, **mandare** + **ti** + **le** becomes **mandartele** and so on.

Grammar Extra!

In English *you* and *one* are used in general statements and questions such as *You don't do it like that; Can you park here?; One has to be careful.*

Use **si** and the reflexive form of the verb in Italian for these kinds of statements and questions.

Si fa così.	This is how you do it.
Si può nuotare qui?	Can you swim here?
Non si sa mai.	You never know.

➪ *For more information on **Reflexive Verbs**, see page 87.*

52 Pronouns

Possessive pronouns

> **What is a possessive pronoun?**
> In English the **possessive pronouns** are *mine, yours, his, hers, ours* and *theirs*.
> You use them instead of a possessive adjective followed by a noun. For example,
> instead of saying *My bag is the blue one*, you say *Mine's the blue one*.

➤ Here are the Italian possessive pronouns; they are exactly the same as Italian
  possessive adjectives, but with the definite article in front of them.

⇨ *For more information on **Possessive adjectives** and the **Definite article**, see pages 34
  and 11.*

Singular		Plural		Meaning
Masculine	**Feminine**	**Masculine**	**Feminine**	
il mio	la mia	i miei	le mie	mine
il tuo	la tua	i tuoi	le tue	yours (*familiar*)
il suo	la sua	i suoi	le sue	his, hers, yours (*polite*)
il nostro	la nostra	i nostri	le nostre	ours
il vostro	la vostra	i vostri	le vostre	yours
il loro	la loro	i loro	le loro	theirs

Tip

There are three ways of saying *yours*, because there are three words for
you – **tu**, **lei** and **voi**.

a bit of consistency!

Questa borsa non è <u>la mia</u>, è <u>la tua</u>.	This bag's not mine, it's yours.
Non è <u>il mio</u>, è <u>il suo</u>, signore.	It's not mine, it's yours, sir.
La nostra casa è piccola, la vostra è grande.	Our house is small, yours is big.
I miei genitori e i suoi si conoscono.	My parents and hers know each other.

ⓘ Note that **i miei**, **i tuoi** and **i suoi** are used to refer to someone's parents.

Vivo con <u>i miei</u>.	I live with my parents.
Cosa hanno detto <u>i tuoi</u>?	What did your parents say?
Lucia è venuta con <u>i suoi</u>.	Lucia came with her parents.

➤ In Italian, possessive pronouns agree with the noun they're used instead of.
  For example **il mio** can only be used to refer to a masculine singular noun.

Key points

✔ Italian possessive pronouns are the same as Italian possessive adjectives.

✔ They are masculine or feminine, singular or plural, depending on what they refer to.

ne and ci

➤ **ne** and **ci** are two extremely useful pronouns which have no single equivalent in English. There are some phrases where you have to use them in Italian.

1 ne

ne is a pronoun with several meanings.

➤ It can refer to amounts and quantities.

- It means *some*, and can be used without a noun, just like English.

Ne vuoi?	Would you like some?
Vuoi del pane? – Ne ho grazie.	Would you like some bread? – I've got some, thanks.

➤ In English, when talking about amounts and quantities, you can say *How much do you want of it?*, or *How much do you want?* and *How many do you want of them?*, or *How many do you want?* **Ne** translates *of it* and *of them* but it is not optional. So you need to remember to use it in sentences of the kind shown below.

Ne ho preso la metà.	I've taken half (of it).
Ne vuoi la metà?	Do you want half (of it/of them)?
Quanti ne vuole?	How many (of them) do you want?
Ne voglio pochi.	I don't want many (of them).

➤ **Ne** also means *about it/them*, *of it/them*, *with it/them*, and so on, when used with Italian adjectives or verbs which are followed by **di**, for example **contento di** (meaning *happy about*), **stufo di** (meaning *fed up with*), **aver paura di** (meaning *to be afraid of*), **scrivere di** (meaning *to write about*).

Ne è molto contenta.	She's very happy about it.
Ne sono conscio.	I'm aware of it.
Ne erano stufi.	They were fed up with it.
Ne sei sicura?	Are you sure (of it)?
Ne hai paura?	Are you afraid of it?
Ne ha scritto sul giornale.	She's written about it in the paper.
Non se ne accorge.	He doesn't realize it.

➤ With adjectives and verbs followed by **di**, **ne** can be used to refer to nouns that have already been mentioned.

Parliamo del futuro. – **Sì, parliamone.**	Let's talk about the future. – Yes, let's talk about it.
Hai bisogno della chiave? – **No, non ne ho più bisogno.**	Do you need the key? – No, I don't need it any more.

⇨ For more information on *di*, see **Prepositions** page 174.

➤ **Ne** usually comes <u>before</u> the verb, except when the verb is an order or the infinitive (the **–re** form of the verb).

➤ When it comes after the verb the final **–e** of the infinitive is dropped.

Volevo parlarne.	I wanted to talk about it.

➤ It follows any other pronoun and is written as one word with it and the verb form.

Dammene uno per favore.	Give me one of them please.
Dagliene due rossi.	Give him two red ones.

[*i*] Note that when joined to **ne**, **mi** becomes **me**, **ti** becomes **te**, **ci** becomes **ce**, **vi** become **ve** and **gli** and **le** become **glie**.

Key points

✔ **ne** can be used to mean *some*.

✔ **ne** can also be used to mean *of it* or *of them* when talking about amounts and quantities. Unlike English, it is not optional.

✔ **ne** is used to mean *about it* or *about them* and so forth with verbs and adjectives followed by **di**.

✔ **ne** usually comes before the verb.

---

2 ci

➤ **Ci** is used with certain verbs to mean *it* or *about it*.

Ripensandoci mi sono pentito.	When I thought it over I was sorry.
Non ci credo per niente.	I don't believe it at all.
Ci penserò.	I'll think about it.
Non ci capisco niente.	I can't understand it at all.
Non so che farci.	I don't know what to do about it.

➤ **Ci** is often used with Italian verbs which are followed by **a**, for example:

- **credere a qualcosa** to believe something, to believe in something

Non ci credo.	I don't believe it.

- **pensare a qualcosa** to think about something

Non voglio nemmeno pensarci.	I don't even want to think about it.

- **far caso a qualcosa** to notice something

Non ci ho fatto caso.	I didn't notice.

[*i*] Note that the equivalent English verb may not be followed by any preposition at all.

➤ With verbs followed by **a**, **ci** can be used to refer to nouns that have already been mentioned.

I fantasmi, non ci credi?	Ghosts – don't you believe in them?
Non pensi mai al futuro? –	Don't you ever think about the
Ci penserò quando sarò più	future? – I'll think about it when
vecchio.	I'm older.

➤ **ci** is used with the verb **entrare** in some common idiomatic phrases.

Cosa c'entra?	What's that got to do with it?
Io non c'entro.	It's nothing to do with me.

➤ Like **ne**, **ci** usually comes <u>before</u> the verb, except when the verb is an order, the infinitive (the **–re** form of the verb) or the –ing form.

Key points

✔ **ci** is used to mean *it* or *about it*.

✔ **ci** is used with verbs which can be followed by the preposition **a**.

✔ **ci** usually comes before the verb.

Indefinite pronouns

> **What is an indefinite pronoun?**
> An **indefinite pronoun** is a word like *everything*, *nobody* and *something* which is used to refer to people or things in a non-specific way.

➤ Some Italian indefinite pronouns always keep the same form:

- **chiunque** anyone

    Attacca discorso con <u>chiunque</u>.   She'll talk to anyone.

- **niente** nothing

    Cosa c'è? – <u>Niente</u>.   What's wrong? – Nothing.

[i] Note that **niente** and **nulla** mean exactly the same, but **niente** is used more often.

- **nulla** nothing

    Che cos'hai comprato? – <u>Nulla</u>.   What did you buy? – Nothing.

- **qualcosa** something, anything

    Ho <u>qualcosa</u> da dirti.   I've got something to tell you.

    Ha bisogno di <u>qualcosa</u>?   Do you need anything?

    Voglio <u>qualcos</u>'altro.   I want something else.

➪ *For more information on **Negatives**, see page 149.*

➤ Other indefinite pronouns are masculine singular words, with a feminine form ending in –**a**:

- **ciascuno, ciascuna** each

    Ne avevamo uno per <u>ciascuno</u>.   We had one each.

    Le torte costano dieci euro <u>ciascuna</u>.   The cakes cost ten euros each.

- **nessuno, nessuna** nobody, anybody; none

    Non è venuto <u>nessuno</u>.   Nobody came.

    Hai visto <u>nessuno</u>?   Did you see anybody?

    <u>Nessuna</u> delle ragazze è venuta.   None of the girls came.

- **ognuno, ognuna** each

    <u>ognuno</u> di voi   each of you

- **qualcuno, qualcuna** somebody; one

    Ha telefonato <u>qualcuno</u>.   Somebody phoned.

    Chiedilo a <u>qualcun</u> altro.   Ask somebody else.

    Conosci <u>qualcuna</u> delle ragazze?   Do you know any of the girls?

- **uno, una** somebody

    Ho incontrato <u>uno</u> che ti conosce.   I met somebody who knows you.

C'è <u>una</u> che ti cerca.	There's somebody (*meaning a woman*) looking for you.

- **alcuni** and **alcune** (meaning *some*) are always used in the plural.

Ci sono posti liberi? – Sì, <u>alcuni</u>.	Are there any empty seats? – Yes, some.
Ci sono ancora delle fragole? – Sì, <u>alcune</u>.	Are there any strawberries left? – Yes, some.

➤ The following pronouns can be singular or plural, masculine or feminine:

- **altro, altra, altri, altre** the other one; another one; other people

L'<u>altro</u> è meno caro.	The other one is cheaper.
Preferisco l'<u>altra</u>.	I prefer the other one.
Non m'interessa quello che dicono gli <u>altri</u>.	I don't care what other people say.
Le <u>altre</u> sono partite.	The others have gone.
Prendine un altro.	Take another one.

[i] Note that **altro** can also mean *anything else*.

Vuole <u>altro</u>?	Do you want anything else?

- **molto, molta, molti, molte** a lot, lots

Ne ha <u>molto</u>.	He's got lots.
<u>molti</u> di noi	a lot of us

- **parecchio, parecchia, parecchi, parecchie** quite a lot

C'è ancora del pane? – Sì, <u>parecchio</u>.	Is there any bread left? – Yes, quite a lot.
Avete avuto problemi? – Sì, <u>parecchi</u>.	Did you have problems? – Yes, a lot.

- **poco, poca, pochi, poche** not much, not many

C'è pane? – <u>Poco</u>.	Is there any bread? – Not much.
Ci sono turisti? – <u>Pochi</u>.	Are there any tourists? – Not many.

- **tanto, tanta, tanti, tante** lots, so much, so many

Hai mangiato? – Sì, <u>tanto</u>!	Have you eaten? – Yes, lots!
Sono <u>tanti</u>!	There are so many of them!

- **troppo, troppa, troppi, troppe** too much, too many

Quanto hai speso? – <u>Troppo</u>!	How much have you spent? – Too much!
Ci sono errori? – Sì, <u>troppi</u>.	Are there any mistakes? – Yes, too many.

- **tutti, tutte** everybody, all

Vengono <u>tutti</u>.	Everybody is coming.
Sono arrivate <u>tutte</u>.	They've all arrived (*they're all women*).

For further explanation of grammatical terms, please see pages viii–xii.

ⓘ Note that in English you can say *Everybody is coming*; *They're all coming*, or *All of them are coming*. All three sentences are translated into Italian in the same way, using **tutti** and a plural verb. **tutti** cannot be followed by **di**, so don't try to translate *all of them* – translate *they all*.

- **tutto** everything, all

Va <u>tutto</u> bene?	Is everything okay?
L'ho finito tutto.	I've finished it all.

Key points

✔ Some indefinite pronouns always have the same form.

✔ Other indefinite pronouns can be masculine or feminine, singular or plural.

Relative pronouns

1 What is a relative pronoun?

➤ In English the relative pronouns are *who, which, that* and *whom*. They are used to specify exactly who or what is being talked about, for example, *The man who has just come in is Anna's boyfriend; The vase that you broke cost a lot of money.*

➤ Relative pronouns can also introduce an extra piece of information, for example, *Peter, who is a brilliant painter, wants to study art; Their house, which was built in 1890, needs a lot of repairs.*

2 che

➤ In English *who, whom* and *that* are used to talk about people and *which* and *that* are used to talk about things. In Italian you use **che** for all of these.

quella signora <u>che</u> ha il piccolo cane nero	that lady who has the little black dog
Mio padre, <u>che</u> ha sessant'anni, va in pensione.	My father, who's sixty, is retiring.
una persona <u>che</u> detesto	a person whom I detest
l'uomo <u>che</u> hanno arrestato	the man that they've arrested
la squadra <u>che</u> ha vinto	the team which *or* that won
il dolce <u>che</u> hai fatto	the pudding you made

➤ In English you can miss out the relative pronoun: *a person I detest; the man they've arrested.* You can <u>never</u> miss out **che**.

the person I admire most → **la persona <u>che</u> ammiro di più**

the money you lent me → **i soldi <u>che</u> mi hai prestato**

➤ Prepositions are sometimes used with relative pronouns: *the man <u>to</u> whom she was talking/the man that she was talking <u>to</u>; the girl who he's going out <u>with</u>.* In English the preposition often goes <u>at the end</u> of the phrase.

➤ In Italian, when you use a preposition with a relative pronoun, use **cui** instead of **che**, and put the preposition in front of it.

la ragazza <u>di cui</u> ti ho parlato	the girl that I told you about
gli amici <u>con cui</u> andiamo in vacanza	the friends who we go on holiday with
la persona <u>a cui</u> si riferiva	the person he was referring to
il quartiere <u>in cui</u> *a*bito	the area in which I live
il film <u>di cui</u> parlavo	the film which I was talking about

Tip

In English *who* is used both as a question word, and as a relative pronoun. In Italian: **chi** is used in questions, and **che** is used as a relative pronoun:

Chi va al concerto?	Who's going to the concert?
la ragazza <u>che</u> hai visto	the girl (that) you saw

➤ In English you often use *which* to refer to a fact or situation that you've just mentioned. In Italian use **il che**.

Loro non pagano nulla, <u>il che</u> non mi sembra giusto.	They don't pay anything, which doesn't seem fair to me.
Dice che non è colpa sua, <u>il che</u> è vero.	She says it's not her fault, which is true.

Grammar Extra!

You may come across **il quale** used to mean *who, which, that* and *whom*. **il quale** is more formal than **che**. **il quale** has feminine and plural forms: **la quale**, **i quali** and **le quali**.

suo padre, <u>il quale</u> è avvocato	his father, who is a lawyer
le sue sorelle, <u>le quali</u> studiano a Roma	his sisters, who study in Rome

il quale, **la quale**, **i quali** and **le quali** are used most often with prepositions.

l'albergo <u>al quale</u> ci siamo fermati	the hotel that we stayed at
la signora <u>con la quale</u> parlavi	the lady you were talking to
gli amici <u>ai quali</u> mando questa cartolina	the friends I'm sending this card to
la medicina <u>della quale</u> hanno bisogno	the medicine they need

➪ For more information about **Prepositions**, see page 172.

---

3 quello che

➤ In English you can put *the one* or *the ones* in front of a relative pronoun such as *who, which, that* and *whom*. For example, *That's the one that I'd like; They're the ones we need.*

➤ To say *the one* in Italian use **quello** to refer to masculine nouns or **quella** to refer to feminine nouns. The relative pronoun is **che**.

È <u>quello</u> che non funziona.	That's the one which isn't working.
È <u>quello</u> che preferisco.	That's the one I prefer.
È <u>quella</u> che parla di più.	She's the one who talks most.

➤ To say *the ones* in Italian use **quelli** for masculine nouns or **quelle** for feminine nouns. The relative pronoun is **che**.

Sono <u>quelli</u> che sono partiti senza pagare.	They're the ones who left without paying.
Queste scarpe sono <u>quelle</u> che ha ordinato.	These shoes are the ones you ordered.

➤ With a preposition use **cui** instead of **che**. Put the preposition in front of **cui**.

È quello a <u>cui</u> parlavo.	He's the one I was talking to.
Sono quelli a <u>cui</u> ti riferivi?	Are they the ones to whom you were referring?
Sono quelli di <u>cui</u> abbiamo bisogno.	They're the ones we need.

i Note that in English the relative pronoun can be left out, for example, *That's the one I want* instead of *That's the one that I want*. In Italian the relative pronoun **che** can <u>never</u> be left out.

Key points

✔ **che** can refer to both people and things in Italian.

✔ The relative pronouns *who*, *which* and *that* can be left out in English, but **che** must always be used.

✔ Use **cui** instead of **che** after a preposition.

✔ **quello**, **quella**, **quelli** and **quelle** are used to say *the one* or *the ones*. They are used with **che**.

Interrogative pronouns

> **What is an interrogative pronoun?**
> In English the **interrogative pronouns** are who...?, which...?, whose...?, whom...? and what...?. They are used without a noun, to ask questions.

1 The interrogative pronouns in Italian

➤ These are the interrogative pronouns in Italian:

Chi?	Who? Whom?
Che?	What?
Cosa?	What?
Che cosa?	What?
Quale?	Which? Which one? What?
Quanto?	How much?
Quanti?	How many?

➤ **Chi**, **che**, **cosa**, and **che cosa** never change their form.

<u>Chi</u> è?	Who is it?
<u>Chi</u> sono?	Who are they?
<u>Che</u> vuoi?	What do you want?
<u>Cosa</u> vuole?	What does he want?
<u>Che cosa</u> vogliono?	What do they want?

[𝑖] Note that there is no difference between **che**, **cosa** and **che cosa**.

➤ **Quale** is used for the masculine and feminine singular, and **quali** is used for masculine and feminine plural.

Conosco sua sorella. – <u>Quale</u>?	I know his sister. – Which one?
Ho rotto dei bicchieri. – <u>Quali</u>?	I broke some glasses. – Which ones?

⇨ *For more information on **Question words**, see page 155.*

➤ **Quanto** and **quanti** have feminine forms.

Farina? Quant<u>a</u> ce ne vuole?	Flour? How much is needed?
Quant<u>e</u> di loro passano la sera a leggere?	How many of them spend the evening reading?

2 che cos'è or qual è?

➤ **che cos'è?** and **qual è?** both mean *what is?* but are used in different ways:

- Use **che cos'è?** or **che cosa sono?** when you're asking someone to explain or identify something.

Che cos'è questo?	What's this?
Che cosa sono questi? –	What are these? –
Sono funghi.	They're mushrooms.

- Use **qual è?** or **quali sono?**, not **che**, when you ask *what is?*, or *what are?* to find out a particular detail, number, name, and so on.

Qual è il suo indirizzo?	What's her address?
Qual è la capitale della Finlandia?	What's the capital of Finland?
Quali sono i loro indirizzi?	What are their addresses?

[*i*] Note that **quale** becomes **qual** in front of a vowel.

3 chi?

➤ Use **chi** for both *who* and *whom*.

Chi ha vinto?	Who won?
Chi hai visto?	Whom did you see?

➤ When there is a preposition in your question put it in front of **chi**.

A chi l'hai dato?	Who did you give it to?
Con chi parlavi?	Who were you talking to?
A chi si riferiva?	To whom was he referring?

➤ Use **di chi è?** or **di chi sono?** to ask who things belong to.

Di chi è questa borsa?	Whose is this bag?
Di chi sono queste chiavi?	Whose are these keys?

Key points

✔ **chi**, **che cosa**, **quale** and **quanto** are the interrogative pronouns in Italian.

✔ Use **chi** for both *who* and *whom*.

Demonstrative pronouns

> **What is a demonstrative pronoun?**
> In English the **demonstrative pronouns** are *this*, *that*, *these* and *those*. They are used instead of a noun to point out people or things, for example, *That's my brother*.

1 Using demonstrative pronouns

➤ These are the demonstrative pronouns in Italian:

	Masculine	Feminine	Meaning
Singular	questo quello	questa quella	this, this one that, that one
Plural	questi quelli	queste quelle	these, these ones those, those ones

➤ The demonstrative pronoun <u>must</u> agree with the noun it is replacing.

<u>Questo</u> è mio marito.	This is my husband.
<u>Questa</u> è camera mia.	This is my bedroom.
<u>Questi</u> sono i miei fratelli.	These are my brothers.
Quali scarpe ti metti? – <u>Queste</u>.	Which shoes are you going to wear? – These ones.
Qual è la sua borsa? – <u>Quella</u>.	Which bag is yours? – That one.
<u>Quelli</u> quanto costano?	How much do those cost?

ⓘ Note that **quello** and **quella** can also be used to mean *that man* and *that woman*.

Dice sempre bugie <u>quello</u>.	That man is always telling lies.
Conosci <u>quella</u>?	Do you know that woman?

⇨ *For more information on **Demonstrative adjectives**, see page 30.*

Key points

✔ The demonstrative pronouns in Italian are **questo** and **quello**.

✔ **Questo** and **quello** have masculine, feminine, singular and plural forms.

✔ They agree with the nouns they replace.

Verbs

> **What is a verb?**
> A **verb** is a word which describes what somebody or something does, what they are, or what happens to them, for example, *play, be, disappear*.

Overview of verbs

➤ Verbs are frequently used with a noun or with somebody's name, for example <u>Children</u> *like stories*; <u>Jason's</u> *playing football*. In English, pronouns such as *I, you* and *she* often come in front of verbs, for example, <u>She</u> *knows my sister*.

➤ Verbs can relate to the present, the past or the future; this is called their <u>tense</u>.

▷ *For more information on* **Nouns** *and* **Pronouns**, *see pages 1 and 40.*

➤ Verbs are either:

• <u>regular</u>: their forms follow the normal rules

OR

• <u>irregular</u>: their forms do not follow the normal rules

➤ Almost all verbs have a form called the <u>infinitive</u> that isn't present, past or future, (for example, *walk, see, hear*). It is used after other verbs, for example, *You should <u>walk</u>; You can <u>see</u>; Kirsty wants <u>to come</u>.* In English, the infinitive is usually shown with the word *to*, for example, *to speak, to eat, to live.*

➤ In Italian the infinitive is always just one word that in most cases ends in either **–are**, **–ere** or **–ire**: for example, **parlare** (meaning *to speak*), **credere** (meaning *to believe*) and **dormire** (meaning *to sleep*).

➤ Regular English verbs can add three endings to the infinitive: *–s* (*walks*), *–ing* (*walking*) and *–ed* (*walked*).

➤ Italian verbs add endings to the verb <u>stem</u>, which is what is left of the verb when you take away the **–are**, **–ere** or **–ire** ending of the infinitive. This means the stem of **parlare** is **parl-**, the stem of **credere** is **cred-**, and the stem of **dormire** is **dorm-**.

➤ Italian verb endings change according to who or what is doing the action. The person or thing that does the action is called the <u>subject</u> of the verb.

➤ In English you nearly always put a noun or a pronoun in front of a verb to show who is doing the action, for example <u>Jack</u> *speaks Italian*; <u>She</u>'s *playing tennis*.

Verbs 67

➤ In Italian, <u>nouns</u> are used as the subject of verbs just as they are in English, but <u>pronouns</u> are used much less often. This is because the ending of an Italian verb often shows you who the subject is.

<u>Mia sorella</u> gioca a tennis.	My sister is playing tennis.
<u>Gioca</u> bene.	She plays well.

⇨ *For more information on **Subject pronouns**, see page 41.*

➤ Italian verb forms also change depending on whether you are talking about the present, past or future: **credo** means *I believe*, **credevo** means *I believed* and **crederò** means *I will believe*.

➤ In English some verbs are <u>irregular</u>, for example, you do not add –ed to *speak*, *go*, or *see* to make the past tense. In the same way, some Italian verbs do not follow the usual patterns. These irregular Italian verbs include some very important and common verbs such as **andare** (meaning *to go*), **essere** (meaning *to be*) and **fare** (meaning *to do* or *to make*).

⇨ *For **Verb tables**, see middle section.*

Key points

✔ Italian verbs have different endings depending on their subject and their tense.

✔ Endings are added to the verb stem.

✔ You often do not need to use a pronoun before a verb in Italian.

The present tenses

> **What are the present tenses?**
> The present tenses are the verb forms that are used to talk about what is true at the moment, what generally happens and what is happening now; for example, *I'm a student; I travel to college by train; The phone's ringing*.

➤ In English there are two tenses you can use to talk about the present:

- the <u>present simple</u> tense
  I <u>live</u> here.
  They always <u>get up</u> early.

- the <u>present continuous</u> tense
  He <u>is eating</u> an apple.
  You <u>aren't</u> <u>listening</u>.

➤ In Italian there is also a <u>present simple</u> and a <u>present continuous</u> tense.

➤ As in English, the <u>present simple</u> tense in Italian is used to talk about:

- things that are generally true
  D'inverno <u>fa</u> freddo.   It'<u>s</u> cold in winter.

- what people and things usually do
  Giulia non <u>mangia</u> la carne.   Giulia <u>doesn't</u> eat meat.
  Queste macchine <u>consumano</u>   These cars <u>use</u> a lot of petrol.
  molta benzina.
  <u>Andiamo</u> spesso al cinema.   We often <u>go</u> to the cinema.

➤ Unlike in English, the <u>present simple</u> tense in Italian can be used to talk about:

- what is happening right now
  Piove.   It'<u>s</u> <u>raining</u>.
  Cosa <u>fai</u>?   What <u>are</u> you <u>doing</u>?

➤ In Italian the <u>present continuous</u> is also used to talk about things that are happening right now.
  Ci <u>sto pensando</u>.   <u>I'm thinking</u> about it.

⇨ *For more information on the use of the **Present tenses**, see pages 69 and 81.*

Tip

You can use the Italian present simple to translate both the English simple present and the English present continuous.

Piove.   It's raining.
Piove molto.   It rains a lot.

⇨ *For more information on **How to use the present simple tense**, see page 77.*

For further explanation of grammatical terms, please see pages viii–xii.

The present simple tense

1 How to make the present simple tense of regular –are verbs

➤ Verbs that have an infinitive ending in **–are**, such as **parlare**, **abitare** and **studiare** have a particular pattern of endings.

➤ To make the present simple tense of regular **–are** verbs take off the **–are** ending to get the <u>stem</u> of the verb.

Infinitive	Meaning	Stem (without –are)
parlare	*to speak*	parl-
abitare	*to live*	abit-
studiare	*to study*	studi-

➤ Then add the correct ending for the person you're talking about.

➤ Here are the present simple endings for regular **–are** verbs:

Present simple endings	Present simple of parlare	Meaning: *to speak*
–o	(io) parl<u>o</u>	I speak/am speaking
–i	(tu) parl<u>i</u>	you speak/are speaking
–a	(lui/lei) parl<u>a</u> (Lei) parl<u>a</u>	he/she/it speaks/is speaking you speak/are speaking
–iamo	(noi) parl<u>iamo</u>	we speak/are speaking
–ate	(voi) parl<u>ate</u>	you speak/are speaking
–ano	(loro) parl<u>ano</u>	they speak/are speaking

Parli inglese?	Do you speak English?
Chi parla?	Who's speaking?
Parlano bene italiano.	They speak good Italian.

Tip

When you are talking about a male, a female or a thing, or are using **lei** as the polite word for *you*, you use the same verb form.

➪ *For more information on **Ways of saying 'you' in Italian**, see page 42.*

---

see page 42.

i Note that in Italian there's often no need to use a subject pronoun such as **io** (meaning *I*) or **tu** (meaning *you*) because the verb ending makes it clear who is doing the action. However, when you're talking about people you can use the pronouns **lui**, **lei** or **loro** with the verb for the sake of emphasis or to make things clearer.

Parla italiano <u>lui</u>?	Does he speak Italian?
<u>Lei</u> parla bene inglese, ma lui no.	She speaks good English, but he doesn't.
<u>Loro</u> non parlano mai.	They never speak.

When you're talking about things you <u>ALWAYS</u> use the verb by itself, with no pronoun.

Vedi l'*autobus*? – Sì, <u>arriva</u>.	Can you see the bus? – Yes, it's coming.
Vuole queste? – No, <u>costano</u> troppo.	Do you want these? – No, they cost too much.

⇨ *For more information on **Subject pronouns**, see page 41.*

Key points

✔ If you take the **–are** ending off the infinitive of a regular verb you get the stem.

✔ You add one of these endings to the stem: **–o**, **–i**, **–a**, **–iamo**, **–ate** or **–ano**.

✔ You only use a pronoun with the verb for emphasis or to be specially clear, but only when talking about people.

---

2 How to make the present simple tense of regular –ere verbs

➤ Verbs that have an infinitive ending in **–ere**, such as **credere**, **ricevere** and **ripetere** have their own pattern of endings.

➤ To make the present simple tense of regular **–ere** verbs take off the **–ere** ending to get the <u>stem</u> and then add the correct ending for the person you're talking about.

Infinitive	Meaning	Stem (without –ere)
credere	*to believe*	**cred-**
ricevere	*to receive*	**ricev-**
ripetere	*to repeat*	**ripet-**

➤ The **io**, **tu** and **noi** endings you add to the stem of **–ere** verbs are the same as **–are** verb endings. The other endings are different.

➤ Here are the present simple endings for regular **–ere** verbs:

Present simple endings	Present simple of credere	Meaning: *to believe*
–o	(io) cred**o**	I believe
–i	(tu) cred**i**	you believe
–e	(lui/lei) cred**e**	he/she believes
	(Lei) cred**e**	you believe
–iamo	(noi) cred**iamo**	we believe
–ete	(voi) cred**ete**	you believe
–ono	(loro) cred**ono**	they believe

Non ci credo.	I don't believe it.
Credi ai fantasmi?	Do you believe in ghosts?
Lo credono tutti.	They all believe it.

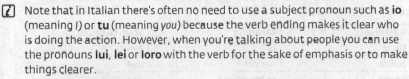

Tip

When you are talking about a male, a female or a thing, or are using **Lei** as the polite word for *you*, you use the same verb form.

ℹ️ Note that in Italian there's often no need to use a subject pronoun such as **io** (meaning *I*) or **tu** (meaning *you*) because the verb ending makes it clear who is doing the action. However, when you're talking about people you can use the pronouns **lui**, **lei** or **loro** with the verb for the sake of emphasis or to make things clearer.

Lui non ci crede.	He doesn't believe it.
Lei crede ai fantasmi, io no.	She believes in ghosts, I don't.
Loro lo credono tutti.	They all believe it.

When you're talking about things you <u>ALWAYS</u> use the verb by itself, with no pronoun.

La minestra? Non sa di nulla.	The soup? It doesn't taste of anything.
Le piante? Crescono bene.	The plants? They're growing well.

⇨ *For more information on **Subject pronouns**, see page 41.*

> **Tip**
>
> Remember that you never use a pronoun in Italian to translate *it* at the beginning of a sentence.
>
> | | |
> |---|---|
> | **Dipende.** | It depends. |
> | **Piove.** | It's raining. |

> **Key points**
>
> ✔ If you take the **–ere** ending off the infinitive of a regular verb you get the stem.
>
> ✔ You add one of these endings to the stem: **–o, –i, –e, –iamo, –ete** or **–ono**.
>
> ✔ You only use a pronoun with the verb for emphasis or to be specially clear, but only when talking about people.

3 How to make the present simple tense of regular –ire verbs

➤ Most verbs that have an infinitive ending in **–ire**, such as **finire** (meaning *to finish*), **pulire** (meaning *to clean*) and **capire** (meaning *to understand*) follow one pattern of endings in the present. Some common verbs such as **dormire** and **servire** have a different pattern.

➤ To make the present simple tense of <u>all</u> **–ire** verbs take off the **–ire** ending to get the <u>stem</u> of the verb.

Infinitive	Meaning	Stem (without –ire)
finire	*to finish*	**fin-**
pulire	*to clean*	**pul-**
capire	*to understand*	**cap-**
dormire	*to sleep*	**dorm-**
servire	*to serve*	**serv-**

➤ Here are the present simple endings for regular **–ire** verbs:

Present simple endings	Present simple of finire	Meaning: *to finish*
–isco	(io) fin**isco**	I finish/am finishing
–isci	(tu) fin**isci**	you finish/are finishing
–isce	(lui/lei) fin**isce** (Lei) fin**isce**	he/she/it finishes/ is finishing you finish/are finishing
–iamo	(noi) fin**iamo**	we finish/are finishing
–ite	(voi) fin**ite**	you finish/are finishing
–iscono	(loro) fin**iscono**	they finish/are finishing

Il film fin**isce** alle dieci.	The film finishes at ten.
Fin**iscono** il lavoro.	They're finishing the work.
Non pul**isco** mai la macchina.	I never clean the car.
Prefer**isci** l'altro?	Do you prefer the other one?
Non cap**iscono**.	They don't understand.

(i) Note that in Italian there's often no need to use a subject pronoun such as **io** (meaning *I*) or **tu** (meaning *you*) because the verb ending makes it clear who is doing the action. However, when you're talking about people you can use the pronouns **lui**, **lei** or **loro** with the verb for the sake of emphasis or to make things clearer.

Lui non pulisce mai la macchina.	He never cleans the car.
Lei mi capisce sempre.	She always understands me.
Loro preferiscono l'altro.	They prefer the other one.

When you're talking about things you <u>ALWAYS</u> use the verb by itself, with no pronoun.

Il primo treno? – <u>Parte</u> alle cinque.	The first train? It goes at five.
Le lezioni quando fin**iscono**? –	When do lessons finish?
Fin**iscono** alle quattro.	They finish at four.

➤ Some common –**ire** verbs do not add –**isc**– to the stem. The most important ones are **dormire** (meaning *to sleep*), **servire** (meaning *to serve*), **aprire** (meaning *to open*), **partire** (meaning *to leave*), **sentire** (meaning *to hear*) and **soffrire** (meaning *to suffer*).

➤ The endings of these verbs are as follows:

Present simple endings	Present simple of dormire	Meaning: *to sleep*
–o	(io) dorm**o**	I sleep/am sleeping
–i	(tu) dorm**i**	you sleep/are sleeping
–e	(lui/lei) dorm**e** (Lei) dorm**e**	he/she/it sleeps/is sleeping you sleep/are sleeping
–iamo	(noi) dorm**iamo**	we sleep/are sleeping
–ite	(voi) dorm**ite**	you sleep/are sleeping
–ono	(loro) dorm**ono**	they sleep/are sleeping

(i) Note that these endings are the same as –**ere** verb endings, except for the second person plural (**voi**).

Dorm**o** sempre bene.	I always sleep well.
A che cosa serv**e**?	What's it for?
Quando part**ite**?	When are you leaving?
Soffr**ono** molto.	They are suffering a lot.

> ### Tip
>
> When you are talking about a male, a female or a thing, or are using **Lei** as the polite word for *you*, you use the same verb form.

Key points

✔ Take the **–ire** ending off the infinitive of a regular verb to get the stem.

✔ For most **–ire** verbs the endings you add to the stem are: **–isco**, **–isci**, **–isce**, **–iamo**, **–ite** or **–iscono**.

✔ A few common **–ire** verbs add these endings to the stem: **–o**, **–i**, **–e**, **–iamo**, **–ite**, **–ono**.

✔ You only use a pronoun with the verb for emphasis or to be specially clear, but only when talking about people.

4 | Infinitives that end in –rre

➤ All regular verbs have infinitives ending in **–are**, **-ere**, or **–ire**.

➤ A few common irregular verbs have infinitives ending in **–rre**. For example:

comporre	to compose	**condurre**	to lead
porre	to put	**produrre**	to produce
proporre	to propose	**ridurre**	to reduce
supporre	to suppose	**tradurre**	to translate

➤ Here are the present simple forms of **comporre**

	Present simple of comporre	Meaning: *to compose*
(io)	compongo	I compose/I am composing
(tu)	componi	you compose/you are composing
(lui/lei) (Lei)	compone	he/she/it composes/is composing you compose/are composing
(noi)	componiamo	we compose/are composing
(voi)	componete	you compose/are composing
(loro)	compongono	they compose/are composing

➤ Here are the present simple forms of **produrre**:

	Present simple of produrre	Meaning: *to produce*
(io)	produco	I produce/I am producing
(tu)	produci	you produce/you are producing
(lui/lei) (Lei)	produce	he/she/it produces/is producing you produce/are producing
(noi)	produciamo	we produce/are producing
(voi)	producete	you produce/are producing
(loro)	producono	they produce/are producing

The present tense of all verbs ending in **–porre** follow the pattern of **comporre**, and all verbs ending in **–durre** follow the pattern of **produrre**.

5 | Where to put the stress when saying the infinitive

➤ When you say the infinitives of **–are** and **–ire** verbs the stress goes on the **a**, or **i** of the ending:

Non vuole parl<u>a</u>re.	He doesn't want to speak.
Non riesco a dorm<u>i</u>re.	I can't sleep.

➤ When you say the infinitive of most **–ere** verbs the stress goes on the syllable that comes <u>before</u> the ending.

D<u>e</u>vono v<u>e</u>ndere la casa.	They've got to sell their house.
Può rip<u>e</u>tere?	Could you repeat that?

➤ However, there are a number of very important irregular **–ere** verbs which have the stress on the first **e** of the ending.

–ere verb	Meaning
av<u>e</u>re	to have
cad<u>e</u>re	to fall
dov<u>e</u>re	to have to
persuad<u>e</u>re	to persuade
pot<u>e</u>re	to be able
riman<u>e</u>re	to remain
ved<u>e</u>re	to see

Fa' attenzione a non cad<u>e</u>re.	Mind you don't fall.
Non puoi av<u>e</u>re il mio.	You can't have mine.

➡ *For more information on the **Infinitive**, see page 138.*

6 | How to make the present simple tense of common irregular verbs

➤ There are many verbs that do not follow the usual patterns. These include some very common and important verbs such as **avere** (meaning *to have*), **fare** (meaning *to do* or *to make*) and **andare** (meaning *to go*).

➤ Here are the present simple forms of **avere**:

	Present simple of avere	Meaning: *to have*
(io)	ho	I have/have got
(tu)	hai	you have
(lui/lei) (Lei)	ha	he/she/it has you have
(noi)	abbiamo	we have
(voi)	avete	you have
(loro)	hanno	they have

Ho due sorelle.	I've got two sisters.
Hai abbastanza soldi?	Have you got enough money?
Abbiamo tempo.	We've got time.
Hanno i capelli biondi.	They have blonde hair.

➤ Here are the present simple forms of **fare**:

	Present simple of fare	Meaning: *to do, to make*
(io)	faccio	I do/am doing, I make/am making
(tu)	fai	you do/are doing, you make/are making
(lui/lei) (Lei)	fa	he/she/it does/is doing, he/she/it makes/is making you do/are doing, you make/are making
(noi)	facciamo	we do/are doing, we make/are making
(voi)	fate	you do/are doing, you make/are making
(loro)	fanno	they do/are doing, they make/are making

Faccio troppi errori.	I make too many mistakes.
Cosa fai stasera?	What are you doing this evening?
Fa caldo.	It's hot.
Fanno quello che possono.	They're doing what they can.

For further explanation of grammatical terms, please see pages viii–xii.

➤ Here are the present simple forms of **andare**:

	Present simple of andare	Meaning: *to go*
(io)	vado	I go/am going
(tu)	vai	you go/are going
(lui/lei) (Lei)	va	he/she/it goes/is going you go/are going
(noi)	andiamo	we go/are going
(voi)	andate	you go/are going
(loro)	vanno	they go/are going

Ci vado spesso.	I often go there.
Dove vai?	Where are you going?
Va bene.	That's okay.
Vanno tutti al concerto.	They're all going to the concert.

⇨ *For other irregular verbs in the present simple tense, see **Verb tables** in the middle section.*

7 How to use the present simple tense in Italian

➤ The present simple tense is often used in Italian in the same way as in English, but there are also some important differences.

➤ As in English, you use the Italian present simple to talk about:
- things that are generally true

La frutta fa bene.	Fruit is good for you.

- current situations

Vivono in Francia.	They live in France.

- what people and things usually do

Litigano sempre.	They always quarrel.
Si blocca spesso.	It often jams.

- fixed arrangements

Comincia domani.	It starts tomorrow.

➤ Unlike in English, the Italian present simple is used to talk about:
- what is happening right now

Arrivo!	I'm coming!
Non mangi niente.	You're not eating anything.

- what you are going to do

È rotto, lo butto via.	It's broken, I'm going to throw it away.
Ci penso io.	I'll see to it.

- predictions

  Se fai così lo rompi.   If you do that you'll break it.

- offers

  Pago io.   I'll pay.

➤ In English the <u>perfect</u> tense is used to say how long someone has been doing something, or how long something has been happening. In Italian you use **da** and the <u>present simple</u> tense for this kind of sentence.

    Aspetto da tre ore.   I've been waiting for three hours.

    Da quanto tempo <u>studi</u> For How long have you been learning
    l'italiano?   Italian?

➡ *For more information on the use of tenses with **da**, see page 174.*

Key points

✔ The present simple tense in Italian is used as in English, and has a few additional uses.

✔ Use the present simple with **da** to talk about how long something has been going on.

---

essere and stare

> In Italian there are two irregular verbs, **essere** and **stare**, that both mean *to be*.
> In the present tense they follow the patterns shown below:

Pronoun	*essere*	stare	Meaning: *to be*
(io)	sono	sto	I am
(tu)	sei	stai	you are
(lui/lei) (Lei)	è	sta	he/she/it is you are
(noi)	siamo	stiamo	we are
(voi)	siete	state	you are
(loro)	sono	stanno	they are

> **essere** is the verb generally used to translate *to be*:

Cosa sono?	What are they?
È italiana.	She's Italian.
Sono io.	It's me.
È un problema.	It's a problem.
Siete pronti?	Are you ready?

> However, **stare** is used for *to be* in some common contexts:
> - to say or ask how someone is

Come stai?	How are you?
Sto bene, grazie.	I'm fine thanks.
Mio nonno sta male.	My grandfather isn't well.

> - to say where someone is

Luigi sta a casa.	Luigi's at home.
Starò a Roma due giorni.	I'll be in Rome for two days.

> - to say where something is situated

La casa sta sulla collina.	The house is on the hill.

> - with the adjectives **zitto** and **solo**

Vuole stare solo.	He wants to be alone.
Sta' zitto!	Be quiet!

> - to make continuous tenses

Sta studiando.	He's studying.
Stavo andando a casa.	I was going home.

⇨ *For more information on the Present continuous, see page 81.*

Key points

✔ **essere** is generally used to translate *to be*.

✔ **stare** is used to talk about health, where people and things are and with some adjectives.

✔ **stare** is also used to make continuous tenses.

The present continuous tense

➤ In Italian the <u>present continuous</u> is used instead of the <u>present simple</u> to talk about what is happening at the moment, when you want to emphasize that it's happening <u>right now</u>.

| Arrivano. | They are coming. |
| Stanno arrivando! | They're coming! |

➤ The Italian present continuous is made with the present tense of **stare** and the <u>gerund</u> of the verb. The gerund is a verb form that ends in **–ando** (for **–are** verbs), or **–endo** (for **–ere** and **–ire** verbs) and is the same as the *–ing* form of the verb in English, for example, *walking*, *swimming*.

<u>Sto cercando</u> il mio passaporto.	I'm looking for my passport.
<u>Sta scrivendo</u>.	He's writing.
<u>Stanno dormendo</u>.	They're sleeping.
Cosa <u>stai facendo</u>?	What are you doing?

⇨ *For more information on* **stare**, *see page 79.*

➤ To make the gerund of an **–are** verb, take off the ending and add **–ando**, for example, **mangiando** (meaning *eating*), **cercando** (meaning *looking for*). To make the gerund of an **–ere** or **–ire** verb, take off the ending and add **–endo**, for example, **scrivendo** (meaning *writing*), **partendo** (meaning *leaving*).

⇨ *For more information on the* **Gerund**, *see page 123.*

Tip

Only use the Italian present continuous to talk about things that are happening at this very minute. Use the present simple tense to talk about things that are continuing, but not necessarily happening at this minute.

| **Studio medicina.** | I'm studying medicine. |

⇨ *For more information on the* **Present simple tense**, *see page 69.*

Key points

✔ Only use the present continuous in Italian for actions that are happening right now.

✔ To make the present continuous, use the present tense of **stare** and the gerund of the main verb.

The imperative

> **What is the imperative?**
> An **imperative** is the form of the verb used to give orders and instructions, for example, *Sit down!*; *Don't go!*; *Let's start!*

1 Using the imperative

➤ In Italian, you use a different form of the imperative depending on whether you are:

- telling someone to do something
- telling someone not to do something
- speaking to one person or more than one person
- speaking to someone you call **tu**
- speaking formally

➤ The pronouns **tu**, **Lei** (the formal way of saying *you*) and **voi** all have their own forms of the imperative, although you don't actually use these pronouns when giving orders and instructions. There is also a formal plural form of the imperative.

- You can also use a form of the imperative to make suggestions. This form is like *let's* in English.

2 How to tell someone to do something

➤ You make the imperative of regular verbs by adding endings to the verb stem, which is what is left when you take away the **–are**, **–ere** or **–ire**. There are different endings for **–are**, **–ere** and **–ire** verbs:

- The endings for **–are** verb imperatives are **–a** (**tu** form), **–i** (**lei** form), **–iamo** (*let's*), **–ate** (**voi** form) and **–ino** (polite plural). For example, **aspettare** → **aspett-** → **aspetta**.

Imperative of aspettare	Example	Meaning: *to wait*
aspetta!	Aspetta, Marco!	Wait, Marco!
aspetti!	Aspetti, signore!	Wait, Sir!
aspettiamo	Aspettiamo qui.	Let's wait here.
aspettate!	Aspettate, ragazzi!	Wait, children!
aspettino!	Aspettino un attimo, signori!	Wait a moment, ladies and gentlemen!

For further explanation of grammatical terms, please see pages viii–xii.

- The endings for **–ere** verb imperatives are **–i** (**tu** form), **–a** (**lei** form), **–iamo** (*let's*), **–ete** (**voi** form) and **–ano** (polite plural).
  For example, **prendere** → prend- → **prendi**.

Imperative of prendere	Example	Meaning: *to take*
prend**i**	**Prendi quello, Marco!**	Take that one, Marco!
prend**a**	**Prenda quello, signore!**	Take that one, Sir!
prend**iamo**	**Prendiamo quello.**	Let's take that one.
prend**ete**	**Prendete quelli, ragazzi!**	Take those ones, children!
prend**ano**	**Prendano quelli, signori!**	Take those ones, ladies and gentlemen!

- The endings for most **–ire** verb imperatives are **–isci** (**tu** form), **–isca** (**lei/Lei** form), **–iamo** (*let's*), **–ite** (**voi** form) and **–iscano** (polite plural).
  For example, **finire** → fin- → **finisci**.

> ℹ️ Note that **sci** is pronounced like *she*; **sca** is pronounced *ska*.

Imperative of finire	Example	Meaning: *to finish*
fin**isci**	**Finisci l'esercizio, Marco!**	Finish the exercise, Marco!
fin**isca**	**Finisca tutto, signore!**	Finish it all, Sir!
fin**iamo**	**Finiamo tutto.**	Let's finish it all.
fin**ite**	**Finite i compiti, ragazzi!**	Finish your homework, children!
fin**iscano**	**Finiscano tutto, signori!**	Finish it all, ladies and gentlemen!

➤ The endings for verbs that do not add **–isc** to the stem, such as **partire** (meaning *to leave*), **dormire** (meaning *to sleep*) **aprire** (meaning *to open*) and **sentire** (meaning *to listen*) are **–i**, **–a**, **–iamo**, **–ite** and **–ano**.

> **Dormi, Giulia!** — Go to sleep, Giulia!
> **Partiamo.** — Let's go.

⇨ *For more information on **Regular –ire verbs**, see page 72.*

➤ Some of the commonest verbs in Italian have irregular imperative forms. Here are the forms for some important verbs:

	dare	dire	essere	fare	andare
(tu)	da'! or dai!	di'!	sii!	fa'! or fai!	va'! or vai!
(lei/lui/Lei)	dia!	dica!	sia!	faccia!	vada!
(noi)	diamo	diciamo	siamo	facciamo	vadano!
(voi) →	date!	dite!	siate!	fate!	andate!
(loro)	diano!	dicano!	siano!	facciano!	vadano!

Sii bravo, Paolo!	Be good, Paolo!
Faccia pure, signore!	Carry on, sir!
Dite la verità, ragazzi!	Tell the truth, children!

⇨ *For more information on the imperatives of Irregular verbs, see **Verb tables** in the middle section.*

Key points

✔ There are familiar and polite forms of the imperative.

✔ The **–iamo** form is used to translate *let's*.

---

3 **Where do pronouns go?**

➤ In English, pronouns such as *me*, *it* and *them* always come after the imperative, for example *Watch me!; Take it!; Give them to me!*

➤ In Italian pronouns come <u>AFTER</u> the imperative in the **tu** and **voi** forms:

- The pronoun joins with the imperative to make one word.

Guardami, mamma!	Look at me, mum!
Aspettateli!	Wait for them!

- When the imperative is only one syllable **mi** becomes **–mmi**, **ti** becomes **–tti**, **lo** becomes **–llo** and so on.

Dimmi!	Tell me!
Fallo subito!	Do it immediately!

- When the pronouns **mi**, **ti**, **ci** and **vi** are followed by another pronoun they become **me-**, **te-**, **ce-** and **ve-**, and **gli** and **le** become **glie-**.

Mandameli.	Send me them.
Daglielo.	Give it to him.

Tip

In Italian you <u>always</u> put the indirect object pronoun first.

⇨ *For more information on **Indirect object pronouns**, see page 46.*

➤ Pronouns also come <u>AFTER</u> the **–iamo** form of the imperative, joining onto it to make one word.

Provi*a*molo!	Let's try it!
Mandiamog*li*ela!	Let's send it to them.

➤ Pronouns come <u>BEFORE</u> the **lei** form of the imperative and the polite plural form.

<u>Mi</u> **dia un chilo d'uva, per favore.**	Give me a kilo of grapes please.
<u>La</u> **prenda, signore.**	Take it, sir.
<u>Ne</u> **ass*a*ggino un po', signori!**	Try a bit, ladies and gentlemen!
<u>Si</u> **accomodi!**	Take a seat!

⇨ *For more information on **Reflexive verbs**, see page 87.*

Key points

✔ Pronouns come after the **tu**, **voi** and **–iamo** forms of the imperative.

✔ Pronouns which come after the imperative join onto it to make one word.

✔ Pronouns come before the polite imperative, and do not join onto it.

---

4 | How to tell someone NOT to do something

➤ When you are telling someone you call **tu** <u>NOT</u> to do something:

- use **non** with the <u>infinitive</u> (the **–are**, **–ere**, **–ire** form) of the verb

Non <u>dire</u> **bugie Andrea!**	Don't tell lies Andrea!
Non <u>dimenticare</u>**!**	Don't forget!

⇨ *For more information on the **Infinitive**, see page 138.*

- if there is also a pronoun, join it onto the infinitive, or put it in front

Non toccar*lo*! OR	
Non <u>lo</u> toccare!	Don't touch it!
Non dirg*li*elo! OR	
Non <u>glielo</u> dire!	Don't tell him about it!
Non far*mi* ridere! OR	
Non <u>mi</u> far ridere!	Don't make me laugh!
Non preoccupar*ti*! OR	
Non <u>ti</u> preoccupare!	Don't worry!
Non bagnar*ti*! OR	
Non <u>ti</u> bagnare!	Don't get wet!

ⓘ Note that the infinitive usually drops the final **e** when the pronoun joins onto it.

➤ In all other cases, to tell someone not to do something:

- use **non** with the imperative

Non dimenticate, ragazzi.	Don't forget, children.
Non abbia paura, signora.	Don't be afraid, madam.
Non esageriamo!	Don't let's go too far!

- join pronouns onto <u>the end of</u> the **voi** and **–iamo** forms of the imperative

Non guardateli!	Don't look at them.
Non ditemelo!	Don't say it to me!
Non mangiamoli tutti.	Don't let's eat them all.
Non diamoglielo.	Don't let's give it to them.

- put pronouns <u>in front of</u> the **lei** and polite plural forms of the imperative

Non li guardi, signora.	Don't look at them, madam.
Non si preoccupino, signori.	Don't worry, ladies and gentlemen.

Key points

✔ To tell a person you call **tu** not to do something, use **non** with the infinitive.

✔ To tell all other people not to do something use **non** with the imperative.

✔ To say *Let's not* use **non** with the **–iamo** form.

Reflexive verbs

What is a reflexive verb?
Reflexive verbs in English are ones where the subject and object are the same, and which use reflexive pronouns such as *myself, yourself* and *themselves*, for example *I've hurt myself; Look after yourself!; They're enjoying themselves.*

---

1 Using reflexive verbs

The basics

➤ There are more reflexive verbs in Italian than in English. The infinitive form of a reflexive verb has **–si** joined onto it, for example, **divertirsi** (meaning *to enjoy oneself*). This is the way reflexive verbs are shown in dictionaries. **si** is a reflexive pronoun and means *himself, herself, itself, themselves* and *oneself.*

➤ Verbs that are reflexive in English, such as *to hurt oneself* or *to enjoy oneself* are reflexive in Italian. In addition, many verbs that include *get*, for example *to get up, to get dressed, to get annoyed, to get bored, to get tanned,* are reflexive verbs in Italian. Here are some important Italian reflexive verbs:

accomodarsi	to sit down; to take a seat
addormentarsi	to go to sleep
alzarsi	to get up
annoiarsi	to get bored; to be bored
arrabbiarsi	to get angry
chiamarsi	to be called
chiedersi	to wonder
divertirsi	to enjoy oneself; to have fun
farsi male	to hurt oneself
fermarsi	to stop
lavarsi	to wash; to get washed
perdersi	to get lost
pettinarsi	to comb one's hair
preoccuparsi	to worry
prepararsi	to get ready
ricordarsi	to remember
sbrigarsi	to hurry
svegliarsi	to wake up
vestirsi	to dress; to get dressed
Si accomodi!	Take a seat!
Mi alzo alle sette.	I get up at seven o'clock.
Come **ti chiami**?	What are you called?
Non **vi preoccupate**!	Don't worry!
Sbrigati!	Hurry up!

Ci prepariamo.	We're getting ready.
Matteo si annoia.	Matteo is getting bored.
Lucia si è fatta male.	Lucia hurt herself.
I bambini **si divertono**.	The children are enjoying themselves.

i Note that in English, you can often add a reflexive pronoun to verbs if you want to, for example, you can say *Don't worry yourself!* or *He didn't hurry himself*. Whenever you can do this in English, the Italian equivalent is likely to be a reflexive verb.

➤ Some Italian verbs can be used both as reflexive verbs, and as ordinary verbs with no reflexive pronoun. If you are talking about getting yourself ready you use **prepararsi**; if you are talking about gettting the dinner ready you use **preparare**.

Mi preparo alla maratona.	I'm getting ready for the marathon.
Sto preparando il pranzo.	I'm getting lunch ready.
Mi chiedo cosa stia facendo.	I wonder what he's doing.
Chiedi a Lidia perché piange.	Ask Lidia why she's crying.

i Note that **chiedersi** literally means *to ask oneself*. *ask myself*

Grammar Extra!

Some reflexive verbs in Italian add the pronoun **ne** after the reflexive pronoun. The most important of these verbs is **andarsene** (meaning *to go away, to leave*).

Me ne vado.	I'm leaving.
Vattene!	Go away!
Ce ne andiamo.	Let's be off.
Se ne sono andati.	They've left.

The pronouns **mi**, **ti**, **si**, **ci** and **vi** become **me**, **te**, **se**, **ce** and **ve** when they are followed by another pronoun, such as **ne**.

---

2 How to make the present tense of reflexive verbs

➤ First, decide which reflexive pronoun to use. You can see how the reflexive pronouns correspond to the subject pronouns in the following table:

Subject pronoun	Reflexive pronoun	Meaning
(io)	mi	myself
(tu)	ti	yourself
(lui), (lei), (Lei), (loro)	si	himself, herself, itself, yourself, themselves
(noi)	ci	ourselves
(voi)	vi	yourselves

For further explanation of grammatical terms, please see pages viii–xii.

Mi alzo presto.	I get up early.
Mia sorella si veste.	My sister's getting dressed.
Si lamentano sempre.	They're always complaining.

➤ The present tense forms of a reflexive verb are just the same as those of an ordinary verb, except for the addition of the reflexive pronoun in front of the verb.

⇨ *For more information on the **Present tense**, see page 68.*

➤ The following table shows the reflexive verb **divertirsi** in full.

Reflexive forms of divertirsi	Meaning
mi diverto	I'm enjoying myself
ti diverti	you're enjoying yourself
si diverte	he is enjoying himself she is enjoying herself you are enjoying yourself
ci divertiamo	we're enjoying ourselves
vi divertite	you're enjoying yourselves
si divertono	they're enjoying themselves

3 | Where to put reflexive pronouns

➤ The reflexive pronoun usually goes in front of the verb, but there are some exceptions. The pronoun goes in front if the verb is:

- an ordinary tense, such as the present simple

| Si diverte signora? | Are you enjoying yourself madam? |
| Mi abituo al lavoro. | I'm getting used to the work. |

⇨ *For more information on the **Present simple tense**, see page 69.*

- the polite imperative   *would have thought this an e but ignore for now.*

| Si avvicini, signore. | Come closer, sir. |

⇨ *For more information on the **Imperative**, see page 82.*

- an imperative telling someone NOT to do something

| Non vi avvicinate troppo, ragazzi. | Don't come too close, children. |
| Non si lamenti, dottore. | Don't complain, doctor. |

➤ The pronoun comes after the verb if it is the **tu** or **voi** form of the imperative, used positively:

| Svegliati! | Wake up! |
| Divertitevi! | Enjoy yourselves! |

but you don't use the ~~imp~~ infinitive, you use the imperative?

➤ In the case of the infinitive, used with **non** to tell someone NOT to do something, the pronoun can either:

- go <u>in front of</u> the infinitive

  OR

- join onto the end of the infinitive

Non ti bruciare! OR **Non bruciarti!**	Don't burn yourself!
Non ti preoccupare! OR **Non preoccuparti!**	Don't worry!

[i] Note that, when telling someone not to do something, you use **non** with the <u>infinitive</u> for people you call **tu**.

➤ There are also two options when you use the infinitive of a reflexive verb after a verb such as *want, must, should* or *can't*. The pronoun can either:

- go in front of the main verb

  OR

- join onto the end of the infinitive

Mi voglio abbronzare. OR **Voglio abbronzarmi.**	I want to get a tan.
Ti devi alzare. OR **Devi alzarti.**	You must get up.
Vi dovreste preparare. OR **Dovreste prepararvi.**	You ought to get ready.
Non mi posso fermare molto. OR **Non posso fermarmi molto.**	I can't stop for long.

➤ In the same way, in <u>continuous tenses</u>, the reflexive pronoun can either:

- go in front of the verb **stare**

  OR

- join onto the gerund

Ti stai annoiando? OR **Stai annoiandoti?**	Are you getting bored?
Si stanno alzando? OR **Stanno alzandosi?**	Are they getting up?

[i] Note that the pronoun is always joined onto the gerund when it is not used in a continuous tense.

Incontrandoci per caso, abbiamo parlato molto.	Meeting by chance, we had a long talk.
Pettinandomi ho trovato un capello bianco.	When I combed my hair I found a white hair.

For further explanation of grammatical terms, please see pages viii–xii.

> **Key points**
> ✔ Reflexive verbs are commoner in Italian than in English.
> ✔ English verbs that include *get* are often translated by an Italian reflexive verb.
> ✔ Reflexive pronouns usually go in front of the verb.

4 | Using reflexive verbs with parts of the body and clothes

➤ In Italian you often talk about actions to do with your body or your clothing using a reflexive verb.

Mi lavo i capelli ogni mattina.	I wash my hair every morning.
Mettiti il cappotto!	Put your coat on!
Si è rotta la gamba.	She's broken her leg.

> *(i)* Note that you do not use possessive adjectives in this kind of sentence. Instead you use the definite article **il**, **la**, **i** and so on with the noun, and a reflexive verb.
>
> **Mi lavo le mani.**   I'm washing my hands.

➪ For more information on **Articles**, see page 10.

5 | How to use reflexive verbs in the perfect tense

➤ The English perfect tense, for example, I *have burnt* myself, and the English simple past, for example I *burnt* myself yesterday, are both translated by the Italian perfect tense.

➪ For more information about the **Perfect tense**, see page 108.

➤ The perfect tense of reflexive verbs is always made with the verb **essere** and the past participle.

Mi sono fatto male.   I've hurt myself.

➤ The past participle used in the perfect tense of reflexive verbs has to agree with the subject of the sentence. You change the **–o** ending of the participle to **–a** if the subject is feminine. The masculine plural ending is **–i**, and the feminine plural is **–e**.

Silvia si è alzata tardi stamattina.	Silvia got up late this morning.
Vi siete divertiti, ragazzi?	Did you have a nice time, children?
Le mie sorelle si sono abbronzate.	My sisters have got suntanned.

> **Tip**
>
> If you are female always use a feminine adjective when you are talking about yourself, and always make the past participle feminine when you are talking about what you have done.
>
> **Mi sono svegliata, mi sono**   I woke up, got up and got dressed.
> **alzata e mi sono vestita.**

6   Other uses of reflexive pronouns

➤ **ci**, **vi** and **si** are used to mean *each other* and *one another*.

     <u>Ci</u> vogliamo molto bene.   We love each other very much.

     <u>Si</u> vede che <u>si</u> odiano.   You can see they hate one another.

     <u>Vi</u> conoscete?   Do you know each other?

> **Tip**
>
> Remember that when *you* is used to mean people in general, it is often translated by **si**.
>
> **Si fa così.**   You do it this way.
>
> **Non si tocca!**   You can't touch them!
>
> **Come <u>si dice</u> "genitori" in inglese?**   How do you say "genitori" in English?

> **Key points**
>
> ✔ The perfect tense of reflexive verbs is made with **essere**, and the past participle agrees with the subject of the verb.
>
> ✔ Reflexive verbs are used with the definite article to talk about washing your hair, breaking your leg, putting on your coat, and so on.

The future tense

> **What is the future tense?**
> The **future tense** is a tense used to talk about something that will happen, or will be true in the future, for example *He'll be here soon; I'll give you a call; It will be sunny tomorrow.*

1 | Using the present tense to talk about the future

➤ Sometimes, both in Italian and in English, you use the <u>present tense</u> to refer to the future.

Il corso <u>comincia</u> domani.	The course <u>starts</u> tomorrow.
Quando <u>partite</u>?	When <u>are you leaving</u>?

➤ In the following cases the <u>present tense</u> is used in Italian, while the <u>future</u> is used in English:

- to say what you're about to do

<u>Pago</u> io.	I'll pay.
<u>Prendo</u> un espresso.	I'll have an espresso.

- to ask for suggestions

Dove lo <u>metto</u>?	Where shall I put it?
Cosa <u>facciamo</u>?	What shall we do?

⇨ *For more information on the **Present simple**, see page 69.*

➤ In Italian the <u>future tense</u> is used after **quando** in cases where *when* is followed by the <u>present</u> in English.

Quando <u>finirò</u>, verrò da te.	When I <u>finish</u> I'll come to yours.
Lo comprerò quando <u>avrò</u> abbastanza denaro.	I'll buy it when <u>I've got</u> enough money.

2 | How to make the future tense

➤ In English we make the future tense by putting *will*, *'ll* or *shall* in front of the verb. In Italian you change the verb endings: **parlo** (meaning *I speak*), becomes **parlerò** (meaning *I will speak*) in the future.

➤ To make the future of regular **–are** and **–ere** verbs take the <u>stem</u>, which is what is left of the verb when you take away the **–are**, **–ere** or **–ire** ending of the infinitive and add the following endings:

- -erò, -erai, -erà, -eremo, -erete, -eranno
  For example, **parlare** → **parl-** → **parlerò**.

➤ The following tables show the future tenses of **parlare** (meaning *to speak*) and **credere** (meaning *to believe*).

Pronoun	Future tense of parlare	Meaning: to speak
(io)	parlerò	I'll speak
(tu)	parlerai	you'll speak
(lui/lei) (Lei)	parlerà	he/she'll speak you'll speak
(noi)	parleremo	we'll speak
(voi)	parlerete	you'll speak
(loro)	parleranno	they'll speak

Gli **parlerò** domani.   I'll speak to him tomorrow.

Pronoun	Future tense of credere	Meaning: to speak
(io)	crederò	I'll believe
(tu)	crederai	you'll believe
(lui/lei) (Lei)	crederà	he/she'll believe you'll believe
(noi)	crederemo	we'll believe
(voi)	crederete	you'll believe
(loro)	crederanno	they'll believe

Non ti **crederanno**.   They won't believe you.

[i] Note that there are accents on the first and third person singular forms, to show that you stress the last vowel.

➤ To make the future of regular –ire verbs take the <u>stem</u> and add the following endings:

- -irò, -irai, -irà, -iremo, -irete, -iranno
  For example, finire → fin- → finirò.

➤ The following table shows the future tense of **finire** (meaning to finish).

Pronoun	Future tense of finire	Meaning: to finish
(io)	finirò	I'll finish
(tu)	finirai	you'll finish
(lui/lei) (Lei)	finirà	he/she'll finish you'll finish
(noi)	finiremo	we'll finish
(voi)	finirete	you'll finish
(loro)	finiranno	they'll finish

Quando **finirai** il lavoro?   When will you finish the work?

For further explanation of grammatical terms, please see pages viii–xii.

➤ Some verbs do not have a vowel before the **r** of the future ending. Their endings are:

- **-rò, -rai, -rà, -remo, -rete, -ranno**

➤ The following table shows the future tense of some of these verbs which you should learn.

Verb	Meaning	io	tu	lui/lei/Lei	noi	voi	loro
andare	to go	andrò	andrai	andrà	andremo	andrete	andranno
cadere	to fall	cadrò	cadrai	cadrà	cadremo	cadrete	cadranno
dire	to say	dirò	dirai	dirà	diremo	direte	diranno
dovere	to have to	dovrò	dovrai	dovrà	dovremo	dovrete	dovranno
fare	to do/make	farò	farai	farà	faremo	farete	faranno
potere	to be able	potrò	potrai	potrà	potremo	potrete	potranno
sapere	to know	saprò	saprai	saprà	sapremo	saprete	sapranno
vedere	to see	vedrò	vedrai	vedrà	vedremo	vedrete	vedranno
vivere	to live	vivrò	vivrai	vivrà	vivremo	vivrete	vivranno

Andrò con loro.	I'll go with them.
Pensi che **diranno** la verità?	Do you think they'll tell the truth?
Non credo che **farà** bel tempo.	I don't think the weather will be nice.
Lo **sapremo** domani.	We'll know tomorrow.

➤ Some verbs have no vowel before the future ending, and they also change their stem, for example:

Verb	Meaning	io	tu	lui/lei/Lei	noi	voi	loro
rimanere	to remain	rimarrò	rimarrai	rimarrà	rimarremo	rimarrete	rimarranno
tenere	to hold	terrò	terrai	terrà	terremo	terrete	terranno
venire	to come	verrò	verrai	verrà	verremo	verrete	verranno
volere	to want	vorrò	vorrai	vorrà	vorremo	vorrete	vorranno

➤ Verbs with infinitives that end in **–ciare** and **–giare**, for example, **parcheggiare** (meaning *to park*), **cominciare** (meaning *to start*), **mangiare** (meaning *to eat*) and **viaggiare** (meaning *to travel*) drop the **i** from the stem in the future. For example, **mangiare → mang- → mangerò**.

Comincerò domani.	I'll start tomorrow.
Mangeranno alle otto.	They'll eat at eight o'clock.

➤ Verbs with infinitives that end in **–care** and **–gare**, for example **cercare** (meaning *to look for*, *to try*), **seccare** (meaning *to annoy*), **pagare** (meaning *to pay*) and **spiegare** (meaning *to explain*) add an **h** before the future ending in the future. For example, **pagare → pagh- → pagherò**.

> **Cercherò di aiutarvi.**   I'll try to help you.
>
> **Mi pagheranno sabato.**   They'll pay me on Saturday.

⇨ *For more information on **Spelling**, see page 191.*

Tip

You use **vero** to translate *will it?* and **vero** or **no** to translate *won't it?* and so on at the end of sentences.

> **Non costerà molto, vero?**   It won't cost much, will it?
>
> **Arriveranno fra poco, no?**   They'll be here soon, won't they?
> OR **vero?**

Grammar Extra!

Will you is used in English to ask someone to do something: *Will you hurry up?*; *Will you stop talking!* You use the Italian imperative, or the verb **volere** (meaning *to want*) to translate this sort of request.

> **Sta' zitto!**   Will you be quiet!
>
> **Vuoi smetterla!**   Will you stop that!

---

3 The future tense of essere and avere

➤ **essere** (meaning *to be*) and **avere** (meaning *to have*) have irregular future forms.

Pronoun	Future tense of essere	Meaning	Future tense of avere	Meaning
(io)	sarò	I'll be	avrò	I'll have
(tu)	sarai	you'll be	avrai	you'll have
(lui/lei) (Lei)	sarà	he/she/it will be you'll be	avrà	he/she/it will have you'll have
(noi)	saremo	we'll be	avremo	we'll have
(voi)	sarete	you'll be	avrete	you'll have
(loro)	saranno	they'll be	avranno	they'll have

Sarà difficile.	It'll be difficult.
Non ne <u>sarai</u> deluso.	You won't be disappointed by it.
Non <u>avrò</u> tempo.	I won't have time.
Lo <u>avrai</u> domani.	You'll have it tomorrow.

Grammar Extra!

In English we sometimes use *will* or *'ll* to say what we think must be true, for example, *You'll be tired after that long journey; It'll be about three miles from here to the town centre.*

The future tense in Italian is used in the same way.

<u>Saranno</u> venti chllometri.	It'll be twenty kilometres.
<u>Avrà</u> cinquant'anni.	He'll be fifty.

Key points

✔ The future endings of regular **–are** and **–ere** verbs are **–erò**, **–erai**, **–erà**, **–eremo**, **–erete**, **–eranno**.

✔ The future endings of regular **–ire** verbs are **–irò**, **–irai**, **–irà**, **–iremo**, **–irete**, **–iranno**.

The conditional

> **What is the conditional?**
> The **conditional** is used to talk about things that would happen or would be true under certain conditions, for example, I _would_ help you if I could.
> It is also used in requests and offers, for example, _Could_ you lend me some money?; I _could_ give you a lift.

1 Using the conditional

➤ In English, when you're talking about what would happen in certain circumstances, or saying what you could or would like to do, you use _would_, '_d_ or _could_ with the infinitive (the base form of the verb).

> I would pay the money back as soon as possible.
> If you asked him he'd probably say yes.
> You could stay here for a while.

➤ In Italian the conditional is used in this kind of sentence. Like the present and the future tenses, you make it by adding endings to the verb stem, which is what is left of the verb when you take away the **–are**, **–ere** or **–ire** ending of the infinitive.

➤ You use the conditional of any Italian verb to say what would happen or would be true.

> **Sarebbe difficile.**   It would be difficult.
> **Farebbe finta di capire.**   He'd pretend to understand.
> **Mia madre non me lo**   My mother wouldn't let me.
> **permetterebbe.**

➤ You use the conditional of the verbs **potere** (meaning _to be able_) and **dovere** (meaning _to have to_) to say what could or should happen or could or should be true.

> **Potremmo andare in Spagna**   We could go to Spain next year.
> **il prossimo anno.**
> **Dovresti studiare di più.**   You should study more.

2 How to make the conditional

➤ To make the conditional of regular **–are** and **–ere** verbs take the stem and add the following endings: **–erei**, **–eresti**, **–erebbe**, **–eremmo**, **–ereste**, **–erebbero**.

➤ The following table shows the conditional of **parlare** (meaning _to speak_) and **credere** (meaning _to believe_).

	Conditional of parlare	Meaning	Conditional of credere	Meaning
(io)	parlerei	I'd speak	crederei	I'd believe
(tu)	parleresti	you'd speak	crederesti	you'd believe
(lui/lei) (Lei)	parlerebbe	he/she'd speak you'd speak	crederebbe	he/she'd believe you'd believe
(noi)	parleremmo	we'd speak	crederemmo	we'd believe
(voi)	parlereste	you'd speak	credereste	you'd believe
(loro)	parlerebbero	they'd speak	crederebbero	they'd believe

Con chi parleresti?   Who would you speak to?
Non ti crederebbe.   He wouldn't believe you.

[i] Note that the same form of the verb is used for the pronouns **lui**, **lei** and **Lei**.

➤ To make the conditional of regular **–ire** verbs take the <u>stem</u> and add the following endings: **–irei**, **–iresti**, **–irebbe**, **–iremmo**, **–ireste**, **–irebbero**.

➤ The following table shows the conditional of **finire** (meaning *to finish*).

(io)	finirei	I'd finish
(tu)	finiresti	you'd finish
(lui/lei) (Lei)	finirebbe	he/she'd finish you'd finish
(noi)	finiremmo	we'd finish
(voi)	finireste	you'd finish
(loro)	finirebbero	they'd finish

Non finiremmo in tempo.   We wouldn't finish in time.

[i] Note that the same form of the verb is used for the pronouns **lui**, **lei** and **Lei**.

---

3 The conditionals of volere, potere and dovere

➤ You use the <u>conditional</u> of the verb **volere** (meaning *to want*) to say what you <u>would like</u>.

     Vorrei un'insalata.   I'd like a salad.

➤ You use the conditional of **volere** with an infinitive to say what you <u>would like</u> to do.

     Vorremmo venire con voi.   We'd like to come with you.
     Vorrebbero rimanere qui.   They'd like to stay here.

Tip

In Italian there are two ways of saying *I'd like to*: **vorrei** and **mi piacerebbe**.

Vorrei vedere quel film. OR   I'd like to see that film.
Mi piacerebbe vedere quel film.

➤ The conditional of **volere** is irregular:

	Conditional of volere	Meaning
(io)	vorrei	I'd like
(tu)	vorresti	you'd like
(lui/lei) (Lei)	vorrebbe	he/she'd like you'd like
(noi)	vorremmo	we'd like
(voi)	vorreste	you'd like
(loro)	vorrebbero	they'd like

Tip

In English, the conditional *What would you like?* is more polite than *What do you want?* In Italian there is no difference in politeness.

Vuoi un gelato?   Would you like OR
                           Do you want an ice cream?

Vuole altro, signora? Would you like anything else,
                           madam?

➤ You use the conditional of the verb **potere** (meaning *to be able*) with an infinitive.

● to say what <u>could</u> be the case, or <u>could</u> happen.

<u>Potresti</u> avere ragione.   You could be right.
<u>Potrebbe</u> essere vero.   It could be true.
<u>Potrebbero</u> vendere la casa.   They could sell the house.

● to ask if somebody <u>could</u> do something.

<u>Potresti</u> chiudere la finestra?   Could you close the window?

For further explanation of grammatical terms, please see pages viii–xii.

➤ The conditional of **potere** is as follows:

	Conditional of potere	Meaning
(io)	potrei	I could
(tu)	potresti	you could
(lui/lei) (Lei)	potrebbe	he/she/it could you could
(noi)	potremmo	we could
(voi)	potreste	you could
(loro)	potrebbero	they could

➤ You use the conditional of **dovere** (meaning *to have to*):

- to say what you or somebody else <u>should</u> do

  Dovrei fare un po' di ginnastica. I should do some exercise.

  Dovresti telefonare al tuoi. You should phone your parents.

- to talk about what <u>should</u> be the case, or <u>should</u> happen.

  Dovrebbe arrivare verso le dieci. He should arrive at around ten.

  Dovrebbe essere bello. This should be good.

➤ The conditional of **dovere** is as follows:

	Conditional of dovere	Meaning
(io)	dovrei	I should
(tu)	dovresti	you should
(lui/lei) (Lei)	dovrebbe	he/she/it should you should
(noi)	dovremmo	we should
(voi)	dovreste	you should
(loro)	dovrebbero	they should

4 Irregular conditionals

➤ Some common verbs do not have a vowel before the **r** of the conditional ending, their endings are **rei, resti, rebbe, remmo, reste, rebbero**.

Verb	Meaning	io	tu	lui/lei/Lei	noi	voi	loro
andare	to go	andrei	andresti	andrebbe	andremmo	andreste	andrebbero
cadere	to fall	cadrei	cadresti	cadrebbe	cadremmo	cadreste	cadrebbero
sapere	to know	saprei	sapresti	saprebbe	sapremmo	sapreste	saprebbero
vedere	to see	vedrei	vedresti	vedrebbe	vedremmo	vedreste	vedrebbero
vivere	to live	vivrei	vivresti	vivrebbe	vivremmo	vivreste	vivrebbero

Non so se <u>andrebbe</u> bene.	I don't know if it would be okay.
<u>Sapreste</u> indicarmi la strada per la stazione?	Could you tell me the way to the station?
Non <u>vivrei</u> mai in un paese caldo.	I'd never live in a hot country.

➤ Some verbs have no vowel before the conditional ending, <u>and</u> change their stem, for example, **rimanere, tenere, venire**:

Verb	Meaning	io	tu	lui/lei/Lei	noi	voi	loro
rimanere	to remain	rimarrei	rimarresti	rimarrebbe	rimarremmo	rimarreste	rimarrebbero
tenere	to hold	terrei	terresti	terrebbe	terremmo	terreste	terrebbero
venire	to come	verrei	verresti	verrebbe	verremmo	verreste	verrebbero

⇨ *For more information on **Verbs which change their stem**, see page 76.*

➤ Verbs such as **cominciare** (meaning *to start*) and **mangiare** (meaning *to eat*), which end in **–ciare** or **–giare**, and which drop the **i** in the future tense also drop the **i** in the conditional.

Quando <u>comincerebbe</u>?	When would it start?
<u>Mangeresti</u> quei funghi?	Would you eat those mushrooms?

⇨ *For more information on the **Future tense**, see page 93.*

➤ Verbs such as **cercare** (meaning *to look for*) and **pagare** (meaning *to pay*), which end in **–care** or **–gare**, and which add an **h** in the future tense also add an **h** in the conditional.

Probabilmente <u>cercherebbe</u> una scusa.	He'd probably look for an excuse.
Quanto mi <u>pagheresti</u>?	How much would you pay me?

⇨ *For more information on **Spelling**, see page 191.*

For further explanation of grammatical terms, please see pages viii–xii.

5 The conditional of essere and avere

➤ **essere** (meaning *to be*) and **avere** (meaning *to have*) have irregular conditionals.

	Conditional of essere	Meaning	Conditional of avere	Meaning
(io)	sarei	I'd be	avrei	I'd have
(tu)	saresti	you'd be	avresti	you'd have
(lui/lei) **(Lei)**	sarebbe	he/she/ it would be you would be	avrebbe	he/she/ it would have you would have
(noi)	saremmo	we'd be	avremmo	we'd have
(voi)	sareste	you'd be	avreste	you'd have
(loro)	sarebbero	they'd be	avrebbero	they'd have

Sarebbe bello.	It would be lovely.
Non so se **sarei** capace di farlo.	I don't know if I'd be able to do it.
Non **avremmo** tempo.	We wouldn't have time.
Avresti paura?	Would you be frightened?

> **Key points**
> ✔ The Italian conditional is often the equivalent of a verb used with *would* in English.
> ✔ *would like*, *could* and *should* are translated by the conditionals of **volere**, **potere** and **dovere**.

Grammar Extra!

The conditional we have looked at so far is the <u>present conditional</u>. There is also the <u>perfect conditional</u>, which is used to talk about what would have happened in the past.

The perfect conditional is made up of the conditional of **avere** or **essere**, and the past participle. Verbs which form their perfect tense with **avere**, such as **fare** (meaning *to do*) and **pagare** (meaning *to pay*) also form their perfect conditional with **avere**. Those forming their perfect with **essere**, such as **andare** (meaning *to go*) also form their perfect conditional with **essere**.

⇨ *For more information about the Perfect tense and the Past participle, see pages 108-109.*

Non **l'avrei fatto** così.	I wouldn't have done it like that.
Non **l'avrebbero pagato**.	They wouldn't have paid it.
Ci **saresti** andato?	Would you have gone?

In Italian, unlike in English, the <u>perfect conditional</u> is used to report what somebody said in the past.

Ha detto che mi **avrebbe aiutato**.	He said he would help me.
Hanno detto che **sarebbero venuti**.	They said they would come.

The imperfect tense

> **What is the imperfect tense?**
> The **imperfect** is a tense used to say what was happening, what used to happen in the past and what things were like in the past, for example, I _was speaking_ to my mother.

1 When to use the imperfect tense

➤ In English various tenses are used to talk about what things were like in the past, for example, It _was raining_; I _used to like_ her; I _didn't know_ what to do. In Italian the imperfect is the tense you use to translate the verbs in all three of these sentences.

➤ Use the Italian imperfect tense:

- to describe what things were like, what people were doing and how people felt in the past.

Faceva caldo.	It was hot.
Aspettavano impazienti.	They were waiting impatiently.
Eravamo tutti felici.	We were all happy.
Avevo fame.	I was hungry.

- to say what people knew, thought or meant in the past.

Non sapevo cosa volevi dire.	I didn't know what you meant.
Pensavo che fosse lui.	I thought it was him.

- to say what used to happen or what people used to do in the past.

Ci trovavamo ogni venerdì.	We met every Friday.
Vendevano le uova al mercato.	They used to sell eggs in the market.

- to describe what was going on when an event took place.

Guardavamo la partita quando è entrato lui.	We were watching the match when he came in.
È successo mentre dormivano.	It happened while they were asleep.
Mentre parlavi mi sono ricordato di qualcosa.	While you were talking I remembered something.

Grammar Extra!

The imperfect continuous is made with the imperfect tense of **stare** and the gerund. The imperfect continuous is used to describe what was going on at a particular moment.

Che stavano facendo?	What were they doing?
Non stava studiando, dormiva.	He wasn't studying, he was asleep.

⇨ _For more information on the **Gerund**, see page 123._

---

2 How to make the imperfect tense

➤ You make the imperfect tense of regular **–are**, **–ere** and **–ire** verbs by knocking off the **–re** from the infinitive to form the <u>stem</u> of the verbs and adding **–vo**, **–vi**, **–va**, **–vamo**, **–vate**, **–vano**.

➤ The following tables show the imperfect tense of three regular verbs: **parlare** (meaning *to speak*), **credere** (meaning *to believe*) and **finire** (meaning *to finish*).

	Imperfect tense of parlare	Meaning	Imperfect tense of credere	Meaning
(io)	parla<u>vo</u>	I was speaking	crede<u>vo</u>	I believed
(tu)	parla<u>vi</u>	you were speaking	crede<u>vi</u>	you believed
(lui/lei) (Lei)	parla<u>va</u>	he/she was speaking you were speaking	crede<u>va</u>	he/she believed you believed
(noi)	parla<u>vamo</u>	we were speaking	crede<u>vamo</u>	we believed
(voi)	parla<u>vate</u>	you were speaking	crede<u>vate</u>	you believed
(loro)	parl<u>avano</u>	they were speaking	crede<u>vano</u>	they believed

	Imperfect tense of finire	Meaning
(io)	fini<u>vo</u>	I was finishing
(tu)	fini<u>vi</u>	you were finishing
(lui/lei) (Lei)	fini<u>va</u>	he/she was finishing you were finishing
(noi)	fini<u>vamo</u>	we were finishing
(voi)	fini<u>vate</u>	you were finishing
(loro)	fini<u>vano</u>	they were finishing

Con chi <u>parlavi</u>?	Who were you talking to?
<u>Credevamo</u> di aver vinto.	We thought we'd won.
Loro si <u>divertivano</u> mentre io <u>lavoravo</u>.	They had fun while I was working.
Una volta <u>costava</u> di più.	It used to cost more.

3 Perfect tense or imperfect tense?

➤ The Italian <u>perfect tense</u> is used for what happened on one occasion.

Oggi <u>ho giocato</u> male.	I played badly today.
<u>Ha finto</u> di non conoscermi.	He pretended not to recognize me.

➤ The Italian <u>imperfect tense</u> is used for repeated actions or for a continuing state of affairs.

Da studente <u>giocavo</u> a calcio.	When I was a student I played football.
<u>Fingevano</u> sempre di avere capito tutto.	They always pretended they'd understood everything.
Mi <u>sentivo</u> male solo a pensarci.	I felt ill just thinking about it.
Non <u>sorrideva</u> mai.	She never smiled.
Ci <u>credevi</u>?	Did you believe it?

4 | Verbs with an irregular imperfect tense

➤ The imperfect of **essere** (meaning *to be*) is irregular:

(io)	ero	I was
(tu)	eri	you were
(lui/lei) (Lei)	era	he/she/it was you were
(noi)	eravamo	we were
(voi)	eravate	you were
(loro)	erano	they were

<u>Era</u> un ragazzo molto simpatico.	He was a very nice boy.
<u>Eravamo</u> in Italia.	We were in Italy.
<u>Erano</u> le quattro.	It was four o'clock.

➤ **bere** (meaning *to drink*), **dire** (meaning *to say*), **fare** (meaning *to do, to make*) and **tradurre** (meaning *to translate*) are the most common verbs which have the normal imperfect endings added onto a stem which is irregular. You just have to learn these.

Verb	(io)	(tu)	(lui/lei/Lei)	(noi)	(voi)	(loro)
bere	bevevo	bevevi	beveva	bevevamo	bevevate	bevevano
dire	dicevo	dicevi	diceva	dicevamo	dicevate	dicevano
fare	facevo	facevi	faceva	facevamo	facevate	facevano
tradurre	traducevo	traducevi	traduceva	traducevamo	traducevate	traducevano

Di solito <u>bevevano</u> solo acqua.	They usually only drank water.
Cosa <u>dicevo</u>?	What was I saying?
<u>Faceva</u> molto freddo.	It was very cold.
<u>Traducevo</u> la lettera.	I was translating the letter.

Grammar Extra!

The Italian imperfect tense is used to translate sentences such as *How long had they known* each other?; They *had been going out* together for a year when they got engaged; He *had been* ill since last year. The words *for* and *since* are translated by **da**.

A quel punto <u>aspettava</u> già **da tre ore.**	By then he'd already been waiting for three hours.
<u>Guidavo</u> **dalle sei di mattina.**	I'd been driving since six in the morning.
Da quanto tempo <u>stava</u> **male?**	How long had he been ill?

➪ *For more information on **da**, see page 174.*

> ### Key points
>
> ✔ You make the imperfect tense of regular verbs by knocking off the final **–re** of the infinitive and adding endings: **–vo, –vi, –va, –vamo, –vate, –vano**.
>
> ✔ The imperfect is used for actions and situations that continued for some time in the past.

The perfect tense

> **What is the perfect tense?**
> In English the **perfect tense** is used to talk about what has or hasn't happened,
> for example *We've won*, *I haven't touched* it.

1 Using the perfect tense

➤ In English the perfect tense is made up of the verb *to have* followed by a <u>past participle</u>, such as *done, broken, worked, arrived*. It is used to talk about:

- what you've done at some time in the past, for example, *We've been to Australia.*
- what you've done so far, for example, *I've eaten half of it.*

➤ In English the <u>simple past</u>, not the <u>perfect</u> is used to say when exactly something happened, for example, *We met last summer; I ate it last night; It rained a lot yesterday.*

➤ In Italian there are two ways of making the perfect tense:

- the present tense of **avere** (meaning *to have*) followed by a past participle
- the present tense of **essere** (meaning *to be*), followed by a past participle.

⇨ *For more information on the **Present tense of avere and essere**, see pages 109 and 112.*

➤ The Italian perfect tense is used to say:

- what you've done at some time in the past.

Ho già visto quel film.	I've already <u>seen</u> that film.
Sono uscita con lui un paio di volte.	I've been out with him a couple of times.

- what you've done so far.

Finora abbiamo fatto solo il presente dei verbi.	So far we've only done the present tense.

➤ Unlike in English, the Italian perfect tense is <u>ALSO</u> used to say what you did at some particular time, or when exactly something happened.

Ho visto quel film sabato scorso.	I saw that film last Saturday.
Sono uscita con lui ieri sera.	I went out with him last night.
È successo ieri.	It happened yesterday.

> *Tip*
>
> Do not use the perfect tense to say since when, or how long you've been doing something – **da** and the present tense is used for this in Italian.
>
> ⇨ *For more information on **da**, see page 174.*

2 | How to make the past participle

➤ The past participle is <u>always</u> part of the perfect tense.

➤ To make the past participle of a regular **–are** verb, take off the **–are** of the infinitive and add **–ato**.

> **parlare** (meaning *to speak*) →**parlato** (*spoken*)

➤ To make the past participle of a regular **–ere** verb, take off the **–ere** of the infinitive and add **–uto**.

> **credere** (meaning *to believe*) → **creduto** (*believed*)

➤ To make the past participle of a regular **–ire** verb, take off the **–ire** of the infinitive and add **–ito**.

> **finire** (meaning *to finish*) → **finito** (*finished*)

3 | How to make the perfect tense with avere

➤ To make the perfect tense with **avere**:

- • choose the present tense form of **avere** that matches the subject of the sentence.
- • add the past participle. <u>Do not</u> change the ending of the participle to make it agree with the subject.

➤ The perfect tense of **parlare** (meaning *to speak*) is as follows:

	Present tense of avere	Past participle of parlare	Meaning
(io)	ho	parlato	I spoke *or* have spoken
(tu)	hai	parlato	you spoke *or* have spoken
(lui/lei) (Lei)	ha	parlato	he/she spoke *or* has spoken you spoke *or* have spoken
(noi)	abbiamo	parlato	we spoke *or* have spoken
(voi)	avete	parlato	you spoke *or* have spoken
(loro)	hanno	parlato	they spoke *or* have spoken

Non gli <u>ho</u> mai <u>parlato</u>.	I've never spoken to him.
Roberta gli <u>ha parlato</u> ieri.	Roberta spoke to him yesterday.

4 | Verbs with irregular past participles

➤ As in English, some very common verbs have irregular past participles. These are some of the most important ones:

aprire (to open)	→	**aperto** (opened)	
ALSO **coprire** (to cover)	→	**coperto** (covered)	
chiudere (to close)	→	**chiuso** (closed)	
decidere (to decide)	→	**deciso** (decided)	
dire (to say)	→	**detto** (said)	
fare (to do, to make)	→	**fatto** (done, made)	
friggere (to fry)	→	**fritto** (fried)	
leggere (to read)	→	**letto** (read)	
mettere (to put)	→	**messo** (put)	
ALSO **promettere** (to promise)	→	**promesso** (promised)	
morire (to die)	→	**morto** (died)	
offrire (to offer)	→	**offerto** (offered)	
prendere (to take)	→	**preso** (taken)	
ALSO **sorprendere** (to surprise)	→	**sorpreso** (surprised)	
rispondere (to reply)	→	**risposto** (replied)	
ALSO **spendere** (to spend)	→	**speso** (spent)	
rompere (to break)	→	**rotto** (broken)	
scegliere (to choose)	→	**scelto** (chosen)	
scrivere (to write)	→	**scritto** (written)	
vincere (to win)	→	**vinto** (won)	
ALSO **convincere** (to convince)	→	**convinto** (convinced)	
vedere (to see)	→	**visto** (seen)	

[i] Note that, as in English, some Italian past participles are also used as adjectives. When they are adjectives they <u>agree</u> with the noun they go with.

patate fritte	fried potatoes
È aperta la banca?	Is the bank open?

⇨ *For more information on **Adjectives**, see page 20.*

5 | When to make the perfect tense with avere

➤ You use **avere** to make the perfect tense of most verbs.

<u>**Ho preso**</u> il treno delle dieci.	I <u>got</u> the ten o'clock train.
<u>**L'hai messo**</u> in frigo?	<u>Have you put</u> it in the fridge?
Perché <u>**l'hai fatto**</u>?	Why <u>did you do</u> it?
Carlo <u>**ha speso**</u> più di me.	Carlo <u>spent</u> more than me.
<u>**Abbiamo comprato**</u> una macchina.	<u>We've bought</u> a car.
Dove <u>**avete parcheggiato**</u>?	Where <u>did you park</u>?
Non <u>**hanno voluto**</u> aiutarmi.	They <u>didn't want</u> to help me.

For further explanation of grammatical terms, please see pages viii–xii.

➤ You <u>do not</u> use **avere** to make the perfect tense of:

- reflexive verbs
- certain verbs that do not take a direct object, such as **andare** (meaning *to go*), **venire** (meaning *to come*) and **diventare** (meaning *to become*).

[*i*] Note that in English the verb *to have* can be used on its own in replies such as *No, he hasn't*, and question phrases such as *haven't you?* – **avere** <u>cannot</u> be used in this way in Italian.

Te l'ha detto? – No.	Has he told you? – No, he hasn't.
Lo hai fatto, vero?	You've done it, haven't you?

⟹ *For more information on **Questions**, see page 152.*

6 When to make the past participle agree

➤ When you make the perfect tense with **avere**, the past participle <u>never</u> agrees with the <u>subject</u>.

➤ You <u>must</u> make the past participle agree with the <u>object pronouns</u> **lo** and **la** (meaning *him, her* and *it*) when they come in front of the verb.

Hai visto Marco? – Sì, <u>l'ho visto</u>.	Have you seen Marco? – Yes, I've seen him.
È un bel film, <u>l'hai visto</u>?	It's a good film, have you seen it?
Hai visto Lucia? – Non <u>l'ho vista</u>.	Have you seen Lucia? – No, I haven't seen her.

➤ You <u>must</u> make the past participle agree with the object pronouns **li** and **le** (meaning *them*) when they come in front of the verb.

I fiammiferi? Non <u>li ho presi</u>.	The matches? I haven't taken them.
Le fragole? <u>Le ho mangiate</u> tutte.	The strawberries? I've eaten them all.

Key points

✔ The Italian perfect tense is used to translate both the English perfect, and the English simple past.

✔ The Italian perfect tense is made with **avere** or **essere** and the past participle.

✔ The past participle does not agree with the subject when the perfect tense is made with **avere**, except when certain object pronouns come in front of the verb.

7 | How to make the perfect tense with *essere*

➤ To make the perfect tense with **essere**:

- choose the present tense form of **essere** that matches the subject of the sentence.
- add the past participle. Make the ending of the participle <u>agree</u> with the subject.

➤ The perfect tense of **andare** (meaning *to go*) is as follows:

	Present tense of *essere*	Past participle of andare	Meaning
(io)	sono	andato *or* andata	I went *or* have gone
(tu)	sei	andato *or* andata	you went *or* have gone
(lui)	è	andato	he/it went *or* has gone
(lei)	è	andata	she/it went *or* has gone
(Lei)	è	andato *or* andata	you went *or* have gone
(noi)	siamo	andati *or* andate	we went *or* have gone
(voi)	siete	andati *or* andate	you went *or* have gone
(loro)	sono	andati *or* andate	they went *or* have gone

Tip

You make past participles agree when they follow the verb **essere**, in the same way that you make adjectives agree.

Sei pront<u>a</u>, Maria?   Are you ready Maria?

Sei andat<u>a</u> anche tu, Maria?   Did you go too, Maria?

⇨ *For more information on* **Adjectives***, see page 20.*

---

8 | When to make the perfect tense with *essere*

➤ Use **essere** to make the perfect tense of certain verbs that <u>do not</u> take a direct object.

⇨ *For more information on* **Direct objects***, see page 44.*

➤ The most important of these verbs are:

andare	to go	**arrivare**	to arrive
diventare	to become	**entrare**	to come in
partire	to leave	**rimanere**	to stay
riuscire	to succeed, manage	**salire**	to go up, get on
scendere	to go down	**succedere**	to happen
stare	to be	**tornare**	to come back
uscire	to go out	**venire**	to come

È rimasta a casa tutto il giorno.	She stayed at home all day.
Siamo riusciti a convincerla.	We managed to persuade her.
Sei mai stata a Bologna, Tina?	Have you ever been to Bologna, Tina?
Le tue amiche sono arrivate.	Your friends have arrived.
Cos'è successo?	What happened?

i Note that **essere** is used to make the perfect tense of **piacere** (meaning literally *to please*). The past participle agrees with the subject of the Italian verb, and not with the subject of the English verb *to like*.

La musica ti è piaciuta, Roberto?	Did you like the music, Robert?
I cioccolatini mi sono piaciuti molto.	I liked the chocolates very much.
Le foto sono piaciute a tutti.	Everyone liked the photos.

➤ Use **essere** to make the perfect tense of all reflexive verbs.

I miei fratelli si sono alzati tardi.	My brothers got up late.
Le ragazze si sono alzate alle sei.	The girls got up at six.

⇨ *For more information on **Reflexive verbs**, see page 87.*

Key points

✔ When the perfect tense is made with **essere** the past participle agrees with the subject of the sentence.

✔ **essere** is used to make the perfect tense of some very common verbs that do not take a direct object.

✔ **essere** is used to make the perfect tense of all reflexive verbs.

The past historic

> **What is the past historic?**
> The **past historic** is equivalent to the English simple past, except that it is only used in written Italian. In spoken Italian the <u>perfect</u> tense is used to talk about the past.

Recognizing the past historic

➤ You do not need to learn the past historic (**il passato remoto**), since you will never need to use it. However, you may come across it in written Italian. To help you recognize it, here are the past historic forms of **essere** (meaning *to be*), **avere** (meaning *to have*), **parlare** (meaning *to speak*), **credere** (meaning *to believe*), and **partire** (meaning *to leave*).

	Past historic of essere	Meaning	Past historic of avere	Meaning
(io)	**fui**	I was	**ebbi**	I had
(tu)	**fosti**	you were	**avesti**	you had
(lui/lei) (Lei)	**fu**	he/she was you were	**ebbe**	he/she had you had
(noi)	**fummo**	we were	**avemmo**	we had
(voi)	**foste**	you were	**aveste**	you had
(loro)	**furono**	they were	**ebbero**	they had

Ci <u>fu</u> un improvviso silenzio quando entrai nella stanza.		There was a sudden silence when I came into the room.	
Non <u>ebbero</u> nessuna speranza.		They had no hope.	

	Past historic of parlare	Meaning	Past historic of credere	Meaning
(io)	**parlai**	I spoke	**credei** or **credetti**	I believed
(tu)	**parlasti**	you spoke	**credesti**	you believed
(lui/lei) (Lei)	**parlò**	he/she spoke you spoke	**credé** or **credette**	he/she believed you believed
(noi)	**parlammo**	we spoke	**credemmo**	we believed
(voi)	**parlaste**	you spoke	**credeste**	you believed
(loro)	**parlarono**	they spoke	**crederono** or **credettero**	they believed

	Past historic of partire	Meaning
(io)	partii	I left
(tu)	partisti	you left
(lui/lei) (Lei)	partì	he/she left you left
(noi)	partimmo	we left
(voi)	partiste	you left
(loro)	partirono	they left

Parlò piano.

He spoke slowly.

Non lo credettero.

They did not believe it.

Partì in fretta.

He left hastily.

Key points

✔ You will come across the past historic in written Italian.

✔ It is translated by the English simple past.

The pluperfect or past perfect tense

> **What is the pluperfect tense?**
> The **pluperfect tense** is used to talk about what had happened or had been true at a point in the past, for example, *I'd forgotten to send her a card.*

1 Using the pluperfect tense

➤ When talking about the past we sometimes refer to things that had already happened previously. In English we use *had* followed by a past participle such as *done, broken, worked, arrived* to do this. This tense is called the pluperfect or past perfect.

➤ The Italian pluperfect tense is used in a similar way, but like the perfect tense, it can be made with either **avere** or **essere**, and the past participle.

⇨ *For more information on **Past participles**, see page 109.*

Avevamo già **mangiato** quando è arrivato.	We'd already eaten when he arrived.
Ovviamente **erano riusciti** a risolvere il problema.	They'd obviously managed to solve the problem.

2 How to make the pluperfect tense with avere

➤ To make the pluperfect tense with **avere**:

- choose the imperfect form of **avere** that matches the subject of the sentence.

- add the past participle. Do not change the ending of the participle to make it agree with the subject.

⇨ *For more information on the **Imperfect tense of avere** and **Past participles**, see pages 106 and 109.*

➤ The pluperfect tense of **parlare** (meaning *to speak*) is as follows:

	Imperfect tense of avere	Past participle of parlare	Meaning
(io)	avevo	parlato	I had spoken
(tu)	avevi	parlato	you had spoken
(lui/lei) (Lei)	aveva	parlato	he/she had spoken you had spoken
(noi)	avevamo	parlato	we had spoken
(voi)	avevate	parlato	you had spoken
(loro)	avevano	parlato	they had spoken

Non gli <u>avevo</u> mai <u>parlato</u> prima.	I'd never spoken to him before.
Sara gli <u>aveva parlato</u> il giorno prima.	Sara had spoken to him the day before.

[i] Note that you use the same form of **avere** for **lui**, **lei** and **Lei**.

⇨ *For more information on **Verbs with irregular past participles**, see page 110.*

Típ

Do not use the pluperfect tense to say since when, or how long you had been doing something – **da** and the imperfect tense is used for this in Italian.

Abitavamo lì dal 1990.   We'd lived there since 1990.

⇨ *For more information on **da**, see **Prepositions** page 174.*

---

3 When to make the pluperfect tense with avere

➤ As with the perfect tense, you use **avere** to make the <u>pluperfect</u> tense of most verbs.

➤ You do <u>not</u> use **avere** to make the pluperfect tense of:

- reflexive verbs
- certain verbs that do not take a direct object, such as **andare** (meaning *to go*), **venire** (meaning *to come*), **diventare** (meaning *to become*).

Ovviamente <u>avevo</u> <u>sbagliato</u>.	I'd obviously made a mistake.
<u>Avevano</u> <u>lavorato</u> molto il giorno prima.	They'd worked hard the day before.

[i] Note that, as with the perfect tense, the past participle agrees with the <u>object</u> <u>pronouns</u> **lo** and **la**, (meaning *him*, *her* and *it*) and **li** and **le** (meaning *them*) when they come before the verb.

Non <u>l'avevo vista</u>.	I hadn't seen her.
<u>Le lettere? Non <u>le aveva</u> mai <u>lette</u>.	The letters? He'd never read them.

⇨ *For more information on **Object pronouns** and the **Perfect tense**, see pages 44 and 108.*

Key points

✔ The pluperfect tense is used to talk about what had already happened in the past.

✔ The Italian pluperfect tense is made with the imperfect of **avere** or **essere**, and the past participle.

✔ **avere** is used to make the pluperfect tense of most verbs.

4 **How to make the pluperfect tense with *essere***

➤ To make the pluperfect tense with ***essere***:
- choose the <u>imperfect</u> form of ***essere*** that matches the subject of the sentence.
- add the past participle. Make the ending of the participle <u>agree</u> with the subject.

➤ The pluperfect tense of **andare** (meaning *to go*) is as follows:

	Imperfect tense of *essere*	Past participle of andare	Meaning
(io)	ero	andato *or* andata	I had gone
(tu)	eri	andato *or* andata	you had gone
(lui)	era	andato	he/it had gone
(lei)	era	andata	she/it had gone
(Lei)	era	andato *or* andata	you had gone
(noi)	eravamo	andati *or* andate	we had gone
(voi)	eravate	andati *or* andate	you had gone
(loro)	erano	andati *or* andate	they had gone

Silvia <u>era andata</u> con loro.	Silvia had gone with them.
Tutti i miei amici <u>erano andati</u> alla festa.	All my friends had gone to the party.

5 **When to make the pluperfect tense with *essere***

➤ When ***essere*** is used to make the perfect tense of a verb, you also use ***essere*** to make the pluperfect.

⇨ *For more information on **Making the perfect tense with essere**, see page 112.*

➤ Use ***essere*** to make the pluperfect of all reflexive verbs, and of certain verbs that do not take a direct object, such as **andare** (meaning *to go*), **venire** (meaning *to come*), **riuscire** (meaning *to succeed*), **diventare** (meaning *to become*) and **piacere** (meaning *to like*).

Ovviamente non gli <u>erano</u> <u>piaciuti</u> i quadri.	He obviously hadn't liked the pictures.
Sono arrivata alle cinque, ma <u>erano</u> già <u>partiti</u>.	I arrived at five, but they'd already gone.
Fortunatamente non si <u>era</u> <u>fatta</u> male.	Luckily she hadn't hurt herself.

Key points

✔ Verbs that make their perfect tense with ***essere*** also make their pluperfect tense with ***essere***.

✔ When the pluperfect tense is made with ***essere*** the past participle agrees with the subject of the sentence.

✔ ***essere*** is used to make the pluperfect tense of reflexive verbs and certain verbs that do not take a direct object.

For further explanation of grammatical terms, please see pages viii–xii.

The passive

> **What is the passive?**
> The **passive** is a verb form that is used when the subject of the verb is the person or thing that is affected by the action, for example, *Everyone was shocked by the incident; Two people were hurt; The house is being demolished.*

1 Using the passive

➤ Verbs can be <u>active</u> or <u>passive</u>.

➤ In a sentence with an <u>active verb</u> the subject of the sentence does the action:

Subject	Active verb	Object
She	does	most of the work.
A dog	bit	him.

➤ In a sentence with a <u>passive</u> verb the action is done by someone or something that is not the subject of the sentence.

Subject	Passive verb	Who/what the action is done by
Most of the work	is done	by her.
He	was bitten	by a dog.

➤ To show who or what is responsible for the action in a passive sentence you use *by* in English.

➤ You use passive rather than active verbs:

- when you want to focus on the person or thing <u>affected</u> by the action
  <u>John</u> was injured in an accident.

- when you don't know who is responsible for the action
  My car was stolen last week.

2 How to make the passive

➤ In English we use the verb *to be* with a <u>past participle</u> (*is done, was bitten*) to make the passive.

➤ In Italian the passive is made in exactly the same way, using **essere** (meaning *to be*) and a <u>past participle</u>.

➡ *For more information on the **Past participle**, see page 109.*

Siamo invitati ad una festa a casa loro.	We're invited to a party at their house.
L'elettricità è stata tagliata ieri.	The electricity was cut off yesterday.
La partita è stata rinviata.	The match has been postponed.
È stato costretto a ritirarsi dalla gara.	He was forced to withdraw from the competition.

➤ When you say who or what is responsible for the action you use **da** (meaning *by*).

I ladri sono stati catturati dalla polizia.	The thieves were caught by the police.

[i] Note that the past participle agrees with the subject of the verb **essere** in the same way an adjective would.

⇨ *For more information on* **Adjectives**, *see page 20.*

➤ Here is the perfect tense of the **–are** verb **invitare** (meaning *to invite*) in its passive form.

(Subject pronoun)		Perfect tense of *essere*	Past Participle	Meaning
(io)	– masculine	sono stato	invitato	I was, have been
	– feminine	sono stata	invitata	invited
(tu)	– masculine	sei stato	invitato	you were, have been
	– feminine	sei stata	invitata	invited
(lui)		è stato	invitato	he was, has been invited
(lei)		è stata	invitata	she was, has been invited
(Lei)	– masculine	è stato	invitato	you were, have been invited
	– feminine	è stata	invitata	you were, have been invited
(noi)	– masculine	siamo stati	invitati	we were, have been invited
	– feminine	siamo state	invitate	we were, have been invited
(voi)	– masculine	siete stati	invitati	you were, have been invited
	– feminine	siete state	invitate	you were, have been invited
(loro)	– masculine	sono stati	invitati	they were, have been invited
	– feminine	sono state	invitate	they were, have been invited

For further explanation of grammatical terms, please see pages viii–xii.

➤ You can change the tense of the verb **essere** to make whatever passive tense you want.

>> **Sarete** tutti invitati.   You'll all be invited.

>> **Non so se sarebbe invitata.**   I don't know if she would be invited.

➤ Some past participles are irregular.

➪ *For more information on* **Irregular past participles**, *see page 110.*

Grammar Extra!

venire (meaning *to come*) and **rimanere** (meaning *to remain*) are sometimes used instead of **essere** to make the passive.

venire is used in the present, imperfect, future and conditional to make passives, but not in the perfect or pluperfect.

>> Quando **vengono cambiate?**   When <u>are they changed</u>?

>> **Venivano controllati** ogni sei mesi.   They <u>were checked</u> every six months.

>> **Verrà criticato** da tutti.   He<u>'ll be criticized</u> by everyone.

>> **Verrebbe scoperto.**   It <u>would be</u> discovered.

rimanere is used very often with **ferito** (meaning *injured*), and with participles describing emotion, such as **stupefatto** (meaning *amazed*) and **deluso** (meaning *disappointed*).

>> **È rimasto ferito** in un incidente stradale.   He <u>was injured</u> in a car accident.

>> **È rimasta stupefatta** dalla scena.   She <u>was amazed</u> by the scene.

---

3 Avoiding the passive

➤ Passives are not as common in Italian as they are in English. In many cases, where we would use a passive verb, one of the following alternatives would be used in Italian:

- an active construction

>> **Due persone sono morte.**   Two people were killed.

>> **Mi hanno rubato la macchina la settimana scorsa.**   My car was stolen last week.

>> **C'erano delle microspie nella stanza.**   The room was bugged.

>> **Dicono che sia molto ambizioso.**   He's said to be very ambitious.

- an ordinary verb made passive by having **si** put in front (this is known as the **si passivante**)

>> **Qui si vende il pane.**   Bread is sold here.

>> **Si parla inglese.**   English spoken.

>> **Dove si trovano i migliori vini?**   Where are the best wines to be found?

In Italia il prosciutto **si mangia** col melone.	In Italy ham is eaten with melon.
Gli spaghetti non **si mangiano** con le dita!	Spaghetti should not be eaten with one's fingers!
"comodo" **si scrive** con una sola m.	"comodo" is spelled with only one m.

(i) Note that wherever the subject comes in the sentence the verb has to agree with it.

- an impersonal construction with **si**

Si dice che non vada molto bene.	It's said not to be going very well.
Non si fa così.	That's not how it's done.

Tip

When you want to say something like *I was told*, or *She was given* use an active construction in Italian: **Mi hanno detto** (meaning *they told me*); **Le hanno dato** (meaning *they gave her*).

Key points

✔ The passive is made using **essere** with the past participle

✔ The past participle must agree with the subject of **essere**.

✔ Alternatives to the passive are often used in Italian.

For further explanation of grammatical terms, please see pages viii–xii.

The gerund

> **What is a gerund?**
> In English the gerund is a verb form ending in *–ing* which is used to make continuous tenses, for example, *What are you <u>doing</u>?* It can also be used as a noun or an adjective, for example, *I love <u>swimming</u>; a <u>skating</u> rink.*

1 Using the gerund

➤ In Italian the gerund is a verb form ending in **–ando** or **–endo**. It is used to make continuous tenses.

Sto <u>lavorando</u>.	I'm working.
Cosa stai <u>facendo</u>?	What are you doing?

● The gerund follows the present tense of **stare** to make the <u>present continuous</u>.

<u>Sto scrivendo</u> una *lettera*.	I'm writing a letter.
<u>Stai cercando</u> lavoro?	Are you looking for a job?

⇨ *For more information on the **Present continuous**, see page 81.*

● The gerund follows the imperfect tense of **stare** to make the <u>past continuous</u>.

Il bambino <u>stava piangendo</u>.	The little boy was crying.
<u>Stavo lavando</u> i piatti.	I was washing the dishes.

[*i*] Note that the Italian <u>past participle</u> is sometimes used where the gerund is used in English: **essere disteso** means *to be lying*; **essere seduto** means *to be sitting* and **essere appoggiato** means *to be leaning*.

<u>Era disteso</u> sul divano.	He was lying on the sofa.
<u>Era seduta</u> accanto a me.	She was sitting next to me.
La scala <u>era appoggiata</u> al muro.	The ladder was leaning against the wall.

➤ The gerund can be used by itself:

● to say when something happened

<u>Entrando</u> ho sentito odore di pesce.	~~When I came~~ coming in I could smell fish.
<u>Ripensandoci</u>, credo che non fosse colpa sua.	Thinking about it, I don't reckon it was his fault.

● to say why something happened

<u>Sentendomi</u> male sono andato a letto.	Because I felt ill I went to bed.
<u>Vedendolo</u> solo, è venuta a parlargli.	Seeing that he was on his own she came to speak to him.

- to say in what circumstances something could happen

Volendo, potremmo comprarne un altro.   If we wanted to, we could buy another one.

Tip

The gerund never changes its form to agree with the subject of the sentence.

2 How to make the gerund

➤ To make the gerund of **–are** verbs, take off the **–are** ending of the infinitive to get the stem, and add **–ando**.

Infinitive	Stem	Gerund	Meaning
lavorare	lavor-	lavorando	working
andare	and-	andando	going
dare	d-	dando	giving
stare	st-	stando	being

ℹ️ Note that the only **–are** verb that does not follow this rule is **fare**, and verbs made of **fare** with a prefix, such as **rifare** (meaning *to do again*) and **disfare** (meaning *to undo*). The gerund of **fare** is **facendo**.

➤ To make the gerund of **–ere** and **–ire** verbs, take off the **–ere** or **–ire** ending of the infinitive to get the stem, and add **–endo**.

Infinitive	Stem	Gerund	Meaning
credere	cred-	credendo	believing
essere	ess-	essendo	being
dovere	dov-	dovendo	having to
finire	fin-	finendo	finishing
dormire	dorm-	dormendo	sleeping

ℹ️ Note that the only **–ire** verb that does not follow this rule is **dire** (and verbs made of **dire** with a prefix, such as **disdire** (meaning *to cancel*) and **contraddire** (meaning *to contradict*) . The gerund of **dire** is **dicendo**.

3 When not to use the gerund

➤ In English the *-ing* form can follow other verbs, for example, *She started crying;*
He insisted on paying; They continued working.

➤ In Italian the gerund is not used in this way. A construction with a preposition and
the infinitive is used instead.

Ha cominciato <u>a ridere</u>.	She started laughing.
Hai finito <u>di mangiare</u>?	Have you finished eating?

➡ *For more information on **Prepositions after verbs**, see page 143.*

➤ In English we often use *-ing* forms as nouns, for example, *driving, skating, cleaning.*

➤ In Italian you cannot use the **-ando** and **-endo** forms like this. When talking
about activities and interests you use nouns, such as **il giardinaggio**
(meaning *gardening*), **la pulizia** (meaning *cleaning*) and **il fumo** (meaning
smoking).

A mia madre piace molto <u>il giardinaggio</u>.	My mother loves gardening.
Facciamo un po' di <u>pulizia</u>.	Let's do a bit of cleaning.
<u>Il fumo</u> fa male.	Smoking is bad for you.

➤ In English you can put an *-ing* noun in front of another noun, for example,
skating rink.

➤ In Italian you can never put one noun in front of another noun .

- Often you link two words together with a preposition:

calzoncini <u>da</u> bagno	swimming trunks
una borsa <u>per</u> la spesa	a shopping bag
un istruttore <u>di</u> guida	a driving instructor

- Sometimes there is one word in Italian for two English words:

la <u>patente</u>	the <u>driving licence</u>
una <u>piscina</u>	a <u>swimming pool</u>

Tip

When you want to translate this kind of English two-word
combination it's a good idea to look it up in a dictionary.

4 | **Where to put pronouns used with the gerund**

➤ Pronouns are usually joined onto the end of the gerund.

Vedendoli è scoppiata in lacrime.	When she saw them she burst into tears.
Ascoltandolo mi sono addormentato.	Listening to him, I fell asleep.
Incontrandosi per caso sono andati al bar.	Meeting each other by chance, they went to a café.

➤ When the gerund is part of a continuous tense the pronoun can either come before **stare** or be joined onto the gerund.

Ti sto parlando OR **Sto parlandoti.**	I'm talking to you.
Si sta vestendo OR **Sta vestendosi.**	He's getting dressed.
Me lo stavano mostrando OR **Stavano mostrandomelo.**	They were showing me it.

Key points

✔ Use the gerund in continuous tenses with **stare**, and by itself to say when or why something happened.

✔ *-ing* forms in English are not always translated by the gerund.

Impersonal verbs

> **What is an impersonal verb?**
> In English an impersonal verb has the subject *it*, but this '*it*'does not refer to any specific thing; for example, *It's going to rain; It's nine o'clock.*

1 Verbs that are always impersonal

➤ Verbs such as **piovere** (meaning *to rain*) and **nevicare** (meaning *to snow*), are always impersonal because there is no person, animal or thing doing the action.

➤ They are used only in the '*it*' form, the infinitive, and as a gerund (the *–ing* form of the verb).

Piove.	It's raining.
Sta piovendo?	Is it raining?
Ha iniziato a piovere.	It started to rain.
Nevicava da due giorni.	It had been snowing for two days.
Pensi che nevicherà?	Do you think it'll snow?

> Note that the perfect and pluperfect tenses of verbs to do with the weather such as **piovere**, **nevicare**, **grandinare** (meaning *to hail*) and **tuonare** (meaning *to thunder*) can be made either with **avere** or **essere**.

<u>Ha</u> piovuto or <u>è</u> piovuto molto ieri.	It rained a lot yesterday.
<u>Aveva</u> nevicato or <u>era</u> nevicato durante la notte.	It had snowed during the night.

2 Verbs that are sometimes impersonal

➤ **fare** is used impersonally to talk about the weather and time of day:

<u>Fa</u> caldo.	It's hot.
<u>Fa</u> freddo.	It's cold.
<u>Faceva</u> bel tempo.	It was good weather. OR The weather was good.
<u>Fa</u> sempre brutto tempo.	The weather's always bad.
<u>Fa</u> notte.	It's getting dark.

> *Tip*
>
> **Fa niente** means *It doesn't matter.*

➤ **è**, and other tenses of **essere** are used impersonally, like *it's* and other tenses of *to be* in English.

<u>È</u> **tardi.**	It's late.
<u>Era</u> **presto.**	It was early.
<u>È</u> **da tre ore che aspettano.**	It's three hours now that they've been waiting.
<u>Era</u> **Pasqua.**	It was Easter.
Non <u>era</u> **da lei fare così.**	It wasn't like her to act like that.

Tip

Just use the verb by itself when talking about the time or the weather. There is no Italian equivalent for "*it*".

➤ **essere** is used in impersonal constructions with adjectives, for example:

- with an adjective followed by an infinitive

<u>È facile capire</u> **che qualcosa non va.**	It's easy to see that something's wrong.
Mi <u>è impossibile andar</u> **via adesso.**	It's impossible for me to leave now.
<u>È stato stupido buttarli</u> **via.**	It was stupid to throw them away.
<u>Sarebbe bello andarci.</u>	It would be nice to go there.

- with an adjective followed by **che**

<u>È vero che</u> **sono stato impaziente.**	It's true that I've been impatient.
<u>Era bello che</u> **ci fossimo tutti.**	It's nice that we were all there.

Grammar Extra!

When an impersonal construction with **che** is used to refer to something that is a possibility rather than a fact, the following verb must be in the <u>subjunctive</u>.

The following impersonal expressions refer to what might, should, or could be the case, rather than what <u>is</u> the case, and therefore they are always followed by the subjunctive:

- **È possibile che...**
  È possibile che *abbia* sbagliato tu.
  It's possible that...
  It's possible that you made a mistake.

- **Non è possibile che...**
  Non è possibile che *sappiano*.
  It's impossible that...
  It's impossible that they should know. OR They can't possibly know.

- **È facile che...**
  È facile che piova.
  It's likely that...
  It's likely that it'll rain. OR It'll probably rain.

- **È difficile che...**
  È difficile che venga.
  It's unlikely that...
  It's unlikely that he'll come.

⇨ *For more information on the **Subjunctive**, see page 130.*

For further explanation of grammatical terms, please see pages viii–xii.

➤ **parere** and **sembrare** (both meaning *to seem*) are often used impersonally.

Sono contenti? – <u>Pare</u> di sì.	Are they happy? – It seems so.
L'ha creduto? – <u>Pare</u> di no.	Did he believe it? – Apparently not.
Forse va tutto bene, ma non <u>sembra</u>.	Maybe everything's okay, but it doesn't look like it.
<u>Pare</u> che sia stato lui.	Apparently it was him.
<u>Sembra</u> che tu *abbia* ragione.	Seemingly you're right.

i Note that the Italian construction with a verb can often be translated by the adverbs *apparently* and *seemingly*.

➤ Other verbs used impersonally are **bastare** (meaning *to be enough*), **bisognare** and **occorrere** (both meaning *to be necessary*), **importare** (meaning *to be important*).

Basta?	Is that enough?
Bisogna prenotare?	Is it necessary to or do you have to book?
Bisogna arrivare un'ora prima.	You have to get there an hour before.
Occorre farlo subito.	It should be done at once.
Oggi o domani, non importa.	Today or tomorrow, it doesn't matter.

i Note that these verbs can be replaced by impersonal constructions with **essere** and an adjective.

È necessario prenotare?	Is it necessary to book?
Sarebbe opportuno farlo subito.	It would be best to do it at once.

Tip

può darsi (meaning *it's possible*), can be used like **forse** (meaning *maybe*).

Vieni? – Può darsi.	Are you coming? – Maybe.
Può darsi che vincano.	It's possible or maybe they'll win.

Key points

✔ Impersonal verbs and expressions can only be used in the 'it' form, the infinitive and the gerund.

✔ Impersonal verbs are often used when talking about the weather.

The subjunctive

> **What is the subjunctive?**
> The **subjunctive** is a verb form that is often used in Italian to express wishes, thoughts and beliefs. In English the subjunctive is only used occasionally, mainly in formal language, for example, *If I were you...; So be it; He asked that they be removed*.

1 Using the subjunctive

➤ If you have the word **che** (meaning *that*) in an Italian sentence you often have to use the subjunctive.

➤ The subjunctive is used after **che**:

- following verbs such as **pensare** (meaning *to think*), **credere** (meaning *to believe/think*) and **sperare** (meaning *to hope*).

Penso che sia giusto.	I think it's fair.
Credo che partano domani.	I think they're leaving tomorrow.
Spero che Luca arrivi in tempo.	I hope Luca arrives in time.

> *Tip*
>
> Whereas in English you can say either *I think...* or *I think that...* in Italian you always say **che**.

- following the verb **volere** (meaning *to want*).

Voglio che i miei ragazzi siano felici.	I want my children to be happy.
Vuole che la aiuti.	She wants me to help her.

2 How to make the present subjunctive

➤ To make the present subjunctive of most verbs, take off the **–o** ending of the **io** form and add endings.

➤ For **–are** verbs the endings are **–i, –i, –i, –iamo, –iate, –ino**.

➤ For **–ere** and **–ire** verbs the endings are **–a, –a, –a, –iamo, –iate, –ano**.

ⓘ Note that in the case of **–ire** verbs which add **–isc** in the **io** form, for example **finisco** (meaning *I finish*) and **pulisco** (meaning *I clean*), **–isc** is not added in the **noi** and **voi** forms. *same then as present*

For further explanation of grammatical terms, please see pages viii–xii.

> **Tip**
>
> The **io**, **tu**, **lui** and **lei** forms of the present subjunctive are all the same.
> The **noi** form of the present subjunctive is the same as the present simple.
>
> ⇨ For more information on the **Present simple**, see page 69.

➤ The following table shows the present subjunctive of three regular verbs:
parlare (meaning *to speak*), **credere** (meaning *to believe*) and **finire** (meaning
to finish).

Infinitive	io, tu, lui, lei, Lei	noi	voi	loro
parlare	parli	parliamo	parliate	parlino
credere	creda	crediamo	crediate	credano
finire	finisca	finiamo	finiate	finiscano

Non voglio che mi <u>parlino</u>.   I don't want them to speak to me.
Può darsi che non ti <u>creda</u>.   Maybe she doesn't believe you.
È meglio che lo <u>finisca</u> io.   It'll be best if I finish it.

➤ Some common verbs that are irregular in the ordinary present tense also have
irregular present subjunctives:

Infinitive	io, tu, lui, lei, Lei	noi	voi	loro
andare *to go*	vada	andiamo	andiate	vadano
avere *to have*	abbia	abbiamo	abbiate	abbiano
dare *to give*	dia	diamo	diate	diano
dire *to say*	dica	diciamo	diciate	dicano
dovere *to have to*	debba	dobbiamo	dobbiate	debbano
essere *to be*	sia	siamo	siate	siano
fare *to do/make*	faccia	facciamo	facciate	facciano
potere *to be able*	possa	possiamo	possiate	possano
scegliere *to choose*	scelga	scegliamo	scegliate	scelgano
stare *to be*	stia	stiamo	stiate	stiano
tenere *to hold*	tenga	teniamo	teniate	tengano
tradurre *to translate*	traduca	traduciamo	traduciate	traducano
uscire *to go out*	esca	usciamo	usciate	escano
venire *to come*	venga	veniamo	veniate	vengano
volere *to want*	voglia	vogliamo	vogliate	vogliano

È meglio che tu te ne <u>vada</u>.	You'd better leave.
Vuoi che lo <u>traduca</u>?	Do you want me to translate it?
È facile che <u>scelgano</u> quelli rossi.	They'll probably choose those red ones.
Spero che tua madre <u>stia</u> meglio ora.	I hope your mother is better now.
Credi che <u>possa</u> essere vero?	Do you think it can be true?

> **Key points**
>
> ✔ When you express a wish, hope, or belief with a verb + **che**, the verb following **che** should be in the subjunctive.
>
> ✔ **che** cannot be missed out in Italian.

3 | When to use the present subjunctive

➤ Use the present subjunctive when you're saying what you think, feel or hope.

➤ The following are common verbs and expressions used to express opinions and hopes. They are used with **che** followed by the subjunctive:

- **pensare che** to think (that)

Pensano <u>che abbia</u> ragione io.	They think I'm right.
Pensi <u>che sia</u> giusto?	Do you think that's fair?

- **credere che** to believe/think (that)

Crede <u>che sia stata</u> una macchina rossa.	He thinks it was a red car.

- **supporre che** to suppose (that)

Suppongo <u>che</u> quello <u>sia</u> il padre.	I suppose he's the father.

- **sperare che** to hope (that)

Spero <u>che vada</u> bene.	I hope it'll be okay.

- **essere contento che** to be glad (that)

Sono contento <u>che faccia</u> bel tempo.	I'm glad the weather's nice.

- **mi dispiace che** I'm sorry (that)

Mi dispiace <u>che</u> non <u>vengano</u>.	I'm sorry they're not coming.

- **è facile che** it's likely (that)

È facile <u>che piova</u>.	It'll probably rain.

For further explanation of grammatical terms, please see pages viii–xii.

- **può darsi che** it's possible (that)

  Può darsi che non **venga**. It's possible that he won't come.

- **è un peccato che** it's a pity (that)

  È un peccato che non **sia potuto venire**. It's a pity he couldn't come.

Tip

It is best to learn the irregular subjunctives of common verbs such as **avere** (meaning *to have*), **essere** (meaning *to be*), **andare** (meaning *to go*) and **fare** (meaning *to make* or *do*).

➤ **che** is not always followed by the subjunctive. Use the ordinary present, future and so on, when you're saying what you know, or are sure of.

So che è tuo.	I know it's yours.
Sa che vale la pena.	She knows it's worth it.
Sono certo che verrà.	I'm sure she'll come.

Key points

✔ Use the present subjunctive + **che** to say what you think, feel or hope.

✔ Do not use the subjunctive + **che** to say what you know or are sure of.

Grammar Extra!

Verbs and verbal expressions that express thoughts and hopes are followed by **di** + the infinitive, instead of **che** + the subjunctive if the subject of the sentence is thinking, hoping or feeling something about themselves.

Compare the following examples: in the sentences on the left side the two verbs have the same subect – I... I... and so on. These use **di** + infinitive. In the sentences on the right the two verbs have different subjects – I... they... and so on. These use **che** + subjunctive.

Infinitive construction	Subjunctive construction
Penso di **poter** venire.	Penso che **possano** venire.
I think I can come.	I think that they can come.
Credo di **aver sbagliato**.	Credo che **abbiamo sbagliato**.
I think I've made a mistake.	I think we've made a mistake.
È contenta di **essere stata promossa**.	Sono contento che **sia stata promossa**.
She's glad she passed.	I'm glad she passed.
Vi dispiace **di partire**?	Ti dispiace che loro **partano**?
Are you sorry you're leaving?	Are you sorry they're leaving?

4 Infinitive or subjunctive after volere?

➤ **volere** can be used with either the infinitive or the subjunctive.

➤ As in English, the infinitive is used in Italian to say what you want to do.

Voglio _essere_ felice.	I want to be happy.
Vogliamo _aiutarla_.	We want to help her.

➤ However, when you're saying what you want someone else to do, or how you want something to be, you use **che** followed by the present subjunctive.

Voglio _che_ tutto _sia_ pronto.	I want everything to be ready.
Vuole _che_ tu _faccia_ del tuo meglio.	He wants you to do your best.
Vogliamo _che_ loro _vadano_ via.	We want them to go away.

➤ When you're saying what you wanted someone else to do in the past, or how you wanted something to be, change the present subjunctive to the imperfect subjunctive.

Volevo _che_ tutto _fosse_ pronto.	I wanted everything to be ready.
Voleva _che_ loro _andassero_ via.	She wanted them to go away.

⇨ _For more information on the **Imperfect subjunctive**, see page 136._

Grammar Extra!

The subjunctive is used after certain conjunctions which include **che**:

- **prima che** before
  Vuoi parlargli _prima che parta_?   Do you want to speak to him before he goes?

☑ Note that **prima di** and the infinitive is used if the two verbs have the same subject:

Mi ha parlato _prima di_ partire.	He spoke to me before he went.
Gli ho parlato _prima di_ partire.	I spoke to him before I went.

- **affinché** so that
  Ti do venti euro _affinché tu possa_ comprarlo.   I'll give you twenty euros so that you can buy it.

- **a meno che** unless
  Lo prendo io, _a meno che_ tu lo _voglia_.   I'll take it, unless you want it.

- **nel caso che** in case
  Ti do il mio numero di telefono _nel caso che tu venga_ a Roma.   I'll give you my phone number in case you come to Rome.

⇨ _For more information on **Conjunctions**, see page 187._

For further explanation of grammatical terms, please see pages viii–xii.

5 | How to make the perfect subjunctive

➤ To make the perfect subjunctive you simply use the subjunctive of **avere** (meaning *to have*) or **essere** (meaning *to be*) with the past participle.

➤ For example, **fare** (meaning *to make* or *to do*) makes its ordinary perfect tense and its perfect subjunctive with **avere**, while **essere** makes its ordinary perfect tense and its perfect subjunctive with **essere**.

⇨ *For more information on the **Perfect tense** and **Past participles**, see pages 108-109.*

		ordinary perfect	perfect subjunctive
fare *to do/make*	io, tu, lui, lei, Lei	ho fatto, hai fatto, ha fatto	*abbia* fatto
	noi	abbiamo fatto	*abbiamo* fatto
	voi	avete fatto	*abbiate* fatto
	loro	hanno fatto	*abbiano* fatto
essere *to be*	io	sono stato, sono stata	sia stato, sia stata
	tu	sei stato, sei stata	sia stato, sia stata
	lui	è stato	sia stato
	lei	è stata	sia stata
	Lei	è stato, è stata	sia stato, sia stata
	noi	siamo stati, siamo state	siamo stati, siamo state
	voi	siete stati, siete state	siate stati, siate state
	loro	sono stati, sono state	siano stati, siano state

Non credo che l'_abbiano fatto_ loro.	I don't think they did it.
È possibile che _sia stato_ un errore.	It might have been a mistake.

6 | When to use the perfect subjunctive

➤ When you want to say what you think or hope about something in the past, use a verb such as **penso che** and **spero che**, followed by the perfect subjunctive.

Penso che _sia stata_ una buona idea.	I think it was a good idea.
Spero che non si _sia fatta_ male.	I hope she didn't hurt herself.
Spero che _abbia detto_ la verità.	I hope you told the truth.
È possibile che _abbiano cambiato_ idea.	It's possible they've changed their minds.

7 | Avoiding the perfect subjunctive

➤ Instead of using expressions such as **penso che** and **è possibile che** with the perfect subjunctive, you can use **secondo me** (meaning *in my opinion*) or **forse** (meaning *perhaps*) with the ordinary perfect tense to say what you think or believe.

Secondo me è stata una buona idea.	In my opinion it was a good idea.
Forse hanno cambiato idea.	Perhaps they've changed their minds.

⇨ *For more information on the **Perfect tense**, see page 108.*

➤ You can also avoid using the perfect subjunctive by saying what you think first, and adding a verb such as **penso**, **credo** or **spero** to the end of the sentence.

Hai detto la verità, <u>spero</u>.	You told the truth, I hope.
Hanno fatto bene, <u>penso</u>.	They did the right thing, I think.

Key points

✔ When you express a wish, hope, or belief about something in the past, the verb following **che** should be in the perfect subjunctive.

✔ You can sometimes reword sentences to avoid using the perfect subjunctive.

---

8 How to make the imperfect subjunctive

➤ The imperfect subjunctive is made by adding endings to the verb <u>stem</u>.

➤ The endings for **–are** verbs are **–assi**, **–assi**, **–asse**, **–assimo**, **–aste**, and **–assero**; the endings for **–ere** verbs are **–essi**, **–essi**, **–esse**, **–essimo**, **–este**, and **–essero**; the endings for **–ire** verbs are **–issi**, **–issi**, **–isse**, **–issimo**, **–iste** and **–issero**.

➤ The following table shows the imperfect subjunctive of three regular verbs: **parlare** (meaning *to speak*), **credere** (meaning *to believe*) and **finire** (meaning *to finish*).

	parlare	credere	finire
(io)	parlassi	credessi	finissi
(tu)	parlassi	credessi	finissi
(lui/lei) (Lei)	parlasse	credesse	finisse
(noi)	parlassimo	credessimo	finissimo
(voi)	parlaste	credeste	finiste
(loro)	parlassero	credessero	finissero

Volevano che <u>parlassi</u> con l'inquilino.	They wanted me to speak to the tenant.
Anche se mi <u>credesse</u>, non farebbe niente.	Even if he believed me he wouldn't do anything.
Se solo <u>finisse</u> prima delle otto!	If only it finished before eight o'clock!

➤ The imperfect subjunctive of **essere** is as follows:

(io)	fossi
(tu)	fossi
(lui/lei)	fosse
(Lei)	fosse
(noi)	fossimo
(voi)	foste
(loro)	fossero

For further explanation of grammatical terms, please see pages viii–xii.

| | | Se <u>fossi</u> in te non lo pagherei. | | If I were you I wouldn't pay it. | |
| Se <u>fosse</u> più furba verrebbe. | | | | If she had more sense she'd come. | |

➤ The imperfect subjunctive of the other important irregular verbs – **bere** (meaning *to drink*), **dare** (meaning *to give*), **dire** (meaning *to say*), **fare** (meaning *to make* or *to do*) and **stare** (meaning *to be*) – is as follows:

	(io)	(tu)	(lui/lei/Lei)	(noi)	(voi)	(loro)
bere	bevessi	bevessi	bevesse	bevessimo	beveste	bevessero
dare	dessi	dessi	desse	dessimo	deste	dessero
dire	dicessi	dicessi	dicesse	dicessimo	diceste	dicessero
fare	facessi	facessi	facesse	facessimo	faceste	facessero
stare	stessi	stessi	stesse	stessimo	steste	stessero

Se solo <u>bevesse</u> meno!	If only he drank less!
Voleva che gli <u>dessero</u> il permesso.	He wanted them to give him permission.

9 When to use the imperfect subjunctive

➤ The imperfect subjunctive is used to talk about what you wanted someone to do in the past, or about how you wanted things to be.

Voleva che <u>fossimo</u> pronti alle otto.	He wanted us to be ready at eight.
Volevano che tutto <u>fosse</u> in ordine.	They wanted everything to be tidy.
Volevo che <u>andasse</u> più veloce.	I wanted him to go faster.

➤ In English, when you are talking about what you would do in an imagined situation, the <u>past tense</u> is used to describe the situation, for example, *What would you do if you <u>won</u> the lottery?*

➤ In Italian the <u>imperfect subjunctive</u> is used for this kind of imagined situation, which is often introduced by **se** (meaning *if*).

Se ne <u>avessi</u> bisogno, te lo darei.	If you needed it I'd give it to you.
Se lo <u>sapesse</u> sarebbe molto deluso.	If he knew he'd be very disappointed.
Se solo <u>avessi</u> più denaro!	If only I had more money!

Key points

✔ The imperfect subjunctive is used when talking about what you wanted someone to do, or how you wanted things to be.

✔ The imperfect subjunctive is used to talk about imagined situations.

The Infinitive

> **What is the infinitive?**
> In English the **infinitive** is the basic form of the verb, for example, *walk*, *see*, *hear*.
> It is used after other verbs such as *should*, *must* and *can*. The infinitive is often
> used with to: *to speak*, *to eat*, *to live*.

1 Using the infinitive

➤ In English the infinitive may be one word, for example, *speak*, or two words,
for example, *to speak*. In Italian the infinitive is always one word, and is the verb
form that ends in **–are**, **–ere**, or **–ire**, for example, **parlare** (meaning *to speak*),
credere (meaning *to believe*), **finire** (meaning *to finish*). The final **–e** of the infinitive
ending is sometimes dropped.

[i] Note that there are a few verbs with infinitives ending in **–urre**, for example,
tradurre (meaning *to translate*), **produrre** (meaning *to produce*) and **ridurre**
(meaning *to reduce*). **–urre** verbs follow the pattern of **produrre**, which you
can find in the verb tables in the middle section of the book.

➤ The infinitive is the form of the verb shown in dictionaries.

➤ In Italian the infinitive is used in the following ways:

- after adjectives and nouns that are followed by **di**

Sono <u>contento di veder</u>ti.	I'm glad to see you.
Sono <u>sorpreso di veder</u>ti qui.	I'm surprised to see you here.
Sono <u>stufo di studiare</u>.	I'm fed up of studying.
Ho <u>voglia di uscire</u>	I feel like going out.
Non c'è <u>bisogno di</u> prenotare.	There's no need to book.

- after another verb

Non <u>devi andar</u>ci se non vuoi.	You don't have to go if you don't want to.
<u>Posso entrare</u>?	Can I come in?
Cosa ti <u>piacerebbe fare</u>?	What would you like to do?
<u>Preferisce spendere</u> i suoi soldi in vestiti.	He prefers to spend his money on clothes.

- to give instructions and orders, particularly on signs, on forms, and in
recipes and manuals

<u>Rallentare</u>.	Slow down.
<u>Spingere</u>.	Push.
<u>Scaldare</u> a fuoco lento per cinque minuti.	Heat gently for five minutes.

For further explanation of grammatical terms, please see pages viii–xii.

- to tell someone you call **tu** not to do something

Non fare sciocchezze!	Don't do anything silly!
Non toccarlo!	Don't touch it!

➪ *For more information on the **Imperative**, see page 82.*

2 | Infinitive or gerund?

➤ In English, prepositions such as *before*, *after* and *without*, are followed by the *-ing* form of the verb, for example, *before leaving*, *after eating*.

➤ In Italian prepositions are followed by the infinitive.

Prima di aprire il pacchetto, leggi le istruzioni.	Before opening the packet, read the instructions.
È andato via **senza dire** niente.	He went away without saying anything.
Dopo aver telefonato è uscita.	After making a phone call she went out.

➤ In English the *-ing* form of the verb can be used as a noun, for example, *They enjoy dancing*. In Italian the infinitive, not the gerund, is used as a noun.

Ascoltare la musica è rilassante.	Listening to music is relaxing.
Camminare fa bene.	Walking is good for you.

> ## Tip
>
> Remember to use the infinitive with **mi piace** when saying what activities you like:
>
> **Mi piace cavalcare.** I like riding.

Grammar Extra!

As well as the ordinary infinitive there is also the perfect infinitive. In English this is made with the infinitive *have* + the past participle, for example *He could have done better; He claims to have seen an eagle*. In Italian the perfect infinitive is made with **avere** or **essere** + the past participle.

Può **aver avuto** un incidente.	He may have had an accident.
Dev'**essere successo** ieri.	It must have happened yesterday.

> ### Key point
>
> ✔ In Italian the infinitive is one word.

3 | Linking verbs together

➤ In English both the infinitive and the *-ing* form can follow after another verb, for example, *Do you want to come?*; *They stopped working*.

➤ In Italian only the infinitive can follow another verb. Verbs are generally linked to the infinitive in one of these three ways:

- directly

  Volete aspettare?   Do you want to wait?

- with the preposition **a**

  Hanno cominciato a ridere.   They started to laugh.

- with the preposition **di**

  Quando sono entrato hanno   When I came in they stopped
  smesso di parlare.   talking.

⇨ *For more information on the* **Prepositions** *a and di, see pages 174 and 176.*

[*i*] Other linking prepositions are sometimes used, for example, **stare per far qualcosa** (meaning to *be about to do something*).

  Stavo per uscire quando ha   I was about to go out when the
  squillato il telefono.   phone rang.

4 | Verbs that are not linked to the infinitive by a preposition

➤ A number of very common verbs are followed directly by the infinitive:

- **dovere** to have to, must

  È dovuto partire.   He had to leave.

  Dev'essere tardi.   It must be late.

- **potere** can, may

  Non posso aiutarti.   I can't help you.

  Potresti aprire la finestra?   Could you open the window?

  Potrebbe essere vero.   It might be true.

- **sapere** to know how to, can

  Sai farlo?   Do you know how to do it?

  Non sapeva nuotare.   He couldn't swim.

- **volere** to want

  Voglio comprare una macchina nuova. I want to buy a new car.

Tip

voler dire (literally *to want to say*) is the Italian for *to mean*.

  Non so che cosa vuol dire.   I don't know what it means.

For further explanation of grammatical terms, please see pages viii–xii.

- verbs such as **piacere**, **dispiacere** and **convenire**

Mi <u>piace andare</u> in bici.	I like cycling.
Ci <u>dispiace andar</u> via.	We're sorry to be leaving.
Ti <u>conviene partire</u> presto.	You'd best set off early.

- **vedere** (meaning *to see*), **ascoltare** (meaning *to listen to*) and **sentire** (meaning *to hear*)

Ci <u>ha visto arrivare</u>.	He saw us arriving.
Ti <u>ho sentito cantare</u>.	I heard you singing.
L'<u>abbiamo ascoltato parlare</u>.	We listened to him talking.

- **fare** (meaning *to make*) and **lasciare** (meaning *to let*)

Non mi <u>far ridere</u>!	Don't make me laugh!
<u>Lascia fare</u> a me.	Let me do it.

[i] Note that **far fare qualcosa** and **farsi fare qualcosa** both mean *to have something done*:

<u>Ho fatto riparare</u> la macchina.	I had the car repaired.
Mi <u>sono fatta tagliare</u> i capelli.	I had my hair cut.

➤ The following common verbs are also followed directly by the infinitive:

bisognare	to be necessary
desiderare	to want
odiare	to hate
preferire	to prefer

<u>Odio alzarmi</u> presto al mattino.	I hate getting up early in the morning.
<u>Desiderava migliorare</u> il suo inglese.	He wanted to improve his English.
<u>Bisogna prenotare</u>.	You need to book.
<u>Preferisco</u> non <u>parlarne</u>.	I prefer not to talk about it.

5 | Verbs followed by a and the infinitive

➤ Some very common verbs can be followed by **a** and the infinitive:

andare a fare qualcosa	to go to do something
venire a fare qualcosa	to come to do something
imparare a fare qualcosa	to learn to do something
cominciare a fare qualcosa	to start doing *or* to do something
continuare a fare qualcosa	to go on doing something
abituarsi a fare qualcosa	to get used to doing something
riuscire a fare qualcosa	to manage to do something

Sono venuti <u>a trovarci</u>.	They came to see us.
Siamo riusciti <u>a convincerla</u>.	We managed to persuade her.
Dovrò abituarmi <u>ad alzarmi</u> presto.	I'll have to get used to getting up early.

➤ As in English, you can put an object between the verb and the infinitive:

aiutare <u>qualcuno</u> a fare qualcosa	to help <u>somebody</u> to do something
invitare <u>qualcuno</u> a fare qualcosa	to invite <u>somebody</u> to do something
insegnare <u>a qualcuno</u> a fare qualcosa	to teach <u>somebody</u> to do something

[i] Note that **insegnare** takes an indirect object.

<u>Hanno invitato Lucia a sedersi</u> <u>al loro ta</u>volo.	They invited Lucia to sit at their table.
<u>Ho aiutato mamma a lavare</u> i piatti.	I helped mum wash up.
<u>Ha insegnato a mio fratello a</u> <u>nuotare.</u>	He taught my brother to swim.

5 | Verbs followed by di and the infinitive

➤ The following are the most common verbs that can be followed by **di** and the infinitive:

cercare di fare qualcosa	to try to do something
decidere di fare qualcosa	to decide to do something
dimenticare di fare qualcosa	to forget to do something
smettere di fare qualcosa	to stop doing something
ricordarsi di aver fatto qualcosa	to remember having done something
negare di aver fatto qualcosa	to deny doing something
Cerca <u>di</u> smettere di fumare.	He's trying to stop smoking.
Ho deciso <u>di</u> non andarci.	I decided not to go.
Non mi ricordo <u>di</u> aver detto una cosa del genere.	I don't remember saying anything like that.
Ho dimenticato <u>di</u> prendere la chiave.	I forgot to take my key.

Tip

Learn the linking preposition that goes with important verbs.

Key points

✔ Italian verbs can be followed by the infinitive, with or without a linking preposition.

✔ Italian verbs are not followed by the gerund.

For further explanation of grammatical terms, please see pages viii–xii.

Prepositions after verbs

➤ English verbs are often followed by prepositions, for example, *I'm relying <u>on</u> you, They'll write <u>to</u> him, He was accused <u>of</u> murder.*

➤ The same is true of Italian verbs, which are often followed by prepositions.

- **entrare in** to go into
  Siamo entrati in aula.   We went into the classroom.

➤ As in English, Italian verbs can be followed by two prepositions.

     parlare <u>a</u> qualcuno <u>di</u> qualcosa   to talk <u>to</u> someone <u>about</u> something

➤ With some verbs the Italian preposition may not be the one you would expect. For example, *to* in English is not always **a** in Italian, **di** is not always translated by *of* and so forth. The most important ones of these are shown in the examples on the following pages.

⮕ *For more information on **Verbs used with a preposition and the infinitive**, see page 141.*

> *Tip*
>
> When you learn a new verb, check if there's a preposition that goes with it, and learn that too.

<u>1</u> **Verbs followed by <u>a</u>**

➤ **a** is used with the indirect object of verbs such as **dire** (meaning *to say*) and **dare** (meaning *to give*).

dare qualcosa <u>a</u> qualcuno	to give something to someone
dire qualcosa <u>a</u> qualcuno	to say something to someone
mandare qualcosa <u>a</u> qualcuno	to send something to someone
scrivere qualcosa <u>a</u> qualcuno	to write something to someone
mostrare qualcosa <u>a</u> qualcuno	to show something to someone

⮕ *For more information about **Indirect objects**, see page 46.*

> *Tip*
>
> In English you can say *to give someone something*. In Italian you <u>cannot</u> leave out the preposition – you have to use **a** with the person who is the indirect object.

➤ Here are some verbs taking **a** in Italian when you might not expect it, since the English equivalent either does not have the preposition *to* or has no preposition at all:

arrivare **a** (una citt**à**)	to arrive at (*a town*)
avvicinarsi **a** qualcuno	to approach someone
chiedere qualcosa **a** qualcuno	to ask someone for something
far male **a** qualcuno	to hurt someone
giocare **a** qualcosa	to play something (*game/sport*)
insegnare qualcosa **a** qualcuno	to teach somebody something
partecipare **a** qualcosa	to take part in something
rispondere **a** qualcuno	to answer someone
rivolgersi **a** qualcuno	to ask someone
somigliare **a** qualcuno	to look like someone
permettere **a** qualcuno di fare qualcosa	to allow someone to do something
proibire **a** qualcuno di fare qualcosa	to forbid someone to do something
rubare qualcosa **a** qualcuno	to steal something from someone
ubbidire **a** qualcuno	to obey someone

Chiedi **a** Lidia come si chiama il suo cane.	Ask Lidia what her dog's called.
Quando arrivi **a** Londra?	When do you arrive in London?
Parteciperai **alla** gara?	Are you going to take part in the competition?
Non permette **a** Luca di uscire.	She doesn't allow Luca to go out.

⇨ *For verbs such as* **piacere**, **mancare** *and* **rincrescere**, *see* **Verbal idioms** *on page 146.*

> *Tip*
>
> Remember that you often have to use a preposition with an Italian verb when there is no preposition in English.

2 | Verbs followed by di

➤ Here are some verbs taking **di** in Italian when the English verb is not followed by *of*:

accorgersi **di** qualcosa	to realize something
aver bisogno **di** qualcosa	to need something
aver voglia **di** qualcosa	to want something
discutere **di** qualcosa	to discuss something
fidarsi **di** qualcosa/qualcuno	to trust something/someone
intendersi **di** qualcosa	to know about something
interessarsi **di** qualcosa	to be interested in something
lamentarsi **di** qualcosa	to complain about something
ricordarsi **di** qualcosa/qualcuno	to remember something/someone

ridere di qualcosa/qualcuno	to laugh at something/someone
stufarsi di qualcosa/qualcuno	to get fed up with something/someone
stupirsi di qualcosa	to be amazed by something
trattare di qualcosa	to be about something
vantarsi di qualcosa	to boast about something
Non mi fido di lui.	I don't trust him.
Ho bisogno di soldi.	I need money.
Discutono spesso di politica.	They often discuss politics.
Mi sono stufato di loro.	I got fed up with them.

3 Verbs followed by da

➤ Here are some verbs taking **da** in Italian when the English verb is not followed by *from*:

dipendere da qualcosa/qualcuno	to depend on something/someone
giudicare da qualcosa	to judge by something
scendere da qualcosa	to get off something (*bus, train, plane*)
sporgersi da qualcosa	to lean out of something
Dipende dal tempo.	It depends on the weather.

4 Verbs that are followed by a preposition in English but not in Italian

➤ Although the English verb is followed by a preposition, you **don't** use a preposition with the following Italian verbs:

guardare qualcosa/qualcuno	to look at something/someone
ascoltare qualcosa/qualcuno	to listen to something/someone
cercare qualcosa/qualcuno	to look for something/someone
chiedere qualcosa	to ask for something
aspettare qualcosa/qualcuno	to wait for something/someone
pagare qualcosa	to pay for something
Guarda la sua faccia.	Look at his face.
Mi stai ascoltando?	Are you listening to me?
Sto cercando la chiave.	I'm looking for my key.
Ha chiesto qualcosa da mangiare.	He asked for something to eat.
Aspettami!	Wait for me!
Ho già pagato il biglietto.	I've already paid for my ticket.

Key points

✔ Many Italian verbs are not followed by the preposition you would expect.

✔ There can be a preposition with a verb in Italian, but not in English, and vice versa.

Verbal Idioms

➤ Some important Italian verbs behave differently from their English equivalent, for example:

Mi piace l'Italia.	I like Italy.
Mi piacciono i cani.	I like dogs.

➤ Both English sentences have the same verb *like*, which agrees with the subject, *I*.

➤ The Italian sentences have different verbs, one singular (**piace**) and the other plural (**piacciono**). This is because the verb **piacere** literally means *to be pleasing*, and in one sentence what's pleasing is singular (**l'Italia**) and in the other it's plural (**i cani**).

➤ If you use this wording in English you also get two different verbs: Italy <u>is</u> pleasing to me; Dogs <u>are</u> pleasing to me.

> *Tip*
>
> Remember to turn the sentence around in this way when talking about what you like in Italian.

<u>**1**</u> **Present tense of piacere**

➤ When talking about likes and dislikes in the present use **piace** if the subject of the verb is singular, and **piacciono** if it is plural.

➤ Use the appropriate indirect pronoun: **mi**, **ti**, **gli**, **le**, **ci**, or **vi**.

[i] Note that **gli** means both *to him*, and *to them*, so it is used to say what he likes, and what they like.

Questo colore non mi <u>piace</u>.	I don't like this colour. (*literally: this colour <u>is</u> not pleasing to me*)
Ti <u>piacciono</u> le mie scarpe?	Do you like my shoes? (*literally: <u>are</u> my shoes pleasing to you?*)
Non gli <u>piacciono</u> i dolci.	He doesn't like desserts. (*literally: desserts <u>are</u> not pleasing to him*)
Le <u>piace</u> l'Italia, signora?	Do you like Italy, madam? (*literally: <u>is</u> Italy pleasing to you?*)
Ci <u>piace</u> il mare.	We like the sea. (*literally: the sea <u>is</u> pleasing to us*)

Vi piacciono le montagne?	Do you like the mountains? (*literally: are the mountains pleasing to you?*)
Sono vecchi, non gli piace questa musica.	They're old, they don't like this music. (*literally: this music isn't pleasing to them*)

➪ For more information on **Indirect object pronouns**, see page 46.

> ## Tip
>
> Use the infinitive, not the gerund, when talking about the activities you like:
>
> | | |
> |---|---|
> | **Mi piace cucinare.** | I like cooking. |
> | **Ci piace camminare.** | We like walking. |

➤ If it is not used with the pronouns **mi**, **ti**, **gli**, **le**, **ci**, or **vi**, **piacere** is followed by the preposition **a**.

Il giardinaggio piace a mia sorella.	My sister likes gardening. (*literally: gardening is pleasing to my sister*)
I suoi film non piacciono a tutti.	Not everyone likes his films. (*literally: his films are not pleasing to everyone*)
L'Italia piace ai tuoi?	Do your parents like Italy? (*literally: Is Italy pleasing to your parents?*)

2 Other tenses of piacere

➤ You can use **piacere** in any tense.

Credi che la casa piacerà a Sara?	Do you think Sara will like the house?
Questo libro ti piacerebbe.	You'd like this book.
Da giovane gli piaceva nuotare.	When he was young he liked swimming.
Il concerto è piaciuto a tutti.	Everyone liked the concert.
Non credo che il calcio piaccia al professore.	I don't think the teacher likes football.

> ## Tip
>
> **Mi dispiace** means *I'm sorry*. Change the pronoun to **gli**, **le**, **ci** and so on if you want to say *He's sorry*, *She's sorry* or *We're sorry*.

3 Other verbs like piacere

➤ There are a number of other important verbs that are used with an indirect pronoun, or are followed by the preposition **a**.

➤ As with **piacere**, the person who is the subject of the verb in English is the indirect object in Italian.

- **convenire** (*literally*) to be advisable

<u>Ti</u> conviene partir presto.	You'd better set off early.
Non conviene <u>a</u> nessuno fare così.	Nobody should behave like that.

- **mancare** (literally) to be missing

Fammi sapere se <u>ti</u> manca qualcosa.	Let me know if you need anything.
<u>Mi</u> manchi.	I miss you.

- **interessare** to be of interest

Se <u>ti</u> interessa puoi venire.	If you're interested you can come.
Pensi che interesserebbe <u>a</u> Luigi?	Do you think Luigi would be interested?

- **importare** to be important

Non <u>mi</u> importa!	I don't care!
Non importa <u>a</u> mio marito.	My husband doesn't care.

- **rincrescere** (*literally*) to make sorry

<u>Ci</u> rincresce di non poterlo fare.	We're sorry we can't do it.
Se non <u>ti</u> rincresce vorrei pensarci su.	If you don't mind I'd like to think it over.

- **restare** to be left

<u>Mi</u> restano cinquanta euro.	I've got fifty euros left.
<u>A</u> Maria restano solo ricordi.	Maria only has memories left.

Key points

✔ Turn the sentence around when using verbs like **piacere**.

✔ Use the preposition **a**, or an indirect object pronoun.

Negatives

> **What is a negative?**
> A negative question or statement is one which contains a word such as *not*, *never* or *nothing*: He's *not* here; I *never* eat meat; She's doing *nothing* about it.

1 | non

➤ The Italian word **non** (meaning *not*) is the one you need to make a statement or a question negative:

Non posso venire.	I can't come.
Non hai la chiave?	Haven't you got the key?
Giuliana **non** abita qui.	Giuliana doesn't live here.

➤ In English *not* or *n't* comes <u>after</u> verbs. In Italian **non** comes <u>in front of</u> verbs.

Non è qui.	It's not here.
Non è venuta.	She didn't come.
I miei **non hanno** la macchina.	My parents haven't got a car.
Lei **non** è molto alta.	She's not very tall.

➤ In English we sometimes make sentences negative by adding *don't*, *doesn't* or *didn't* before the main verb, but in Italian you always just add **non** to the verb.

Positive		Negative	
Lavorano.	They work.	**Non** lavorano.	They don't work.
Lo vuole.	He wants it.	**Non** lo vuole.	He doesn't want it.

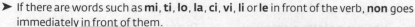

> *Tip*
> NEVER use the verb **fare** to translate *don't*, *doesn't* or *didn't* in negatives.

➤ If there are words such as **mi**, **ti**, **lo**, **la**, **ci**, **vi**, **li** or **le** in front of the verb, **non** goes immediately <u>in front of</u> them.

Non l'ho visto.	I didn't see it.
Non mi piace il calcio.	I don't like football.

➤ If you have a phrase consisting of *not* with another word or phrase, such as *not now*, or *not yet*, use **non** before the other word.

non adesso	not now
non ancora	not yet
non sempre	not always
non dopo sabato	not after Saturday

➤ BUT, if you want to be more emphatic, or to make a contrast, use **no** instead of **non**, and put it <u>after</u> the other word.

<u>Sempre no</u>, qualche volta.	Not ALWAYS, but sometimes.

➤ You use **no** instead of **non** in certain phrases:

● In the phrase **o no** (meaning *or not*)

Vieni <u>o no</u>?	Are you coming or not?
che gli piaccia <u>o no</u>	whether he likes it or not

● In the phrase **di no** after some verbs:

Credo <u>di no</u>.	I don't think so.
Spero <u>di no</u>.	I hope not.
Ha detto <u>di no</u>.	He said not.

---

2 | Other negative phrases

➤ In English you only use one negative word in a sentence: *I haven't ever seen him.*
In Italian you use **non** followed by another negative word such as **niente** (meaning *nothing*), or **mai**, (meaning *never*).

<u>Non</u> succede <u>mai</u>.	It never happens.
<u>Non</u> ha detto <u>niente</u>.	She didn't say anything.

➤ The following are the most common phrases of this kind.

● **non ... mai** never *or* not ever

<u>Non</u> la vedo <u>mai</u>.	I never see her.

> ### Tip
>
> You put **mai** between the two parts of the perfect tense.
>
> | | |
> |---|---|
> | Non l'<u>ho mai vista</u>. | I've never seen her. |
> | Non ci <u>siamo mai stati</u>. | We've never been there. |

● **non ... niente** nothing *or* not ...anything

<u>Non</u> hanno fatto <u>niente</u>.	They didn't do anything.

● **non ... nessuno** nobody *or* not ... anybody

<u>Non</u> ho visto <u>nessuno</u>.	I didn't see anybody.

● **non ... da nessuna parte** nowhere *or* not ... anywhere

<u>Non</u> riuscivo a trovarlo <u>da nessuna parte</u>.	I couldn't find it anywhere.

For further explanation of grammatical terms, please see pages viii–xii.

- **non ... nessuno/nessuna** + *noun*   no *or* not ... any

  Non c'è **nessun** bisogno di andare.   There's no need to go. *or*
  There isn't any need to go.

- **non ... più**   no longer *or* not ... any more

  Non escono **più** insieme.   They're not going out together any more.

- **non ...né ... né ...**   neither ... nor

  Non verranno **né** Chiara   Neither Chiara nor Donatella
  né Donatella.   are coming.

➤ If you <u>begin</u> a sentence with a negative word such as **nessuno** or **niente**, do not use **non** with the verb that comes after it.

  Nessuno è venuto.   Nobody came.
  Niente è cambiato.   Nothing has changed.
  BUT
  Non è venuto nessuno.
  Non è cambiato niente.

➤ In Italian you can have more than one negative word following a negative verb.

  Non fanno **mai niente**.   They never do anything.
  Non si confida **mai** con **nessuno**.   He never confides in anyone.

➤ As in English, negative words can be used on their own to answer a question.

  Cos'hai comprato? – <u>Niente</u>.   What did you buy? – Nothing.
  Chi ti accompagna? – <u>Nessuno</u>.   Who's going with you? – Nobody.

Key points

✔ To make a verb negative put **non** in front of it.

✔ Unlike English, in Italian it is good grammar to follow **non** with another negative word.

QUESTIONS

What is a question?
A **question** is a sentence which is used to ask someone about something and which often has the verb in front of the subject.

Different types of questions

➤ Some questions can be answered by <u>yes</u> or <u>no</u>. They are sometimes called <u>yes/no questions</u>. When you ask this type of question your voice goes up at the end of the sentence.

>
> Is it raining?
> Do you like olives?
> You're leaving tomorrow?

➤ Other questions begin with <u>question words</u> such as *why*, *where* and *when* and have to be answered with specific information.

>
> Why are you late?
> Where have you been?
> When did they leave?

1 | How to ask yes/no questions in Italian

➤ If you are expecting the answer *yes* or *no*, make your voice go up at the end of the question.

Tip

In Italian you can turn an adjective or a verb into a question simply by making your voice go up on the last syllable.

Basta?	Is that enough?
Piove?	Is it raining?
Chiaro?	Is that clear?
Buono?	Is it nice?

For further explanation of grammatical terms, please see pages viii–xii.

➤ If you are asking about a person, place or thing using a noun, put the noun at the <u>end</u> of the question.

È partita <u>tua sorella</u>?	Has your sister gone?
È bella <u>la Calabria</u>?	Is Calabria beautiful?
Sono <u>buoni gli spaghetti</u>?	Is the spaghetti nice?

➤ If the English question has a pronoun such as *you, they* or *he* in it, you:

- keep to normal word order
- don't translate the pronoun into Italian unless you want to stress it

Parlano italiano?	Do they speak Italian?
Ha francobolli?	Have you got stamps?
È caro?	Is it expensive?
C'è tempo?	Is there time?
Fa l'avvocato?	Is he a lawyer?
Va bene?	Is that okay?

➤ If you do want to stress *you, he, they* and so on, use a pronoun in Italian, and put it at the <u>end</u> of the sentence.

Parla italiano <u>Lei</u>?	Do <u>you</u> speak Italian?
Viene anche <u>lui</u>?	Is <u>he</u> coming too?
L'hanno fatto <u>loro</u>?	Did <u>they</u> do it?

⇨ *For more information on **Pronouns**, see page 40.*

2 How to answer yes/no questions

➤ In English you can answer questions simply by saying *yes* or *no*. If this doesn't seem quite enough you add a short phrase, using the verb that starts the question.

<u>Do</u> you speak Italian?	Yes, I <u>do</u>.
<u>Can</u> he swim?	Yes, he <u>can</u>.
<u>Have</u> you been to Rome?	No, I <u>haven't</u>.
<u>Are</u> they leaving now?	No, they'<u>re</u> not.

➤ In Italian you can very often answer just with **sì** or **no**.

Stai bene? – <u>Sì</u>.	Are you okay? – Yes.
Ti piace? – <u>No</u>.	Do you like it? – No.

➤ If you don't want to answer this sort of question with a definite *yes* or *no* you can use phrases such as:

Penso di sì.	I think so.
Spero di sì.	I hope so.
Credo di no.	I don't think so.
Spero di no.	I hope not.

➤ If you want to answer more fully you have to repeat the verb that's in the Italian question.

Sai nuotare? – Sì, <u>so</u> nuotare.	Can you swim? – Yes, I can (swim).
Piove? – Sì, <u>piove</u>.	Is it raining? – Yes, it's raining OR Yes, it is.
Capisci? – No, non <u>capisco</u>.	Do you understand? – No, I don't (understand).

ⓘ Note that there is no Italian equivalent for answers using short phrases such as *Yes, I do; No, I don't; No, they haven't.*

Key points

✔ Make your voice go up at the end of questions.

✔ Put nouns and stressed pronouns at the end of the question.

✔ If you want to answer more fully, repeat the verb that is used in the question.

Question words

1 How to ask questions using question words

➤ The following are common question words which never change their form:

- **dove?** where?

  Dove abiti?   Where do you live?

- **come?** how?

  Come si fa?   How do you do it?

[*i*] Note that **come** can be translated by *what?* when it is used to mean *pardon?*

  Scusi, come ha detto?   Sorry, what did you say?

- **quando?** when

  Quando parti?   When are you leaving?

- **perché?** why

  Perché non vieni?   Why don't you come?

[*i*] Note that **perché** also means *because.*

  Lo mangio perché ho fame.   I'm eating it because I'm hungry.

- **chi?** who?

  Chi è?   Who is it?
  Chi sono?   Who are they?

- **che?** what?

  Che giorno è oggi?   What day is it today?

- **cosa?** what?

  Cosa vuoi?   What do you want?

- **che cosa?** what?

  Che cosa fanno?   What are they doing?

⟹ *For more information on **Conjunctions**, see page 187.*

Tip

Remember to shorten **che cosa** (meaning *what*) and **come** (meaning *how, what*) to **che cos'** and **com'** when they are followed by a vowel.

  Che cos'è?   What is it?
  Com'è successo?   How did it happen?

➤ Some question words do sometimes change their form.

➤ You can use **quale** to ask for precise information about people or things. It has a plural form **quali**, and a singular form **qual** which is used in front of a vowel:

- Use **quale** with a singular noun when you want to ask *which* or *what*.

Per **quale** motivo?	For what reason?
Quale stanza preferisci?	Which room do you prefer?

- Use the singular form **qual** when the next word starts with a vowel.

Qual è il tuo colore preferito?	What's your favourite colour?
Qual è la tua *camera*?	Which is your room?

- Use **quali** with plural nouns.

Quali programmi hai?	What plans have you got?
Quali sono i tuoi sport preferiti?	Which are your favourite sports?

- Use **quale** by itself when you want to ask *which one*.

Quale vuoi?	Which one would you like?

- Use **quali** by itself when you want to ask *which ones*.

Quali sono i migliori?	Which ones are the best?

➤ You can use **quanto** or the feminine form **quanta** to ask *how much*:

- Use **quanto** by itself to ask *how much*?

Quanto costa?	How much does it cost?
Quanta ne vuoi?	How much do you want?

- Use **quanto** as an adjective with masculine nouns and **quanta** with feminine nouns.

Quanto tempo hai?	How much time have you got?
Quanta stoffa ti serve?	How much material do you need?

➤ Use **quanti** to ask *how many*. Use **quanti** as an adjective with masculine nouns and **quante** with feminine nouns.

Quanti ne vuoi?	How many do you want?
Quanti giorni?	How many days?
Quante notti?	How many nights?

➪ *For more information on **Adjectives**, see page 20.*

🛈 Note that some very common questions do not start with the Italian question word you might expect.

Quanti anni hai?	How old are you?
Come si chiama?	What's he called?
Com'è?	What's it like?

2   How to answer questions which use question words

➤ If someone asks you a question such as **Chi è?** or **Quanto costa?**, you answer using the same verb.

Chi è? – È Giulia.	Who's that? – That's Giulia.
Quanto <u>costa</u>? – <u>Costa</u> molto.	How much does it cost? – It costs a lot.

➤ When you don't know the answer you say **Non lo so**, or **Non so** followed by the original question.

Chi è? – <u>Non lo so</u>.	Who's that? – I don't know.
<u>Non so</u> chi è.	I don't know who it is.
Quanto costa? – <u>Non lo so</u>.	How much does it cost? – I don't know.
<u>Non so</u> quanto costa.	I don't know how much it costs.

Grammar Extra!

The question word *what* can be either a <u>pronoun</u> or an <u>adjective</u>. In the sentence *What do you want?* it's a <u>pronoun</u> and you can use **che**, **cosa**, or **che cosa** to translate it.

When *what* is an <u>adjective</u>, and is used with a noun, for example *What day is it today?* you translate it by **che**, and NOT by **cosa**, or **che cosa**.

Che giorno è?	What day is it?

[ℤ] Note that when *what?* means *pardon?* it is translated by **come**?

⇨ *For more information on **Adjectives** and **Pronouns**, see pages 20 and 40.*

---

3   Where does the question word come in the sentence?

➤ In English, question words like *who*, *what*, *where* and *when* nearly always come at the beginning of the sentence.

<u>Who</u> are you?

<u>Who</u> does it belong to?

<u>Where</u> do you come from?

<u>What</u> do you think?

➤ Italian question words often come first in the sentence, but this is by no means always the case. Here are some exceptions:

● If you want to emphasize the person or thing you are asking about, you can put a noun or pronoun first.

<u>Tu</u> chi sei?	Who are <u>you</u>?
<u>Lei</u> cosa dice?	What do <u>you</u> think?
<u>La mia borsa</u> dov'è?	Where's <u>my bag</u>?

- If there is a preposition such as *with*, *for*, *from* or *to* at the end of the English question, you <u>MUST</u> put the Italian preposition at the start of the question.

<u>Di</u> **dove sei?**	Where do you come <u>from</u>?
<u>Con</u> **chi parlavi?**	Who were you talking <u>to</u>?
<u>A</u> **che cosa serve?**	What's it <u>for</u>?

i Note that when you ask someone what time they do something, the question starts with **a che ora**.

<u>A che ora</u> **ti alzi?**	What time do you get up?

⇨ *For more information on **Prepositions**, see page 172.*

- When you are asking about the colour, make, or type of something you must start the question with **di**.

<u>Di</u> **che colore è?**	What colour is it?
<u>Di</u> **che marca è?**	What make is it?

- When you are asking who owns something start the question in Italian with **di**.

<u>Di</u> **chi è questa borsa?**	Whose bag is this?
<u>Di</u> **chi sono quelle scarpe rosse?**	Who do those red shoes belong to?

Key points

✔ Most question words don't change their form.

✔ Question words do not always come first in Italian questions.

✔ If there is a preposition in the Italian question you MUST put it first.

---

4 **Questions which end with question phrases**

➤ In English you add a question phrase (like <u>aren't you?</u>, <u>isn't it?</u>, <u>didn't I</u> and so on) to the end of a sentence to check that an idea you have is true. You expect the person you're speaking to will agree by saying *yes* (or *no*, if your idea is negative).

This is the house, isn't it?

You won't tell anyone, will you?

➤ In Italian, when you expect someone to say *yes* to your idea, you put either **no**, or **vero** at the end of the sentence and make your voice go up as you say the word.

Mi scriverai, <u>no</u>?	You'll write to me, won't you?
Vieni anche tu, <u>no</u>?	You're coming too, aren't you?
Hai finito, <u>no</u>?	You've finished, haven't you?

For further explanation of grammatical terms, please see pages viii–xii.

Questa è la tua macchina, <u>vero</u>?	This is your car, isn't it?
Ti piace la cioccolata, <u>vero</u>?	You like chocolate, don't you?

➤ When you expect someone to agree with you by saying *no*, use **vero** only.

Non sono partiti, <u>vero</u>?	They haven't gone, have they?
Non fa molto male, <u>vero</u>?	It doesn't hurt much, does it?

Grammar Extra!

Questions such as *Where are you going?* and *Why did he do that?* are <u>direct questions</u>.

Sometimes this type of question is phrased in a more roundabout way, for example:

Tell me where you are going.

Would you mind telling me where you are going?

Can you tell me why he did that?

I'd like to know why he did that.

I wonder why he did that.

This type of question is called an <u>indirect question</u>. It is very simple to ask indirect questions in Italian: you simply add a phrase to the beginning of the direct question, for example, you could add **Può dirmi** (meaning *Can you tell me*) to the question **Dove va?** (meaning *where are you going?*).

Può dirmi dove va?	Can you tell me where you're going?

The following are other phrases that introduce an indirect question:

Dimmi...	Tell me...
Vorrei sapere...	I'd like to know...
Mi domando...	I wonder...
Non capisco...	I don't understand...
<u>Dimmi</u> perché l'hai fatto.	Tell me why you did it.
<u>Vorrei sapere</u> quanto costa.	I'd like to know how much it costs.
<u>Mi domando</u> cosa pensano.	I wonder what they think.
<u>Non capisco</u> che vuol dire.	I don't understand what it means.

Adverbs

What is an adverb?
An **adverb** is a word used with verbs to give information on where, when or how an action takes place, for example, *here, today, quickly*. An adverb can also add information to adjectives and other adverbs, for example, *extremely quick, very quickly*.

How adverbs are used

➤ You use adverbs:

- with verbs: *He's never there; She smiled happily*.
- with adjectives: *She's rather ill; I feel a lot happier*.
- with other adverbs: *He drives really slowly; I'm very well*.

➤ Adverbs are also used at the start of a sentence to give an idea of what the speaker is thinking or feeling.

Luckily, nobody was hurt.

Surprisingly, he made no objection.

How to form adverbs

1 The basics

➤ In English you can make an adverb from the adjective *slow* by adding –*ly*. You can do a similar kind of thing in Italian.

➤ Here are some guidelines:

- if the adjective ends in –**o** in the masculine, take the feminine form, ending in –**a**, and add –**mente**

Masculine adjective	Feminine adjective	Adverb	Meaning
lento	lenta	lentamente	slowly
fortunato	fortunata	fortunatamente	luckily

Cammina molto lentamente.	He walks very slowly.
Fortunatamente non ha piovuto.	Luckily, it didn't rain.

- if the adjective ends in **–e** for both masculine and feminine, just add **–mente**

Adjective	Adverb	Meaning
veloce	velocemente	quickly, fast
corrente	correntemente	fluently

Parla correntemente l'italiano.   She speaks Italian fluently.

- if the adjective ends in **–le**, or **–re**, you drop the final **e** before adding **–mente**

Adjective	Adverb	Meaning
facile	facilmente	easily
particolare	particolarmente	particularly

Puoi farlo facilmente.   You can easily do it.
Non è particolarmente buono.   It's not particularly nice.

> *Tip*
>
> Don't try to make adverbs agree with anything – they always keep the same form.

2 Irregular adverbs

➤ In Italian there are two kinds of adverbs which do not behave in the way just described. They are:

- adverbs which are completely different from the adjective
- adverbs which are exactly the same as the masculine adjective

➤ The adverb related to **buono** (meaning *good*) is **bene** (meaning *well*). The adverb related to **cattivo** (meaning *bad*) is **male** (meaning *badly*).

Parlano bene l'italiano.   They speak Italian well.
Ho giocato male.   I played badly.

➤ Words such as *fast* and *hard* can be both adjectives and adverbs:

a fast car
You're driving too fast.
a hard question
He works very hard.

➤ The same kind of thing happens in Italian: some adverbs are the same as the masculine adjective. The following are the most common ones:

- **chiaro** (adjective: *clear*; adverb: *clearly*)

Il significato è chiaro.   The meaning is clear.
Giulia parla chiaro.   Giulia speaks clearly.

- **giusto** (adjective: *right, correct*; adverb: *correctly, right*)

il momento giusto.	the right moment.
Marco ha risposto giusto.	Marco answered correctly.

- **vicino** (adjective: *near, close*; adverb: *nearby, near here*)

È molto vicino.	He's very close.
I miei amici abitano vicino.	My friends live nearby.
C'è una piscina vicino?	Is there a swimming pool near here?

- **diritto** (adjective: *straight*; adverb: *straight on*)

Il bordo non è diritto.	The edge is not straight.
Siamo andati sempre diritto.	We kept straight on.

- **certo** (adjective: *sure, certain*; adverb: *of course*)

Non ne sono certo.	I'm not sure.
Vieni stasera? – Certo!	Are you coming this evening? – Of course!

- **solo** (adjective: *alone, lonely*; adverb: *only*)

Si sente solo.	He feels lonely.
L'ho incontrata solo due volte.	I've only met her twice.

- **forte** (adjective: *strong, hard*; adverb: *fast, hard*)

È più forte di me.	He's stronger than me.
Correva forte.	He was running fast.

- **molto** (adjective: *a lot of*; adverb: *a lot, very, very much*)

Non hanno molto denaro.	They haven't got a lot of money.
Quel quadro mi piace molto.	I like that picture a lot.

- **poco** (adjective: *little, not very much*; adverb *not very much, not very*)

Hai mangiato poco riso.	You haven't eaten very much rice.
Viene in ufficio poco spesso.	She doesn't come to the office very often.

[i] Note that although these adverbs look like adjectives, they NEVER change their form.

Key points

✔ You generally make adverbs by adding **–mente** to adjectives.

✔ Adverbs never agree with anything.

✔ Some adverbs have the same form as the masculine adjective.

Making comparisons using adverbs

➤ In English, there are two major ways of comparing things using an adverb.

- To express the idea of 'more' or 'less' you either put **–er** on the end of the adverb, or *more* or *less* in front of it: *earlier*, *sooner*, *more/less* often. This way of comparing things is called the comparative.

- To express the idea of 'the most' or 'the least' you either put **–est** on the end, or *most* or *least* in front of it: *earliest*, *soonest*, *most/least* often. This way of comparing things is called the superlative.

---

1 Comparatives and superlatives of adverbs

➤ In Italian you make comparisons expressing the idea of 'more' or 'less' by putting **più** (meaning *more*) and **meno** (meaning *less*) in front of the adverb.

più spesso	more often
più lentamente	more slowly
meno velocemente	less quickly

➤ You use **di** to say *than*.

Correva più forte di me.	He was running faster than me.
Viene meno spesso di lui.	She comes less often than he does.
Luca parla più correttamente l'inglese di me.	Luca speaks English more correctly than I do.
Ha agito più prudentemente di me.	She's acted more sensibly than I have.
Loro lavorano più sodo di prima.	They work harder than before.

➤ In Italian you can make comparisons expressing the idea of 'the most' or 'the least' by putting **più** (meaning *more*) or **meno** (meaning *less*) in front of the adverb and by putting **di tutti** (meaning *of all*) after it.

Cammina più piano di tutti.	She walks the slowest (of all).
L'ha fatto meno volentieri di tutti.	He did it the least willingly.
Mia madre ci veniva più spesso di tutti.	My mother came most often.

➡️ *For more information on **Adjectives** see page 20.*

2 | Irregular comparatives and superlatives of adverbs

➤ Some very common Italian adverbs have irregular comparatives and superlatives. Here are the commonest ones.

Adverb	Meaning	Comparative	Meaning	Superlative	Meaning
bene	well	meglio	better	meglio di tutti	best (of all)
male	badly	peggio	worse	peggio di tutti	worst (of all)
molto	a lot	più	more	più di tutti	most (of all)
poco	not much	meno	less	meno di tutti	least (of all)

Loro hanno giocato _meglio_ di noi.	They played better than us.
Si sono comportati _peggio_ del solito.	They behaved worse than usual.
Ho speso _più_ di dieci sterline.	I spent more than ten pounds.
Andrea ha giocato _meglio di tutti_.	Andrea played best of all.

3 | più di..., meno di...: di più, di meno

➤ These are very common phrases, meaning *more* and *less*, which are used in rather different ways.

● You use **più di** and **meno di** to say *more than* and *less than* when comparing things where you would use *than* in English.

Paolo le piace _più di_ Marco.	She likes Paolo more than Marco.
Leggo _meno di_ te.	I read less than you.
Non guadagna _più di_ me.	He doesn't earn more than I do.
Pesa _meno di_ Luca.	He weighs less than Luca.

● If there is no *than* in the sentence in English use **di più** and **di meno**.

Costa _di più_.	It costs more.
Quello mi piace _di meno_.	I like that one less.
Ho speso _di meno_.	I spent less.

[handwritten margin note: the only difference here is that one is used sparingly]

● **di più** and **di meno** are also used to mean *most* and *least*.

la cosa che temeva _di più_	the thing she feared most
quello che mi piace _di meno_	the one I like least
Sono quelli che guadagnano _di meno_.	They're the ones who earn least.

[handwritten note: not so clear]

Grammar Extra!

To say that something is getting *better and better, worse and worse, slower and slower*, and so on, use **sempre** with the comparative adverb.

Le cose vanno sempre meglio.	Things are going better and better.
Mio nonno sta sempre peggio.	My grandfather's getting worse and worse.
Cammina sempre più lento.	He's walking slower and slower.

Key points

- ✔ To express the idea of 'more' and 'most' with adverbs use **più**.
- ✔ To express the idea of 'less' and 'least' use **meno**.
- ✔ Use **di** to mean 'than'.

Some common adverbs

1 Adverbs to use in everyday conversation

➤ Just as in English, you can often answer a question simply by using an adverb.

Vieni alla festa? – <u>Forse</u>.	Are you coming to the party? – <u>Maybe</u>.
Deve proprio partire? –	Do you really have to go? –
Sì, <u>purtroppo</u>.	Yes, <u>unfortunately</u>.

➤ The following are particularly useful adverbs:

● **ecco**   here

<u>Ecco</u> l'*au*tobus!	Here's the bus!
<u>Ecco</u> la sua birra!	Here's your beer!

i Note that you can say **ecco** (meaning *here you are*) when you hand somebody something. **Ecco** combines with the pronouns **lo**, **la**, **li** and **le** to mean *Here she is*, *Here they are* and so forth:

Dov'è Carla? – <u>Eccola</u>!	Where's Carla? – Here she is!
Non vedo i libri – Ah, <u>eccoli</u>!	I can't see the books – Oh, here they are!
<u>Eccolo</u>!	Here he is!

● **anche**   too

È venuta <u>anche</u> mia sorella.	My sister came too.

● **certo**   certainly, of course

<u>Certo</u> che puoi.	Of course you can.
<u>Certo</u> che sì.	Certainly.

● **così**   so, like this, like that

È <u>così</u> simp*a*tica!	She's so nice!
Si apre <u>così</u>.	It opens like this.
Non si fa <u>così</u>.	You don't do it like that.

● **davvero**   really

È successo <u>davvero</u>.	It really happened.

● **forse**   perhaps, maybe

<u>Forse</u> hanno ragione.	Maybe they're right.

● **proprio**   really

Sono <u>proprio</u> stanca.	I'm really tired.

● **purtroppo**   unfortunately

<u>Purtroppo</u> non posso venire.	Unfortunately I can't come.

Tip

These adverbs are such common words that it's a good idea to learn as many as possible.

---

2 Adverbs that tell you HOW MUCH

➤ **molto**, **poco**, **troppo** and **tanto** are used with adjectives, verbs and other adverbs;

- Use **molto** to mean *very* or *very much*.

Sono <u>molto</u> stanca.	I'm very tired.
Ti piace? – Sì, <u>molto</u>.	Do you like it? – Yes, very much.
Ora mi sento <u>molto</u> meglio.	I feel much better now.

- Use **poco** to mean *not very* or *not very much*.

Questa mela è <u>poco</u> buona.	This apple isn't very nice.
Mi piacciono <u>poco</u>.	I don't like them very much.
Ci vado <u>poco</u> spesso.	I don't go there very often.

- Use **tanto** to mean *so* or *so much*.

Questo libro è <u>tanto</u> noioso.	This book is so boring.
Tu mi manchi <u>tanto</u>.	I miss you so much.
Mi sento <u>tanto</u> meglio.	I feel so much better.

- Use **troppo** to mean *too* or *too much*.

È <u>troppo</u> caro.	It's too expensive.
Parlano <u>troppo</u>.	They talk too much.
Le sei? È <u>troppo</u> presto.	Six o'clock? That's too early.

ℹ Note that **molto**, **poco**, **troppo** and **tanto** can also be used as adjectives. When you use them as adverbs they do NOT agree with anything.

3 Adverbs that tell you TO WHAT EXTENT

- **abbastanza** quite, enough

È <u>abbastanza</u> alta.	She's quite tall.
Non studia <u>abbastanza</u>.	He doesn't study enough.

- **appena** just, only just

L'ho <u>appena</u> fatto.	I've just done it.
L'indirizzo ere <u>appena</u> leggibile.	The address was only just legible.

- piuttosto quite, rather
  - Fa **piuttosto** caldo oggi. — It's quite warm today.
  - È **piuttosto** lontano. — It's rather a long way.

- quasi nearly
  - Sono **quasi** pronta. — I'm nearly ready.
  - Hanno **quasi** finito. — They've nearly finished.

4 Adverbs that tell you WHEN

- adesso now
  - Non posso farlo **adesso**. — I can't do it now.

- ancora still, yet
  - Sei **ancora** a letto? — Are you still in bed?
  - Silvia non è **ancora** arrivata. — Silvia's not here yet.

- domani tomorrow
  - Ci vediamo **domani**. — See you tomorrow.

- dopo after, later
  - Ci vediamo **dopo**. — See you later.

- già already
  - Te l'ho **già** detto. — I've already told you.

- ieri yesterday
  - **Ieri** ha piovuto molto. — It rained a lot yesterday.

- mai never, ever
  - Non sono **mai** stato in America. — I've never been to America.
  - Sei **mai** stato in America? — Have you ever been to America?

- oggi today
  - **Oggi** andiamo al mare. — We're going to the seaside today.

- ora now
  - **Ora** cosa facciamo? — What are we going to do now?

- poi then
  - E **poi** che cos'è successo? — And then what happened?

- presto soon, early
  - Arriverà **presto**. — He'll be here soon.
  - Mi alzo sempre **presto**. — I always get up early.

- **prima** before
  Prima non lo sapevo.   I didn't know that before.

- **spesso** often
  Vanno **spesso** in centro.   They often go into town.

- **subito** at once
  Fallo **subito**!   Do it at once.

- **tardi** late
  Oggi mi sono alzata **tardi**.   I got up late today.

5   Adverbs that tell you WHERE

- **là** there
  Vieni via di **là**.   Come away from there.

- **laggiù** down there, over there
  È **laggiù** da qualche parte.   It's down there somewhere.
  È apparso **laggiù** in lontananza.   It appeared over there in the distance.

- **lassù** up there
  un paesino **lassù** in montagna   a little village up there in the mountains

- **lì** there
  Mettilo **lì**.   Put it there.

- **qua** here
  Eccomi **qua**!   I'm here!

- **qui** here
  Vieni **qui**.   Come here.

[*i*] Note that **lì** has an accent to distinguish it from the pronoun **li** (meaning *them*)
and **là** has an accent to distinguish it from **la** (meaning *the, her* or *it*).

⇨ *For more information on* **Articles** *and* **Pronouns**, *see pages 10 and 40.*

- **ci** there
  Ci sei mai stato?   Have you ever been there?

- **dappertutto** everywhere
  Ho cercato **dappertutto**.   I looked everywhere.

- **lontano** a long way away
  Abita **lontano**.   He lives a long way away.

- **sotto** underneath, downstairs
  Porta una giacca con una   He's wearing a jacket with a t-shirt
  maglietta **sotto**.   underneath.
  Il bagno è **sotto**.   The bathroom is downstairs.

- **sopra** up, on top

  qui **sopra** — up here

  Il dizion*ario* è **sopra** quella pila di libri. — The dictionary is on top of that pile of books.

- **fuori** outside

  Ti aspetto **fuori**. — I'll wait for you outside.

- **dentro** inside

  Vai **dentro**. — Go inside.

- **indietro** back

  Torniamo **indietro**. — Let's turn back.

- **davanti** at the front

  V*o*glio sedermi **davanti**. — I want to sit at the front.

6 | Adverbs consisting of more than one word

➤ In English you sometimes use a phrase instead of a single word to give information about time, place and so on, and the same is true in Italian.

- **una volta** once

  una volta la settimana — once a week

- **due volte** twice

  Ho provato **due volte**. — I tried twice.

- **molte volte** many times

  L'ho fatto **molte volte**. — I've done it many times.

- **da qualche parte** somewhere

  Ho lasciato le chiavi **da qualche parte**. — I've left my keys somewhere.

- **qualche volta** sometimes

  Qualche volta arriva in ritardo. — She sometimes arrives late.

- **di solito** usually

  Di solito arrivo prima. — I usually get here earlier.

Where to put adverbs

1 Adverbs with verbs

➤ You normally put adverbs immediately after the verb.

Non posso farlo <u>adesso</u>.	I can't do it now.
Parli <u>bene</u> l'italiano.	You speak Italian well.
Non torno <u>più</u>.	I'm not coming back.

➤ If you want to emphasize the adverb you can put it at the beginning of the sentence.

<u>Ora</u> non posso.	I can't do it just now.
<u>Prima</u> non lo sapevo.	I didn't know that before.

> ## Tip
>
> In English adverbs can come between the subject and the verb:
> It *often* changes. Adverbs can NEVER come in this position in Italian.
>
> | | |
> |---|---|
> | **Marco viene sempre.** | Marco always comes. |
> | **Di solito vince Jessica.** | Jessica usually wins. |

➤ When you are using adverbs such as **mai** (meaning *never*), **sempre** (meaning *always*), **già** (meaning *already*), **più** (meaning *again*) and **appena** (meaning *just*) with verbs in the perfect tense, you put the adverb between the two parts of the verb:

Non sono <u>mai</u> stata a Milano.	I've never been to Milan.
È <u>sempre</u> venuto con me.	He always came with me.
L'ho <u>già</u> letto.	I've already read it.

⇨ For more information on the **Perfect tense**, see page 108.

2 Adverbs with adjectives and adverbs

➤ Put the adverb in front of the adjective or other adverb, as you do in English.

Fa <u>troppo</u> freddo.	It's too cold.
Vai <u>più</u> piano.	Go more slowly.

> ### Key points
>
> ✔ Some adverbs are very common in Italian, and it's a good idea to learn as many as possible.
> ✔ You usually put adverbs after the verb.
> ✔ If you want to emphasize the adverb, you put it at the beginning of the sentence.
> ✔ Adverbs go before adjectives or other adverbs.

Prepositions

What is a preposition?
A preposition is one word such as *at, for, with, into* or *from*, or words such as *in front of* or *near to*, which are usually followed by a noun or a pronoun.

Prepositions show how people and things relate to the rest of the sentence, for example, *She's at home; It's for you; You'll get into trouble; It's in front of you.*

Using prepositions

1 Where they go

➤ Prepositions are used in front of nouns and pronouns to show the relationship between the noun or pronoun and the rest of the sentence.

Andiamo a Roma.	We're going to Rome.
Vieni con me.	Come with me.

➤ In English you can separate a preposition from its noun or pronoun and put it at the end of a question, or at the end of part of a sentence, for example, *Who were you talking to?; the people I came with.*

➤ In Italian prepositions always go in front of another word and never at the end of a question or part of a sentence:

Con chi sei venuto?	Who did you come with?
la ragazza alla quale ho dato la chiave	the girl I gave the key to

2 Which preposition to use

➤ In English certain adjectives and verbs are always followed by particular prepositions, for example, *happy with, afraid of, talk to, smile at.* The same is true in Italian.

Sono deluso del voto che ho preso.	I'm disappointed with the mark I got.
Andiamo in Italia.	We're going to Italy.

ⓘ Note that when a preposition is used in front of the –ing form in English, a preposition is used in front of the infinitive (the **–re** form of the verb) in Italian.

È andato via senza salutarci.	He went away without saying goodbye to us.
Sono stufo di studiare.	I'm fed up of studying.

For further explanation of grammatical terms, please see pages viii–xii.

➤ The prepositions used in Italian may not be what you expect, for example, the Italian preposition **in** is used for both the following:

I miei sono in Italia.	My parents are <u>in</u> Italy.
I miei vanno in Italia.	My parents are going <u>to</u> Italy.

➤ You sometimes need to use a preposition in Italian when there is no preposition in English.

Hai bisogno <u>di</u> qualcosa?	Do you need anything?
Chiedi <u>a</u> Lidia cosa vuole.	Ask Lidia what she wants.

⇨ *For more information on **Prepositions after verbs**, see page 143.*

> ## *Tip*
>
> When you look up a verb in the dictionary, take note of any preposition that is shown with the translation.
>
> | | |
> |---|---|
> | **congratularsi <u>con</u>** | to congratulate |
> | **dire qualcosa <u>a</u> qualcuno** | to tell someone something |

3 | Prepositions that combine with the definite article

➤ When the prepositions **a**, **di**, **da**, **in** and **su** are followed by the <u>definite article</u> – **il**, **la**, **i**, **le** and so on, they combine with it to make one word.

	+ il	+ lo	+ la	+ l'	+ i	+ gli	+ le
a	al	allo	alla	all'	ai	agli	alle
di	del	dello	della	dell'	dei	degli	delle
da	dal	dallo	dalla	dall'	dai	dagli	dalle
in	nel	nello	nella	nell'	nei	negli	nelle
su	sul	sullo	sulla	sull'	sui	sugli	sulle

⇨ *For more information on **Articles**, see page 10.*

Si guardava <u>allo</u> specchio.	He was looking at himself <u>in the</u> mirror.
la cima <u>del</u> monte	the top <u>of the</u> mountain
Sto <u>dai</u> miei.	I live <u>with</u> my parents.
Cos'hai <u>nella</u> tasca?	What have you got <u>in</u> your pocket?
I soldi sono <u>sul</u> tavolo.	The money's <u>on the</u> table.

> ### Key points
>
> ✔ Italian prepositions are always used in front of another word.
>
> ✔ The preposition used in Italian may not be what you expect.
>
> ✔ Italian prepositions combine with the definite article to make one word.

a, di, da, in, su and per

1 a

➤ **a** is used with nouns to tell you <u>where</u>.

<u>alla</u> porta	<u>at</u> the door
<u>al</u> sole	<u>in</u> the sun
<u>all'</u>ombra	<u>in</u> the shade
Vivo <u>al</u> terzo piano.	I live <u>on</u> the third floor.
È <u>a</u> letto.	He's <u>in</u> bed.
<u>alla</u> radio	<u>on</u> the radio
<u>alla</u> tivù	<u>on</u> TV

➤ Use **a** to mean *to* when you're talking about <u>going to a place</u>.

Andiamo <u>al</u> cinema?	Shall we go <u>to</u> the cinema?
Sei mai stato <u>a</u> New York?	Have you ever been <u>to</u> New York?

ℹ️ Note that if the place is a country, use **in** in Italian.

Andrò <u>in</u> Germania quest'estate.	I'm going <u>to</u> Germany this summer.

➤ Use **a** to mean *at* when you're talking about <u>being at a place</u>.

Devo essere <u>all'</u>aeroporto alle dieci.	I've got to be <u>at</u> the airport at ten.
Scendo <u>alla</u> prossima fermata.	I'm getting off <u>at</u> the next stop.
Luigi è <u>a</u> casa.	Luigi is <u>at</u> home.

➤ Use **a** to mean *in* when you're talking about being <u>in a town</u>.

Abitano <u>a</u> Bologna.	They live <u>in</u> Bologna.

ℹ️ Note that if the place is a country, use **in** in Italian.

Vivo <u>in</u> Scozia.	I live <u>in</u> Scotland.
Vive <u>in</u> Canada.	He lives <u>in</u> Canada.

➤ Use **a** to mean *away* when you're talking about distances.

<u>a</u> tre chilometri da qui	three kilometres <u>away</u> from here
<u>a</u> due ore di distanza in macchina	two hours <u>away</u> by car

ℹ️ Note that *away* can be left out of this kind of phrase, but **a** has to be used in Italian.

L'albergo è <u>ad</u> un chilometro dalla spiaggia.	The hotel is a kilometre from the beach.

➤ **a** is used with nouns to tell you <u>when</u>.

<u>a</u> volte	<u>at</u> times
<u>a</u> tempo	<u>on</u> time
<u>alla</u> fine	<u>in</u> the end

For further explanation of grammatical terms, please see pages viii–xii.

➤ Use **a** to mean *at* with <u>times and festivals</u>.

<u>alle</u> cinque	<u>at</u> five o'clock
<u>a</u> mezzogiorno	<u>at</u> midday
<u>al</u> fine settimana	<u>at</u> the weekend
<u>a</u> Pasqua	<u>at</u> Easter
<u>a</u> Natale	<u>at</u> Christmas

Tip

Remember that questions beginning *What time ...* must start with the preposition **a** in Italian.

A che ora parti?	What time are you leaving?

● Use **a** with <u>months</u> to mean *in*.

Sono nata a maggio.	I was born <u>in</u> May.

➤ **a** is used with nouns to tell you <u>how</u>.

<u>a</u> piedi	<u>on</u> foot
<u>a</u> mano	<u>by</u> hand
<u>a</u> poco <u>a</u> poco	little <u>by</u> little

● Use **a** with <u>flavours</u>.

un gelato <u>alla</u> fragola	a strawberry ice cream
una torta <u>al</u> cioccolato	a chocolate cake
gli spaghetti <u>al</u> pomodoro	spaghetti with tomato sauce

➤ **a** is used with <u>nouns and pronouns</u> after some verbs.

L'ho dato a Selene.	I gave it to Selene.
Piace a me, ma a mia sorella no.	I like it, but my sister doesn't.
A che cosa stai pensando?	What are you thinking about?

⇨ *For more information on **Prepositions after verbs**, see page 143.*

ⓘ Note that the unstressed pronouns **mi**, **ti**, **gli**, **le**, **ci** and **vi** come in front of the verb and are not used with **a**.

Ti ha parlato?	Did she speak to you?
Gliel'ho dato.	I gave it to her.
Mi piace.	I like it.

⇨ *For more information on **Indirect pronouns**, see page 46.*

➤ **a** is used with the <u>infinitive</u> (the **–re** form of the verb) to say what your purpose is.

Sono uscita a fare due passi.	I went out for a little walk.
Sono andati a fare il bagno.	They've gone to have a swim.

2 di

➤ **di** is used to talk about who or what something belongs to.

il nome <u>del</u> ristorante	the name of the restaurant
il capitano <u>della</u> squadra	the captain of the team
È <u>di</u> Marco.	It belongs to Marco.
<u>Di</u> chi è?	Whose is it?

➤ Use **di** to refer to the person who made something.

un quadro <u>di</u> Picasso	a picture <u>by</u> Picasso
una commedia <u>di</u> Shakespeare	a play <u>by</u> Shakespeare
un film <u>di</u> Fellini	a Fellini film

➤ In English, ownership can be shown by using a noun with 's, or s' added to it, for example the *child's name, the boys' teacher*. In Italian you change the word order and use **di** to translate this sort of phrase.

la macchina <u>di</u> mia madre	my mother's car
	(*literally: the car of my mother*)
la casa <u>dei</u> miei amici	my friends' house
l'Otello di Verdi	Verdi's Othello

⇨ *For more information on **Possessive adjectives** and **Possessive pronouns**, see pages 34 and 52.*

➤ In English, when there is a connection between two things, one noun can be used in front of another, for example the <u>car</u> keys, the <u>bathroom</u> window. In Italian you change the word order and use **di** to translate this sort of phrase.

il tavolo <u>della</u> cucina	the kitchen table
il periodo <u>delle</u> vacanze	the holiday season
il professore <u>di</u> inglese	the English teacher
il campione <u>del</u> mondo	the world champion

➤ When a noun such as *cotton, silver, paper* is used as an adjective, use **di** in Italian.

una maglietta <u>di</u> cotone	a cotton T-shirt
una collana <u>d'</u>argento	a silver necklace
dei tovaglioli <u>di</u> carta	paper napkins

➤ **di** sometimes means *from*.

È <u>di</u> Firenze.	He's <u>from</u> Florence.
<u>Di</u> dove sei?	Where are you <u>from</u>?

➤ **di** is used to say what something contains or what it is made of.

un gruppo <u>di</u> studenti	a group <u>of</u> students
un bicchiere <u>di</u> vino	a glass <u>of</u> wine
È fatto <u>di</u> plastica.	It's made <u>of</u> plastic.

➤ **di** is used after **milione** (meaning *million*), and words for approximate numbers, such as **un migliaio** (meaning *about a thousand*) and **una ventina** (meaning *about twenty*).

un milione **di** dollari	a million dollars
un migliaio **di** persone	about a thousand people
una ventina **di** macchine	about twenty cars

➤ **di** is used after certain verbs and adjectives.

Ti ricordi di Laura?	Do you remember Laura?
Sto tentando di concentrarmi.	I'm trying to concentrate.
Le arance sono ricche di vitamina C.	Oranges are rich in vitamin C.
Era pieno di gente.	It was full of people.

➡ For more information on **Prepositions after verbs** and **Adjectives**, see pages 143 and 20.

> ## Tip
>
> Remember that some verbs are single words in English, but in Italian they are phrases ending with **di**, for example, **aver bisogno di** (meaning *to need*) and **aver voglia di** (meaning *to want*).
>
> | | |
> |---|---|
> | **Non ho bisogno di niente.** | I don't <u>need</u> anything. |
> | **Non ho voglia di andare a letto.** | I don't <u>want</u> to go to bed. |

➤ **di** is used with nouns to say <u>when</u>.

di domenica	<u>on</u> Sundays
di notte	<u>at</u> night
di giorno	<u>during</u> the day

➤ Use **di** to mean *in* with seasons and parts of the day.

d'estate	<u>in</u> summer
d'inverno	<u>in</u> winter

ℹ Note that **in** can also be used with seasons, for example, **in estate** (meaning *in summer*).

di mattina	<u>in</u> the morning
di sera	<u>in</u> the evening

➤ **di** is used in comparisons to mean *than*.

È più alto di me.	He's taller <u>than</u> me.
È più brava di lui.	She's better <u>than</u> him.

➤ Use **di** to mean *in* after a superlative.

il più grande del mondo	the biggest <u>in</u> the world
la più brava della classe	the best <u>in</u> the class
il migliore d'Italia	the best <u>in</u> Italy

➡ For more information on **Superlatives**, see page 27.

Típ

È più bravo di tutti and **è più brava di tutti** are ways of saying
He's the best and *She's the best.*

> **del**, **della**, **dei**, **delle** and so on (**di** combined with the definite article) are used
> to mean *some.*

C'era <u>della</u> gente che aspettava.	There were <u>some</u> people waiting.
Vuoi <u>dei</u> biscotti?	Would you like <u>some</u> biscuits?

> **di** is used with the <u>infinitive</u> (the **–re** form of the verb) when it is used as a noun.

Ho paura <u>di</u> volare.	I'm afraid of flying.
Non ho voglia <u>di</u> mangiare.	I don't feel like eating.

3 | **da**

> **da** is used with places to mean *from.*

a tre chilometri <u>da</u> qui	three kilometres <u>from</u> here.
Viene <u>da</u> Roma.	He comes <u>from</u> Rome.

> Use **da** to talk about getting, jumping or falling <u>off</u> something, or getting or falling
> <u>out of</u> something.

Chiara è scesa <u>dal</u> treno.	Chiara got <u>off</u> the train.
Il vaso è cascato <u>dal</u> terrazzo.	The plant pot fell <u>off</u> the balcony.
Il gatto è saltato <u>dal</u> muro.	The cat jumped <u>off</u> the wall.
È scesa <u>dalla</u> macchina.	She got <u>out of</u> the car.
Sono cascato <u>dal</u> letto.	I fell <u>out of</u> bed.

i Note that **da … a…** means *from … to…*

<u>da</u> cima <u>a</u> fondo	<u>from</u> top <u>to</u> bottom
<u>dalle</u> otto <u>alle</u> dieci	<u>from</u> eight <u>to</u> ten

> Use **da** with **andare** to say you're going <u>to</u> a shop, or <u>to</u> someone's house or
> workplace.

<u>Vado dal</u> giornalaio.	I'm going <u>to</u> the paper shop.
È <u>andato dal</u> dentista.	He's gone <u>to</u> the dentist's.
<u>Andiamo da</u> Gabriele?	Shall we go <u>to</u> Gabriele's house?

> Use **da** with **essere** to say you're <u>at</u> a shop, or <u>at</u> someone's house or workplace.

Laura è <u>dal</u> parucchiere.	Laura's <u>at</u> the hairdresser's.
Sono <u>da</u> Anna.	I'm <u>at</u> Anna's house.

For further explanation of grammatical terms, please see pages viii–xii.

➤ **da** is used to talk about <u>how long</u> something has been happening.

- Use **da** with periods of time to mean *for*.

  Vivo qui <u>da</u> un anno.   I've been living here <u>for</u> a year.

- Use **da** with points in time to mean *since*.

  <u>da</u> allora   <u>since</u> then

  Ti aspetto <u>dalle</u> tre.   I've been waiting for you <u>since</u> three o'clock.

i   Note that the present tense is used in Italian to talk about what has been happening for a period, or since a certain time.

     È a Londra <u>da</u> martedì.   He's been in London <u>since</u> Tuesday.

⇨ *For more information on the **Present tense**, see page 69.*

➤ **da** is used with passive verbs to mean *by*.

     dipinto <u>da</u> un grande artista   painted <u>by</u> a great artist

     I ladri sono stati catturati <u>dalla</u> polizia.   The thieves were caught <u>by</u> the police.

⇨ *For more information on the **Passive**, see page 119.*

➤ **da** is used with the <u>infinitive</u> (the **–re** form of the verb) when you're talking about things to do.

     C'è molto <u>da</u> fare.   There's lots to do.

     È un film <u>da</u> vedere.   It's a film that you've got to see.

     Non c'è niente <u>da</u> mangiare.   There's nothing to eat.

     E <u>da</u> bere?   And what would you like to drink?

➤ In English you can say what something is used for by putting one noun in front of another, for example *a <u>racing</u> car, an <u>evening</u> dress*. In Italian change the word order and use **da**.

     un nuovo paio di scarpe <u>da</u> corsa   a new pair of running shoes

     Paolo non ha il costume <u>da</u> bagno.   Paolo hasn't got his swimming trunks.

➤ **da** is used when describing someone or something.

     una ragazza <u>dagli</u> occhi azzurri   a girl with blue eyes

     un vestito <u>da</u> cento euro   a dress costing a hundred euros

➤ **da** is used with nouns to mean *as*.

     <u>Da</u> bambino avevo paura del buio.   <u>As</u> a child I was afraid of the dark.

4 **in**

➤ Use **in** with **essere** to mean *in* when you are talking about where someone or something is – except in the case of towns.

Vive **in** Canada.	He lives in Canada.
È **nel** cassetto.	It's in the drawer.

ⓘ Note that in the case of towns you use **a** in Italian.

Abitano **a** Bologna.	They live in Bologna.

> *Tip*
>
> You don't use **in** with adverbs such as **qui** (meaning *here*) and **lì** (meaning *there*).
>
> | | |
> |---|---|
> | **qui** dentro | in here |
> | **lì** dentro | in there |

➤ Use **in** with **andare** to mean *to* when you're talking about where someone or something is going *to*, except in the case of towns.

Andrò **in** Germania quest'estate.	I'm going to Germany this summer.
È andato **in** ufficio.	He's gone to the office.

ⓘ Note that in the case of towns you use **a** in Italian.

Sei mai stato **a** New York?	Have you ever been to New York?

> *Tip*
>
> **essere in vacanza** means *to be on holiday*, **andare in vacanza** means *to go on holiday*.

➤ Use **in** to mean *into* when you're talking about getting *into* something, or putting something *into* something.

Su, sali **in** macchina.	Come on, get into the car.
Come sono penetrati **in** banca?	How did they get into the bank?
L'ha gettato **in** acqua.	He threw it into the water.

ⓘ Note that **in** is also used with verbs such as **dividere** (meaning *to divide*) and **tagliare** (meaning *to cut*).

L'ha tagliato **in** due.	She cut it into two.

➪ *For more information on **Prepositions after verbs**, see page 143.*

➤ Use **in** to mean *in* with years, seasons and months.

nel duemilasedici	in two thousand and sixteen
in estate	in summer
in ottobre	in October

For further explanation of grammatical terms, please see pages viii–xii.

i Note that you can also use **di** with seasons (**d'estate**) and **a** with months (**ad ottobre**).

➤ **in** is used with periods of time to mean *in*.

L'ha fatto **in** sei mesi.	He did it **in** six months.
Puoi finirlo **in** trenta minuti.	You can finish it **in** thirty minutes.

➤ **in** is used with modes of transport to mean *by*.

Siamo andati **in** treno.	We went **by** train.
È meglio andare **in** bici.	It's better to go **by** bike.

➤ **in** is used to say <u>how</u> something is done.

Camminavano **in** silenzio.	They walked in silence.
È scritto **in** tedesco.	It's written in German.

5 **su**

➤ Use **su** to mean *on*.

Il tuo telefonino è **sul** pavimento.	Your mobile phone is <u>on</u> the floor.
Mettilo **sulla** sedia.	Put it <u>on</u> the chair.
È **sulla** sinistra.	It's <u>on</u> the left.

i Note that **sul giornale** means *in the newspaper*.

L'ho letto **sul** giornale.	I read it in the newspaper.

> ## Tip
>
> **qui su** and **qua su** mean *up here*. **là** combines with **su** to make one word with a double s: **lassù** (meaning *up there*).
>
> | | |
> |---|---|
> | Siamo **qui su**. | We're <u>up here</u>. |
> | Eccoli **lassù**. | They're <u>up there</u>. |

➤ **su** is used with topics to mean *about*.

un libro **sugli** animali	a book <u>about</u> animals

➤ **su** is used with numbers:

- to talk about ratios

in tre casi **su** dieci	in three cases <u>out of</u> ten
due giorni **su** tre	two days <u>out of</u> three

- with an article and a number to indicate an approximate amount

È costato **sui** cinquecento euro.	It cost <u>around</u> five hundred euros.
È **sulla** trentina.	She's <u>about</u> thirty.

6 per

➤ **per** often means *for*.

Questo è per te.	This is for you.
È troppo difficile per lui.	It's too difficult for him.
L'ho comprato per trenta euro.	I bought it for thirty euros.
Ho guidato per trecento chilometri.	I drove for three hundred kilometres.

🛈 Note that when you are talking about how long you have been doing something you use **da**.

Aspetto da un pezzo.	I've been waiting for a while.

➤ **per** is used with destinations.

il volo per Londra	the flight to London
il treno per Roma	the train to Rome

➤ **per** is used with verbs of movement to mean *through*.

I ladri sono entrati per la finestra.	The burglars got in through the window.
Siamo passati per Birmingham.	We went through Birmingham.

➤ **per** is used to indicate how something is transported or communicated.

per posta	by post
per via aerea	by airmail
per email	by email
per ferrovia	by rail
per telefono	by *or* on the phone

🛈 Note that **per** is NOT used when referring to means of transport for people, **in** is used instead.

in macchina	by car

➤ **per** is used to explain the reason for something.

L'ho fatto per aiutarti.	I did it to help you.
L'abbiamo fatto per ridere.	We did it for a laugh.
Ci sono andato per abitudine.	I went out of habit.
Non l'ho fatto per pigrizia.	I didn't do it out of laziness.
È successo per errore.	It happened by mistake.

➤ **per** is used in some very common phrases.

uno per uno	one by one
giorno per giorno	day by day
una per volta	one at a time
due per tre	two times three

For further explanation of grammatical terms, please see pages viii–xii.

Some other common prepositions

1 One- word and two-word prepositions

➤ As in English, Italian prepositions can be one word or consist of more than one word, for example **vicino a** (meaning *near*) and **prima di** (meaning *before*).

The following are some of the commonest prepositions in Italian:

- **prima di** before, until

prima di me	before me
prima delle sette	before seven o'clock
Non sarà pronto prima delle otto.	It won't be ready until eight o'clock.

> *Tip*
>
> When a preposition includes **a** or **di** remember to combine these words with definite articles such as **il**, **la** and **le**.

i Note that **prima di**, like many other Italian prepositions, can be used in front of an infinitive (the **–re** form of the verb).

Dobbiamo informarci prima di cominciare.	We need to find out before starting or before we start.

- **dopo** after

Ci vediamo dopo le vacanze.	See you after the holidays.
Dopo aver mandato messaggino ha spento il telefonino.	After sending or after she'd sent the text she switched off the phone.

i Note that **dopo di** is used with pronouns.

Loro sono arrivati dopo di noi.	They arrived after us.

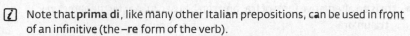

⇨ *For more information on* **Pronouns**, *see page 40.*

- **fino a** until, as far as

Resto fino a venerdì.	I'm staying until Friday.
Vengo con te fino alla posta.	I'll come with you as far as the post office.

i Note that **Fino a quando?** (meaning literally *until when*) is used to ask *How long?*

Fino a quando puoi rimanere?	How long can you stay?

> *Tip*
>
> When a preposition includes **a** or **di** remember to combine these words with definite articles such as **il**, **la** and **le**.

- **fra** in, between, among

Torno <u>fra</u> un'ora.	I'll be back <u>in</u> an hour.
Era seduto <u>fra</u> il padre e lo zio.	He was sitting <u>between</u> his father and his uncle.
<u>Fra</u> i sopravvissuti c'era anche il pilota.	The pilot was <u>among</u> the survivors.

[i] Note that **fra di** is used with pronouns.

<u>Fra di</u> noi ci sono alcuni mancini.	There are some left-handers <u>among us</u>.

⇨ *For more information on **Pronouns**, see page 40.*

Tip

fra poco means *in a short time*, or *soon*.

Lo sapremo <u>fra poco</u>.	We'll <u>soon</u> know.

- **tra** is an alternative form of **fra**, and can be used in exactly the same way

<u>tra</u> un'ora	<u>in</u> an hour
<u>tra</u> poco	soon
<u>tra</u> il padre e lo zio	<u>between</u> his father and his uncle
<u>tra</u> i feriti	<u>among</u> the injured

- **durante** during

<u>durante</u> la notte	<u>during</u> the night

- **con** with, to

Ci andrò <u>con</u> lei.	I'll go <u>with</u> her.
Hai parlato <u>con</u> lui?	Have you spoken <u>to</u> him?

- **senza** without

Esci <u>senza</u> cappotto?	Are you going out <u>without</u> a coat?

[i] Note that **senza di** is used with pronouns.

Non posso vivere <u>senza di lui</u>.	I can't live <u>without him</u>.

⇨ *For more information on **Pronouns**, see page 40.*

- **contro** against

Sono <u>contro</u> la caccia.	I'm <u>against</u> hunting.

[i] Note that **contro di** is used with pronouns.

Non ho niente <u>contro di lui</u>.	I've got nothing <u>against him</u>.

- **davanti a** in front of, opposite
  Era seduta <u>davanti a</u> me nell'aereo.   She was sitting <u>in front of</u> me in the plane.
  la casa <u>davanti alla</u> mia   the house <u>opposite</u> mine

---

> *Tip*
>
> When a preposition includes **a** or **di** remember to combine these words with definite articles such as **il**, **la** and **le**.

- **dietro** behind
  <u>dietro</u> la porta   <u>behind</u> the door

[*i*] Note that **dietro di** is used with pronouns.
  Sono seduti <u>dietro di me</u>.   They're sitting <u>behind me</u>.

⇨ *For more information on Pronouns, see page 40.*

- **sotto** under, below
  Il gatto si è nascosto <u>sotto</u> il letto.   The cat hid <u>under</u> the bed.
  cinque gradi <u>sotto</u> zero   five degrees <u>below</u> zero

- **sopra** over, above, on top of
  le donne <u>sopra</u> i sessant'anni   women <u>over</u> sixty
  cento metri <u>sopra</u> il livello del mare   a hundred metres <u>above</u> sea level
  <u>sopra</u> l'armadio   <u>on top of</u> the cupboard

- **accanto a** next to
  Siediti <u>accanto a</u> me.   Sit <u>next to</u> me.

> *Tip*
>
> When a preposition includes **a** or **di** remember to combine these words with definite articles such as **il**, **la** and **le**.

- **verso** towards, around
  Correva <u>verso</u> l'uscita.   He was running <u>towards</u> the exit.
  Arriverò <u>verso</u> le sette.   I'll arrive <u>around</u> seven.

[*i*] Note that **verso di** is used with pronouns.
  Correvano <u>verso di lui</u>.   They were running <u>towards him</u>.

⇨ *For more information on Pronouns, see page 40.*

- **a causa di** because of
  L'aeroporto è chiuso <u>a causa della</u> nebbia.   The airport is closed <u>because of</u> fog.

> ## Tip
> When a preposition includes **a** or **di** remember to combine these words
> with definite articles such as **il**, **la** and **le**.

- **malgrado** in spite of

  **Malgrado tutto siamo ancora   We're still friends in spite of
  amici.**   everything.

2 | Preposition or adverb?

➤ In English some words can be used both as <u>adverbs</u>, which describe verbs,
and as <u>prepositions</u>, which go in front of nouns and pronouns.

➤ The word *before* is an <u>adverb</u> in the sentence *We've met before* and a <u>preposition</u>
in the phrase *before dinner*.

⇨ *For more information on **Adverbs**, see page 160.*

➤ In Italian you <u>don't</u> usually use exactly the same word as both an adverb and
a preposition:

- **prima** and **davanti** are <u>adverbs</u>

  **Perché non me l'hai detto prima?   Why didn't you tell me before?
  la casa davanti   the house opposite.

- **prima di** and **davanti a** are <u>prepositions</u>

  **Ne ho bisogno prima di giovedì.   I need it before Thursday.
  Ero seduto davanti a lui a cena.   I was sitting opposite him at dinner.

Key points

✔ **dopo**, **senza**, **fra**, **dietro**, **contro**, **verso** are used without **di**, except
when followed by a pronoun.

✔ Italian prepositions often have **di** or **a** as their second element; Italian
adverbs are not followed by **di** or **a**.

Conjunctions

> **What is a conjunction?**
> A **conjunction** is a word such as *and*, *but*, *or*, *so*, *if* and *because*, that links two
> words or phrases, or two parts of a sentence, for example, *Diane <u>and</u> I have been
> friends for years; I left <u>because</u> I was bored.*

e, ma, anche, o, perché, che and se

➤ These common Italian conjunctions correspond to common English conjunctions,
such as *and* and *but*. However they are sometimes used differently from their
English counterparts, for example, **Ma no!** (literally, *But no!*) means *No!*, or
Of course not!

➤ Shown below are the common Italian conjunctions **e**, **anche**, **o**, **ma**, **perché**,
che and **se** and how they are used:

- **e** and, but, what about

io <u>e</u> Giovanni	Giovanni <u>and</u> I
tu <u>ed</u> io	you <u>and</u> me
Lo credevo simpatico <u>e</u> non lo è.	I thought he was nice, <u>but</u> he isn't.
Io non ci vado, <u>e</u> tu?	I'm not going, <u>what about</u> you?

📝 Note that you use **di** or **a**, not the conjunction **e**, to translate *try <u>and</u>*, *go <u>and</u>*
and so on.

Cerca <u>di</u> capire!	Try and understand!
Vado <u>a</u> vedere.	I'll go and see.

⇨ For more information on *di* and *a*, see page 174.

- **ma** but

strano <u>ma</u> vero	strange <u>but</u> true
Dice così, <u>ma</u> non ci credo.	That's what he says, <u>but</u> I don't believe it.

📝 Note that **ma** is used for emphasis with **sì** and **no**.

Ti dispiace? – <u>Ma</u> no!	Do you mind? – <u>Of course</u> not.
Non ti piace? – <u>Ma</u> sì!	Don't you like it? – Yes <u>of course</u> I do.

- **anche** also, too, even

Parla tedesco e <u>anche</u> francese.	She speaks German and <u>also</u> French.
Ho fame. – <u>Anch'</u>io!	I'm hungry. – Me <u>too</u>!
Lo saprebbe fare <u>anche</u> un bambino.	<u>Even</u> a child could do it.

- **o** or

due <u>o</u> tre volte	two <u>or</u> three times

> ## Tip
>
> **oppure** is another word for *or*. It is used to join two parts of a sentence when you're talking about alternatives.
>
> | | |
> |---|---|
> | **Possiamo guardare la TV oppure ascoltare musica.** | We can watch TV <u>or</u> listen to music. |

- **perché** because

Non posso uscire <u>perché</u> ho molto da fare.	I can't go out <u>because</u> I've got a lot to do.

i Note that **perché** also means *why*.

<u>Perché</u> vai via? – Perché è tardi.	<u>Why</u> are you going? – Because it's late.

- **che** that

Ha detto <u>che</u> farà tardi.	He said <u>that</u> he'll be late.
Penso <u>che</u> sia il migliore.	I think <u>that</u> it's the best.

⇨ *For more information on* **che** *followed by the* **Subjunctive**, *see page 130.*

> ## Tip
>
> In English you can say either *He says he loves me* or *He says <u>that</u> he loves me*. In Italian **che** is <u>NOT</u> optional in this way.
>
> | | |
> |---|---|
> | **So <u>che</u> le piace la cioccolata.** | I know (that) she likes chocolate. |

- **se** if, whether

Fammi sapere <u>se</u> c'è qualche problema.	Let me know <u>if</u> there are any problems.
<u>Se</u> fosse più furbo verrebbe.	<u>If</u> he had more sense he'd come.
Non so <u>se</u> dirglielo o no.	I don't know <u>whether</u> to tell him or not.

⇨ *For more information on* **se** *followed by the* **Subjunctive**, *see page 130.*

Some other common conjunctions

➤ The following conjunctions are used a lot in colloquial Italian:

- **allora** so, right then

<u>Allora</u>, cosa pensi?	<u>So</u>, what do you think?
<u>Allora</u>, cosa facciamo stasera?	<u>Right then</u>, what shall we do this evening?

- **dunque** so, well

Ha sbagliato lui, <u>dunque</u> è giusto che paghi.	It was his mistake, <u>so</u> it's right he should pay.
<u>Dunque</u>, come dicevo...	<u>Well</u>, as I was saying...

- **quindi** so

L'ho già visto, <u>quindi</u> non vado.	I've already seen it, <u>so</u> I'm not going.

- **però** but, however, though

Mi piace, <u>però</u> è troppo caro.	I like it – <u>but</u> it's too expensive.
Non è l'ideale, <u>però</u> può andare.	It's not ideal, <u>however</u> it'll do.
Sì, lo so – strano <u>però</u>.	Yes, I know – it's odd <u>though</u>.

- **invece** actually

Ero un po' pessimista, ma <u>invece</u> è andato tutto bene.	I wasn't too hopeful, but <u>actually</u> it all went fine.

Tip

invece is often used for emphasis in Italian – it isn't always translated in English.

Ho pensato che fosse lui, ma <u>invece</u> no.	I thought it was him but it wasn't.

- **anzi** in fact

Non mi dispiace, <u>anzi</u> sono contento.	I don't mind, <u>in fact</u> I'm glad.

- **quando** when

Giocano fuori <u>quando</u> fa bel tempo.	They play outside <u>when</u> the weather's nice.

ⓘ Note that in sentences referring to the future, the future tense is used after **quando**.

Lo farò <u>quando</u> <u>avrò</u> tempo.	I'll do it <u>when</u> I <u>have</u> time.

⇨ *For more information on the **Future tense**, see page 93.*

- **mentre** while

È successo <u>mentre</u> eri fuori.	It happened <u>while</u> you were out.

- **come** as

Ho fatto <u>come</u> hai detto tu.	I did <u>as</u> you told me.

ⓘ Note that **quando** and **mentre** tell you <u>WHEN</u> something happens; **come** tells you <u>HOW</u> something happens.

Split conjunctions

➤ English split conjunctions such as *either ... or* and *both ... and* are translated by split conjunctions in Italian.

- **o ... o** either ... or

o oggi o domani	either today or tomorrow
Ti accompagneranno o Carlo o Marco.	Either Carlo or Marco will go with you.

- **né ... né** neither ... nor, either ... or

Non mi hanno chiamato né Claudio né Luca.	Neither Claudio nor Luca has phoned me.
Non avevo né guanti né scarponi.	I didn't have either gloves or boots.

- **sia ... che** both ... and

Verranno sia Luigi che suo fratello.	Both Luigi and his brother are coming.

[*i*] Note that in English a singular verb is used in sentences that have split conjunctions. In Italian a plural verb is used in sentences with split conjunctions if the two people or things involved are both the subject of the verb.

Non vengono né lui né sua moglie.	Neither he nor his wife is coming.

Spelling

1 How to spell words that have a hard k or g sound

➤ In Italian the [k] sound you have in the English words *kite* and *car* is spelled in two different ways, depending on the following vowel:

- **c** before **a**, **o** and **u**
- **ch** before **e** and **i**

➤ This means that the Italian word for *singer* is spelled **cantante** (pronounced [*kan-tan-tay*]; the word for *necklace* is spelled **collana** (pronounced [*kol-la-na*]), and the word for *cure* is spelled **cura** (pronounced [*koo-ra*]).

➤ However, the Italian word for *that* is spelled **che** (pronounced [*kay*]) and the word for *chemistry* is spelled **chimica** (pronounced [*kee-mee-ka*].

Tip

Remember that the Italian words for *kilo* and *kilometre* are spelled with **ch**:

due chili	two kilos
cento chilometri	a hundred kilometres

➤ In the same way, the hard [g] sound that you have in the English word *gas* is also spelled two ways in Italian:

- **g** before **a**, **o** and **u**
- **gh** before **e** and **i**

➤ This means that the Italian word for *cat* is spelled **gatto** (pronounced [*ga-toe*]; the word for *elbow* is spelled **gomito** (pronounced [*go-mee-toe*]), and the word for *taste* is spelled **gusto** (pronounced [*goos-toe*]).

➤ However, the Italian word for *leagues* is spelled **leghe** (pronounced [*lay-gay*]) and the word for *lakes* is spelled **laghi** (pronounced [*lah-ghee*].

2 How to pronounce c + a vowel

➤ As we have seen, the Italian letter **c** is pronounced like a [k] when it's followed by **a**, **o**, or **u**.

➤ When **c** is followed by **e** or **i** it is pronounced like the [ch] in *children*. This means that **centro** (meaning *centre*) is pronounced [*chen-tro*] and **città** (meaning *city*) is pronounced [*chee-tah*].

3 | How to pronounce g + a vowel

➤ The Italian letter **g** is pronounced like the [g] in *gas* when it's followed by **a**, **o**, or **u**. When an Italian **g** is followed by **e** or **i**, however, it's pronounced like the [j] in *jet*. This means that **gente** (meaning *people*) is pronounced [*jen-tay*] and **giorno** (meaning *day*) is pronounced [*jor-no*].

4 | How to spell verb endings which have c or g + vowel

➤ When an Italian verb has a hard [k] or [g] sound before the infinitive ending, for example **cercare** (meaning *to look for*) and **pagare** (meaning *to pay*), you have to change the spelling to **ch** and **gh** in forms of the verb that have endings starting with **e** or **i**.

➤ Here are the present and future tenses of **cercare** and **pagare**, showing how the spelling changes.

Vowel that follows c/g	Present of cercare	Meaning	Present of pagare	Meaning
o	cerco	I look for	pago	I pay
i	cerchi	you look for	paghi	you pay
a	cerca	he/she looks for	paga	he/she pays
i	cerchiamo	we look for	paghiamo	we pay
a	cercate	you look for	pagate	you pay
a	cercano	they look for	pagano	they pay

Vowel that follows c/g	Future of cercare	Meaning	Future of pagare	Meaning
e	cercherò	I'll look for	pagherò	I'll pay
e	cercherai	you'll look for	pagherai	you'll pay
e	cercherà	he/she will look for	pagherà	he/she will pay
e	cercheremo	we'll look for	pagheremo	we'll pay
e	cercherete	you'll look for	pagherete	you'll pay
e	cercheranno	they'll look for	pagheranno	they'll pay

Cosa cerchi? – Cerco le chiavi.   What are you looking for?
                                        – I'm looking for my keys.

Pago io. – No, paghiamo noi.   I'll pay. – No, we'll pay.

For further explanation of grammatical terms, please see pages viii–xii.

➤ When an Italian verb has a [sh] or [j] sound before the infinitive ending, for example **lasciare** (meaning *to leave*) and **mangiare** (meaning *to eat*), you drop the **i** of the stem before endings starting with **e** or **i**.

➤ This means that you spell the **tu** form of the present tense of these verbs **lasci** and **mangi**.

La<u>sci</u> la finestra aperta?	Are you leaving the window open?
Cosa man<u>gi</u>?	What are you eating?

➤ The futures of the two verbs are spelled **lascerò, lascerai, lascerà, lasceremo, lascerete, lasceranno** and **mangerò, mangerai, mangerà, mangeremo, mangerete, mangeranno**.

Fa caldo, la<u>sc</u>erò a casa il maglione.	It's hot, I'll leave my jumper at home.
Domani man<u>g</u>eremo meno.	We'll eat less tomorrow.

> *Tip*
>
> Although the spelling of some verb endings changes, the pronunciation stays the same.

---

5 **How to spell plurals of nouns and adjectives ending in –ca or –ga**

➤ When a feminine noun or adjective has a hard [k] or [g] sound before the singular ending **–a**, you add an **h** to the plural ending.

Singular	Meaning	Plural	Meaning
amica	friend	amiche	friends
riga	line	righe	lines
ricca	rich	ricche	rich
lunga	long	lunghe	long

una sua amica ricca	a rich friend of hers
le sue ami<u>ch</u>e ric<u>ch</u>e	her rich friends
una riga sotto le parole	a line under the words
Ne ho letto solo po<u>ch</u>e ri<u>gh</u>e.	I just read a few lines of it.

> *Tip*
>
> Feminine nouns and adjectives always keep their hard [k] and [g] sounds in the plural.

6 | How to spell plurals of nouns and adjectives ending in –co or –go

➤ There is not a fixed rule for the sound of the consonants **c** and **g** in the plural of masculine nouns and adjectives ending in **–co** and **–go**.

➤ Some words keep the hard sound of their **c** or **g** in the plural, and add an **h** to the spelling.

Singular	Meaning	Plural	Meaning
fuoco	fire	**fuochi**	fires
albergo	hotel	**alberghi**	hotels
ricco	rich	**ricchi**	rich
lungo	long	**lunghi**	long

È un albergo per ricchi.	It's a hotel for rich people.
Ho i capelli lunghi.	I've got long hair.

➤ The plurals of many other words, however, change from the hard [k] sound to the [ch] sound, or from the hard [g] to [j]. This means their plurals are not spelled with an added **h**.

Singular	Meaning	Plural	Meaning
amico	friend	**amici**	friends
astrologo	astrologer	**astrologi**	astrologers
greco	Greek	**greci**	Greek
psicologico	psychological	**psicologici**	psychological

un astrologo greco	a Greek astrologer
i miei amici e i loro problemi psicologici	my friends and their psychological problems

7 | How to spell plurals of nouns ending in –io

➤ When the **i** of the **–io** ending is stressed, as it is in **zio** (meaning *uncle*) and **invio** (meaning *dispatch*), the plural is spelled with double **i**: **zii**, **invii**.

Ho sei zii e sette zie.	I've got six uncles and seven aunts.

➤ If the **i** of the **–io** ending is not stressed you spell the plural ending with only one **i**, for example **figlio → figli**; **occhio → occhi**.

Ha gli occhi azzurri.	He's got blue eyes.

8 | How to spell plurals of nouns ending in –cia and –gia

➤ The spelling of the plurals of these words also depends on whether the **i** of the ending is stressed.

For further explanation of grammatical terms, please see pages viii–xii.

➤ In some words, such words as **farmacia** (meaning *chemist's*) and **bugia** (meaning *lie*), the stress is on the **i**, and the plurals keep the **i**: **farmacie**; **bugie**.

> **Non dire bugie.**   Don't tell lies.

➤ In others, such as **faccia** (meaning *face*) and **spiaggia** (meaning *beach*) the **i** of the singular ending is not stressed, and the plural is not spelled with **i**: **facce**; **spiagge**.

> **le nostre spiagge preferite**   our favourite beaches

9 How to use accents

➤ Accents have two main uses: one is to show that a word is stressed on the last syllable, which is not normal In Italian, for example **città** (meaning *city*), **università** (meaning *university*), **perché** (meaning *why/because*), **cercherò** (meaning *I will look for*).

➡ *For more information on **Stress**, see page 196.*

➤ The second use of accents is to distinguish between words that have Identical pronunciations and spellings.

Without an accent		With an accent	
da	from	dà	he/she/it gives
e	and	è	is
la	the/It	là	there
li	them	lì	there
ne	of it/them	né	neither
se	if	sé	himself
si	hImself/herself/one	sì	yes
te	you	tè	tea

> **Mettila là.**   Put it there.
> **Non so se l'ha fatto da sé.**   I don't know if he made it himself.

Tip

The words **può**, **già**, **ciò**, **più** and **giù** are spelled with an accent.

Key points

✔ Spelling changes are sometimes necessary to keep the consonants **c** and **g** hard.

✔ Accents show that the last syllable of a word is stressed.

Stress

Which syllable to stress

➤ Most Italian words have two or more <u>syllables</u>, (units containing a vowel sound). In this section syllables are shown divided by | and the stressed vowel is in italic.

➤ Most words are stressed on the next to the last syllable, for example, **fi|ne|stra**.

➤ Some words are stressed on the last vowel, and this is always shown by an accent, for example, **u|ni|ver|si|tà**.

➤ Some words have their stress on an unexpected vowel, but are not spelled with an accent, for example, **mac|chi|na** (meaning *car*).

➤ If a word has the stress on a vowel you wouldn't expect, the stressed vowel is in italics, for example, **vogliono** (meaning *they want*), **vendere** (meaning *to sell*), **quindici** (meaning *fifteen*), **medico** (meaning *doctor*).

➤ This book also marks the stress in words in which **i** before another vowel is pronounced like **y**, for example **Lidia**.

1 Words that are stressed on the next to last syllable

➤ Two-syllable words <u>always</u> stress the first vowel, unless the final vowel has an accent:

ca|sa	house	**gior|no**	day
bel|la	beautiful	**du|e**	two
so|no	I am	**spes|so**	often
lu |i	he	**og|gi**	today

➤ Words with three or more syllables <u>generally</u> have the stress on the next to the last vowel:

in|gle|se	English	**par|la|vo**	I was speaking
gen|ti|le	nice	**an|dreb|be**	he'd go
set|ti|ma|na	week	**par|le|re|mo**	we'll speak
sta|zio|ne	station	**su|per|mer|ca|to**	supermarket
stra|or|di|na|ria|men|te	extraordinarily		

2 Words that stress the last syllable

➤ There are a number of nouns in Italian that have the stress on the final syllable and are spelled with an accent. They sometimes correspond to English nouns that end with *ty*, such as *university* and *faculty*.

For further explanation of grammatical terms, please see pages viii–xii.

re|al|tà	reality	u|ni|ver|si|tà	university
fe|li|ci|tà	happiness, felicity	fe|del|tà	fidelity
cu|rio|si|tà	curiosity	fa|col|tà	faculty
bon|tà	goodness	cit|tà	city
cru|del|tà	cruelty	e|tà	age
ti|vù	TV	me|tà	half

➤ There are some common adverbs and conjunctions that have the stress on the final syllable and are spelled with an accent, for example, per\|ché, co\|sì, and pe\|rò.

⇨ *For more information about **Spelling**, see page 191.*

---

3 **Words that stress an unexpected syllable**

➤ Some words have the stress on a syllable which is neither the last, nor the next to the last.

u|ti|le	useful	por|ta|ti|le	portable
dif|fi|ci|le	difficult	su|bi|to	suddenly
nu|me|ro	number	pen|to|la	saucepan
ca|me|ra	bedroom	com|pi|to	homework
mo|du|lo	form		

ℹ️ Note that past participles such as fi\|ni\|to (meaning *finished*) and par\|ti\|to (meaning *left*) always have the stress on the next to last syllable, but there are similar-looking words, such as su\|bi\|to (meaning *immediately*) and com\|pi\|to (meaning *homework*), that are not past participles, and that have the stress on a syllable you wouldn't expect.

> ## *Tip*
> When learning new vocabulary, check in the dictionary where the stress goes.

---

4 **Stress in verb forms**

➤ In the present tense, the **loro** form always has the stress on the same vowel as the **io** form:

io form		loro form	
par|lo	I speak	par|la|no	they speak
con|si|de|ro	I consider	con|si|de|ra|no	they consider
mi al|le|no	I'm training	si al|le |na|no	they're training

➤ In the future tense of all verbs the stress is on the last syllable of the **io** form and the **lui/lei** form. These two verb forms are spelled with an accent on the stressed vowel.

Future	
sa|rò	I will be
la|vo|re|rò	I will work
fi|ni|rà	it will finish
as|pet|te|rà	she'll wait

➤ The infinitive of –are verbs <u>always</u> has the stress on the **a** of the ending, for example **in\|vi\|ta\|re** (meaning *to invite*) and **cam\|mi\|na\|re** (meaning *to walk*). The infinitive of –ire verbs always has the stress on the **i** of the ending, for example **par\|ti\|re** (meaning *to leave*) and **fi\|ni\|re** (meaning *to finish*).

➤ The infinitive of **–ere** verbs <u>sometimes</u> has the stress on the first **e** of the ending, for example, **ve\|de\|re** (meaning *to see*) and **av\|e\|re** (meaning *to have*). However, these verbs **often** stress a syllable before the **–ere** ending, for example **ven\|de\|re** (meaning *to sell*), **di\|vi\|de\|re** (meaning *to divide*) and **es\|se\|re** (meaning *to be*).

Tip

Remember that **–ere** verbs do not always stress the **e** of the ending, and take note of the stress when learning a new verb.

5 Different stress for different meanings

➤ In a few cases one word has two pronunciations, depending on its meaning. The following are some examples:

Normal stress	Meaning	Unusual stress	Meaning
an|co|ra	again	an|co|ra	anchor
ca|pi|ta|no	captain	ca|pi|ta|no	they happen
me|tro	meter	me|trò	metro

Key points

✔ Two-syllable words are stesssed on the first syllable, unless there's an accent.

✔ Longer words are usually stressed on the next to the last syllable.

✔ If the stress is on an unexpected vowel you need to learn it.

For further explanation of grammatical terms, please see pages viii–xii.

Numbers

1	uno (un, una)	31	trentuno
2	due	40	quaranta
3	tre	41	quarantuno
4	quattro	50	cinquanta
5	cinque	58	cinquantotto
6	sei	60	sessanta
7	sette	63	sessantatré
8	otto	70	settanta
9	nove	75	settantacinque
10	dieci	80	ottanta
11	undici	81	ottantuno
12	dodici	90	novanta
13	tredici	99	novantanove
14	quattordici	100	cento
15	quindici	101	centouno
16	sedici	200	duecento
17	diciassette	203	duecentotré
18	diciotto	300	trecento
19	diciannove	400	quattrocento
20	venti	500	cinquecento
21	ventuno	600	seicento
22	ventidue	700	settecento
23	ventitré	800	ottocento
24	ventiquattro	900	novecento
25	venticinque	1000	mille
26	ventisei	1001	milleuno
27	ventisette	2000	duemila
28	ventotto	2500	duemilacinquecento
29	ventinove	1.000.000	un milione
30	trenta		(in English 1,000,000)

a pagina diciannove	on page nineteen
nel capitolo sette	in chapter seven
dieci per cento	ten per cent
seicento euro	six hundred euros
tremila persone	three thousand people

i Note that in the numbers 21, 31, 41 and so on, the final vowel of **venti**, **trenta** and **quaranta** is lost: **ventuno**, **trentuno**, **quarantuno**. The same thing happens with the numbers 28, 38, 48 and so on: **ventotto**, **trentotto**, **quarantotto**. When **tre** is combined with another number it takes an accent: **trentatré** (33), **centotré** (103), **milletré** (1003).

1 uno, un or una?

➤ In Italian the same word – **uno** – is used for the number *one* and the indefinite article *a*.

➤ When using **uno** as a number in front of a noun, follow the same rules as for the indefinite article.

un uomo	one man
uno scienzato	one scientist
una ragazza	one girl
un'*anatra*	one duck

➡ *For more information on the* **Indefinite article**, *see page 17.*

➤ When replying to a question, use **uno** if what's referred to is masculine, and **una** if it's feminine.

Quanti giorni? – Uno.	How many days? – One.
Quante notti? – Una.	How many nights? – One.

➤ Use **uno** when counting, unless referring to something or someone feminine.

➤ Do NOT use **un** to translate *one hundred*, or *one thousand*.

cento metri	one hundred metres
mille euro	one thousand euros

➤ You do use **un** with **milione** (meaning *million*) and **miliardo** (meaning *thousand million*).

Quante persone? – Un milione.	How many people? – One million.
un milione di dollari	one million dollars
un miliardo di euro	one thousand million euros

[i] Note that when **un milione** and **un miliardo** are followed by a noun, **di** is added.

2 Which numbers have plurals?

➤ The only numbers which have plurals are **mille**, **milione**, and **miliardo**. **Due**, **tre**, **quattro** and so on are added to **mila** to make **duemila** (meaning *two thousand*), **tremila** (meaning *three thousand*) and **quattromila** (meaning *four thousand*).

mille euro	one thousand euros
diecimila euro	ten thousand euros
un milione di dollari	one million dollars
venti milioni di dollari	twenty million dollars
un miliardo di sterline	one thousand million pounds
due miliardi di sterline	two thousand million pounds

For further explanation of grammatical terms, please see pages viii–xii.

3 | Full stop or comma?

➤ Use a full stop, not a comma, to separate thousands and millions in figures.

700.000 (settecentomila)	700,000 (seven hundred thousand)
5.000.000 (cinque milioni)	5,000,000 (five million)

➤ Use a comma instead of a decimal point to show decimals in Italian.

0,5 (zero virgola cinque)	0.5 (nought point five)
3,4 (tre virgola quattro)	3.4 (three point four)

1st	primo (1°)
2nd	secondo (2°)
3rd	terzo (3°)
4th	quarto (4°)
5th	quinto (5°)
6th	sesto (6°)
7th	settimo (7°)
8th	ottavo (8°)
9th	nono (9°)
10th	decimo (10°)
11th	undicesimo (11°)
18th	diciottesimo (18°)
21st	ventunesimo (21°)
33rd	trentatreesimo (33°)
100th	centesimo (100°)
101st	centunesimo (101°)
1000th	millesimo (1000°)

> **Tip**
>
> Learn the first ten of these numbers.

➤ To make the others, take numbers such as **venti** and **trentotto**, drop the final vowel and add **–esimo**. If the number ends in **tre**, DON'T drop the final **e** before adding **–esimo**.

la ventesima settimana	the twentieth week
il trentottesimo anno	the thirty-eighth year
il loro trentatreesimo anniversario di matrimonio	their thirty-third anniversary

➤ These numbers are adjectives and can be made masculine or feminine, singular or plural.

il quindicesimo piano	the fifteenth floor
la terza lezione	the third lesson
i primi piatti	the first courses
le loro seconde scelte	their second choices

ⓘ Note that when writing these numbers in figures you should use a little °, or ª, depending on whether what's referred to is masculine or feminine.

il 15° piano	the 15th floor
la 24ª giornata	the 24th day

➤ Roman numerals are often used for centuries, popes and monarchs.

il XIV *secolo*	the 14th century
Paolo VI	Paul VI
Enrico III	Henry III

⇨ *For more information on **Numbers used in dates**, see page 204.*

L'ORA

Che ora è? *or* Che ore sono?

È l'una meno venti.
È l'una meno un quarto.
È l'una.
È l'una e dieci.
È l'una e un quarto.
È l'una e mezza.
Sono le due meno venticinque.
Sono le due meno un quarto.
Sono le due.
Sono le due e dieci.
Sono le due e un quarto.
Sono le due e mezza.
Sono le tre.

THE TIME

What time is it?

It's twenty to one.
It's a quarter to one.
It's one o'clock.
It's ten past one.
It's a quarter past one.
It's half past one.
It's twenty-five to two.
It's a quarter to two.
It's two o'clock.
It's ten past two.
It's a quarter past two.
It's half past two.
It's three o'clock.

Tip

Use **sono le** for all times not involving **una** (meaning *one*).

A che ora?

Arrivano oggi. – A che ora?

(At) what time?

They're arriving today. – What time?

ℹ Note that *at* is optional in English when asking what time something happens, but **a** must always be used in Italian.

a mezzanotte
a mezzogiorno
all'una (del pomeriggio)
alle otto (di sera)
alle 9:25 *or* alle nove e
venticinque
alle 16:50 *or* alle sedici e
cinquanta

at midnight
at midday
at one o'clock (in the afternoon)
at eight o'clock (in the evening)
at twenty-five past nine

at 16:50 *or* sixteen fifty

ℹ Note that the twenty-four hour clock is often used in Italy.

LA DATA	THE DATE
I giorni della settimana	**The days of the week**

lunedì	Monday
martedì	Tuesday
mercoledì	Wednesday
giovedì	Thursday
venerdì	Friday
sabato	Saturday
domenica	Sunday

Quando?	**When?**
lunedì	on Monday
di lunedì	on Mondays
tutti i lunedì	every Monday
martedì scorso	last Tuesday
venerdì prossimo	next Friday
sabato della settimana prossima	a week on Saturday
sabato tra due settimane	two weeks on Saturday

(i) Note that days of the week <u>DON'T</u> have a capital letter in Italian.

I mesi dell'anno	**The months of the year**
gennaio	January
febbraio	February
marzo	March
aprile	April
maggio	May
giugno	June
luglio	July
agosto	August
settembre	September
ottobre	October
novembre	November
dicembre	December

Quando?	**When?**
in *or* a febbraio	in February
il primo dicembre	on December 1st
il due dicembre	on December 2nd
nel 1969 (millenovecento-sessantanove)	in 1969 (in nineteen sixty-nine)
il primo dicembre 2016	on December 1st 2016
nel duemilasei	in two thousand and six

(i) Note that months of the year <u>DON'T</u> have a capital letter in Italian.

For further explanation of grammatical terms, please see pages viii–xii.

> ## Tip
>
> In Italian you use **il primo** for the first day of the month. For all the other days you use the equivalent of *two, three, four* and so on.
>
> **il tre maggio**   the third of May

FRASI UTILI	USEFUL PHRASES
Quando?	**When?**
oggi	today
stamattina	this morning
stasera	this evening
Ogni quanto?	**How often?**
ogni giorno	every day
ogni due giorni	every other day
una volta alla settimana	once a week
due volte alla settimana	twice a week
una volta al mese	once a month
Quando è successo?	**When did it happen?**
di mattina	in the morning
di sera	in the evening
ieri	yesterday
ieri mattina	yesterday morning
ieri sera	yesterday evening/last night
ieri notte	last night
l'altro ieri	the day before yesterday
una settimana fa	a week ago
due settimane fa	two weeks ago
la settimana scorsa	last week
l'anno scorso	last year
Quando succederà?	**When is it going to happen?**
domani	tomorrow
domani mattina	tomorrow morning
domani sera	tomorrow evening/night
dopodomani	the day after tomorrow
fra *or* tra due giorni	in two days' time
fra *or* tra una settimana	in a week's time
fra *or* tra quindici giorni	in two weeks' time
il mese prossimo	next month
l'anno prossimo	next year

Main Index

Verb Tables

Introduction

The **Verb Tables** in the following section contain 120 tables of Italian verbs (some regular and some irregular) in alphabetical order. Each table shows you the following forms: **Present**, **Present Subjunctive**, **Perfect**, **Imperfect**, **Future**, **Conditional**, **Past Historic**, **Pluperfect**, **Imperative** and the **Past Participle** and **Gerund**. For more information on these tenses and how they are formed, when they are used and so on, you should look at the section on Verbs on pages 66–148.

In order to help you use the verbs shown in Verb Tables correctly, there are also a number of example phrases at the bottom of each page to show the verb as it is used in context.

In Italian there are **regular** verbs (their forms follow the regular patterns of **-are**, **-ere** or **-ire** verbs), and **irregular** verbs (their forms do not follow the normal rules). Examples of regular verbs in these tables are:

> **parlare** (regular **-are** verb, Verb Table 346)
> **credere** (regular **-ere** verb, Verb Table 264)
> **capire** (regular **-ire** verb, Verb Table 240)

Some irregular verbs are irregular in most of their forms, while others may only have a couple of irregular forms.

The **Verb Index** at the end of this section contains over 1000 verbs, each of which is cross-referred to one of the verbs given in the Verb Tables. The table shows the patterns that the verb listed in the index follows.

accadere (to happen)

PRESENT		PRESENT SUBJUNCTIVE	
io	–	io	–
tu	–	tu	–
lui/lei/Lei	accade	lui/lei/Lei	accada
noi	–	noi	–
voi	–	voi	–
loro	accadono	loro	accadano

PERFECT		IMPERFECT	
io	–	io	–
tu	–	tu	–
lui/lei/Lei	è accaduto/a	lui/lei/Lei	accadeva
noi	–	noi	–
voi	–	voi	–
loro	sono accaduti/e	loro	accadevano

GERUND
accadendo

PAST PARTICIPLE
accaduto

EXAMPLE PHRASES

All'epoca questo **accadeva** spesso. At that time this often happened.

Stanno **accadendo** molte cose strane. A lot of strange things are happening.

Remember that subject pronouns are not used very often in Italian.

accadere

FUTURE

io	–
tu	–
lui/lei/Lei	accadrà
noi	–
voi	–
loro	accadranno

CONDITIONAL

io	–
tu	–
lui/lei/Lei	accadrebbe
noi	–
voi	–
loro	accadrebbero

PAST HISTORIC

io	–
tu	–
lui/lei/Lei	accadde
noi	–
voi	–
loro	accaddero

PLUPERFECT

io	–
tu	–
lui/lei/Lei	era accaduto/a
noi	–
voi	–
loro	erano accaduti/e

IMPERATIVE

–

EXAMPLE PHRASES

Che cosa ti **accadrà**? What will happen to you?

Non sappiamo cosa ci **accadrebbe**. We don't know what would happen to us.

Accadde un fatto meraviglioso. A wonderful thing happened.

Non capivamo ciò che **era accaduto**. We couldn't understand what had happened.

Italic letters in Italian words show where stress does not follow the usual rules.

accendere (to light)

PRESENT		PRESENT SUBJUNCTIVE	
io	accendo	io	accenda
tu	accendi	tu	accenda
lui/lei/Lei	accende	lui/lei/Lei	accenda
noi	accendiamo	noi	accendiamo
voi	accendete	voi	accendiate
loro	accendono	loro	accendano

PERFECT		IMPERFECT	
io	ho acceso	io	accendevo
tu	hai acceso	tu	accendevi
lui/lei/Lei	ha acceso	lui/lei/Lei	accendeva
noi	abbiamo acceso	noi	accendevamo
voi	avete acceso	voi	accendevate
loro	hanno acceso	loro	accendevano

GERUND
accendendo

PAST PARTICIPLE
acceso

EXAMPLE PHRASES

Abbiamo acceso le candeline. We lit the candles.

Appena entrava in casa **accendeva** sempre la radio. He always switched on the radio as soon as he came into the house.

Mi stavo **accendendo** una sigaretta quando è arrivato il bus. I was lighting a cigarette when the bus arrived.

Mi fai **accendere**? Have you got a light?

Remember that subject pronouns are not used very often in Italian.

accendere

FUTURE

io	**accenderò**
tu	**accenderai**
lui/lei/Lei	**accenderà**
noi	**accenderemo**
voi	**accenderete**
loro	**accenderanno**

CONDITIONAL

io	**accenderei**
tu	**accenderesti**
lui/lei/Lei	**accenderebbe**
noi	**accenderemmo**
voi	**accendereste**
loro	**accenderebbero**

PAST HISTORIC

io	**accesi**
tu	**accendesti**
lui/lei/Lei	**accese**
noi	**accendemmo**
voi	**accendeste**
loro	**accesero**

PLUPERFECT

io	**avevo acceso**
tu	**avevi acceso**
lui/lei/Lei	**aveva acceso**
noi	**avevamo acceso**
voi	**avevate acceso**
loro	**avevano acceso**

IMPERATIVE

accendi
accendiamo
accendete

EXAMPLE PHRASES

Appena arrivati **accenderemo** un fuoco. We'll light a fire as soon as we arrive.
Accendi la TV. Turn on the TV.
Accese una candela in chiesa. She lit a candle in church. ?

ha accessa

Italic letters in Italian words show where stress does not follow the usual rules.

accorgersi (to realize)

PRESENT

io	**mi accorgo**
tu	**ti accorgi**
lui/lei/Lei	**si accorge**
noi	**ci accorgiamo**
voi	**vi accorgete**
loro	**si accorgono**

PRESENT SUBJUNCTIVE

io	**mi accorga**
tu	**ti accorga**
lui/lei/Lei	**si accorga**
noi	**ci accorgiamo**
voi	**vi accorgiate**
loro	**si accorgano**

PERFECT

io	**mi sono accorto/a**
tu	**ti sei accorto/a**
lui/lei/Lei	**si è accorto/a**
noi	**ci siamo accorti/e**
voi	**vi siete accorti/e**
loro	**si sono accorti/e**

IMPERFECT

io	**mi accorgevo**
tu	**ti accorgevi**
lui/lei/Lei	**si accorgeva**
noi	**ci accorgevamo**
voi	**vi accorgevate**
loro	**si accorgevano**

GERUND

accorgendosi

PAST PARTICIPLE

accorto

EXAMPLE PHRASES

Avvisami se non **mi accorgo** che è tardi. Warn me if I don't notice it's getting late.

Mi sono accorto subito che qualcosa non andava. I immediately realized something was wrong.

Si è accorto del furto solo il giorno dopo. He only noticed it had been stolen the next day.

Remember that subject pronouns are not used very often in Italian.

accorgersi

FUTURE

io	**mi accorgerò**
tu	**ti accorgerai**
lui/lei/Lei	**si accorgerà**
noi	**ci accorgeremo**
voi	**vi accorgerete**
loro	**si accorgeranno**

CONDITIONAL

io	**mi accorgerei**
tu	**ti accorgeresti**
lui/lei/Lei	**si accorgerebbe**
noi	**ci accorgeremmo**
voi	**vi accorgereste**
loro	**si accorgerebbero**

PAST HISTORIC

io	**mi accorsi**
tu	**ti accorgesti**
lul/lel/Lel	**si accorse**
noi	**ci accorgemmo**
vol	**vi accorgeste**
loro	**si accorsero**

PLUPERFECT

io	**mi ero accorto/a**
tu	**ti eri accorto/a**
lui/lei/Lei	**si era accorto/a**
noi	**ci eravamo accorti/e**
voi	**vi eravate accorti/e**
loro	**si erano accorti/e**

IMPERATIVE

accorgiti
accorgiamoci
accorgetevi

EXAMPLE PHRASES

Un giorno si **accorgerà** di te. Some day he'll notice you.

Se tu mi ingannassi, **me ne accorgerei**. If you were tricking me I'd notice.

Era malato ma nessuno se ne **accorse**. He was ill, but nobody noticed.

Non si **erano accorti** che ero nella stanza. They hadn't noticed that I was in the room.

È difficile **accorgersi** degli errori di battitura. It's difficult to notice typing errors.

Italic letters in Italian words show where stress does not follow the usual rules.

addormentarsi (to go to sleep)

PRESENT

io	**mi addormento**
tu	**ti addormenti**
lui/lei/Lei	**si addormenta**
noi	**ci addormentiamo**
voi	**vi addormentate**
loro	**si addormentano**

PRESENT SUBJUNCTIVE

io	**mi addormenti**
tu	**ti addormenti**
lui/lei/Lei	**si addormenti**
noi	**ci addormentiamo**
voi	**vi addormentiate**
loro	**si addormentino**

PERFECT

io	**mi sono addormentato/a**
tu	**ti sei addormentato/a**
lui/lei/Lei	**si è addormentato/a**
noi	**ci siamo addormentati/e**
voi	**vi siete addormentati/e**
loro	**si sono addormentati/e**

IMPERFECT

io	**mi addormentavo**
tu	**ti addormentavi**
lui/lei/Lei	**si addormentava**
noi	**ci addormentavamo**
voi	**vi addormentavate**
loro	**si addormentavano**

GERUND

addormentando

PAST PARTICIPLE

addormentato

EXAMPLE PHRASES

Mio padre **si addormenta** sempre davanti alla TV. My father always goes to sleep in front of the TV.

Mi **si è addormentato** un piede. My foot has gone to sleep.

Non riesco ad **addormentarmi**. I can't get to sleep.

Non voleva **addormentarsi**. He didn't want to go to sleep.

Remember that subject pronouns are not used very often in Italian.

addormentarsi

FUTURE

io	mi addormenterò
tu	ti addormenterai
lui/lei/Lei	si addormenterà
noi	ci addormenteremo
voi	vi addormenterete
loro	si addormenteranno

CONDITIONAL

io	mi addormenterei
tu	ti addormenteresti
lui/lei/Lei	si addormenterebbe
noi	ci addormenteremmo
voi	vi addormentereste
loro	si addormenterebbero

PAST HISTORIC

io	mi addormentai
tu	ti addormentasti
lui/lei/Lei	si addormentò
noi	ci addormentammo
voi	vi addormentaste
loro	si addormentarono

PLUPERFECT

io	mi ero addormentato/a
tu	ti eri addormentato/a
lul/lei/Lei	si era addormentato/a
noi	ci eravamo addormentati/e
voi	vi eravate addormentati/e
loro	si erano addormentati/e

IMPERATIVE

addormentati
addormentiamoci
addormentatevi

EXAMPLE PHRASES

Leggo sempre prima di **addormentarmi**. I always read before I go to sleep.

Sono stanco: stasera **mi addormenterò** subito. I'm tired: I'll go to sleep immediately tonight.

Non mi accorsi che **si era addormentata**. I didn't realize she'd gone to sleep.

Italic letters in Italian words show where stress does not follow the usual rules.

andare (to go)

PRESENT

io	**vado**
tu	**vai**
lui/lei/Lei	**va**
noi	**andiamo**
voi	**andate**
loro	**vanno**

PRESENT SUBJUNCTIVE

io	**vada**
tu	**vada**
lui/lei/Lei	**vada**
noi	**andiamo**
voi	**andiate**
loro	**vadano**

PERFECT

io	**sono andato/a**
tu	**sei andato/a**
lui/lei/Lei	**è andato/a**
noi	**siamo andati/e**
voi	**siete andati/e**
loro	**sono andati/e**

IMPERFECT

io	**andavo**
tu	**andavi**
lui/lei/Lei	**andava**
noi	**andavamo**
voi	**andavate**
loro	**andavano**

GERUND

andando

PAST PARTICIPLE

andato

EXAMPLE PHRASES

Su, **andiamo**! Come on, let's go!

Come **va**? – Bene, grazie! How are you? – Fine, thanks!

La mamma vuole che tu **vada** a fare la spesa. Mum wants you to go and do the shopping.

Questo mese non **sono** ancora **andata** al cinema. I haven't been to the cinema yet this month.

Com'**è andata**? How did it go?

L'anno scorso **andavo** sempre a dormire tardi. Last year I always went to bed late.

Remember that subject pronouns are not used very often in Italian.

andare

FUTURE

io	**andrò**
tu	**andrai**
lui/lei/Lei	**andrà**
noi	**andremo**
voi	**andrete**
loro	**andranno**

CONDITIONAL

io	**andrei**
tu	**andresti**
lui/lei/Lei	**andrebbe**
noi	**andremmo**
voi	**andreste**
loro	**andrebbero**

PAST HISTORIC

io	**andai**
tu	**andasti**
lui/lei/Lei	**andò**
noi	**andammo**
voi	**andaste**
loro	**andarono**

PLUPERFECT

io	**ero andato/a**
tu	**eri andato/a**
lui/lei/Lei	**era andato/a**
noi	**eravamo andati/e**
voi	**eravate andati/e**
loro	**erano andati/e**

IMPERATIVE

vai
andiamo
andate

EXAMPLE PHRASES

Andremo in Grecia quest'estate. We're going *to* Greece this summer.

Stasera **andrei** volentieri al ristorante. I'd like to go to a restaurant this evening.

Andarono a trovare la nonna. They went to see their grandmother.

Era **andato** in biblioteca per l'accesso gratuito al wifi. He'd gone to the library for the free wifi access.

Italic letters in Italian words show where stress does not follow the usual rules.

apparire (to appear)

PRESENT

io	**appaio**
tu	**appari**
lui/lei/Lei	**appare**
noi	**appariamo**
voi	**apparite**
loro	**appaiono**

PRESENT SUBJUNCTIVE

io	**appaia**
tu	**appaia**
lui/lei/Lei	**appaia**
noi	**appaiamo**
voi	**appaiate**
loro	**appaiano**

PERFECT

io	**sono apparso/a**
tu	**sei apparso/a**
lui/lei/Lei	**è apparso/a**
noi	**siamo apparsi/e**
voi	**siete apparsi/e**
loro	**sono apparsi/e**

IMPERFECT

io	**apparivo**
tu	**apparivi**
lui/lei/Lei	**appariva**
noi	**apparivamo**
voi	**apparivate**
loro	**apparivano**

GERUND
apparendo

PAST PARTICIPLE
apparso

EXAMPLE PHRASES

Oggi Mario **appare** turbato. Mario seems upset today.

Aspettiamo che **appaia** la luce del faro. Let's wait until we see the beam of the lighthouse.

Il fantasma **appariva** ogni sera a mezzanotte. The ghost appeared every night at twelve o'clock.

Finalmente una nave **apparve** all'orizzonte. At last a ship appeared on the horizon.

Remember that subject pronouns are not used very often in Italian.

apparire

FUTURE

io	apparirò
tu	apparirai
lui/lei/Lei	apparirà
noi	appariremo
voi	apparirete
loro	appariranno

CONDITIONAL

io	apparirei
tu	appariresti
lui/lei/Lei	apparirebbe
noi	appariremmo
voi	apparireste
loro	apparirebbero

PAST HISTORIC

io	apparvi
tu	apparisti
lui/lei/Lei	apparve
noi	apparimmo
voi	appariste
loro	apparvero

PLUPERFECT

io	ero apparso/a
tu	eri apparso/a
lui/lei/Lei	era apparso/a
noi	eravamo apparsi/e
voi	eravate apparsi/e
loro	erano apparsi/e

IMPERATIVE

appari
appariamo
apparite

EXAMPLE PHRASES

Tra poco il sole **apparirà** in cielo. The sun will soon appear in the sky.

Con quel vestito **appariresti** ridicolo. You'd look silly in that suit.

I soldati si fermarono: i banditi **erano apparsi** tra le rocce. The soldiers halted: the bandits had appeared from among the rocks.

Non vorrei **apparire** maleducato. I wouldn't want to seem rude.

Italic letters in Italian words show where stress does not follow the usual rules.

aprire (to open)

PRESENT

io	**apro**
tu	**apri**
lui/lei/Lei	**apre**
noi	**apriamo**
voi	**aprite**
loro	*aprono*

PRESENT SUBJUNCTIVE

io	**apra**
tu	**apra**
lui/lei/Lei	**apra**
noi	**apriamo**
voi	**apriate**
loro	*aprano*

PERFECT

io	**ho aperto**
tu	**hai aperto**
lui/lei/Lei	**ha aperto**
noi	**abbiamo aperto**
voi	**avete aperto**
loro	**hanno aperto**

IMPERFECT

io	**aprivo**
tu	**aprivi**
lui/lei/Lei	**apriva**
noi	**aprivamo**
voi	**aprivate**
loro	**aprivano**

GERUND

aprendo

PAST PARTICIPLE

aperto

EXAMPLE PHRASES

Posso **aprire** la finestra? Can I open the window?

Dai, non **apri** il pacco? Come on, aren't you going to open the package?

Non **ha aperto** bocca. She didn't say a word.

Non voglio che **apriate** i regali prima di Natale. I don't want you to open your presents before Christmas.

Si è tagliato **aprendo** una scatola di tonno. He cut himself opening a tin of tuna.

Remember that subject pronouns are not used very often in Italian.

aprire

FUTURE

io	**aprirò**
tu	**aprirai**
lui/lei/Lei	**aprirà**
noi	**apriremo**
voi	**aprirete**
loro	**apriranno**

CONDITIONAL

io	**aprirei**
tu	**apriresti**
lui/lei/Lei	**aprirebbe**
noi	**apriremmo**
voi	**aprireste**
loro	**aprirebbero**

PAST HISTORIC

io	**aprii**
tu	**apristi**
lui/lei/Lei	**aprì**
noi	**aprimmo**
voi	**apriste**
loro	**aprirono**

PLUPERFECT

io	**avevo aperto**
tu	**avevi aperto**
lui/lei/Lei	**aveva aperto**
noi	**avevamo aperto**
voi	**avevate aperto**
loro	**avevano aperto**

IMPERATIVE

apri
apriamo
aprite

EXAMPLE PHRASES

Aprirono lo champagne e festeggiarono. They opened the champagne and celebrated.

Aveva aperto la busta per leggere la lettera. She'd opened the envelope to read the letter.

Apri il rubinetto e innaffia il giardino. Turn on the tap and water the garden.

Polizia! **Aprite** questa porta! Police! Open the door!

Italic letters in Italian words show where stress does not follow the usual rules.

arrivare (to arrive)

PRESENT

io	arrivo
tu	arrivi
lui/lei/Lei	arriva
noi	arriviamo
voi	arrivate
loro	arrivano

PRESENT SUBJUNCTIVE

io	arrivi
tu	arrivi
lui/lei/Lei	arrivi
noi	arriviamo
voi	arriviate
loro	arrivino

PERFECT

io	sono arrivato/a
tu	sei arrivato/a
lui/lei/Lei	è arrivato/a
noi	siamo arrivati/e
voi	siete arrivati/e
loro	sono arrivati/e

IMPERFECT

io	arrivavo
tu	arrivavi
lui/lei/Lei	arrivava
noi	arrivavamo
voi	arrivavate
loro	arrivavano

GERUND

arrivando

PAST PARTICIPLE

arrivato

EXAMPLE PHRASES

Come si **arriva** al castello? How do you get to the castle?

A che ora **arrivi** a scuola? What time do you get to school?

Sono arrivato a Londra alle sette. I arrived in London at seven.

È troppo in alto, non ci **arrivo**. It's too high, I can't reach it.

Non **arrivava** mai in orario. He never arrived on time.

Aspettami, sto **arrivando**! Wait, I'm coming!

Remember that subject pronouns are not used very often in Italian.

arrivare

FUTURE

io	**arriverò**
tu	**arriverai**
lui/lei/Lei	**arriverà**
noi	**arriveremo**
voi	**arriverete**
loro	**arriveranno**

CONDITIONAL

io	**arriverei**
tu	**arriveresti**
lui/lei/Lei	**arriverebbe**
noi	**arriveremmo**
voi	**arrivereste**
loro	**arriverebbero**

PAST HISTORIC

io	**arrivai**
tu	**arrivasti**
lui/lei/Lei	**arrivò**
noi	**arrivammo**
voi	**arrivaste**
loro	**arrivarono**

PLUPERFECT

io	**ero arrivato/a**
tu	**eri arrivato/a**
lui/lei/Lei	**era arrivato/a**
noi	**eravamo arrivati/e**
voi	**eravate arrivati/e**
loro	**erano arrivati/e**

IMPERATIVE

arriva
arriviamo
arrivate

EXAMPLE PHRASES

Arriveremo in ritardo per colpa del traffico. We'll get there late because
of the traffic.

Arrivammo al rifugio molto stanchi. We were very tired when we got to the
mountain refuge.

Dopo due giorni di viaggio **era** finalmente **arrivata**. After two days' travelling
he'd at last arrived.

Italic letters in Italian words show where stress does not follow the usual rules.

assumere (to take on, to employ)

PRESENT

io	assumo
tu	assumi
lui/lei/Lei	assume
noi	assumiamo
voi	assumete
loro	assumono

PRESENT SUBJUNCTIVE

io	assuma
tu	assuma
lui/lei/Lei	assuma
noi	assumiamo
voi	assumiate
loro	assumano

PERFECT

io	ho assunto
tu	hai assunto
lui/lei/Lei	ha assunto
noi	abbiamo assunto
voi	avete assunto
loro	hanno assunto

IMPERFECT

io	assumevo
tu	assumevi
lui/lei/Lei	assumeva
noi	assumevamo
voi	assumevate
loro	assumevano

GERUND

assumendo

PAST PARTICIPLE

assunto

EXAMPLE PHRASES

La ditta **assumeva** e ho presentato il curriculum. The company was taking on staff and I sent in my CV.

Sua moglie vuole **assumere** una badante. His wife wants to employ a carer.

C'è troppo lavoro: **assumiamo** del personale. There's too much work: let's take on some more staff.

È stata **assunta** come programmatrice. She's got a job as a programmer.

DOUBLE PAST
PARTICIPLE

Remember that subject pronouns are not used very often in Italian.

assumere

FUTURE

io	assumerò
tu	assumerai
lui/lei/Lei	assumerà
noi	assumeremo
voi	assumerete
loro	assumeranno

CONDITIONAL

io	assumerei
tu	assumeresti
lui/lei/Lei	assumerebbe
noi	assumeremmo
voi	assumereste
loro	assumerebbero

PAST HISTORIC

io	assunsi
tu	assumesti
lui/lei/Lei	assunse
noi	assumemmo
voi	assumeste
loro	assunsero

PLUPERFECT

io	avevo assunto
tu	avevi assunto
lui/lei/Lei	aveva assunto
noi	avevamo assunto
voi	avevate assunto
loro	avevano assunto

IMPERATIVE

assumi
assumiamo
assumete

EXAMPLE PHRASES

L'azienda **assumerà** due operai. The company is going to take on two workers.

Sei bravo: ti **assumerei** come assistente. You're good: I'd give you a job as an assistant.

Italic letters in Italian words show where stress does not follow the usual rules.

avere (to have)

PRESENT

io	**ho**
tu	**hai**
lui/lei/Lei	**ha**
noi	**abbiamo**
voi	**avete**
loro	**hanno**

PRESENT SUBJUNCTIVE

io	*abbia*
tu	*abbia*
lui/lei/Lei	*abbia*
noi	**abbiamo**
voi	**abbiate**
loro	*abbiano*

PERFECT

io	**ho avuto**
tu	**hai avuto**
lui/lei/Lei	**ha avuto**
noi	**abbiamo avuto**
voi	**avete avuto**
loro	**hanno avuto**

IMPERFECT

io	**avevo**
tu	**avevi**
lui/lei/Lei	**aveva**
noi	**avevamo**
voi	**avevate**
loro	**avevano**

GERUND
avendo

PAST PARTICIPLE
avuto

EXAMPLE PHRASES

All'inizio **ha avuto** un sacco di problemi. He had a lot of problems at first.

Ho già mangiato. I've already eaten.

Ora **ha** uno smartphone. Now she's got a smartphone.

Non penso che tu *abbia* il coraggio necessario per farlo. I don't think you're
   brave enough to do it.

Quanti ne **abbiamo** oggi? What's the date today?

Aveva la mia età. He was the same age as me.

Remember that subject pronouns are not used very often in Italian.

avere

FUTURE

io	**avrò**
tu	avrai
lui/lei/Lei	**avrà**
noi	avremo
voi	avrete
loro	avranno

CONDITIONAL

io	avrei
tu	avresti
lui/lei/Lei	avrebbe
noi	avremmo
voi	avreste
loro	avrebbero

PAST HISTORIC

io	**ebbi**
tu	avesti
lui/lei/Lei	ebbe
noi	avemmo
voi	aveste
loro	ebbero

PLUPERFECT

io	avevo avuto
tu	avevi avuto
lui/lei/Lei	aveva avuto
noi	avevamo avuto
voi	avevate avuto
loro	avevano avuto

IMPERATIVE

abbi
abbiamo
abbiate

EXAMPLE PHRASES

Quanti anni **avrà**? How old do you think she is?

Quando **ebbe** fame, mangiò. When he was hungry he had something to eat.

Prima di atterrare **avevano avuto** veramente paura. Before the plane landed they'd been really frightened.

Abbi pazienza, non ho ancora finito! Be patient, I've not finished yet!

Italic letters in Italian words show where stress does not follow the usual rules.

bere (to drink)

PRESENT

io	**bevo**
tu	**bevi**
lui/lei/Lei	**beve**
noi	**beviamo**
voi	**bevete**
loro	**bevono**

PRESENT SUBJUNCTIVE

io	**beva**
tu	**beva**
lui/lei/Lei	**beva**
noi	**beviamo**
voi	**beviate**
loro	**bevano**

PERFECT

io	**ho bevuto**
tu	**hai bevuto**
lui/lei/Lei	**ha bevuto**
noi	**abbiamo bevuto**
voi	**avete bevuto**
loro	**hanno bevuto**

IMPERFECT

io	**bevevo**
tu	**bevevi**
lui/lei/Lei	**beveva**
noi	**bevevamo**
voi	**bevevate**
loro	**bevevano**

GERUND

bevendo

PAST PARTICIPLE

bevuto

EXAMPLE PHRASES

Vuoi **bere** qualcosa? Would you like something to drink?

Chi porta da **bere**? Who's going to bring the drinks?

Ho l'impressione che tu **beva** troppo. I've a feeling you drink too much.

Mai **bevuto** un vino così! I've never tasted a wine like this!

Beveva sei caffè al giorno, ma ora ha smesso. He used to drink six cups
of coffee a day, but he's stopped now.

Bevendo così si ubriacherà di sicuro. If he drinks like that he'll be bound
to get drunk.

Remember that subject pronouns are not used very often in Italian.

bere

FUTURE

io	**berrò**
tu	**berrai**
lui/lei/Lei	**berrà**
noi	**berremo**
voi	**berrete**
loro	**berranno**

CONDITIONAL

io	**berrei**
tu	**berresti**
lui/lei/Lei	**berrebbe**
noi	**berremmo**
voi	**berreste**
loro	**berrebbero**

PAST HISTORIC

io	**bevvi**
tu	**bevesti**
lui/lei/Lei	**bevve**
noi	**bevemmo**
voi	**beveste**
loro	**bevvero**

PLUPERFECT

io	**avevo bevuto**
tu	**avevi bevuto**
lui/lei/Lei	**aveva bevuto**
noi	**avevamo bevuto**
voi	**avevate bevuto**
loro	**avevano bevuto**

IMPERATIVE

bevi
beviamo
bevete

EXAMPLE PHRASES

Berrei volentieri un bicchiere di vino bianco. I'd love a glass of white wine.

Non sono potuti tornare in auto perché **avevano bevuto**. They couldn't drive back because they'd been drinking.
— non potevano

Beviamo alla salute degli sposi! Let's drink to the health of the bride and groom!

Italic letters in Italian words show where stress does not follow the usual rules.

cadere (to fall)

PRESENT		PRESENT SUBJUNCTIVE	
io	cado	io	cada
tu	cadi	tu	cada
lui/lei/Lei	cade	lui/lei/Lei	cada
noi	cadiamo	noi	cadiamo
voi	cadete	voi	cadiate
loro	cadono	loro	cadano

PERFECT		IMPERFECT	
io	sono caduto/a	io	cadevo
tu	sei caduto/a	tu	cadevi
lui/lei/Lei	è caduto/a	lui/lei/Lei	cadeva
noi	siamo caduti/e	noi	cadevamo
voi	siete caduti/e	voi	cadevate
loro	sono caduti/e	loro	cadevano

GERUND	PAST PARTICIPLE
cadendo	caduto

EXAMPLE PHRASES

Il mio compleanno **cade** di lunedì. My birthday is on a Monday.

Ti **è caduta** la sciarpa. You've dropped your scarf.

Ho inciampato e **sono caduta**. I tripped and fell.

È caduta la linea. We were cut off.

Attento che fai **cadere** il bicchiere. Mind you don't knock over your glass.

Ha fatto **cadere** il vassoio. She dropped the tray.

Si è fatta male **cadendo** con i pattini. She fell and hurt herself when she was skating.

Remember that subject pronouns are not used very often in Italian.

cadere

FUTURE

io	cadrò
tu	cadrai
lui/lei/Lei	cadrà
noi	cadremo
voi	cadrete
loro	cadranno

CONDITIONAL

io	cadrei
tu	cadresti
lui/lei/Lei	cadrebbe
noi	cadremmo
voi	cadreste
loro	cadrebbero

PAST HISTORIC

io	caddi
tu	cadesti
lui/lei/Lei	cadde
noi	cademmo
voi	cadeste
loro	caddero

PLUPERFECT

io	ero caduto/a
tu	eri caduto/a
lui/lei/Lei	era caduto/a
noi	eravamo caduti/e
voi	eravate caduti/e
loro	erano caduti/e

IMPERATIVE

cadi
cadiamo
cadete

EXAMPLE PHRASES

Quando glielo diremo **cadranno** dalle nuvole. When we tell them they'll
be amazed.
Cadde dalla bicicletta. She fell off her bike.

Italic letters in Italian words show where stress does not follow the usual rules.

cambiare (to change)

PRESENT		PRESENT SUBJUNCTIVE	
io	cambio	io	cambi
tu	cambi	tu	cambi
lui/lei/Lei	cambia	lui/lei/Lei	cambi
noi	cambiamo	noi	cambiamo
voi	cambiate	voi	cambiate
loro	cambiano	loro	cambino

PERFECT		IMPERFECT	
io	ho cambiato	io	cambiavo
tu	hai cambiato	tu	cambiavi
lui/lei/Lei	ha cambiato	lui/lei/Lei	cambiava
noi	abbiamo cambiato	noi	cambiavamo
voi	avete cambiato	voi	cambiavate
loro	hanno cambiato	loro	cambiavano

GERUND
cambiando

PAST PARTICIPLE
cambiato

EXAMPLE PHRASES

È necessario che **cambiate** atteggiamento. You need to change your attitude.

Era confuso e **cambiava** opinione in continuazione. He was confused and kept changing his mind.

Ultimamente è molto **cambiato**. He's changed a lot recently.

Vorrei **cambiare** questi euro in sterline. I'd like to change these euros into pounds.

Remember that subject pronouns are not used very often in Italian.

cambiare

FUTURE

io	**cambierò**
tu	**cambierai**
lui/lei/Lei	**cambierà**
noi	**cambieremo**
voi	**cambierete**
loro	**cambieranno**

CONDITIONAL

io	**cambierei**
tu	**cambieresti**
lui/lei/Lei	**cambierebbe**
noi	**cambieremmo**
voi	**cambiereste**
loro	**cambierebbero**

PAST HISTORIC

io	**cambiai**
tu	**cambiasti**
lui/lei/Lei	**cambiò**
noi	**cambiammo**
voi	**cambiaste**
loro	**cambiarono**

PLUPERFECT

io	**avevo cambiato**
tu	**avevi cambiato**
lui/lei/Lei	**aveva cambiato**
noi	**avevamo cambiato**
voi	**avevate cambiato**
loro	**avevano cambiato**

IMPERATIVE

cambia
cambiamo
cambiate

EXAMPLE PHRASES

Cambieremo casa il mese prossimo. We're moving house next month.

Cambiammo idea e prendemmo quell'altro. We changed our mind and took the other one.

Ci **cambiammo** prima di uscire. We got changed before we went out.

Aveva cambiato l'auto poco prima del furto. She'd changed the car shortly before it was stolen.

Cambiamo argomento. Let's change the subject.

Italic letters in Italian words show where stress does not follow the usual rules.

capire (to understand)

PRESENT

io	capisco
tu	capisci
lui/lei/Lei	capisce
noi	capiamo
voi	capite
loro	capiscono

PRESENT SUBJUNCTIVE

io	capisca
tu	capisca
lui/lei/Lei	capisca
noi	capiamo
voi	capiate
loro	capiscano

PERFECT

io	ho capito
tu	hai capito
lui/lei/Lei	ha capito
noi	abbiamo capito
voi	avete capito
loro	hanno capito

IMPERFECT

io	capivo
tu	capivi
lui/lei/Lei	capiva
noi	capivamo
voi	capivate
loro	capivano

GERUND

capendo

PAST PARTICIPLE

capito

EXAMPLE PHRASES

Va bene, **capisco**. OK, I understand.

È necessario che **capiate** bene le istruzioni. You've got to understand the instructions properly.

Non **ho capito** una parola. I didn't understand a word.

Non **ho capito**, puoi ripetere? I *don't* understand, could you say it again?

Fammi **capire**... Let me get this straight...

Capivamo le sue ragioni, ma aveva torto. We understood his motives, but he was wrong.

Remember that subject pronouns are not used very often in Italian.

capire

FUTURE

io	capirò
tu	capirai
lui/lei/Lei	capirà
noi	capiremo
voi	capirete
loro	capiranno

CONDITIONAL

io	capirei
tu	capiresti
lui/lei/Lei	capirebbe
noi	capiremmo
voi	capireste
loro	capirebbero

PAST HISTORIC

io	capii
tu	capisti
lui/lei/Lei	capì
noi	capimmo
voi	capiste
loro	capirono

PLUPERFECT

io	avevo capito
tu	avevi capito
lui/lei/Lei	aveva capito
noi	avevamo capito
voi	avevate capito
loro	avevano capito

IMPERATIVE

capisci

capiamo

capite

EXAMPLE PHRASES

Non ti **capirò** mai. I'll never understand you.

Se mi volessi bene, mi **capiresti**. If you loved me, you'd understand me.

Capirono che era ora di andarsene. They realized it was time to go.

Avevamo capito male le sue intenzioni. We'd misunderstood his intentions.

Italic letters in Italian words show where stress does not follow the usual rules.

cercare (to look for)

PRESENT		PRESENT SUBJUNCTIVE	
io	cerco	io	cerchi
tu	cerchi	tu	cerchi
lui/lei/Lei	cerca	lui/lei/Lei	cerchi
noi	cerchiamo	noi	cerchiamo
voi	cercate	voi	cerchiate
loro	cercano	loro	cerchino

PERFECT		IMPERFECT	
io	ho cercato	io	cercavo
tu	hai cercato	tu	cercavi
lui/lei/Lei	ha cercato	lui/lei/Lei	cercava
noi	abbiamo cercato	noi	cercavamo
voi	avete cercato	voi	cercavate
loro	hanno cercato	loro	cercavano

GERUND
cercando

PAST PARTICIPLE
cercato

EXAMPLE PHRASES

Io non **cerco** guai. I'm not looking for trouble.

È bene che **cerchiate** di essere puntuali. You'd do well to try to be punctual.

Le **ho cercate** dappertutto. I've looked for them everywhere.

Stai **cercando** lavoro? Are you looking for a job?

Sta **cercando** di imparare l'inglese. He's trying to learn English.

Remember that subject pronouns are not used very often in Italian.

cercare

FUTURE

io	cercherò
tu	cercherai
lui/lei/Lei	cercherà
noi	cercheremo
voi	cercherete
loro	cercheranno

CONDITIONAL

io	cercherei
tu	cercheresti
lui/lei/Lei	cercherebbe
noi	cercheremmo
voi	cerchereste
loro	cercherebbero

PAST HISTORIC

io	cercai
tu	cercasti
lui/lei/Lei	cercò
noi	cercammo
voi	cercaste
loro	cercarono

PLUPERFECT

io	avevo cercato
tu	avevi cercato
lui/lei/Lei	aveva cercato
noi	avevamo cercato
voi	avevate cercato
loro	avevano cercato

IMPERATIVE

cerca
cerchiamo
cercate

EXAMPLE PHRASES

Mi cercheresti il suo numero nell'agenda? Would you look for his number in your diary?

Cercammo di spiegargli il motivo. We tried to explain the reason to him.

Cerca di non fare tardi. Try not to be late.

Italic letters in Italian words show where stress does not follow the usual rules.

chiedere (to ask)

PRESENT

io	chiedo
tu	chiedi
lui/lei/Lei	chiede
noi	chiediamo
voi	chiedete
loro	chiedono

PRESENT SUBJUNCTIVE

io	chieda
tu	chieda
lui/lei/Lei	chieda
noi	chiediamo
voi	chiediate
loro	chiedano

PERFECT

io	ho chiesto
tu	hai chiesto
lui/lei/Lei	ha chiesto
noi	abbiamo chiesto
voi	avete chiesto
loro	hanno chiesto

IMPERFECT

io	chiedevo
tu	chiedevi
lui/lei/Lei	chiedeva
noi	chiedevamo
voi	chiedevate
loro	chiedevano

GERUND

chiedendo

PAST PARTICIPLE

chiesto

EXAMPLE PHRASES

Non **chiedo** mai favori a nessuno. I never ask anyone for favours.

Mi **ha chiesto** l'ora. He asked me the time.

Se non lo sai, basta **chiedere**. If you don't know, just ask.

Remember that subject pronouns are not used very often in Italian.

chiedere

FUTURE

io	**chiederò**
tu	**chiederai**
lui/lei/Lei	**chiederà**
noi	**chiederemo**
voi	**chiederete**
loro	**chiederanno**

CONDITIONAL

io	**chiederei**
tu	**chiederesti**
lui/lei/Lei	**chiederebbe**
noi	**chiederemmo**
voi	**chiedereste**
loro	**chiederebbero**

PAST HISTORIC

io	**chiesi**
tu	**chledesti**
lui/lei/Lei	**chiese**
noi	**chledemmo**
voi	**chiedeste**
loro	**chiesero**

PLUPERFECT

io	**avevo chiesto**
tu	**avevi chiesto**
lui/lei/Lei	**aveva chiesto**
noi	**avevamo chiesto**
voi	**avevate chiesto**
loro	**avevano chiesto**

IMPERATIVE

chiedi
chiediamo
chiedete

EXAMPLE PHRASES

Chiederemo agli amici di ospitarci. We'll ask our friends to put us up.

Chiederesti a Giulia di spostarsi un po'? Would you ask Giulia to move a bit?

Chiedemmo la strada per la stazione. We asked the way to the station.

Avevo chiesto il conto al cameriere, ma è sparito. I'd asked the waiter for the bill, but he disappeared.

Chiedi a Lidia come si chiama il suo cane. Ask Lidia what her dog's called.

Italic letters in Italian words show where stress does not follow the usual rules.

chiudere (to close)

PRESENT

io	chiudo
tu	chiudi
lui/lei/Lei	chiude
noi	chiudiamo
voi	chiudete
loro	chiudono

PRESENT SUBJUNCTIVE

io	chiuda
tu	chiuda
lui/lei/Lei	chiuda
noi	chiudiamo
voi	chiudiate
loro	chiudano

PERFECT

io	ho chiuso
tu	hai chiuso
lui/lei/Lei	ha chiuso
noi	abbiamo chiuso
voi	avete chiuso
loro	hanno chiuso

IMPERFECT

io	chiudevo
tu	chiudevi
lui/lei/Lei	chiudeva
noi	chiudevamo
voi	chiudevate
loro	chiudevano

GERUND

chiudendo

PAST PARTICIPLE

chiuso

EXAMPLE PHRASES

Un momento! **Chiudo** casa e scendo. I'll just be a minute. I'll lock the door and come down.

È meglio che tu **chiuda** a chiave. You'd better lock the door.

La fabbrica **ha chiuso** due anni fa. The factory closed two years ago.

Con lui **ho chiuso**. I've finished with him.

Remember that subject pronouns are not used very often in Italian.

chiudere

FUTURE

io	chiuderò
tu	chiuderai
lui/lei/Lei	chiuderà
noi	chiuderemo
voi	chiuderete
loro	chiuderanno

CONDITIONAL

io	chiuderei
tu	chiuderesti
lui/lei/Lei	chiuderebbe
noi	chiuderemmo
voi	chiudereste
loro	chiuderebbero

PAST HISTORIC

io	chiusi
tu	chiudesti
lui/lei/Lei	chiuse
noi	chiudemmo
voi	chiudeste
loro	chiusero

PLUPERFECT

io	avevo chiuso
tu	avevi chiuso
lui/lei/Lei	aveva chiuso
noi	avevamo chiuso
voi	avevate chiuso
loro	avevano chiuso

IMPERATIVE

chiudi
chiudiamo
chiudete

EXAMPLE PHRASES

A che ora **chiuderà** il negozio? What time will the shop shut?

La porta si **chiuse**. The door closed.

L'ho sgridato perché non **aveva chiuso** il gas. I told him off because he'd not turned the gas off.

Chiudi bene il rubinetto. Turn the tap off properly.

Italic letters in Italian words show where stress does not follow the usual rules.

cogliere (to pick)

PRESENT		PRESENT SUBJUNCTIVE	
io	colgo	io	colga
tu	cogli	tu	colga
lui/lei/Lei	coglie	lui/lei/Lei	colga
noi	cogliamo	noi	cogliamo
voi	cogliete	voi	cogliate
loro	colgono	loro	colgano

PERFECT		IMPERFECT	
io	ho colto	io	coglievo
tu	hai colto	tu	coglievi
lui/lei/Lei	ha colto	lui/lei/Lei	coglieva
noi	abbiamo colto	noi	coglievamo
voi	avete colto	voi	coglievate
loro	hanno colto	loro	coglievano

GERUND	PAST PARTICIPLE
cogliendo	colto

EXAMPLE PHRASES

Colgo l'occasione per augurarvi buon Natale. May I take this opportunity to wish you a happy Christmas.

L'**ho colto** sul fatto. I caught him red-handed.

Stavamo **cogliendo** dei fiori quando arrivò il temporale. We were picking flowers when the storm started.

Remember that subject pronouns are not used very often in Italian.

cogliere

FUTURE

io	**coglierò**
tu	**coglierai**
lui/lei/Lei	**coglierà**
noi	**coglieremo**
voi	**coglierete**
loro	**coglieranno**

CONDITIONAL

io	**coglierei**
tu	**coglieresti**
lui/lei/Lei	**coglierebbe**
noi	**coglieremmo**
voi	**cogliereste**
loro	**coglierebbero**

PAST HISTORIC

io	**colsi**
tu	**cogliesti**
lui/lei/Lei	**colse**
noi	**cogliemmo**
voi	**coglieste**
loro	**colsero**

PLUPERFECT

io	**avevo colto**
tu	**avevi colto**
lui/lei/Lei	**aveva colto**
noi	**avevamo colto**
voi	**avevate colto**
loro	**avevano colto**

IMPERATIVE

cogli
cogliamo
cogliete

EXAMPLE PHRASES

Tra qualche giorno **coglieranno** le fragole. In a few days' time they'll be picking the strawberries.

Colsi una mela dall'albero. I picked an apple off the tree.

Andiamo in campagna a **cogliere** la frutta. Let's go into the countryside and pick some fruit.

Italic letters in Italian words show where stress does not follow the usual rules.

cominciare (to start)

PRESENT		PRESENT SUBJUNCTIVE	
io	comincio	io	cominci
tu	cominci	tu	cominci
lui/lei/Lei	comincia	lui/lei/Lei	cominci
noi	cominciamo	noi	cominciamo
voi	cominciate	voi	cominciate
loro	cominciano	loro	comincino

PERFECT		IMPERFECT	
io	ho cominciato	io	cominciavo
tu	hai cominciato	tu	cominciavi
lui/lei/Lei	ha cominciato	lui/lei/Lei	cominciava
noi	abbiamo cominciato	noi	cominciavamo
voi	avete cominciato	voi	cominciavate
loro	hanno cominciato	loro	cominciavano

GERUND	PAST PARTICIPLE
cominciando	cominciato

EXAMPLE PHRASES

Il film **comincia** con un'esplosione. The film starts with an explosion.

Hai cominciato il libro che ti ho prestato? Have you started the book
  I lent you?

Faceva freddo e **cominciava** a nevicare. It was cold and starting to snow.

Cominciando oggi, dovrei finire lunedì. If I start today I should finish
  on Monday.

Remember that subject pronouns are not used very often in Italian.

cominciare

FUTURE

io	comincerò
tu	comincerai
lui/lei/Lei	comincerà
noi	cominceremo
voi	comincerete
loro	cominceranno

CONDITIONAL

io	comincerei
tu	cominceresti
lui/lei/Lei	comincerebbe
noi	cominceremmo
voi	comincereste
loro	comincerebbero

PAST HISTORIC

io	cominciai
tu	cominciasti
lui/lei/Lei	cominciò
noi	cominciammo
voi	cominciaste
loro	cominciarono

PLUPERFECT

io	avevo cominciato
tu	avevi cominciato
lui/lei/Lei	aveva cominciato
noi	avevamo cominciato
voi	avevate cominciato
loro	avevano cominciato

IMPERATIVE

comincia
cominciamo
cominciate

EXAMPLE PHRASES

Adesso **cominceranno** di sicuro a lamentarsi. Now they're sure to start
complaining.

Cominciarono tutti a ridere. They all started to laugh.

Non **avevo** ancora **cominciato** che lui mi interruppe. I hadn't even started and
he interrupted me.

Cominciamo bene! This is a fine start!

Italic letters in Italian words show where stress does not follow the usual rules.

compiere (to complete)

PRESENT

io	compio
tu	compi
lui/lei/Lei	compie
noi	compiamo
voi	compite
loro	compiono

PRESENT SUBJUNCTIVE

io	compia
tu	compia
lui/lei/Lei	compia
noi	compiamo
voi	compiate
loro	compiano

PERFECT

io	ho compiuto
tu	hai compiuto
lui/lei/Lei	ha compiuto
noi	abbiamo compiuto
voi	avete compiuto
loro	hanno compiuto

IMPERFECT

io	compivo
tu	compivi
lui/lei/Lei	compiva
noi	compivamo
voi	compivate
loro	compivano

GERUND
compiendo

PAST PARTICIPLE
compiuto

EXAMPLE PHRASES

Quando **compi** gli anni? When is your birthday?

Quanti anni **compi**? How old will you be?

Ho compiuto sedici anni il mese scorso. I was sixteen last month.

Per essere maggiorenne devi **compiere** 18 anni. To be of age you have to be 18.

Remember that subject pronouns are not used very often in Italian.

compiere

FUTURE

io	compirò
tu	compirai
lui/lei/Lei	compirà
noi	compiremo
voi	compirete
loro	compiranno

CONDITIONAL

io	compirei
tu	compiresti
lui/lei/Lei	compirebbe
noi	compiremmo
voi	compireste
loro	compirebbero

PAST HISTORIC

io	compii
tu	compisti
lui/lei/Lei	compì
noi	compimmo
voi	compiste
loro	compirono

PLUPERFECT

io	avevo compiuto
tu	avevi compiuto
lui/lei/Lei	aveva compiuto
noi	avevamo compiuto
voi	avevate compiuto
loro	avevano compiuto

IMPERATIVE

compi
compiamo
compite

EXAMPLE PHRASES

Quando **compirai** gli anni faremo una bella festa. When it's your birthday we'll have a great party.

Aveva compiuto 18 anni e gli regalarono l'auto. He was 18 and they gave him a car.

Italic letters in Italian words show where stress does not follow the usual rules.

confondere (to mix up)

PRESENT

io	confondo
tu	confondi
lui/lei/Lei	confonde
noi	confondiamo
voi	confondete
loro	confondono

PRESENT SUBJUNCTIVE

io	confonda
tu	confonda
lui/lei/Lei	confonda
noi	confondiamo
voi	confondiate
loro	confondano

PERFECT

io	ho confuso
tu	hai confuso
lui/lei/Lei	ha confuso
noi	abbiamo confuso
voi	avete confuso
loro	hanno confuso

IMPERFECT

io	confondevo
tu	confondevi
lui/lei/Lei	confondeva
noi	confondevamo
voi	confondevate
loro	confondevano

GERUND

confondendo

PAST PARTICIPLE

confuso

EXAMPLE PHRASES

Ho confuso le date. I mixed up the dates.

No, scusa, mi **sono confuso**: era ieri. No, sorry, I've got mixed up: it was yesterday.

Maria **confondeva** sempre i sogni e la realtà. Maria always mixed up dreams and reality.

Tutti questi discorsi mi **confondono le idee.** All this talk is getting me confused.

Non starai **confondendo** i nomi? You're not mixing up the names, are you?

Remember that subject pronouns are not used very often in Italian.

confondere

FUTURE

io	**confonderò**
tu	**confonderai**
lui/lei/Lei	**confonderà**
noi	**confonderemo**
voi	**confonderete**
loro	**confonderanno**

CONDITIONAL

io	**confonderei**
tu	**confonderesti**
lui/lei/Lei	**confonderebbe**
noi	**confonderemmo**
voi	**confondereste**
loro	**confonderebbero**

PAST HISTORIC

io	**confusi**
tu	**confondesti**
lui/lei/Lei	**confuse**
noi	**confondemmo**
voi	**confondeste**
loro	**confusero**

PLUPERFECT

io	**avevo confuso**
tu	**avevi confuso**
lui/lei/Lei	**aveva confuso**
noi	**avevamo confuso**
voi	**avevate confuso**
loro	**avevano confuso**

IMPERATIVE

confondi
confondiamo
confondete

EXAMPLE PHRASES

All'esame di storia **confonderò** di certo le date. In the history exam I'm sure to mix up the dates.

Se fossi stanca come me, ti **confonderesti** anche tu. If you were as tired as I am, you'd get mixed up too.

Avevate confuso i dati e l'esperimento è fallito. You had got the data mixed up and the experiment was a failure.

Italic letters in Italian words show where stress does not follow the usual rules.

connettere (to connect)

PRESENT

io	connetto
tu	connetti
lui/lei/Lei	connette
noi	connettiamo
voi	connettete
loro	connettono

PRESENT SUBJUNCTIVE

io	connetta
tu	connetta
lui/lei/Lei	connetta
noi	connettiamo
voi	connettiate
loro	connettano

PERFECT

io	ho connesso
tu	hai connesso
lui/lei/Lei	ha connesso
noi	abbiamo connesso
voi	avete connesso
loro	hanno connesso

IMPERFECT

io	connettevo
tu	connettevi
lui/lei/Lei	connetteva
noi	connettevamo
voi	connettevate
loro	connettevano

GERUND

connettendo

PAST PARTICIPLE

connesso

EXAMPLE PHRASES

Non **connetti** più: hai bisogno di un caffè. You're not thinking straight: you need a coffee.

Non **hanno connesso** il suo buon umore con l'arrivo di Carla. They didn't make the connection between his good mood and Carla's arrival.

Sta **connettendo** il computer alla presa elettrica. She's plugging the computer into the socket.

La mattina non riesco a **connettere**. I can't think straight in the morning.

Remember that subject pronouns are not used very often in Italian.

connettere

FUTURE

io	connetterò
tu	connetterai
lui/lei/Lei	connetterà
noi	connetteremo
voi	connetterete
loro	connetteranno

CONDITIONAL

io	connetterei
tu	connetteresti
lui/lei/Lei	connetterebbe
noi	connetteremmo
voi	connettereste
loro	connetterebbero

PAST HISTORIC

io	connettei
tu	connettesti
lui/lei/Lei	connetté
noi	connettemmo
voi	connetteste
loro	connetterono

PLUPERFECT

io	avevo connesso
tu	avevi connesso
lui/lei/Lei	aveva connesso
noi	avevamo connesso
voi	avevate connesso
loro	avevano connesso

IMPERATIVE

connetti
connettiamo
connettete

EXAMPLE PHRASES

Attento ai cortocircuiti quando **connetterai** la batteria. Mind you don't get a short-circuit when you connect the battery.

Non **avevo connesso** i due fatti. I hadn't connected the two facts.

Italic letters in Italian words show where stress does not follow the usual rules.

conoscere (to know)

PRESENT

io	conosco
tu	conosci
lui/lei/Lei	conosce
noi	conosciamo
voi	conoscete
loro	conoscono

PRESENT SUBJUNCTIVE

io	conosca
tu	conosca
lui/lei/Lei	conosca
noi	conosciamo
voi	conosciate
loro	conoscano

PERFECT

io	ho conosciuto
tu	hai conosciuto
lui/lei/Lei	ha conosciuto
noi	abbiamo conosciuto
voi	avete conosciuto
loro	hanno conosciuto

IMPERFECT

io	conoscevo
tu	conoscevi
lui/lei/Lei	conosceva
noi	conoscevamo
voi	conoscevate
loro	conoscevano

GERUND

conoscendo

PAST PARTICIPLE

conosciuto

EXAMPLE PHRASES

Non **conosco** bene la città. I don't know the town well.

Ci **conosciamo** da poco tempo. We haven't known each other long.

Voglio che tu **conosca** i miei. I'd like you to meet my parents.

Ci siamo **conosciuti** a Firenze. We first met in Florence. *conoscere = to meet ???*

Lo **conoscevamo** solo di vista. We only knew him by sight.

Remember that subject pronouns are not used very often in Italian.

conoscere

FUTURE

io	conoscerò
tu	conoscerai
lui/lei/Lei	conoscerà
noi	conosceremo
voi	conoscerete
loro	conosceranno

CONDITIONAL

io	conoscerei
tu	conosceresti
lui/lei/Lei	conoscerebbe
noi	conosceremmo
voi	conoscereste
loro	conoscerebbero

PAST HISTORIC

io	conobbi
tu	conoscesti
lui/lei/Lei	conobbe
noi	conoscemmo
voi	conosceste
loro	conobbero

PLUPERFECT

io	avevo conosciuto
tu	avevi conosciuto
lui/lei/Lei	aveva conosciuto
noi	avevamo conosciuto
voi	avevate conosciuto
loro	avevano conosciuto

IMPERATIVE

conosci
conosciamo
conoscete

EXAMPLE PHRASES

Viaggeremo e **conosceremo** posti nuovi. We'll travel and get to know new places.

Ci **conoscemmo** in vacanza. We met on holiday.

Conoscendoti, credo che farai la scelta giusta. Knowing you, I think you'll make the right choice.

Italic letters in Italian words show where stress does not follow the usual rules.

correggere (to correct)

PRESENT		PRESENT SUBJUNCTIVE	
io	correggo	io	corregga
tu	correggi	tu	corregga
lui/lei/Lei	corregge	lui/lei/Lei	corregga
noi	correggiamo	noi	correggiamo
voi	correggete	voi	correggiate
loro	correggono	loro	correggano

PERFECT		IMPERFECT	
io	ho corretto	io	correggevo
tu	hai corretto	tu	correggevi
lui/lei/Lei	ha corretto	lui/lei/Lei	correggeva
noi	abbiamo corretto	noi	correggevamo
voi	avete corretto	voi	correggevate
loro	hanno corretto	loro	correggevano

GERUND
correggendo

PAST PARTICIPLE
corretto

EXAMPLE PHRASES

Correggimi se faccio un errore. Correct me if I make a mistake.

Non **ha** ancora **corretto** i compiti di ieri. She hasn't corrected yesterday's homework yet.

Non **correggevano** mai gli errori del figlio. They never corrected their son's mistakes.

Si migliora **correggendo** i propri errori. You improve by correcting your own mistakes.

Remember that subject pronouns are not used very often in Italian.

correggere

FUTURE

io	correggerò
tu	correggerai
lui/lei/Lei	correggerà
noi	correggeremo
voi	correggerete
loro	correggeranno

CONDITIONAL

io	correggerei
tu	correggeresti
lui/lei/Lei	correggerebbe
noi	correggeremmo
voi	correggereste
loro	correggerebbero

PAST HISTORIC

io	corressi
tu	correggesti
lui/lei/Lei	corresse
noi	correggemmo
voi	correggeste
loro	corressero

PLUPERFECT

io	avevo corretto
tu	avevi corretto
lui/lei/Lei	aveva corretto
noi	avevamo corretto
voi	avevate corretto
loro	avevano corretto

IMPERATIVE

correggi
correggiamo
correggete

EXAMPLE PHRASES

Se non ti sforzi, non **correggerai** mai la tua pronuncia. If you don't make an effort you'll never get your pronunciation right.

Si è offeso perché lo **avevo corretto**. He took offence because I'd corrected him.

Se sbaglia, lo **correggiamo**. If he makes a mistake we correct him.

Italic letters in Italian words show where stress does not follow the usual rules.

correre (to run)

PRESENT		PRESENT SUBJUNCTIVE	
io	**corro**	io	**corra**
tu	**corri**	tu	**corra**
lui/lei/Lei	**corre**	lui/lei/Lei	**corra**
noi	**corriamo**	noi	**corriamo**
voi	**correte**	voi	**corriate**
loro	**corrono**	loro	**corrano**

PERFECT		IMPERFECT	
io	**ho corso**	io	**correvo**
tu	**hai corso**	tu	**correvi**
lui/lei/Lei	**ha corso**	lui/lei/Lei	**correva**
noi	**abbiamo corso**	noi	**correvamo**
voi	**avete corso**	voi	**correvate**
loro	**hanno corso**	loro	**correvano**

GERUND	PAST PARTICIPLE
correndo	**corso**

EXAMPLE PHRASES

Corre troppo in macchina. He drives too fast.

Non voglio che **corriate** dei rischi. I don't want you to take risks.

Abbiamo corso come pazzi per non perdere il treno. We ran like mad to catch the train.

Sono inciampato mentre **correvo**. I tripped when I was running.

Sono corso subito fuori. I immediately rushed outside.

Remember that subject pronouns are not used very often in Italian.

correre

FUTURE

io	**correrò**
tu	**correrai**
lui/lei/Lei	**correrà**
noi	**correremo**
voi	**correrete**
loro	**correranno**

CONDITIONAL

io	**correrei**
tu	**correresti**
lui/lei/Lei	**correrebbe**
noi	**correremmo**
voi	**correreste**
loro	**correrebbero**

PAST HISTORIC

io	**corsi**
tu	**corresti**
lui/lei/Lei	**corse**
noi	**corremmo**
voi	**correste**
loro	**corsero**

PLUPERFECT

io	**avevo corso**
tu	**avevi corso**
lul/lei/Lei	**aveva corso**
noi	**avevamo corso**
voi	**avevate corso**
loro	**avevano corso**

IMPERATIVE

corri
corriamo
correte

EXAMPLE PHRASES

Paola **correrà** i cento metri. Paola is going to run the hundred metres.

È prudente: non **correrebbe** mai rischi inutili. She's sensible: she'd never take unnecessary risks.

Aveva corso e ansimava ancora. He'd been running and was still out of breath.

Corri o perdiamo l'*au*tobus! Run or we'll miss the bus!

Italic letters in Italian words show where stress does not follow the usual rules.

credere (to believe)

	PRESENT		PRESENT SUBJUNCTIVE
io	credo	io	creda
tu	credi	tu	creda
lui/lei/Lei	crede	lui/lei/Lei	creda
noi	crediamo	noi	crediamo
voi	credete	voi	crediate
loro	credono	loro	credano

	PERFECT		IMPERFECT
io	ho creduto	io	credevo
tu	hai creduto	tu	credevi
lui/lei/Lei	ha creduto	lui/lei/Lei	credeva
noi	abbiamo creduto	noi	credevamo
voi	avete creduto	voi	credevate
loro	hanno creduto	loro	credevano

GERUND

credendo

PAST PARTICIPLE

creduto

EXAMPLE PHRASES

Non ci **credo**! I don't believe it!

Non dirmi che **credi** ai fantasmi! Don't tell me you believe in ghosts!

Non voglio che lei **creda** che sono un bugiardo. I don't want her to think I'm a liar.

Non **ha** mai **creduto** nell'astrologia. She's never believed in astrology.

Non **credeva** ai suoi occhi. She couldn't believe her eyes.

Remember that subject pronouns are not used very often in Italian.

credere

FUTURE

io	**crederò**
tu	**crederai**
lui/lei/Lei	**crederà**
noi	**crederemo**
voi	**crederete**
loro	**crederanno**

CONDITIONAL

io	**crederei**
tu	**crederesti**
lui/lei/Lei	**crederebbe**
noi	**crederemmo**
voi	**credereste**
loro	**crederebbero**

PAST HISTORIC

io	**credetti** *or* **credei**
tu	**credesti**
lui/lei/Lei	**credette**
noi	**credemmo**
voi	**credeste**
loro	**credettero**

PLUPERFECT

io	**avevo creduto**
tu	**avevi creduto**
lui/lei/Lei	**aveva creduto**
noi	**avevamo creduto**
voi	**avevate creduto**
loro	**avevano creduto**

IMPERATIVE

credi
crediamo
credete

EXAMPLE PHRASES

Non ti **crederò** mai più. I'll never believe you again.

Ci **credereste**? Ho comprato casa. Would you believe it! I've bought a house.

Stento a **crederci**! I can hardly believe it!

Credemmo di aver perso le chiavi. We thought we'd lost our keys.

Italic letters in Italian words show where stress does not follow the usual rules.

crescere (to grow)

PRESENT

io	cresco
tu	cresci
lui/lei/Lei	cresce
noi	cresciamo
voi	crescete
loro	crescono

PRESENT SUBJUNCTIVE

io	cresca
tu	cresca
lui/lei/Lei	cresca
noi	cresciamo
voi	cresciate
loro	crescano

PERFECT

io	sono cresciuto/a
tu	sei cresciuto/a
lui/lei/Lei	è cresciuto/a
noi	siamo cresciuti/e
voi	siete cresciuti/e
loro	sono cresciuti/e

IMPERFECT

io	crescevo
tu	crescevi
lui/lei/Lei	cresceva
noi	crescevamo
voi	crescevate
loro	crescevano

GERUND

crescendo

PAST PARTICIPLE

cresciuto

EXAMPLE PHRASES

Tuo figlio **cresce** a vista d'occhio. Your son is growing very fast.

Più lavora e più **cresce** la sua insoddisfazione. The harder she works the more dissatisfied she becomes.

Com'**è cresciuto** tuo fratello! Hasn't your brother grown!

È cresciuto in campagna. He grew up in the country.

Si sta facendo **crescere** i capelli. She's growing her hair.

Le tue piante stanno **crescendo** molto bene. Your plants are growing very well.

Remember that subject pronouns are not used very often in Italian.

crescere

FUTURE

io	crescerò
tu	crescerai
lui/lei/Lei	crescerà
noi	cresceremo
voi	crescerete
loro	cresceranno

CONDITIONAL

io	crescerei
tu	cresceresti
lui/lei/Lei	crescerebbe
noi	cresceremmo
voi	crescereste
loro	crescerebbero

PAST HISTORIC

io	crebbi
tu	crescesti
lui/lei/Lei	crebbe
noi	crescemmo
voi	cresceste
loro	crebbero

PLUPERFECT

io	ero cresciuto/a
tu	eri cresciuto/a
lui/lei/Lei	era cresciuto/a
noi	eravamo cresciuti/e
voi	eravate cresciuti/e
loro	erano cresciuti/e

IMPERATIVE

cresci
cresciamo
crescete

EXAMPLE PHRASES

I prezzi **cresceranno** durante le feste. Prices will go up during the holiday season.

Era molto **cresciuta** e non la riconoscevo. She'd grown a lot and I didn't recognize her.

Italic letters in Italian words show where stress does not follow the usual rules.

cucire (to sew)

	PRESENT			PRESENT SUBJUNCTIVE
io	cucio		io	cucia
tu	cuci		tu	cucia
lui/lei/Lei	cuce		lui/lei/Lei	cucia
noi	cuciamo		noi	cuciamo
voi	cucite		voi	cuciate
loro	cuciono		loro	cuciano

	PERFECT			IMPERFECT
io	ho cucito		io	cucivo
tu	hai cucito		tu	cucivi
lui/lei/Lei	ha cucito		lui/lei/Lei	cuciva
noi	abbiamo cucito		noi	cucivamo
voi	avete cucito		voi	cucivate
loro	hanno cucito		loro	cucivano

GERUND
cucendo

PAST PARTICIPLE
cucito

EXAMPLE PHRASES

Bisogna che entro domani **cucia** il vestito. She has to finish sewing the dress by tomorrow.

Mi piacciono le toppe che **hai cucito** sulla giacca. I like the patches you've sewn on your jacket.

Si è punta con l'ago mentre **cuciva**. She pricked her finger with the needle while she was sewing.

Sta **cucendo** uno strappo alla gonna. She's mending a tear in her skirt.

Remember that subject pronouns are not used very often in Italian.

cucire

FUTURE

io	**cucirò**
tu	**cucirai**
lui/lei/Lei	**cucirà**
noi	**cuciremo**
voi	**cucirete**
loro	**cuciranno**

CONDITIONAL

io	**cucirei**
tu	**cuciresti**
lui/lei/Lei	**cucirebbe**
noi	**cuciremmo**
voi	**cucireste**
loro	**cucirebbero**

PAST HISTORIC

io	**cucii**
tu	**cucisti**
lui/lei/Lei	**cucì**
noi	**cucimmo**
voi	**cuciste**
loro	**cucirono**

PLUPERFECT

Io	**avevo cucito**
tu	**avevi cucito**
lui/lei/Lei	**aveva cucito**
noi	**avevamo cucito**
voi	**avevate cucito**
loro	**avevano cucito**

IMPERATIVE

cuci
cuciamo
cucite

EXAMPLE PHRASES

Domani **cucirò** i bottoni sul vestito. I'll sew the buttons on the dress tomorrow.

Non so **cucire**. I can't sew.

Italic letters in Italian words show where stress does not follow the usual rules.

cuocere (to cook)

PRESENT

io	**cuocio**
tu	**cuoci**
lui/lei/Lei	**cuoce**
noi	**cuociamo**
voi	**cuocete**
loro	**cuociono**

PRESENT SUBJUNCTIVE

io	**cuocia**
tu	**cuocia**
lui/lei/Lei	**cuocia**
noi	**cuociamo**
voi	**cuociate**
loro	**cuociano**

PERFECT

io	**ho cotto**
tu	**hai cotto**
lui/lei/Lei	**ha cotto**
noi	**abbiamo cotto**
voi	**avete cotto**
loro	**hanno cotto**

IMPERFECT

io	**cuocevo**
tu	**cuocevi**
lui/lei/Lei	**cuoceva**
noi	**cuocevamo**
voi	**cuocevate**
loro	**cuocevano**

GERUND
cuocendo

PAST PARTICIPLE
cotto

EXAMPLE PHRASES

Si è bruciato **cuocendo** la pizza. He burnt himself when he was baking
the pizza.

La carne **cuoceva** sulla brace. The meat was cooking on the barbecue.

Mi piace la carne **cotta** sulla piastra. I like meat cooked on the hotplate.

Remember that subject pronouns are not used very often in Italian.

cuocere

FUTURE

io	**cuocerò**
tu	**cuocerai**
lui/lei/Lei	**cuocerà**
noi	**cuoceremo**
voi	**cuocerete**
loro	**cuoceranno**

CONDITIONAL

io	**cuocerei**
tu	**cuoceresti**
lui/lei/Lei	**cuocerebbe**
noi	**cuoceremmo**
voi	**cuocereste**
loro	**cuocerebbero**

PAST HISTORIC

io	**cossi**
tu	**cuocesti**
lui/lei/Lei	**cosse**
noi	**cuocemmo**
voi	**cuoceste**
loro	**cossero**

PLUPERFECT

io	**avevo cotto**
tu	**avevi cotto**
lui/lei/Lei	**aveva cotto**
noi	**avevamo cotto**
voi	**avevate cotto**
loro	**avevano cotto**

IMPERATIVE

cuoci
cuociamo
cuocete

EXAMPLE PHRASES

Stasera, il pesce, lo **cuocerò** alla griglia. This evening I'll grill the fish.

Come lo **cuocerai**? How are you going to cook it?

Avevamo cotto troppo la torta: era immangiabile. We'd left the cake in the oven too long: it was inedible.

Cuocilo per mezz'ora. Cook it for half an hour.

Italic letters in Italian words show where stress does not follow the usual rules.

dare (to give)

PRESENT		PRESENT SUBJUNCTIVE	
io	**do**	io	**dia**
tu	**dai**	tu	**dia**
lui/lei/Lei	**dà**	lui/lei/Lei	**dia**
noi	**diamo**	noi	**diamo**
voi	**date**	voi	**diate**
loro	**danno**	loro	**diano**

PERFECT		IMPERFECT	
io	**ho dato**	io	**davo**
tu	**hai dato**	tu	**davi**
lui/lei/Lei	**ha dato**	lui/lei/Lei	**dava**
noi	**abbiamo dato**	noi	**davamo**
voi	**avete dato**	voi	**davate**
loro	**hanno dato**	loro	**davano**

GERUND

dando

PAST PARTICIPLE

dato

EXAMPLE PHRASES

Può **darsi** che sia malata. She may be ill.

La mia finestra **dà** sul giardino. My window looks onto the garden.

Gli **ho dato** un libro. I gave him a book.

Dandoti da fare, potresti ottenere molto di più. If you exerted yourself you could achieve a lot more.

Remember that subject pronouns are not used very often in Italian.

dare

FUTURE

io	**darò**
tu	**darai**
lui/lei/Lei	**darà**
noi	**daremo**
voi	**darete**
loro	**daranno**

CONDITIONAL

io	**darei**
tu	**daresti**
lui/lei/Lei	**darebbe**
noi	**daremmo**
voi	**dareste**
loro	**darebbero**

PAST HISTORIC

io	**diedi** or **detti**
tu	**desti**
lui/lei/Lei	**diede** or **dette**
noi	**demmo**
voi	**deste**
loro	**diedero** or **dettero**

PLUPERFECT

io	**avevo dato**
tu	**avevi dato**
lui/lei/Lei	**aveva dato**
noi	**avevamo dato**
voi	**avevate dato**
loro	**avevano dato**

IMPERATIVE

dai or **da'**
diamo
date

EXAMPLE PHRASES

Domani sera **daranno** un bel film in TV. There's a good film on TV tomorrow evening.

Quanti anni gli **daresti**? How old would you say he was?

Ci **diede** l'impressione di essere molto infelice. We got the impression he was very unhappy.

Lo ringraziai perché mi aveva **dato** una mano. I thanked him for giving me a hand.

Ricordami di **darti** la lista della spesa. Remind me to give you the shopping list.

Dammelo. Give it to me.

Italic letters in Italian words show where stress does not follow the usual rules.

decidere (to decide)

PRESENT

io	decido
tu	decidi
lui/lei/Lei	decide
noi	decidiamo
voi	decidete
loro	decidono

PRESENT SUBJUNCTIVE

io	decida
tu	decida
lui/lei/Lei	decida
noi	decidiamo
voi	decidiate
loro	decidano

PERFECT

io	ho deciso
tu	hai deciso
lui/lei/Lei	ha deciso
noi	abbiamo deciso
voi	avete deciso
loro	hanno deciso

IMPERFECT

io	decidevo
tu	decidevi
lui/lei/Lei	decideva
noi	decidevamo
voi	decidevate
loro	decidevano

GERUND

decidendo

PAST PARTICIPLE

deciso

EXAMPLE PHRASES

Quand'è che si **decidono** a venirci a trovare? When will they decide to come and see us?

Hai deciso? Have you decided?

Allora ci vai? – Non so, sto ancora **decidendo**. So, are you going? – I don't know, I'm still trying to decide.

Non so **decidermi**. I can't decide.

Remember that subject pronouns are not used very often in Italian.

decidere

FUTURE

io	deciderò
tu	deciderai
lui/lei/Lei	deciderà
noi	decideremo
voi	deciderete
loro	decideranno

CONDITIONAL

io	deciderei
tu	decideresti
lui/lei/Lei	deciderebbe
noi	decideremmo
voi	decidereste
loro	deciderebbero

PAST HISTORIC

io	decisi
tu	decidesti
lui/lei/Lei	decise
noi	decidemmo
voi	decideste
loro	decisero

PLUPERFECT

io	avevo deciso
tu	avevi deciso
lui/lei/Lei	aveva deciso
noi	avevamo deciso
voi	avevate deciso
loro	avevano deciso

IMPERATIVE

decidi
decidiamo
decidete

EXAMPLE PHRASES

Deciderai quando sarai sicura. You'll decide when you're sure.

Decidemmo di non andarci. We decided not to go.

Aveva deciso di smettere di fumare, ma non ce l'ha fatta. She'd decided to stop smoking, but she didn't manage to.

Non so scegliere: **decidi** tu al posto mio. I don't know which to choose: you decide for me.

Italic letters in Italian words show where stress does not follow the usual rules.

deludere (to disappoint)

PRESENT

io	deludo
tu	deludi
lui/lei/Lei	delude
noi	deludiamo
voi	deludete
loro	deludono

PRESENT SUBJUNCTIVE

io	deluda
tu	deluda
lui/lei/Lei	deluda
noi	deludiamo
voi	deludiate
loro	deludano

PERFECT

io	ho deluso
tu	hai deluso
lui/lei/Lei	ha deluso
noi	abbiamo deluso
voi	avete deluso
loro	hanno deluso

IMPERFECT

io	deludevo
tu	deludevi
lui/lei/Lei	deludeva
noi	deludevamo
voi	deludevate
loro	deludevano

GERUND
deludendo

PAST PARTICIPLE
deluso

EXAMPLE PHRASES

Spero proprio che tu non mi **deluda**. I really hope you won't disappoint me.

Il suo ultimo film mi **ha deluso**. His last film was disappointing.

Non vorrei **deluderti**, ma l'esame è andato male. I hate to disappoint you, but the exam didn't go well.

Remember that subject pronouns are not used very often in Italian.

deludere

FUTURE

io	**deluderò**
tu	**deluderai**
lui/lei/Lei	**deluderà**
noi	**deluderemo**
voi	**deluderete**
loro	**deluderanno**

CONDITIONAL

io	**deluderei**
tu	**deluderesti**
lui/lei/Lei	**deluderebbe**
noi	**deluderemmo**
voi	**deludereste**
loro	**deluderebbero**

PAST HISTORIC

io	**delusi**
tu	**deludesti**
lui/lei/Lei	**deluse**
noi	**deludemmo**
voi	**deludeste**
loro	**delusero**

PLUPERFECT

io	**avevo deluso**
tu	**avevi deluso**
lui/lei/Lei	**aveva deluso**
noi	**avevamo deluso**
voi	**avevate deluso**
loro	**avevano deluso**

IMPERATIVE

deludi
deludiamo
deludete

EXAMPLE PHRASES

So che vi **deluderò**, ma ormai ho deciso. I know you're going to be disappointed, but I've made up my mind.

Se lo facessero mi **deluderebbero** molto. If they did that I'd be very disappointed in them.

Mi **deluse** molto. It disappointed me very much.

Ci **aveva deluso** e non gli parlammo più. He'd let us down and we didn't speak to him any more.

Italic letters in Italian words show where stress does not follow the usual rules.

dire (to say)

PRESENT

io	**dico**
tu	**dici**
lui/lei/Lei	**dice**
noi	**diciamo**
voi	**dite**
loro	**dicono**

PRESENT SUBJUNCTIVE

io	**dica**
tu	**dica**
lui/lei/Lei	**dica**
noi	**diciamo**
voi	**diciate**
loro	**dicano**

PERFECT

io	**ho detto**
tu	**hai detto**
lui/lei/Lei	**ha detto**
noi	**abbiamo detto**
voi	**avete detto**
loro	**hanno detto**

IMPERFECT

io	**dicevo**
tu	**dicevi**
lui/lei/Lei	**diceva**
noi	**dicevamo**
voi	**dicevate**
loro	**dicevano**

GERUND
dicendo

PAST PARTICIPLE
detto

EXAMPLE PHRASES

Come si **dice** "quadro" in inglese? How do you say "quadro" in English?

Ha detto che verrà. He said he'll come.

Era una persona generosa: **diceva** sempre di sì a tutti. She was a generous person: she always said yes to everyone.

Che ne **diresti** di farci un selfie? Shall we take a selfie?

Che cosa stai **dicendo**? What are you saying?

Remember that subject pronouns are not used very often in Italian.

dire

FUTURE

io	**dirò**
tu	**dirai**
lui/lei/Lei	**dirà**
noi	**diremo**
voi	**direte**
loro	**diranno**

CONDITIONAL

io	**direi**
tu	**diresti**
lui/lei/Lei	**direbbe**
noi	**diremmo**
voi	**direste**
loro	**direbbero**

PAST HISTORIC

io	**dissi**
tu	**dicesti**
lui/lei/Lei	**disse**
noi	**dicemmo**
voi	**diceste**
loro	**dissero**

PLUPERFECT

io	**avevo detto**
tu	**avevi detto**
lui/lei/Lei	**aveva detto**
noi	**avevamo detto**
voi	**avevate detto**
loro	**avevano detto**

IMPERATIVE

di'
diciamo
dite

EXAMPLE PHRASES

Ti **dirò** un segreto. I'll tell you a secret.

Non **disse** una parola. She didn't say a word.

Gli **avevo detto** di andarsene. I'd told him to go away.

Dimmi dov'è. Tell me where it is.

Dovete **dire** la verità. You must tell the truth.

Italic letters in Italian words show where stress does not follow the usual rules.

dirigere (to direct)

PRESENT

io	**dirigo**
tu	**dirigi**
lui/lei/Lei	**dirige**
noi	**dirigiamo**
voi	**dirigete**
loro	**dirigono**

PRESENT SUBJUNCTIVE

io	**diriga**
tu	**diriga**
lui/lei/Lei	**diriga**
noi	**dirigiamo**
voi	**dirigiate**
loro	**dirigano**

PERFECT

io	**ho diretto**
tu	**hai diretto**
lui/lei/Lei	**ha diretto**
noi	**abbiamo diretto**
voi	**avete diretto**
loro	**hanno diretto**

IMPERFECT

io	**dirigevo**
tu	**dirigevi**
lui/lei/Lei	**dirigeva**
noi	**dirigevamo**
voi	**dirigevate**
loro	**dirigevano**

GERUND

dirigendo

PAST PARTICIPLE

diretto

EXAMPLE PHRASES

I vigili **dirigono** il traffico. The police are directing the traffic.

Voglio che tu **diriga** il progetto. I want you to manage the project.

Ha diretto l'orchestra con grande abilità. He conducted the orchestra with great skill.

Si **è diretto** verso la porta. He headed for the door.

Prima **dirigeva** una ditta. Before that he managed a company.

Remember that subject pronouns are not used very often in Italian.

dirigere

FUTURE

io	dirigerò
tu	dirigerai
lui/lei/Lei	dirigerà
noi	dirigeremo
voi	dirigerete
loro	dirigeranno

CONDITIONAL

io	dirigerei
tu	dirigeresti
lui/lei/Lei	dirigerebbe
noi	dirigeremmo
voi	dirigereste
loro	dirigerebbero

PAST HISTORIC

io	diressi
tu	dirigesti
lui/lei/Lei	diresse
noi	dirigemmo
voi	dirigeste
loro	diressero

PLUPERFECT

io	avevo diretto
tu	avevi diretto
lui/lei/Lei	aveva diretto
noi	avevamo diretto
voi	avevate diretto
loro	avevano diretto

IMPERATIVE

dirigi
dirigiamo
dirigete

EXAMPLE PHRASES

Chi **dirigerà** i lavori? Who'll be in charge of the work?

Prima dell'incidente **erano diretti** a nord. Before the accident they'd been heading north.

Dirigiamoci verso sud. Let's head south.

Italic letters in Italian words show where stress does not follow the usual rules.

discutere (to discuss)

PRESENT

io	**discuto**
tu	**discuti**
lui/lei/Lei	**discute**
noi	**discutiamo**
voi	**discutete**
loro	**discutono**

PRESENT SUBJUNCTIVE

io	**discuta**
tu	**discuta**
lui/lei/Lei	**discuta**
noi	**discutiamo**
voi	**discutiate**
loro	**discutano**

PERFECT

io	**ho discusso**
tu	**hai discusso**
lui/lei/Lei	**ha discusso**
noi	**abbiamo discusso**
voi	**avete discusso**
loro	**hanno discusso**

IMPERFECT

io	**discutevo**
tu	**discutevi**
lui/lei/Lei	**discuteva**
noi	**discutevamo**
voi	**discutevate**
loro	**discutevano**

GERUND
discutendo

PAST PARTICIPLE
discusso

EXAMPLE PHRASES

Discutono spesso di politica. They often discuss politics.

Ho discusso a lungo con lui. I had a long discussion with him.

C'è stato un periodo in cui **discutevano** sempre. There was a time when they argued constantly.

Il problema non si risolverà solo **discutendo**. Just talking about it won't solve the problem.

Remember that subject pronouns are not used very often in Italian.

discutere

FUTURE

io	**discuterò**
tu	**discuterai**
lui/lei/Lei	**discuterà**
noi	**discuteremo**
voi	**discuterete**
loro	**discuteranno**

CONDITIONAL

io	**discuterei**
tu	**discuteresti**
lui/lei/Lei	**discuterebbe**
noi	**discuteremmo**
voi	**discutereste**
loro	**discuterebbero**

PAST HISTORIC

io	**discussi**
tu	**discutesti**
lui/lei/Lei	**discusse**
noi	**discutemmo**
voi	**discuteste**
loro	**discussero**

PLUPERFECT

io	**avevo discusso**
tu	**avevi discusso**
lui/lei/Lei	**aveva discusso**
noi	**avevamo discusso**
voi	**avevate discusso**
loro	**avevano discusso**

IMPERATIVE

discuti
discutiamo
discutete

EXAMPLE PHRASES

Discuteremo della questione più tardi. We'll discuss the matter later.

Discussero a fondo della possibilità di trasferirsi. They had a detailed discussion about the possibility of moving.

Mi ha ubbidito senza **discutere**. He obeyed me without question.

È inutile che **discutiamo**: ho ragione io. There's no point arguing: I'm right.

Italic letters in Italian words show where stress does not follow the usual rules.

distinguere (to see)

PRESENT

io	distinguo
tu	distingui
lui/lei/Lei	distingue
noi	distinguiamo
voi	distinguete
loro	distinguono

PRESENT SUBJUNCTIVE

io	distingua
tu	distingua
lui/lei/Lei	distingua
noi	distinguiamo
voi	distinguiate
loro	distinguano

PERFECT

io	ho distinto
tu	hai distinto
lui/lei/Lei	ha distinto
noi	abbiamo distinto
voi	avete distinto
loro	hanno distinto

IMPERFECT

io	distinguevo
tu	distinguevi
lui/lei/Lei	distingueva
noi	distinguevamo
voi	distinguevate
loro	distinguevano

GERUND

distinguendo

PAST PARTICIPLE

distinto

EXAMPLE PHRASES

Non li **distinguo** tra loro. I can't tell the difference between them.

Mi pare che tu non **distingua** bene i colori. I think you have difficulty telling one colour from another.

Non **distinguevo** il numero dell'autobus. I couldn't see the number of the bus.

Si è **distinto** per efficienza. He's exceptionally efficient.

Remember that subject pronouns are not used very often in Italian.

distinguere

FUTURE

io	**distinguerò**
tu	**distinguerai**
lui/lei/Lei	**distinguerà**
noi	**distingueremo**
voi	**distinguerete**
loro	**distingueranno**

CONDITIONAL

io	**distinguerei**
tu	**distingueresti**
lui/lei/Lei	**distinguerebbe**
noi	**distingueremmo**
voi	**distinguereste**
loro	**distinguerebbero**

PAST HISTORIC

io	**distinsi**
tu	**distinguesti**
lui/lei/Lei	**distinse**
noi	**distinguemmo**
voi	**distingueste**
loro	**distinsero**

PLUPERFECT

io	**avevo distinto**
tu	**avevi distinto**
lui/lei/Lei	**aveva distinto**
noi	**avevamo distinto**
voi	**avevate distinto**
loro	**avevano distinto**

IMPERATIVE

distingui
distinguiamo
distinguete

EXAMPLE PHRASES

È una copia perfetta: non **distinguerei** il falso dall'originale. It's a perfect copy:
I couldn't tell the fake from the original.

Distinguemmo nella nebbia la sagoma della nave. Through the mist we could
see the outline of the ship.

Non sa **distinguere** sogni e realtà. She can't tell the difference between dreams
and reality.

Italic letters in Italian words show where stress does not follow the usual rules.

dividere (to divide)

PRESENT

io	**divido**
tu	**dividi**
lui/lei/Lei	**divide**
noi	**dividiamo**
voi	**dividete**
loro	**dividono**

PRESENT SUBJUNCTIVE

io	**divida**
tu	**divida**
lui/lei/Lei	**divida**
noi	**dividiamo**
voi	**dividiate**
loro	**dividano**

PERFECT

io	**ho diviso**
tu	**hai diviso**
lui/lei/Lei	**ha diviso**
noi	**abbiamo diviso**
voi	**avete diviso**
loro	**hanno diviso**

IMPERFECT

io	**dividevo**
tu	**dividevi**
lui/lei/Lei	**divideva**
noi	**dividevamo**
voi	**dividevate**
loro	**dividevano**

GERUND
dividendo

PAST PARTICIPLE
diviso

EXAMPLE PHRASES

Il libro si **divide** in tre parti. The book is divided into three parts.

L'**ho diviso** in tre parti. I've divided it into three parts.

Abit*a*vano insieme e **divid*e*vano** le spese. They lived together and shared expenses.

Otto **diviso** quattro fa due. Eight divided by four is two.

Dividendo il lavoro, faremo prima. If we share the work we'll get it done sooner.

Remember that subject pronouns are not used very often in Italian.

dividere

FUTURE

io	**dividerò**
tu	**dividerai**
lui/lei/Lei	**dividerà**
noi	**divideremo**
voi	**dividerete**
loro	**divideranno**

CONDITIONAL

io	**dividerei**
tu	**divideresti**
lui/lei/Lei	**dividerebbe**
noi	**divideremmo**
voi	**dividereste**
loro	**dividerebbero**

PAST HISTORIC

io	**divisi**
tu	**dividesti**
lui/lei/Lei	**divise**
noi	**dividemmo**
voi	**divideste**
loro	**divisero**

PLUPERFECT

io	**avevo diviso**
tu	**avevi diviso**
lui/lei/Lei	**aveva diviso**
noi	**avevamo diviso**
voi	**avevate diviso**
loro	**avevano diviso**

IMPERATIVE

dividi
dividiamo
dividete

EXAMPLE PHRASES

È egoista e non **dividerebbe** mai nulla con nessuno. He's selfish and would never share anything with anyone.

Li **avevano divisi** perché litigavano sempre. They had separated them because they quarrelled all the time.

Dividi la cioccolata con tuo fratello. Share the chocolate with your brother.

Italic letters in Italian words show where stress does not follow the usual rules.

dormire (to sleep)

PRESENT		PRESENT SUBJUNCTIVE	
io	**dormo**	io	**dorma**
tu	**dormi**	tu	**dorma**
lui/lei/Lei	**dorme**	lui/lei/Lei	**dorma**
noi	**dormiamo**	noi	**dormiamo**
voi	**dormite**	voi	**dormiate**
loro	**dormono**	loro	**dormano**

PERFECT		IMPERFECT	
io	**ho dormito**	io	**dormivo**
tu	**hai dormito**	tu	**dormivi**
lui/lei/Lei	**ha dormito**	lui/lei/Lei	**dormiva**
noi	**abbiamo dormito**	noi	**dormivamo**
voi	**avete dormito**	voi	**dormivate**
loro	**hanno dormito**	loro	**dormivano**

GERUND	PAST PARTICIPLE
dormendo	dormito

EXAMPLE PHRASES

Era così stanco che **dormiva** in piedi. He was so tired he was asleep on his feet.

Dormivo e non ti ho sentita entrare. I was asleep and didn't hear you come in.

Sta **dormendo**. She's sleeping.

Vado a **dormire**. I'm going to bed.

Remember that subject pronouns are not used very often in Italian.

dormire

FUTURE

io	dormirò
tu	dormirai
lui/lei/Lei	dormirà
noi	dormiremo
voi	dormirete
loro	dormiranno

CONDITIONAL

io	dormirei
tu	dormiresti
lui/lei/Lei	dormirebbe
noi	dormiremmo
voi	dormireste
loro	dormirebbero

PAST HISTORIC

io	dormii
tu	dormisti
lui/lei/Lei	dormì
noi	dormimmo
voi	dormiste
loro	dormirono

PLUPERFECT

io	avevo dormito
tu	avevi dormito
lui/lei/Lei	aveva dormito
noi	avevamo dormito
voi	avevate dormito
loro	avevano dormito

IMPERATIVE

dormi
dormiamo
dormite

EXAMPLE PHRASES

Stanotte **dormirò** come un ghiro. I'll sleep like a log tonight.

Se potessi **dormirei** fino a tardi. If I could I'd have a lie-in.

Dormimmo profondamente e ci svegliammo riposati. We slept soundly and woke up refreshed.

Aveva dormito male ed era nervoso. He hadn't slept well and was irritable.

Italic letters in Italian words show where stress does not follow the usual rules.

dovere (to have to)

PRESENT		PRESENT SUBJUNCTIVE	
io	**devo**	io	**debba**
tu	**devi**	tu	**debba**
lui/lei/Lei	**deve**	lui/lei/Lei	**debba**
noi	**dobbiamo**	noi	**dobbiamo**
voi	**dovete**	voi	**dobbiate**
loro	**devono**	loro	**debbano**

PERFECT		IMPERFECT	
io	**ho dovuto**	io	**dovevo**
tu	**hai dovuto**	tu	**dovevi**
lui/lei/Lei	**ha dovuto**	lui/lei/Lei	**doveva**
noi	**abbiamo dovuto**	noi	**dovevamo**
voi	**avete dovuto**	voi	**dovevate**
loro	**hanno dovuto**	loro	**dovevano**

GERUND	PAST PARTICIPLE
dovendo	**dovuto**

EXAMPLE PHRASES

Ora **devo** proprio andare. I've really got to go now.

Devi finire i compiti prima di uscire. You must finish your homework before you go out.

Dev'essere tardi. It must be late.

Non è che si **debba** sempre dire la verità. You don't always have to tell the truth.

Gli **dovevo** 30 euro e così l'ho invitato a cena. I owed him 30 euros so I took him out to dinner.

È **dovuto** partire. He had to leave.

Remember that subject pronouns are not used very often in Italian.

dovere

FUTURE

io	dovrò
tu	dovrai
lui/lei/Lei	dovrà
noi	dovremo
voi	dovrete
loro	dovranno

CONDITIONAL

io	dovrei
tu	dovresti
lui/lei/Lei	dovrebbe
noi	dovremmo
voi	dovreste
loro	dovrebbero

PAST HISTORIC

io	dovetti
tu	dovesti
lui/lei/Lei	dovette
noi	dovemmo
voi	doveste
loro	dovettero

PLUPERFECT

io	avevo dovuto
tu	avevi dovuto
lui/lei/Lei	aveva dovuto
noi	avevamo dovuto
voi	avevate dovuto
loro	avevano dovuto

IMPERATIVE

–

EXAMPLE PHRASES

Per correre la maratona **dovranno** allenarsi molto. They'll have to do a lot of training to run the marathon.

Dovrebbe arrivare alle dieci. He should arrive at ten.

Dovemmo partire all'improvviso. We had to leave unexpectedly.

Dovendo scegliere, preferisco la giacca blu. If I have to choose, I prefer the blue jacket.

Italic letters in Italian words show where stress does not follow the usual rules.

escludere (to exclude)

PRESENT		PRESENT SUBJUNCTIVE	
io	**escludo**	io	**escluda**
tu	**escludi**	tu	**escluda**
lui/lei/Lei	**esclude**	lui/lei/Lei	**escluda**
noi	**escludiamo**	noi	**escludiamo**
voi	**escludete**	voi	**escludiate**
loro	**escludono**	loro	**escludano**

PERFECT		IMPERFECT	
io	**ho escluso**	io	**escludevo**
tu	**hai escluso**	tu	**escludevi**
lui/lei/Lei	**ha escluso**	lui/lei/Lei	**escludeva**
noi	**abbiamo escluso**	noi	**escludevamo**
voi	**avete escluso**	voi	**escludevate**
loro	**hanno escluso**	loro	**escludevano**

GERUND	PAST PARTICIPLE
escludendo	**escluso**

EXAMPLE PHRASES

Escludo che possa essere stato lui. I certainly don't think it could have been him.

Una cosa non **esclude** l'altra. The one doesn't rule out the other.

È stato **escluso** dalla gara. He was excluded from the competition.

Non conosceva nessuno e si sentiva **esclusa**. She didn't know anyone and felt excluded.

Escludendo il pesce, mangio di tutto. Apart from fish, I eat everything.

Remember that subject pronouns are not used very often in Italian.

escludere

FUTURE

io	**escluderò**
tu	**escluderai**
lui/lei/Lei	**escluderà**
noi	**escluderemo**
voi	**escluderete**
loro	**escluderanno**

CONDITIONAL

io	**escluderei**
tu	**escluderesti**
lui/lei/Lei	**escluderebbe**
noi	**escluderemmo**
voi	**escludereste**
loro	**escluderebbero**

PAST HISTORIC

io	**esclusi**
tu	**escludesti**
lui/lei/Lei	**escluse**
noi	**escludemmo**
voi	**escludeste**
loro	**esclusero**

PLUPERFECT

io	**avevo escluso**
tu	**avevi escluso**
lui/lei/Lei	**aveva escluso**
noi	**avevamo escluso**
voi	**avevate escluso**
loro	**avevano escluso**

IMPERATIVE

escludi
escludiamo
escludete

EXAMPLE PHRASES

Non **escluderei** questa possibilità. I wouldn't rule out this possibility.

Italic letters in Italian words show where stress does not follow the usual rules.

esigere (to require)

PRESENT		PRESENT SUBJUNCTIVE	
io	**esigo**	io	**esiga**
tu	**esigi**	tu	**esiga**
lui/lei/Lei	**esige**	lui/lei/Lei	**esiga**
noi	**esigiamo**	noi	**esigiamo**
voi	**esigete**	voi	**esigiate**
loro	**esigono**	loro	**esigano**

PERFECT		IMPERFECT	
io	–	io	**esigevo**
tu	–	tu	**esigevi**
lui/lei/Lei	–	lui/lei/Lei	**esigeva**
noi	–	noi	**esigevamo**
voi	–	voi	**esigevate**
loro	–	loro	**esigevano**

GERUND	PAST PARTICIPLE
esigendo	–

EXAMPLE PHRASES

Il proprietario **esige** il pagamento immediato. The owner is demanding immediate payment.

È un lavoro che **esige** molta concentrazione. It's a job which demands a lot of concentration.

Il capufficio **esigeva** sempre la perfezione. The head clerk always demanded perfection.

Remember that subject pronouns are not used very often in Italian.

esigere

FUTURE

io	**esigerò**
tu	**esigerai**
lui/lei/Lei	**esigerà**
noi	**esigeremo**
voi	**esigerete**
loro	**esigeranno**

CONDITIONAL

io	**esigerei**
tu	**esigeresti**
lui/lei/Lei	**esigerebbe**
noi	**esigeremmo**
voi	**esigereste**
loro	**esigerebbero**

PAST HISTORIC

Io	**esigetti**
tu	**esigesti**
lui/lei/Lei	**esigette**
noi	**esigemmo**
voi	**esigeste**
loro	**esigettero**

PLUPERFECT

io	–
tu	–
lui/lei/Lei	–
noi	–
voi	–
loro	–

IMPERATIVE

esigi
esigiamo
esigete

EXAMPLE PHRASES

Esigerò sempre il massimo dagli studenti. I'll always demand the maximum from my students.

Devi **esigere** sempre rispetto dagli altri. You must always demand respect from other people.

Esigemmo una risposta immediata. We demanded an immediate reply.

Italic letters in Italian words show where stress does not follow the usual rules.

esistere (to exist)

PRESENT

io	esisto
tu	esisti
lui/lei/Lei	esiste
noi	esistiamo
voi	esistete
loro	esistono

PRESENT SUBJUNCTIVE

io	esista
tu	esista
lui/lei/Lei	esista
noi	esistiamo
voi	esistiate
loro	esistano

PERFECT

io	sono esistito/a
tu	sei esistito/a
lui/lei/Lei	è esistito/a
noi	siamo esistiti/e
voi	siete esistiti/e
loro	sono esistiti/e

IMPERFECT

io	esistevo
tu	esistevi
lui/lei/Lei	esisteva
noi	esistevamo
voi	esistevate
loro	esistevano

GERUND

esistendo

PAST PARTICIPLE

esistito

EXAMPLE PHRASES

Babbo Natale non **esiste**. Father Christmas doesn't exist.

Non **esiste**! No way!

In Italia **esistono** molte tradizioni religiose. There are many religious traditions in Italy.

Non sappiamo se **esista** la vita su altri pianeti. We do not know if life exists on other planets.

Il 221b di Baker Street non **è** mai **esistito**. There never was a 221b Baker Street.

Un tempo qui **esisteva** una grande città. At one time there was a great city here.

Remember that subject pronouns are not used very often in Italian.

esistere

FUTURE

io	**esisterò**
tu	**esisterai**
lui/lei/Lei	**esisterà**
noi	**esisteremo**
voi	**esisterete**
loro	**esisteranno**

CONDITIONAL

io	**esisterei**
tu	**esisteresti**
lui/lei/Lei	**esisterebbe**
noi	**esisteremmo**
voi	**esistereste**
loro	**esisterebbero**

PAST HISTORIC

io	**esistei**
tu	**esistesti**
lui/lei/Lei	**esistette**
noi	**esistemmo**
voi	**esisteste**
loro	**esistettero**

PLUPERFECT

io	**ero esistito/a**
tu	**eri esistito/a**
lui/lei/Lei	**era esistito/a**
noi	**eravamo esistiti/e**
voi	**eravate esistiti/e**
loro	**erano esistiti/e**

IMPERATIVE

esisti
esistiamo
esistite

EXAMPLE PHRASES

Non disperare: **esisterà** pure una soluzione al problema! Don't despair:
there's sure to be a solution to the problem!

Secondo alcuni **esisterebbe** una quarta dimensione. Some people think there's
a fourth dimension.

Italic letters in Italian words show where stress does not follow the usual rules.

espellere (to expel)

PRESENT		PRESENT SUBJUNCTIVE	
io	espello	io	espella
tu	espelli	tu	espella
lui/lei/Lei	espelle	lui/lei/Lei	espella
noi	espelliamo	noi	espelliamo
voi	espellete	voi	espelliate
loro	espellono	loro	espellano

PERFECT		IMPERFECT	
io	ho espulso	io	espellevo
tu	hai espulso	tu	espellevi
lui/lei/Lei	ha espulso	lui/lei/Lei	espelleva
noi	abbiamo espulso	noi	espellevamo
voi	avete espulso	voi	espellevate
loro	hanno espulso	loro	espellevano

GERUND

espellendo

PAST PARTICIPLE

espulso

EXAMPLE PHRASES

Non va a scuola perché l'**hanno espulso**. He doesn't go to school because he's been expelled.

Tutt'e due i calciatori **sono** stati **espulsi**. Both players were sent off.

Remember that subject pronouns are not used very often in Italian.

espellerre

FUTURE

io	**espellerò**
tu	**espellerai**
lui/lei/Lei	**espellerà**
noi	**espelleremo**
voi	**espellerete**
loro	**espelleranno**

CONDITIONAL

io	**espellerei**
tu	**espelleresti**
lui/lei/Lei	**espellerebbe**
noi	**espelleremmo**
voi	**espellereste**
loro	**espellerebbero**

PAST HISTORIC

io	**espulsi**
tu	**espellesti**
lui/lei/Lei	**espulse**
noi	**espellemmo**
voi	**espelleste**
loro	**espulsero**

PLUPERFECT

io	**avevo espulso**
tu	**avevi espulso**
lui/lei/Lei	**aveva espulso**
noi	**avevamo espulso**
voi	**avevate espulso**
loro	**avevano espulso**

IMPERATIVE

espelli
espelliamo
espellete

EXAMPLE PHRASES

Espellerò chi non rispetta la disciplina. I will expel anyone who doesn't obey the rules.

Se farai un altro fallo ti **espelleranno**. If you commit another foul you'll be sent off.

Lo **espulsero** dalla scuola. He was expelled from the school.

Dopo mezz'ora l'arbitro **aveva** già **espulso** due giocatori. After half an hour the referee had already sent two players off.

Italic letters in Italian words show where stress does not follow the usual rules.

esplodere (to explode)

PRESENT

io	**esplodo**
tu	**esplodi**
lui/lei/Lei	**esplode**
noi	**esplodiamo**
voi	**esplodete**
loro	**esplodono**

PRESENT SUBJUNCTIVE

io	**esploda**
tu	**esploda**
lui/lei/Lei	**esploda**
noi	**esplodiamo**
voi	**esplodiate**
loro	**esplodano**

PERFECT

io	**sono esploso/a**
tu	**sei esploso/a**
lui/lei/Lei	**è esploso/a**
noi	**siamo esplosi/e**
voi	**siete esplosi/e**
loro	**sono esplosi/e**

IMPERFECT

io	**esplodevo**
tu	**esplodevi**
lui/lei/Lei	**esplodeva**
noi	**esplodevamo**
voi	**esplodevate**
loro	**esplodevano**

GERUND
esplodendo

PAST PARTICIPLE
esploso

EXAMPLE PHRASES

La nitroglicerina **esplode** facilmente. Nitroglycerin explodes easily.

L'ordigno **è esploso** uccidendo tre persone. The bomb exploded, killing three people.

Tutt'intorno **esplodevano** i colpi di cannone. Guns were firing on all sides.

Remember that subject pronouns are not used very often in Italian.

esplodere

FUTURE

io	**esploderò**
tu	**esploderai**
lui/lei/Lei	**esploderà**
noi	**esploderemo**
voi	**esploderete**
loro	**esploderanno**

CONDITIONAL

io	**esploderei**
tu	**esploderesti**
lui/lei/Lei	**esploderebbe**
noi	**esploderemmo**
voi	**esplodereste**
loro	**esploderebbero**

PAST HISTORIC

io	**esplosi**
tu	**esplodesti**
lui/lei/Lei	**esplose**
noi	**esplodemmo**
voi	**esplodeste**
loro	**esplosero**

PLUPERFECT

io	**ero esploso/a**
tu	**eri esploso/a**
lui/lei/Lei	**era esploso/a**
noi	**eravamo esplosi/e**
voi	**eravate esplosi/e**
loro	**erano esplosi/e**

IMPERATIVE

esplodi
esplodiamo
esplodete

EXAMPLE PHRASES

Cerca di trattenersi, ma prima o poi **esploderà**. He's trying to control himself, but sooner or later he'll explode.

Una bomba **esplose** vicino alla trincea. A bomb exploded near the trench.

Le mina **era esplosa** senza ferire nessuno. The mine exploded without injuring anyone.

esprimere (to express)

PRESENT

io	**esprimo**
tu	**esprimi**
lui/lei/Lei	**esprime**
noi	**esprimiamo**
voi	**esprimete**
loro	**esprimono**

PRESENT SUBJUNCTIVE

io	**esprima**
tu	**esprima**
lui/lei/Lei	**esprima**
noi	**esprimiamo**
voi	**esprimiate**
loro	**esprimano**

PERFECT

io	**ho espresso**
tu	**hai espresso**
lui/lei/Lei	**ha espresso**
noi	**abbiamo espresso**
voi	**avete espresso**
loro	**hanno espresso**

IMPERFECT

io	**esprimevo**
tu	**esprimevi**
lui/lei/Lei	**esprimeva**
noi	**esprimevamo**
voi	**esprimevate**
loro	**esprimevano**

GERUND

esprimendo

PAST PARTICIPLE

espresso

EXAMPLE PHRASES

Non **esprime** mai la sua opinione. He never expresses his own opinion.

Se non conosco la lingua, mi **esprimo** a gesti. If I don't know the language, I use gestures.

È meglio che tu non **esprima** le tue idee. You'd better not express your ideas.

Abbiamo espresso i nostri dubbi. We expressed our doubts.

Remember that subject pronouns are not used very often in Italian.

esprimere

FUTURE

io	esprimer*ò*
tu	esprimerai
lui/lei/Lei	esprimer*à*
noi	esprimeremo
voi	esprimerete
loro	esprimeranno

CONDITIONAL

io	esprimerei
tu	esprimeresti
lui/lei/Lei	esprimerebbe
noi	esprimeremmo
voi	esprimereste
loro	esprimer*e*bbero

PAST HISTORIC

io	espressi
tu	esprimesti
lui/lei/Lei	espresse
noi	esprimemmo
voi	esprimeste
loro	espr*e*ssero

PLUPERFECT

io	avevo espresso
tu	avevi espresso
lui/lei/Lei	aveva espresso
noi	avevamo espresso
voi	avevate espresso
loro	avevano espresso

IMPERATIVE

esprimi
esprimiamo
esprimete

EXAMPLE PHRASES

Il Parlamento si **espresse** a favore della proposta di legge. Parliament
approved the legislation.

Avevano espresso il desiderio di uscire. They had expressed a desire to go out.

Trovo difficile **esprimermi** in inglese. I find it difficult to express myself
in English.

Dai, **esprimi** un desiderio! Go on, make a wish!

Italic letters in Italian words show where stress does not follow the usual rules.

essere (to be)

PRESENT

io	**sono**
tu	**sei**
lui/lei/Lei	**è**
noi	**siamo**
voi	**siete**
loro	**sono**

PRESENT SUBJUNCTIVE

io	**sia**
tu	**sia**
lui/lei/Lei	**sia**
noi	**siamo**
voi	**siate**
loro	**siano**

PERFECT

io	**sono stato/a**
tu	**sei stato/a**
lui/lei/Lei	**è stato/a**
noi	**siamo stati/e**
voi	**siete stati/e**
loro	**sono stati/e**

IMPERFECT

io	**ero**
tu	**eri**
lui/lei/Lei	**era**
noi	**eravamo**
voi	**eravate**
loro	**erano**

GERUND

essendo

PAST PARTICIPLE

stato

EXAMPLE PHRASES

Sono italiana. I'm Italian.

Mario **è** appena partito. Mario has just left.

Siete mai **stati** in Africa? Have you ever been to Africa?

Quando è arrivato **erano** le quattro. When he arrived it was four o'clock.

La foto **era** già virale. The photo had already gone viral.

Essendo così tardi, dubito che verranno. As it's so late I doubt they'll
  be coming.

Remember that subject pronouns are not used very often in Italian.

essere

FUTURE

io	**sarò**
tu	**sarai**
lui/lei/Lei	**sarà**
noi	**saremo**
voi	**sarete**
loro	**saranno**

CONDITIONAL

io	**sarei**
tu	**saresti**
lui/lei/Lei	**sarebbe**
noi	**saremmo**
voi	**sareste**
loro	**sarebbero**

PAST HISTORIC

io	**fui**
tu	**fosti**
lul/lei/Lei	**fu**
noi	**fummo**
voi	**foste**
loro	**furono**

PLUPERFECT

io	**ero stato/a**
tu	**eri stato/a**
lui/lei/Lei	**era stato/a**
noi	**eravamo stati/e**
voi	**eravate stati/e**
loro	**erano stati/e**

IMPERATIVE

sii
siamo
siate

EXAMPLE PHRASES

Alla festa ci **saranno** tutti i miei amici. All my friends will be at the party.

Saresti così gentile da aiutarmi? Would you be kind enough to help me?

Quando **fui** pronto, chiusi la valigia e partii. When I was ready I fastened my case and left.

Non **era** mai **stato** così preoccupato in vita sua. He'd never been so worried in his life.

Siate onesti, e ammettete il vostro errore. Be honest and admit your mistake.

Italic letters in Italian words show where stress does not follow the usual rules.

fare (to do, to make)

PRESENT		PRESENT SUBJUNCTIVE	
io	faccio	io	faccia
tu	fai	tu	faccia
lui/lei/Lei	fa	lui/lei/Lei	faccia
noi	facciamo	noi	facciamo
voi	fate	voi	facciate
loro	fanno	loro	facciano

PERFECT		IMPERFECT	
io	ho fatto	io	facevo
tu	hai fatto	tu	facevi
lui/lei/Lei	ha fatto	lui/lei/Lei	faceva
noi	abbiamo fatto	noi	facevamo
voi	avete fatto	voi	facevate
loro	hanno fatto	loro	facevano

GERUND

facendo

PAST PARTICIPLE

fatto

EXAMPLE PHRASES

Due più due **fa** quattro. Two and two makes four.

Fa il medico. He is a doctor.

Fa caldo. It's hot.

Ho fatto un errore. I made a mistake.

Cosa stai **facendo**? What are you doing?

Remember that subject pronouns are not used very often in Italian.

fare

FUTURE

io	farò
tu	farai
lui/lei/Lei	farà
noi	faremo
voi	farete
loro	faranno

CONDITIONAL

io	farei
tu	faresti
lui/lei/Lei	farebbe
noi	faremmo
voi	fareste
loro	farebbero

PAST HISTORIC

io	feci
tu	facesti
lui/lei/Lei	fece
noi	facemmo
voi	faceste
loro	fecero

PLUPERFECT

io	avevo fatto
tu	avevi fatto
lui/lei/Lei	aveva fatto
noi	avevamo fatto
voi	avevate fatto
loro	avevano fatto

IMPERATIVE

fai *or* fa'
facciamo
fate

EXAMPLE PHRASES

Domani si **farà** tagliare i capelli. He's going to get his hair cut tomorrow.

Mi **faresti** un piacere? Would you do me a favour?

Fecero una stupenda vacanza al mare. They had a wonderful holiday at the seaside.

Le **aveva fatto** male la testa tutto il pomeriggio. She'd had a headache all afternoon.

Fammi un favore, ti prego. Please do me a favour.

Italic letters in Italian words show where stress does not follow the usual rules.

fingere (to pretend)

PRESENT

io	fingo
tu	fingi
lui/lei/Lei	finge
noi	fingiamo
voi	fingete
loro	fingono

PRESENT SUBJUNCTIVE

io	finga
tu	finga
lui/lei/Lei	finga
noi	fingiamo
voi	fingiate
loro	fingano

PERFECT

io	ho finto
tu	hai finto
lui/lei/Lei	ha finto
noi	abbiamo finto
voi	avete finto
loro	hanno finto

IMPERFECT

io	fingevo
tu	fingevi
lui/lei/Lei	fingeva
noi	fingevamo
voi	fingevate
loro	fingevano

GERUND

fingendo

PAST PARTICIPLE

finto

EXAMPLE PHRASES

Ha finto di non conoscermi. He pretended he didn't recognize me.

Si **è finto** ubriaco. He pretended he was drunk.

Fingevano sempre di avere capito tutto. They always pretended they'd understood everything.

Non risposi, **fingendo** di non ricordare. I didn't answer, pretending I couldn't remember.

Remember that subject pronouns are not used very often in Italian.

fingere

FUTURE

io	fingerò
tu	fingerai
lui/lei/Lei	fingerà
noi	fingeremo
voi	fingerete
loro	fingeranno

CONDITIONAL

io	fingerei
tu	fingeresti
lui/lei/Lei	fingerebbe
noi	fingeremmo
voi	fingereste
loro	fingerebbero

PAST HISTORIC

io	finsi
tu	fingesti
lui/lei/Lei	finse
noi	fingemmo
voi	fingeste
loro	finsero

PLUPERFECT

io	avevo finto
tu	avevi finto
lui/lei/Lei	aveva finto
noi	avevamo finto
voi	avevate finto
loro	avevano finto

IMPERATIVE

fingi
fingiamo
fingete

EXAMPLE PHRASES

Fingeremo di avere molto da fare. We'll pretend we've got a lot to do.

La spia **finse** di *e*ssere un turista. The spy pretended to be a tourist.

Non devi **fingere** sentimenti che non provi. You mustn't pretend you have feelings that you don't have.

Fingiamo di dormire. Let's pretend we're asleep.

Italic letters in Italian words show where stress does not follow the usual rules.

fuggire (to run away)

PRESENT

io	**fuggo**
tu	**fuggi**
lui/lei/Lei	**fugge**
noi	**fuggiamo**
voi	**fuggite**
loro	**fuggono**

PRESENT SUBJUNCTIVE

io	**fugga**
tu	**fugga**
lui/lei/Lei	**fugga**
noi	**fuggiamo**
voi	**fuggiate**
loro	**fuggano**

PERFECT

io	**sono fuggito/a**
tu	**sei fuggito/a**
lui/lei/Lei	**è fuggito/a**
noi	**siamo fuggiti/e**
voi	**siete fuggiti/e**
loro	**sono fuggiti/e**

IMPERFECT

io	**fuggivo**
tu	**fuggivi**
lui/lei/Lei	**fuggiva**
noi	**fuggivamo**
voi	**fuggivate**
loro	**fuggivano**

GERUND
fuggendo

PAST PARTICIPLE
fuggito

EXAMPLE PHRASES

È **fuggita** di casa. She ran away from home.

Non è **fuggendo** che si risolvono i problemi. You won't solve problems by running away from them.

Il ladro stava **fuggendo** su un'auto sportiva. The robber was escaping in a sports car.

Remember that subject pronouns are not used very often in Italian.

fuggire

FUTURE

io	**fuggirò**
tu	**fuggirai**
lui/lei/Lei	**fuggirà**
noi	**fuggiremo**
voi	**fuggirete**
loro	**fuggiranno**

CONDITIONAL

io	**fuggirei**
tu	**fuggiresti**
lui/lei/Lei	**fuggirebbe**
noi	**fuggiremmo**
voi	**fuggireste**
loro	**fuggirebbero**

PAST HISTORIC

io	**fuggii**
tu	**fuggisti**
lui/lei/Lei	**fuggì**
noi	**fuggimmo**
voi	**fuggiste**
loro	**fuggirono**

PLUPERFECT

io	**ero fuggito/a**
tu	**eri fuggito/a**
lui/lei/Lei	**era fuggito/a**
noi	**eravamo fuggiti/e**
voi	**eravate fuggiti/e**
loro	**erano fuggiti/e**

IMPERATIVE

fuggi
fuggiamo
fuggite

EXAMPLE PHRASES

Non c'è bisogno che tu leghi il cane alla sedia: non, **fuggirà**. There is no need
 for you to tie your dog to the chair: it won't run off.

Se ci scopriranno, **fuggiremo**. If they find us we'll run for it.

Fuggirono di prigione. They escaped from prison.

La polizia! **Fuggiamo**! It's the police! Run for it!

Italic letters in Italian words show where stress does not follow the usual rules.

immergere (to immerse)

PRESENT

io	immergo
tu	immergi
lui/lei/Lei	immerge
noi	immergiamo
voi	immergete
loro	immergono

PRESENT SUBJUNCTIVE

io	immerga
tu	immerga
lui/lei/Lei	immerga
noi	immergiamo
voi	immergiate
loro	immergano

PERFECT

io	ho immerso
tu	hai immerso
lui/lei/Lei	ha immerso
noi	abbiamo immerso
voi	avete immerso
loro	hanno immerso

IMPERFECT

io	immergevo
tu	immergevi
lui/lei/Lei	immergeva
noi	immergevamo
voi	immergevate
loro	immergevano

GERUND

immergendo

PAST PARTICIPLE

immerso

EXAMPLE PHRASES

Ha immerso il metallo incandescente nell'acqua. He plunged the red-hot metal into the water.

Non la disturbare: **è immersa** nel lavoro. Don't disturb her: she's deep in her work.

Si **immergevano** nello studio ogni sera. They immersed themselves in their studies every night.

Ha scoperto il relitto **immergendosi** poco lontano. He discovered the wreck when he was diving not far away.

Remember that subject pronouns are not used very often in Italian.

immergere

FUTURE

io	immergerò
tu	immergerai
lui/lei/Lei	immergerà
noi	immergeremo
voi	immergerete
loro	immergeranno

CONDITIONAL

io	immergerei
tu	immergeresti
lui/lei/Lei	immergerebbe
noi	immergeremmo
voi	immergereste
loro	immergerebbero

PAST HISTORIC

io	immersi
tu	immergesti
lui/lei/Lei	immerse
noi	immergemmo
voi	immergeste
loro	immersero

PLUPERFECT

io	avevo immerso
tu	avevi immerso
lui/lei/Lei	aveva immerso
noi	avevamo immerso
voi	avevate immerso
loro	avevano immerso

IMPERATIVE

immergi
immergiamo
immergete

EXAMPLE PHRASES

Ci **immergeremo** nelle acque dell'Adriatico. We'll dive in the waters of the
Adriatic.

Il sottomarino si **immerse**. The submarine submerged.

Italic letters in Italian words show where stress does not follow the usual rules.

intendere (to understand) ℓ

PRESENT

io	**intendo**
tu	**intendi**
lui/lei/Lei	**intende**
noi	**intendiamo**
voi	**intendete**
loro	**intendono**

PRESENT SUBJUNCTIVE

io	**intenda**
tu	**intenda**
lui/lei/Lei	**intenda**
noi	**intendiamo**
voi	**intendiate**
loro	**intendano**

PERFECT

io	**ho inteso**
tu	**hai inteso**
lui/lei/Lei	**ha inteso**
noi	**abbiamo inteso**
voi	**avete inteso**
loro	**hanno inteso**

IMPERFECT

io	**intendevo**
tu	**intendevi**
lui/lei/Lei	**intendeva**
noi	**intendevamo**
voi	**intendevate**
loro	**intendevano**

GERUND

intendendo

PAST PARTICIPLE

inteso

EXAMPLE PHRASES

Dipende da cosa **intendi** per "giustizia". It depends what you mean by "justice".

Si **intende** di fotografia. She knows about photography.

Non riusciamo a capire che cosa **intendano**. We don't know what they mean.

Siamo sicuri che si **intenda** di automobili? Can we be sure he knows about cars?

Ci **siamo intesi**? Is that clear?

Cosa **intendevi**? What did you mean?

Remember that subject pronouns are not used very often in Italian.

intendere

FUTURE

io	intenderò
tu	intenderai
lui/lei/Lei	intenderà
noi	intenderemo
voi	intenderete
loro	intenderanno

CONDITIONAL

io	intenderei
tu	intenderesti
lui/lei/Lei	intenderebbe
noi	intenderemmo
voi	intendereste
loro	intenderebbero

PAST HISTORIC

io	intesi
tu	intendesti
lui/lei/Lei	intese
noi	intendemmo
voi	intendeste
loro	intesero

PLUPERFECT

io	avevo inteso
tu	avevi inteso
lui/lei/Lei	aveva inteso
noi	avevamo inteso
voi	avevate inteso
loro	avevano inteso

IMPERATIVE

intendi
intendiamo
intendete

EXAMPLE PHRASES

Noi due non ci **intenderemo** mai. We two will never agree.

Intenderesti dire che ho sbagliato? Are you saying I made a mistake?

Italic letters in Italian words show where stress does not follow the usual rules.

invadere (to invade)

PRESENT

io	invado
tu	invadi
lui/lei/Lei	invade
noi	invadiamo
voi	invadete
loro	invadono

PRESENT SUBJUNCTIVE

io	invada
tu	invada
lui/lei/Lei	invada
noi	invadiamo
voi	invadiate
loro	invadano

PERFECT

io	ho invaso
tu	hai invaso
lui/lei/Lei	ha invaso
noi	abbiamo invaso
voi	avete invaso
loro	hanno invaso

IMPERFECT

io	invadevo
tu	invadevi
lui/lei/Lei	invadeva
noi	invadevamo
voi	invadevate
loro	invadevano

GERUND

invadendo

PAST PARTICIPLE

invaso

EXAMPLE PHRASES

La folla **invade** la piazza. The crowd is streaming into the square.

I tifosi **hanno invaso** il campo. The fans invaded the pitch.

L'esercito stava **invadendo** la città. The army was taking possession of the city.

Remember that subject pronouns are not used very often in Italian.

invadere

FUTURE		CONDITIONAL	
io	invaderò	io	invaderei
tu	invaderai	tu	invaderesti
lui/lei/Lei	invaderà	lui/lei/Lei	invaderebbe
noi	invaderemo	noi	invaderemmo
voi	invaderete	voi	invadereste
loro	invaderanno	loro	invaderebbero

PAST HISTORIC		PLUPERFECT	
io	invasi	io	avevo invaso
tu	invadesti	tu	avevi invaso
lui/lei/Lei	invase	lui/lei/Lei	aveva invaso
noi	invademmo	noi	avevamo invaso
voi	invadeste	voi	avevate invaso
loro	invasero	loro	avevano invaso

IMPERATIVE

invadi
invadiamo
invadete

EXAMPLE PHRASES

Senza steccati le pecore **invaderebbero** i campi. Without fences the sheep would overrun the fields.

Il virus **invase** il mio computer. The virus infected my computer.

Italic letters in Italian words show where stress does not follow the usual rules.

invecchiare (to get old)

PRESENT

io	invecchio
tu	invecchi
lui/lei/Lei	invecchia
noi	invecchiamo
voi	invecchiate
loro	invecchiano

PRESENT SUBJUNCTIVE

io	invecchi
tu	invecchi
lui/lei/Lei	invecchi
noi	invecchiamo
voi	invecchiate
loro	invecchino

PERFECT

io	sono invecchiato/a
tu	sei invecchiato/a
lui/lei/Lei	è invecchiato/a
noi	siamo invecchiati/e
voi	siete invecchiati/e
loro	sono invecchiati/e

IMPERFECT

io	invecchiavo
tu	invecchiavi
lui/lei/Lei	invecchiava
noi	invecchiavamo
voi	invecchiavate
loro	invecchiavano

GERUND

invecchiando

PAST PARTICIPLE

invecchiato

EXAMPLE PHRASES

La barba ti **invecchia**. The beard makes you look older.

Tutti **invecchiano** prima o poi. Everyone gets old sooner or later.

Questo vino **è invecchiato** in botti di rovere. This wine is aged in oak casks.

Invecchiava a vista d'occhio. He was visibly ageing.

Il vino migliora **invecchiando**. Wine gets better with age.

Molti hanno paura di **invecchiare**. A lot of people are afraid of getting old.

Remember that subject pronouns are not used very often in Italian.

invecchiare

FUTURE

io	**invecchierò**
tu	**invecchierai**
lui/lei/Lei	**invecchierà**
noi	**invecchieremo**
voi	**invecchierete**
loro	**invecchieranno**

CONDITIONAL

io	**invecchierei**
tu	**invecchieresti**
lui/lei/Lei	**invecchierebbe**
noi	**invecchieremmo**
voi	**invecchiereste**
loro	**invecchierebbero**

PAST HISTORIC

io	**invecchiai**
tu	**invecchiasti**
lui/lei/Lei	**invecchiò**
noi	**invecchiammo**
voi	**invecchiaste**
loro	**invecchiarono**

PLUPERFECT

io	**ero invecchiato/a**
tu	**eri invecchiato/a**
lui/lei/Lei	**era invecchiato/a**
noi	**eravamo invecchiati/e**
voi	**eravate invecchiati/e**
loro	**erano invecchiati/e**

IMPERATIVE

invecchia
invecchiamo
invecchiate

EXAMPLE PHRASES

Quando la rividi **era** molto **invecchiata**. When I saw her again she'd aged a lot.

inviare (to send)

PRESENT

io	**invio**
tu	**invii**
lui/lei/Lei	**invia**
noi	**inviamo**
voi	**inviate**
loro	**inviano**

PRESENT SUBJUNCTIVE

io	**invii**
tu	**invii**
lui/lei/Lei	**invii**
noi	**inviamo**
voi	**inviate**
loro	**inviino**

PERFECT

io	**ho inviato**
tu	**hai inviato**
lui/lei/Lei	**ha inviato**
noi	**abbiamo inviato**
voi	**avete inviato**
loro	**hanno inviato**

IMPERFECT

io	**inviavo**
tu	**inviavi**
lui/lei/Lei	**inviava**
noi	**inviavamo**
voi	**inviavate**
loro	**inviavano**

GERUND

inviando

PAST PARTICIPLE

inviato

EXAMPLE PHRASES

Per prenotare è necessario che tu **invii** una mail. You have to send an email to book.

Non **ho** ancora **inviato** la domanda di iscrizione. I haven't sent the enrolment form off yet.

Il figlio le **inviava** un sms tutte le sere. Her son texted her every evening.

Potete partecipare **inviando** il video. You can take part by sending a videoclip.

Remember that subject pronouns are not used very often in Italian.

inviare

FUTURE

io	**invierò**
tu	**invierai**
lui/lei/Lei	**invierà**
noi	**invieremo**
voi	**invierete**
loro	**invieranno**

CONDITIONAL

io	**invierei**
tu	**invieresti**
lui/lei/Lei	**invierebbe**
noi	**invieremmo**
voi	**inviereste**
loro	**invierebbero**

PAST HISTORIC

io	**inviai**
tu	**inviasti**
lui/lei/Lei	**inviò**
noi	**inviammo**
voi	**inviaste**
loro	**inviarono**

PLUPERFECT

io	**avevo inviato**
tu	**avevi inviato**
lui/lei/Lei	**aveva inviato**
noi	**avevamo inviato**
voi	**avevate inviato**
loro	**avevano inviato**

IMPERATIVE

invia
inviamo
inviate

EXAMPLE PHRASES

Vi **invieremo** ulteriori dettagli in seguito. We will send you further details later.

Ti **invierei** le informazioni, ma non ho la tua mail. I'd send you the information, but I haven't got your email address.

Quando arrivi, **inviami** un sms. Text me when you arrive.

Italic letters in Italian words show where stress does not follow the usual rules.

lasciare (to leave)

PRESENT

io	**lascio**
tu	**lasci**
lui/lei/Lei	**lascia**
noi	**lasciamo**
voi	**lasciate**
loro	**lasciano**

PRESENT SUBJUNCTIVE

io	**lasci**
tu	**lasci**
lui/lei/Lei	**lasci**
noi	**lasciamo**
voi	**lasciate**
loro	**lascino**

PERFECT

io	**ho lasciato**
tu	**hai lasciato**
lui/lei/Lei	**ha lasciato**
noi	**abbiamo lasciato**
voi	**avete lasciato**
loro	**hanno lasciato**

IMPERFECT

io	**lasciavo**
tu	**lasciavi**
lui/lei/Lei	**lasciava**
noi	**lasciavamo**
voi	**lasciavate**
loro	**lasciavano**

GERUND

lasciando

PAST PARTICIPLE

lasciato

EXAMPLE PHRASES

Mio padre non mi **lascia** uscire fino a tardi. My father doesn't let me stay out late.

È meglio che tu **lasci** acceso il vivavoce. You'd better leave the loudspeaker on.

I miei si **sono lasciati** un anno fa. My parents split up a year ago.

La madre non lo **lasciava** mai solo un minuto. His mother never left him alone for a single minute.

Remember that subject pronouns are not used very often in Italian.

lasciare

FUTURE

io	**lascerò**
tu	**lascerai**
lui/lei/Lei	**lascerà**
noi	**lasceremo**
voi	**lascerete**
loro	**lasceranno**

CONDITIONAL

io	**lascerei**
tu	**lasceresti**
lui/lei/Lei	**lascerebbe**
noi	**lasceremmo**
voi	**lascereste**
loro	**lascerebbero**

PAST HISTORIC

io	**lasciai**
tu	**lasciasti**
lui/lei/Lei	**lasciò**
noi	**lasciammo**
voi	**lasciaste**
loro	**lasciarono**

PLUPERFECT

io	**avevo lasciato**
tu	**avevi lasciato**
lui/lei/Lei	**aveva lasciato**
noi	**avevamo lasciato**
voi	**avevate lasciato**
loro	**avevano lasciato**

IMPERATIVE

lascia
lasciamo
lasciate

EXAMPLE PHRASES

Fa caldo, **lascerò** a casa il maglione. It's hot, so I'll leave my jumper at home.

Il marito la **lasciò** per un'altra. Her husband left her for another woman.

Lascia fare a me. Let me do it.

Lasciamo stare, non vale la pena arrabbiarsi. Let's forget it, it's not worth getting angry about.

Italic letters in Italian words show where stress does not follow the usual rules.

leggere (to read)

PRESENT

io	**leggo**
tu	**leggi**
lui/lei/Lei	**legge**
noi	**leggiamo**
voi	**leggete**
loro	**leggono**

PRESENT SUBJUNCTIVE

io	**legga**
tu	**legga**
lui/lei/Lei	**legga**
noi	**leggiamo**
voi	**leggiate**
loro	**leggano**

PERFECT

io	**ho letto**
tu	**hai letto**
lui/lei/Lei	**ha letto**
noi	**abbiamo letto**
voi	**avete letto**
loro	**hanno letto**

IMPERFECT

io	**leggevo**
tu	**leggevi**
lui/lei/Lei	**leggeva**
noi	**leggevamo**
voi	**leggevate**
loro	**leggevano**

GERUND

leggendo

PAST PARTICIPLE

letto

EXAMPLE PHRASES

Legge il giornale tutti i giorni. She reads the paper every day.

Non **ho** ancora **letto** quel libro. I haven't read that book yet.

Leggevo molto prima di iniziare a lavorare. I read a lot before I started working.

Non li disturbiamo: stanno **leggendo**. Don't let's disturb them, they're reading.

Le piace molto **leggere**. She loves reading.

Remember that subject pronouns are not used very often in Italian.

leggere

FUTURE

io	**leggerò**
tu	**leggerai**
lui/lei/Lei	**leggerà**
noi	**leggeremo**
voi	**leggerete**
loro	**leggeranno**

CONDITIONAL

io	**leggerei**
tu	**leggeresti**
lui/lei/Lei	**leggerebbe**
noi	**leggeremmo**
voi	**leggereste**
loro	**leggerebbero**

PAST HISTORIC

io	**lessi**
tu	**leggesti**
lui/lei/Lei	**lesse**
noi	**leggemmo**
voi	**leggeste**
loro	**lessero**

PLUPERFECT

io	**avevo letto**
tu	**avevi letto**
lui/lei/Lei	**aveva letto**
noi	**avevamo letto**
voi	**avevate letto**
loro	**avevano letto**

IMPERATIVE

leggi
leggiamo
leggete

EXAMPLE PHRASES

Durante le vacanze **leggerò** un romanzo. I'll read a novel during the holidays.

Mi **leggeresti** le istruzioni? Sono senza occhiali. Could you read me the instructions? I haven't got my glasses.

Leggete a voce alta, per favore. Read aloud please.

Italic letters in Italian words show where stress does not follow the usual rules.

mangiare (to eat)

PRESENT

io	**mangio**
tu	**mangi**
lui/lei/Lei	**mangia**
noi	**mangiamo**
voi	**mangiate**
loro	**mangiano**

PRESENT SUBJUNCTIVE

io	**mangi**
tu	**mangi**
lui/lei/Lei	**mangi**
noi	**mangiamo**
voi	**mangiate**
loro	**mangino**

PERFECT

io	**ho mangiato**
tu	**hai mangiato**
lui/lei/Lei	**ha mangiato**
noi	**abbiamo mangiato**
voi	**avete mangiato**
loro	**hanno mangiato**

IMPERFECT

io	**mangiavo**
tu	**mangiavi**
lui/lei/Lei	**mangiava**
noi	**mangiavamo**
voi	**mangiavate**
loro	**mangiavano**

GERUND

mangiando

PAST PARTICIPLE

mangiato

EXAMPLE PHRASES

Non **mangio** carne. I don't eat meat.

Si **mangia** bene in quel ristorante. The food is good in that restaurant.

Chi **ha mangiato** l'ultima fetta di torta? Who ate the last slice of cake?

Ultimamente sto **mangiando** troppo. I've been eating too much lately.

Remember that subject pronouns are not used very often in Italian.

mangiare

FUTURE

io	mangerò
tu	mangerai
lui/lei/Lei	mangerà
noi	mangeremo
voi	mangerete
loro	mangeranno

CONDITIONAL

io	mangerei
tu	mangeresti
lui/lei/Lei	mangerebbe
noi	mangeremmo
voi	mangereste
loro	mangerebbero

PAST HISTORIC

io	mangiai
tu	mangiasti
lui/lei/Lei	mangiò
noi	mangiammo
voi	mangiaste
loro	mangiarono

PLUPERFECT

io	avevo mangiato
tu	avevi mangiato
lui/lei/Lei	aveva mangiato
noi	avevamo mangiato
voi	avevate mangiato
loro	avevano mangiato

IMPERATIVE

mangia
mangiamo
mangiate

EXAMPLE PHRASES

Domani **mangeremo** pesce. We'll have fish tomorrow.

Mangerei volentieri del gelato. I'd like some ice cream.

Mangiarono troppo e fecero indigestione. They ate too much and got indigestion.

Mangia che la minestra si raffredda. Eat your soup, it's getting cold.

Italic letters in Italian words show where stress does not follow the usual rules.

mettere (to put)

PRESENT		PRESENT SUBJUNCTIVE	
io	metto	io	metta
tu	metti	tu	metta
lui/lei/Lei	mette	lui/lei/Lei	metta
noi	mettiamo	noi	mettiamo
voi	mettete	voi	mettiate
loro	mettono	loro	mettano

PERFECT		IMPERFECT	
io	ho messo	io	mettevo
tu	hai messo	tu	mettevi
lui/lei/Lei	ha messo	lui/lei/Lei	metteva
noi	abbiamo messo	noi	mettevamo
voi	avete messo	voi	mettevate
loro	hanno messo	loro	mettevano

GERUND

mettendo

PAST PARTICIPLE

messo

EXAMPLE PHRASES

Non **metto** più quelle scarpe. I don't wear those shoes any more.

È meglio che tu **metta** la sveglia. You'd better set the alarm.

Hai messo i bambini a letto? Have you put the children to bed?

Quanto tempo ci **hai messo**? How long did it take you?

Si **metteva** sempre un vecchio maglione blu. She always wore an old blue jumper.

Remember that subject pronouns are not used very often in Italian.

mettere

FUTURE

io	**metterò**
tu	**metterai**
lui/lei/Lei	**metterà**
noi	**metteremo**
voi	**metterete**
loro	**metteranno**

CONDITIONAL

io	**metterei**
tu	**metteresti**
lui/lei/Lei	**metterebbe**
noi	**metteremmo**
voi	**mettereste**
loro	**metterebbero**

PAST HISTORIC

io	**misi**
tu	**mettesti**
lui/lei/Lei	**mise**
noi	**mettemmo**
voi	**metteste**
loro	**misero**

PLUPERFECT

io	**avevo messo**
tu	**avevi messo**
lui/lei/Lei	**aveva messo**
noi	**avevamo messo**
voi	**avevate messo**
loro	**avevano messo**

IMPERATIVE

metti
mettiamo
mettete

EXAMPLE PHRASES

Metterò un annuncio sul giornale. I'll put an advert in the paper.

Quanto ci **metteresti** lavorando giorno e notte? How long would it take you if you worked day and night?

Si **misero** a sedere e aspettarono. They sat down and waited.

Mettiti là e aspetta. Wait there.

Italic letters in Italian words show where stress does not follow the usual rules.

morire (to die)

PRESENT

io	**muoio**
tu	**muori**
lui/lei/Lei	**muore**
noi	**moriamo**
voi	**morite**
loro	**muoiono**

PRESENT SUBJUNCTIVE

io	**muoia**
tu	**muoia**
lui/lei/Lei	**muoia**
noi	**moriamo**
voi	**moriate**
loro	**muoiano**

PERFECT

io	**sono morto/a**
tu	**sei morto/a**
lui/lei/Lei	**è morto/a**
noi	**siamo morti/e**
voi	**siete morti/e**
loro	**sono morti/e**

IMPERFECT

io	**morivo**
tu	**morivi**
lui/lei/Lei	**moriva**
noi	**morivamo**
voi	**morivate**
loro	**morivano**

GERUND

morendo

PAST PARTICIPLE

morto

EXAMPLE PHRASES

Muoio di sete. I'm parched.

Sono morti in un incidente. They were killed in an accident.

Sta **morendo** di fame. She's starving.

Moriva dalla voglia di raccontarle tutto. He was dying to tell her everything.

Remember that subject pronouns are not used very often in Italian.

morire

FUTURE

io	**morirò**
tu	**morirai**
lui/lei/Lei	**morirà**
noi	**moriremo**
voi	**morirete**
loro	**moriranno**

CONDITIONAL

io	**morirei**
tu	**moriresti**
lui/lei/Lei	**morirebbe**
noi	**moriremmo**
voi	**morireste**
loro	**morirebbero**

PAST HISTORIC

io	**morii**
tu	**moristi**
lui/lei/Lei	**morì**
noi	**morimmo**
voi	**moriste**
loro	**morirono**

PLUPERFECT

io	**ero morto/a**
tu	**eri morto/a**
lui/lei/Lei	**era morto/a**
noi	**eravamo morti/e**
voi	**eravate morti/e**
loro	**erano morti/e**

IMPERATIVE

muori
moriamo
morite

EXAMPLE PHRASES

Morirei di paura, ma lo farei. I'd be scared to death, but I'd do it.

Morì nel 1857. He died in 1857.

Il padre **era morto** in un incidente stradale. His father had been killed in a car crash.

Italic letters in Italian words show where stress does not follow the usual rules.

muovere (to move)

PRESENT

io	**muovo**
tu	**muovi**
lui/lei/Lei	**muove**
noi	**muoviamo**
voi	**muovete**
loro	**muovono**

PRESENT SUBJUNCTIVE

io	**muova**
tu	**muova**
lui/lei/Lei	**muova**
noi	**muoviamo**
voi	**muoviate**
loro	**muovano**

PERFECT

io	**ho mosso**
tu	**hai mosso**
lui/lei/Lei	**ha mosso**
noi	**abbiamo mosso**
voi	**avete mosso**
loro	**hanno mosso**

IMPERFECT

io	**muovevo**
tu	**muovevi**
lui/lei/Lei	**muoveva**
noi	**muovevamo**
voi	**muovevate**
loro	**muovevano**

GERUND

muovendo

PAST PARTICIPLE

mosso

EXAMPLE PHRASES

Non si **muove**. It won't move.

Ho mosso l'alfiere per dare scacco al re. I moved the bishop to check the king.

Ti **sei mosso** e la foto è sfocata. You moved and the photo is out of focus.

Non **muovevo** più la gamba per il dolore. I could no longer move my leg because of the pain.

Il meccanismo si aziona **muovendo** la leva. You work the mechanism by moving the lever.

Remember that subject pronouns are not used very often in Italian.

muovere

FUTURE

io	muoverò
tu	muoverai
lui/lei/Lei	muoverà
noi	muoveremo
voi	muoverete
loro	muoveranno

CONDITIONAL

io	muoverei
tu	muoveresti
lui/lei/Lei	muoverebbe
noi	muoveremmo
voi	muovereste
loro	muoverebbero

PAST HISTORIC

io	mossi
tu	muovesti
lui/lei/Lei	mosse
noi	muovemmo
voi	muoveste
loro	mossero

PLUPERFECT

io	avevo mosso
tu	avevi mosso
lui/lei/Lei	aveva mosso
noi	avevamo mosso
voi	avevate mosso
loro	avevano mosso

IMPERATIVE

muovi
muoviamo
muovete

EXAMPLE PHRASES

Non ti **muovere**! Don't move!

Muoviti, o perdiamo il treno! Hurry up, or we'll miss the train!

Italic letters in Italian words show where stress does not follow the usual rules.

nascere (to be born)

	PRESENT		PRESENT SUBJUNCTIVE
io	nasco	io	nasca
tu	nasci	tu	nasca
lui/lei/Lei	nasce	lui/lei/Lei	nasca
noi	nasciamo	noi	nasciamo
voi	nascete	voi	nasciate
loro	nascono	loro	nascano

	PERFECT		IMPERFECT
io	sono nato/a	io	nascevo
tu	sei nato/a	tu	nascevi
lui/lei/Lei	è nato/a	lui/lei/Lei	nasceva
noi	siamo nati/e	noi	nascevamo
voi	siete nati/e	voi	nascevate
loro	sono nati/e	loro	nascevano

GERUND

nascendo

PAST PARTICIPLE

nato

EXAMPLE PHRASES

Speriamo che il bambino **nasca** dopo il trasloco. We're hoping the baby will be born after the move.

Sono nata il 28 aprile. I was born on the 28th of April.

È nato nel 1998. He was born in 1998.

Remember that subject pronouns are not used very often in Italian.

nascere

FUTURE

io	**nascerò**
tu	**nascerai**
lui/lei/Lei	**nascerà**
noi	**nasceremo**
voi	**nascerete**
loro	**nasceranno**

CONDITIONAL

io	**nascerei**
tu	**nasceresti**
lui/lei/Lei	**nascerebbe**
noi	**nasceremmo**
voi	**nascereste**
loro	**nascerebbero**

PAST HISTORIC

io	**nacqui**
tu	**nascesti**
lui/lei/Lei	**nacque**
noi	**nascemmo**
voi	**nasceste**
loro	**nacquero**

PLUPERFECT

io	**ero nato/a**
tu	**eri nato/a**
lui/lei/Lei	**era nato/a**
noi	**eravamo nati/e**
voi	**eravate nati/e**
loro	**erano nati/e**

IMPERATIVE

nasci
nasciamo
nascete

EXAMPLE PHRASES

Il bambino **nascerà** tra due settimane. The baby is due in two weeks.

Franz Kafka **nacque** nel 1883. Franz Kafka was born in 1883.

Lasciò molto presto la casa dove **era nato**. Very soon he left the house where he was born.

Italic letters in Italian words show where stress does not follow the usual rules.

nuocere (to harm)

PRESENT

io	**nuoccio**
tu	**nuoci**
lui/lei/Lei	**nuoce**
noi	**nuociamo**
voi	**nuocete**
loro	**nuocciono**

PRESENT SUBJUNCTIVE

io	**nuoccia**
tu	**nuoccia**
lui/lei/Lei	**nuoccia**
noi	**nuociamo**
voi	**nuociate**
loro	**nuocciano**

PERFECT

io	**ho nuociuto**
tu	**hai nuociuto**
lui/lei/Lei	**ha nuociuto**
noi	**abbiamo nuociuto**
voi	**avete nuociuto**
loro	**hanno nuociuto**

IMPERFECT

io	**nuocevo**
tu	**nuocevi**
lui/lei/Lei	**nuoceva**
noi	**nuocevamo**
voi	**nuocevate**
loro	**nuocevano**

GERUND

nuocendo

PAST PARTICIPLE

nuociuto

EXAMPLE PHRASES

Il fumo **nuoce** alla salute. Smoking is bad for your health.

Si pensa che **nuoccia** all'ambiente. It is thought to be bad for the environment.

Le cattive conoscenze **hanno nuociuto** alla sua reputazione. His disreputable associates have damaged his reputation.

Anche se gli **nuoceva**, continuava a bere. Despite the harm it was doing him, he went on drinking.

Remember that subject pronouns are not used very often in Italian.

nuocere

FUTURE

io	**nuocerò**
tu	**nuocerai**
lui/lei/Lei	**nuocerà**
noi	**nuoceremo**
voi	**nuocerete**
loro	**nuoceranno**

CONDITIONAL

io	**nuocerei**
tu	**nuoceresti**
lui/lei/Lei	**nuocerebbe**
noi	**nuoceremmo**
voi	**nuocereste**
loro	**nuocerebbero**

PAST HISTORIC

io	**nocqui**
tu	**nuocesti**
lui/lei/Lei	**nocque**
noi	**nuocemmo**
voi	**nuoceste**
loro	**nocquero**

PLUPERFECT

io	**avevo nuociuto**
tu	**avevi nuociuto**
lui/lei/Lei	**aveva nuociuto**
noi	**avevamo nuociuto**
voi	**avevate nuociuto**
loro	**avevano nuociuto**

IMPERATIVE

nuoci
nuociamo
nuocete

EXAMPLE PHRASES

Un po' di vino non ti **nuocerà**. A drop of wine won't do you any harm.

Una settimana al mare non mi **nuocerebbe**. A week at the seaside would do me no harm.

Italic letters in Italian words show where stress does not follow the usual rules.

offendere (to offend)

PRESENT

io	offendo
tu	offendi
lui/lei/Lei	offende
noi	offendiamo
voi	offendete
loro	offendono

PRESENT SUBJUNCTIVE

io	offenda
tu	offenda
lui/lei/Lei	offenda
noi	offendiamo
voi	offendiate
loro	offendano

PERFECT

io	ho offeso
tu	hai offeso
lui/lei/Lei	ha offeso
noi	abbiamo offeso
voi	avete offeso
loro	hanno offeso

IMPERFECT

io	offendevo
tu	offendevi
lui/lei/Lei	offendeva
noi	offendevamo
voi	offendevate
loro	offendevano

GERUND

offendendo

PAST PARTICIPLE

offeso

EXAMPLE PHRASES

Se non vieni mi **offendo**. I'll be offended if you don't come.

Si è **offeso** per non essere stato invitato. He took offence because they didn't invite him.

Da piccolo si **offendeva** per un nonnulla. When he was a little boy he got upset over the slightest thing.

Cambia tono: mi stai **offendendo**! Don't talk like that: I find it offensive.

Non avevo intenzione di **offenderti**. I didn't mean to insult you.

Remember that subject pronouns are not used very often in Italian.

offendere

FUTURE

io	**offenderò**
tu	**offenderai**
lui/lei/Lei	**offenderà**
noi	**offenderemo**
voi	**offenderete**
loro	**offenderanno**

CONDITIONAL

io	**offenderei**
tu	**offenderesti**
lui/lei/Lei	**offenderebbe**
noi	**offenderemmo**
voi	**offendereste**
loro	**offenderebbero**

PAST HISTORIC

io	**offesi**
tu	**offendesti**
lui/lei/Lei	**offese**
noi	**offendemmo**
voi	**offendeste**
loro	**offesero**

PLUPERFECT

io	**avevo offeso**
tu	**avevi offeso**
lui/lei/Lei	**aveva offeso**
noi	**avevamo offeso**
voi	**avevate offeso**
loro	**avevano offeso**

IMPERATIVE

offendi
offendiamo
offendete

EXAMPLE PHRASES

Dimmi tutto: prometto che non mi **offenderò**. Tell me everything: I promise
I won't be offended.

Se glielo dicessi, si **offenderebbe**. If I told him that he'd be offended.

L'**avevamo offeso** e non ci parlava più. We'd offended him and he wouldn't
speak to us any more.

Italic letters in Italian words show where stress does not follow the usual rules.

offrire (to offer)

PRESENT

io	**offro**
tu	**offri**
lui/lei/Lei	**offre**
noi	**offriamo**
voi	**offrite**
loro	**offrono**

PRESENT SUBJUNCTIVE

io	**offra**
tu	**offra**
lui/lei/Lei	**offra**
noi	**offriamo**
voi	**offriate**
loro	**offrano**

PERFECT

io	**ho offerto**
tu	**hai offerto**
lui/lei/Lei	**ha offerto**
noi	**abbiamo offerto**
voi	**avete offerto**
loro	**hanno offerto**

IMPERFECT

io	**offrivo**
tu	**offrivi**
lui/lei/Lei	**offriva**
noi	**offrivamo**
voi	**offrivate**
loro	**offrivano**

GERUND

offrendo

PAST PARTICIPLE

offerto

EXAMPLE PHRASES

Offro io, questa volta! I'll pay this time!

Spero si **offrano** di aiutarci. I hope they'll offer to help us.

Mi **ha offerto** un passaggio. He offered me a lift.

Nessuno si **è offerto** volontario. Nobody volunteered.

Offriva sempre il suo aiuto a tutti. She always offered help to everyone.

Remember that subject pronouns are not used very often in Italian.

offrire

FUTURE

io	**offrirò**
tu	**offrirai**
lui/lei/Lei	**offrirà**
noi	**offriremo**
voi	**offrirete**
loro	**offriranno**

CONDITIONAL

io	**offrirei**
tu	**offriresti**
lui/lei/Lei	**offrirebbe**
noi	**offriremmo**
voi	**offrireste**
loro	**offrirebbero**

PAST HISTORIC

io	**offrii**
tu	**offristi**
lui/lei/Lei	**offrì**
noi	**offrimmo**
voi	**offriste**
loro	**offrirono**

PLUPERFECT

Io	**avevo offerto**
tu	**avevi offerto**
lui/lei/Lei	**aveva offerto**
noi	**avevamo offerto**
voi	**avevate offerto**
loro	**avevano offerto**

IMPERATIVE

offri
offriamo
offrite

EXAMPLE PHRASES

L'università **offrirà** consulenza e orientamento. The university will provide guidance and advice.

Mi **offriresti** una sigaretta? Could you let me have a cigarette?

Le **offrirono** un lavoro. They offered her a job.

Offri da bere agli amici! Offer our friends a drink!

Italic letters in Italian words show where stress does not follow the usual rules.

pagare (to pay)

PRESENT

io	**pago**
tu	**paghi**
lui/lei/Lei	**paga**
noi	**paghiamo**
voi	**pagate**
loro	**pagano**

PRESENT SUBJUNCTIVE

io	**paghi**
tu	**paghi**
lui/lei/Lei	**paghi**
noi	**paghiamo**
voi	**paghiate**
loro	**paghino**

PERFECT

io	**ho pagato**
tu	**hai pagato**
lui/lei/Lei	**ha pagato**
noi	**abbiamo pagato**
voi	**avete pagato**
loro	**hanno pagato**

IMPERFECT

io	**pagavo**
tu	**pagavi**
lui/lei/Lei	**pagava**
noi	**pagavamo**
voi	**pagavate**
loro	**pagavano**

GERUND

pagando

PAST PARTICIPLE

pagato

EXAMPLE PHRASES

Pago io. I'll pay.

Hai pagato il conto? Have you paid the bill?

Quando uscivamo insieme **pagava** sempre lui. When we went out together he always paid.

Pagando si ottiene tutto. You can get anything if you pay for it.

Avevo finito di **pagare** la macchina il giorno dell'incidente. I'd finished paying for the car on the day of the accident.

Remember that subject pronouns are not used very often in Italian.

pagare

FUTURE

io	pagherò
tu	pagherai
lui/lei/Lei	pagherà
noi	pagheremo
voi	pagherete
loro	pagheranno

CONDITIONAL

io	pagherei
tu	pagheresti
lui/lei/Lei	pagherebbe
noi	pagheremmo
voi	paghereste
loro	pagherebbero

PAST HISTORIC

io	pagai
tu	pagasti
lui/lei/Lei	pagò
noi	pagammo
voi	pagaste
loro	pagarono

PLUPERFECT

io	avevo pagato
tu	avevi pagato
lui/lei/Lei	aveva pagato
noi	avevamo pagato
voi	avevate pagato
loro	avevano pagato

IMPERATIVE

paga
paghiamo
pagate

EXAMPLE PHRASES

La **pagherai**! You'll pay for this!

Pagherei io, ma non accettano carte di credito. I'd pay, but they don't accept credit cards.

Pagò un conto salatissimo. She paid an enormous bill.

Paga tu stavolta! You pay this time!

Italic letters in Italian words show where stress does not follow the usual rules.

parere (to appear)

	PRESENT		PRESENT SUBJUNCTIVE
io	paio	io	paia
tu	pari	tu	paia
lui/lei/Lei	pare	lui/lei/Lei	paia
noi	pariamo	noi	paiamo
voi	parete	voi	paiate
loro	paiono	loro	paiano

	PERFECT		IMPERFECT
io	sono parso/a	io	parevo
tu	sei parso/a	tu	parevi
lui/lei/Lei	è parso/a	lui/lei/Lei	pareva
noi	siamo parsi/e	noi	parevamo
voi	siete parsi/e	voi	parevate
loro	sono parsi/e	loro	parevano

GERUND

parendo

PAST PARTICIPLE

parso

EXAMPLE PHRASES

Mi **pare** che sia già arrivato. I think he's already here.

Ci **è parso** che foste stanchi. We thought you were tired.

Faceva solo ciò che gli **pareva**. He did just what he liked.

parere

FUTURE

io	**parrò**
tu	**parrai**
lui/lei/Lei	**parrà**
noi	**parremo**
voi	**parrete**
loro	**parranno**

CONDITIONAL

io	**parrei**
tu	**parresti**
lui/lei/Lei	**parrebbe**
noi	**parremmo**
voi	**parreste**
loro	**parrebbero**

PAST HISTORIC

io	**parvi**
tu	**paresti**
lui/lei/Lei	**parve**
noi	**paremmo**
voi	**pareste**
loro	**parvero**

PLUPERFECT

io	**ero parso/a**
tu	**eri parso/a**
lui/lei/Lei	**era parso/a**
noi	**eravamo parsi/e**
voi	**eravate parsi/e**
loro	**erano parsi/e**

IMPERATIVE

pari
pariamo
parete

EXAMPLE PHRASES

Mi **parrebbe** di disturbare. I wouldn't want to be a nuisance.

Gli **parve** che non lo volessero con loro. He thought they didn't want him with them.

Quella sera mi **parvero** tutti ubriachi. They all seemed drunk that night.

Mi **era parso** che volessi da bere. I'd thought you wanted something to drink.

Italic letters in Italian words show where stress does not follow the usual rules.

parlare (to speak)

PRESENT

io	parlo
tu	parli
lui/lei/Lei	parla
noi	parliamo
voi	parlate
loro	parlano

PRESENT SUBJUNCTIVE

io	parli
tu	parli
lui/lei/Lei	parli
noi	parliamo
voi	parliate
loro	parlino

PERFECT

io	ho parlato
tu	hai parlato
lui/lei/Lei	ha parlato
noi	abbiamo parlato
voi	avete parlato
loro	hanno parlato

IMPERFECT

io	parlavo
tu	parlavi
lui/lei/Lei	parlava
noi	parlavamo
voi	parlavate
loro	parlavano

GERUND

parlando

PAST PARTICIPLE

parlato

EXAMPLE PHRASES

Pronto, chi **parla**? Hello, who's speaking?

Di cosa **parla** quel libro? What is that book about?

Lascia che gli **parli** io. Let me talk to him.

Abbiamo parlato per ore. We talked for hours.

Passammo il pomeriggio **parlando** del più e del meno. We spent the afternoon talking about this and that.

Remember that subject pronouns are not used very often in Italian.

parlare

FUTURE

io	parlerò
tu	parlerai
lui/lei/Lei	parlerà
noi	parleremo
voi	parlerete
loro	parleranno

CONDITIONAL

io	parlerei
tu	parleresti
lui/lei/Lei	parlerebbe
noi	parleremmo
voi	parlereste
loro	parlerebbero

PAST HISTORIC

io	parlai
tu	parlasti
lui/lei/Lei	parlò
noi	parlammo
voi	parlaste
loro	parlarono

PLUPERFECT

io	avevo parlato
tu	avevi parlato
lui/lei/Lei	aveva parlato
noi	avevamo parlato
voi	avevate parlato
loro	avevano parlato

IMPERATIVE

parla
parliamo
parlate

EXAMPLE PHRASES

Gli **parlerò** di te. I'll talk to him about you.

Non **parlerei** mai male dei miei amici. I'd never speak ill of my friends.

Mi **avevano** già **parlato** di te. They'd already talked to me about you.

Non **parliamone** più. Let's just forget about it.

Italic letters in Italian words show where stress does not follow the usual rules.

pescare (to fish)

PRESENT

io	pesco
tu	peschi
lui/lei/Lei	pesca
noi	peschiamo
voi	pescate
loro	pescano

PRESENT SUBJUNCTIVE

io	peschi
tu	peschi
lui/lei/Lei	peschi
noi	peschiamo
voi	peschiate
loro	peschino

PERFECT

io	ho pescato
tu	hai pescato
lui/lei/Lei	ha pescato
noi	abbiamo pescato
voi	avete pescato
loro	hanno pescato

IMPERFECT

io	pescavo
tu	pescavi
lui/lei/Lei	pescava
noi	pescavamo
voi	pescavate
loro	pescavano

GERUND

pescando

PAST PARTICIPLE

pescato

EXAMPLE PHRASES

Ho pescato un pesce enorme. I caught an enormous fish.

Dove diavolo **hai pescato** quella giacca? Where on earth did you get that jacket?

Ti insegnerò a **pescare**. I'll teach you how to fish.

Remember that subject pronouns are not used very often in Italian.

pescare

FUTURE

io	**pescherò**
tu	**pescherai**
lui/lei/Lei	**pescherà**
noi	**pescheremo**
voi	**pescherete**
loro	**pescheranno**

CONDITIONAL

io	**pescherei**
tu	**pescheresti**
lui/lei/Lei	**pescherebbe**
noi	**pescheremmo**
voi	**peschereste**
loro	**pescherebbero**

PAST HISTORIC

io	**pescai**
tu	**pescasti**
lui/lei/Lei	**pescò**
noi	**pescammo**
voi	**pescaste**
loro	**pescarono**

PLUPERFECT

io	**avevo pescato**
tu	**avevi pescato**
lui/lei/Lei	**aveva pescato**
noi	**avevamo pescato**
voi	**avevate pescato**
loro	**avevano pescato**

IMPERATIVE

pesca
peschiamo
pescate

EXAMPLE PHRASES

Io **pescherò** il pesce e tu lo cucinerai. I'll catch the fish and you can cook it.

Pescammo tutto il giorno. We fished all day.

Avevano pescato molto pesce per la cena. They'd caught a lot of fish for dinner.

Italic letters in Italian words show where stress does not follow the usual rules.

piacere (to be pleasing)

PRESENT

io	**piaccio**
tu	**piaci**
lui/lei/Lei	**piace**
noi	**piacciamo**
voi	**piacete**
loro	**piacciono**

PRESENT SUBJUNCTIVE

io	**piaccia**
tu	**piaccia**
lui/lei/Lei	**piaccia**
noi	**piacciamo**
voi	**piacciate**
loro	**piacciano**

PERFECT

io	**sono piaciuto/a**
tu	**sei piaciuto/a**
lui/lei/Lei	**è piaciuto/a**
noi	**siamo piaciuti/e**
voi	**siete piaciuti/e**
loro	**sono piaciuti/e**

IMPERFECT

io	**piacevo**
tu	**piacevi**
lui/lei/Lei	**piaceva**
noi	**piacevamo**
voi	**piacevate**
loro	**piacevano**

GERUND

piacendo

PAST PARTICIPLE

piaciuto

EXAMPLE PHRASES

Questa musica non mi **piace**. I don't like this music.

Spero che il regalo vi **piaccia**. I hope you like the present.

La birra non le è mai **piaciuta**. She's never liked beer.

Da piccola non mi **piacevano** i ragni. I didn't like spiders when I was little.

Remember that subject pronouns are not used very often in Italian.

piacere

FUTURE

io	**piacerò**
tu	**piacerai**
lui/lei/Lei	**piacerà**
noi	**piaceremo**
voi	**piacerete**
loro	**piaceranno**

CONDITIONAL

io	**piacerei**
tu	**piaceresti**
lui/lei/Lei	**piacerebbe**
noi	**piaceremmo**
voi	**piacereste**
loro	**piacerebbero**

PAST HISTORIC

io	**piacqui**
tu	**piacesti**
lui/lei/Lei	**piacque**
noi	**piacemmo**
voi	**piaceste**
loro	**piacquero**

PLUPERFECT

io	**ero piaciuto/a**
tu	**eri piaciuto/a**
lui/lei/Lei	**era piaciuto/a**
noi	**eravamo piaciuti/e**
voi	**eravate piaciuti/e**
loro	**erano piaciuti/e**

IMPERATIVE

piaci
piacciamo
piacete

EXAMPLE PHRASES

La nuova casa ti **piacerà**, vedrai. You'll like the new house, you'll see.

Cosa ti **piacerebbe** fare? What would you like to do?

Mi **piacque** appena la vidi. I liked her as soon as I saw her.

Vi **era piaciuto** il film? Did you like the film?

Italic letters in Italian words show where stress does not follow the usual rules.

piovere (to rain)

PRESENT
piove

PRESENT SUBJUNCTIVE
piova

PERFECT
ha *or* è piovuto

IMPERFECT
pioveva

GERUND
piovendo

PAST PARTICIPLE
piovuto

EXAMPLE PHRASES

Piove. It's raining.

Speriamo che non **piova**. Let's hope it doesn't rain.

Ha piovuto tutto il giorno. It's rained all day.

Quando sono uscita **pioveva**. When I went out it was raining.

Sta **piovendo**: prendi l'ombrello. It's raining – take your umbrella.

Remember that subject pronouns are not used very often in Italian.

piovere

FUTURE
piover*à*

CONDITIONAL
pioverebbe

PAST HISTORIC
plovve

PLUPERFECT
era *or* aveva piovuto

IMPERATIVE
-

EXAMPLE PHRASES

Guarda che nubi: **piover*à*** di certo. Look at those clouds – it's going to rain for sure.

Piovve tutta la notte. It rained all night.

Aveva piovuto e le strade *e*rano bagnate. It had been raining and the roads were wet.

Italic letters in Italian words show where stress does not follow the usual rules.

potere (to be able)

PRESENT		PRESENT SUBJUNCTIVE	
io	posso	io	possa
tu	puoi	tu	possa
lui/lei/Lei	può	lui/lei/Lei	possa
noi	possiamo	noi	possiamo
voi	potete	voi	possiate
loro	possono	loro	possano

PERFECT		IMPERFECT	
io	ho potuto	io	potevo
tu	hai potuto	tu	potevi
lui/lei/Lei	ha potuto	lui/lei/Lei	poteva
noi	abbiamo potuto	noi	potevamo
voi	avete potuto	voi	potevate
loro	hanno potuto	loro	potevano

GERUND	PAST PARTICIPLE
potendo	potuto

EXAMPLE PHRASES

Si **può** visitare il castello tutti i giorni dell'anno. You can visit the castle any day of the year.

Può aver avuto un incidente. She may have had an accident.

Speriamo che voi **possiate** aiutarci. We hope you can help us.

Non è **potuto** venire. He couldn't come.

Non sono venuti perché non **potevano**. They didn't come because they weren't able to.

Potendo, eviterei di partire domani. I'd avoid setting off tomorrow if I could.

Remember that subject pronouns are not used very often in Italian.

potere

FUTURE

io	**potrò**
tu	**potrai**
lui/lei/Lei	**potrà**
noi	**potremo**
voi	**potrete**
loro	**potranno**

CONDITIONAL

io	**potrei**
tu	**potresti**
lui/lei/Lei	**potrebbe**
noi	**potremmo**
voi	**potreste**
loro	**potrebbero**

PAST HISTORIC

io	**potei**
tu	**potesti**
lui/lei/Lei	**poté**
noi	**potemmo**
voi	**poteste**
loro	**poterono**

PLUPERFECT

io	**avevo potuto**
tu	**avevi potuto**
lui/lei/Lei	**aveva potuto**
noi	**avevamo potuto**
voi	**avevate potuto**
loro	**avevano potuto**

IMPERATIVE

–

EXAMPLE PHRASES

Non **potrò** venire domani. I won't be able to come tomorrow.

Potresti aprire la finestra? Could you open the window?

Potrebbe essere vero. It could be true.

Era dispiaciuto perché non **aveva potuto** aiutarci. He was sorry he hadn't been able to help us.

Italic letters in Italian words show where stress does not follow the usual rules.

prefiggersi (to set oneself)

PRESENT

io	mi prefiggo
tu	ti prefiggi
lui/lei/Lei	si prefigge
noi	ci prefiggiamo
voi	vi prefiggete
loro	si prefiggono

PRESENT SUBJUNCTIVE

io	mi prefigga
tu	ti prefigga
lui/lei/Lei	si prefigga
noi	ci prefiggiamo
voi	vi prefiggiate
loro	si prefiggano

PERFECT

io	mi sono prefisso/a
tu	ti sei prefisso/a
lui/lei/Lei	si è prefisso/a
noi	ci siamo prefissi/e
voi	vi siete prefissi/e
loro	si sono prefissi/e

IMPERFECT

io	mi prefiggevo
tu	ti prefiggevi
lui/lei/Lei	si prefiggeva
noi	ci prefiggevamo
voi	vi prefiggevate
loro	si prefiggevano

GERUND

prefiggendosi

PAST PARTICIPLE

prefisso

EXAMPLE PHRASES

Si **prefiggono** sempre obiettivi irrealizzabili. They always set themselves goals they can't achieve.

Voglio che tu ti **prefigga** un obiettivo. I want you to set yourself a goal.

Mi **prefiggevo** di finire il libro entro domenica. I was aiming to finish the book by Sunday.

Remember that subject pronouns are not used very often in Italian.

prefiggersi

FUTURE

io	**mi prefiggerò**
tu	**ti prefiggerai**
lui/lei/Lei	**si prefiggerà**
noi	**ci prefiggeremo**
voi	**vi prefiggerete**
loro	**si prefiggeranno**

CONDITIONAL

io	**mi prefiggerei**
tu	**ti prefiggeresti**
lui/lei/Lei	**si prefiggerebbe**
noi	**ci prefiggeremmo**
voi	**vi prefiggereste**
loro	**si prefiggerebbero**

PAST HISTORIC

io	**mi prefissi**
tu	**ti prefiggesti**
lui/lei/Lei	**si prefisse**
noi	**ci prefiggemmo**
voi	**vi prefiggeste**
loro	**si prefissero**

PLUPERFECT

io	**mi ero prefisso/a**
tu	**ti eri prefisso/a**
lui/lei/Lei	**si era prefisso/a**
noi	**ci eravamo prefissi/e**
voi	**vi eravate prefissi/e**
loro	**si erano prefissi/e**

IMPERATIVE

prefiggiti
prefiggiamoci
prefiggetevi

EXAMPLE PHRASES

Che cosa ti **prefiggerai** per il prossimo anno? What are your aims for next year?

Fossi in te, non mi **prefiggerei** una meta così ambiziosa. If I were you I wouldn't set myself such an ambitious target.

Hai raggiunto i risultati che ti **eri prefisso**? Have you achieved the results you were aiming for?

Questo era lo scopo che mi **ero prefissa**. This was the goal that I had set myself.

Italic letters in Italian words show where stress does not follow the usual rules.

prendere (to take)

PRESENT

io	prendo
tu	prendi
lui/lei/Lei	prende
noi	prendiamo
voi	prendete
loro	prendono

PRESENT SUBJUNCTIVE

io	prenda
tu	prenda
lui/lei/Lei	prenda
noi	prendiamo
voi	prendiate
loro	prendano

PERFECT

io	ho preso
tu	hai preso
lui/lei/Lei	ha preso
noi	abbiamo preso
voi	avete preso
loro	hanno preso

IMPERFECT

io	prendevo
tu	prendevi
lui/lei/Lei	prendeva
noi	prendevamo
voi	prendevate
loro	prendevano

GERUND

prendendo

PAST PARTICIPLE

preso

EXAMPLE PHRASES

Per chi mi **prendi**? Who do you think I am?

Prende qualcosa da bere? Would you like something to drink?

Non so quanto **prenda** per una traduzione. I don't know how much she charges for a translation.

Ho preso un bel voto. I got a good mark.

Remember that subject pronouns are not used very often in Italian.

prendere

FUTURE		CONDITIONAL	
io	prenderò	io	prenderei
tu	prenderai	tu	prenderesti
lui/lei/Lei	prenderà	lui/lei/Lei	prenderebbe
noi	prenderemo	noi	prenderemmo
voi	prenderete	voi	prendereste
loro	prenderanno	loro	prenderebbero

PAST HISTORIC		PLUPERFECT	
io	presi	io	avevo preso
tu	prendesti	tu	avevi preso
lui/lei/Lei	prese	lui/lei/Lei	aveva preso
noi	prendemmo	noi	avevamo preso
voi	prendeste	voi	avevate preso
loro	presero	loro	avevano preso

IMPERATIVE
prendi
prendiamo
prendete

EXAMPLE PHRASES

Copriti o **prenderai** il raffreddore. Cover yourself up or you'll catch a cold.

Quanto **prenderemo** per quel lavoro? How much will we get for that job?

Prenderei volentieri un caffè. I'd love a coffee.

Quella volta **prendemmo** una bella paura. That time we got a real fright.

Aveva preso un grosso pesce e lo cucinò. He'd caught a big fish so he cooked it.

Prendi quella borsa. Take that bag.

Italic letters in Italian words show where stress does not follow the usual rules.

prevedere (to foresee)

PRESENT

io	prevedo
tu	prevedi
lui/lei/Lei	prevede
noi	prevediamo
voi	prevedete
loro	prevedono

PRESENT SUBJUNCTIVE

io	preveda
tu	preveda
lui/lei/Lei	preveda
noi	prevediamo
voi	prevediate
loro	prevedano

PERFECT

io	ho previsto
tu	hai previsto
lui/lei/Lei	ha previsto
noi	abbiamo previsto
voi	avete previsto
loro	hanno previsto

IMPERFECT

io	prevedevo
tu	prevedevi
lui/lei/Lei	prevedeva
noi	prevedevamo
voi	prevedevate
loro	prevedevano

GERUND

prevedendo

PAST PARTICIPLE

previsto

EXAMPLE PHRASES

Si **prevede** maltempo per il fine settimana. Bad weather is forecast for
the weekend.

Come **previsto**, arriveremo in orario. As we planned, we'll get there on time.

È **previsto** per martedì. It's planned for Tuesday.

Prevedevamo che arrivaste più tardi. We thought the plan was for you to
arrive later.

Non possiamo **prevedere** cosa succederà. We can't foresee what will happen.

Remember that subject pronouns are not used very often in Italian.

prevedere

FUTURE

io	prevederò
tu	prevederai
lui/lei/Lei	prevederà
noi	prevederemo
voi	prevederete
loro	prevederanno

CONDITIONAL

io	prevederei
tu	prevederesti
lui/lei/Lei	prevederebbe
noi	prevederemmo
voi	prevedereste
loro	prevederebbero

PAST HISTORIC

io	previdi
tu	prevedesti
lui/lei/Lei	previde
noi	prevedemmo
voi	prevedeste
loro	previdero

PLUPERFECT

io	avevo previsto
tu	avevi previsto
lui/lei/Lei	aveva previsto
noi	avevamo previsto
voi	avevate previsto
loro	avevano previsto

IMPERATIVE

prevedi
prevediamo
prevedete

EXAMPLE PHRASES

Il mago **previde** il nostro incontro. The clairvoyant foresaw that we'd meet.

Non **avevano previsto** questi cambiamenti. They hadn't foreseen these changes.

È un ansioso che vuole **prevedere** tutto. He's a worrier who wants to plan everything ahead.

Italic letters in Italian words show where stress does not follow the usual rules.

procedere (to move along)

PRESENT		PRESENT SUBJUNCTIVE	
io	procedo	io	proceda
tu	procedi	tu	proceda
lui/lei/Lei	procede	lui/lei/Lei	proceda
noi	procediamo	noi	procediamo
voi	procedete	voi	procediate
loro	procedono	loro	procedano

PERFECT		IMPERFECT	
io	sono proceduto/a	io	procedevo
tu	sei proceduto/a	tu	procedevi
lui/lei/Lei	è proceduto/a	lui/lei/Lei	procedeva
noi	siamo proceduti/e	noi	procedevamo
voi	siete proceduti/e	voi	procedevate
loro	sono proceduti/e	loro	procedevano

GERUND	PAST PARTICIPLE
procedendo	proceduto

EXAMPLE PHRASES

Come **procede** il lavoro? How's the work getting on?

Gli affari **procedono** bene. Business is going well.

Voglio che tutto **proceda** senza intoppi. I want everything to go ahead without any hitches.

I miei studi **procedevano** con lentezza. My studies were making slow progress.

Il traffico sta **procedendo** lentamente. The traffic is moving slowly.

Remember that subject pronouns are not used very often in Italian.

procedere

FUTURE

io	procederò
tu	procederai
lui/lei/Lei	procederà
noi	procederemo
voi	procederete
loro	procederanno

CONDITIONAL

io	procederei
tu	procederesti
lui/lei/Lei	procederebbe
noi	procederemmo
voi	procedereste
loro	procederebbero

PAST HISTORIC

io	procedetti
tu	procedesti
lul/lel/Lei	procedette
noi	procedemmo
voi	procedeste
loro	procedettero

PLUPERFECT

io	ero proceduto/a
tu	eri proceduto/a
lui/lei/Lei	era proceduto/a
noi	eravamo proceduti/e
voi	eravate proceduti/e
loro	erano proceduti/e

IMPERATIVE

procedi
procediamo
procedete

EXAMPLE PHRASES

Procedettero lungo il corridoio. They moved along the corridor.
La strada è ghiacciata, **procedete** con cautela. The road is icy, drive
  with caution.

Italic letters in Italian words show where stress does not follow the usual rules.

produrre (to produce)

PRESENT

io	**produco**
tu	**produci**
lui/lei/Lei	**produce**
noi	**produciamo**
voi	**producete**
loro	**producono**

PRESENT SUBJUNCTIVE

io	**produca**
tu	**produca**
lui/lei/Lei	**produca**
noi	**produciamo**
voi	**produciate**
loro	**producano**

PERFECT

io	**ho prodotto**
tu	**hai prodotto**
lui/lei/Lei	**ha prodotto**
noi	**abbiamo prodotto**
voi	**avete prodotto**
loro	**hanno prodotto**

IMPERFECT

io	**producevo**
tu	**producevi**
lui/lei/Lei	**produceva**
noi	**producevamo**
voi	**producevate**
loro	**producevano**

GERUND
producendo

PAST PARTICIPLE
prodotto

EXAMPLE PHRASES

La ditta **produce** scarpe. The company produces shoes.

Questa soluzione non **ha prodotto** buoni risultati. This solution did not produce good results.

Questi macchinari **sono prodotti** in Giappone. This machinery is produced in Japan.

L'Italia **produceva** molto grano. Italy used to produce a lot of wheat.

Si sono arricchiti **producendo** maglie. They got rich by manufacturing knitwear.

Remember that subject pronouns are not used very often in Italian.

produrre

FUTURE

io	produrrò
tu	produrrai
lui/lei/Lei	produrrà
noi	produrremo
voi	produrrete
loro	produrranno

CONDITIONAL

io	produrrei
tu	produrresti
lui/lei/Lei	produrrebbe
noi	produrremmo
voi	produrreste
loro	produrrebbero

PAST HISTORIC

io	produssi
tu	producesti
lul/lei/Lei	produsse
noi	producemmo
voi	produceste
loro	produssero

PLUPERFECT

io	avevo prodotto
tu	avevi prodotto
lui/lei/Lei	aveva prodotto
noi	avevamo prodotto
voi	avevate prodotto
loro	avevano prodotto

IMPERATIVE

produci
produciamo
producete

EXAMPLE PHRASES

Se lavorerai sodo, **produrrai** di più. If you work hard you'll produce more.

Avevamo prodotto articoli di grande successo. We'd manufactured very
   successful products.

Italic letters in Italian words show where stress does not follow the usual rules.

proporre (to suggest)

PRESENT

io	propongo
tu	proponi
lui/lei/Lei	propone
noi	proponiamo
voi	proponete
loro	propongono

PRESENT SUBJUNCTIVE

io	proponga
tu	proponga
lui/lei/Lei	proponga
noi	proponiamo
voi	proponiate
loro	propongano

PERFECT

io	ho proposto
tu	hai proposto
lui/lei/Lei	ha proposto
noi	abbiamo proposto
voi	avete proposto
loro	hanno proposto

IMPERFECT

io	proponevo
tu	proponevi
lui/lei/Lei	proponeva
noi	proponevamo
voi	proponevate
loro	proponevano

GERUND

proponendo

PAST PARTICIPLE

proposto

EXAMPLE PHRASES

Che cosa **propone** lo chef? What does the chef recommend?

Ho proposto di andare al cinema. I suggested going to the cinema.

Maria **proponeva** una pizza, ma non ne ho voglia. Maria suggested a pizza, but I don't feel like one.

Remember that subject pronouns are not used very often in Italian.

proporre

FUTURE

io	**proporrò**
tu	**proporrai**
lui/lei/Lei	**proporrà**
noi	**proporremo**
voi	**proporrete**
loro	**proporranno**

CONDITIONAL

io	**proporrei**
tu	**proporresti**
lui/lei/Lei	**proporrebbe**
noi	**proporremmo**
voi	**proporreste**
loro	**proporrebbero**

PAST HISTORIC

io	**proposi**
tu	**proponesti**
lui/lei/Lei	**propose**
noi	**proponemmo**
voi	**proponeste**
loro	**proposero**

PLUPERFECT

io	**avevo proposto**
tu	**avevi proposto**
lui/lei/Lei	**aveva proposto**
noi	**avevamo proposto**
voi	**avevate proposto**
loro	**avevano proposto**

IMPERATIVE

proponi
proponiamo
proponete

EXAMPLE PHRASES

Non **proporrei** mai una cosa del genere. I'd never suggest something like that.

Propose un brindisi alla salute dell'invitato. He proposed a toast to the guest.

Avevano proposto di fermarci, ma continuammo. They'd suggested we should stop, but we continued.

Forza, **proponete** qualcosa di nuovo per stasera. Go on, suggest something new for this evening.

Italic letters in Italian words show where stress does not follow the usual rules.

raggiungere (to reach)

	PRESENT		PRESENT SUBJUNCTIVE
io	raggiungo	io	raggiunga
tu	raggiungi	tu	raggiunga
lui/lei/Lei	raggiunge	lui/lei/Lei	raggiunga
noi	raggiungiamo	noi	raggiungiamo
voi	raggiungete	voi	raggiungiate
loro	raggiungono	loro	raggiungano

	PERFECT		IMPERFECT
io	ho raggiunto	io	raggiungevo
tu	hai raggiunto	tu	raggiungevi
lui/lei/Lei	ha raggiunto	lui/lei/Lei	raggiungeva
noi	abbiamo raggiunto	noi	raggiungevamo
voi	avete raggiunto	voi	raggiungevate
loro	hanno raggiunto	loro	raggiungevano

GERUND
raggiungendo

PAST PARTICIPLE
raggiunto

EXAMPLE PHRASES

La temperatura può **raggiungere** i quaranta gradi. The temperature can reach forty degrees.

Vi **raggiungo** più tardi. I'll join you later.

Non **ho** ancora **raggiunto** il mio scopo. I haven't yet achieved my aim.

Remember that subject pronouns are not used very often in Italian.

raggiungere

FUTURE

io	raggiungerò
tu	raggiungerai
lui/lei/Lei	raggiungerà
noi	raggiungeremo
voi	raggiungerete
loro	raggiungeranno

CONDITIONAL

io	raggiungerei
tu	raggiungeresti
lui/lei/Lei	raggiungerebbe
noi	raggiungeremmo
voi	raggiungereste
loro	raggiungerebbero

PAST HISTORIC

io	raggiunsi
tu	raggiungesti
lui/lei/Lei	raggiunse
noi	raggiungemmo
voi	raggiungeste
loro	raggiunsero

PLUPERFECT

io	avevo raggiunto
tu	avevi raggiunto
lui/lei/Lei	aveva raggiunto
noi	avevamo raggiunto
voi	avevate raggiunto
loro	avevano raggiunto

IMPERATIVE

raggiungi
raggiungiamo
raggiungete

EXAMPLE PHRASES

Vi **raggiungeremo** in albergo. We'll meet you in the hotel.

Ci rincorsero e ci **raggiunsero**. They ran after us and caught us up.

Il fiume **aveva raggiunto** il livello di guardia. The river had reached the high-water mark.

I tuoi amici ti aspettano: **raggiungili**. Your friends are waiting for you: go and join them.

Italic letters in Italian words show where stress does not follow the usual rules.

rendere (to make)

PRESENT		PRESENT SUBJUNCTIVE	
io	rendo	io	renda
tu	rendi	tu	renda
lui/lei/Lei	rende	lui/lei/Lei	renda
noi	rendiamo	noi	rendiamo
voi	rendete	voi	rendiate
loro	rendono	loro	rendano

PERFECT		IMPERFECT	
io	ho reso	io	rendevo
tu	hai reso	tu	rendevi
lui/lei/Lei	ha reso	lui/lei/Lei	rendeva
noi	abbiamo reso	noi	rendevamo
voi	avete reso	voi	rendevate
loro	hanno reso	loro	rendevano

GERUND
rendendo

PAST PARTICIPLE
reso

EXAMPLE PHRASES

Forse non ti **rendi** conto di quanto sia pericoloso. Maybe you don't realize how dangerous it is.

Scusa, non mi **ero reso** conto di averti offeso. I'm sorry, I didn't realize I'd upset you.

Non si **è** mai **resa** conto dei suoi limiti. She's never recognized her limitations.

Potresti **rendermi** la penna? Could you give me back my pen?

Remember that subject pronouns are not used very often in Italian.

rendere

FUTURE

io	renderò
tu	renderai
lui/lei/Lei	renderà
noi	renderemo
voi	renderete
loro	renderanno

CONDITIONAL

io	renderei
tu	renderesti
lui/lei/Lei	renderebbe
noi	renderemmo
voi	rendereste
loro	renderebbero

PAST HISTORIC

io	resi
tu	rendesti
lui/lei/Lei	rese
noi	rendemmo
voi	rendeste
loro	resero

PLUPERFECT

io	avevo reso
tu	avevi reso
lui/lei/Lei	aveva reso
noi	avevamo reso
voi	avevate reso
loro	avevano reso

IMPERATIVE

rendi
rendiamo
rendete

EXAMPLE PHRASES

Questa crema **renderà** i capelli luminosi. This cream will make your hair shiny.

Un po' di diplomazia **renderebbe** tutto più facile. A bit of diplomacy would make everything easier.

Il ladro **rese** la refurtiva. The burglar returned the stolen goods.

Fai qualcosa! **Renditi** utile! Do something! Make yourself useful!

Italic letters in Italian words show where stress does not follow the usual rules.

restare (to stay)

PRESENT

io	resto
tu	resti
lui/lei/Lei	resta
noi	restiamo
voi	restate
loro	restano

PRESENT SUBJUNCTIVE

io	resti
tu	resti
lui/lei/Lei	resti
noi	restiamo
voi	restiate
loro	restino

PERFECT

io	sono restato/a
tu	sei restato/a
lui/lei/Lei	è restato/a
noi	siamo restati/e
voi	siete restati/e
loro	sono restati/e

IMPERFECT

io	restavo
tu	restavi
lui/lei/Lei	restava
noi	restavamo
voi	restavate
loro	restavano

GERUND

restando

PAST PARTICIPLE

restato

EXAMPLE PHRASES

Ne **restano** solo due. There are only two left.

Sono restato a casa tutto il giorno. I stayed at home all day.

Restava solo da pulire la cucina. The only thing left to do was cleaning the kitchen.

Remember that subject pronouns are not used very often in Italian.

restare

FUTURE

io	**resterò**
tu	**resterai**
lui/lei/Lei	**resterà**
noi	**resteremo**
voi	**resterete**
loro	**resteranno**

CONDITIONAL

io	**resterei**
tu	**resteresti**
lui/lei/Lei	**resterebbe**
noi	**resteremmo**
voi	**restereste**
loro	**resterebbero**

PAST HISTORIC

io	**restai**
tu	**restasti**
lui/lei/Lei	**restò**
noi	**restammo**
voi	**restaste**
loro	**restarono**

PLUPERFECT

io	**ero restato/a**
tu	**eri restato/a**
lui/lei/Lei	**era restato/a**
noi	**eravamo restati/e**
voi	**eravate restati/e**
loro	**erano restati/e**

IMPERATIVE

resta
restiamo
restate

EXAMPLE PHRASES

Resterò in Italia per tutta l'estate. I'll stay in Italy for the whole summer.

Resterei, ma ho da fare. I'd stay, but I've got things to do.

Mi **restarono** solo cinquanta sterline. I only had fifty pounds left.

Era restato da solo tutta la sera. He'd been alone all evening.

Dai, **resta** ancora un po'. Go on, stay a bit longer.

Italic letters in Italian words show where stress does not follow the usual rules.

ridere (to laugh)

PRESENT

io	**rido**
tu	**ridi**
lui/lei/Lei	**ride**
noi	**ridiamo**
voi	**ridete**
loro	**ridono**

PRESENT SUBJUNCTIVE

io	**rida**
tu	**rida**
lui/lei/Lei	**rida**
noi	**ridiamo**
voi	**ridiate**
loro	**ridano**

PERFECT

io	**ho riso**
tu	**hai riso**
lui/lei/Lei	**ha riso**
noi	**abbiamo riso**
voi	**avete riso**
loro	**hanno riso**

IMPERFECT

io	**ridevo**
tu	**ridevi**
lui/lei/Lei	**rideva**
noi	**ridevamo**
voi	**ridevate**
loro	**ridevano**

GERUND

ridendo

PAST PARTICIPLE

riso

EXAMPLE PHRASES

Perché **ridi**? Why are you laughing?

Abbiamo riso per tutto lo spettacolo. We laughed all through the show.

State **ridendo** di me? Are you laughing at me?

Tutti sono scoppiati a **ridere**. They all burst out laughing.

Non c'è niente da **ridere**. It's not funny.

Remember that subject pronouns are not used very often in Italian.

ridere

FUTURE

io	riderò
tu	riderai
lui/lei/Lei	riderà
noi	rideremo
voi	riderete
loro	rideranno

CONDITIONAL

io	riderei
tu	rideresti
lui/lei/Lei	riderebbe
noi	rideremmo
voi	ridereste
loro	riderebbero

PAST HISTORIC

Io	risi
tu	ridesti
lui/lei/Lei	rise
noi	ridemmo
voi	rideste
loro	risero

PLUPERFECT

io	avevo riso
tu	avevi riso
lui/lei/Lei	aveva riso
noi	avevamo riso
voi	avevate riso
loro	avevano riso

IMPERATIVE

ridi
ridiamo
ridete

EXAMPLE PHRASES

Rideresti meno se sapessi la verità. You wouldn't laugh so much if you knew the truth.

Non **avevo** mai **riso** tanto in vita mia. I'd never laughed so much in all my life.

Italic letters in Italian words show where stress does not follow the usual rules.

riempire (to fill)

PRESENT

io	riempio
tu	riempi
lui/lei/Lei	riempie
noi	riempiamo
voi	riempite
loro	riempiono

PRESENT SUBJUNCTIVE

io	riempia
tu	riempia
lui/lei/Lei	riempia
noi	riempiamo
voi	riempiate
loro	riempiano

PERFECT

io	ho riempito
tu	hai riempito
lui/lei/Lei	ha riempito
noi	abbiamo riempito
voi	avete riempito
loro	hanno riempito

IMPERFECT

io	riempivo
tu	riempivi
lui/lei/Lei	riempiva
noi	riempivamo
voi	riempivate
loro	riempivano

GERUND
riempiendo

PAST PARTICIPLE
riempito

EXAMPLE PHRASES

Vedervi ci **riempie** di gioia. It's always a joy to see you.

È meglio che tu **riempia** la borraccia prima di partire. You'd better fill your water bottle before you set off.

Tieni, **ho riempito** il termos di caffè, va bene? Here, I've filled the flask with coffee, okay?

Remember that subject pronouns are not used very often in Italian.

riempire

FUTURE

io	**riempirò**
tu	**riempirai**
lui/lei/Lei	**riempirà**
noi	**riempiremo**
voi	**riempirete**
loro	**riempiranno**

CONDITIONAL

io	**riempirei**
tu	**riempiresti**
lui/lei/Lei	**riempirebbe**
noi	**riempiremmo**
voi	**riempireste**
loro	**riempirebbero**

PAST HISTORIC

io	**riempii**
tu	**riempisti**
lui/lei/Lei	**riempì**
noi	**riempimmo**
voi	**riempiste**
loro	**riempirono**

PLUPERFECT

io	**avevo riempito**
tu	**avevi riempito**
lui/lei/Lei	**aveva riempito**
noi	**avevamo riempito**
voi	**avevate riempito**
loro	**avevano riempito**

IMPERATIVE

riempi
riempiamo
riempite

EXAMPLE PHRASES

Riempiremo tutte le bottiglie col vino del nonno. We're going to fill all the bottles with granddad's wine.

Mi **riempì** la testa di sciocchezze. She filled my head with nonsense.

Riempi il modulo, per favore. Fill in the form, please.

Italic letters in Italian words show where stress does not follow the usual rules.

riflettere (to think)

PRESENT		PRESENT SUBJUNCTIVE	
io	rifletto	io	rifletta
tu	rifletti	tu	rifletta
lui/lei/Lei	riflette	lui/lei/Lei	rifletta
noi	riflettiamo	noi	riflettiamo
voi	riflettete	voi	riflettiate
loro	riflettono	loro	riflettano

PERFECT		IMPERFECT	
io	ho riflettuto	io	riflettevo
tu	hai riflettuto	tu	riflettevi
lui/lei/Lei	ha riflettuto	lui/lei/Lei	rifletteva
noi	abbiamo riflettuto	noi	riflettevamo
voi	avete riflettuto	voi	riflettevate
loro	hanno riflettuto	loro	riflettevano

GERUND
riflettendo

PAST PARTICIPLE
riflettuto

EXAMPLE PHRASES

È una persona cauta: **riflette** molto prima di agire. He's a cautious person: he thinks a lot before he does anything.

Ci **ho riflettuto** su e ho deciso di accettare. I've thought about it and have decided to accept.

Guardavo la TV mentre **riflettevo** sul da farsi. I watched TV while I thought about what should be done.

Riflettendo un po', troveremo la soluzione. If we think a bit we'll find a solution.

Agisce senza **riflettere**. He does things without thinking.

Remember that subject pronouns are not used very often in Italian.

riflettere

FUTURE

io	**rifletterò**
tu	**rifletterai**
lui/lei/Lei	**rifletterà**
noi	**rifletteremo**
voi	**rifletterete**
loro	**rifletteranno**

CONDITIONAL

io	**rifletterei**
tu	**rifletteresti**
lui/lei/Lei	**rifletterebbe**
noi	**rifletteremmo**
voi	**riflettereste**
loro	**rifletterebbero**

PAST HISTORIC

io	**riflettei**
tu	**riflettesti**
lui/lei/Lei	**rifletté**
noi	**riflettemmo**
voi	**rifletteste**
loro	**rifletterono**

PLUPERFECT

io	**avevo riflettuto**
tu	**avevi riflettuto**
lui/lei/Lei	**aveva riflettuto**
noi	**avevamo riflettuto**
voi	**avevate riflettuto**
loro	**avevano riflettuto**

IMPERATIVE

rifletti
riflettiamo
riflettete

EXAMPLE PHRASES

Io **rifletterei** un po' prima di fare una simile scelta. I'd think a bit before
   I made a choice like that.
Rifletti prima di parlare! Think before you speak!

Italic letters in Italian words show where stress does not follow the usual rules.

rimanere (to stay)

PRESENT

io	rimango
tu	rimani
lui/lei/Lei	rimane
noi	rimaniamo
voi	rimanete
loro	rimangono

PRESENT SUBJUNCTIVE

io	rimanga
tu	rimanga
lui/lei/Lei	rimanga
noi	rimaniamo
voi	rimaniate
loro	rimangano

PERFECT

io	sono rimasto/a
tu	sei rimasto/a
lui/lei/Lei	è rimasto/a
noi	siamo rimasti/e
voi	siete rimasti/e
loro	sono rimasti/e

IMPERFECT

io	rimanevo
tu	rimanevi
lui/lei/Lei	rimaneva
noi	rimanevamo
voi	rimanevate
loro	rimanevano

GERUND

rimanendo

PAST PARTICIPLE

rimasto

EXAMPLE PHRASES

Temo che **rimanga** poco tempo. I'm afraid she won't stay long.

Sono rimasto a casa tutto il giorno. I stayed at home all day.

Rimanevano sempre indietro. They were always behind.

Mi piacerebbe **rimanere** qualche altro giorno. I'd like to stay a few more days.

Remember that subject pronouns are not used very often in Italian.

rimanere

FUTURE		CONDITIONAL	
io	**rimarrò**	io	**rimarrei**
tu	**rimarrai**	tu	**rimarresti**
lui/lei/Lei	**rimarrà**	lui/lei/Lei	**rimarrebbe**
noi	**rimarremo**	noi	**rimarremmo**
voi	**rimarrete**	voi	**rimarreste**
loro	**rimarranno**	loro	**rimarrebbero**

PAST HISTORIC		PLUPERFECT	
io	**rimasi**	io	**ero rimasto/a**
tu	**rimanesti**	tu	**eri rimasto/a**
lui/lei/Lei	**rimase**	lui/lei/Lei	**era rimasto/a**
noi	**rimanemmo**	noi	**eravamo rimasti/e**
voi	**rimaneste**	voi	**eravate rimasti/e**
loro	**rimasero**	loro	**erano rimasti/e**

IMPERATIVE

rimani
rimaniamo
rimanete

EXAMPLE PHRASES

Rimarrete senza parole. You'll be speechless.
Ci **rimarrebbero** molto male. They'd be very hurt. *rimanere?*
Ne **rimase** solo uno. There was only one left.
Eravamo rimasti senza pane, così andai a comprarlo. We had no bread left,
  so I went to get some. *rimanere?*

Italic letters in Italian words show where stress does not follow the usual rules.

risolvere (to solve)

PRESENT

io	risolvo
tu	risolvi
lui/lei/Lei	risolve
noi	risolviamo
voi	risolvete
loro	risolvono

PRESENT SUBJUNCTIVE

io	risolva
tu	risolva
lui/lei/Lei	risolva
noi	risolviamo
voi	risolviate
loro	risolvano

PERFECT

io	ho risolto
tu	hai risolto
lui/lei/Lei	ha risolto
noi	abbiamo risolto
voi	avete risolto
loro	hanno risolto

IMPERFECT

io	risolvevo
tu	risolvevi
lui/lei/Lei	risolveva
noi	risolvevamo
voi	risolvevate
loro	risolvevano

GERUND

risolvendo

PAST PARTICIPLE

risolto

EXAMPLE PHRASES

Così non **risolvi** nulla. You won't solve the problems that way.

Ho risolto l'indovinello! I've worked out the riddle!

Remember that subject pronouns are not used very often in Italian.

risolvere

FUTURE

io	risolver**ò**
tu	risolverai
lui/lei/Lei	risolver**à**
noi	risolveremo
voi	risolverete
loro	risolveranno

CONDITIONAL

io	risolverei
tu	risolveresti
lui/lei/Lei	risolverebbe
noi	risolveremmo
voi	risolvereste
loro	risolverebbero

PAST HISTORIC

Io	risolsi
tu	risolvesti
lui/lei/Lei	risolse
noi	risolvemmo
voi	risolveste
loro	risolsero

PLUPERFECT

io	avevo risolto
tu	avevi risolto
lui/lei/Lei	aveva risolto
noi	avevamo risolto
voi	avevate risolto
loro	avevano risolto

IMPERATIVE

risolvi
risolviamo
risolvete

EXAMPLE PHRASES

Solo se ti calmerai **risolverai** i tuoi problemi. You'll only solve your problems if you calm down.

Una tua parola **risolverebbe** molte questioni. If you said something it would resolve many issues.

Il suo intervento **risolse** la controversia. His intervention settled the dispute.

Aveva risolto un'equazione difficilissima. He'd worked out a very difficult equation.

Italic letters in Italian words show where stress does not follow the usual rules.

rispondere (to answer)

PRESENT

io	rispondo
tu	rispondi
lui/lei/Lei	risponde
noi	rispondiamo
voi	rispondete
loro	rispondono

PRESENT SUBJUNCTIVE

io	risponda
tu	risponda
lui/lei/Lei	risponda
noi	rispondiamo
voi	rispondiate
loro	rispondano

PERFECT

io	ho risposto
tu	hai risposto
lui/lei/Lei	ha risposto
noi	abbiamo risposto
voi	avete risposto
loro	hanno risposto

IMPERFECT

io	rispondevo
tu	rispondevi
lui/lei/Lei	rispondeva
noi	rispondevamo
voi	rispondevate
loro	rispondevano

GERUND

rispondendo

PAST PARTICIPLE

risposto

EXAMPLE PHRASES

Cosa vuoi che ti **risponda**? What do you want me to say?

Ho telefonato ma non **ha risposto** nessuno. I phoned, but nobody answered.

Rispondeva sempre di sì a tutti. She always said yes to everyone.

Remember that subject pronouns are not used very often in Italian.

rispondere

FUTURE

io	**risponderò**
tu	**risponderai**
lui/lei/Lei	**risponderà**
noi	**risponderemo**
voi	**risponderete**
loro	**risponderanno**

CONDITIONAL

io	**risponderei**
tu	**risponderesti**
lui/lei/Lei	**risponderebbe**
noi	**risponderemmo**
voi	**rispondereste**
loro	**risponderebbero**

PAST HISTORIC

Io	**risposi**
tu	**rispondesti**
lui/lei/Lei	**rispose**
noi	**rispondemmo**
voi	**rispondeste**
loro	**risposero**

PLUPERFECT

io	**avevo risposto**
tu	**avevi risposto**
lui/lei/Lei	**aveva risposto**
noi	**avevamo risposto**
voi	**avevate risposto**
loro	**avevano risposto**

IMPERATIVE

rispondi
rispondiamo
rispondete

EXAMPLE PHRASES

Risponderai di tutti i tuoi crimini. You will answer for all your crimes.

Cosa **rispondereste** a una domanda simile? How would you answer
a question like that?

Rispose di no. He said no.

Avevate risposto alle sue lettere? Had you replied to her letters?

Rispondi alla mia domanda. Answer my question.

Italic letters in Italian words show where stress does not follow the usual rules.

rivolgere (to turn)

PRESENT

io	rivolgo
tu	rivolgi
lui/lei/Lei	rivolge
noi	rivolgiamo
voi	rivolgete
loro	rivolgono

PRESENT SUBJUNCTIVE

io	rivolga
tu	rivolga
lui/lei/Lei	rivolga
noi	rivolgiamo
voi	rivolgiate
loro	rivolgano

PERFECT

io	ho rivolto
tu	hai rivolto
lui/lei/Lei	ha rivolto
noi	abbiamo rivolto
voi	avete rivolto
loro	hanno rivolto

IMPERFECT

io	rivolgevo
tu	rivolgevi
lui/lei/Lei	rivolgeva
noi	rivolgevamo
voi	rivolgevate
loro	rivolgevano

GERUND

rivolgendo

PAST PARTICIPLE

rivolto

EXAMPLE PHRASES

Sono due giorni che non mi **rivolge** la parola. She hasn't spoken to me for two days.

È meglio che si **rivolga** all'impiegato laggiù. You'd better go and ask the man over there.

Si **è rivolta** a me per un consiglio. She came to me for advice.

Remember that subject pronouns are not used very often in Italian.

rivolgere

FUTURE

io	**rivolgerò**
tu	**rivolgerai**
lui/lei/Lei	**rivolgerà**
noi	**rivolgeremo**
voi	**rivolgerete**
loro	**rivolgeranno**

CONDITIONAL

io	**rivolgerei**
tu	**rivolgeresti**
lui/lei/Lei	**rivolgerebbe**
noi	**rivolgeremmo**
voi	**rivolgereste**
loro	**rivolgerebbero**

PAST HISTORIC

io	**rivolsi**
tu	**rivolgesti**
lui/lei/Lei	**rivolse**
noi	**rivolgemmo**
voi	**rivolgeste**
loro	**rivolsero**

PLUPERFECT

io	**avevo rivolto**
tu	**avevi rivolto**
lui/lei/Lei	**aveva rivolto**
noi	**avevamo rivolto**
voi	**avevate rivolto**
loro	**avevano rivolto**

IMPERATIVE

rivolgi
rivolgiamo
rivolgete

EXAMPLE PHRASES

Ci **rivolgeremo** alle autorità. We'll go to the authorities

In caso di problemi, ci **rivolgevamo** a lui. If there was a problem we went to him.

Non mi **rivolgerei** mai a te per avere aiuto. I'd never come to you for help.

Si **rivolse** a me in tono aggressivo. She spoke to me aggressively.

Rivolgetevi all'ufficio informazioni. Go to the information office.

Non so a chi **rivolgermi**. I don't know who to go to.

Italic letters in Italian words show where stress does not follow the usual rules.

rompere (to break)

PRESENT

io	**rompo**
tu	**rompi**
lui/lei/Lei	**rompe**
noi	**rompiamo**
voi	**rompete**
loro	**rompono**

PRESENT SUBJUNCTIVE

io	**rompa**
tu	**rompa**
lui/lei/Lei	**rompa**
noi	**rompiamo**
voi	**rompiate**
loro	**rompano**

PERFECT

io	**ho rotto**
tu	**hai rotto**
lui/lei/Lei	**ha rotto**
noi	**abbiamo rotto**
voi	**avete rotto**
loro	**hanno rotto**

IMPERFECT

io	**rompevo**
tu	**rompevi**
lui/lei/Lei	**rompeva**
noi	**rompevamo**
voi	**rompevate**
loro	**rompevano**

GERUND
rompendo

PAST PARTICIPLE
rotto

EXAMPLE PHRASES
Uffa quanto **rompi**! What a pain you are!
Ho rotto un bicchiere! I've broken a glass!
Il piatto si **è rotto**. The plate broke.
Da piccolo **rompeva** tutto quello che toccava. When he was little he broke
   everything he touched.

Remember that subject pronouns are not used very often in Italian.

rompere

FUTURE

io	**romperò**
tu	**romperai**
lui/lei/Lei	**romperà**
noi	**romperemo**
voi	**romperete**
loro	**romperanno**

CONDITIONAL

io	**romperei**
tu	**romperesti**
lui/lei/Lei	**romperebbe**
noi	**romperemmo**
voi	**rompereste**
loro	**romperebbero**

PAST HISTORIC

io	**ruppi**
tu	**rompesti**
lui/lei/Lei	**ruppe**
noi	**rompemmo**
voi	**rompeste**
loro	**ruppero**

PLUPERFECT

io	**avevo rotto**
tu	**avevi rotto**
lui/lei/Lei	**aveva rotto**
noi	**avevamo rotto**
voi	**avevate rotto**
loro	**avevano rotto**

IMPERATIVE

rompi
rompiamo
rompete

EXAMPLE PHRASES

Rischia troppo: si **romperà** una gamba. She takes too many risks: she'll
   break her leg.

La corda si **romperebbe** se tirassi troppo. The rope would break if I pulled
   too hard.

La macchina si **ruppe** sull'autostrada. The car broke down on the motorway.

Italic letters in Italian words show where stress does not follow the usual rules.

salire (to go up)

PRESENT

io	**salgo**
tu	**sali**
lui/lei/Lei	**sale**
noi	**saliamo**
voi	**salite**
loro	**salgono**

PRESENT SUBJUNCTIVE

io	**salga**
tu	**salga**
lui/lei/Lei	**salga**
noi	**saliamo**
voi	**saliate**
loro	**salgano**

PERFECT

io	**sono salito/a**
tu	**sei salito/a**
lui/lei/Lei	**è salito/a**
noi	**siamo saliti/e**
voi	**siete saliti/e**
loro	**sono saliti/e**

IMPERFECT

io	**salivo**
tu	**salivi**
lui/lei/Lei	**saliva**
noi	**salivamo**
voi	**salivate**
loro	**salivano**

GERUND
salendo

PAST PARTICIPLE
salito

EXAMPLE PHRASES

Sali tu o scendo io? Are you coming up or shall I come down?

Non voglio che i tuoi amici **salgano** in casa. I don't want your friends to come into the house.

I prezzi **sono saliti**. Prices have gone up.

Mentre **saliva** verso la cima, si sentì senza forze. As she climbed up to the summit she felt weak.

Remember that subject pronouns are not used very often in Italian.

salire

FUTURE

io	**salirò**
tu	**salirai**
lui/lei/Lei	**salirà**
noi	**saliremo**
voi	**salirete**
loro	**saliranno**

CONDITIONAL

io	**salirei**
tu	**saliresti**
lui/lei/Lei	**salirebbe**
noi	**saliremmo**
voi	**salireste**
loro	**salirebbero**

PAST HISTORIC

io	**salii**
tu	**salisti**
lui/lei/Lei	**salì**
noi	**salimmo**
voi	**saliste**
loro	**salirono**

PLUPERFECT

io	**ero salito/a**
tu	**eri salito/a**
lui/lei/Lei	**era salito/a**
noi	**eravamo saliti/e**
voi	**eravate saliti/e**
loro	**erano saliti/e**

IMPERATIVE

sali
saliamo
salite

EXAMPLE PHRASES

Dopo cena **salirai** in camera tua. After dinner you'll go up to your room.

Non **salirei** mai su un aereo. I'd never go on a plane.

Salì sull'albero per raccogliere le ciliegie. She climbed up the tree to pick the cherries.

Sali in macchina e partiamo. Get in the car and we'll be off.

Italic letters in Italian words show where stress does not follow the usual rules.

sapere (to know)

PRESENT		PRESENT SUBJUNCTIVE	
io	**so**	io	**sappia**
tu	**sai**	tu	**sappia**
lui/lei/Lei	**sa**	lui/lei/Lei	**sappia**
noi	**sappiamo**	noi	**sappiamo**
voi	**sapete**	voi	**sappiate**
loro	**sanno**	loro	**sappiano**

PERFECT		IMPERFECT	
io	**ho saputo**	io	**sapevo**
tu	**hai saputo**	tu	**sapevi**
lui/lei/Lei	**ha saputo**	lui/lei/Lei	**sapeva**
noi	**abbiamo saputo**	noi	**sapevamo**
voi	**avete saputo**	voi	**sapevate**
loro	**hanno saputo**	loro	**sapevano**

GERUND	PAST PARTICIPLE
sapendo	saputo

EXAMPLE PHRASES

Sai dove abita? Do you know where he lives?

Non ne **so** nulla. I don't know anything about it.

Sa di fragola. It tastes of strawberries.

Sa di pesce. It smells of fish.

Non **abbiamo** più **saputo** nulla di lui. We didn't hear anything more about him.

Non **sapeva** andare in bicicletta. He couldn't ride a bike.

Remember that subject pronouns are not used very often in Italian.

sapere

FUTURE

io	saprò
tu	saprai
lui/lei/Lei	saprà
noi	sapremo
voi	saprete
loro	sapranno

CONDITIONAL

io	saprei
tu	sapresti
lui/lei/Lei	saprebbe
noi	sapremmo
voi	sapreste
loro	saprebbero

PAST HISTORIC

io	seppi
tu	sapesti
lui/lei/Lei	seppe
noi	sapemmo
voi	sapeste
loro	seppero

PLUPERFECT

io	avevo saputo
tu	avevi saputo
lui/lei/Lei	aveva saputo
noi	avevamo saputo
voi	avevate saputo
loro	avevano saputo

IMPERATIVE

sappi
sappiamo
sappiate

EXAMPLE PHRASES

Come **saprete**, abbiamo deciso di traslocare. As you know, we've decided to move.

Sapreste indicarmi la strada per la stazione? Could you tell me the way to the station?

Solo dopo molti anni **sapemmo** che era emigrato. Only after many years did we hear that he'd emigrated.

Sappi che non sono disposto a perdonarti. I want you to know that I'm not prepared to forgive you.

Italic letters in Italian words show where stress does not follow the usual rules.

sbagliare (to make a mistake)

PRESENT

io	**sbaglio**
tu	**sbagli**
lui/lei/Lei	**sbaglia**
noi	**sbagliamo**
voi	**sbagliate**
loro	**sbagliano**

PRESENT SUBJUNCTIVE

io	**sbagli**
tu	**sbagli**
lui/lei/Lei	**sbagli**
noi	**sbagliamo**
voi	**sbagliate**
loro	**sbaglino**

PERFECT

io	**ho sbagliato**
tu	**hai sbagliato**
lui/lei/Lei	**ha sbagliato**
noi	**abbiamo sbagliato**
voi	**avete sbagliato**
loro	**hanno sbagliato**

IMPERFECT

io	**sbagliavo**
tu	**sbagliavi**
lui/lei/Lei	**sbagliava**
noi	**sbagliavamo**
voi	**sbagliavate**
loro	**sbagliavano**

GERUND
sbagliando

PAST PARTICIPLE
sbagliato

EXAMPLE PHRASES

Mi dispiace, **avete sbagliato**. I'm sorry, you've made a mistake.

Scusi, **ho sbagliato** numero. Sorry, I've got the wrong number.

Pensavo fosse lei, ma mi **sono sbagliato**. I thought it was her, but I was wrong.

Ci eravamo persi e **sbagliavamo** sempre strada. We were lost and kept taking the wrong road.

Sbagliando s'impara. You learn by your mistakes.

Remember that subject pronouns are not used very often in Italian.

sbagliare

FUTURE

io	sbaglierò
tu	sbaglierai
lui/lei/Lei	sbaglierà
noi	sbaglieremo
voi	sbaglierete
loro	sbaglieranno

CONDITIONAL

io	sbaglierei
tu	sbaglieresti
lui/lei/Lei	sbaglierebbe
noi	sbaglieremmo
voi	sbagliereste
loro	sbaglierebbero

PAST HISTORIC

io	sbagliai
tu	sbagliasti
lui/lei/Lei	sbagliò
noi	sbagliammo
voi	sbagliaste
loro	sbagliarono

PLUPERFECT

io	avevo sbagliato
tu	avevi sbagliato
lui/lei/Lei	aveva sbagliato
noi	avevamo sbagliato
voi	avevate sbagliato
loro	avevano sbagliato

IMPERATIVE

sbaglia
sbagliamo
sbagliate

EXAMPLE PHRASES

Mi **sbaglierò**, ma per me questa è la risposta giusta. I may be mistaken,
but I think this is the right answer.

Sbaglieresti, se pensassi che non mi importa. You'd be wrong if you thought I
didn't care.

Aveva sbagliato e non voleva ammetterlo. He'd been wrong but didn't want
to admit it.

Italic letters in Italian words show where stress does not follow the usual rules.

scegliere (to choose)

PRESENT

io	scelgo
tu	scegli
lui/lei/Lei	sceglie
noi	scegliamo
voi	scegliete
loro	scelgono

PRESENT SUBJUNCTIVE

io	scelga
tu	scelga
lui/lei/Lei	scelga
noi	scegliamo
voi	scegliate
loro	scelgano

PERFECT

io	ho scelto
tu	hai scelto
lui/lei/Lei	ha scelto
noi	abbiamo scelto
voi	avete scelto
loro	hanno scelto

IMPERFECT

io	sceglievo
tu	sceglievi
lui/lei/Lei	sceglieva
noi	sceglievamo
voi	sceglievate
loro	sceglievano

GERUND

scegliendo

PAST PARTICIPLE

scelto

EXAMPLE PHRASES

Chi **sceglie** il vino? Who's going to choose the wine?

Hai scelto il regalo per lei? Have you chosen her present?

Sceglievano sempre il vino più costoso. They always chose the most expensive wine.

Stavo **scegliendo** le pesche più mature. I was choosing the ripest peaches.

Remember that subject pronouns are not used very often in Italian.

scegliere

FUTURE

io	sceglierò
tu	sceglierai
lui/lei/Lei	sceglierà
noi	sceglieremo
voi	sceglierete
loro	sceglieranno

CONDITIONAL

io	sceglierei
tu	sceglieresti
lui/lei/Lei	sceglierebbe
noi	sceglieremmo
voi	scegliereste
loro	sceglierebbero

PAST HISTORIC

io	scelsi
tu	scegliesti
lui/lei/Lei	scelse
noi	scegliemmo
voi	sceglieste
loro	scelsero

PLUPERFECT

io	avevo scelto
tu	avevi scelto
lui/lei/Lei	aveva scelto
noi	avevamo scelto
voi	avevate scelto
loro	avevano scelto

IMPERATIVE

scegli
scegliamo
scegliete

EXAMPLE PHRASES

Non sa ancora quale *a*bito **sceglier***à*. She hasn't decided yet which dress
  she'll choose.
Il cappello che **aveva scelto** con tanta cura ora non le piace più. She no longer
  likes the hat she'd chosen with such care.
Scegli la pizza che vuoi. Choose which pizza you want.

Italic letters in Italian words show where stress does not follow the usual rules.

scendere (to go down)

PRESENT

io	scendo
tu	scendi
lui/lei/Lei	scende
noi	scendiamo
voi	scendete
loro	scendono

PRESENT SUBJUNCTIVE

io	scenda
tu	scenda
lui/lei/Lei	scenda
noi	scendiamo
voi	scendiate
loro	scendano

PERFECT

io	sono sceso/a
tu	sei sceso/a
lui/lei/Lei	è sceso/a
noi	siamo scesi/e
voi	siete scesi/e
loro	sono scesi/e

IMPERFECT

io	scendevo
tu	scendevi
lui/lei/Lei	scendeva
noi	scendevamo
voi	scendevate
loro	scendevano

GERUND
scendendo

PAST PARTICIPLE
sceso

EXAMPLE PHRASES

Sali tu o **scendo** io? Are you coming up or shall I come down?

Scendo subito! I'm coming!

La temperatura **è scesa** di due gradi. The temperature fell by two degrees.

Scendevo le scale quando sono inciampata. I tripped coming down the stairs.

Si è storto una caviglia **scendendo** dalla macchina. He twisted his ankle getting out of the car.

Remember that subject pronouns are not used very often in Italian.

scendere

FUTURE

io	scenderò
tu	scenderai
lui/lei/Lei	scenderà
noi	scenderemo
voi	scenderete
loro	scenderanno

CONDITIONAL

io	scenderei
tu	scenderesti
lui/lei/Lei	scenderebbe
noi	scenderemmo
voi	scendereste
loro	scenderebbero

PAST HISTORIC

io	scesi
tu	scendesti
lui/lei/Lei	scese
noi	scendemmo
voi	scendeste
loro	scesero

PLUPERFECT

io	ero sceso/a
tu	eri sceso/a
lui/lei/Lei	era sceso/a
noi	eravamo scesi/e
voi	eravate scesi/e
loro	erano scesi/e

IMPERATIVE

scendi
scendiamo
scendete

EXAMPLE PHRASES

Dopo le feste i prezzi **scenderanno**. After the holidays prices will come down.

Sono arrivati. **Scendi** ad aprire la porta. They're here. Go down and open the door.

Italic letters in Italian words show where stress does not follow the usual rules.

sciare (to ski)

PRESENT

io	**scio**
tu	**scii**
lui/lei/Lei	**scia**
noi	**sciamo**
voi	**sciate**
loro	**sciano**

PRESENT SUBJUNCTIVE

io	**scii**
tu	**scii**
lui/lei/Lei	**scii**
noi	**sciamo**
voi	**sciate**
loro	**sciino**

PERFECT

io	**ho sciato**
tu	**hai sciato**
lui/lei/Lei	**ha sciato**
noi	**abbiamo sciato**
voi	**avete sciato**
loro	**hanno sciato**

IMPERFECT

io	**sciavo**
tu	**sciavi**
lui/lei/Lei	**sciava**
noi	**sciavamo**
voi	**sciavate**
loro	**sciavano**

GERUND

sciando

PAST PARTICIPLE

sciato

EXAMPLE PHRASES

Scia come un campione. He skis like a champion.

Sai **sciare**? Can you ski?

Abbiamo sciato tutto il giorno. We skied all day.

Si è rotto la gamba **sciando**. He broke his leg when he was skiing.

Remember that subject pronouns are not used very often in Italian.

sciare

FUTURE

io	**scierò**
tu	**scierai**
lui/lei/Lei	**scierà**
noi	**scieremo**
voi	**scierete**
loro	**scieranno**

CONDITIONAL

io	**scierei**
tu	**scieresti**
lui/lei/Lei	**scierebbe**
noi	**scieremmo**
voi	**sciereste**
loro	**scierebbero**

PAST HISTORIC

io	**sciai**
tu	**sciasti**
lui/lei/Lei	**sciò**
noi	**sciammo**
voi	**sciaste**
loro	**sciarono**

PLUPERFECT

io	**avevo sciato**
tu	**avevi sciato**
lui/lei/Lei	**aveva sciato**
noi	**avevamo sciato**
voi	**avevate sciato**
loro	**avevano sciato**

IMPERATIVE

scia
sciamo
sciate

EXAMPLE PHRASES

Se seguirai i miei consigli **scierai** meglio. If you follow my advice you'll
  ski better.

Adoro la montagna: **scierei** sempre. I love the mountains: I'd like to spend
  all my time skiing.

Sciò molto bene e vinse la gara. She skied very well and won the competition.

Avevamo sciato a lungo ed eravamo stanchi. We'd been skiing for a long
  time and were tired.

Italic letters in Italian words show where stress does not follow the usual rules.

sciogliere (to melt)

PRESENT

io	sciolgo
tu	sciogli
lui/lei/Lei	scioglie
noi	sciogliamo
voi	sciogliete
loro	sciolgono

PRESENT SUBJUNCTIVE

io	sciolga
tu	sciolga
lui/lei/Lei	sciolga
noi	sciogliamo
voi	sciogliate
loro	sciolgano

PERFECT

io	ho sciolto
tu	hai sciolto
lui/lei/Lei	ha sciolto
noi	abbiamo sciolto
voi	avete sciolto
loro	hanno sciolto

IMPERFECT

io	scioglievo
tu	scioglievi
lui/lei/Lei	scioglieva
noi	scioglievamo
voi	scioglievate
loro	scioglievano

GERUND
sciogliendo

PAST PARTICIPLE
sciolto

EXAMPLE PHRASES

Nell'acqua il sale si **scioglie**. Salt dissolves in water.

Fai attenzione che i nodi non si **sciolgano**. Be careful that the knots don't come undone.

Il sole **ha sciolto** la neve. The sun has melted the snow.

La neve si **è sciolta** al sole. The snow melted in the sun.

Remember that subject pronouns are not used very often in Italian.

sciogliere

FUTURE

io	scioglierò
tu	scioglierai
lui/lei/Lei	scioglierà
noi	scioglieremo
voi	scioglierete
loro	scioglieranno

CONDITIONAL

io	scioglierei
tu	scioglieresti
lui/lei/Lei	scioglierebbe
noi	scioglieremmo
voi	sciogliereste
loro	scioglierebbero

PAST HISTORIC

io	sciolsi
tu	sciogliesti
lui/lei/Lei	sciolse
noi	sciogliemmo
voi	scioglieste
loro	sciolsero

PLUPERFECT

io	avevo sciolto
tu	avevi sciolto
lui/lei/Lei	aveva sciolto
noi	avevamo sciolto
voi	avevate sciolto
loro	avevano sciolto

IMPERATIVE

sciogli
sciogliamo
sciogliete

EXAMPLE PHRASES

Si **sciolse** i capelli. She undid her hair.

Sciogli la barca che salpiamo! Untie the boat so we can move off.

Facevamo esercizi per **sciogliere** i muscoli. We did exercises to loosen up our muscles.

Italic letters in Italian words show where stress does not follow the usual rules.

sconfiggere (to defeat)

PRESENT

io	sconfiggo
tu	sconfiggi
lui/lei/Lei	sconfigge
noi	sconfiggiamo
voi	sconfiggete
loro	sconfiggono

PRESENT SUBJUNCTIVE

io	sconfigga
tu	sconfigga
lui/lei/Lei	sconfigga
noi	sconfiggiamo
voi	sconfiggiate
loro	sconfiggano

PERFECT

io	ho sconfitto
tu	hai sconfitto
lui/lei/Lei	ha sconfitto
noi	abbiamo sconfitto
voi	avete sconfitto
loro	hanno sconfitto

IMPERFECT

io	sconfiggevo
tu	sconfiggevi
lui/lei/Lei	sconfiggeva
noi	sconfiggevamo
voi	sconfiggevate
loro	sconfiggevano

GERUND

sconfiggendo

PAST PARTICIPLE

sconfitto

EXAMPLE PHRASES

Hanno finalmente **sconfitto** la malattia. They have at last conquered the disease.

Li **hanno sconfitti** uno a zero. They beat them one nil.

La mia squadra **è** stata **sconfitta**. My team was beaten.

Remember that subject pronouns are not used very often in Italian.

sconfiggere

FUTURE

io	sconfiggerò
tu	sconfiggerai
lui/lei/Lei	sconfiggerà
noi	sconfiggeremo
voi	sconfiggerete
loro	sconfiggeranno

CONDITIONAL

io	sconfiggerei
tu	sconfiggeresti
lui/lei/Lei	sconfiggerebbe
noi	sconfiggeremmo
voi	sconfiggereste
loro	sconfiggerebbero

PAST HISTORIC

io	sconfissi
tu	sconfiggesti
lui/lei/Lei	sconfisse
noi	sconfiggemmo
voi	sconfiggeste
loro	sconfissero

PLUPERFECT

io	avevo sconfitto
tu	avevi sconfitto
lui/lei/Lei	aveva sconfitto
noi	avevamo sconfitto
voi	avevate sconfitto
loro	avevano sconfitto

IMPERATIVE

sconfiggi
sconfiggiamo
sconfiggete

EXAMPLE PHRASES

Quel candidato **sconfiggerà** certamente tutti gli altri. This candidate is sure to defeat all the others.

Se fossi in forma non mi **sconfiggeresti** mai. If I was fit you'd never beat me.

L'esercito **sconfisse** i nemici. The army defeated the enemy.

Era triste perché lo **avevano sconfitto**. He was unhappy because they'd beaten him.

Attacchiamo e **sconfiggiamoli**! Let's attack and defeat them!

Italic letters in Italian words show where stress does not follow the usual rules.

scrivere (to write)

PRESENT

io	scrivo
tu	scrivi
lui/lei/Lei	scrive
noi	scriviamo
voi	scrivete
loro	scrivono

PRESENT SUBJUNCTIVE

io	scriva
tu	scriva
lui/lei/Lei	scriva
noi	scriviamo
voi	scriviate
loro	scrivano

PERFECT

io	ho scritto
tu	hai scritto
lui/lei/Lei	ha scritto
noi	abbiamo scritto
voi	avete scritto
loro	hanno scritto

IMPERFECT

io	scrivevo
tu	scrivevi
lui/lei/Lei	scriveva
noi	scrivevamo
voi	scrivevate
loro	scrivevano

GERUND

scrivendo

PAST PARTICIPLE

scritto

EXAMPLE PHRASES

Scrivo molti sms ai miei amici. I write lots of text messages to my friends.

Come si **scrive**? How do you spell it?

Ho scritto una mail a Luca. I sent Luca an email.

A Natale ci **scrivevano** sempre. They always wrote to us at Christmas.

Non so **scrivere** velocemente al computer. I can't type fast on the computer.

Sta **scrivendo** la tesi di laurea. She's writing her thesis.

Remember that subject pronouns are not used very often in Italian.

scrivere

FUTURE

io	scriverò
tu	scriverai
lui/lei/Lei	scriverà
noi	scriveremo
voi	scriverete
loro	scriveranno

CONDITIONAL

io	scriverei
tu	scriveresti
lui/lei/Lei	scriverebbe
noi	scriveremmo
voi	scrivereste
loro	scriverebbero

PAST HISTORIC

io	scrissi
tu	scrivesti
lui/lei/Lei	scrisse
noi	scrivemmo
voi	scriveste
loro	scrissero

PLUPERFECT

io	avevo scritto
tu	avevi scritto
lui/lei/Lei	aveva scritto
noi	avevamo scritto
voi	avevate scritto
loro	avevano scritto

IMPERATIVE

scrivi
scriviamo
scrivete

EXAMPLE PHRASES

Avevo scritto un appunto ma l'ho perso. I'd written a note but lost it.

Scrivimi presto. Write to me soon.

Italic letters in Italian words show where stress does not follow the usual rules.

scuotere (to shake)

PRESENT

io	**scuoto**
tu	**scuoti**
lui/lei/Lei	**scuote**
noi	**scuotiamo**
voi	**scuotete**
loro	**scuotono**

PRESENT SUBJUNCTIVE

io	**scuota**
tu	**scuota**
lui/lei/Lei	**scuota**
noi	**scuotiamo**
voi	**scuotiate**
loro	**scuotano**

PERFECT

io	**ho scosso**
tu	**hai scosso**
lui/lei/Lei	**ha scosso**
noi	**abbiamo scosso**
voi	**avete scosso**
loro	**hanno scosso**

IMPERFECT

io	**scuotevo**
tu	**scuotevi**
lui/lei/Lei	**scuoteva**
noi	**scuotevamo**
voi	**scuotevate**
loro	**scuotevano**

GERUND
scuotendo

PAST PARTICIPLE
scosso

EXAMPLE PHRASES

È sul terrazzo che **scuote** i tappeti. She's on the balcony shaking the rugs.

Ha scosso la testa. He shook his head.

Scuoteva la scatola per capire cosa conteneva. He shook the box to see what was in it.

Stava **scuotendo** la borsa per farne uscire il contenuto. She was shaking the contents out of the bag.

Se ne andò **scuotendo** la testa senza parlare. She went off, shaking her head but saying nothing.

Remember that subject pronouns are not used very often in Italian.

scuotere

FUTURE

io	**scuoterò**
tu	**scuoterai**
lui/lei/Lei	**scuoterà**
noi	**scuoteremo**
voi	**scuoterete**
loro	**scuoteranno**

CONDITIONAL

io	**scuoterei**
tu	**scuoteresti**
lui/lei/Lei	**scuoterebbe**
noi	**scuoteremmo**
voi	**scuotereste**
loro	**scuoterebbero**

PAST HISTORIC

io	**scossi**
tu	**scuotesti**
lui/lei/Lei	**scosse**
noi	**scuotemmo**
voi	**scuoteste**
loro	**scossero**

PLUPERFECT

io	**avevo scosso**
tu	**avevi scosso**
lui/lei/Lei	**aveva scosso**
noi	**avevamo scosso**
voi	**avevate scosso**
loro	**avevano scosso**

IMPERATIVE

scuoti
scuotiamo
scuotete

EXAMPLE PHRASES

Quel rumore mi **scosse** i nervi. That noise drove me mad.

Italic letters in Italian words show where stress does not follow the usual rules.

sedere (to sit)

PRESENT

io	**siedo**
tu	**siedi**
lui/lei/Lei	**siede**
noi	**sediamo**
voi	**sedete**
loro	**siedono**

PRESENT SUBJUNCTIVE

io	**sieda**
tu	**sieda**
lui/lei/Lei	**sieda**
noi	**sediamo**
voi	**sediate**
loro	**siedano**

PERFECT

io	**sono seduto/a**
tu	**sei seduto/a**
lui/lei/Lei	**è seduto/a**
noi	**siamo seduti/e**
voi	**siete seduti/e**
loro	**sono seduti/e**

IMPERFECT

io	**sedevo**
tu	**sedevi**
lui/lei/Lei	**sedeva**
noi	**sedevamo**
voi	**sedevate**
loro	**sedevano**

GERUND

sedendo

PAST PARTICIPLE

seduto

EXAMPLE PHRASES

Si **siede** sempre in ultima fila. She always sits in the back row.

Prego, si **sieda** qui accanto. Please sit here beside me.

Si **è seduto** per terra. He sat on the floor.

Sono stato **seduto** tutto il giorno. I've been sitting down all day.

Sedevano in silenzio e leggevano. They were sitting in silence reading.

Remember that subject pronouns are not used very often in Italian.

sedere

FUTURE

io	**sederò**
tu	**sederai**
lui/lei/Lei	**sederà**
noi	**sederemo**
voi	**sederete**
loro	**sederanno**

CONDITIONAL

io	**sederei**
tu	**sederesti**
lui/lei/Lei	**sederebbe**
noi	**sederemmo**
voi	**sedereste**
loro	**sederebbero**

PAST HISTORIC

io	**sedetti**
tu	**sedesti**
lui/lei/Lei	**sedette**
noi	**sedemmo**
voi	**sedeste**
loro	**sedettero**

PLUPERFECT

io	**ero seduto/a**
tu	**eri seduto/a**
lui/lei/Lei	**era seduto/a**
noi	**eravamo seduti/e**
voi	**eravate seduti/e**
loro	**erano seduti/e**

IMPERATIVE
siedi
sediamo
sedete

EXAMPLE PHRASES

Si **sedettero** a tavola e iniziarono la cena. They sat down at the table and started dinner.

Era seduta accanto a me. She was sitting beside me.

Siediti qui! Sit here!

Italic letters in Italian words show where stress does not follow the usual rules.

soddisfare (to satisfy)

PRESENT		PRESENT SUBJUNCTIVE	
io	soddisfo	io	soddisfi
tu	soddisfi	tu	soddisfi
lui/lei/Lei	soddisfa	lui/lei/Lei	soddisfi
noi	soddisfiamo	noi	soddisfiamo
voi	soddisfate	voi	soddisfiate
loro	soddisfano	loro	soddisfino

PERFECT		IMPERFECT	
io	ho soddisfatto	io	soddisfacevo
tu	hai soddisfatto	tu	soddisfacevi
lui/lei/Lei	ha soddisfatto	lui/lei/Lei	soddisfaceva
noi	abbiamo soddisfatto	noi	soddisfacevamo
voi	avete soddisfatto	voi	soddisfacevate
loro	hanno soddisfatto	loro	soddisfacevano

GERUND	PAST PARTICIPLE
soddisfacendo	soddisfatto

EXAMPLE PHRASES

Il mio lavoro non mi **soddisfa**. My job doesn't satisfy me.

Soddisfaceva ogni desiderio della moglie. He satisfied his wife's every wish.

Remember that subject pronouns are not used very often in Italian.

soddisfare

FUTURE

io	soddisfer*ò*
tu	soddisferai
lui/lei/Lei	soddisfer*à*
noi	soddisferemo
voi	soddisferete
loro	soddisferanno

CONDITIONAL

io	soddisferei
tu	soddisferesti
lui/lei/Lei	soddisferebbe
noi	soddisferemmo
voi	soddisfereste
loro	soddisferebbero

PAST HISTORIC

io	soddisfeci
tu	soddisfacesti
lui/lei/Lei	soddisfece
noi	soddisfacemmo
voi	soddisfaceste
loro	soddisfecero

PLUPERFECT

Io	avevo soddisfatto
tu	avevi soddisfatto
lui/lei/Lei	aveva soddisfatto
noi	avevamo soddisfatto
voi	avevate soddisfatto
loro	avevano soddisfatto

IMPERATIVE

soddisfa
soddisfiamo
soddisfate

EXAMPLE PHRASES

Questo libro **soddisfer*à*** i lettori più esigenti. This book will please the most demanding readers.

Questa soluzione non ci **soddisferebbe**. We wouldn't be satisfied by this solution.

La sua scelta non li **aveva soddisfatti**. They hadn't been pleased with her choice.

Italic letters in Italian words show where stress does not follow the usual rules.

sognare (to dream)

PRESENT		PRESENT SUBJUNCTIVE	
io	**sogno**	io	**sogni**
tu	**sogni**	tu	**sogni**
lui/lei/Lei	**sogna**	lui/lei/Lei	**sogni**
noi	**sogniamo**	noi	**sogniamo**
voi	**sognate**	voi	**sogniate**
loro	**sognano**	loro	**sognino**

PERFECT		IMPERFECT	
io	**ho sognato**	io	**sognavo**
tu	**hai sognato**	tu	**sognavi**
lui/lei/Lei	**ha sognato**	lui/lei/Lei	**sognava**
noi	**abbiamo sognato**	noi	**sognavamo**
voi	**avete sognato**	voi	**sognavate**
loro	**hanno sognato**	loro	**sognavano**

GERUND
sognando

PAST PARTICIPLE
sognato

EXAMPLE PHRASES

Stanotte ti **ho sognato**. I dreamt about you last night.

Tutte le notti **sognavo** la stessa cosa. I had the same dream every night.

Stavo **sognando** ad occhi aperti. I was daydreaming.

Remember that subject pronouns are not used very often in Italian.

sognare

FUTURE

io	**sognerò**
tu	**sognerai**
lui/lei/Lei	**sognerà**
noi	**sogneremo**
voi	**sognerete**
loro	**sogneranno**

CONDITIONAL

io	**sognerei**
tu	**sogneresti**
lui/lei/Lei	**sognerebbe**
noi	**sogneremmo**
voi	**sognereste**
loro	**sognerebbero**

PAST HISTORIC

io	**sognai**
tu	**sognasti**
lui/lei/Lei	**sognò**
noi	**sognammo**
voi	**sognaste**
loro	**sognarono**

PLUPERFECT

io	**avevo sognato**
tu	**avevi sognato**
lui/lei/Lei	**aveva sognato**
noi	**avevamo sognato**
voi	**avevate sognato**
loro	**avevano sognato**

IMPERATIVE

sogna
sogniamo
sognate

EXAMPLE PHRASES

Non ci **sogneremmo** mai di chiedere una cosa simile. We'd never dream
   of asking for something like that.
Sognai di essere sulla luna. I dreamt I was on the moon.
Avevo sempre **sognato** una casa così. I'd always dreamt of a house like that.
Smetti di **sognare** e sii realista. Stop dreaming and be realistic.
Ve lo **sognate**! You can forget it!

Italic letters in Italian words show where stress does not follow the usual rules.

sparire (to disappear)

PRESENT		PRESENT SUBJUNCTIVE	
io	sparisco	io	sparisca
tu	sparisci	tu	sparisca
lui/lei/Lei	sparisce	lui/lei/Lei	sparisca
noi	spariamo	noi	spariamo
voi	sparite	voi	spariate
loro	spariscono	loro	spariscano

PERFECT		IMPERFECT	
io	sono sparito/a	io	sparivo
tu	sei sparito/a	tu	sparivi
lui/lei/Lei	è sparito/a	lui/lei/Lei	spariva
noi	siamo spariti/e	noi	sparivamo
voi	siete spariti/e	voi	sparivate
loro	sono spariti/e	loro	sparivano

GERUND	PAST PARTICIPLE
sparendo	sparito

EXAMPLE PHRASES

Sparisce ogni volta che c'è bisogno di lui. He disappears whenever he's needed.

La nave **è sparita** all'orizzonte. The ship disappeared over the horizon.

Dov'**è sparita** la mia penna? Where has my pen gone?

Remember that subject pronouns are not used very often in Italian.

sparire

FUTURE

io	**sparirò**
tu	**sparirai**
lui/lei/Lei	**sparirà**
noi	**spariremo**
voi	**sparirete**
loro	**spariranno**

CONDITIONAL

io	**sparirei**
tu	**spariresti**
lui/lei/Lei	**sparirebbe**
noi	**spariremmo**
voi	**sparireste**
loro	**sparirebbero**

PAST HISTORIC

io	**sparii**
tu	**sparisti**
lui/lei/Lei	**sparì**
noi	**sparimmo**
voi	**spariste**
loro	**sparirono**

PLUPERFECT

io	**ero sparito/a**
tu	**eri sparito/a**
lui/lei/Lei	**era sparito/a**
noi	**eravamo spariti/e**
voi	**eravate spariti/e**
loro	**erano spariti/e**

IMPERATIVE

sparisci
spariamo
sparite

EXAMPLE PHRASES

Spariranno dopo cena, come al solito. They'll go off after dinner, as usual.

Sparì senza salutare nessuno. He went off without saying goodbye to anyone.

Erano spariti senza lasciare traccia. They had disappeared without trace.

Sparisci e non farti più vedere! Be off with you and don't show your face around here again!

Italic letters in Italian words show where stress does not follow the usual rules.

spegnere (to put out)

PRESENT

io	**spengo**
tu	**spegni**
lui/lei/Lei	**spegne**
noi	**spegniamo**
voi	**spegnete**
loro	**spengono**

PRESENT SUBJUNCTIVE

io	**spenga**
tu	**spenga**
lui/lei/Lei	**spenga**
noi	**spegniamo**
voi	**spegniate**
loro	**spengano**

PERFECT

io	**ho spento**
tu	**hai spento**
lui/lei/Lei	**ha spento**
noi	**abbiamo spento**
voi	**avete spento**
loro	**hanno spento**

IMPERFECT

io	**spegnevo**
tu	**spegnevi**
lui/lei/Lei	**spegneva**
noi	**spegnevamo**
voi	**spegnevate**
loro	**spegnevano**

GERUND

spegnendo

PAST PARTICIPLE

spento

EXAMPLE PHRASES

L'ultimo **spenga** la luce e chiuda la porta. Will the last person turn off the light and shut the door.

Hai spento la sigaretta? Have you put your cigarette out?

La luce si è **spenta** all'improvviso. The light went off suddenly.

La candela si stava **spegnendo** lentamente. The candle was slowly going out.

what exactly is the polite Atino word?

Remember that subject pronouns are not used very often in Italian.

spegnere

FUTURE

io	spegnerò
tu	spegnerai
lui/lei/Lei	spegnerà
noi	spegneremo
voi	spegnerete
loro	spegneranno

CONDITIONAL

io	spegnerei
tu	spegneresti
lui/lei/Lei	spegnerebbe
noi	spegneremmo
voi	spegnereste
loro	spegnerebbero

PAST HISTORIC

io	spensi
tu	spegnesti
lui/lei/Lei	spense
noi	spegnemmo
voi	spegneste
loro	spensero

PLUPERFECT

io	avevo spento
tu	avevi spento
lui/lei/Lei	aveva spento
noi	avevamo spento
voi	avevate spento
loro	avevano spento

IMPERATIVE

spegni
spegniamo
spegnete

EXAMPLE PHRASES

Senza ossigeno il fuoco si **spegnerebbe**. Without oxygen the fire would go out.

Il motore si **spense** al semaforo. The engine stalled at the traffic lights.

Spegnete le luci che guardiamo il film. Turn off the lights and we'll watch
   the film.

Italic letters in Italian words show where stress does not follow the usual rules.

spendere (to spend)

PRESENT

io	spendo
tu	spendi
lui/lei/Lei	spende
noi	spendiamo
voi	spendete
loro	spendono

PRESENT SUBJUNCTIVE

io	spenda
tu	spenda
lui/lei/Lei	spenda
noi	spendiamo
voi	spendiate
loro	spendano

PERFECT

io	ho speso
tu	hai speso
lui/lei/Lei	ha speso
noi	abbiamo speso
voi	avete speso
loro	hanno speso

IMPERFECT

io	spendevo
tu	spendevi
lui/lei/Lei	spendeva
noi	spendevamo
voi	spendevate
loro	spendevano

GERUND

spendendo

PAST PARTICIPLE

speso

EXAMPLE PHRASES

Si mangia bene e si **spende** poco. The food's good and it doesn't cost much.

Quanto **hai speso**? How much did you spend?

Spendeva tutto quello che guadagnava. He spent all he earned.

Ultimamente stiamo **spendendo** troppo. We've been spending too much lately.

Remember that subject pronouns are not used very often in Italian.

spendere

FUTURE

io	**spenderò**
tu	**spenderai**
lui/lei/Lei	**spenderà**
noi	**spenderemo**
voi	**spenderete**
loro	**spenderanno**

CONDITIONAL

io	**spenderei**
tu	**spenderesti**
lui/lei/Lei	**spenderebbe**
noi	**spenderemmo**
voi	**spendereste**
loro	**spenderebbero**

PAST HISTORIC

io	**spesi**
tu	**spendesti**
lui/lei/Lei	**spese**
noi	**spendemmo**
voi	**spendeste**
loro	**spesero**

PLUPERFECT

io	**avevo speso**
tu	**avevi speso**
lui/lei/Lei	**aveva speso**
noi	**avevamo speso**
voi	**avevate speso**
loro	**avevano speso**

IMPERATIVE

spendi
spendiamo
spendete

EXAMPLE PHRASES

Lì **spenderete** poco e starete bene. You won't have to pay much there, and you'll be comfortable.

Non **spenderei** mai una cifra simile. I'd never spend as much as that.

Entrò nel negozio e **spese** tutto ciò che aveva. She went into the shop and spent all she had.

Aveva speso tutto al gioco e si è indebitato. He'd spent all his money gambling and was in debt.

Italic letters in Italian words show where stress does not follow the usual rules.

sporgersi (to lean out)

PRESENT

io	**mi sporgo**
tu	**ti sporgi**
lui/lei/Lei	**si sporge**
noi	**ci sporgiamo**
voi	**vi sporgete**
loro	**si sporgono**

PRESENT SUBJUNCTIVE

io	**mi sporga**
tu	**ti sporga**
lui/lei/Lei	**si sporga**
noi	**ci sporgiamo**
voi	**vi sporgiate**
loro	**si sporgano**

PERFECT

io	**mi sono sporto/a**
tu	**ti sei sporto/a**
lui/lei/Lei	**si è sporto/a**
noi	**ci siamo sporti/e**
voi	**vi siete sporti/e**
loro	**si sono sporti/e**

IMPERFECT

io	**mi sporgevo**
tu	**ti sporgevi**
lui/lei/Lei	**si sporgeva**
noi	**ci sporgevamo**
voi	**vi sporgevate**
loro	**si sporgevano**

GERUND
sporgendosi

PAST PARTICIPLE
sporto

EXAMPLE PHRASES
Sporgendoti, vedrai meglio. If you lean out you'll see better.

sporgersi

FUTURE

io	**mi sporgerò**
tu	**ti sporgerai**
lui/lei/Lei	**si sporgerà**
noi	**ci sporgeremo**
voi	**vi sporgerete**
loro	**si sporgeranno**

CONDITIONAL

io	**mi sporgerei**
tu	**ti sporgeresti**
lui/lei/Lei	**si sporgerebbe**
noi	**ci sporgeremmo**
voi	**vi sporgereste**
loro	**si sporgerebbero**

PAST HISTORIC

io	**mi sporsi**
tu	**ti sporgesti**
lui/lei/Lei	**si sporse**
noi	**ci sporgemmo**
voi	**vi sporgeste**
loro	**si sporsero**

PLUPERFECT

io	**mi ero sporto/a**
tu	**ti eri sporto/a**
lui/lei/Lei	**si era sporto/a**
noi	**ci eravamo sporti/e**
voi	**vi eravate sporti/e**
loro	**si erano sporti/e**

IMPERATIVE

sporgiti
sporgiamoci
sporgetevi

EXAMPLE PHRASES

Si **sporsero** per guardare la sfilata. They leaned out to watch the parade.

Si **era sporto** per salutare. He'd leant out to say hello.

Non **sporgerti** dal finestrino. Don't lean out of the window.

Italic letters in Italian words show where stress does not follow the usual rules.

stare (to be)

PRESENT

io	**sto**
tu	**stai**
lui/lei/Lei	**sta**
noi	**stiamo**
voi	**state**
loro	**stanno**

PRESENT SUBJUNCTIVE

io	**stia**
tu	**stia**
lui/lei/Lei	**stia**
noi	**stiamo**
voi	**stiate**
loro	**stiano**

PERFECT

io	**sono stato/a**
tu	**sei stato/a**
lui/lei/Lei	**è stato/a**
noi	**siamo stati/e**
voi	**siete stati/e**
loro	**sono stati/e**

IMPERFECT

io	**stavo**
tu	**stavi**
lui/lei/Lei	**stava**
noi	**stavamo**
voi	**stavate**
loro	**stavano**

GERUND

stando

PAST PARTICIPLE

stato

EXAMPLE PHRASES

Come **stai**? How are you?

Sta a te decidere. It's up to you to decide.

Sei mai **stato** in Francia? Have you ever been to France?

Stavo per uscire quando ha squillato il telefono. I was about to go out when the phone rang.

Stavo andando a casa. I was going home.

Stando così le cose, non voglio aiutarti. In this situation I don't want to help you.

Remember that subject pronouns are not used very often in Italian.

stare

FUTURE

io	**starò**
tu	**starai**
lui/lei/Lei	**starà**
noi	**staremo**
voi	**starete**
loro	**staranno**

CONDITIONAL

io	**starei**
tu	**staresti**
lui/lei/Lei	**starebbe**
noi	**staremmo**
voi	**stareste**
loro	**starebbero**

PAST HISTORIC

io	**stetti**
tu	**stesti**
lui/lei/Lei	**stette**
noi	**stemmo**
voi	**steste**
loro	**stettero**

PLUPERFECT

io	**ero stato/a**
tu	**eri stato/a**
lui/lei/Lei	**era stato/a**
noi	**eravamo stati/e**
voi	**eravate stati/e**
loro	**erano stati/e**

IMPERATIVE

stai
stiamo
state

EXAMPLE PHRASES

A Londra **starò** da amici. I'll be staying with friends in London.

Ci **stareste** a fare uno scherzo a Monica? Do you want to play a trick on Monica?

Era stata zitta tutta la sera. She'd been silent all evening.

Stai ancora un po'! Stay a bit longer!

Italic letters in Italian words show where stress does not follow the usual rules.

storcere (to twist)

PRESENT		PRESENT SUBJUNCTIVE	
io	storco	io	storca
tu	storci	tu	storca
lui/lei/Lei	storce	lui/lei/Lei	storca
noi	storciamo	noi	storciamo
voi	storcete	voi	storciate
loro	storcono	loro	storcano

PERFECT		IMPERFECT	
io	ho storto	io	storcevo
tu	hai storto	tu	storcevi
lui/lei/Lei	ha storto	lui/lei/Lei	storceva
noi	abbiamo storto	noi	storcevamo
voi	avete storto	voi	storcevate
loro	hanno storto	loro	storcevano

GERUND
storcendo

PAST PARTICIPLE
storto

EXAMPLE PHRASES

Storce sempre il naso se c'è da lavorare. He always turns up his nose if there's any work to be done.

È inutile che tu **storca** il naso. There's no point turning up your nose.

Le **ha storto** un braccio. He twisted her arm.

Mi **sono storto** una caviglia. I've twisted my ankle.

Remember that subject pronouns are not used very often in Italian.

storcere

FUTURE

io	**storcerò**
tu	**storcerai**
lui/lei/Lei	**storcerà**
noi	**storceremo**
voi	**storcerete**
loro	**storceranno**

CONDITIONAL

io	**storcerei**
tu	**storceresti**
lui/lei/Lei	**storcerebbe**
noi	**storceremmo**
voi	**storcereste**
loro	**storcerebbero**

PAST HISTORIC

io	**storsi**
tu	**storcesti**
lui/lei/Lei	**storse**
noi	**storcemmo**
voi	**storceste**
loro	**storsero**

PLUPERFECT

io	**avevo storto**
tu	**avevi storto**
lui/lei/Lei	**aveva storto**
noi	**avevamo storto**
voi	**avevate storto**
loro	**avevano storto**

IMPERATIVE

storci
storciamo
storcete

EXAMPLE PHRASES

Non **storceresti** il naso se fossi meno schizzinoso. You wouldn't turn up your nose if you weren't so fussy.

Guardò il cibo e **storse** il naso. He looked at the food and turned up his nose.

Italic letters in Italian words show where stress does not follow the usual rules.

stringere (to tighten)

PRESENT		PRESENT SUBJUNCTIVE	
io	**stringo**	io	**stringa**
tu	**stringi**	tu	**stringa**
lui/lei/Lei	**stringe**	lui/lei/Lei	**stringa**
noi	**stringiamo**	noi	**stringiamo**
voi	**stringete**	voi	**stringiate**
loro	**stringono**	loro	**stringano**

PERFECT		IMPERFECT	
io	**ho stretto**	io	**stringevo**
tu	**hai stretto**	tu	**stringevi**
lui/lei/Lei	**ha stretto**	lui/lei/Lei	**stringeva**
noi	**abbiamo stretto**	noi	**stringevamo**
voi	**avete stretto**	voi	**stringevate**
loro	**hanno stretto**	loro	**stringevano**

GERUND
stringendo

PAST PARTICIPLE
stretto

EXAMPLE PHRASES

La gonna è larga: bisogna che la **stringa**. The skirt is too loose: I'll have to take it in.

Ho stretto la cintura perché sono dimagrita. I've tightened my belt because I've lost weight.

Ci **siamo stretti** la mano. We shook hands.

Le scarpe **stringevano** e ho dovuto cambiarle. The shoes were too tight so I had to change them.

Remember that subject pronouns are not used very often in Italian.

stringere

FUTURE

io	**stringerò**
tu	**stringerai**
lui/lei/Lei	**stringerà**
noi	**stringeremo**
voi	**stringerete**
loro	**stringeranno**

CONDITIONAL

io	**stringerei**
tu	**stringeresti**
lui/lei/Lei	**stringerebbe**
noi	**stringeremmo**
voi	**stringereste**
loro	**stringerebbero**

PAST HISTORIC

io	**strinsi**
tu	**stringesti**
lui/lei/Lei	**strinse**
noi	**stringemmo**
voi	**stringeste**
loro	**strinsero**

PLUPERFECT

io	**avevo stretto**
tu	**avevi stretto**
lui/lei/Lei	**aveva stretto**
noi	**avevamo stretto**
voi	**avevate stretto**
loro	**avevano stretto**

IMPERATIVE

stringi
stringiamo
stringete

EXAMPLE PHRASES

Se ci **stringeremo** ci staremo tutti. If we squeeze up we'll all get in.

Stringiamo i denti e continuiamo. Let's grit our teeth and carry on.

Italic letters in Italian words show where stress does not follow the usual rules.

succedere (to happen)

PRESENT

io	–
tu	–
lui/lei/Lei	**succede**
noi	–
voi	–
loro	**succedono**

PRESENT SUBJUNCTIVE

io	–
tu	–
lui/lei/Lei	**succeda**
noi	–
voi	–
loro	**succedano**

PERFECT

io	–
tu	–
lui/lei/Lei	**è successo/a**
noi	–
voi	–
loro	**sono successi/e**

IMPERFECT

io	–
tu	–
lui/lei/Lei	**succedeva**
noi	–
voi	–
loro	**succedevano**

GERUND

succedendo

PAST PARTICIPLE

successo

EXAMPLE PHRASES

Sono cose che **succedono**. These things happen.

Non capisco cosa **succeda**. I don't know what might be happening.

Cos'**è successo**? What happened?

Dev'essergli **successo** qualcosa. Something must have happened to him.

Remember that subject pronouns are not used very often in Italian.

succedere

FUTURE

io	–
tu	–
lui/lei/Lei	**succederà**
noi	–
voi	–
loro	**succederanno**

CONDITIONAL

io	–
tu	–
lui/lei/Lei	**succederebbe**
noi	–
voi	–
loro	**succederebbero**

PAST HISTORIC

io	–
tu	–
lui/lei/Lei	**successe**
noi	–
voi	–
loro	**successero**

PLUPERFECT

io	–
tu	–
lui/lei/Lei	**era successo/a**
noi	–
voi	–
loro	**erano successi/e**

IMPERATIVE

–

EXAMPLE PHRASES

Ho paura di ciò che **succederà**. I'm afraid of what will happen.

Cosa **succederebbe** se lui tornasse? What would happen if he came back?

Dalla sua partenza erano **successe** molte cose. A lot of things happened as a consequence of his departure.

Successe il finimondo. All hell broke loose.

Italic letters in Italian words show where stress does not follow the usual rules.

tacere (to be quiet)

PRESENT

io	taccio
tu	taci
lui/lei/Lei	tace
noi	tacciamo
voi	tacete
loro	tacciono

PRESENT SUBJUNCTIVE

io	taccia
tu	taccia
lui/lei/Lei	taccia
noi	tacciamo
voi	tacciate
loro	tacciano

PERFECT

io	ho taciuto
tu	hai taciuto
lui/lei/Lei	ha taciuto
noi	abbiamo taciuto
voi	avete taciuto
loro	hanno taciuto

IMPERFECT

io	tacevo
tu	tacevi
lui/lei/Lei	taceva
noi	tacevamo
voi	tacevate
loro	tacevano

GERUND

tacendo

PAST PARTICIPLE

taciuto

EXAMPLE PHRASES

È meglio che **tacciate**. It's best if you say nothing.

Tacevano e si guardavano. They said nothing and looked at each other.

Pur **tacendo**, gli fece capire che sbagliava. Even though she didn't say anything, she made him realize he was wrong.

Remember that subject pronouns are not used very often in Italian.

tacere

FUTURE

io	**tacerò**
tu	**tacerai**
lui/lei/Lei	**tacerà**
noi	**taceremo**
voi	**tacerete**
loro	**taceranno**

CONDITIONAL

io	**tacerei**
tu	**taceresti**
lui/lei/Lei	**tacerebbe**
noi	**taceremmo**
voi	**tacereste**
loro	**tacerebbero**

PAST HISTORIC

io	**tacqui**
tu	**tacesti**
lui/lei/Lei	**tacque**
noi	**tacemmo**
voi	**taceste**
loro	**tacquero**

PLUPERFECT

io	**avevo taciuto**
tu	**avevi taciuto**
lui/lei/Lei	**aveva taciuto**
noi	**avevamo taciuto**
voi	**avevate taciuto**
loro	**avevano taciuto**

IMPERATIVE

taci
tacciamo
tacete

EXAMPLE PHRASES

Improvvisamente **tacque** e sorrise. He suddenly stopped talking and smiled.
Avevo taciuto a lungo prima di parlare. I'd been silent a long time before
  I spoke.
Taci! Be quiet!

Italic letters in Italian words show where stress does not follow the usual rules.

tenere (to hold)

PRESENT

io	**tengo**
tu	**tieni**
lui/lei/Lei	**tiene**
noi	**teniamo**
voi	**tenete**
loro	**tengono**

PRESENT SUBJUNCTIVE

io	**tenga**
tu	**tenga**
lui/lei/Lei	**tenga**
noi	**teniamo**
voi	**teniate**
loro	**tengano**

PERFECT

io	**ho tenuto**
tu	**hai tenuto**
lui/lei/Lei	**ha tenuto**
noi	**abbiamo tenuto**
voi	**avete tenuto**
loro	**hanno tenuto**

IMPERFECT

io	**tenevo**
tu	**tenevi**
lui/lei/Lei	**teneva**
noi	**tenevamo**
voi	**tenevate**
loro	**tenevano**

GERUND

tenendo

PAST PARTICIPLE

tenuto

EXAMPLE PHRASES

Tiene la racchetta con la sinistra. He holds the racket with his left hand.

La mamma **tiene** in braccio il bambino. The mother is holding the baby.

Ecco i soldi, **tenga** pure il resto. Here's the money, keep the change.

Si **tenevano** per mano. They were holding hands.

Remember that subject pronouns are not used very often in Italian.

tenere

FUTURE

io	**terrò**
tu	**terrai**
lui/lei/Lei	**terrà**
noi	**terremo**
voi	**terrete**
loro	**terranno**

CONDITIONAL

io	**terrei**
tu	**terresti**
lui/lei/Lei	**terrebbe**
noi	**terremmo**
voi	**terreste**
loro	**terrebbero**

PAST HISTORIC

io	**tenni**
tu	**tenesti**
lui/lei/Lei	**tenne**
noi	**tenemmo**
voi	**teneste**
loro	**tennero**

PLUPERFECT

io	**avevo tenuto**
tu	**avevi tenuto**
lui/lei/Lei	**aveva tenuto**
noi	**avevamo tenuto**
voi	**avevate tenuto**
loro	**avevano tenuto**

IMPERATIVE

tieni
teniamo
tenete

EXAMPLE PHRASES

Se non ti serve, lo **terrò** io. If you don't need it I'll keep it.

Mi **terresti** il posto? Torno subito. Could you keep my place for me? I'll be right back.

Ci dettero una parte dei soldi e **tennero** il resto per sé. They gave us some of the money and kept the rest for themselves.

Tieni, questo è per te. Here, this is for you.

Tieniti pronta per le cinque. Be ready by five.

Tieniti forte! Hold on tight!

Italic letters in Italian words show where stress does not follow the usual rules.

togliere (to take off)

PRESENT

io	tolgo
tu	togli
lui/lei/Lei	toglie
noi	togliamo
voi	togliete
loro	tolgono

PRESENT SUBJUNCTIVE

io	tolga
tu	tolga
lui/lei/Lei	tolga
noi	togliamo
voi	togliate
loro	tolgano

PERFECT

io	ho tolto
tu	hai tolto
lui/lei/Lei	ha tolto
noi	abbiamo tolto
voi	avete tolto
loro	hanno tolto

IMPERFECT

io	toglievo
tu	toglievi
lui/lei/Lei	toglieva
noi	toglievamo
voi	toglievate
loro	toglievano

GERUND

togliendo

PAST PARTICIPLE

tolto

EXAMPLE PHRASES

Avevo caldo e mi **sono tolto** la giacca. I was hot and took my jacket off.

Ho tolto il poster dalla parete. I took the poster off the wall.

Stavo **togliendo** i vestiti dall'armadio quando mi hanno chiamato. I was taking clothes out of the cupboard when they phoned me.

Remember that subject pronouns are not used very often in Italian.

togliere

FUTURE

io	**toglierò**
tu	**toglierai**
lui/lei/Lei	**toglierà**
noi	**toglieremo**
voi	**toglierete**
loro	**toglieranno**

CONDITIONAL

io	**toglierei**
tu	**toglieresti**
lui/lei/Lei	**toglierebbe**
noi	**toglieremmo**
voi	**togliereste**
loro	**toglierebbero**

PAST HISTORIC

io	**tolsi**
tu	**togliesti**
lui/lei/Lei	**tolse**
noi	**togliemmo**
voi	**toglieste**
loro	**tolsero**

PLUPERFECT

io	**avevo tolto**
tu	**avevi tolto**
lui/lei/Lei	**aveva tolto**
noi	**avevamo tolto**
voi	**avevate tolto**
loro	**avevano tolto**

IMPERATIVE

togli
togliamo
togliete

EXAMPLE PHRASES

Mi **toglieranno** due denti. I'm going to have two teeth out.

Lo riconobbi solo quando si **tolse** il cappello. I only recognized him when he took his hat off.

Togliti il cappotto. Take off your coat.

Italic letters in Italian words show where stress does not follow the usual rules.

trarre (to draw)

PRESENT		PRESENT SUBJUNCTIVE	
io	traggo	io	tragga
tu	trai	tu	tragga
lui/lei/Lei	trae	lui/lei/Lei	tragga
noi	traiamo	noi	traiamo
voi	traete	voi	traiate
loro	traggono	loro	traggano

PERFECT		IMPERFECT	
io	ho tratto	io	traevo
tu	hai tratto	tu	traevi
lui/lei/Lei	ha tratto	lui/lei/Lei	traeva
noi	abbiamo tratto	noi	traevamo
voi	avete tratto	voi	traevate
loro	hanno tratto	loro	traevano

GERUND
traendo

PAST PARTICIPLE
tratto

EXAMPLE PHRASES

Il suo modo di fare **trae** in inganno. His manner is misleading.

Sono stati **tratti** in salvo dai vigili del fuoco. They were rescued by the firemen.

Un film **tratto** da un romanzo di Agatha Christie. A film based on a novel by Agatha Christie.

Dalla ricerca **hanno tratto** conclusioni interessanti. They've drawn some interesting conclusions from the research.

Traeva tutti in inganno con la sua falsa modestia. She deceived everyone with her false modesty.

Remember that subject pronouns are not used very often in Italian.

trarre

FUTURE

io	**trarrò**
tu	**trarrai**
lui/lei/Lei	**trarrà**
noi	**trarremo**
voi	**trarrete**
loro	**trarranno**

CONDITIONAL

io	**trarrei**
tu	**trarresti**
lui/lei/Lei	**trarrebbe**
noi	**trarremmo**
voi	**trarreste**
loro	**trarrebbero**

PAST HISTORIC

io	**trassi**
tu	**traesti**
lui/lei/Lei	**trasse**
noi	**traemmo**
voi	**traeste**
loro	**trassero**

PLUPERFECT

io	**avevo tratto**
tu	**avevi tratto**
lui/lei/Lei	**aveva tratto**
noi	**avevamo tratto**
voi	**avevate tratto**
loro	**avevano tratto**

IMPERATIVE

trai
traiamo
traete

EXAMPLE PHRASES

Non **trarrei** delle conclusioni così affrettate. I wouldn't draw such hasty conclusions.

Trassero in salvo l'alpinista ferito. They rescued the injured climber.

Italic letters in Italian words show where stress does not follow the usual rules.

uscire (to go out)

PRESENT

io	esco
tu	esci
lui/lei/Lei	esce
noi	usciamo
voi	uscite
loro	escono

PRESENT SUBJUNCTIVE

io	esca
tu	esca
lui/lei/Lei	esca
noi	usciamo
voi	usciate
loro	escano

PERFECT

io	sono uscito/a
tu	sei uscito/a
lui/lei/Lei	è uscito/a
noi	siamo usciti/e
voi	siete usciti/e
loro	sono usciti/e

IMPERFECT

io	uscivo
tu	uscivi
lui/lei/Lei	usciva
noi	uscivamo
voi	uscivate
loro	uscivano

GERUND

uscendo

PAST PARTICIPLE

uscito

EXAMPLE PHRASES

La rivista **esce** di lunedì. The magazine comes out on Mondays.

I suoi non sono contenti che **esca** tutte le sere. Her parents aren't happy with the fact she goes out every evening.

È uscita a comprare il giornale. She's gone out to buy a newspaper.

Li ho incontrati **uscendo**. I met them as I was going out.

L'ho incontrata che **usciva** dalla farmacia. I met her coming out of the chemist's.

Remember that subject pronouns are not used very often in Italian.

uscire

FUTURE

io	**uscirò**
tu	**uscirai**
lui/lei/Lei	**uscirà**
noi	**usciremo**
voi	**uscirete**
loro	**usciranno**

CONDITIONAL

io	**uscirei**
tu	**usciresti**
lui/lei/Lei	**uscirebbe**
noi	**usciremmo**
voi	**uscireste**
loro	**uscirebbero**

PAST HISTORIC

io	**uscii**
tu	**uscisti**
lui/lei/Lei	**uscì**
noi	**uscimmo**
voi	**usciste**
loro	**uscirono**

PLUPERFECT

io	**ero uscito/a**
tu	**eri uscito/a**
lui/lei/Lei	**era uscito/a**
noi	**eravamo usciti/e**
voi	**eravate usciti/e**
loro	**erano usciti/e**

IMPERATIVE

esci
usciamo
uscite

EXAMPLE PHRASES

Uscirà dall'ospedale domani. He's coming out of hospital tomorrow.
Usciresti con me stasera? Would you go out with me this evening?
La macchina **uscì** di strada. The car came off the road.
Quando siamo arrivati **era** appena **uscita**. When we arrived she'd just left.
Uscite di qui immediatamente! Get out of here this minute!

Italic letters in Italian words show where stress does not follow the usual rules.

valere (to be worth)

PRESENT		PRESENT SUBJUNCTIVE	
io	**valgo**	io	**valga**
tu	**vali**	tu	**valga**
lui/lei/Lei	**vale**	lui/lei/Lei	**valga**
noi	**valiamo**	noi	**valiamo**
voi	**valete**	voi	**valiate**
loro	**valgono**	loro	**valgano**

PERFECT		IMPERFECT	
io	**sono valso/a**	io	**valevo**
tu	**sei valso/a**	tu	**valevi**
lui/lei/Lei	**è valso/a**	lui/lei/Lei	**valeva**
noi	**siamo valsi/e**	noi	**valevamo**
voi	**siete valsi/e**	voi	**valevate**
loro	**sono valsi/e**	loro	**valevano**

GERUND	PAST PARTICIPLE
valendo	valso

EXAMPLE PHRASES

L'auto **vale** tremila euro. The car is worth three thousand euros.

Non ne **vale** la pena. It's not worth it.

È stato difficile, ma ne **è valsa** la pena. It was difficult, but it was worth it.

Non **valeva** la pena arrabbiarsi tanto. It wasn't worth getting so angry.

Valendo poco, questa moto è difficile da vendere. Since it's worth so little, this bike is difficult to sell.

Remember that subject pronouns are not used very often in Italian.

valere

FUTURE

io	**varrò**
tu	**varrai**
lui/lei/Lei	**varrà**
noi	**varremo**
voi	**varrete**
loro	**varranno**

CONDITIONAL

io	**varrei**
tu	**varresti**
lui/lei/Lei	**varrebbe**
noi	**varremmo**
voi	**varreste**
loro	**varrebbero**

PAST HISTORIC

io	**valsi**
tu	**valesti**
lui/lei/Lei	**valse**
noi	**valemmo**
voi	**valeste**
loro	**valsero**

PLUPERFECT

io	**ero valso/a**
tu	**eri valso/a**
lui/lei/Lei	**era valso/a**
noi	**eravamo valsi/e**
voi	**eravate valsi/e**
loro	**erano valsi/e**

IMPERATIVE

vali
valiamo
valete

EXAMPLE PHRASES

Senza il giardino la casa non **varrebbe** niente. Without the garden the house
wouldn't be worth anything.

Italic letters in Italian words show where stress does not follow the usual rules.

vedere (to see)

PRESENT

io	**vedo**
tu	**vedi**
lui/lei/Lei	**vede**
noi	**vediamo**
voi	**vedete**
loro	**vedono**

PRESENT SUBJUNCTIVE

io	**veda**
tu	**veda**
lui/lei/Lei	**veda**
noi	**vediamo**
voi	**vediate**
loro	**vedano**

PERFECT

io	**ho visto**
tu	**hai visto**
lui/lei/Lei	**ha visto**
noi	**abbiamo visto**
voi	**avete visto**
loro	**hanno visto**

IMPERFECT

io	**vedevo**
tu	**vedevi**
lui/lei/Lei	**vedeva**
noi	**vedevamo**
voi	**vedevate**
loro	**vedevano**

GERUND

vedendo

PAST PARTICIPLE

visto

EXAMPLE PHRASES

Non ci **vedo** senza occhiali. I can't see without my glasses.

Ci **vediamo** domani! See you tomorrow!

Non **vedevo** l'ora di conoscerla. I couldn't wait to meet her.

Avete visto Marco? Have you seen Marco?

Non **vedendovi** arrivare, ce ne siamo andati. As we didn't see you arriving, we went away.

Remember that subject pronouns are not used very often in Italian.

vedere

FUTURE

io	**vedrò**
tu	**vedrai**
lui/lei/Lei	**vedrà**
noi	**vedremo**
voi	**vedrete**
loro	**vedranno**

CONDITIONAL

io	**vedrei**
tu	**vedresti**
lui/lei/Lei	**vedrebbe**
noi	**vedremmo**
voi	**vedreste**
loro	**vedrebbero**

PAST HISTORIC

io	**vidi**
tu	**vedesti**
lui/lei/Lei	**vide**
noi	**vedemmo**
voi	**vedeste**
loro	**videro**

PLUPERFECT

io	**avevo visto**
tu	**avevi visto**
lui/lei/Lei	**aveva visto**
noi	**avevamo visto**
voi	**avevate visto**
loro	**avevano visto**

IMPERATIVE

vedi
vediamo
vedete

EXAMPLE PHRASES

Stasera **vedremo** un film in TV. We're going to watch a film on TV this evening.

Finalmente **vedemmo** una nave all'orizzonte. At last we saw a ship on the horizon.

Non **avevo** mai **visto** una cosa simile. I'd never seen such a thing.

Vediamo un po' il tuo tema. Let's have a look at your essay.

Italic letters in Italian words show where stress does not follow the usual rules.

venire (to come)

PRESENT

io	**vengo**
tu	**vieni**
lui/lei/Lei	**viene**
noi	**veniamo**
voi	**venite**
loro	**vengono**

PRESENT SUBJUNCTIVE

io	**venga**
tu	**venga**
lui/lei/Lei	**venga**
noi	**veniamo**
voi	**veniate**
loro	**vengano**

PERFECT

io	**sono venuto/a**
tu	**sei venuto/a**
lui/lei/Lei	**è venuto/a**
noi	**siamo venuti/e**
voi	**siete venuti/e**
loro	**sono venuti/e**

IMPERFECT

io	**venivo**
tu	**venivi**
lui/lei/Lei	**veniva**
noi	**venivamo**
voi	**venivate**
loro	**venivano**

GERUND
venendo

PAST PARTICIPLE
venuto

EXAMPLE PHRASES

Da dove **vieni**? Where do you come from?

Quanto **viene**? How much is it?

È venuto in macchina. He came by car.

Era depressa e le **veniva** sempre da piangere. She was depressed and always felt like crying.

La casa sta **venendo** bene. The house is taking shape.

Remember that subject pronouns are not used very often in Italian.

venire

FUTURE

io	**verrò**
tu	**verrai**
lui/lei/Lei	**verrà**
noi	**verremo**
voi	**verrete**
loro	**verranno**

CONDITIONAL

io	**verrei**
tu	**verresti**
lui/lei/Lei	**verrebbe**
noi	**verremmo**
voi	**verreste**
loro	**verrebbero**

PAST HISTORIC

io	**venni**
tu	**venisti**
lui/lei/Lei	**venne**
noi	**venimmo**
voi	**veniste**
loro	**vennero**

PLUPERFECT

io	**ero venuto/a**
tu	**eri venuto/a**
lui/lei/Lei	**era venuto/a**
noi	**eravamo venuti/e**
voi	**eravate venuti/e**
loro	**erano venuti/e**

IMPERATIVE

vieni
veniamo
venite

EXAMPLE PHRASES

A forza di bere gli **verrà** il mal di testa. He'll get a headache if he drinks like that.

Verresti a cena da me domani? Would you come to dinner tomorrow?

Mi **venne** un'idea. I had an idea.

Erano venuti per parlare con te, ma non c'eri. They'd come to talk to you, but you weren't there.

Vieni a trovarci. Come and see us!

Italic letters in Italian words show where stress does not follow the usual rules.

vincere (to defeat)

PRESENT		PRESENT SUBJUNCTIVE	
io	vinco	io	vinca
tu	vinci	tu	vinca
lui/lei/Lei	vince	lui/lei/Lei	vinca
noi	vinciamo	noi	vinciamo
voi	vincete	voi	vinciate
loro	vincono	loro	vincano

PERFECT		IMPERFECT	
io	ho vinto	io	vincevo
tu	hai vinto	tu	vincevi
lui/lei/Lei	ha vinto	lui/lei/Lei	vinceva
noi	abbiamo vinto	noi	vincevamo
voi	avete vinto	voi	vincevate
loro	hanno vinto	loro	vincevano

GERUND

vincendo

PAST PARTICIPLE

vinto

EXAMPLE PHRASES

Quando giochiamo **vince** sempre lui. When we play he always wins.

Che **vinca** il migliore! May the best man win!

Ieri **abbiamo vinto** la partita. We won the match yesterday.

Vincendo l'incontro, si sono aggiudicati il campionato. By winning the match they won the championship.

Remember that subject pronouns are not used very often in Italian.

vincere

FUTURE

io	**vincerò**
tu	**vincerai**
lui/lei/Lei	**vincerà**
noi	**vinceremo**
voi	**vincerete**
loro	**vinceranno**

CONDITIONAL

io	**vincerei**
tu	**vinceresti**
lui/lei/Lei	**vincerebbe**
noi	**vinceremmo**
voi	**vincereste**
loro	**vincerebbero**

PAST HISTORIC

io	**vinsi**
tu	**vincesti**
lui/lei/Lei	**vinse**
noi	**vincemmo**
voi	**vinceste**
loro	**vinsero**

PLUPERFECT

io	**avevo vinto**
tu	**avevi vinto**
lui/lei/Lei	**aveva vinto**
noi	**avevamo vinto**
voi	**avevate vinto**
loro	**avevano vinto**

IMPERATIVE

vinci
vinciamo
vincete

EXAMPLE PHRASES

Stavolta **vincerò** io. I'm going to win this time.

Non **vincerebbero** mai senza di lui in squadra. They'd never win without
  him in the team.

Vinsero la lotteria e cambiarono vita. They won the lottery and changed
  their lives.

vivere (to live)

PRESENT

io	**vivo**
tu	**vivi**
lui/lei/Lei	**vive**
noi	**viviamo**
voi	**vivete**
loro	**vivono**

PRESENT SUBJUNCTIVE

io	**viva**
tu	**viva**
lui/lei/Lei	**viva**
noi	**viviamo**
voi	**viviate**
loro	**vivano**

PERFECT

io	**ho vissuto**
tu	**hai vissuto**
lui/lei/Lei	**ha vissuto**
noi	**abbiamo vissuto**
voi	**avete vissuto**
loro	**hanno vissuto**

IMPERFECT

io	**vivevo**
tu	**vivevi**
lui/lei/Lei	**viveva**
noi	**vivevamo**
voi	**vivevate**
loro	**vivevano**

GERUND
vivendo

PAST PARTICIPLE
vissuto

EXAMPLE PHRASES

Vivevano in una piccola casa di periferia. They lived in a small house in the suburbs.

Vivendo in città si respira molto smog. If you live in a city you breathe a lot of smog.

Remember that subject pronouns are not used very often in Italian.

vivere

FUTURE

io	**vivrò**
tu	**vivrai**
lui/lei/Lei	**vivrà**
noi	**vivremo**
voi	**vivrete**
loro	**vivranno**

CONDITIONAL

io	**vivrei**
tu	**vivresti**
lui/lei/Lei	**vivrebbe**
noi	**vivremmo**
voi	**vivreste**
loro	**vivrebbero**

PAST HISTORIC

io	**vissi**
tu	**vivesti**
lui/lei/Lei	**visse**
noi	**vivemmo**
voi	**viveste**
loro	**vissero**

PLUPERFECT

io	**avevo vissuto**
tu	**avevi vissuto**
lui/lei/Lei	**aveva vissuto**
noi	**avevamo vissuto**
voi	**avevate vissuto**
loro	**avevano vissuto**

IMPERATIVE

vivi
viviamo
vivete

EXAMPLE PHRASES

Non **vivrei** mai in un Paese caldo. I'd never live in a hot country.

Vivemmo un'esperienza indimenticabile. We had an unforgettable experience.

Non **avevo** mai **vissuto** prima in campagna. I'd never lived in the countryside before.

Vivi la tua vita giorno per giorno. Live your life day by day.

Italic letters in Italian words show where stress does not follow the usual rules.

volere (to want)

PRESENT		PRESENT SUBJUNCTIVE	
io	**voglio**	io	**voglia**
tu	**vuoi**	tu	**voglia**
lui/lei/Lei	**vuole**	lui/lei/Lei	**voglia**
noi	**vogliamo**	noi	**vogliamo**
voi	**volete**	voi	**vogliate**
loro	**vogliono**	loro	**vogliano**

PERFECT		IMPERFECT	
io	**ho voluto**	io	**volevo**
tu	**hai voluto**	tu	**volevi**
lui/lei/Lei	**ha voluto**	lui/lei/Lei	**voleva**
noi	**abbiamo voluto**	noi	**volevamo**
voi	**avete voluto**	voi	**volevate**
loro	**hanno voluto**	loro	**volevano**

GERUND
volendo

PAST PARTICIPLE
voluto

EXAMPLE PHRASES

Voglio comprare una macchina nuova. I want to buy a new car.

Devo pagare subito o posso pagare domani? – Come **vuole**. Do I have to pay now or can I pay tomorrow? – As you prefer.

La campanella **voleva** dire che la lezione era finita. The bell meant the lesson was finished.

Anche **volendo** non posso invitarti: la festa è sua. I'd like to, but I can't invite you: it's his party.

Remember that subject pronouns are not used very often in Italian.

volere

FUTURE

io	**vorrò**
tu	**vorrai**
lui/lei/Lei	**vorrà**
noi	**vorremo**
voi	**vorrete**
loro	**vorranno**

CONDITIONAL

io	**vorrei**
tu	**vorresti**
lui/lei/Lei	**vorrebbe**
noi	**vorremmo**
voi	**vorreste**
loro	**vorrebbero**

PAST HISTORIC

io	**volli**
tu	**volesti**
lui/lei/Lei	**volle**
noi	**volemmo**
voi	**voleste**
loro	**vollero**

PLUPERFECT

io	**avevo voluto**
tu	**avevi voluto**
lui/lei/Lei	**aveva voluto**
noi	**avevamo voluto**
voi	**avevate voluto**
loro	**avevano voluto**

IMPERATIVE

–

EXAMPLE PHRASES

Quanto ci **vorrà** prima che finiate? How long will it take you to finish?

Ci **vorrà** una app per scaricare la musica. You'll need an app to download music.

Mi chiedo che cosa **vorrà** dire tutto ciò. I wonder what it all will mean.

Che cosa **vorresti** che faccia? What would you like me to do?

Volle pagare lui a tutti i costi. He wanted to pay at all costs.

Il figlio **aveva voluto** la macchina come regalo di laurea. Their son had wanted a car as a graduation present.

Italic letters in Italian words show where stress does not follow the usual rules.

How to use the Verb Index

The verbs in bold are the model verbs which you will find in the verb tables. All the other verbs follow one of these patterns, so the number next to each verb indicates which pattern fits this particular verb. For example, **divertire** (*to amuse*) follows the same pattern as **dormire** (*to sleep*), which is number 288 in the verb tables.

All the verbs are in alphabetical order. Superior numbers ([1], [2] etc) refer you to notes on page 459. These notes explain any differences between the verbs and their model.

With the exception of reflexive verbs which *always* take **essere**, all verbs have the same auxiliary (**essere** or **avere**) as their model verbs. There are a few exceptions which are indicated by superior numbers [1] to [4]. An asterisk (*) means that the verb takes **avere** when it is used with a direct object, and **essere** when it isn't.

*For more information on verbs that take either **avere** or **essere**, see pages 108–113.*

abbaiare	238	acquistare	346	allontanare	346	arrabbiarsi	238
abbandonare	346	**addormentarsi**	**220**	allungare	342	arrangiarsi	326
abbassare	346	adoperare	346	amare	346	arrendersi	370
abbattere	264	adorare	346	ambientare	346	arrestare	346
abboccare	242	adottare	346	ammazzare	346	**arrivare**	**228**
abbonarsi	346	affacciarsi	250	ammettere	328	arrotondare	346
abitare	346	afferrare	346	amministrare	346	arruolarsi	346
abituarsi	346	affibbiare	238	ammirare	346	asciugare	342
abolire	240	affidare	346	ammonire	240	ascoltare	346
abusare	346	affittare	346	ammucchiare[1]	318	aspettare	346
accadere	**214**	affogare[2]	342	**andare**	**222**	assaggiare	326
accantonare	346	affondare*	346	annaffiare	238	assicurare	346
accarezzare	346	affrettarsi	346	annegare*	342	assistere[1]	296
accavallare	346	affrontare	346	annoiare	238	assolvere	382
accelerare	346	agganciare	250	annotare	346	assomigliare[2]	394
accendere	**216**	aggiungere	368	annullare	346	**assumere**	**230**
accennare	346	aggiustare	346	annunciare	250	attaccare	242
accertarsi	346	aggrapparsi	346	annusare	346	atterrare[3]	346
accettare	346	aggravare	346	appannarsi	346	attirare	346
acchiappare	346	aggredire	240	apparecchiare[1]	318	attraversare	346
accingersi	308	agire	240	**apparire**	**224**	aumentare*	346
accludere	292	agitare	346	appartenere[2]	434	autorizzare	346
accogliere	248	aiutare	346	appendere	420	avanzare	228
accomodarsi	346	allacciare	250	appiccicare	242	**avere**	**232**
accompagnare	414	allagare	342	applaudire	288	avvenire	446
accontentare	346	allargare	342	appoggiare	326	avvertire	288
accorciare	250	allarmare	346	approfittare	346	avvicinare	346
accordare	346	allegare	342	approfondire	240	avvolgere	386
accorgersi	**218**	allenare	346	approvare	346	azzardarsi	346
accudire	240	allineare	346	**aprire**	**226**	azzeccare	242
accusare	346	alloggiare	326	archiviare	238	baciare	250

Notes

[1] Auxiliary = **avere**.
[2] Auxiliary = **_essere_**.
[3] Auxiliary = either **_essere_** or **avere**.
[4] Past participle of this verb is rare.

Vocabulary

contents

464 contents

This section is divided into 50 topics, arranged in alphabetical order. This thematic approach enables you to learn related words and phrases together, so that you can become confident in using particular vocabulary in context.

Vocabulary within each topic is divided into nouns and useful phrases which are aimed at helping you to express yourself in idiomatic Italian. Vocabulary within each topic is graded to help you prioritize your learning. Essential words include the basic words you will need to be able to communicate effectively, important words help expand your knowledge, and useful words provide additional vocabulary which will enable you to express yourself more fully.

Nouns are grouped by gender: masculine ("il") nouns are given on the left-hand page, and feminine ("la") nouns on the right-hand page, enabling you to memorize words according to their gender. In addition, all feminine forms of adjectives are shown, as are irregular, invariable and gender-changing noun plurals.

At the end of the section you will find a list of supplementary vocabulary, grouped according to part of speech – adjective, verb, noun and so on. This is vocabulary which you will come across in many everyday situations.

ABBREVIATIONS

adj	adjective
adv	adverb
conj	conjunction
f	feminine
inv	invariable
m	masculine
m+f	masculine and feminine form
n	noun
pl	plural
pl inv	invariable, with no change to noun in the plural
prep	preposition
qc	qualcosa
qn	qualcuno
sb	somebody
sing	singular
sth	something

The swung dash ~ is used to indicate no change to a word in the plural of a compound noun.

GENDER

In Italian, nouns are either masculine or feminine. Most masculine nouns take the article il. This article becomes l' when the noun begins with a vowel and becomes lo when the noun begins with s+consonant (eg sc, sp, st), or begins gn, pn, ps, x, y or z.
Feminine nouns take la or l' (when the noun begins with a vowel).

Many masculine nouns end in o; many feminine nouns end in a. Both masculine and feminine nouns can end in e.

PLURAL

Unlike English, where you generally add letters (s or es) to make nouns plural, in Italian you change the final letter.
o > i (il post**o** > i post**i**)
a > e (la pizz**a** > le pizz**e**)
e > i (il padr**e**, la madr**e** > i padr**i**, le madr**i**)
Articles change as follows:
masculine: il > i l' > gli lo > gli
feminine: la > le l' > le
Nouns that are imported into Italian (such as bar, computer, menù, sport) stay the same in the plural (*pl inv*). They are generally masculine:
il bar > i bar, il computer > I computer, il menù > i menù, lo sport > gli sport.

PLURAL SPELLING CHANGES

Most nouns ending -co, -ca, -go and -ga often require an h inserting in the plural to retain the hard 'kuh' and 'guh' sounds:
il parco > i parchi, la banca > le banche
il lago > i laghi, la targa > le targhe
Where spelling changes occur in the plural we have included the plural ending.

ESSENTIAL WORDS *(masculine)*

un	aereo	plane
un	aeroplano	aeroplane
un	aeroporto	airport
un	agente di viaggio	travel agent
l'	arrivo	arrival
il	bagaglio	luggage
il	bagaglio a mano	hand luggage
il	banco	desk
il	biglietto	ticket
il	carrello	trolley
il	check-in	check in
il	doganiere	customs officer
l'	imbarco	boarding
il	noleggio auto	car hire
il	numero	number
un	orario	timetable
il	passaporto	passport
il	passeggero	passenger
il	prezzo del biglietto	fare
il	ritardo	delay
il	taxi *(pl inv)*	taxi
il	turista	tourist; holiday maker
il	viaggiatore	traveller
il	viaggio	trip
il	volo	flight

USEFUL PHRASES

viaggiare in aereo to travel by plane
un biglietto di sola andata a one-way ticket
un biglietto di andata e ritorno a return ticket
prenotare un biglietto aereo to book a plane ticket
fare il check-in del bagaglio to check in luggage
l'aereo è decollato/atterrato the plane has taken off/landed
il tabellone degli arrivi/delle partenze the arrivals/departures board
il volo numero 776 proveniente da Roma/diretto a Roma flight number
776 from Rome/to Rome

ESSENTIAL WORDS (feminine)

un'	**agente di viaggio**	travel agent
la	**borsa**	bag
la	**cancellazione**	cancellation
la	**carta d'identità**	ID card
la	**carta d'imbarco**	boarding card
la	**coincidenza**	connection
la	**dogana**	customs
la	**doganiera**	customs officer
l'	**entrata**	entrance
le	**informazioni**	information desk; information
la	**partenza**	departure
la	**passeggera**	passenger
la	**prenotazione**	reservation
la	**tarlffa**	fare
le	**toilette**	toilets
la	**turista**	tourist; holiday maker
l'	**uscita**	exit; gate
l'	**uscita d'emergenza**	emergency exit
l'	**uscita d'imbarco**	departure gate
la	**valigia** (pl -gie or -ge)	bag; suitcase
la	**viaggiatrice**	traveller

USEFUL PHRASES

ho perso la coincidenza I missed my connection
ritirare la valigia to collect one's luggage
"ritiro bagagli" "baggage reclaim"
passare per la dogana to go through customs
ho qualcosa da dichiarare I have something to declare
non ho niente da dichiarare I have nothing to declare
controllare il bagaglio to search the luggage
voli nazionali/internazionali domestic/international flights

IMPORTANT WORDS *(masculine)*

il	**biglietto elettronico**	e-ticket
il	**corridoio**	aisle
un	**elicottero**	helicopter
il	**finestrino**	window
un	**incidente aereo**	plane crash
il	**mal d'aria**	airsickness
il	**pilota**	pilot

USEFUL WORDS *(masculine)*

un	**assistente di volo**	flight attendant
un	**atterraggio**	landing
i	**comandi**	controls
il	**controllo di sicurezza**	security check
il	**controllore del traffico aereo**	air-traffic controller
il	**decollo**	take-off
i	**diritti di dogana**	customs duty
un	**equipaggio**	crew
l'	**imbarco** *(pl -chi)*	boarding
il	**jumbo** *(pl inv)*	jumbo jet
il	**metal detector** *(pl inv)*	metal detector
il	**nastro trasportatore**	carousel
un	**orario**	timetable
il	**paracadute** *(pl inv)*	parachute
il	**posto (a sedere)**	seat
il	**radar** *(pl inv)*	radar
il	**reattore**	jet engine
lo	**scalo**	stopover
lo	**steward** *(pl inv)*	steward
il	**terminal** *(pl inv)*	terminal
il	**vuoto d'aria**	air pocket

USEFUL PHRASES

a bordo on board; **"vietato fumare"** "no smoking"
in ritardo delayed; **in orario** on time
"allacciare le cinture di sicurezza" "fasten your seat belts"
stiamo volando sopra Londra we are flying over London
ho la nausea I am feeling sick; **fare un dirottamento aereo** to hijack a plane

IMPORTANT WORDS (*feminine*)

la	**cintura di sicurezza**	seat belt
la	**durata**	length; duration
la	**mappa**	map
la	**sala d'imbarco**	departure lounge
la	**velocità** (*pl inv*)	speed

USEFUL WORDS (*feminine*)

un'	**ala**	wing
l'	**altezza**	height
l'	**altitudine**	altitude
un'	**assistente di volo**	flight attendant
la	**barriera del suono**	sound barrier
un'	**elica** (*pl -che*)	propeller
un'	**etichetta**	label
la	**hostess** (*pl inv*)	air hostess
la	**linea aerea**	airline
la	**pista (d'atterraggio)**	runway
la	**rivista**	magazine
la	**scala mobile**	escalator
la	**scatola nera**	black box
la	**torre di controllo**	control tower
la	**turbolenza**	turbulence

USEFUL PHRASES

"i passeggeri del volo AB251 con destinazione Roma sono pregati di procedere all'imbarco all'uscita 51" "flight AB251 to Rome now boarding at gate 51"

abbiamo fatto scalo a New York we stopped over in New York

un atterraggio d'emergenza an emergency landing

un atterraggio di fortuna a crash landing

ESSENTIAL WORDS (*masculine*)

un	agnello	lamb
un	animale	animal
il	bue (*pl* buoi)	ox
il	cane	dog
il	cavallo	horse
il	cinghiale	wild boar
il	coniglio	rabbit
il	criceto	hamster
il	cucciolo	puppy
un	elefante	elephant
il	gattino	kitten
il	gatto	cat
il	giardino zoologico	zoo
un	insetto	insect
il	leone	lion
il	maiale	pig
il	pelo	coat, hair
il	pesce	fish
il	topo	mouse
un	uccello	bird
il	vitello	calf
lo	zoo (*pl inv*)	zoo

USEFUL PHRASES

mi piacciono i gatti, odio i serpenti, preferisco i cani I like cats, I hate snakes, I prefer dogs

in casa abbiamo 12 animali we have 12 pets in our house

non abbiamo animali in casa we have no pets in our house

gli animali selvatici wild animals

gli animali domestici pets

il bestiame livestock

mettere un animale in gabbia to put an animal in a cage

liberare un animale to set an animal free

ESSENTIAL WORDS (feminine)

la	**cagna**	dog (female)
la	**gatta**	cat (female)
la	**mucca** (pl -che)	cow
la	**pecora**	ewe
la	**pelliccia** (pl -ce)	fur
la	**scimmia**	monkey
la	**tartaruga** (pl -ghe)	tortoise
la	**tigre**	tiger
la	**volpe**	fox

IMPORTANT WORDS (feminine)

la	**caccia**	hunting
la	**coda**	tail
la	**gabbia**	cage
la	**zampa**	paw

USEFUL PHRASES

il cane abbaia the dog barks; **ringhia** it growls
il gatto miagola the cat miaows; **fa le fusa** it purrs
mi piace l'equitazione or **andare a cavallo** I like horse-riding
a cavallo on horseback
"attenti al cane" "beware of the dog"
"è vietato introdurre cani" "no dogs allowed"
"a cuccia!" (to dog) "down!"
i diritti degli animali animal rights
andare a caccia to go hunting

USEFUL WORDS *(masculine)*

un	artiglio	claw *(of lion, tiger)*
un	asino	donkey
il	cammello	camel
il	canguro	kangaroo
il	canile	kennel
il	caprone	billy goat
il	carapace	shell *(of tortoise)*
il	cervo	deer, stag
il	coccodrillo	crocodile
il	corno	horn
il	guinzaglio	dog lead
un	ippopotamo	hippopotamus
il	lupo	wolf
il	maiale	pig
il	marsupio	pouch *(of kangaroo)*
il	mulo	mule
il	muso	muzzle; snout
il	negozio di animali	pet shop
un	orso	bear
un	orso polare	polar bear
il	pipistrello	bat
il	pony *(pl inv)*	pony
il	porcellino d'india	guinea pig
il	puledro	foal
il	ratto	rat
il	riccio	hedgehog
il	rinoceronte	rhinoceros
il	rospo	toad
lo	scoiattolo	squirrel
il	serpente	snake
lo	squalo	shark
il	toro	bull
lo	zoccolo	hoof

USEFUL WORDS *(feminine)*

la	**balena**	whale
la	**biscia** *(pl -sce)*	snake
la	**bocca** *(pl -che)*	mouth
la	**capra**	(nanny) goat
la	**cavalla**	mare
la	**cavia**	guinea pig
la	**cerva**	doe
le	**corna**	antlers; horns
la	**criniera**	mane
la	**foca** *(pl -che)*	seal
la	**giraffa**	giraffe
la	**gobba**	hump *(of camel)*
la	**leonessa**	lioness
la	**lepre**	hare
la	**lucertola**	lizard
la	**mula**	mule
la	**pelle**	hide *(of cow, elephant etc)*
la	**proboscide**	trunk *(of elephant)*
la	**rana**	frog
le	**strisce**	stripes *(of zebra)*
la	**talpa**	mole
la	**tigre**	tigress
la	**trappola**	trap
la	**vipera**	viper; adder
la	**volpe**	fox
la	**zanna**	tusk
la	**zebra**	zebra

ESSENTIAL WORDS (*masculine*)

il **casco** (*pl* -chi)	helmet
il **ciclismo**	cycling
il **ciclista**	cyclist
il **fanale**	lamp
il **freno**	brake

IMPORTANT WORDS (*masculine*)

il **pedale**	pedal
il **sellino**	saddle

USEFUL WORDS (*masculine*)

il **cambio**	derailleur; gears
il **campanello**	bell
il **catarifrangente**	reflector
il **cestino**	pannier
il **Giro d'Italia**	Tour of Italy
il **kit** (*pl inv*) **per riparare le gomme**	puncture repair kit
il **lucchetto**	padlock
il **manubrio**	handlebars
il **mozzo**	hub
il **parafango** (*pl* -ghi)	mudguard
il **portapacchi** (*pl inv*)	carrier
il **raggio**	spoke
il **telaio**	frame
il **tubolare**	tyre

USEFUL PHRASES

andare in bici(cletta) to go by bike, to cycle
sono venuto in bici(cletta) I came by bike
pedalare to pedal
a tutta velocità at full speed
cambiare marcia to change gear
fermarsi to stop
frenare bruscamente to brake suddenly

ESSENTIAL WORDS (feminine)

la	**bici** (pl inv)	bike
la	**bicicletta**	bicycle
la	**ciclista**	cyclist
la	**city bike** (pl inv)	city bike
la	**mountain bike** (pl inv)	mountain bike
la	**sella**	saddle

IMPORTANT WORDS (feminine)

la	**camera d'aria**	inner tube
la	**discesa**	descent
la	**foratura**	puncture
la	**gomma**	tyre
la	**marcia** (pl -ce)	gear
la	**pista ciclabile**	cycle lane
la	**pompa**	pump
la	**ruota**	wheel
la	**salita**	climb
la	**velocità** (pl inv)	speed

USEFUL WORDS (feminine)

la	**caduta**	fall
la	**canna superiore**	crossbar
la	**catena**	chain
la	**cima**	top (of hill)
la	**dinamo** (pl inv)	dynamo
la	**luce anteriore**	front light
la	**valvola**	valve

USEFUL PHRASES

fare un giro in bici(cletta) to go for a bike ride
bucare to have a puncture
riparare una gomma to mend a puncture
la ruota anteriore/posteriore the front/back wheel
gonfiare le ruote to blow up the tyres
lucido(a) shiny
fluorescente fluorescent

ESSENTIAL WORDS *(masculine)*

il	**cielo**	sky
il	**gallo**	cock
il	**pappagallino**	budgie
il	**pappagallo**	parrot
il	**tacchino**	turkey
un	**uccello**	bird

USEFUL WORDS *(masculine)*

un	**avvoltoio**	vulture
il	**becco** *(pl -chi)*	beak
il	**canarino**	canary
il	**cigno**	swan
il	**corvo**	raven
il	**cuculo**	cuckoo
il	**fagiano**	pheasant
il	**falcone**	falcon
il	**gabbiano**	seagull
il	**gallo cedrone**	grouse
il	**gufo**	owl
il	**martin pescatore**	kingfisher
il	**merlo**	blackbird
il	**nido**	nest
il	**passero**	sparrow
il	**pavone**	peacock
il	**pettirosso**	robin
il	**picchio**	woodpecker
il	**piccione**	pigeon
il	**pinguino**	penguin
lo	**scricciolo**	wren
lo	**storno**	starling
lo	**struzzo**	ostrich
il	**tordo**	thrush
un	**uccello rapace**	bird of prey
un	**uovo** *(pl f* **uova***)*	egg
un	**usignolo**	nightingale

ESSENTIAL WORDS (feminine)

un'	**ala**	wing
un'	**anatra**	duck
la	**gallina**	hen
un'	**oca** (pl -che)	goose

USEFUL WORDS (feminine)

un'	**allodola**	lark
un'	**aquila**	eagle
la	**cicogna**	stork
la	**cinciarella**	bluetit
la	**colomba**	dove
la	**gabbia**	cage
l'	**influenza aviaria**	bird flu
la	**gazza**	magpie
la	**pernice**	partridge
la	**piuma**	feather
la	**quaglia**	quail
la	**rondine**	swallow
la	**taccola**	jackdaw
le	**uova**	eggs

USEFUL PHRASES

volare to fly
volare via to fly away
costruire un nido to build a nest
fischiare to whistle
cantare to sing
la gente li mette in gabbia people put them in cages
covare un uovo to sit on an egg
un uccello migratore a migratory bird

ESSENTIAL WORDS *(masculine)*

il	**braccio** *(pl f* **braccia)**	arm
i	**capelli**	hair
il	**corpo**	body
il	**cuore**	heart
il	**dente**	tooth
il	**dito** *(pl f* **dita)**	finger
il	**ginocchio** *(pl f* **ginocchia)**	knee
il	**naso**	nose
un	**occhio**	eye
un	**orecchio** *(pl f* **orecchie)**	ear
il	**pelo**	hair
il	**piede**	foot
lo	**stomaco**	stomach
il	**viso**	face

IMPORTANT WORDS *(masculine)*

il	**collo**	neck
il	**mento**	chin
il	**petto**	chest; bust
il	**pollice**	thumb
il	**sangue**	blood
il	**sopracciglio** *(pl f* **sopracciglia)**	eyebrow

USEFUL PHRASES

in piedi standing
seduto(a) sitting
disteso(a) lying

ESSENTIAL WORDS (feminine)

la	**bocca** (pl -che)	mouth
le	**braccia**	arms
le	**dita**	fingers
la	**gamba**	leg
le	**ginocchia**	knees
la	**gola**	throat
la	**mano** (pl **mani**)	hand
la	**narice**	nostril
la	**schiena**	back
la	**testa**	head

IMPORTANT WORDS (feminine)

la	**caviglia**	ankle
la	**faccia** (pl -ce)	face
la	**fronte**	forehead
la	**guancia** (pl -ce)	cheek
la	**lingua**	tongue
le	**orecchie**	ears
la	**pelle**	skin
le	**sopracciglia**	eyebrows
la	**spalla**	shoulder
la	**voce**	voice

USEFUL PHRASES

grande big
alto(a) tall
piccolo(a) small
basso(a) short
grasso(a) fat
magro(a) skinny
snello(a) slim
bello(a) beautiful; handsome
carino(a) pretty; cute
brutto(a) ugly

USEFUL WORDS *(masculine)*

l'	alluce	the big toe
il	cervello	brain
il	ciglio *(pl f ciglia)*	eyelash
il	dito del piede	toe
il	fegato	liver
il	fianco	hip
il	gesto	gesture
il	gomito	elbow
un	indice	forefinger
il	labbro *(pl f labbra)*	lip
i	lineamenti	features
il	muscolo	muscle
un	osso *(pl f ossa)*	bone
il	polmone	lung
il	polpaccio	calf *(of leg)*
il	polso	wrist
il	pugno	fist
il	rene	kidney
lo	scheletro	skeleton
il	sedere	bottom
il	seno	breast
il	tallone	heel
il	tratto	feature

USEFUL PHRASES

soffiarsi il naso to blow one's nose
tagliarsi le unghie to cut one's nails
tagliarsi i capelli to have one's hair cut
scrollare le spalle to shrug one's shoulders
fare cenno di sì con il capo to nod one's head *(say yes)*
fare cenno di no con il capo to shake one's head *(say no)*
vedere to see; **sentire** to hear; to feel
annusare to smell; **toccare** to touch; **assaggiare** to taste
stringere la mano a qn to shake hands with sb
salutare qn con la mano to wave at sb
indicare qc to point at sth

USEFUL WORDS *(feminine)*

un'	anca *(pl -che)*	hip
un'	arteria	artery
la	carnagione	skin, complexion
la	carne	flesh
le	ciglia	eyelashes
la	colonna vertebrale	spine
la	coscia *(pl -sce)*	thigh
la	costola	rib
le	dita del piede	toes
la	fronte	temple *(of head)*
le	labbra	lips
la	mandibola	jaw
la	nuca *(pl -che)*	nape of the neck
le	ossa	bones
la	palpebra	eyelid
la	pianta del piede	sole of the foot
la	pupilla	pupil *(of the eye)*
la	taglia	size
un'	unghia	nail
la	vena	vein
la	vita	waist

USEFUL PHRASES

(misura dei) fianchi hip measurement
giro vita waist measurement
(misura del) petto chest measurement
sordo(a) deaf
cieco(a) blind
disabile disabled
persona con problema di udito person with hearing problems
lui è più alto di te he is taller than you
Sara è cresciuta molto Sara has grown a lot
sono in sovrappeso I am overweight
è ingrassata/dimagrita she has put on weight/lost weight
è alta 1 metro e 47 she is 1.47 metres tall
pesa 40 chili he/she weighs 40 kilos

SEASONS

la	**primavera**	spring
l'	**estate** (f)	summer
l'	**autunno** (m)	autumn
l'	**inverno** (m)	winter

MONTHS

gennaio	January	**luglio**	July
febbraio	February	**agosto**	August
marzo	March	**settembre**	September
aprile	April	**ottobre**	October
maggio	May	**novembre**	November
giugno	June	**dicembre**	December

DAYS OF THE WEEK

lunedì	Monday
martedì	Tuesday
mercoledì	Wednesday
giovedì	Thursday
venerdì	Friday
sabato	Saturday
domenica	Sunday

USEFUL PHRASES

in primavera/estate/autunno/inverno in spring/summer/autumn/winter
in maggio in May
il 10 luglio 2016 on 10 July 2016
è il 3 dicembre it's 3rd December
di sabato vado in piscina on Saturdays I go to the swimming pool
sabato sono andato in piscina on Saturday I went to the swimming pool
il prossimo sabato/sabato scorso next/last Saturday
il sabato prima/dopo the previous/following Saturday

un	**anno**	year
il	**calendario**	calendar
i	**giorni della settimana**	days of the week
il	**giorno**	day
il	**giorno festivo**	public holiday
il	**mese**	month
la	**settimana**	week
la	**stagione**	season

USEFUL PHRASES

fare ponte to take a long weekend
Il primo aprile the first of April, April Fools' Day
il pesce d'aprile April Fools' trick
il primo maggio Labour day
il carnevale carnival period prior to Lent
l'Epifania Epiphany (6 January)
Ferragosto August 15 (Bank Holiday in Italy)
San Valentino St Valentine's Day
Ognissanti All Saints' Day
Pasqua Easter
Domenica di Pasqua Easter Sunday
Pasquetta or **Lunedì di Pasqua** Easter Monday
Mercoledì delle Ceneri Ash Wednesday
Venerdì Santo Good Friday
la Quaresima Lent
la Pasqua ebraica Passover
il Ramadan Ramadan
Hanukkah Hanukkah *or* Hanukah
la vigilia di Natale Christmas Eve
Natale Christmas
il giorno di Natale Christmas Day
San Silvestro New Year's Eve
Capodanno New Year's Day; New Year's Eve
il cenone/la festa di Capodanno New Year's Eve dinner/party

ESSENTIAL WORDS (masculine)

un	anniversario di matrimonio	wedding anniversary
un	appuntamento	appointment, date
il	biglietto d'auguri	greetings card
il	compleanno	birthday
il	divorzio	divorce
il	matrimonio	marriage; wedding
un	onomastico	saint's day
il	regalo	present

IMPORTANT WORDS (masculine)

il	falò (pl inv)	bonfire
il	fidanzamento	engagement
i	fuochi d'artificio	fireworks; firework display
il	parco (pl -chi) dei divertimenti	fun fair

USEFUL WORDS (masculine)

il	battesimo	christening
il	cimitero	cemetery
il	funerale	funeral
il	regalo di Natale	Christmas present
il	testimone di nozze	witness (at a wedding)

USEFUL PHRASES

festeggiare il compleanno to celebrate one's birthday
mia sorella è nata nel 1995 my sister was born in 1995
ha appena compiuto 17 anni he/she has just turned 17
mi ha fatto un regalo he/she gave me a present
te lo regalo! I'm giving it to you!
grazie thank you
divorziare to get divorced
sposarsi to get married
fidanzarsi (con qn) to get engaged (to sb)
mio padre è morto due anni fa my father died two years ago
seppellire to bury

ESSENTIAL WORDS (feminine)

la	**data**	date
la	**festa**	party; birthday
la	**morte**	death
la	**nascita**	birth
le	**nozze**	wedding

IMPORTANT WORDS (feminine)

le	**feste**	festivities
la	**fiera**	fair
la	**sagra**	festival

USEFUL WORDS (feminine)

la	**cerimonia**	ceremony
la	**damigella (d'onore)**	bridesmaid
la	**luna di miele**	honeymoon
la	**participazione (di nozze)**	wedding invitation
la	**pensione**	retirement
la	**prima comunione**	first communion
la	**processione**	procession
la	**testimone**	witness

USEFUL PHRASES

nozze d'oro/argento/diamante silver/golden/diamond wedding anniversary

fare gli auguri di Buon Anno a qn to wish sb a happy New Year

dare una festa to have a party

invitare gli amici to invite friends

scegliere un regalo to choose a gift

Buon Natale! Happy Christmas!

Buon compleanno! happy birthday!

auguri best wishes

ESSENTIAL WORDS *(masculine)*

il **bidone della spazzatura**	dustbin
il **campeggiatore**	camper
il **campeggio**	camping; campsite
il **camper** *(pl inv)*	camper van
il **coltello**	knife
il **cucchiaio**	spoon
il **fiammifero**	match
il **gas** *(pl inv)*	gas
il **piatto**	plate
il **picchetto**	tent peg
il **posto**	place; vacancy
i **servizi**	washrooms; toilets
lo **specchio**	mirror
il **supplemento**	extra charge
il **tavolino**	table
il **temperino**	penknife
il **veicolo**	vehicle

IMPORTANT WORDS *(masculine)*

un **apribottiglie** *(pl inv)*	corkscrew
un **apriscatole** *(pl inv)*	tin-opener
il **barbecue** *(pl inv)*	barbecue
il **bucato**	washing
il **detersivo**	washing powder
il **fango** *(pl -ghi)*	mud
il **fornello**	stove
un **igloo** *(pl inv)*	dome tent
il **martello**	hammer
il **materassino gonfiabile**	airbed
il **regolamento**	rules
il **sacco a pelo**	sleeping bag
lo **zaino**	rucksack

USEFUL PHRASES
andare in campeggio to go camping
accamparsi to camp
ben attrezzato(a) well equipped

ESSENTIAL WORDS (feminine)

l'	acqua (non) potabile	(non-)drinking water
la	bombola del gas	gas cylinder
la	brandina	camp bed
la	campeggiatrice	camper
la	cassa	box
la	doccia (pl -ce)	shower
la	forchetta	fork
la	lattina	can, tin
la	lavatrice	washing machine
la	notte	night
la	piazzola	pitch, site
la	pila	torch, flashlight; battery
la	piscina	swimming pool
la	roulotte (pl inv)	caravan
la	scatola	box, tin
la	(sedia a) sdraio	deckchair
la	sedia pieghevole	folding chair
la	stanza	room
la	tenda (da campeggio)	tent
le	toilette	toilets

IMPORTANT WORDS (feminine)

la	lavanderia	launderette
l'	ombra	shade; shadow
la	presa di corrente	socket
la	sala giochi	games room

USEFUL PHRASES
montare una tenda to pitch a tent
fare salsicce alla griglia to grill sausages

ESSENTIAL WORDS *(masculine)*

un	agente di polizia	police officer
un	assistente di volo	flight attendant
il	capo	boss
il	carabiniere	police officer
il	cassiere	check-out assistant
il	commercio	trade
il	commesso	sales assistant, shop assistant
il	consulente professionale	careers adviser
il	datore di lavoro	employer
il	dipendente	employee
il	disegnatore di pagine web	web designer
il	dottore	doctor
un	elettricista	electrician
il	farmacista	chemist
un	impiegato	clerk
un	infermiere	nurse
un	ingegnere	engineer
un	insegnante	teacher
il	lavoro	job; work
il	macchinista	train driver
il	meccanico	mechanic
il	medico	doctor
il	poliziotto	police officer
il	pompiere	fire fighter
il	postino	postman
il	professore	teacher
il	programmatore	computer programmer
il	redattore	editor
il	soldato	soldier
lo	steward *(pl inv)*	steward
un	ufficio	office
il	vigile	traffic warden

USEFUL PHRASES

interessante/poco interessante interesting/not very interesting
fa il postino he is a postman; **fa il medico** he/she is a doctor
lavorare to work; **diventare** to become

ESSENTIAL WORDS *(feminine)*

un'	**ambizione**	ambition
un'	**assistente di volo**	flight attendant
la	**banca**	bank
la	**cassiera**	check-out assistant
la	**commessa**	sales assistant, shop assistant
la	**consulente professionale**	careers adviser
la	**dipendente**	employee
la	**dottoressa**	doctor
la	**fabbrica** *(pl -che)*	factory
la	**hostess** *(pl inv)*	stewardess
un'	**impiegata**	clerk
un'	**infermiera**	nurse
un'	**insegnante**	teacher
la	**paga**	wages
la	**pensione**	retirement
la	**postina**	postwoman
la	**professione**	profession
la	**professoressa**	teacher
la	**programmatrice**	computer programmer
la	**receptionist** *(pl inv)*	receptionist
la	**redattrice**	editor
la	**segretaria**	secretary
la	**star** *(m+f pl inv)*	film star
la	**vita**	life
la	**vita lavorativa**	working life

USEFUL PHRASES

lavorare per guadagnarsi da vivere to work for one's living
che lavoro fa? what do you do (for a living)?
cosa vuoi fare da grande? what do you want to do when you grow up?
fare domanda di lavoro to apply for a job

IMPORTANT WORDS *(masculine)*

gli	**affari**	business
l'	**apprendistato**	apprenticeship
un	**aumento**	rise
un	**autore**	author
il	**barbiere**	barber
il	**bidello**	caretaker, janitor *(at school)*
il	**collega** *(pl -ghi)*	colleague
il	**commerciante**	shopkeeper
il	**contratto**	contract
il	**cuoco** *(pl -chi)*	cook
il	**custode**	caretaker *(of building)*
il	**dirigente**	manager
il	**disoccupato**	unemployed person
il	**futuro**	future
un	**idraulico**	plumber
un	**imbianchino**	decorator
un	**impiego** *(pl -ghi)*	job; situation
un	**interinale**	temp
il	**lavoratore**	worker
il	**manager** *(pl inv)*	manager
il	**mercato del lavoro**	job market
un	**operaio**	worker
un	**ottico**	optician
il	**parrucchiere**	hairdresser
il	**pilota**	pilot
il	**pittore**	painter
il	**pompiere**	fire fighter
il	**posto di lavoro**	job
il	**presidente**	president; chairperson
lo	**sciopero**	strike
il	**sindacato**	trade union
un	**uomo d'affari**	businessman

USEFUL PHRASES

essere disoccupato(a) to be unemployed
licenziare qn per esubero di personale to make sb redundant
un contratto a tempo indeterminato a permanent contract
un contratto a tempo determinato temporary contract

IMPORTANT WORDS *(feminine)*

un'	agenzia di collocamento	job centre
un'	agenzia di lavoro interinale	temping agency
la	biblioteca *(pl -che)*	library
la	bidella	caretaker, janitor *(at school)*
la	carriera	career
la	collega *(pl -ghe)*	colleague
la	cuoca *(pl -che)*	cook
la	custode	caretaker *(of building)*
la	dirigente	manager
la	disoccupazione	unemployment
la	domanda (di lavoro)	(job) application
la	donna d'affari	businesswoman
la	donna delle pulizie	cleaner
un'	interinale	temp
la	lettera d'accompagnamento	covering letter
la	manager *(pl inv)*	manager
un'	operaia	worker
la	parrucchiera	hairdresser
la	pittrice	painter
la	politica	politics
la	presidente	president; chairperson

USEFUL PHRASES

"domande di impiego" "situations wanted"
"offerte di impiego" "situations vacant"
appartenere ad un sindacato to be in a union
guadagnare 1000 euro al mese to earn 1000 euros per month
un aumento (di paga) a pay rise
scioperare *or* fare sciopero to go on strike
essere in sciopero to be on strike
lavorare a tempo pieno/lavorare part-time to work full-time/to work
   part-time
fare lo straordinario to work overtime
riduzione delle ore lavorative reduction in working hours

USEFUL WORDS (*masculine*)

un **agricoltore**	farmer (*crops*)
un **allevatore**	farmer (*animals*)
un **architetto**	architect
un **artista**	artist
un **avvocato**	lawyer; solicitor
il **chirurgo** (*pl* -ghi)	surgeon
il **colloquio (di lavoro)**	(job) interview
il **contabile**	accountant
il **corso di formazione**	training course
il **cosmonauta**	cosmonaut
il **deputato**	MP
il **direttore amministrativo**	company secretary
un **elettrauto**	car electrician
il **falegname**	joiner, carpenter
il **fotografo**	photographer
il **funzionario**	civil servant
il **giornalista**	journalist
il **giudice**	judge
un **ingegnere**	engineer
un **interprete**	interpreter
il **marinaio**	sailor
il **minatore**	miner
il **modello**	model
il **muratore**	bricklayer; mason
il **notaio**	notary
il **personale**	staff
il **politico**	politician
il **prete**	priest
il **rappresentante**	sales rep
un **ricercatore**	researcher
lo **scrittore**	writer
lo **stilista**	fashion designer
il **sussidio di disoccupazione**	unemployment benefit
il **tassista**	taxi driver
il **tirocinio**	apprenticeship; training
il **traduttore**	translator
il **veterinario**	vet
il **viticoltore**	wine grower

USEFUL WORDS *(feminine)*

un'	**agente di polizia**	police officer
un'	**amministrazione**	administration
un'	**annunciatrice**	announcer
un'	**artista**	artist
la	**casalinga** *(pl -ghe)*	housewife, home maker
la	**cassa integrazione**	redundancy payment
la	**contabile**	accountant
la	**deputata**	MP
la	**direttrice amministrativa**	company secretary
la	**ditta**	business
la	**formazione**	training
la	**giornalista**	journalist
un'	**impresa**	company; business
un'	**interprete**	interpreter
la	**modella**	model
la	**monaca** *(pl -che)*	nun
la	**poliziotta**	police officer
la	**rappresentante**	rep; sales rep
la	**sarta**	dressmaker
la	**società** *(pl inv)*	company
la	**suora**	nun
la	**traduttrice**	translator
la	**vigile**	traffic warden

USEFUL PHRASES

un lavoro stagionale seasonal work
un lavoro temporaneo/fisso a temporary/permanent job
un lavoro part-time a part-time job
essere assunto(a) to be taken on; **essere licenziato(a)** to be dismissed
licenziare qn to give sb the sack
cercare lavoro to look for work
fare un corso di formazione professionale to go on a training course
timbrare il cartellino to clock in/out
lavorare con un orario flessibile to work flexi-time

ESSENTIAL WORDS *(masculine)*

l'	**acceleratore**	accelerator
un	**agente di polizia**	police officer
un	**autista**	driver; chauffeur
un	**autovelox** *(pl inv)*	speed camera
il	**box** *(pl inv)*	garage *(for parking car)*
il	**cambio**	gear, gearbox
il	**chilometro**	kilometre
il	**ciclista**	cyclist
il	**distributore di benzina**	filling station; petrol pump
i	**fari**	headlights
il	**freno**	brake
il	**garage** *(pl inv)*	garage *(for parking car)*
il	**gasolio**	diesel
il	**GPL**	LPG fuel
il	**guidatore**	driver
un	**incrocio**	crossroads
un	**ingorgo** *(pl -ghi)*	traffic jam
il	**libretto di circolazione**	(car) registration document
il	**litro**	litre
il	**meccanico**	mechanic
il	**motore**	engine
l'	**olio**	oil
il	**parcheggio**	car park
il	**pedaggio**	toll
il	**pedone**	pedestrian
lo	**pneumatico**	tyre
il	**semaforo**	traffic lights
lo	**svincolo autostradale**	motorway exit, junction
il	**viaggio**	journey

USEFUL PHRASES
frenare bruscamente to brake suddenly
100 chilometri all'ora 100 kilometres an hour
ha la patente? do you have a driving licence?
andiamo a fare un giro (in macchina) we're going for a drive (in the car)

ESSENTIAL WORDS *(feminine)*

l'	**acqua**	water
un'	**assicurazione**	insurance
un'	**autista**	driver; chauffeur
un'	**autorimessa**	garage *(for repairs)*
un'	**autostrada**	motorway
la	**benzina**	petrol
la	**benzina senza piombo**	unleaded petrol
la	**carta stradale**	street map
la	**deviazione**	diversion
la	**direzione**	direction
la	**distanza**	distance
la	**gomma**	tyre
la	**guidatrice**	driver
le	**indicazioni**	directions
la	**macchina**	car
la	**patente**	driving licence
la	**polizia**	police
la	**polizza di assicurazione**	insurance policy
la	**roulotte** *(pl inv)*	caravan
la	**stazione di servizio**	service station
la	**strada**	road
la	**strada principale**	main road
la	**strada statale**	main road; A road
la	**targa** *(pl -ghe)*	number plate
un'	**uscita (autostradale)**	motorway exit, junction

USEFUL PHRASES

il pieno, per favore fill it up please
prendere la strada per Lecco to take the road to Lecco
è un viaggio di tre ore it's a 3-hour journey
buon viaggio! have a good journey!
andiamo! let's go!
lungo la strada abbiamo visto ... on the way we saw ...
sorpassare una macchina to overtake a car

IMPORTANT WORDS *(masculine)*

un	**autolavaggio**	car wash
un	**automobilista**	motorist
l'	**autostop**	hitch-hiking
un	**autostoppista**	hitch-hiker
il	**bagagliaio**	boot
il	**benzinaio**	petrol pump attendant
il	**camionista**	lorry driver
il	**carro attrezzi**	breakdown van
il	**cartello stradale**	road sign
il	**clacson** *(pl inv)*	horn
il	**codice della strada**	highway code
il	**confine**	border
il	**cruscotto**	dashboard
il	**danno**	damage
i	**documenti (della macchina)**	official papers
il	**faro**	headlight
il	**guasto**	breakdown
un	**incidente (stradale)**	(road) accident
il	**motociclista**	motorcyclist
il	**parcheggio**	parking
il	**pezzo di ricambio**	spare part
lo	**scontro**	collision
il	**traffico**	traffic

USEFUL PHRASES

accendere il motore to switch on the engine
il motore parte the engine starts up
il motore non parte the engine won't start
accelerare to accelerate; **proseguire** to continue
ridurre la velocità to slow down
fermarsi to stop; **parcheggiare (la macchina)** to park (the car)
spegnere il motore to switch off the engine
fermarsi con il semaforo rosso to stop at the red light

IMPORTANT WORDS *(feminine)*

un'	**automobile**	car
un'	**automobilista**	motorist
un'	**autoscuola**	driving school
un'	**autostoppista**	hitch-hiker
la	**batteria**	battery
la	**carrozzeria**	body work
la	**cintura di sicurezza**	seat belt
la	**collisione**	collision
la	**foratura**	puncture
la	**frizione**	clutch
la	**marca** *(pl -che)*	make *(of car)*
la	**marcia** *(pl -ce)*	gear
la	**motociclista**	motorcyclist
la	**pompa di benzina**	petrol pump
la	**portiera**	(car) door
la	**prova del palloncino**	Breathalyser® test
la	**revisione**	MOT test
la	**rotatoria**	roundabout
la	**rotonda**	roundabout
la	**ruota di scorta**	spare tyre
la	**scuola guida**	driving school
la	**strada a senso unico**	one-way street
la	**velocità**	speed
la	**zona a traffico limitato**	controlled traffic zone
la	**zona pedonale**	pedestrian zone

USEFUL PHRASES

c'è stato un incidente there's been an accident
nell'incidente sono rimaste ferite sei persone six people were injured in the accident
favorisca i documenti, per cortesia? may I see your papers please?
forare to have a puncture; **riparare** to fix
avere un'avaria to break down
sono rimasto senza benzina I've run out of petrol

USEFUL WORDS (*masculine*)

il	**carabiniere**	police officer
il	**carburatore**	carburettor
il	**catalizzatore**	catalytic converter
il	**centro abitato**	built-up area
il	**certificato di assicurazione**	insurance certificate
il	**cofano**	bonnet
il	**consumo di benzina**	petrol consumption
il	**contachilometri** (*pl inv*)	speedometer
un	**istruttore di guida**	driving instructor
il	**lavaggio auto**	car-wash
il	**limite di velocità**	speed limit
il	**parabrezza** (*pl inv*)	windscreen
il	**paraurti** (*pl inv*)	bumper
il	**parchimetro**	parking meter
il	**pedale**	pedal
il	**portapacchi** (*pl inv*)	roof rack
il	**principiante**	learner driver
il	**pulsante di avvio**	starter
il	**rimorchio**	trailer
il	**servosterzo**	power steering
il	**(sistema di navigazione) GPS**	satellite navigation system
lo	**spartitraffico** (*pl inv*)	central reservation
lo	**specchietto retrovisore**	rear-view mirror
il	**tergicristalli** (*pl inv*)	windscreen wiper
il	**vigile**	traffic warden
il	**volante**	steering wheel

USEFUL PHRASES

a rimorchio on tow
nell'ora di punta at rush hour
ha ricevuto una multa di 100 euro he got a 100-euro fine
è assicurato? are you insured?
non dimentichi di allacciare le cinture di sicurezza don't forget to put on your seat belts
al confine at the border
fare l'autostop to hitch-hike

USEFUL WORDS *(feminine)*

un'	**area di servizio**	service station
la	**rampa d'accesso**	slip road
la	**circonvallazione**	ring road
la	**corsia**	lane
la	**corsia d'emergenza**	hard shoulder
la	**curva**	bend
la	**deviazione**	detour
la	**freccia** *(pl -ce)*	indicator
la	**frenata improvvisa**	emergency stop
un'	**infrazione stradale**	traffic offence
la	**lezione di guida**	driving lesson
la	**multa**	fine
la	**piazzola di sosta**	lay-by
la	**pressione**	pressure
la	**stazione di servizio**	service station
la	**via**	street
la	**vigile**	traffic warden
la	**vittima**	casualty

USEFUL PHRASES

la ruota anteriore/posteriore the front/back wheel

dobbiamo fare una deviazione we have to make a detour

una multa per eccesso di velocità a fine for speeding

accosti per favore pull in please

"dare la precedenza" "give way to the right"

"tenere la destra" "keep to the right"

"vietato l'accesso" "no entry"

"divieto di sosta" "no parking"

"lavori in corso" "roadworks"

ESSENTIAL WORDS (masculine)

l'	**abito**	suit; dress
il	**bottone**	button
il	**calzino**	sock
i	**calzoni**	trousers
il	**cappello**	hat
il	**cappotto**	coat
i	**collant**	tights
il	**costume da bagno**	swimming trunks; swimsuit
il	**fazzoletto**	handkerchief
un	**impermeabile**	raincoat
i	**jeans**	jeans
il	**maglione**	jumper
il	**numero (di scarpe)**	(shoe) size
un	**ombrello**	umbrella
i	**pantaloncini**	shorts
i	**pantaloni**	trousers
il	**pigiama**	pyjamas
il	**reggiseno**	bra
gli	**slip** (pl inv)	knickers; underpants
il	**soprabito**	overcoat
i	**vestiti**	clothes
il	**vestito**	suit; dress; costume

IMPORTANT WORDS (masculine)

un	**accappatoio**	bathrobe
il	**cappuccio**	hood
il	**giaccone**	heavy jacket
il	**golf** (pl inv)	cardigan
il	**guanto**	glove
i	**pantaloni corti**	shorts
il	**sandalo**	sandal
lo	**scarpone**	boot
gli	**shorts**	shorts
lo	**stivale**	boot

ESSENTIAL WORDS (feminine)

la	**biancheria intima**	underwear
la	**borsa**	bag
la	**borsetta**	handbag
la	**camicia**	shirt
la	**camicia da notte**	nightdress
la	**cravatta**	tie
la	**felpa**	sweatshirt
la	**giacca** (pl -che)	jacket
la	**giacca** (pl -che) **a vento**	anorak
la	**gonna**	skirt
la	**maglietta**	T-shirt
la	**moda**	fashion
le	**mutande**	underpants; knickers
la	**scarpa**	shoe
la	**taglia**	size
la	**vita**	waist

IMPORTANT WORDS (feminine)

la	**blusa**	blouse
la	**canottiera**	vest
la	**ciabatta**	slipper
la	**cintura**	belt
la	**roba da vestire**	clothes
la	**tasca**	pocket
un'	**uniforme**	uniform
la	**vestaglia**	dressing gown

USEFUL PHRASES

di mattina mi vesto in the morning I get dressed
di sera mi spoglio in the evening I get undressed
quando torno a casa mi cambio when I get home I get changed
indossare or **avere addosso** to wear
mettersi to put on
è molto elegante that's very smart

USEFUL WORDS *(masculine)*

gli	**accessori**	accessories
il	**bastone (da passeggio)**	walking stick
i	**bermuda**	Bermuda shorts
il	**berretto**	cap; beret
il	**bucato**	washing
il	**camice**	overalls
il	**colletto**	collar
il	**fiocco** *(pl -chi)*	bow
il	**foulard** *(pl inv)*	scarf
il	**gilè** *(pl inv)*	waistcoat
il	**grembiule**	apron
gli	**infradito**	flip flops
i	**lacci**	(shoe)laces
il	**nastro**	ribbon
un	**occhiello**	buttonhole
il	**papillon** *(pl inv)*	bow tie
lo	**spogliatoio**	changing room
il	**vestito da sera**	evening dress
il	**vestito da sposa**	wedding dress

USEFUL PHRASES

ti sta bene that suits you
che taglia porti (or porta)? what size do you take?
che numero di scarpe porti (or porta)? what shoe size do you take?
ho il 38 di piede I take size 38 in shoes

USEFUL WORDS *(feminine)*

l'	**alta moda**	haute couture
la	**(borsa a) tracolla**	shoulder bag
le	**bretelle**	braces
le	**calze**	stockings; socks
la	**canotta**	tank top
la	**chiusura lampo** *(pl -e ~)*	zip
la	**felpa**	sweatshirt
la	**gonna pantalone**	culottes
la	**maglia con il cappuccio**	hooded top
la	**maglietta senza maniche**	tank top
la	**manica** *(pl -che)*	sleeve
la	**polo** *(pl inv)*	polo shirt
la	**pulitura a secco**	dry-cleaning
la	**salopette** *(pl inv)*	dungarees
le	**scarpe basse**	flat shoes
le	**scarpe con i tacchi**	high heels
le	**scarpe da ginnastica**	trainers
la	**sfilata di moda**	fashion show
la	**sottogonna**	underskirt
la	**tuta da ginnastica**	tracksuit
la	**zip** *(pl inv)*	zip

USEFUL PHRASES

lungo(a) long; **corto(a)** short
un vestito con le maniche corte/lunghe a short-sleeved/long-sleeved dress
stretto(a) tight
largo(a) loose
una gonna attillata a tight skirt
a strisce striped; **a quadretti** checked; **a pallini** spotted
vestiti sportivi casual clothes
in pigiama in pyjamas
alla moda fashionable; **moderno(a)** trendy
fuori moda old-fashioned

arancione	orange
azzurro(a)	light blue
beige *(pl inv)*	beige
bianco(a)	white
blu *(pl inv)*	blue
blu marina *(pl inv)*	navy blue
blu scuro *(pl inv)*	dark blue
bordeaux *(pl inv)*	maroon
celeste	sky blue
d'argento *(pl inv)*	silver
dorato(a)	golden
d'oro *(pl inv)*	gold
giallo(a)	yellow
grigio(a)	grey
malva *(pl inv)*	mauve
marrone	brown
naturale	natural
nero(a)	black
rosa *(pl inv)*	pink
rosso(a)	red
rosso fuoco *(pl inv)*	bright red
turchese	turquoise
verde	green
viola *(pl inv)*	purple
violetto(a)	violet

USEFUL PHRASES

il colore colour
di che colore hai (*or* **ha**) **gli occhi/i capelli?** what colour are your eyes/ is your hair?
il blu ti sta bene blue suits you
quello blu ti sta bene the blue one suits you
dipingere qc di blu to paint sth blue
le scarpe blu blue shoes
le scarpe azzurre light blue shoes
ha gli occhi verdi she/he has green eyes
cambiare colore to change colour
la Casa Bianca the White House
bianco come la neve as white as snow
Biancaneve Snow White
Cappuccetto Rosso Little Red Riding Hood
diventare rosso(a) to turn red, to blush
rosso(a) come un peperone as red as a beetrot
chiaro(a)/scuro(a) light/dark
nero(a) come il carbone as brown as a berry
un occhio nero a black eye
un (romanzo) giallo a crime novel
un romanzo rosa a romantic novel
Pagine Gialle Yellow pages®
una notte in bianco a sleepless night
riso/pasta in bianco plain rice/pasta
la benzina verde unleaded petrol
numero verde freephone
essere al verde to be broke
essere di umore nero to be in a very bad mood

ESSENTIAL WORDS (*masculine*)

il **computer** (*pl inv*)	computer
il **mouse** (*pl inv*)	mouse
il **programma**	program

USEFUL WORDS (*masculine*)

l' **ADSL**	broadband
il **backup** (*pl inv*)	back-up
il **browser** (*pl inv*)	browser
il **CD-ROM** (*pl inv*)	CD-ROM
il **computer fisso**	desktop computer
il **correttore ortografico**	spellchecker
il **cursore**	cursor
il **data base** (*pl inv*)	database
i **dati**	data
il **disco esterno** (*pl -chi -i*)	external disk
il **disco rigido**	hard disk
il **documento**	document
il **file** (*pl inv*)	file
il **foglio di calcolo**	spreadsheet
il **gioco per il computer**	computer game
un **indirizzo di posta elettronica**	e-mail address
Internet	internet
il **lettore DVD**	DVD player
il **masterizzatore DVD**	DVD writer
il **menu** (*pl inv*)	menu
il **messaggio di posta elettronica**	email message
il **modem** (*pl inv*)	modem
il **monitor** (*pl inv*)	monitor
il **navigatore internet**	internet user
il **pirata informatico**	hacker
il **portatile**	laptop
il **router wifi** (*pl inv*)	wifi router
lo **schermo**	screen
il **sito web**	website
il **software** (*pl inv*)	software
il **tasto**	key (*on keyboard*)
il **virus** (*pl inv*)	virus
il **Web**	Web

ESSENTIAL WORDS (feminine)

l'	**informatica**	computer science; computer studies
la	**stampante**	printer

USEFUL WORDS (feminine)

un'	**applicazione**	program
la	**banda larga**	broadband
la	**cartuccia d'inchiostro**	ink cartridge
la	**chiavetta USB**	USB key
la	**copia di sicurezza**	back-up
la	**finestra**	window
la	**funzione**	function
la	**home page** (pl inv)	home page
un'	**icona**	icon
un'	**interfaccia** (pl -ce)	interface
la	**mail** (pl inv)	email (message)
la	**memoria**	memory
la	**(memoria) RAM**	RAM, random-access memory
la	**(memoria) ROM**	ROM, read-only Memory
la	**navigatrice internet**	Internet user
la	**password** (pl inv)	password
la	**posta elettronica**	email
la	**rete**	network
la	**scheda di memoria**	memory stick
la	**stampa**	print-out
la	**tastiera**	keyboard
un'	**unità disco** (pl inv)	disk drive
la	**webcam** (pl inv)	webcam

USEFUL PHRASES

copiare to copy; **cancellare** to delete
allegare alla mail to attach an email
scaricare/caricare un file to download/upload a file
salvare to save; **stampare** to print; **digitare** to key
visualizzare to view
navigare in Internet to surf the internet

ESSENTIAL WORDS (*masculine*)

il	**Belgio**	Belgium
il	**Canada**	Canada
il	**Galles**	Wales
il	**paese**	country; village
i	**Paesi Bassi**	Netherlands
il	**Regno Unito**	United Kingdom
gli	**Stati Uniti**	United States
il	**Sudamerica**	South America
gli	**USA**	USA

USEFUL WORDS (*masculine*)

il	**Brasile**	Brazil
El	**Salvador**	El Salvador
il	**Giappone**	Japan
il	**Marocco**	Morocco
il	**Messico**	Mexico
il	**Pakistan**	Pakistan
il	**Perù**	Peru
il	**Terzo Mondo**	Third World

USEFUL PHRASES

il mio paese d'origine my native country
la capitale italiana the capital of Italy
di che paese sei? what country do you come from?
sono italiano/canadese I am Italian/Canadian
sono nato in Scozia I was born in Scotland
vado nei Paesi Bassi I'm going to the Netherlands
sono appena tornato dagli Stati Uniti I've just come back from the United States
sei mai stato in Italia? have you ever been to Italy?
i paesi in via di sviluppo the developing countries
i paesi di lingua spagnola Spanish-speaking countries

ESSENTIAL WORDS *(feminine)*

l'	**America**	America
l'	**Europa**	Europe
la	**Francia**	France
la	**Germania**	Germany
la	**Gran Bretagna**	Great Britain
l'	**Inghilterra**	England
l'	**Irlanda (del Nord)**	(Northern) Ireland
l'	**Italia**	Italy
l'	**Olanda**	Holland
la	**Scozia**	Scotland
la	**Spagna**	Spain
la	**Svizzera**	Switzerland

USEFUL WORDS *(feminine)*

l'	**Africa**	Africa
l'	**Algeria**	Algeria
l'	**America del sud**	South America
l'	**Asia**	Asia
l'	**Australia**	Australia
l'	**Austria**	Austria
la	**Cina**	China
la	**Croazia**	Croatia
la	**Finlandia**	Finland
la	**Grecia**	Greece
l'	**India**	India
la	**Norvegia**	Norway
la	**Nuova Zelanda**	New Zealand
la	**Russia**	Russia
la	**Slovenia**	Slovenia
la	**Tunisia**	Tunisia
l'	**Ungheria**	Hungary
l'	**Unione europea, la UE**	the European Union, the EU

ESSENTIAL WORDS *(masculine)*

un	**americano**	an American
un	**belga**	a Belgian
un	**britannico**	a Briton
un	**canadese**	a Canadian
un	**europeo**	a European
un	**francese**	a Frenchman
un	**gallese**	a Welshman
un	**inglese**	an Englishman
un	**irlandese**	an Irishman
un	**italiano**	an Italian
un	**olandese**	a Dutchman
un	**pachistano**	a Pakistani
uno	**scozzese**	a Scot
uno	**spagnolo**	a Spaniard
uno	**svizzero**	a Swiss (man *or* boy)
un	**tedesco** *(pl* **-chi***)*	a German
un	**ungherese**	a Hungarian

USEFUL PHRASES

è irlandese he/she is Irish
la campagna irlandese the Irish countryside
una città irlandese an Irish town

ESSENTIAL WORDS *(feminine)*

un'	**americana**	an American
una	**belga**	a Belgian
una	**britannica** *(pl -che)*	a Briton, a British woman *or* girl
una	**canadese**	a Canadian
un'	**europea**	a European
una	**francese**	a Frenchwoman, a French girl
una	**gallese**	a Welshwoman, a Welsh girl
un'	**inglese**	an Englishwoman, an English girl
un'	**irlandese**	an Irishwoman, an Irish girl
un'	**italiana**	an Italian
un'	**olandese**	a Dutchwoman, a Dutch girl
una	**pachistana**	a Pakistani
una	**scozzese**	a Scot
una	**spagnola**	a Spaniard
una	**svizzera**	a Swiss woman *or* girl
una	**tedesca** *(pl -che)*	a German
un'	**ungherese**	a Hungarian

USEFUL PHRASES
parlo inglese I speak English
sono scozzese I am Scottish
uno(a) straniero(a) a foreigner
all'estero abroad
la nazionalità nationality

USEFUL WORDS *(masculine)*

un	**africano**	an African
un	**albanese**	an Albanian
un	**arabo**	an Arab
un	**argentino**	an Argentinian
un	**asiatico** *(pl -chi)*	an Asian
un	**australiano**	an Australian
un	**caraibico** *(pl -chi)*	a West Indian
un	**ceco** *(pl -chi)*	a Czech
un	**cinese**	a Chinese
un	**giapponese**	a Japanese
un	**indiano**	an Indian
un	**neozelandese**	a New Zealander
un	**portoghese**	a Portuguese
un	**polacco** *(pl -chi)*	a Pole
un	**russo**	a Russian
uno	**slovacco** *(pl -chi)*	a Slovakian
un	**turco** *(pl -chi)*	a Turk
un	**ucraino**	a Ukranian

USEFUL WORDS *(feminine)*

un'	**africana**	an African
un'	**albanese**	an Albanian
un'	**araba**	an Arab
un'	**argentina**	an Argentinian
un'	**asiatica** *(pl -che)*	an Asian
un'	**australiana**	an Australian
una	**caraibica** *(pl -che)*	a West Indian
una	**ceca** *(pl -che)*	a Czech
una	**cinese**	a Chinese
una	**giapponese**	a Japanese
un'	**indiana**	an Indian
una	**neozelandese**	a New Zealander
una	**polacca** *(pl -che)*	a Pole
una	**portoghese**	a Portuguese
una	**russa**	a Russian
una	**slovacca** *(pl -che)*	a Slovakian
una	**turca** *(pl -che)*	a Turk
un'	**ucraina**	a Ukranian

ESSENTIAL WORDS *(masculine)*

un	**agriturismo**	farmhouse holiday accommodation
un	**albero**	tree
un	**allevatore**	farmer *(raising animals)*
il	**bastone (da passeggio)**	walking stick
il	**bosco** *(pl -chi)*	wood; forest
il	**cacciatore**	hunter
il	**campo**	field
il	**cancello**	gate
il	**castello**	castle
il	**contadino**	farmer *(growing crops)*
il	**fiume**	river
il	**mercato**	market
un	**ostello della gioventù**	youth hostel
il	**paesaggio**	scenery
il	**paese**	village
il	**picnic** *(pl inv)*	picnic
il	**ponte**	bridge
il	**prato**	meadow
il	**rifugio**	mountain hostel
il	**rumore**	noise
il	**ruscello**	stream
il	**sasso**	stone, pebble
il	**sentiero**	path; track
lo	**steccato**	fence
il	**suolo**	ground
il	**terreno**	land; ground
il	**turista**	tourist

USEFUL PHRASES
all'aria aperta in the open air
so come arrivare al paese I know the way to the village
andare in bicicletta to go cycling
gli abitanti del posto the locals
siamo andati a fare un picnic we went for a picnic

ESSENTIAL WORDS *(feminine)*

un'	**allevatrice**	farmer *(raising animals)*
l'	**aria**	air
la	**cacciatrice**	hunter
la	**campagna**	country; countryside
la	**contadina**	farmer *(growing crops)*
un'	**escursione**	hike
la	**fattoria**	farm, farmhouse
la	**montagna**	mountain
la	**passeggiata**	walk
la	**pietra**	stone
la	**regione**	district
la	**roccia** *(pl* **-ce)**	rock
la	**strada**	way; road
la	**terra**	land; earth; soil; ground
la	**torre**	tower
la	**turista**	tourist
la	**valle**	valley

USEFUL PHRASES

in campagna in the country
andare in campagna to go into the country
vivere in campagna to live in the country
coltivare la terra to cultivate the land

IMPORTANT WORDS (*masculine*)

il	**fienile**	barn
il	**fiore**	flower
il	**lago** (*pl* -ghi)	lake
il	**podere**	farm; holding
gli	**stivali di gomma**	(wellington) boots
il	**vigneto**	vineyard

USEFUL WORDS (*masculine*)

un	**agriturismo**	farmhouse holiday accommodation
un	**arbusto**	bush
il	**bastone**	stick
il	**binocolo**	binoculars
il	**borgo**	hamlet
il	**cartello segnaletico**	signpost
il	**cespuglio**	bush
il	**ciottolo**	pebble
il	**fango**	mud
il	**fieno**	hay
il	**fossato**	ditch
il	**grano**	grain; wheat
il	**mulino (a vento)**	(wind)mill
il	**palo della luce**	telegraph pole
il	**pozzo**	well
il	**prato**	meadow
il	**raccolto**	crop; harvest
lo	**stagno**	pond
un	**ulivo**	olive tree

USEFUL PHRASES

agricolo(a) agricultural
tranquillo(a) peaceful
in cima alla collina at the top of the hill
cadere in trappola to fall into a trap

IMPORTANT WORDS *(feminine)*

l'	**agricoltura**	agriculture
la	**cima**	top *(of hill)*
la	**collina**	hill
la	**foglia**	leaf
la	**gente di campagna**	country people
la	**pace**	peace, tranquillity
la	**polvere**	dust
la	**proprietà**	property; estate
la	**stalla**	stable
la	**tranquillità**	tranquillity, peace
la	**trattoria**	restaurant *(in country)*
la	**vigna**	vineyard
la	**vista**	view

USEFUL WORDS *(feminine)*

la	**brughiera**	moor
la	**caccia**	hunting
la	**cascata**	waterfall
la	**cava**	quarry
l'	**erica** *(pl -che)*	heather
la	**fonte**	spring; source
la	**grotta**	cave
la	**palude**	marsh
la	**pianura**	plain
la	**pozzanghera**	puddle
la	**riva**	bank *(of river)*
le	**rovine**	ruins
la	**siepe**	hedge
la	**trappola**	trap
la	**vendemmia**	grape harvest

USEFUL PHRASES
perdersi to lose one's way; to get lost
raccogliere frutta/grano to harvest fruit/grain
vendemmiare, fare la vendemmia to harvest the grapes

ESSENTIAL WORDS (masculine)

un	aspetto	appearance
i	baffi	moustache
i	capelli	hair
il	colore	colour
il	naso	nose
gli	occhi	eyes

USEFUL PHRASES

allegro(a) cheerful
alto(a) tall
antipatico(a) unpleasant
anziano(a) elderly
basso(a) short
bello handsome; **bella** beautiful (person)
beneducato(a) well-behaved
brutto(a) ugly
buono(a) kind
calvo(a) bald
carino(a) pretty; cute
cattivo(a) naughty
con la barba bearded, with a beard
dinamico(a) dynamic
divertente amusing, entertaining; funny
educato(a) polite
felice happy
giovane young
grasso(a) fat
infelice unhappy
inquieto(a) agitated
intelligente intelligent
lungo(a) long
magro(a) thin
maleducato(a) rude
nervoso(a) nervous
orribile hideous

ESSENTIAL WORDS (feminine)

la	**barba**	beard
l'	**età**	age
l'	**identità**	identity
gli	**occhiali**	glasses
la	**persona**	person
la	**pettinatura**	hairstyle
la	**statura**	height
la	**taglia**	size

USEFUL PHRASES

ottimista/pessimista optimistic/pessimistic
piccolo(a) small, little
serio(a) serious
sfortunato(a) unfortunate
simpatico(a) nice
snello(a) slim
stupendo(a) great
stupido(a) stupid
teso(a) tense
timido(a) shy
tranquillo(a) calm
vecchio(a) old
ha un'aria triste he/she looks sad
stava piangendo he/she was crying
stava sorridendo he/she was smiling
aveva le lacrime agli occhi he/she had tears in his eyes
un uomo di statura media a man of average height
sono alto 1 metro e 70 or **uno e settanta** I am 1 metre 70 tall
di che colore hai (or **ha**) **gli occhi/i capelli?** what colour are your eyes/is your hair?
ho i capelli chiari I have fair hair
ho gli occhi azzurri/verdi I have blue/green eyes
capelli castano chiaro light brown hair; **capelli ricci** curly hair; **con i capelli rossi** red-haired
capelli neri/grigi black/grey hair
capelli scuri/castani dark/brown hair
capelli tinti dyed hair

IMPORTANT WORDS (masculine)

il	**brufolo**	spot; pimple
il	**carattere**	character; nature
lo	**sguardo**	look
il	**sorriso**	smile
l'	**umore**	mood

USEFUL WORDS (masculine)

il	**difetto**	fault
il	**foruncolo**	spot, zit; boil
il	**gesto**	gesture
il	**gigante**	giant
il	**neo**	mole, beauty spot
il	**peso**	weight
il	**ricci**	curls

USEFUL PHRASES

ha un buon carattere he/she is goodnatured
avere la carnagione chiara to have a pale complexion
portare gli occhiali to wear glasses
portare le lenti a contatto to wear contact lenses

IMPORTANT WORDS *(feminine)*

un'	abitudine	habit
la	bellezza	beauty
la	bruttezza	ugliness
la	carnagione	complexion
la	curiosità	curiosity
un'	espressione	expression
le	lenti a contatto	contact lenses
la	qualità	(good) quality
la	vita	waist
la	voce	voice

USEFUL WORDS *(feminine)*

la	cicatrice	scar
la	dentiera	false teeth
la	fossetta	dimple
la	frangia	fringe
le	lentiggini	freckles
la	rassomiglianza	resemblance
le	rughe	wrinkles
la	timidezza	shyness

USEFUL PHRASES

sono sempre di buon umore I am always in a good mood
è di cattivo umore he/she is in a bad mood
si è arrabbiato he got angry
assomiglia a sua madre he/she looks like his/her mother
si mangia le unghie he/she bites his/her nails

ESSENTIAL WORDS (masculine)

l'	alfabeto	alphabet
un	alunno	pupil; schoolboy
un	amico	friend
un	asilo	nursery school
il	compagno di classe	classmate
i	compiti (per casa)	homework
il	compito	task; test
il	computer (pl inv)	computer
il	concerto	concert
il	disegno	drawing
il	dormitorio	dormitory
un	errore	mistake
un	esame	exam
un	esperimento	experiment
il	francese	French
il	giorno	day
il	gruppo	group
l'	inglese	English
l'	insegnamento	education; teaching
l'	intervallo	break; playtime
un	istituto (scolastico)	school; institute
l'	italiano	Italian
il	laboratorio	laboratory
i	lavori manuali	handicrafts
il	lavoro	work
il	libro	book
il	liceo	secondary school (14 to 18 year olds)
il	maestro	primary school teacher
il	nuoto	swimming
un	orario	timetable
il	premio	prize
il	preside	headmaster
il	professore	teacher
il	progresso	progress
il	quaderno	exercise book
il	refettorio	dining hall

ESSENTIAL WORDS *(feminine)*

un'	**alunna**	pupil; schoolgirl
un'	**amica** *(pl -che)*	friend
un'	**aula**	classroom
la	**biologia**	biology
la	**carta geografica** *(pl -e -che)*	map
la	**chimica**	chemistry
la	**classe**	class; year; classroom
la	**compagna di classe**	school friend
la	**domanda**	question
l'	**educazione fisica**	PE
l'	**elettronica**	electronics
un'	**escursione**	trip; outing
la	**fisica**	physics
la	**frase**	sentence
la	**geografia**	geography
la	**ginnastica**	PE, gymnastics
la	**gomma (da cancellare)**	rubber
l'	**informatica**	computer studies
un'	**interrogazione**	oral test
la	**lavagna**	blackboard
la	**lavagna bianca**	whiteboard
la	**lavagna interattiva**	interactive whiteboard
la	**lettura**	reading
la	**lezione**	lesson
le	**lingue straniere**	(modern) languages
la	**maestra**	primary school teacher
la	**matematica**	mathematics, maths
la	**materia (scolastica)**	(school) subject
la	**matita**	pencil
la	**mensa**	canteen
la	**musica**	music
la	**palestra**	gym
la	**parola**	word
la	**penna**	pen
la	**piscina**	swimming pool
la	**preside**	headmistress
la	**professoressa**	teacher
la	**ricreazione**	break; playtime

ESSENTIAL WORDS *(masculine continued)*

il	**risultato**	result
lo	**sbaglio**	mistake
lo	**scambio**	exchange
lo	**scolaro**	schoolboy
il	**semestre**	semester
lo	**spagnolo**	Spanish
lo	**studente**	student
gli	**studi**	studies
lo	**studio**	study
il	**tedesco**	German
il	**tirocinio**	apprenticeship
il	**voto**	mark

USEFUL PHRASES

imparare to learn

studiare to study

da quanto tempo studi l'italiano? how long have you been learning Italian?

imparare qc a memoria to learn sth off by heart

ho compiti da fare tutti i giorni I have homework every day

la mia sorellina va alle elementari, io frequento la scuola secondaria my little sister goes to primary school – I go to secondary school

insegnare l'italiano to teach Italian

il professore/la professoressa di tedesco the German teacher

ho fatto progressi *or* **ho migliorato in matematica** I have made progress in maths

fare il compito di matematica to do a maths test

dare un esame to sit an exam

passare un esame to pass an exam

non passare un esame to fail an exam

essere interrogato(a) to have an oral test

prendere la sufficienza to get a pass mark

ESSENTIAL WORDS (feminine continued)

la	**risposta**	answer; reply
la	**sala professori**	staffroom
le	**scienze**	science
la	**scolara**	schoolgirl
la	**scuola**	school
la	**scuola secondaria**	secondary school
la	**scuola (secondaria) superiore**	secondary school (14 to 19 year olds)
la	**scuola elementare** or **primaria**	primary school
la	**scuola materna**	nursery school
la	**scuola media** or **secondaria inferiore**	secondary school (11 to 14 year olds)
la	**storia**	history; story
la	**studentessa**	student
un'	**università**	university
le	**vacanze**	holidays
le	**vacanze estive**	summer holidays

USEFUL PHRASES

facile easy; **difficile** difficult
interessante interesting
noioso(a) boring
leggere to read; **scrivere** to write
ascoltare to listen (to)
guardare to look at, watch
ripetere to repeat
rispondere to reply
parlare to speak
è la prima or **la migliore della classe** she is top of the class
è la peggiore della classe she is bottom of the class
entrare in classe to go into the classroom
fare un errore or **uno sbaglio** to make a mistake
correggere to correct
ho fatto un errore di grammatica I made a grammatical error
ho ricevuto un bel voto I got a good mark
rispondete alla domanda! answer the question!
alzate la mano! put your hand up!

IMPORTANT WORDS (*masculine*)

un	**astuccio portapenne**	pencil case
il	**certificato**	certificate
il	**corridoio**	corridor
il	**cortile (per la ricreazione)**	playground
il	**diploma**	diploma
il	**diploma di scuola secondaria**	higher school-leaving course/ certificate
un	**esame di ammissione**	entrance exam
l'	**esame di maturità**	school-leaving examination
un	**esame orale**	oral exam
un	**esame scritto**	written exam
il	**foglio di carta**	sheet of paper
il	**giorno libero**	day off
il	**regolamento scolastico**	school rules
il	**righello**	ruler
un	**ufficio**	office
lo	**zaino**	rucksack; school bag

USEFUL PHRASES

il mio amico sta preparando l'esame di ammissione all'università my friend is sitting his university entrance exam

ripassare (la lezione) to revise

ripasserò la lezione ancora una volta domani I'll go over the lesson again tomorrow

IMPORTANT WORDS *(feminine)*

un'	**assenza**	absence
la	**carta**	paper
la	**cartella**	folder; file; schoolbag
la	**laurea**	university degree
la	**lezione (universitaria)**	lecture
la	**pagella**	school report
la	**regola**	rule
la	**scuola privata**	private school
la	**scuola statale**	state school
la	**traduzione**	translation

USEFUL PHRASES

al secondo anno in year two
al primo anno della scuola media in year seven
al secondo anno della scuola media in year eight
al terzo anno della scuola media in year nine
al primo anno della scuola superiore in year ten
al secondo anno della scuola superiore in year eleven

presente present
assente absent
punire un alunno/un'alunna to punish a pupil
silenzio! be quiet!

USEFUL WORDS (masculine)

un	**alunno interno**	boarder
il	**banco** (pl -chi)	(pupil's) desk
il	**bidello**	janitor
il	**bloc-notes** (pl inv)	jotter
il	**collegio**	boarding school
il	**comportamento**	behaviour
il	**dizionario**	dictionary
un	**esaminatore**	examiner
un	**esercizio**	exercise
un	**evidenziatore**	highlighter
i	**gabinetti**	lavatories; cloakroom
il	**gesso**	chalk
il	**greco**	Greek
l'	**inchiostro**	ink
un	**insegnante di sostegno**	support teacher
un	**ispettore scolastico**	school inspector
il	**latino**	Latin
il	**libretto delle assenze**	absence sheet
il	**libro di testo**	textbook
il	**liquido correttore**	correction fluid
il	**pennarello**	felt-tip pen
il	**quadrimestre**	term (4 months)
il	**supplente**	supply teacher
il	**tema**	essay; class exam
il	**temperamatite** (pl inv)	pencil sharpener
il	**test** (pl inv)	test
il	**trimestre**	term (3 months)
il	**tutor** (pl inv)	form tutor
il	**vocabolario**	vocabulary; dictionary

USEFUL WORDS *(feminine)*

un'	**alunna interna**	boarder
l'	**algebra**	algebra
l'	**aritmetica**	arithmetic
la	**bidella**	janitor
la	**biro** *(pl inv)*	Biro®
la	**brutta copia**	rough copy
la	**calcolatrice**	calculator
la	**calligrafia**	handwriting
la	**cattedra**	teacher's desk
la	**facoltà** *(pl inv)*	faculty
la	**fila**	row *(of seats etc)*
la	**geometria**	geometry
la	**grammatica**	grammar
un'	**insegnante di sostegno**	support teacher
un'	**ispettrice scolastica** *(pl -i -che)*	school inspector
la	**macchia**	blot
l'	**ortografia**	spelling
la	**poesia**	poetry; poem
la	**prova**	test
la	**religione**	religion; religious education, RE
le	**scienze naturali**	natural science
la	**scuola professionale**	technical college
la	**somma**	sum
la	**sufficienza**	pass mark; average mark
la	**supplente**	supply teacher

ESSENTIAL WORDS *(masculine)*

gli **abitanti**	inhabitants
gli **alberi**	trees
l' **ambiente**	environment
gli **animali**	animals
il **bosco** *(pl* -chi*)*	woods; forest
il **combustibile fossile**	fossil fuel
un **ecologista**	environmentalist
il **fiore**	flower
il **gas** *(pl inv)*	gas
i **gas di scarico**	exhaust fumes
il **gasolio**	diesel
l' **inquinamento**	pollution
il **mare**	sea
il **mondo**	world
i **pesci**	fish
il **tempo**	weather; time
i **Verdi**	the Greens
il **vetro**	glass

IMPORTANT WORDS *(masculine)*

un **agente inquinante**	pollutant
l' **alluminio**	aluminium
un **avvenimento**	event
il **buco** *(pl* -chi*)*	hole
il **calore**	heat
il **clima**	climate
il **danno**	damage
il **detersivo**	detergent; washing powder
il **fiume**	river
il **futuro**	future
il **governo**	government
il **lago** *(pl* -ghi*)*	lake
il **pannello solare**	solar panel
il **pianeta**	planet
i **prodotti eco solidali**	fair trade products

ESSENTIAL WORDS *(feminine)*

l'	**acqua**	water
l'	**aria**	air
un'	**automobile**	car
la	**benzina**	petrol
le	**bottiglie**	bottles
la	**campagna**	country
la	**carta geografica** *(pl -e -che)*	map
la	**costa**	coast
l'	**ecologia**	ecology
l'	**energia sostenibile**	renewable energy
la	**fabbrica** *(pl -che)*	factory
la	**frutta**	fruit
un'	**isola**	island
la	**macchina**	car
la	**montagna**	mountain
la	**pianta**	plant
la	**pioggia** *(pl -ge)*	rain
la	**questione**	question
la	**regione**	region; area
la	**specie** *(pl inv)*	species
la	**spiaggia** *(pl -ge)*	beach
la	**temperatura**	temperature
la	**terra**	earth; soil; ground
la	**verdura**	vegetables

IMPORTANT WORDS *(feminine)*

la	**centrale eolica** *(pl -i -che)*	windfarm
la	**centrale nucleare**	nuclear plant
la	**crisi** *(pl inv)*	crisis
la	**foresta**	forest
la	**giungla**	jungle
un'	**imposta**	tax
la	**soluzione**	solution
la	**tassa**	tax
la	**turbina eolica**	wind turbine
la	**zona**	zone

USEFUL WORDS *(masculine)*

il	**buco dell'ozono**	ozone hole
il	**canale**	canal
i	**CFC (clorofluorocarburi)**	CFCs
i	**cibi biologici**	organic food
il	**combustibile**	fuel
il	**continente**	continent
il	**deserto**	desert
l'	**ecosistema**	ecosystem
il	**fertilizzante**	(artificial) fertilizer
un	**inceneritore**	incinerator
l'	**inquinamento acustico**	noise pollution
un	**oceano**	ocean
un	**OGM (organismo geneticamente modificato)**	GMO
i	**prodotti chimici**	chemicals
il	**prodotto**	product
il	**ricercatore**	researcher
il	**riciclaggio**	recycling
il	**riscaldamento globale**	global warming
gli	**scienziati**	scientists
lo	**strato di ozono**	ozone layer
lo	**sviluppo sostenibile**	sustainable development
l'	**universo**	universe

USEFUL PHRASES

ha molto rispetto per l'ambiente he's/she's very environmentally-minded
un prodotto ecologico an eco-friendly product
in futuro in the future
distruggere to destroy
inquinare to pollute; **contaminare** to contaminate
vietare to ban
salvare to save
riciclare to recycle
verde green

USEFUL WORDS *(feminine)*

le	**acque di scolo**	sewage
la	**bomboletta**	aerosol
la	**catastrofe**	disaster
la	**chiazza di petrolio**	oil slick
la	**contaminazione**	contamination
la	**discarica** *(pl -che)*	dumping ground
l'	**energia eolica**	wind power
l'	**energia nucleare**	nuclear power
l'	**energia rinnovabile**	renewable energy
la	**foresta pluviale**	rainforest
la	**luna**	moon
la	**marmitta catalitica**	catalytic converter
la	**pioggia acida**	acid rain
la	**popolazione**	population
la	**raccolta differenziata (dei rifiuti)**	separate collection of different types of household waste
le	**scorie nucleari/ industriali**	nuclear/industrial waste

USEFUL PHRASES

biodegradabile biodegradable

dannoso(a) per l'ambiente harmful to the environment

biologico(a) organic; biological

ecologico(a) environment-friendly

benzina senza piombo unleaded petrol

le specie in via di estinzione endangered species

ESSENTIAL WORDS (*masculine*)

gli	**adulti**	adults
il	**bambino**	child; baby; little boy
il	**cognome**	surname
il	**cognome da ragazza**	maiden name
il	**cugino**	cousin
il	**fidanzato**	fiancé
il	**figlio**	son
il	**fratello**	brother
i	**genitori**	parents
il	**giovane**	youth, young man
i	**giovani**	young people
i	**grandi**	grown-ups
il	**marito**	husband
il	**nome**	name
il	**nome (di battesimo)**	first *or* Christian name
i	**nonni**	grandparents
il	**nonno**	grandfather
il	**padre**	father
il	**papà** (*pl inv*)	daddy
il	**parente**	relative
il	**ragazzo**	boy; boyfriend
un	**uomo** (*pl* **uomini**)	man
lo	**zio** (*pl* **zii**)	uncle

USEFUL PHRASES

quanti anni hai (or** ha)?** how old are you?
ho 15 anni; ha 40 anni I'm 15 – he/she is 40
come ti chiami (or** si chiama)?** what is your name?
mi chiamo Daniela my name is Daniela
si chiama Paolo his name is Paolo
fidanzato(a) engaged; **sposato(a)** married
divorziato(a) divorced; **separato(a)** separated
sposarsi con qn to marry sb
sposarsi to get married; **divorziare** to get divorced

ESSENTIAL WORDS *(feminine)*

la	**bambina**	child; baby girl; little girl
la	**cugina**	cousin
la	**donna**	woman
l'	**età** *(pl inv)*	age
la	**famiglia**	family
la	**fidanzata**	fiancée
la	**figlia**	daughter
la	**gente**	people
la	**gioventù**	youth
la	**madre**	mother
la	**mamma**	mummy
la	**moglie**	wife
la	**nonna**	grandmother
la	**persona**	person
la	**ragazza**	girl; girlfriend
la	**signora**	lady
la	**sorella**	sister
la	**zia**	aunt

USEFUL PHRASES

più giovane/vecchio(a) di me younger/older than me
hai (*or* **ha**) **fratelli o sorelle?** do you have any brothers or sisters?
ho un fratello e una sorella I have one brother and one sister
non ho fratelli I don't have any brothers or sisters
sono figlio(a) unico(a) I am an only child
tutta la famiglia the whole family
crescere to grow
invecchiare, diventare vecchio(a) to get old
vado d'accordo con i miei genitori I get on well with my parents
mia madre lavora my mother works

IMPORTANT WORDS *(masculine)*

un	**adolescente**	teenager
un	**assegno familiare**	child benefit
il	**bimbo**	child; baby; little boy
il	**neonato**	newborn baby
i	**nipoti**	grandchildren; nieces and nephews
il	**nipote**	grandson; nephew
il	**patrigno**	stepfather
lo	**scapolo**	bachelor
il	**single** *(pl inv)*	single man
il	**suocero**	father-in-law
il	**vedovo**	widower
il	**vicino**	neighbour

USEFUL WORDS *(masculine)*

il	**cognato**	brother-in-law
il	**figliastro**	stepson
il	**figlioccio**	godson
il	**fratellastro**	stepbrother
i	**gemelli**	twins
il	**genero**	son-in-law
un	**orfano**	orphan
il	**padrino**	godfather
il	**pensionato**	pensioner
il	**soprannome**	nickname
gli	**sposi novelli**	newlyweds
lo	**sposo**	bridegroom
un	**uomo anziano** *(pl* **uomini anziani**)	old man
il	**vecchio**	old man

USEFUL PHRASES

nascere to be born; **vivere** to live; **morire** to die
sono nato nel 1990 I was born in 1990
mia nonna è morta my grandmother is dead
è morta nel 1995 she died in 1995

IMPORTANT WORDS *(feminine)*

un'	**adolescente**	teenager
la	**bimba**	child; baby girl; little girl
la	**matrigna**	stepmother
la	**neonata**	newborn baby
la	**nipote**	granddaughter; niece
la	**ragazza alla pari**	au pair girl
la	**ragazza madre**	single mother
la	**single** *(pl inv)*	single woman
la	**suocera**	mother-in-law
la	**vedova**	widow
la	**vicina**	neighbour

USEFUL WORDS *(feminine)*

la	**baby sitter** *(pl inv)*	baby sitter; nanny
la	**casalinga** *(pl -ghe)*	housewife
la	**cognata**	sister-in-law
la	**coppia**	couple
la	**donna anziana**	old woman
la	**figliastra**	stepdaughter
la	**figlioccia** *(pl -ce)*	goddaughter
le	**gemelle**	twins
la	**madrina**	godmother
la	**nuora**	daughter-in-law
un'	**orfana**	orphan
la	**pensionata**	pensioner
la	**persona anziana**	old person
la	**sorellastra**	stepsister
la	**sposa**	bride
la	**vecchia**	old woman
la	**vecchiaia**	old age

USEFUL PHRASES

è single he/she is single

è vedovo he is a widower; **è vedova** she is a widow

sono la più giovane I am the youngest; **sono la più grande/vecchia** I am the eldest

la mia sorella maggiore my older sister

adottare un bambino to adopt a child

prendere un bambino in affidamento to foster a child

ESSENTIAL WORDS *(masculine)*

un	**agricoltore**	farmer *(cultivating crops)*
un	**allevatore**	farmer *(raising animals)*
un	**animale**	animal
il	**bosco** *(pl -chi)*	woods; forest
il	**bue** *(pl buoi)*	ox
il	**campo**	field
il	**cancello**	gate
il	**cane**	dog
il	**cane pastore**	sheepdog
il	**capretto**	kid
il	**cavallo**	horse
il	**contadino**	farmer *(cultivating crops)*
il	**furgone**	van
il	**gatto**	cat
il	**maiale**	pig
il	**paese**	village
il	**pollo**	chicken
il	**tacchino**	turkey
il	**vitello**	calf

IMPORTANT WORDS *(masculine)*

un	**agnello**	lamb
il	**fattore**	farmer
il	**gallo**	cock
il	**trattore**	tractor

USEFUL PHRASES

un campo di grano a cornfield
l'agricoltura biologica organic farming
polli ruspanti free range chickens
uova di galline da cortile free range eggs
badare agli animali to look after the animals
raccogliere to harvest
raccogliere frutta/il grano to harvest fruit/grain

ESSENTIAL WORDS (feminine)

un'	**anatra**	duck
la	**campagna**	country
la	**cavalla**	mare
la	**contadina**	farmer (crops)
la	**fattoria**	farm; farmhouse
la	**gallina**	hen
la	**mucca** (pl -che)	cow
la	**pecora**	sheep; ewe
la	**scrofa**	sow
la	**serra**	greenhouse
la	**terra**	ground; soil; earth
la	**vacca** (pl -che)	cow

IMPORTANT WORDS (feminine)

la	**collina**	hill
la	**forca** (pl -che)	fork
la	**vanga** (pl -ghe)	spade
la	**zappa**	hoe

USEFUL PHRASES
vivere in campagna to live in the country
lavorare in una fattoria to work on a farm
raccogliere il fieno to make hay

USEFUL WORDS *(masculine)*

un	allevamento	farm *(with livestock)*
un	aratro	plough
un	ariete	ram
un	asino	donkey
il	bestiame	cattle
il	capanno	shed
il	carro	cart
il	cereale	cereal
il	concime	manure; fertilizer
il	covone	haystack
il	fango	mud
il	fertilizzante	fertilizer
il	fienile	hayloft
il	fieno	hay
il	fossato	ditch
il	granaio	barn
il	grano	corn; wheat
il	gregge	flock *(sheep)*
il	letame	manure
il	mais	maize
il	mercato	market
il	montone	ram
il	mulino (a vento)	(wind)mill
l'	orzo	barley
il	paesaggio	landscape
il	pastore	shepherd
il	pollaio	henhouse
il	porcile	pigsty
il	pulcino	chick
il	puledro	foal
il	raccolto	crop; harvest
il	seme	seed
il	solco *(pl -chi)*	furrow
lo	spaventapasseri *(pl inv)*	scarecrow
lo	stagno	pond
il	suolo	ground, soil
il	toro	bull
il	vino	vine

USEFUL WORDS (feminine)

un'	**aia**	farmyard
l'	**avena**	oats
la	**brughiera**	moor, heath
la	**capra**	goat
la	**capretta**	kid
la	**falce**	sickle
la	**lana**	wool
la	**mandria**	herd (cattle)
la	**mietitrebbia**	combine harvester
un'	**oca** (pl -che)	goose
la	**paglia**	straw
la	**scala**	ladder
la	**segale**	rye
la	**stalla**	cow shed; stable
l'	**uva**	grapes
la	**vendemmia**	grape harvest, grape picking

USEFUL PHRASES
coltivare to grow (crops etc)
mungere una vacca to milk a cow
macellare to slaughter (animal)

ESSENTIAL WORDS *(masculine)*

i **frutti di mare**	seafood
il **pesce**	fish
il **pesce rosso**	goldfish

IMPORTANT WORDS *(masculine)*

il **granchio**	crab
un **insetto**	insect

USEFUL WORDS *(masculine)*

un **acquario**	aquarium
il **baco da seta**	silkworm
il **bruco** *(pl -chi)*	caterpillar
il **calabrone**	hornet
il **calamaro**	squid
un **eglefino**	haddock
il **gambero**	shrimp
il **gambero d'acqua dolce**	crayfish
il **girino**	tadpole
il **grillo**	cricket
il **luccio**	pike
il **merluzzo**	cod
il **moscerino**	midge
il **polpo**	octopus
il **ragno**	spider
il **salmone**	salmon
gli **scampi**	scampi
lo **scarafaggio**	cockroach
lo **squalo**	shark
il **tonno**	tuna
il **verme**	worm

USEFUL PHRASES

nuotare to swim
volare to fly
stiamo andando a pescare we're going fishing

ESSENTIAL WORDS (feminine)

l' **acqua**	water

IMPORTANT WORDS (feminine)

la **mosca** (pl -che)	fly
la **sardina**	sardine
la **trota**	trout

USEFUL WORDS (feminine)

un' **ala**	wing
un' **allergia**	allergy
un' **anguilla**	eel
un' **ape**	bee
un' **aragosta**	lobster
un' **aringa** (pl -ghe)	herring
la **cavalletta**	grasshopper
la **cicala**	cicada
la **cimice**	bed bug
la **coccinella**	ladybird
la **cozza**	mussel
la **falena**	moth
la **farfalla**	butterfly
la **formica** (pl -che)	ant
la **libellula**	dragonfly
la **medusa**	jellyfish
un' **ostrica** (pl -che)	oyster
la **pulce**	flea
la **rana**	frog
la **sogliola**	sole
la **tarma**	moth (clothes)
la **vespa**	wasp
la **zanzara**	mosquito

USEFUL PHRASES
una puntura di vespa a wasp sting
una ragnatela a spider's web

ESSENTIAL WORDS (masculine)

l'	aceto	vinegar
gli	antipasti	starters
un	aperitivo	aperitif
un	arrosto	roast
il	bar *(pl inv)*	café-bar
il	bicchiere	glass
il	brodo	(clear) soup, bouillon
il	burro	butter
il	caffè *(pl inv)*	coffee; café
il	caffelatte *(pl inv)*	coffee with milk
il	cameriere	waiter
i	cereali	cereal
il	cibo	food
il	cibo in scatola	tinned food
il	coltello	knife
il	conto	bill
il	cornetto	croissant
il	cucchiaino	teaspoon
il	cucchiaio	spoon
il	cuoco *(pl -chi)*	cook
il	dessert *(pl inv)*	dessert
il	dolce	sweet, dessert
il	filetto	steak
il	filoncino	French stick
il	formaggio	cheese
i	frutti di mare	seafood
il	frutto *(pl f frutta)*	piece of fruit
il	gelato	ice cream
un	hamburger *(pl inv)*	hamburger
il	latte	milk
il	litro	litre
il	maiale	pork
il	menù *(pl inv)*	menu
il	menù a prezzo fisso	fixed-price menu
l'	olio	oil
il	pane	bread
il	pane tostato	toast
il	panino	bread roll; sandwich

ESSENTIAL WORDS (feminine)

l'	**acqua (minerale)**	(mineral) water
la	**bibita**	soft drink
la	**birra**	beer
la	**birra alla spina**	draught beer
la	**bistecca** (pl -che)	steak
la	**bottiglia**	bottle
le	**caramelle**	sweets
la	**carne**	meat
la	**carne di manzo**	beef
la	**cena**	dinner
la	**cioccolata (calda)**	(hot) chocolate
la	**Coca Cola®** (pl -che -e)	Coke®
la	**colazione**	breakfast
la	**crêpe** (pl inv)	pancake
la	**fame**	hunger
la	**fetta**	slice
la	**forchetta**	fork
la	**frutta**	fruit
un'	**insalata**	salad
un'	**insalata mista**	mixed salad
la	**lattina**	can
la	**limonata**	lemonade
la	**marmellata**	jam
la	**marmellata d'arance**	marmalade
la	**minestra**	soup
un'	**oliva**	olive
un'	**omelette** (pl inv)	omelette
la	**pasta**	pastry; small cake
la	**pasticceria**	cake shop
le	**patatine**	crisps
le	**patatine fritte**	chips, fries
la	**pescheria**	fish shop
la	**salsiccia** (pl -ce)	sausage
la	**scatola**	tin, can; box
la	**sete**	thirst
le	**stoviglie**	dishes

ESSENTIAL WORDS *(masculine continued)*

il	**pasto pronto**	ready-made meal
il	**pesce**	fish
il	**piatto**	plate; dish; course
il	**piatto del giorno**	today's special
il	**picnic** *(pl inv)*	picnic
il	**pollo (arrosto)**	(roast) chicken
il	**pranzo**	lunch
il	**primo (piatto)**	first course
il	**prosciutto**	ham
il	**prosciutto cotto**	cooked ham
il	**prosciutto crudo**	cured ham
un	**quarto**	quarter *(bottle/litre etc)*
il	**riso**	rice
il	**ristorante**	restaurant
il	**salame**	salami
il	**sale**	salt
il	**secondo (piatto)**	main course
il	**servizio**	service
il	**succo di frutta**	fruit juice
il	**tè** *(pl inv)*	tea
il	**toast** *(pl inv)*	toasted sandwich
un	**uovo** *(pl f uova)*	egg
un	**uovo alla coque**	soft-boiled egg
un	**uovo sodo**	hard-boiled egg
il	**vino**	wine
il	**vitello**	veal
lo	**yogurt** *(pl inv)*	yoghurt
lo	**zucchero**	sugar

USEFUL PHRASES

cucinare to cook; **mangiare** to eat
bere to drink; **inghiottire** to swallow
il mio piatto preferito my favourite dish
cosa vuoi *or* **vuole da bere?** what are you having to drink?
è buono it's nice
avere fame, essere affamato(a) to be hungry
avere sete, essere assetato(a) to be thirsty

ESSENTIAL WORDS *(feminine continued)*

la	**tavola**	table
la	**tazza**	cup
la	**torta**	cake
la	**trattoria**	restaurant
le	**uova**	eggs
le	**verdure**	vegetables
la	**zuppa**	soup

IMPORTANT WORDS *(feminine)*

la	**brocca** *(pl -che)*	jug
la	**cameriera**	waitress
la	**capocuoca** *(pl -che)*	chef
la	**caraffa**	carafe
la	**carne alla griglia**	grilled meat
la	**carne macinata**	mince
la	**cotoletta di maiale**	pork chop
la	**crostata**	tart
la	**cuoca** *(pl -che)*	cook
la	**farina**	flour
le	**lumache**	snails
la	**maionese**	mayonnaise
la	**mancia** *(pl -ce)*	tip
la	**mensa**	canteen
la	**merendina**	snack
la	**panna**	cream
la	**pizza**	pizza
la	**ricetta**	recipe
la	**scelta**	choice
la	**scodella**	bowl
la	**senape**	mustard
la	**teiera**	teapot
la	**vaniglia**	vanilla

IMPORTANT WORDS *(masculine)*

l' **aglio**	garlic
un **agnello**	lamb
il **bricco** *(pl -chi)* **del latte**	milk jug
il **capocuoco** *(pl -chi)*	chef
il **carrello**	trolley
lo **chef** *(pl inv)*	chef
il **coniglio**	rabbit
il **coperto**	cover charge; place setting
il **cordiale**	cordial
il **cucchiaio da portata**	tablespoon
il **digestivo**	after-dinner liqueur
il **gusto**	taste; flavour
il **montone**	mutton
un **odore**	smell
il **peperone**	bell pepper
il **prezzo fisso**	set price
il **prezzo tutto compreso**	inclusive price
il **sapore**	flavour
lo **sciroppo**	syrup
lo **spuntino**	snack, bite to eat
il **supplemento**	extra charge
il **vitello**	veal

USEFUL WORDS *(masculine)*

l' **apribottiglie** *(pl inv)*	bottle opener
l' **apriscatole** *(pl inv)*	tin opener
il **brandy** *(pl inv)*	brandy
il **cacao**	cocoa
il **cavatappi** *(pl inv)*	corkscrew
lo **champagne** *(pl inv)*	champagne
il **cibo**	food
il **cubetto di ghiaccio**	ice cube
il **fegato**	liver
il **ketchup** *(pl inv)*	ketchup
il **miele**	honey
il **panettone**	cake eaten at Christmas
il **panino dolce**	sweet bun

USEFUL WORDS *(feminine)*

la **briciola**	crumb
la **cannuccia** *(pl* -**ce**)	straw
la **carta dei vini**	wine list
la **cotoletta**	chop
le **cozze**	mussels
la **crema**	custard
la **fetta di pane tostato**	Melba toast
la **gelatina**	jelly
la **limonata**	freshly-squeezed lemon juice
la **margarina**	margarine
la **pancetta**	bacon
la **panna montata**	whipped cream
la **panna per cucina**	cream for cooking
la **pasta**	pasta
la **pasta in bianco**	plain pasta *(with butter/oil)*
la **pasta in brodo**	pasta in broth
la **pastasciutta**	pasta in a sauce
la **roba da mangiare**	food
la **salsa**	sauce
la **selvaggina**	game
la **tisana**	herbal tea
la **tovaglia**	tablecloth
la **trippa**	tripe

USEFUL PHRASES

lavare i piatti to do the dishes

quando torniamo da scuola pranziamo we have lunch when we get back from school

fare colazione to have breakfast

delizioso(a) delicious; **disgustoso(a)** disgusting

buon appetito! enjoy your meal!; **salute!** cheers!

il conto, per favore! the bill please!

lasciamo la mancia? shall we leave a tip?

mangiare fuori to eat out

invitare qn a pranzo to invite sb to lunch

prendere qualcosa da bere to have drinks

USEFUL WORDS *(masculine continued)*

il	**parmigiano**	parmesan cheese
il	**pasticcino**	petit four; fancy cake
il	**pasto**	meal
il	**pâté** *(pl inv)*	pâté
il	**pesto**	pesto sauce
il	**piattino**	saucer
il	**pollame**	poultry
il	**proprietario**	owner
il	**puré di patate**	mashed potatoes
il	**risotto**	risotto
il	**roastbeef** *(pl inv)*	roast beef
il	**rognone**	kidneys
il	**sandwich** *(pl inv)*	sandwich
il	**self-service** *(pl inv)*	self-service restaurant
il	**sidro**	cider
lo	**spiedino**	kebab; skewer
lo	**stufato**	stew
il	**sugo** *(pl -ghi)* **di carne**	gravy
il	**tappo**	cork
il	**thermos** *(pl inv)*	flask
il	**tovagliolo**	napkin
il	**vassoio**	tray
il	**whisky** *(pl inv)*	whisky

USEFUL PHRASES

apparecchiare la tavola to set the table
sparecchiare la tavola to clear the table
pranzare to have lunch
cenare to have dinner
assaggiare qc to taste sth
che buon profumo! that smells good!
vino bianco/rosso/rosato white/red wine/rosé
una bistecca al sangue/a media cottura/ben cotta a rare/medium/well-
    done steak
un toast con formaggio e prosciutto a ham and cheese toastie

SMOKING

un	**accendino**	lighter
il	**cerino**	match *(made of wax)*
il	**fiammifero**	match
il	**fumatore**	smoker
la	**fumatrice**	smoker
il	**pacchetto di sigarette**	packet of cigarettes
la	**pipa**	pipe
il	**portacenere** *(pl inv)*	ashtray
la	**sigaretta**	cigarette
il	**sigaro**	cigar
il	**tabaccaio**	tobacconist's
il	**tabacco**	tobacco

USEFUL PHRASES

una scatola di fiammiferi a box of matches
hai (*or* **ha**) **da accendere?** do you have a light?
accendere una sigaretta to light up
"vietato fumare" "no smoking"
non fumo I don't smoke
ho smesso di fumare I've stopped smoking
fumare fa molto male alla salute smoking is very bad for you

ESSENTIAL WORDS *(masculine)*

un	**amico** *(pl -ci)* **di penna**	pen friend
il	**ballo**	dance
il	**biglietto**	ticket
il	**calcetto**	table football
il	**cantante**	singer
il	**canto**	singing
il	**CD** *(pl inv)*	CD
il	**cellulare**	mobile phone
il	**cinema** *(pl inv)*	cinema
il	**concerto**	concert
il	**decoder** *(pl inv)*	digibox
il	**dépliant** *(pl inv)*	leaflet
il	**disco** *(pl -chi)*	record
il	**divertimento**	entertainment; pastime
il	**DVD** *(pl inv)*	DVD
il	**film** *(pl inv)*	film *(movie)*
il	**fine settimana** *(pl inv)*	weekend
il	**fumetto**	comic strip
il	**gioco** *(pl -chi)*	game
il	**giornale**	newspaper
un	**hobby** *(pl inv)*	hobby
	Internet	internet
un	**iPod®** *(pl inv)*	iPod®
il	**lettore CD/DVD/MP3**	CD/DVD/MP3 player
il	**museo**	museum; art gallery
il	**passatempo**	hobby
il	**programma**	programme
il	**romanzo**	novel
il	**romanzo giallo**	detective novel
gli	**scacchi**	chess
lo	**schermo al plasma**	plasma screen
il	**socio**	member *(of club)*
lo	**spettacolo**	show
lo	**sport** *(pl inv)*	sport
il	**teatro**	theatre
il	**telegiornale**	TV news
il	**tempo libero**	free time
il	**videogioco** *(pl -chi)*	video game

ESSENTIAL WORDS *(feminine)*

un'	**amica** *(pl -che)* **di penna**	pen friend
un'	**antenna parabolica** *(pl -e -che)*	satellite dish
la	**cantante**	singer
la	**canzone**	song
le	**carte da gioco**	cards
la	**console per videogiochi** *(pl inv)*	games console
la	**discoteca** *(pl -che)*	disco; night club
un'	**escursione**	trip; outing; hike
la	**festa**	party
la	**foto** *(pl inv)*	photo
la	**lettura**	reading
la	**macchina fotografica** *(pl -e -che)*	camera
la	**musica (pop/classica)**	(pop/classical) music
la	**paghetta**	pocket money
la	**passeggiata**	walk
la	**pellicola**	film *(for camera)*
la	**pista di pattinaggio**	skating rink
la	**pubblicità** *(pl inv)*	publicity; advert
la	**radio** *(pl inv)*	radio
la	**rivista**	magazine
la	**stampa**	the press
la	**star** *(m+f pl inv)*	film star
la	**televisione**	television
la	**TV** *(pl inv)*	TV
la	**TV satellitare**	satellite TV

USEFUL PHRASES

esco con i miei amici I go out with my friends
leggo il giornale I read the newspaper
guardo la televisione I watch television
gioco a calcio/tennis/carte I play football/tennis/cards
fare bricolage to do DIY
fare il/la baby sitter to baby-sit
fare zapping to channel-hop
andare in discoteca to go clubbing

IMPORTANT WORDS *(masculine)*

gli	**annunci (sul giornale)**	adverts; small ads
il	**cartone animato**	cartoon
il	**computer** *(pl inv)*	computer
il	**concorso**	competition
il	**disegno**	drawing
il	**giocattolo**	toy
un	**incontro**	meeting
un	**manifesto**	notice; poster
il	**masterizzatore CD/DVD**	CD/DVD writer
il	**messaggino**	text message
il	**PC** *(pl inv)*	PC
il	**quadro**	painting
il	**ragazzo**	boy; boyfriend
il	**sito web**	website
lo	**smartphone** *(pl inv)*	smartphone
un	**sms** *(pl inv)*	text message

USEFUL WORDS *(masculine)*

il	**blog** *(pl inv)*	blog
il	**campeggio**	campsite; holiday camp
il	**coro**	choir
il	**cruciverba** *(pl inv)*	crossword puzzle(s)
il	**fan** *(pl inv)*	fan
il	**gioco** *(pl -chi)* **da tavolo**	board game
il	**monopattino**	scooter
il	**night club** *(pl inv)*	night club
i	**pattini in linea**	rollerblades
lo	**scout** *(pl inv)*	scout
lo	**skateboard** *(pl inv)*	skateboard

USEFUL PHRASES

emozionante exciting
noioso(a) boring
divertente funny
lavorare a maglia to knit
cucire to sew

IMPORTANT WORDS *(feminine)*

la **collezione**	collection
la **macchina fotografica digitale**	digital camera
la **mostra**	exhibition
la **notte**	evening; night
la **pittura**	painting
la **ragazza**	girl; girlfriend
la **sera**	evening
la **serie televisiva**	serial
la **telenovela** *(pl inv)*	soap (opera)
la **videocamera**	camcorder

USEFUL WORDS *(feminine)*

la **chat** *(pl inv)*	chat; chatroom
la **diapositiva**	slide
la **fan** *(pl Inv)*	fan
la **fotografia**	photograph; photography
la **hit parade** *(pl inv)*	charts
le **parole crociate**	crossword puzzle(s)
la **scout** *(pl inv)*	girl scout

USEFUL PHRASES

non è male it's not bad
abbastanza bello(a) quite good
ballare to dance
fare fotografie to take photos
mi annoio I'm bored
ci vediamo di venerdì we meet on Fridays
sto risparmiando per comprare un iPad® I'm saving up to buy an iPad®
mi piacerebbe fare il giro del mondo I'd like to go round the world

ESSENTIAL WORDS (*masculine*)

un **ananas** (*pl inv*)	pineapple
il **frutto** (*pl f* **frutta**)	(piece of) fruit
il **lampone**	raspberry
il **limone**	lemon
il **pomodoro**	tomato
il **pompelmo**	grapefruit

IMPORTANT WORDS (*masculine*)

un **albero da frutta**	fruit tree
il **melone**	melon

USEFUL WORDS (*masculine*)

un **avocado** (*pl inv*)	avocado
il **dattero**	date
il **fico** (*pl* **-chi**)	fig
il **kiwi** (*pl inv*)	kiwi fruit
il **mandarino**	tangerine
il **mirtillo**	blueberry
il **nocciolo**	stone (*in fruit*)
il **rabarbaro**	rhubarb
il **ribes** (*pl inv*) **nero**	blackcurrant
il **ribes** (*pl inv*) **rosso**	redcurrant
il **semino**	pip (*in fruit*)

USEFUL PHRASES
maturo(a) ripe
acerbo(a) unripe
un chilo di a kilo of
mezzo chilo di half a kilo of
un cestino di lamponi a punnet of raspberries

ESSENTIAL WORDS (feminine)

un' **albicocca** (pl-**che**)	apricot
un' **arancia** (pl-**ce**)	orange
la **banana**	banana
la **buccia** (pl-**ce**)	skin
la **caldarrosta**	(roasted) chestnut
la **castagna**	chestnut
la **ciliegia** (pl-**gie** or-**ge**)	cherry
la **fragola**	strawberry
la **frutta**	fruit
la **mela**	apple
la **pera**	pear
la **pesca** (pl-**che**)	peach
la **pescanoce**	nectarine
l' **uva**	grapes
l' **uvetta**	raisin

USEFUL WORDS (feminine)

un' **arachide**	peanut
la **bacca** (pl-**che**)	berry
la **melagrana**	pomegranate
la **mora**	blackberry
la **nocciola**	hazelnut
la **noce**	walnut
la **noce di anacardo**	cashew nut
la **noce di cocco**	coconut
la **prugna**	plum
la **prugna secca** (pl-**e** -**che**)	prune
l' **uva spina**	gooseberry
la **vite**	vine

USEFUL PHRASES

un succo d'arancia/d'ananas an orange/a pineapple juice
un grappolo d'uva a bunch of grapes
sbucciare un frutto to peel a fruit
scivolare su una buccia di banana to slip on a banana skin

ESSENTIAL WORDS (masculine)

un **armadietto**	cupboard
un **armadio**	wardrobe
il **calorifero**	radiator
il **congelatore**	freezer
il **fornello (elettrico/a gas)**	(electric/gas) cooker
il **frigo** (pl -ghi)	fridge
il **frigorifero**	refrigerator
il **guardaroba** (pl inv)	wardrobe
il **letto**	bed
il **mobile**	piece of furniture
i **mobili**	furniture
un **orologio**	clock
il **paralume** (pl inv)	lampshade
lo **scaffale**	shelf
lo **specchio**	mirror
il **tavolo**	table
il **telefono**	telephone

IMPORTANT WORDS (masculine)

il **baule**	chest
il **bollitore**	kettle
il **cellulare**	mobile phone
il **divano**	sofa
un **elettrodomestico**	domestic appliance
il **ferro da stiro**	iron
il **forno a microonde**	microwave oven
il **lettore di CD/DVD**	CD/DVD player
il **monolocale**	studio flat
il **piano(forte)**	piano
il **quadro**	painting, picture
il **tavolino**	coffee table
il **(telefono) cordless**	cordless phone
(pl i **(telefoni) cordless**)	

ESSENTIAL WORDS *(feminine)*

la	**lampada**	lamp
la	**lavastoviglie** *(pl inv)*	dishwasher
la	**lavatrice**	washing machine
la	**poltrona**	armchair
la	**radio** *(pl inv)*	radio
la	**radiosveglia**	radio alarm
la	**sedia**	chair
la	**stanza**	room
la	**stufa**	heater
la	**tavola**	table
la	**televisione**	television

IMPORTANT WORDS *(feminine)*

un'	**asciugatrice**	tumble-dryer
un'	**aspirapolvere** *(pl inv)*	vacuum cleaner
la	**credenza**	sideboard
la	**libreria**	bookcase
la	**radio digitale**	digital radio
la	**scrivania**	(writing) desk

USEFUL WORDS *(masculine)*

un **addetto ai traslochi**	removal man
un **altoparlante**	loudspeaker
un **asciugacapelli** *(pl inv)*	hairdryer
il **camion dei traslochi** *(pl inv)*	removal van
il **carrello**	trolley
il **cassetto**	drawer
il **cassettone**	chest of drawers
il **comodino**	bedside table
il **computer** *(pl inv)*	computer
il **forno**	oven
i **letti a castello**	bunk beds
il **lettino**	cot
il **letto a una piazza**	single bed
il **letto matrimoniale**	double bed
il **materasso**	mattress
i **mobili**	furniture
il **portaombrelli** *(pl inv)*	umbrella stand
lo **sgabello**	stool
lo **stereo compatto**	music centre
il **tappeto**	rug
il **telecomando**	remote control
il **trasloco**	move
il **tritatutto** *(pl inv)*	food processor

USEFUL PHRASES

un appartamento ammobiliato a furnished flat
accendere/spegnere la stufa to switch the heater on/off
ho rifatto il mio letto I've made my bed
sedersi to sit down
mettere qc in forno to put sth in the oven
tirare le tende to draw the curtains
chiudere le imposte to close the shutters

USEFUL WORDS (feminine)

un'	**antenna**	aerial
un'	**antenna parabolica** (pl -e -che)	satellite dish
la	**bilancia** (pl -ce)	scales
la	**cornice**	frame
la	**culla**	cradle
le	**imposte**	shutters
la	**lampada a stelo**	standard lamp
la	**lampada alogena**	halogen lamp
la	**macchina per cucire**	sewing machine
la	**moquette**	fitted carpet
la	**piantana**	standard lamp
la	**piastra per capelli**	hair straighteners
la	**scala a libretto**	step ladder
la	**segreteria telefonica** (pl -e -che)	answering machine
la	**tapparella**	blind
la	**tavola da stiro**	ironing board
la	**toilette**	toilet; dressing table
la	**TV a schermo panoramico**	widescreen TV
la	**videocamera**	camcorder

USEFUL PHRASES
è un appartamento di 4 stanze it's a 4-roomed flat
la colazione/la cena è pronta! breakfast/dinner is ready!
il pranzo è pronto! lunch is ready!

ESSENTIAL WORDS

le	**Alpi**	the Alps
gli	**Appennini**	Apennines
l'	**Atlantico**	the Atlantic
	Bruxelles	Brussels
la	**Costa Azzurra**	Côte d'Azur
le	**Dolomiti**	Dolomites
l'	**est** (*m*)	the east
l'	**estero** (*m*)	foreign countries; abroad
	Firenze	Florence
la	**Germania**	Germany
	Genova	Genoa
	Livorno	Livorno, Leghorn
la	**Lombardia**	Lombardy
	Londra	London
	Marsiglia	Marseilles
il	**Mediterraneo**	the Mediterranean
il	**Meridione**	the South
	Milano	Milan
la	**montagna**	mountain
il	**Monte Bianco**	Mont Blanc
	Napoli	Naples
il	**nord**	the north
l'	**ovest** (*m*)	the west
	Parigi	Paris
il	**passo**	pass (*mountain*)
il	**Piemonte**	Piedmont
	Roma	Rome
la	**Sardegna**	Sardinia
la	**Sicilia**	Sicily
il	**sud**	the south
il	**Tevere**	the Tiber
	Torino	Turin
la	**Toscana**	Tuscany
il	**Vaticano**	the Vatican
	Venezia	Venice

IMPORTANT WORDS

Edimburgo *(f)*	Edinburgh
il **Tamigi**	the Thames

USEFUL WORDS

Atene	Athens
Berlino	Berlin
il **canale della Manica, la Manica**	English Channel
la **capitale**	capital
l' **Estremo Oriente**	the Far East
Ginevra	Geneva
le **isole britanniche**	the British Isles
L'Aia	The Hague
Lisbona	Lisbon
il **Medio Oriente**	the Middle East
Mosca	Moscow
il **Pacifico**	the Pacific
Pechino	Beijing
il **Polo Nord/Sud**	the North/South Pole
la **provincia** *(pl* **-ce)**	province
Varsavia	Warsaw

USEFUL PHRASES

andare a Londra/Roma to go to London/Rome
andare in Lombardia to go to Lombardy
vengo da Milano/dal sud I come from Milan/from the south
all'estero abroad

a nord in *or* to the north
a sud in *or* to the south
a est in *or* to the east
a ovest in *or* to the west

l'Italia del sud *or* **meridionale** southern Italy
l'Italia del nord *or* **settentrionale** northern Italy

GREETINGS

ciao hello, hi; bye
come stai (*or*sta)? how are you?
come va? how are you?
bene fine *(in reply)*
piacere (di conoscerla) pleased to meet you
pronto hello *(on telephone)*
buonasera good afternoon; good evening
buonanotte good night
arrivederci goodbye
ci vediamo domani see you tomorrow
ci vediamo più tardi see you later

BEST WISHES

buon compleanno happy birthday
buon Natale merry Christmas
felice anno nuovo *or*buon anno happy New Year
buona Pasqua happy Easter
saluti best wishes
auguri best wishes
benvenuto(a) welcome
congratulazioni congratulations
buon appetito enjoy your meal
cari saluti all the best
divertiti (*or*si diverta) enjoy yourself
buona fortuna good luck
buon viaggio safe journey
salute bless you *(after a sneeze)*; cheers
alla tua (*or*alla vostra, *etc*)**!** your health!

SURPRISE

mio Dio my goodness
cosa? what?
come? what?
capisco oh, I see
ma dai! really?
beh... well...
veramente? really?
stai scherzando? are you kidding?
che fortuna! how lucky!

POLITENESS

scusa (*or* **mi scusi**) I'm sorry; excuse me
per favore please
grazie thank you
no, grazie no thank you
sì, grazie yes please
di niente not at all, don't mention it, you're welcome
volentieri gladly

AGREEMENT

sì yes
naturalmente of course
d'accordo OK
va bene fine

DISAGREEMENT

no no
certo che no of course not
non esiste no way
per niente not at all
al contrario on the contrary
questa poi! well I never
che faccia tosta what a cheek
bada agli affari tuoi mind your own business

DIFFICULTIES

aiuto! help!
al fuoco! fire!
ahi! ouch!
scusa (or **scusi**) (I'm) sorry, excuse me, I beg your pardon
mi dispiace I'm sorry
che peccato what a pity
che seccatura what a nuisance
che noia how boring
sono stufo(a) I'm fed up
non lo sopporto più I can't stand it any more
mamma mia oh dear
è terribile how awful

ORDERS

attento(a) be careful
fermati (or si fermi) stop
ehi, tu hey, you there
fuori di qui clear off
silenzio shh
basta that's enough
vietato fumare no smoking
andiamo let's go
continua go ahead, go on

OTHERS

non ne ho idea no idea
forse perhaps, maybe
non so I don't know
posso aiutarti (or aiutarla)? can I help you?
eccoti qua there you are
ecco tieni (or tenga) here you are; take this
arrivo just coming
non preoccuparti don't worry
non ne vale la pena it's not worth it
a proposito by the way
caro(a) darling
poverino(a) poor thing
tanto meglio so much the better
non importa I don't mind; it doesn't matter
per me è lo stesso (or è uguale) it's all the same to me
che sfortuna too bad; bad luck!
dipende it depends
cosa devo fare? what shall I do?
a che scopo? what's the point?
mi dà fastidio it annoys me
mi dà ai nervi it gets on my nerves

ESSENTIAL WORDS *(masculine)*

un	**appuntamento**	appointment
il	**dentista**	dentist
il	**dottore**	doctor
un	**incidente**	accident
un	**infermiere**	(male) nurse
il	**letto**	bed
il	**medico**	doctor
un	**ospedale**	hospital
il	**paziente**	patient
lo	**stomaco**	stomach

IMPORTANT WORDS *(masculine)*

un	**antisettico**	antiseptic
il	**caldo**	heat
il	**cerotto**	(sticking) plaster
il	**cotone idrofilo**	cotton wool
il	**cucchiaio**	spoon; spoonful
il	**dolore**	pain
il	**farmacista**	chemist
il	**farmaco**	medicine, drug
il	**freddo**	cold
il	**gesso**	plaster cast
un	**intervento chirurgico**	operation, surgery
il	**Pronto Soccorso**	Accident and Emergency, A&E
il	**sangue**	blood
lo	**sciroppo**	syrup
lo	**studio medico**	surgery
un	**unguento**	ointment

USEFUL PHRASES

c'è stato un incidente there's been an accident
essere ricoverato(a) in ospedale to be admitted to hospital
devi (*or* **deve**) **stare a letto** you must stay in bed
essere malato(a) to be ill; **sentirsi meglio** to feel better
mi sono fatto male I have hurt myself
mi sono tagliato un dito I have cut my finger
mi sono slogato la caviglia I have sprained my ankle
si è rotto un braccio he has broken his arm

ESSENTIAL WORDS (feminine)

un'	**aspirina**	aspirin
la	**dentista**	dentist
la	**dottoressa**	doctor
la	**farmacia**	chemist's (shop)
la	**farmacista**	chemist, pharmacy
la	**febbre**	temperature
un'	**infermiera**	nurse
la	**pasticca** (pl -che)	tablet, pill
la	**pastiglia**	tablet, pill
la	**paziente**	patient
la	**pillola**	pill
la	**salute**	health

IMPORTANT WORDS (feminine)

un'	**ambulanza**	ambulance
un'	**assicurazione**	Insurance
la	**barella**	stretcher
la	**clinica** (pl -che)	clinic
la	**compressa**	tablet
la	**diarrea**	diarrhoea
la	**fascia** (pl -sce)	bandage
la	**ferita**	wound
un'	**influenza**	flu
un'	**ingessatura**	plaster cast
un'	**iniezione**	injection
un'	**insolazione**	sunstroke
la	**malattia**	illness
la	**medicina**	medicine
un'	**operazione**	operation
la	**ricetta**	prescription
la	**scottatura**	burn; scald

USEFUL PHRASES

mi sono ustionato I have burnt myself
mi fa male la gola/la testa/lo stomaco I've got a sore throat/
  a headache/a stomach ache
avere la febbre to have a temperature

USEFUL WORDS *(masculine)*

un	**ascesso**	abscess
un	**attacco** *(pl -chi)*	fit
un	**attacco cardiaco** *(pl -chi -ci)*	heart attack
i	**batteri**	germs, bacteria
il	**cancro**	cancer
il	**capogiro**	dizziness
il	**graffio**	scratch
il	**livido**	bruise
il	**mal di gola**	sore throat
il	**microbo**	germ
il	**morbillo**	measles
il	**nervo**	nerve
gli	**orecchioni**	mumps
il	**polso**	pulse
il	**preservativo**	condom
il	**ricostituente**	tonic
il	**riposo**	rest
lo	**shock** *(pl inv)*	shock
lo	**stress** *(pl inv)*	stress
lo	**svenimento**	fainting
il	**vaiolo**	smallpox
il	**veleno**	poison

USEFUL PHRASES

ho sonno I'm sleepy
ho la nausea I feel sick
dimagrire to lose weight
ingrassare to put on weight
inghiottire to swallow
sanguinare to bleed
vomitare to vomit
essere in forma to be in good shape
riposare to rest

USEFUL WORDS (feminine)

l'	**appendicite**	appendicitis
l'	**AIDS**	AIDS
l'	**articolazione**	joint
la	**ASL (Azienda Sanitaria Locale)**	local health centre
la	**cassetta del pronto soccorso**	first aid kit
la	**cicatrice**	scar
la	**dentiera**	false teeth
la	**dieta**	diet
un'	**emicrania**	migraine
un'	**epidemia**	epidemic
la	**fasciatura**	dressing
la	**febbre da fieno**	hay fever
la	**gravidanza**	pregnancy
la	**guarigione**	recovery
un'	**infiammazione**	inflammation
la	**nausea**	nausea
la	**pomata**	ointment
la	**radiografia**	X-ray
la	**rosolia**	German measles
la	**scheggia** (pl -ge)	splinter
la	**sedia a rotelle**	wheelchair
la	**stampella**	crutch
la	**tonsillite**	tonsillitis
la	**tosse**	cough
la	**tosse canina**	whooping cough
la	**trasfusione (di sangue)**	blood transfusion
la	**varicella**	chickenpox

USEFUL PHRASES

curare to cure; to treat; **stare meglio** to get better
gravemente ferito(a) seriously injured
sei (or **è**) **assicurato(a)?** are you insured?
sono raffreddato(a) I have a cold
mi fa male! that hurts!; it hurts!
respirare to breathe; **svenire** to faint; **tossire** to cough
morire to die
perdere conoscenza to lose consciousness
avere il braccio al collo to have one's arm in a sling

ESSENTIAL WORDS (*masculine*)

un	**albergo** (*pl* -ghi)	hotel
un	**ascensore**	lift
un	**assegno**	cheque
i	**bagagli**	luggage
il	**bagno**	bathroom
il	**balcone**	balcony
il	**bar** (*pl inv*)	bar
il	**cameriere**	waiter
il	**conto**	bill
il	**direttore**	manager
il	**facchino**	porter
un	**hotel** (*pl inv*)	hotel
i	**letti gemelli**	twin beds
il	**letto matrimoniale**	double bed
il	**modulo**	form
il	**numero**	number
un	**ospite**	guest
il	**passaporto**	passport
il	**pasto**	lunch; meal
il	**piano**	floor; storey
il	**pianoterra**	ground floor
il	**pranzo**	lunch
il	**prezzo**	price
un	**receptionist** (*pl inv*)	receptionist
il	**ristorante**	restaurant
il	**rumore**	noise
il	**soggiorno**	stay
gli	**spiccioli**	change, loose coins
il	**telefono**	telephone

USEFUL PHRASES

vorrei prenotare una camera I would like to book a room
una camera con doccia/bagno a room with a shower/bathroom
una camera singola/matrimoniale a single/double room
una camera a due letti a twin-bedded room

ESSENTIAL WORDS *(feminine)*

la	**camera**	room
la	**cameriera**	waitress; chambermaid
la	**caparra**	deposit
la	**carta di credito**	credit card
la	**chiave**	key
la	**colazione**	breakfast
la	**comodità** *(pl inv)*	comfort; convenience
la	**data**	date
la	**direttrice**	manager
la	**doccia** *(pl -ce)*	shower
la	**mezza pensione**	half board
la	**notte**	night
un'	**ospite**	guest
la	**pensione**	guest house
la	**pensione completa**	full board
la	**piscina**	swimming pool
la	**reception** *(pl inv)*	reception
la	**receptionist** *(pl inv)*	receptionist
la	**scala**	ladder; staircase
la	**tariffa**	rate, rates
la	**televisione**	television
la	**valigia** *(pl -gie or -ge)*	suitcase
la	**vista**	view
le	**toilette**	toilets
un'	**uscita d'emergenza**	fire escape

USEFUL PHRASES

ha un documento di identità? do you have any ID?
a che ora è servita la colazione? what time is breakfast served?
pulire la stanza to clean the room
"non disturbare" "do not disturb"

IMPORTANT WORDS *(masculine)*

un	**asciugamano**	towel
il	**bagno**	bathroom
il	**benvenuto**	welcome
un	**interruttore**	switch
il	**lavandino**	washbasin
il	**prezzo tutto compreso**	all inclusive price
il	**reclamo**	complaint
il	**rumore**	noise

USEFUL WORDS *(masculine)*

l'	**atrio**	foyer
il	**capocameriere**	head waiter
il	**cuoco** *(pl -chi)*	cook
il	**cuscino**	pillow
il	**rubinetto**	tap
il	**sommellier** *(pl inv)*	wine waiter

USEFUL PHRASES

occupato(a) occupied
libero(a) vacant
pulito(a) clean
sporco(a) dirty
dormire to sleep
svegliarsi to wake up
"con tutte le comodità" "with all facilities"
potrei avere la sveglia domani mattina alle sette, per favore? I'd like a 7 o'clock alarm call tomorrow morning, please
una camera con vista sul mare a room overlooking the sea

IMPORTANT WORDS (feminine)

l'	**acqua calda**	hot water
la	**fattura**	bill; invoice
la	**guida turistica** (pl **-e -che**)	guidebook
la	**mancia** (pl **-ce**)	tip
la	**ricevuta**	receipt
la	**saponetta**	bar of soap
la	**vasca** (pl **-che**) **da bagno**	bathtub

USEFUL WORDS (feminine)

la	**cassaforte** (pl **casseforti**)	safe
la	**carta igienica**	toilet paper
la	**coperta**	blanket
la	**corrente d'aria**	draught
la	**cuoca** (pl **-che**)	cook

USEFUL PHRASES

una camera con mezza pensione room with half board

ci sediamo fuori? shall we sit outside?

abbiamo cenato all'aperto we were served dinner outside

un albergo a tre stelle a three-star hotel

IVA inclusa inclusive of VAT

ESSENTIAL WORDS (*masculine*)

un	**(appezzamento di) terreno**	plot of land
un	**appartamento**	flat, apartment
un	**ascensore**	lift
· il	**bagno**	bathroom
il	**balcone**	balcony
il	**box** (*pl inv*)	garage
il	**cancello**	gate
il	**condominio**	block of flats
il	**cortile**	(court)yard
un	**edificio**	building
l'	**esterno**	exterior
il	**garage** (*pl inv*)	garage
· il	**giardino**	garden
un	**indirizzo**	address
l'	**interno**	interior
· il	**mobile**	piece of furniture
i	**mobili**	furniture
il	**numero di telefono**	phone number
· il	**paese**	village
il	**parcheggio**	car park; parking space
il	**piano**	floor, storey; piano
il	**pianoterra**	ground floor
il	**pianterreno**	ground floor
il	**quartiere residenziale**	housing estate
il	**riscaldamento (centralizzato)**	(central) heating
il	**seminterrato**	basement
· il	**soggiorno**	living room
il	**viale**	avenue
il	**vialetto d'accesso**	drive

USEFUL PHRASES

quando vado a casa when I go home
guardare fuori dalla finestra to look out of the window
a casa mia/tua/nostra at my/your/our house
traslocare to move house
affittare un appartamento to rent a flat

ESSENTIAL WORDS *(feminine)*

la	**camera da letto**	bedroom
la	**cantina**	cellar
la	**casa**	house
la	**chiave**	key
la	**città** *(pl inv)*	town; city
la	**cucina**	kitchen
la	**doccia** *(pl -ce)*	shower
un'	**entrata**	entrance
la	**finestra**	window
la	**parete**	wall
la	**porta**	door
la	**porta d'ingresso**	front door
la	**sala da pranzo**	dining room
le	**scale**	stairs
la	**stanza**	room
la	**via**	street
la	**vista**	view

USEFUL PHRASES

vivo in una casa/un appartamento I live in a house/flat
(al piano) di sopra upstairs
(al piano) di sotto downstairs
al primo piano on the first floor
al pianoterra on the ground floor
in casa at home

IMPORTANT WORDS (masculine)

l'	affitto	rent
• l'	alloggio	accommodation
un	appartamento ammobiliato	furnished flat
il	bilocale	two-roomed flat
il	caminetto	fireplace
il	camino	chimney
• il	corridoio	corridor
' il	gabinetto	lavatory
il	lavandino	washbasin
il	mobilio	furniture
il	monolocale	studio flat
‹ il	padrone di casa	landlord; owner
il	pianerottolo	landing
il	portinaio	caretaker; concierge
il	prato	lawn
• il	proprietario	owner; landlord
il	solaio	attic
il	tetto	roof
il	trasloco (pl -chi)	move
⌐ il	vicino (di casa)	neighbour

USEFUL WORDS (masculine)

un	attico	penthouse; loft apartment
il	campanello	door bell
l'	ingresso	hall; entrance
, un	inquilino	tenant; lodger
il	lucernario	skylight
il	muro	wall
il	parquet (pl inv)	parquet floor
il	pavimento	floor
lo	scaldabagno (elettrico)	(electric) water heater
lo	scalino	step
il	soffitto	ceiling
lo	studio	study
il	tubo	pipe
il	vetro	window pane

IMPORTANT WORDS *(feminine)*

la	**casetta di campagna**	cottage
la	**donna delle pulizie**	cleaner
la	**legnaia**	lumber room
la	**manutenzione**	upkeep; maintenance
la	**padrona di casa**	landlady; owner
la	**portinaia**	caretaker; concierge
la	**proprietaria**	owner; landlady
la	**vicina (di casa)**	neighbour

USEFUL WORDS *(feminine)*

un'	**antenna**	aerial
la	**caldaia**	boiler
la	**camera degli ospiti**	spare room
la	**casa popolare**	council flat or house
la	**casalinga** *(pl -ghe)*	housewife
la	**decorazione**	decoration
la	**facciata**	front (of house)
un'	**imposta**	shutter
un'	**inquilina**	tenant; lodger
la	**mattonella**	tile
la	**persiana**	blind; shutter
la	**piastrella**	tile
la	**portafinestra**	French window
la	**portineria**	caretaker's room
la	**siepe**	hedge
la	**soffitta**	attic
la	**soglia**	doorstep
la	**tegola**	roof tile; slate
la	**tubatura**	pipe
la	**villetta**	detached house
le	**villette a schiera**	terraced houses

USEFUL PHRASES
bussare alla porta to knock at the door
ha suonato il campanello the doorbell's just gone
dall'esterno from the outside
dentro on the inside
fino al tetto up to the ceiling

ESSENTIAL WORDS (*masculine*)

un	**armadietto**	cupboard
un	**armadio**	wardrobe
un	**asciugacapelli** (*pl inv*)	hair dryer
un	**asciugamano**	towel
il	**bidone della spazzatura**	dustbin
il	**cuscino**	pillow; cushion
il	**dentifricio**	toothpaste
il	**forno**	oven
il	**frigo** (*pl inv*)	fridge
il	**frigorifero**	refrigerator
il	**gas**	gas
un	**interruttore**	switch
il	**lavabo**	washbasin
il	**lavandino**	sink
il	**lenzuolo** (*pl f* **lenzuola**)	sheet
i	**piatti**	dishes
il	**portacenere** (*pl inv*)	ashtray
il	**poster** (*pl inv*)	poster
il	**quadro**	picture
il	**radiatore**	radiator
il	**rubinetto**	tap
il	**sapone**	soap
lo	**specchio**	mirror
lo	**spremiagrumi** (*pl inv*)	juicer
lo	**strofinaccio**	dishtowel, tea towel
il	**tappeto**	carpet, rug
il	**televisore**	television set
il	**tovagliolo**	napkin
il	**vassoio**	tray

USEFUL PHRASES

farsi un bagno to have a bath
farsi una doccia to have a shower
fare le pulizie to do the housework
mi piace cucinare I like cooking

ESSENTIAL WORDS (feminine)

l'	acqua	water
la	bilancia (pl -ce)	scales
la	caffettiera	coffee maker
la	casseruola	saucepan
la	cassetta delle lettere	letterbox
la	coperta	blanket
la	doccia (pl -ce)	shower
l'	elettricità	electricity
la	foto (pl inv)	photo
la	lampada	lamp
la	lavatrice	washing machine
le	lenzuola	sheets
la	luce	light
la	pentola	saucepan
la	radio (pl inv)	radio
la	spazzola	brush
le	stoviglie	dishes
la	sveglia	alarm clock
la	televisione	television
le	tende	curtains
la	vasca (pl -che)	bath

USEFUL PHRASES

guardare la televisione to watch television
alla televisione on television
accendere/spegnere la TV to switch on/off the TV
gettare qc nel bidone della spazzatura to throw sth in the dustbin
lavare i piatti to do the dishes

IMPORTANT WORDS (*masculine*)

un	aspirapolvere (*pl inv*)	vacuum cleaner
il	bidé (*pl inv*)	bidet
il	bucato	(clean) washing
il	calorifero	radiator
il	detersivo (in polvere)	washing powder
il	detersivo per piatti	washing-up liquid
il	fornello	stove
il	termosifone	heater
il	ventilatore	electric fan

USEFUL WORDS (*masculine*)

il	cestino	wastepaper basket
il	coperchio	lid
il	ferro da stiro	iron
il	forno a microonde	microwave oven
il	frullatore	blender
il	guanciale	pillow
il	macinacaffè (*pl inv*)	coffee grinder
il	mestolo	ladle
il	piumone	duvet
il	secchio	bucket
il	soprammobile	ornament
lo	straccio per la polvere	duster
lo	strofinaccio	dishcloth
il	tostapane (*pl inv*)	toaster
il	vaso	vase

USEFUL PHRASES

collegare/scollegare un elettrodomestico to plug in/to unplug an
   appliance
passare l'aspirapolvere to hoover
fare il bucato to do the washing

IMPORTANT WORDS *(feminine)*

la	**donna delle pulizie**	cleaner
la	**lampadina**	light bulb
la	**lavastoviglie** *(pl inv)*	dishwasher
la	**padella**	frying pan
la	**piastra**	hob
la	**pittura**	paint; painting
la	**polvere**	dust
la	**presa (di corrente)**	socket
la	**prolunga** *(pl -ghe)*	extension
la	**ricetta**	recipe
la	**roba sporca**	(dirty) washing, laundry
la	**serratura**	lock
la	**spina elettrica**	plug *(electric)*
la	**stufa**	heater

USEFUL WORDS *(feminine)*

la	**carta da parati**	wallpaper
la	**cera**	floor polish
la	**coperta elettrica** *(pl -e -che)*	electric blanket
la	**gruccia** *(pl -ce)*	coat hanger
l'	**immondizia**	rubbish
la	**maniglia**	door handle
la	**moquette** *(pl inv)*	fitted carpet
la	**pentola a pressione**	pressure cooker
la	**ringhiera**	bannister
la	**scala**	ladder; staircase
la	**scopa**	broom
la	**spugna**	sponge
la	**tappezzeria**	upholstery
la	**tavola da stiro**	ironing board

USEFUL PHRASES

scopare to sweep (up)
pulire to clean
mettere via le cose to tidy away things
lasciare in giro i giocattoli to leave toys lying about

ESSENTIAL WORDS *(masculine)*

un	acconto	deposit
un	assegno	cheque
il	Bancomat® *(pl inv)*	debit card; cashpoint, ATM
il	cambio	exchange
il	centesimo (di euro)	euro cent
il	codice postale	postcode
il	contratto telefonico	phone contract
il	documento (d'identità)	ID card
un	errore	mistake
un	euro *(pl inv)*	euro
il	fax *(pl inv)*	fax; fax machine
il	francobollo	postage stamp
un	impiegato (allo sportello)	counter clerk
un	indirizzo	address
il	modulo	form
il	numero	number
il	pacchetto	parcel
il	passaporto	passport
il	postino	postman
il	prefisso telefonico	dialling code
il	prezzo	price
il	segnale di libero	dialling tone
un	sms *(pl inv)*	text message
lo	sportello	counter
gli	spiccioli	small change
il	telefono	telephone
un	ufficio informazioni turistiche	tourist information office
un	ufficio postale	post office

USEFUL PHRASES

la banca più vicina the nearest bank

vorrei incassare un assegno/cambiare del denaro I would like to cash a cheque/to change some money

dov'è il Bancomat® più vicino? where is the nearest cashpoint?

ESSENTIAL WORDS (feminine)

la	**banca** (pl -che)	bank
la	**banconota**	banknote
la	**biro** (pl inv)	Biro®
la	**buca** (pl -che) **delle lettere**	postbox
la	**busta**	envelope
la	**carta di credito**	credit card
la	**carta di debito**	debit card
la	**carta d'identità**	ID card
la	**cartolina**	postcard
la	**cassa**	check-out
la	**chiamata**	call
la	**compagnia telefonica** (pl -e -che)	phone company
la	**firma**	signature
un'	**impiegata (allo sportello)**	counter clerk
le	**informazioni**	information
la	**lettera**	letter
la	**penna**	pen
la	**posta elettronica**	email (service)
la	**postina**	postwoman
la	**risposta**	reply
la	**sterlina**	pound (sterling)

USEFUL PHRASES

una chiamata telefonica a phone call
telefonare a qn to phone sb
alzare la cornetta to lift the receiver
comporre il numero to dial (the number)
pronto – sono il signor Rossi hello, this is Mr Rossi
la linea è occupata the line is engaged
attenda in linea hold the line
ho sbagliato numero I got the wrong number
riattaccare to hang up
attivare il roaming to activate roaming
vorrei fare una chiamata internazionale I'd like to make an international
   phone call

IMPORTANT WORDS *(masculine)*

l'	**ADSL**	broadband
il	**cellulare**	mobile (phone)
il	**conto (in banca)**	(bank) account
il	**credito**	credit
il	**domicilio**	home address
un	**internet caffè** *(pl inv)*	internet café
il	**libretto degli assegni**	cheque book
il	**messaggio di posta elettronica**	email
il	**numero verde**	freephone
un	**operatore telefonico**	operator
il	**pagamento**	payment
il	**portafoglio**	wallet
il	**portamonete** *(pl inv)*	purse
il	**tasso di cambio**	exchange rate
il	**telefono fisso**	landline
il	**traveller's cheque** *(pl inv)*	traveller's cheque
un	**ufficio oggetti smarriti**	lost property office

USEFUL WORDS *(masculine)*

un	**allegato**	attachment
il	**destinatario**	addressee
il	**login** *(pl inv)*	login
il	**mittente**	sender
il	**ricevente**	receiver
un	**ufficio cambio**	bureau de change
il	**vaglia** *(pl inv)* **postale**	postal order

USEFUL PHRASES

**sara punto smith chiocciola anywhere punto com
(sara.smith@anywhere.com)** sara dot smith at anywhere dot com
(sara.smith@anywhere.com)

voo voo voo punto workspace punto com (www.workspace.com)
www dot workspace dot com (www.workspace.com)

IMPORTANT WORDS *(feminine)*

la	**banda larga**	broadband
la	**cabina telefonica** *(pl -e -che)*	phone box
la	**carta da lettera**	writing paper
la	**chiamata telefonica** *(pl -e -che)*	phone call
la	**guida telefonica** *(pl -e -che)*	telephone directory
un'	**imposta**	tax
la	**levata (della posta)**	collection
la	**mail** *(pl inv)*	email
un'	**operatrice telefonica** *(pl -i -che)*	operator
la	**password** *(pl inv)*	password
la	**posta**	mail
la	**ricarica** *(pl -che)*	top-up (card)
la	**ricompensa**	reward
la	**scheda telefonica** *(pl -e -che)*	phonecard
la	**scheda telefonica prepagata**	prepaid phonecard
la	**segreteria telefonica**	voicemail; answering machine
la	**spesa extra** *(pl -i ~)*	extra charge
le	**spese**	expenses
la	**tassa**	tax

USEFUL WORDS *(feminine)*

la	**carta da regalo**	wrapping paper
la	**casella postale**	PO box
la	**chiamata internazionale**	international call
la	**destinataria**	addressee
la	**lettera raccomandata**	registered letter
la	**mittente**	sender
la	**SIM**	SIM card
la	**suoneria**	ringtone

USEFUL PHRASES

ho perso il portafoglio I've lost my wallet
riempire un modulo to fill in a form
in stampatello in block letters
fare una chiamata a carico del destinatario to make a reverse charge call

GENERAL SITUATIONS

qual è il tuo (*or* **suo**) **indirizzo?** what is your address?
come si scrive? how do you spell that?
puoi (*or* **può**) **cambiarmi 100 euro?** do you have change of 100 euros?
scrivere to write
rispondere to reply
firmare to sign
puoi (*or* **può**) **aiutarmi per favore?** can you help me please?
qual è la strada per la stazione? how do I get to the station?
dritto straight on
a destra to (*or* on) the right; **a sinistra** to (*or* on) the left

LETTERS

Caro Carlo Dear Carlo
Cara Anna Dear Anna
Egr. Sig. Dear Sir
Gent. Sig.ra Dear Madam
saluti best wishes
un abbraccio da love from
baci da love from
cordiali saluti kind regards
distinti saluti yours faithfully; yours sincerely
baci e abbracci love and kisses
% PTO

INTERNET & E-MAILS

chattare to chat
fare una (video)chiamata con Skype® to make a (video) call with Skype®
mandare una mail a qn to email sb

MOBILES

farsi un selfie to take a selfie
mandare un sms a qn to text sb

PRONUNCIATION GUIDE

Pronounced approximately as:

A	ah
B	bee
C	chee
D	dee
E	ay
F	ef-fay
G	djee
H	ak-ka
I	ee
J	ee loonga
K	kap-pa
L	el-lay
M	em-may
N	en-nay
O	oh
P	pee
Q	koo
R	er-ray
S	es-say
T	tee
U	oo
V	voo
W	dop-pya voo
X	eeks
Y	eepsilon
Z	dzay-ta

ESSENTIAL WORDS (*masculine*)

un	**avvocato**	lawyer
i	**documenti**	papers
il	**furto**	burglary; theft
un	**incendio**	fire
un	**incidente**	accident
il	**passaporto**	passport
il	**problema**	problem

IMPORTANT WORDS (*masculine*)

un	**aggressore**	mugger
il	**carabiniere**	police officer
il	**colpevole**	culprit
il	**commissariato (di polizia)**	police station
il	**consolato**	consulate
il	**danno** *or* **i danni**	damage
un	**esercito**	army
il	**governo**	government
il	**ladro**	burglar; thief
il	**morto**	dead man
il	**permesso**	permission
il	**poliziotto**	police officer
il	**posto di blocco**	checkpoint; roadblock
il	**proprietario**	owner
il	**rapinatore**	robber
il	**rapinatore a mano armata**	armed robber
il	**testimone**	witness

USEFUL PHRASES

rubare to steal; **rubare in casa** to burgle; **rapinare** to rob
mi hanno rubato il portafoglio! someone has stolen my wallet!
illegale illegal; **innocente** innocent
non è colpa mia it's not my fault
aiuto! help!; **al ladro!** stop thief!
al fuoco! fire!; **mani in alto!** hands up!
rapinare una banca to rob a bank
mandare qn in prigione to send sb to prison; **fuggire** to escape
evadere to escape from prison

ESSENTIAL WORDS (feminine)

la	**carta d'identità**	ID card
la	**colpa**	fault
l'	**identità** (pl inv)	identity
la	**polizia**	police
la	**poliziotta**	police officer
la	**verità** (pl inv)	truth

IMPORTANT WORDS (feminine)

un'	**aggressione**	mugging
la	**banda**	gang
la	**borsetta**	handbag
la	**colpevole**	culprit
la	**denuncia** (pl -ce)	report
l'	**imposta sul reddito**	income tax
la	**ladra**	thief; burglar
la	**manifestazione**	demonstration
la	**morta**	dead woman
la	**morte**	death
la	**multa**	fine
la	**pena di morte**	death penalty
la	**polizza di assicurazione**	insurance policy
la	**proprietaria**	owner
la	**rapina**	hold-up, robbery
la	**rapinatrice**	robber
la	**ricompensa**	reward
la	**spia**	spy
le	**tasse**	taxes
la	**testimone**	witness

USEFUL PHRASES

una rapina a mano armata a hold-up
rapire un bambino to abduct a child
un gruppo di teppisti a bunch of hooligans
in prigione in prison
picchiarsi to fight; **arrestare** to arrest; **accusare** to charge
essere in custodia cautelare to be remanded in custody
accusare qn di qc to accuse sb of sth; to charge sb with sth

USEFUL WORDS (*masculine*)

un	**arresto**	arrest
un	**assassinio**	murder
il	**bottino**	loot
il	**cadavere**	corpse
il	**carcere**	prison
un	**clandestino**	illegal immigrant; stowaway
il	**criminale**	criminal
il	**delitto**	crime
il	**detective** (*pl inv*) **privato**	private detective
il	**detenuto**	prisoner
il	**dirottamento aereo**	hijacking
il	**dirottatore**	hijacker
il	**drogato**	drug addict
il	**gangster** (*pl inv*)	gangster
il	**giudice**	judge
un	**imbroglione**	crook
un	**immigrato clandestino**	illegal immigrant
un	**omicida**	murderer
un	**omicidio**	murder
un	**ostaggio**	hostage
il	**piromane**	arsonist
il	**poliziotto**	police officer
il	**prigioniero**	prisoner
il	**processo**	trial
il	**rapitore**	kidnapper
il	**riscatto**	ransom
il	**salvataggio**	rescue
lo	**sbirro**	cop
il	**sequestro**	kidnapping
lo	**spacciatore (di droga)**	drugs pusher
lo	**sparo**	(gun) shot
il	**tentativo**	attempt
un	**teppista**	hooligan
il	**terrorismo**	terrorism
il	**terrorista**	terrorist
il	**tossicodipendente**	drug addict
il	**trafficante di droga**	drug dealer
il	**tribunale**	court

USEFUL WORDS *(feminine)*

l'	**accusa**	the prosecution; charge
un'	**assassina**	murderer
la	**bomba**	bomb
la	**clandestina**	illegal immigrant; stowaway
la	**criminale**	criminal
la	**custodia cautelare**	custody
la	**delinquente**	criminal
la	**detective** *(pl inv)* **privata**	private detective
la	**detenuta**	prisoner
la	**detenzione**	imprisonment
la	**dichiarazione**	statement
la	**difesa**	defence
la	**dirottatrice**	hijacker
la	**droga** *(pl -ghe)*	drug
la	**drogata**	drug addict
la	**fuga** *(pl -ghe)*	escape
la	**giuria**	jury
la	**guardia**	guard; warden
un'	**immigrata clandestina**	illegal immigrant
un'	**inchiesta**	inquiry
un'	**insurrezione**	uprising
la	**legge**	law
la	**lite**	quarrel, argument
la	**multa**	fine
un'	**omicida**	murderer
la	**piromane**	arsonist
la	**pistola**	gun
la	**poliziotta**	police officer
la	**prigione**	prison
la	**prova**	proof; evidence
la	**rapitrice**	kidnapper
la	**retata**	raid
la	**rivolta**	uprising
la	**spacciatrice (di droga)**	drugs pusher
la	**teppista**	hooligan
la	**terrorista**	terrorist
la	**tossicodipendente**	drug addict
la	**trafficante di droga**	drug dealer

ESSENTIAL WORDS (*masculine*)

l'	acciaio	steel
l'	argento	silver
il	cotone	cotton
il	cristallo	crystal
il	cuoio	leather
il	ferro	iron
il	gas	gas
il	gasolio	diesel
il	legno	wood
il	metallo	metal
l'	oro	gold
il	vetro	glass

IMPORTANT WORDS (*masculine*)

l'	acciaio inossidabile	stainless steel
l'	alluminio	aluminium
il	cartone	cardboard
il	ferro battuto	wrought iron
il	mattone	brick
lo	stato	condition
il	tessuto	fabric

USEFUL PHRASES

una sedia di legno a wooden chair
una cassa di plastica a plastic box
un anello d'oro a gold ring
in buone condizioni in good condition
in cattive condizioni in bad condition

ESSENTIAL WORDS (*feminine*)

la	**gomma**	rubber
la	**lana**	wool
la	**pelle**	leather
la	**pietra**	stone
la	**plastica**	plastic

IMPORTANT WORDS (*feminine*)

la	**carta**	paper
la	**fibra sintetica** (*pl* -e -che)	synthetic fibre
la	**seta**	silk
la	**stoffa**	fabric

USEFUL PHRASES
una pelliccia a fur coat
una medaglia d'oro a gold medal
un maglione di lana a woollen jumper
arrugginito(a) rusty

USEFUL WORDS (*masculine*)

l'	**acrilico**	acrylic
il	**bronzo**	bronze
il	**carbone**	coal
il	**cemento**	concrete
il	**filo (di cotone)**	thread
il	**filo di ferro**	wire
il	**gesso**	plaster
il	**lino**	linen
il	**liquido**	liquid
il	**marmo**	marble
il	**materiale**	material
l'	**ottone**	brass
il	**piombo**	lead
il	**pizzo**	lace
il	**rame**	copper
il	**raso**	satin
lo	**stagno**	tin
il	**tweed**	tweed
il	**velluto**	velvet
il	**velluto a coste**	corduroy
il	**vimini**	wickerwork

USEFUL WORDS *(feminine)*

l'	**argilla**	clay
la	**cera**	wax
la	**ceramica** *(pl -che)*	ceramics; pottery
la	**colla**	glue
la	**corda**	string
la	**creta**	clay
la	**gommapiuma**	foam rubber
la	**latta**	tinplate
la	**paglia**	straw
la	**pelle scamosciata**	suede
la	**porcellana**	china
la	**tela**	canvas

ESSENTIAL WORDS (*masculine*)

il	direttore d'orchestra	conductor
il	gruppo	band
il	musicista	musician
il	pianoforte	piano
lo	strumento musicale	musical instrument
il	violino	violin

USEFUL WORDS (*masculine*)

un	accordo	chord
un	archetto	bow
un	astuccio	case
il	basso	bass guitar
il	clarinetto	clarinet
il	contrabbasso	double bass
il	fagotto	bassoon
il	flauto	flute
il	flauto dolce	recorder
un	impianto di amplificazione	PA system
il	jazz	jazz
il	leggio (*pl* -gii)	music stand
il	microfono	microphone
il	mixer (*pl inv*)	mixing deck
un	oboe	oboe
un	organo	organ
gli	ottoni	brass
i	piatti	cymbals
il	sassofono	saxophone
il	solista	soloist
lo	studio di registrazione	recording studio
gli	strumenti a corda	string instruments
gli	strumenti a fiato	wind instruments
gli	strumenti a percussione	percussion instruments
il	tamburello	tambourine
il	tamburo	drum
il	tasto (del piano)	(piano) key
il	trombone	trombone
il	violoncello	cello

ESSENTIAL WORDS (feminine)

la	**batteria**	drums, drum kit
la	**chitarra**	guitar
la	**direttrice d'orchestra**	conductor
la	**musica**	music
la	**musicista**	musician
un'	**orchestra**	orchestra

USEFUL WORDS (feminine)

un'	**armonica** (pl -che)	harmonica
un'	**arpa**	harp
la	**bacchetta**	conductor's baton
la	**banda**	brass band
la	**composizione**	composition
la	**corda**	string
la	**cornamusa**	bagpipes
la	**custodia**	case
la	**grancassa**	bass drum
la	**fisarmonica** (pl -che)	accordion
la	**nota**	note
la	**registrazione digitale**	digital recording
la	**solista**	soloist
la	**tromba**	trumpet; bugle
la	**viola**	viola

USEFUL PHRASES

suonare un pezzo to play a piece
suonare forte/piano to play loudly/softly
essere intonato(a)/stonato(a) to sing in tune/out of tune
suonare il piano/la chitarra to play the piano/the guitar
suonare la batteria to play drums
Paolo alla batteria Paolo on drums
esercitarsi al pianoforte to practise the piano
suoni in un gruppo? do you play in a band?
una nota falsa a wrong note

CARDINAL NUMBERS

zero	0	zero
uno (m), una (f)	1	one
due	2	two
tre	3	three
quattro	4	four
cinque	5	five
sei	6	six
sette	7	seven
otto	8	eight
nove	9	nine
dieci	10	ten
undici	11	eleven
dodici	12	twelve
tredici	13	thirteen
quattordici	14	fourteen
quindici	15	fifteen
sedici	16	sixteen
diciassette	17	seventeen
diciotto	18	eighteen
diciannove	19	nineteen
venti	20	twenty
ventuno	21	twenty-one
ventidue	22	twenty-two
ventitré	23	twenty-three
trenta	30	thirty
trentuno	31	thirty-one
trentadue	32	thirty-two
quaranta	40	forty
cinquanta	50	fifty
sessanta	60	sixty
settanta	70	seventy
ottanta	80	eighty
novanta	90	ninety
cento	100	one hundred

CARDINAL NUMBERS (continued)

centouno	101	a hundred and one
centodue	102	a hundred and two
centodieci	110	a hundred and ten
centottantadue	182	a hundred and eighty-two
duecento	200	two hundred
duecentouno	201	two hundred and one
duecentodue	202	two hundred and two
trecento	300	three hundred
quattrocento	400	four hundred
cinquecento	500	five hundred
seicento	600	six hundred
settecento	700	seven hundred
ottocento	800	eight hundred
novecento	900	nine hundred
mille	1000	one thousand
milleuno(a)	1001	a thousand and one
milledue	1002	a thousand and two
duemila	2000	two thousand
duemilasedici	2016	two thousand and sixteen
diecimila	10000	ten thousand
centomila	100000	one hundred thousand
un milione	1000000	one million
due milioni	2000000	two million

USEFUL PHRASES
mille euro a thousand euros; **duemila euro** two thousand euros
un milione di dollari one million dollars
tre virgola due (3,2) three point two (3.2)

ORDINAL NUMBERS

primo(a)	1°, 1^a	first
secondo(a)	2°, 2^a	second
terzo(a)	3°, 3^a	third
quarto(a)	4°, 4^a	fourth
quinto(a)	5°, 5^a	fifth
sesto(a)	6°, 6^a	sixth
settimo(a)	7°, 7^a	seventh
ottavo(a)	8°, 8^a	eighth
nono(a)	9°, 9^a	ninth
decimo(a)	10°, 10^a	tenth
undicesimo(a)	11°, 11^a	eleventh
dodicesimo(a)	12°, 12^a	twelfth
tredicesimo(a)	13°, 13^a	thirteenth
quattordicesimo(a)	14°, 14^a	fourteenth
quindicesimo(a)	15°, 15^a	fifteenth
sedicesimo(a)	16°, 16^a	sixteenth
diciassettesimo(a)	17°, 17^a	seventeenth
diciottesimo(a)	18°, 18^a	eighteenth
diciannovesimo(a)	19°, 19^a	nineteenth
ventesimo(a)	20°, 20^a	twentieth
millesimo(a)	1000°, 1000^a	thousandth
duemillesimo(a)	2000°, 2000^a	two thousandth

FRACTIONS

(un) mezzo/(una) mezza	½	a half
uno(a) e mezzo	1½	one and a half
due e mezzo	2½	two and a half
un terzo	⅓	a third
due terzi	⅔	two thirds
un quarto	¼	a quarter
tre quarti	¾	three quarters
un sesto	⅙	a sixth
tre e cinque sesti	3⅚	three and five sixths
un settimo	⅐	a seventh
un ottavo	⅛	an eighth
un nono	⅑	a ninth
un decimo	⅒	a tenth
un undicesimo	1/11	an eleventh
un dodicesimo	1/12	a twelfth
sette dodicesimi	7/12	seven twelfths
un centesimo	1/100	a hundredth
un millesimo	1/1000	a thousandth

USEFUL PHRASES

un barattolo di a jar of; a tin *or* can of
un barile di a barrel of
un bicchiere di a glass of
un boccone di a mouthful of
una bottiglia di a bottle of
una cassa di a box of
centinaia di hundreds of
un centinaio di (about) a hundred
un chilo di a kilo of
una cucchiaiata di a spoonful of
una decina di persone about ten people
diversi(e) several
a diversi chilometri da a few kilometres from
una dozzina di (about) a dozen
entrambi both of them
un etto di a hundred grams of
una fetta di pane a slice of bread
una fetta di prosciutto a slice of ham
una (gran) quantità di lots of
un gregge di a flock of
un gruppo di a group of
un litro di a litre of
la maggior parte di, gran parte di most (of)
una mandria di a herd of

USEFUL PHRASES

un metro di a metre of
mezza dozzina half a dozen
mezzo(a) half (of)
mezzo litro di half a litre of
migliaia di thousands of
molti(e) many; a lot of
molto(a) a lot (of); much
un mucchio di a pile of; loads of
un pacchetto di a packet of
un paio di a pair of
un pezzo di carta a piece of paper
un pezzo di pane a piece of bread
un piatto di a plate of
a pochi metri da a few metres from
un poco di a little; some
una porzione di a portion of
un pugno di a handful of
un quarto di a quarter of
tre quarti di three quarters of
una scatola di a tin or can of
una scodella di a bowl of
una tazza di a cup of
tutti(e) e due both of them
una zolletta di zucchero a lump of sugar

ESSENTIAL WORDS (*masculine*)

un	**anello**	ring
il	**braccialetto**	bracelet
il	**deodorante**	deodorant
il	**gioiello**	jewel
un	**orologio**	watch
il	**pettine**	comb
il	**profumo**	perfume
il	**rasoio**	razor
il	**rasoio elettrico**	electric shaver
lo	**shampoo** (*pl inv*)	shampoo
lo	**spazzolino da denti**	toothbrush
lo	**specchio**	mirror
il	**trucco**	make-up

USEFUL WORDS (*masculine*)

l'	**acetone**	nail varnish remover
un	**asciugacapelli** (*pl inv*)	hairdryer
il	**bigodino**	roller
il	**ciondolo**	pendant
il	**dentifricio**	toothpaste
il	**diamante**	diamond
il	**dopobarba** (*pl inv*)	aftershave
gli	**effetti personali**	personal effects
il	**fard** (*pl inv*)	(powder) compact
il	**fazzoletto di carta**	tissue
il	**fondotinta** (*pl inv*)	foundation
il	**gemello**	cufflink
il	**maquillage** (*pl inv*)	make-up
il	**mascara** (*pl inv*)	mascara
il	**nécessaire da toilette** (*pl inv*)	toilet bag
un	**ombretto**	eye shadow
un	**orecchino**	earring
il	**pennello da barba**	shaving brush
il	**portachiavi** (*pl inv*)	key-ring; key holder
il	**rossetto**	lipstick
lo	**smalto per unghie**	nail varnish

ESSENTIAL WORDS *(feminine)*

l'	**acqua di colonia**	eau de cologne
la	**catenina**	chain
la	**crema per il viso**	face cream
la	**spazzola**	brush

USEFUL WORDS *(feminine)*

un'	**acconciatura**	hairstyle
la	**carta igienica**	toilet paper
la	**cipria**	face powder
la	**collana**	necklace
la	**crema da barba**	shaving cream
la	**fede (nuziale)**	wedding ring
la	**manicure** *(pl inv)*	manicure
la	**perla**	pearl
la	**pettinatura**	hairstyle
la	**schiuma da barba**	shaving foam
la	**spilla**	brooch
la	**spugna**	sponge

USEFUL PHRASES

truccarsi to put on one's make-up
struccarsi to take off one's make-up
farsi un'acconciatura to do one's hair
pettinarsi to comb one's hair
spazzolarsi i capelli to brush one's hair
radersi to shave
lavarsi i denti to clean *or* brush one's teeth

ESSENTIAL WORDS (masculine)

un	albero	tree
il	fiore	flower
il	giardinaggio	gardening
il	giardiniere	gardener
il	giardino	garden
gl	ortaggi	vegetables
il	prato	lawn
il	ramo	branch
il	sole	sun
il	terreno	land; soil; ground

IMPORTANT WORDS (masculine)

il	cancello	gate
il	cespuglio	bush
il	mazzo di fiori	bunch of flowers
il	recinto	fence
il	vialetto	path; drive

USEFUL PHRASES

piantare to plant
togliere le erbacce to weed
regalare a qn un mazzo di fiori to give sb a bunch of flowers
tagliare l'erba to mow the lawn
"non calpestare" "keep off the grass"
a mio padre piace fare giardinaggio my father likes gardening

ESSENTIAL WORDS *(feminine)*

un'	**aiuola**	flower bed
l'	**erba**	grass
la	**foglia**	leaf
la	**pianta**	plant
la	**pioggia** *(pl -ge)*	rain
la	**rosa**	rose
la	**terra**	soil; ground

IMPORTANT WORDS *(feminine)*

un'	**ape**	bee
la	**coltivazione**	cultivation
le	**erbacce**	weeds
l'	**ombra**	shade; shadow
la	**panchina**	bench
la	**radice**	root
la	**vespa**	wasp

USEFUL PHRASES
i fiori stanno crescendo the flowers are growing
sottoterra underground
bagnare i fiori to water the flowers
raccogliere fiori to pick flowers
andare all'ombra to go into the shade
rimanere all'ombra to remain in the shade
all'ombra di un albero in the shade of a tree

USEFUL WORDS *(masculine)*

l'	autunno	autumn
un	annaffiatoio	watering can
un	attrezzo	tool
il	bocciolo	bud
il	bucaneve *(pl inv)*	snowdrop
il	caprifoglio	honeysuckle
il	ciclamino	cyclamen
il	crisantemo	chrysanthemum
il	croco *(pl -chi)*	crocus
il	dente di leone	dandelion
il	fogliame	leaves
il	garofano	carnation
il	geranio	geranium
il	giacinto	hyacinth
il	giglio	lily
il	girasole	sunflower
l'	inverno	winter
il	lillà *(pl inv)*	lilac
il	mughetto	lily of the valley
il	narciso	daffodil
un	oleandro	oleander
un	orto	vegetable garden
il	papavero	poppy
il	raccolto	crop
il	ranuncolo	buttercup
il	rastrello	rake
il	roseto	rose bush
il	seme	seed
lo	stagno	pond
lo	stelo	stalk
il	suolo	ground; soil
il	tagliaerba *(pl inv)*	lawnmower
il	tagliasiepe *(pl inv)*	hedgecutter
il	tronco *(pl -chi)*	trunk *(of tree)*
il	tubo per annaffiare	(garden) hose
il	tulipano	tulip
il	verme	worm

plants and gardens 613

USEFUL WORDS (*feminine*)

l' **azalea**	azalea
l' **estate**	summer
la **bacca** (*pl* -**che**)	berry
la **begonia**	begonia
la **campanula**	campanula, bellflower
la **carriola**	wheelbarrow
un' **edera**	ivy
la **farfalla**	butterfly
la **margherita**	daisy
un' **orchidea**	orchid
un' **ortensia**	hydrangea
la **peonia**	peony
la **primavera**	spring
la **primula**	primrose
la **rugiada**	dew
la **serra**	greenhouse
la **siepe**	hedge
la **spina**	thorn
la **stella di Natale**	poinsettia
la **viola del pensiero**	pansy
la **violetta**	violet

ESSENTIAL WORDS (masculine)

un	**asciugamano**	towel
il	**bagnante**	swimmer
il	**battello**	passenger boat
il	**bikini** (pl inv)	bikini
il	**catamarano**	catamaran
il	**costume da bagno**	swimming trunks; swimsuit
il	**mare**	sea
il	**molo**	quay
il	**nuoto**	swimming
gli	**occhiali da sole**	sunglasses
il	**pescatore**	fisherman
il	**porto**	port, harbour
il	**remo**	oar

IMPORTANT WORDS (masculine)

il	**castello di sabbia**	sandcastle
il	**fondo**	bottom
il	**granchio**	crab
il	**lettino**	sun lounger
il	**mal di mare**	seasickness
il	**materassino gonfiabile**	airbed, lilo
l'	**orizzonte**	horizon
il	**turista**	tourist; holiday-maker
il	**windsurf** (pl inv)	surfboard; windsurfing

USEFUL PHRASES

in spiaggia at or on the beach
al mare at the seaside; at or on the beach
all'orizzonte on the horizon
ha il mal di mare he/she is seasick
nuotare to swim; **affogare** to drown
vado a fare una nuotata I'm going for a swim
tuffarsi in acqua to dive into the water
galleggiare to float

ESSENTIAL WORDS *(feminine)*

l'	**abbronzatura**	suntan
l'	**acqua**	water
la	**bagnante**	swimmer
la	**barca** *(pl -che)*	boat
la	**costa**	coast
un'	**isola**	island
la	**nave**	ship
la	**pietra**	stone
la	**sabbia**	sand
la	**scottatura solare**	sunburn
la	**spiaggia** *(pl -ge)*	beach

IMPORTANT WORDS *(feminine)*

la	**brandina**	sun lounger
la	**crema solare**	suncream
la	**sedia a sdraio**	deckchair
la	**tavola da windsurf**	surfboard
la	**traversata**	crossing
la	**turista**	tourist; holiday-maker

USEFUL PHRASES

in fondo al mare at the bottom of the sea
fare la traversata in barca to cross by boat
abbronzarsi to get a suntan
essere abbronzato(a) to be tanned
sa nuotare he/she can swim

USEFUL WORDS *(masculine)*

un	acquascooter *(pl inv)*	jet ski
l'	albero	mast
un	aliscafo	hydrofoil
il	bagnino	lifeguard
il	binocolo	binoculars
il	cannocchiale	telescope
il	cargo *(pl inv)*	cargo
il	ciottolo	pebble
l'	equipaggio	crew
un	estuario	estuary
il	faro	lighthouse
il	gabbiano	seagull
il	marinaio	sailor
il	motoscafo	speedboat
il	naufragio	shipwreck
un	oceano	ocean
un	ombrellone	beach umbrella
un	parasole *(pl inv)*	parasol
il	pedalò *(pl inv)*	pedalo
il	ponte	bridge
il	pontile	pier, jetty
il	promontorio	headland
il	salvagente *(pl inv)*	lifebelt
il	secchiello	bucket
il	timone	rudder
il	traghetto	ferry

USEFUL WORDS *(feminine)*

le	**alghe**	seaweed
un'	**ancora**	anchor
l'	**aria di mare**	sea air
la	**bagnina**	lifeguard
la	**baia**	bay
la	**balneazione**	bathing
la	**bandiera**	flag
la	**barca** *(pl -che)* **da diporto**	pleasure craft
la	**boa**	buoy
la	**brezza di mare**	sea breeze
la	**conchiglia**	shell
la	**corrente**	current
la	**crociera**	cruise
la	**duna di sabbia**	sand dune
la	**foce**	mouth *(of river)*
un'	**insolazione**	sunstroke
la	**marea**	tide
la	**marina**	navy; marina
la	**marinaia**	sailor
un'	**onda**	wave
la	**paletta**	spade
la	**passerella**	gangway
la	**riva**	shore
la	**roccia** *(pl -ce)*	rock
la	**schiuma**	foam
la	**scogliera**	cliff
la	**vela**	sail; sailing
la	**zattera**	raft

USEFUL PHRASES

mi sono preso un'insolazione I had sunstroke
con l'alta/la bassa marea at low/high tide
fare vela to go sailing

ESSENTIAL WORDS (*masculine*)

un	**assegno**	cheque
il	**Bancomat®** (*pl inv*)	debit card; cashpoint, ATM
il	**centesimo**	cent
il	**centro commerciale**	shopping centre
il	**cliente**	customer
il	**codice a barre**	barcode
il	**commesso**	shop assistant, sales assistant
il	**denaro**	money
un	**euro** (*pl inv*)	euro
il	**fioraio**	flower shop; florist
il	**fruttivendolo**	greengrocer's
i	**grandi magazzini**	department store
un	**ipermercato**	super store
il	**libretto degli assegni**	cheque book
il	**mercato**	market
il	**negozio**	shop
un	**outlet**	retail outlet
il	**prezzo**	price
il	**regalo**	present, gift
il	**reparto**	department
il	**resto**	change
il	**ribasso**	reduction
i	**saldi**	sales
lo	**sconto**	discount
i	**soldi**	money
il	**supermercato**	supermarket
il	**tabaccaio**	tobacconist's; tobacconist
il	**venditore**	salesman

USEFUL PHRASES

comprare/vendere to buy/to sell
quanto costa? how much does it cost?
a quanto ammonta? how much does it come to?
l'ho pagato 20 euro I paid 20 euros for it
in macelleria/panetteria at the butcher's/bakery

ESSENTIAL WORDS *(feminine)*

un'	**agenzia di viaggio**	travel agent's
l'	**alimentazione**	food
la	**banconota**	banknote
la	**carta di credito**	credit card
la	**carta di credito del negozio**	store card
la	**carta di debito**	debit card
la	**carta fedeltà**	loyalty card
la	**cassa**	checkout; cash desk
la	**cassa automatica**	self-service checkout
la	**cliente**	customer
la	**commessa**	shop assistant, sales assistant
la	**farmacia**	chemist's
la	**lista**	list
la	**macelleria**	butcher's
la	**panetteria**	bakery
la	**pasticceria**	cake shop
la	**pescheria**	fishmonger's
la	**posta**	post office
la	**profumeria**	perfume shop
la	**salumeria**	delicatessen
la	**tabaccheria**	tobacconist's
la	**taglia**	size
la	**venditrice**	saleswoman

IMPORTANT WORDS (*masculine*)

un	**articolo**	article
il	**banco** (*pl* -chi)	counter
il	**calzolaio**	cobbler
il	**commerciante**	shopkeeper
il	**commercio**	trade
il	**commercio equo e solidale**	fair trade
il	**direttore**	manager
il	**giornalaio**	newsagent
il	**macellaio**	butcher; butcher's
il	**mercatino**	street market
il	**mercatino delle pulci**	flea market
il	**negozio di generi alimentari**	grocer's
il	**negozio di scarpe**	shoe shop
il	**numero di scarpe**	shoe size
il	**panettiere**	baker
il	**parrucchiere**	hairdresser; hairdresser's
il	**pasticciere**	confectioner
il	**pescivendolo**	fishmonger
il	**portafoglio**	wallet
il	**portamonete** (*pl inv*)	purse
il	**reclamo**	complaint
lo	**scontrino**	receipt

USEFUL PHRASES

sto dando un'occhiata I'm just looking

è troppo caro it's too expensive

qualcosa di più economico something cheaper

è a buon prezzo it's cheap

"pagare alla cassa" "pay at the cash desk"

vuole che le faccia un pacchetto regalo? would you like it gift-wrapped?

ci dev'essere un errore there must be some mistake

IMPORTANT WORDS *(feminine)*

la	**borsetta**	handbag
la	**calcolatrice**	calculator
la	**commerciante**	shopkeeper
la	**direttrice**	manager
un'	**enoteca** *(pl* **-che***)*	wine shop
la	**fruttivendola**	fruit shop; greengrocer's
la	**giornalaia**	newsagent
la	**libreria**	bookshop
la	**macellaia**	butcher
la	**marca** *(pl* **-che***)*	brand
la	**panetteria**	bakery
la	**panettiera**	baker
la	**parrucchiera**	hairdresser
la	**pasticcera**	confectioner
la	**pasticceria**	confectioner's
la	**pescivendola**	fishmonger
la	**promozione**	special offer
la	**pulitura (a secco)**	dry-cleaner's
la	**ricevuta**	receipt
la	**scala mobile**	escalator
la	**tintoria**	dry-cleaner's
la	**vetrina**	display case; shop window

USEFUL PHRASES

qualcos'altro? anything else?

i saldi the sales

quando cominciano i saldi? when do the sales start?

"in vendita qui" "on sale here"

una macchina usata a used car

in offerta on special offer

il caffè del commercio equo e solidale fair-trade coffee

USEFUL WORDS *(masculine)*

l'	abbigliamento	clothes
gli	acquisti	shopping
un	affare	deal
un	agente immobiliare	estate agent
i	beni	goods
il	colore	colour
il	gerente	manager
il	gioielliere	jeweller's
il	libraio	bookseller
il	negozio di dolciumi	sweetshop
un	orologiaio	watchmaker; clockmaker
un	ottico	optician
i	prodotti	produce; products
il	prodotto	product
lo	sconto	discount
il	videonoleggio	video shop

USEFUL PHRASES

andare a fare un giro per vetrine to go window shopping
orario di apertura opening hours
comprare online to shop online
pagare in contanti to pay cash
pagare con la carta di credito to pay by credit card

USEFUL WORDS *(feminine)*

un'	**agente immobiliare**	estate agent
un'	**agenzia di viaggio**	travel agent's
un'	**agenzia immobiliare**	estate agent's
le	**calzature**	footwear
le	**caramelle**	sweets
la	**cartoleria**	stationery shop
la	**cassa di risparmio**	savings bank
la	**coda**	queue
la	**commissione**	errand; commission
la	**drogheria**	grocer's
la	**ferramenta**	ironmonger
la	**fila**	queue
la	**filiale**	branch
la	**gerente**	manager
la	**gioielleria**	jewellery
la	**lavanderia automatica**	launderette
la	**libraia**	bookseller
le	**merci**	goods
un'	**orologeria**	watchmaker's; clockmaker's
un'	**orologiaia**	watchmaker; clockmaker
la	**spesa**	purchase; shopping
la	**taglia del collo**	collar size
la	**vendita**	sale

USEFUL PHRASES

in vetrina in the window
andare a fare acquisti to go shopping
fare la spesa to do the shopping
spendere to spend

ESSENTIAL WORDS *(masculine)*

il	basket	basketball
il	biliardo	billiards
il	calcio	football; kick
il	campionato	championship
il	campione	champion
il	campo	field; pitch; course; court
il	campo da golf	golf course
il	campo da tennis	tennis court
il	campo di calcio	football pitch
il	campo sportivo	sports field
il	ciclismo	cycling
il	cricket	cricket
il	ginnasta	gymnast
il	giocatore	player
il	gioco *(pl -chi)*	game; play
il	gol *(pl inv)*	goal
il	golf	golf
l'	hockey	hockey
il	nuoto	swimming
il	pallone	ball *(large)*; football
il	risultato	result
il	rugby	rugby
gli	scacchi	chess
lo	sci *(pl inv)*	skiing; ski
lo	sci d'acqua	water skiing
lo	sport *(pl inv)*	sport
lo	stadio	stadium
il	tennis	tennis
il	windsurf *(pl inv)*	windsurfing; surfboard

USEFUL PHRASES
giocare a calcio/tennis to play football/tennis
segnare un gol/un punto to score a goal/a point
tenere il punteggio to keep the score
il campione/la campionessa del mondo the world champion
vincere/perdere una partita to win/lose a match
il mio sport preferito my favourite sport

ESSENTIAL WORDS *(feminine)*

l'	**acquagym**	aquarobics
la	**campionessa**	champion
l'	**equitazione**	horse-riding
la	**ginnasta**	gymnast
la	**ginnastica**	gymnastics
la	**giocatrice**	player
la	**marcia**	racewalking
la	**palla**	ball
la	**pallacanestro**	basketball
la	**pallavolo**	volleyball
la	**partita**	match, game
la	**pesca**	fishing
la	**piscina**	swimming pool
la	**pista**	track
la	**rete**	net; goal
la	**squadra**	team
la	**vela**	sailing; sail

USEFUL PHRASES

pareggiare to equalize; to draw
correre to run; **saltare** to jump; **lanciare** to throw
battere qn to beat sb
allenarsi to train
il Liverpool conduce per 2 a 1 Liverpool is leading by 2 goals to 1
un partita a tennis a game of tennis
è socio di un club he belongs to a club
andare a pesca to go fishing
andare in piscina to go to the swimming pool
sai (*or* sa) nuotare? can you swim?
fare sport to do sport
andare in bicicletta to go cycling
fare vela to go sailing
fare jogging/alpinismo to go jogging/climbing
pattini da ghiaccio/a rotelle (ice) skate/roller skates
pattini in linea Rollerblades®
tiro con l'arco/al bersaglio archery/target practice

IMPORTANT WORDS (*masculine*)

un	**arbitro**	referee; umpire (*tennis*)
un	**incontro**	match
il	**punteggio**	score
il	**torneo**	tournament

USEFUL WORDS (*masculine*)

un	**allenatore**	trainer; coach
l'	**alpinismo**	mountaineering
un	**avversario**	opponent
il	**canottaggio**	rowing
il	**cronometro**	stopwatch
il	**giavellotto**	javelin
i	**Giochi Olimpici**	Olympic Games
l'	**intervallo**	half-time
l'	**ippodromo**	race course
il	**jogging**	jogging
il	**parapendio**	paragliding
il	**pattinaggio su ghiaccio**	(ice) skating
il	**pattino**	skate
il	**perdente**	loser
il	**portiere**	goalkeeper
il	**principiante**	beginner
il	**pugilato**	boxing
il	**punto**	point
il	**remo**	oar
il	**salto in alto**	high jump
il	**salto in lungo**	long jump
lo	**spettatore**	spectator
lo	**squash**	squash
i	**tempi supplementari**	extra time
il	**tiro**	shooting
i	**tuffi**	diving
il	**vincitore**	winner
il	**volano**	shuttlecock; badminton

IMPORTANT WORDS *(feminine)*

l'	**atletica**	athletics
le	**bocce**	pétanque
la	**boxe**	boxing
la	**Coppa del Mondo**	World Cup
la	**corsa**	race
le	**corse dei cavalli**	horse-racing
la	**difesa**	defence
l'	**ippica**	horse-racing
le	**Olimpiadi**	Olympic Games
la	**pallina**	ball *(small)*
la	**pista da sci**	ski slope
la	**slitta**	sledge

USEFUL WORDS *(feminine)*

un'	**allenatrice**	trainer, coach
un'	**avversaria**	opponent
la	**canna da pesca**	fishing rod
un'	**eliminatoria**	heat
la	**finale**	final
la	**lotta libera**	wrestling
la	**maglietta**	jersey, shirt
la	**perdente**	loser
la	**pesca**	fishing
la	**pista da pattinaggio**	skating rink
la	**pista da pattinaggio su ghiaccio**	ice rink
la	**principiante**	beginner
la	**racchetta da ping pong**	ping pong bat
la	**racchetta da sci**	ski pole
la	**racchetta da tennis**	tennis racket
le	**scarpe da ginnastica**	sports shoes; trainers
le	**scarpe da tennis**	tennis shoes
la	**scherma**	fencing
la	**spettatrice**	spectator
la	**stazione sciistica**	ski resort
la	**tappa**	stage
la	**tribuna**	stand
la	**vincitrice**	winner

ESSENTIAL WORDS (masculine)

un **attore**	actor
un **auditorium** (pl inv)	auditorium
il **biglietto**	ticket
il **botteghino**	box office
il **cinema** (pl inv)	cinema
il **circo** (pl -chi)	circus
il **clown** (pl inv)	clown
il **comico**	comedian
il **costume**	costume
il **film** (pl inv)	film
il **pagliaccio**	clown
il **posto (a sedere)**	seat
il **programma**	programme
il **pubblico**	audience; public
il **sipario**	curtain
lo **spettacolo**	show; performance; showing
il **teatro**	theatre
il **western** (pl inv)	western

IMPORTANT WORDS (masculine)

il **balletto**	ballet
il **cartellone**	poster; playbill
un **intervallo**	interval
il **primo attore**	leading man

USEFUL PHRASES

andare a teatro/al cinema to go to the theatre/to the cinema
prenotare un posto to book a seat
una poltrona in platea a seat in the stalls
il mio attore preferito/la mia attrice preferita my favourite actor/actress
durante l'intervallo during the interval
entrare in scena to come on stage
interpretare la parte di to play the part of

ESSENTIAL WORDS (feminine)

l'	**atmosfera**	atmosphere
un'	**attrice**	actress
la	**colonna sonora**	soundtrack
la	**commedia**	play; comedy
la	**galleria**	the circle
la	**musica** (pl -che)	music
l'	**opera**	opera
un'	**orchestra**	orchestra
la	**pagliaccia** (pl -ce)	clown
la	**pellicola**	film
la	**platea**	stalls
la	**poltrona**	seat
la	**prima galleria**	dress circle
la	**proiezione**	screening (of film)
la	**sala**	screen (of cinema)
la	**star** (m+f pl inv)	film star
la	**tragedia**	tragedy
un'	**uscita**	exit

USEFUL PHRASES

recitare to play
ballare to dance
cantare to sing
girare un film to shoot a film
"versione originale" "original version"
"con sottotitoli" "subtitled"
"tutto esaurito" "sold out"
applaudire to clap
bis! encore!
bravo! bravo!
un film di fantascienza/d'amore a science fiction film/a romance
un film d'avventura/dell'orrore an adventure/horror film

IMPORTANT WORDS *(masculine continued)*

il	**protagonista**	protagonist; star
il	**sottotitolo**	subtitle
il	**titolo**	title
il	**trucco** *(pl* **-chi**)	make-up; trick

USEFUL WORDS *(masculine)*

gli	**applausi**	applause
il	**cast** *(pl inv)*	cast
il	**commediografo**	playwright
il	**copione**	script
il	**critico**	critic
il	**direttore artistico**	artistic director
il	**direttore di scena**	stage manager
il	**drammaturgo** *(pl* **-ghi**)	playwright
il	**guardaroba** *(pl inv)*	cloakroom
il	**loggione**	the "gods"
il	**musical** *(pl inv)*	musical
il	**palco** *(pl* **-chi**)	box
il	**palco(scenico)**	stage
il	**personaggio**	character
il	**produttore**	producer
il	**reality** *(pl inv)*	reality show
il	**regista**	director *(cinema)*; producer *(TV)*
il	**ridotto**	foyer
il	**riflettore**	spotlight
il	**ruolo**	part
il	**serial** *(pl inv)*	serial
lo	**scenario**	scenery; set
lo	**sceneggiatore**	scriptwriter
lo	**schermo**	screen
lo	**spettatore**	member of the audience
il	**suggeritore**	prompter

IMPORTANT WORDS *(feminine)*

la	**locandina**	poster
un'	**imbeccata**	cue; prompt
la	**maschera**	usher; usherette
la	**prenotazione**	booking
la	**prima attrice**	leading lady
la	**protagonista**	protagonist; star

USEFUL WORDS *(feminine)*

la	**biglietteria**	ticket office
la	**buca** *(pl -che)* **dell'orchestra**	orchestra pit
la	**commediografa**	playwright
la	**critica** *(pl -che)*	review; critics
la	**direttrice di scena**	stage manager
la	**drammaturga** *(pl -ghe)*	playwright
la	**farsa**	farce
le	**luci della ribalta**	footlights
la	**messa in scena**	production
la	**parte**	part
la	**piccionaia**	the "gods"
la	**prima**	first night, premiere
la	**produttrice**	producer
la	**produzione**	production
le	**prove**	(dress) rehearsal
le	**quinte**	wings
la	**rappresentazione**	performance
la	**recitazione**	acting
la	**regista**	director *(cinema)*; producer *(TV)*
la	**scena**	scene
la	**sceneggiatrice**	scriptwriter
la	**sceneggiatura**	script
la	**scenografia**	set design
la	**serie** *(pl inv)*	series
la	**soap** *(pl inv)*	soap (opera)
la	**spettatrice**	member of the audience
la	**suggeritrice**	prompter
la	**trama**	plot
la	**videoclip** *(pl inv)*	music video

ESSENTIAL WORDS *(masculine)*

un	**anno**	year
il	**fine settimana** *(pl inv)*	weekend
il	**giorno**	day
un	**istante**	moment; instant
il	**mattino**	morning
il	**mese**	month
il	**minuto**	minute
il	**momento**	moment
un	**orologio**	watch; clock
il	**pomeriggio**	afternoon; evening
il	**quarto d'ora**	quarter of an hour
il	**secolo**	century
il	**secondo**	second
il	**tempo**	time

USEFUL PHRASES

a mezzogiorno at midday
a mezzanotte at midnight
oggi today
domani tomorrow
dopodomani the day after tomorrow
ieri yesterday
ieri sera last night, yesterday evening
l'altroieri the day before yesterday
due giorni fa 2 days ago
tra due giorni in 2 days
una settimana a week
quindici giorni a fortnight
ogni giorno every day
che giorno è oggi? what day is it?; what's the date?
al momento at the moment
le tre meno un quarto a quarter to 3
le tre e un quarto a quarter past 3
oggigiorno nowadays
il ventunesimo secolo the 21st century

ESSENTIAL WORDS *(feminine)*

la	**giornata**	day
la	**mattina**	morning
la	**mezzora**	half an hour
la	**notte**	night
un'	**ora**	hour
la	**sera**	night; evening
la	**serata**	evening
la	**settimana**	week
la	**sveglia**	alarm clock

USEFUL PHRASES

l'anno scorso/prossimo last/next year
la prossima settimana next week
entro mezzora in half an hour
una volta once
due/tre volte two/three times
diverse volte several times
tre volte all'anno three times a year
nove volte su dieci nine times out of ten
c'era una volta once upon a time there was
dieci alla volta ten at a time
che ore sono? what time is it?
sai (*or* sa) che ore sono? have you got the time?
sono le sei/le sei meno dieci/le sei e mezza it is 6 o'clock/10 to 6/half past 6
sono le due in punto it is 2 o'clock exactly
poco fa a while ago
tra un po' in a while
presto early
tardi late
stanotte last night *(past)*; tonight *(to come)*

IMPORTANT WORDS (*masculine*)

il	**futuro**	future; future tense
il	**giorno dopo**	next day
il	**passato**	past; past tense
il	**presente**	present (*time*); present tense
il	**ritardo**	delay

USEFUL WORDS (*masculine*)

un	**anno bisestile**	leap year
il	**calendario**	calendar
il	**cronometro**	stopwatch
il	**decennio**	decade
il	**Medio Evo**	the Middle Ages
un	**orologio a pendolo**	grandfather clock
un	**orologio da polso**	wristwatch
il	**quadrante**	face (*of clock*)
il	**sorgere del sole**	sunrise
il	**tramonto**	sunset

USEFUL PHRASES

due giorni dopo two days later
il giorno prima the day before
ogni secondo giorno every other day
in futuro in the future
un giorno di ferie a day off
un giorno festivo a public holiday
un giorno lavorativo a weekday
in un giorno di pioggia on a rainy day
all'alba at dawn
la mattina/sera seguente the following morning/evening
adesso now

USEFUL WORDS *(feminine)*

l'	**alba**	dawn
un'	**epoca** *(pl* **-che***)*	time; era
le	**lancette**	hands *(of clock)*
la	**vigilia**	eve

USEFUL PHRASES

sei (*or* **è**) **in ritardo** you are late
sei (*or* **è**) **in anticipo** you are early
quest'orologio va avanti/indietro this watch is fast/slow
arrivare puntuale to arrive on time
quanto tempo? how long?
nel terzo millennio the third millennium
dormire fino a tardi to have a lie-in
da un momento all'altro any minute now
tra una settimana in a week's time
lunedì otto a week on Monday
la notte prima the night before
a quel tempo at that time

ESSENTIAL WORDS (masculine)

il	**bricolage**	DIY
il	**fai da te**	DIY
un	**attrezzo**	tool

USEFUL WORDS (masculine)

un	**ago** (pl -ghi)	needle
il	**badile**	spade
il	**cacciavite** (pl inv)	screwdriver
il	**chiodo**	nail
un	**elastico**	rubber band
il	**filo spinato**	(barbed) wire
il	**forcone**	(garden) fork
il	**lucchetto**	padlock
il	**martello**	hammer
il	**martello pneumatico**	pneumatic drill
il	**metro a nastro**	tape measure
il	**nastro adesivo**	sticky tape
il	**pennello**	paintbrush
il	**piccone**	pickaxe
lo	**scalpello**	chisel
lo	**scotch** (pl inv)	Sellotape®
il	**secchio**	bucket
il	**trapano**	drill
il	**tuttofare** (pl inv)	handyman

USEFUL PHRASES
fare qualche lavoretto to do odd jobs
battere un chiodo con il martello to hammer in a nail
"pittura fresca" "wet paint"
pitturare to paint
mettere la carta da parati to wallpaper

ESSENTIAL WORDS *(feminine)*

la **chiave**	key
la **chiave inglese**	spanner
la **corda**	rope
la **macchina**	machine
un' **officina**	workshop

USEFUL WORDS *(feminine)*

la **batteria**	battery
la **carta vetrata**	sandpaper
la **cassetta degli attrezzi**	toolbox
la **colla**	glue
le **forbici**	scissors
un' **impalcatura**	scaffolding
la **lima**	file
la **molla**	spring
la **pala**	shovel
la **pila**	battery *(in radio etc)*; torch
le **pinze**	pliers
la **puntina da disegno**	drawing pin
la **scala (a libretto)**	(step)ladder
la **sega** *(pl -ghe)*	saw
la **serratura**	lock
la **tavola (di legno)**	plank
la **tuttofare** *(pl inv)*	handywoman
la **vernice**	varnish
la **vite**	screw

USEFUL PHRASES

"lavori in corso: vietato l'accesso" "construction site: keep out"
pratico(a) handy
tagliare to cut
riparare to mend
avvitare to screw (in)
svitare to unscrew

ESSENTIAL WORDS *(masculine)*

un	**abitante**	inhabitant
un	**albergo** *(pl -ghi)*	hotel
un	**angolo**	corner
un	**autobus** *(pl inv)*	bus
il	**caffè** *(pl inv)*	café; coffee
il	**centro (della città)**	town centre
il	**cinema** *(pl inv)*	cinema
il	**commissariato di polizia**	police station
il	**comune**	town hall
il	**condominio**	block of flats
i	**dintorni**	surroundings
il	**distributore di benzina**	petrol station
il	**duomo**	cathedral
un	**edificio**	building
il	**giro**	tour
l'	**inquinamento (dell'aria)**	(air) pollution
il	**mercato**	market
il	**municipio**	town hall
il	**museo**	museum; art gallery
il	**negozio**	shop
il	**parcheggio**	car park; parking space
il	**parco** *(pl -chi)*	park
il	**pedone**	pedestrian
il	**poliziotto**	police officer
il	**ponte**	bridge
il	**posteggio dei taxi**	taxi rank
il	**quartiere**	district
il	**quartiere degradato**	slum area
il	**ristorante**	restaurant
il	**sobborgo** *(pl -ghi)*	suburb
il	**taxi** *(pl inv)*	taxi
il	**teatro**	theatre
il	**turista**	tourist
un	**ufficio**	office
un	**ufficio postale**	post office

ESSENTIAL WORDS *(feminine)*

un'	**abitante**	inhabitant
un'	**automobile**	car
la	**banca** *(pl -che)*	bank
la	**casa popolare**	council house
la	**cattedrale**	cathedral
la	**città** *(pl inv)*	town, city
la	**corriera**	bus; coach
la	**fabbrica** *(pl -che)*	factory
la	**fermata dell'autobus**	bus stop
la	**lavanderia automatica**	launderette
la	**macchina**	car
la	**metropolitana**	underground, subway
la	**panchina**	bench
la	**piazza**	square
la	**piscina**	swimming pool
la	**polizia**	police
la	**poliziotta**	police officer
la	**posta**	post office
la	**stazione (ferroviaria)**	(train) station
la	**stazione delle corriere**	bus station
la	**strada**	road
la	**torre**	tower
la	**turista**	tourist
la	**via**	street
la	**vista**	view

USEFUL PHRASES

vado in città I'm going into town
in centro in the town centre
nella piazza in the square
una strada a senso unico a one-way street
"vietato l'accesso" "no entry"
attraversare la strada to cross the road

IMPORTANT WORDS *(masculine)*

un	abbonamento	season ticket
un	agente di polizia	police officer
il	cartello	notice; sign
il	castello	castle
il	centro storico	old town
il	distributore di biglietti	ticket machine
il	giardino pubblico	park
il	giornalaio	news stand
un	incrocio	crossroads
un	ingorgo *(pl -ghi)*	traffic jam
un	internet caffè *(pl inv)*	internet café
il	marciapiede	pavement
il	monumento	monument
il	parchimetro	parking meter
il	parco *(pl -chi)*	park
il	passante	passer-by
il	posto	place
il	semaforo	traffic lights
il	sindaco	mayor
il	supermercato	supermarket
il	traffico	traffic
lo	zoo *(pl inv)*	zoo

USEFUL PHRASES

all'angolo della strada at the corner of the street
vivere in periferia to live on the outskirts
camminare to walk
prendere l'autobus/la metropolitana to take the bus/the underground
comprare un biglietto multicorse to buy a multiple-journey ticket
timbrare il biglietto to punch the ticket

IMPORTANT WORDS *(feminine)*

un'	agente di polizia	police officer
la	biblioteca (pl -che)	library
la	chiesa	church
la	circolazione	traffic
la	città vecchia	old town
la	deviazione	diversion
un'	edicola	newspaper kiosk
la	moschea	mosque
la	passante	passer-by
la	pinacoteca	art gallery
la	sinagoga (pl -ghe)	synagogue
la	stazione di servizio	petrol station
la	via principale	main street
la	zona	zone; area
la	zona a traffico limitato	restricted traffic zone
la	zona industriale	industrial estate
la	zona pedonale	pedestrian precinct

USEFUL PHRASES
industriale industrial
storico(a) historic
bello(a) pretty
brutto(a) ugly
pulito(a) clean
sporco(a) dirty

USEFUL WORDS *(masculine)*

un	**attraversamento pedonale**	pedestrian crossing
il	**bar** *(pl inv)*	café-bar
il	**bastione**	rampart
il	**caffè** *(pl inv)*	coffee shop, café
il	**carcere**	prison
il	**cartello stradale**	road sign
il	**cimitero**	cemetery
il	**ciottolo**	cobblestone
il	**cittadino**	citizen
il	**consiglio comunale**	town council
il	**dépliant** *(pl inv)*	leaflet
il	**distretto**	district
il	**furgone dei traslochi**	delivery van
il	**grattacielo**	skyscraper
il	**lampione**	street lamp
i	**luoghi d'interesse**	sights, places of interest
il	**manifestino**	leaflet
il	**passeggino**	pushchair
il	**quartiere residenziale**	residential area
il	**sondaggio d'opinione**	opinion poll
il	**vicolo cieco** *(pl -i -chi)*	cul-de-sac, dead end
il	**volantino**	flyer, leaflet

USEFUL WORDS (feminine)

la	**carrozzina**	pram
la	**caserma dei pompieri**	fire station
la	**cittadina**	citizen
la	**coda**	queue
la	**curva**	bend
la	**fermata dell'autobus**	bus stop
la	**fognatura**	sewer
la	**folla**	crowd
la	**freccia** (pl -ce)	arrow
la	**galleria d'arte**	art gallery
un'	**isola pedonale**	traffic island
la	**periferia**	outskirts
la	**pista ciclabile**	cycle path; cycle lane
la	**popolazione**	population
la	**prigione**	prison
la	**processione**	procession
la	**sfilata**	parade
la	**statua**	statue
la	**strada senza uscita**	cul-de-sac, dead end
le	**strisce pedonali**	zebra crossing
la	**superficie stradale**	road surface

ESSENTIAL WORDS *(masculine)*

un	**armadietto per i bagagli**	left-luggage locker
l'	**arrivo**	arrival
il	**bagaglio**	luggage
il	**bar della stazione**	station bar
il	**biglietto**	ticket
il	**biglietto di andata e ritorno**	return ticket
il	**biglietto di sola andata**	single ticket
il	**binario**	platform; track
il	**buffet della stazione** *(pl inv)*	station bar
il	**deposito bagagli**	left-luggage office
il	**doganiere**	customs officer
il	**facchino**	porter
il	**freno**	brake
un	**intercity** *(pl inv)*	intercity train
il	**numero**	number
un	**orario**	timetable
il	**parcheggio dei taxi**	taxi rank
il	**passaporto**	passport
il	**ponte**	bridge
il	**portafoglio**	wallet
il	**posto (a sedere)**	seat
il	**ritardo**	delay
lo	**scompartimento**	compartment
lo	**scontrino**	ticket; receipt
il	**supplemento**	extra charge *(to be paid on intercity)*
il	**taxi** *(pl inv)*	taxi
il	**treno**	train
il	**treno ad alta velocità**	high-speed train
il	**treno regionale**	local stopping train
un	**ufficio oggetti smarriti**	lost property office
il	**vagone**	carriage
il	**viaggiatore**	traveller
il	**viaggio**	journey

ESSENTIAL WORDS *(feminine)*

la	**bici** *(pl inv)*	bike
la	**bicicletta**	bicycle
la	**biglietteria**	ticket office
la	**borsa**	bag
la	**borsetta**	handbag
la	**cartina stradale**	map
la	**classe**	class
la	**coincidenza**	connection
la	**direzione**	direction
la	**dogana**	customs
la	**doganiera**	customs officer
la	**fermata della metropolitana**	underground station
le	**informazioni**	information
la	**linea**	line
la	**metropolitana**	underground, subway
la	**partenza**	departure
la	**prenotazione**	reservation
la	**riduzione**	reduction
la	**sala d'aspetto**	waiting room
la	**stazione**	station
la	**tariffa**	fare
la	**valigia** *(pl -gie or -ge)*	suitcase
la	**viaggiatrice**	traveller

USEFUL PHRASES
prenotare un posto to book a seat
pagare un supplemento to pay an extra charge, to pay a surcharge
fare/disfare i bagagli to pack/unpack

IMPORTANT WORDS (*masculine*)

un	**allarme**	alarm
il	**cancello**	barrier
il	**carnet di biglietti** (*pl inv*)	book of tickets
il	**confine**	border
il	**controllore**	ticket collector
il	**guidatore**	driver
il	**vagone letto** (*pl* **-i ~**)	sleeping car
il	**vagone ristorante** (*pl* **-i ~**)	dining car

USEFUL WORDS (*masculine*)

un	**abbonamento**	season ticket
il	**bagagliaio**	trunk
il	**capostazione** (*pl* **capistazione**)	stationmaster
il	**deragliamento**	derailment
il	**fischietto**	whistle
il	**macchinista**	engine-driver
il	**passaggio a livello**	level crossing
il	**tabellone**	noticeboard
il	**treno merci** (*pl* **-i ~**)	goods train
il	**vagone**	carriage
il	**viaggio**	journey; trip

USEFUL PHRASES

prendere il treno to take the train
perdere il treno to miss the train
convalidare il biglietto to date stamp a ticket
salire in treno to get on the train
scendere dal treno to get off the train
è libero questo posto? is this seat free?
il treno è in ritardo the train is late
"è vietato sporgersi dal finestrino" "do not lean out of the window"

IMPORTANT WORDS *(feminine)*

la **carrozza**	carriage
la **cuccetta**	couchette
la **destinazione**	destination
la **durata**	length (of time)
la **ferrovia**	railway
la **frontiera**	border
la **mancia** *(pl -ce)*	tip
la **scala mobile**	escalator
la **tariffa**	fare
Trenitalia	Italian Railway

USEFUL WORDS *(feminine)*

la **capostazione** *(pl inv)*	stationmaster
un' **etichetta**	label
la **locomotiva**	locomotive
la **macchinista**	engine-driver
le **rotaie**	rails

USEFUL PHRASES

vengo con te alla stazione I'll go to the station with you
ti accompagno alla stazione I'll take you to the station
vengo a prenderti alla stazione I'll come and pick you up at the station
il treno delle dieci diretto a/proveniente da Roma the 10 o'clock train to/
from Rome

ESSENTIAL WORDS *(masculine)*

un	**albero**	tree
il	**bosco** *(pl -chi)*	wood
il	**ramo**	branch

USEFUL WORDS *(masculine)*

un	**abete**	fir tree
un	**acero**	maple
un	**agrifoglio**	holly
un	**albero da frutta**	fruit tree
un	**albicocco** *(pl -chi)*	apricot tree
un	**arancio**	orange tree; orange
un	**arbusto**	shrub
il	**fico** *(pl -chi)*	fig tree; fig
il	**leccio**	ilex, holm oak
il	**banano**	banana tree
il	**biancospino**	hawthorn
il	**bocciolo**	bud
il	**bosso**	box tree
il	**castagno**	chestnut tree
il	**cespuglio**	bush
il	**ciliegio**	cherry tree
il	**faggio**	beech
il	**fogliame**	foliage
il	**frassino**	ash
il	**limone**	lemon tree; lemon
il	**melo**	apple tree
il	**noce**	walnut tree
un	**olmo**	elm
un	**orto**	orchard
il	**pero**	pear tree
il	**pesco** *(pl -chi)*	peach tree
il	**pino**	pine
il	**pioppo**	poplar
il	**platano**	plane tree
il	**rovere**	oak
il	**salice piangente**	weeping willow
il	**tiglio**	lime tree
il	**tronco** *(pl -chi)*	trunk

ESSENTIAL WORDS *(feminine)*

la	**foglia**	leaf
la	**foresta**	forest
la	**foresta pluviale**	rain forest
la	**palma**	palm tree

USEFUL WORDS *(feminine)*

la	**bacca** *(pl -che)*	berry
la	**betulla**	birch
la	**corteccia** *(pl -ce)*	bark
la	**foresta**	forest
la	**gemma**	bud
la	**radice**	root
la	**vigna**	vineyard

ESSENTIAL WORDS *(masculine)*

l'	**aglio**	garlic
il	**cavolfiore**	cauliflower
i	**fagiolini**	French beans
i	**funghi**	mushrooms
gli	**ortaggi**	vegetables
il	**peperone**	pepper
i	**piselli**	peas
il	**pomodoro**	tomato

USEFUL WORDS *(masculine)*

gli	**asparagi**	asparagus
il	**basilico**	basil
i	**broccoli**	broccoli
il	**carciofo**	artichoke
i	**cavoletti di Bruxelles**	Brussels sprouts
il	**cavolo**	cabbage
i	**ceci**	chickpeas
il	**cetriolo**	cucumber
il	**cipollotto**	spring onion
i	**fagioli**	beans
i	**fagioli bianchi**	haricot beans
i	**(fagioli) borlotti**	kidney beans
i	**legumi**	pulses
il	**mais**	sweetcorn
il	**porro**	leek
il	**prezzemolo**	parsley
il	**ravanello**	radish
il	**sedano**	celery
gli	**spinaci**	spinach

USEFUL PHRASES
coltivare ortaggi to grow vegetables
una pannocchia bollita corn on the cob

ESSENTIAL WORDS *(feminine)*

la	**carota**	carrot
la	**cipolla**	onion
l'	**insalata**	salad
la	**patata**	potato
le	**verdure**	vegetables

USESFUL WORDS *(feminine)*

la	**barbabietola**	beetroot
la	**cicoria**	chicory
l'	**indivia**	endive
la	**lattuga**	lettuce
le	**lenticchie**	lentils
la	**melanzana**	aubergine
la	**rapa**	turnip
la	**scarola**	curly endive
la	**zucca** *(pl* **-che)**	pumpkin
la	**zucchina**	courgette

USEFUL PHRASES

carote grattugiate grated carrot
biologico(a) organic
vegano(a) vegan
vegetariano(a) vegetarian

ESSENTIAL WORDS *(masculine)*

un **aereo**	plane
un **aeroplano**	aeroplane
un **autobus** *(pl inv)*	bus
il **camion** *(pl inv)*	lorry
il **camper** *(pl inv)*	camper van
il **casco** *(pl -chi)*	helmet
il **ciclomotore**	moped
un **elicottero**	helicopter
il **ferry** *(pl inv)*	ferry
il **furgone**	van
il **mezzo di trasporto**	means of transport
il **motorino**	moped
il **prezzo del biglietto**	fare
lo **scooter** *(pl inv)*	scooter
il **taxi** *(pl inv)*	taxi
il **tir** *(pl inv)*	heavy goods vehicle
il **traghetto**	ferry
i **trasporti pubblici**	public transport
il **treno**	train
il **veicolo**	vehicle
il **veliero**	sailing ship

IMPORTANT WORDS *(masculine)*

il **camion** *(pl inv)* **dei pompieri**	fire engine
il **carro attrezzi**	breakdown van

USEFUL PHRASES

viaggiare to travel

ha preso un aereo per Palermo he/she flew to Palermo

prendere l'autobus/la metropolitana/il treno to take the bus/the subway/the train

andare in bicicletta to go cycling

ci si può andare in macchina you can go there by car

ESSENTIAL WORDS *(feminine)*

un' **auto** *(pl inv)*	car
un' **automobile**	car
la **barca** *(pl -che)*	boat
la **barca** *(pl -che)* **a remi**	rowing boat
la **barca** *(pl -che)* **a vela**	sailing boat
la **bici** *(pl inv)*	bike
la **bicicletta**	bicycle
la **corriera**	coach
la **distanza**	distance
la **funicolare**	funicular railway
la **macchina**	car
la **metropolitana**	underground, subway
la **moto** *(pl inv)*	motorbike
la **motocicletta**	motorcycle, motorbike
la **parte anteriore**	front
la **parte posteriore**	back
la **roulotte** *(pl inv)*	caravan
la **vespa**®	vespa®

IMPORTANT WORDS *(feminine)*

un' **ambulanza**	ambulance
un' **autopompa**	fire engine

USEFUL PHRASES

riparare la macchina a qn to repair sb's car
una macchina a noleggio a hire car
una macchina sportiva a sports car
una macchina da corsa a racing car
la macchina della ditta the company car
"auto usate" "used cars"
partire to start, to move off
sedersi davanti/dietro to sit in the front/back

USEFUL WORDS *(masculine)*

un	**aliante**	glider
un	**aliscafo**	hydrofoil
un	**autoarticolato**	articulated lorry
un	**autocarro**	lorry
il	**bulldozer** *(pl inv)*	bulldozer
il	**camion cisterna** *(pl inv)*	tanker lorry
il	**carro**	cart
il	**carro armato**	tank
il	**disco volante** *(pl -chi -i)*	flying saucer
il	**fuoristrada** *(pl inv)*	jeep, off-road vehicle
il	**furgone dei traslochi**	delivery van
il	**gommone**	rubber dinghy
un	**hovercraft** *(pl inv)*	hovercraft
un	**idrovolante**	seaplane
il	**motore**	engine
il	**motoscafo**	speedboat
il	**passeggino**	pushchair
il	**razzo**	rocket
il	**rimorchiatore**	tug
il	**rimorchio**	trailer
il	**sottomarino**	submarine
il	**suv** *(pl inv)*	suv
il	**tram** *(pl inv)*	tram
il	**trattore**	tractor
un	**ufo** *(pl inv)*	UFO *(unidentified flying object)*
lo	**yacht** *(pl inv)*	yacht

USEFUL WORDS *(feminine)*

un'	**astronave**	spaceship
una	**barca** *(pl -che)* **da diporto**	pleasure boat
la	**canoa**	canoe
la	**carrozzina**	pram
la	**chiatta**	barge
la	**funivia**	cable car
un'	**imbarcazione**	boat
la	**jeep** *(pl inv)*	jeep
la	**lancia** *(pl -ce)*	launch
la	**lancia** *(pl -ce)* **di salvataggio**	lifeboat
la	**locomotiva**	locomotive
la	**macchina familiare**	estate car
la	**monovolume** *(pl inv)*	people carrier
la	**nave**	ship
la	**nave cisterna** *(pl -i ~)*	tanker (ship); water supply ship
la	**navetta**	shuttle bus
la	**petroliera**	oil tanker *(ship)*
la	**portaerei** *(pl inv)*	aircraft carrier
la	**seggiovia**	chairlift
la	**station wagon** *(pl inv)*	estate car

ESSENTIAL WORDS *(masculine)*

l'	**autunno**	autumn
il	**bollettino meteo**	weather report
il	**calore**	heat
il	**cielo**	sky
il	**clima** *(pl inv)*	climate
l'	**est**	east
il	**freddo**	cold
il	**grado**	degree
il	**ghiaccio**	ice
l'	**inverno**	winter
il	**meteo** *(pl inv)*	weather report
il	**nord**	north
l'	**ovest**	west
un	**ombrello**	umbrella
il	**sole**	sun; sunshine
il	**sud**	south
il	**tempo**	weather
il	**vento**	wind

USEFUL PHRASES

che tempo fa? what's the weather like?

fa caldo/freddo it's hot/cold

è una bella giornata it's a lovely day

è una brutta giornata it's a horrible day

all'aria aperta in the open air

c'è nebbia it's foggy

30° all'ombra 30° in the shade

ascoltare le previsioni del tempo to listen to the weather forecast

piovere to rain

nevicare to snow

c'è il sole it's sunny

c'è vento it's windy

piove it's raining

nevica it's snowing

ESSENTIAL WORDS *(feminine)*

l'	**aria**	air
l'	**estate**	summer
la	**nebbia**	fog
la	**neve**	snow
la	**nuvola**	cloud
la	**pioggia** *(pl -ge)*	rain
le	**previsioni del tempo**	(weather) forecast
la	**primavera**	spring
la	**regione**	region, area
la	**stagione**	season
la	**temperatura**	temperature

USEFUL PHRASES

brilla il sole the sun is shining
soffia il vento the wind is blowing
si gela it's freezing
gelare to freeze
c'è stata una gelata there's been a frost
sciogliersi to melt
una giornata di sole a sunny day
una giornata di pioggia a rainy day
tempestoso(a) stormy
fresco(a) cool
variabile changeable
umido(a) humid
è coperto the sky is overcast

IMPORTANT WORDS (*masculine*)

il **buio**	darkness
il **fumo**	smoke
il **rovescio**	shower

USEFUL WORDS (*masculine*)

un **acquazzone**	downpour
un **arcobaleno**	rainbow
il **barometro**	barometer
il **cambiamento**	change
il **chiaro di luna**	moonlight
il **crepuscolo**	nightfall, dusk
il **cumulo di neve**	snowdrift
il **disgelo**	thaw
il **fiocco** (*pl* -**chi**) **di neve**	snowflake
il **fulmine**	flash of lightning
il **ghiacciolo**	icicle
il **miglioramento**	improvement
il **parafulmine** (*pl inv*)	lightning conductor
il **raggio di sole**	ray of sunshine
lo **spazzaneve** (*pl inv*)	snowplough
il **temporale**	thunderstorm
il **tramonto**	sunset
il **tuono**	thunder
un **uragano**	hurricane

IMPORTANT WORDS *(feminine)*

la	burrasca *(pl -che)*	storm
la	polvere	dust
le	precipitazioni	rainfall
la	schiarita	sunny spell
la	tempesta	storm
la	tormenta	storm
la	tromba d'aria	whirlwind
la	visibilità	visibility

USEFUL WORDS *(feminine)*

l'	alba	dawn, daybreak
un'	alluvione	flood
l'	atmosfera	atmosphere
la	brezza	breeze
la	brina	frost *(on the ground)*
la	corrente (d'aria)	draught
la	foschia	mist
la	gelata	frost
la	goccia di pioggia	raindrop
la	grandine	hail
un'	inondazione	flood
la	nevicata	snowfall
un'	ondata di caldo	heatwave
l'	oscurità	darkness
la	pozzanghera	puddle
la	raffica di vento	gust of wind
la	rugiada	dew
la	siccità	drought

ESSENTIAL WORDS (masculine)

il	bagno	bathroom
il	bidone delle immondizie	dustbin
il	dormitorio	dormitory
i	gabinetti	lavatories
il	lenzuolo *(pl f* lenzuola*)*	sheet
i	letti a castello	bunk bed
il	letto	bed
il	listino dei prezzi	price list
un	ospite	visitor
un	ostello della gioventù	youth hostel
il	pasto	meal
il	rifugio	mountain hostel
i	servizi	toilets
il	silenzio	silence
il	soggiorno	stay; living room
un	ufficio	office

IMPORTANT WORDS (masculine)

il	lavandino	washbasin
il	regolamento	rules
il	sacco *(pl* -chi*)* a pelo	sleeping bag
lo	zaino	rucksack

ESSENTIAL WORDS (feminine)

la	**cartina**	map
la	**colazione**	breakfast
la	**cucina**	kitchen; cooking
la	**doccia** (pl -ce)	shower
le	**lenzuola**	sheets
la	**notte**	night
un'	**ospite**	visitor
la	**sala giochi**	games room
la	**sala da pranzo**	dining room
la	**tariffa**	rate
le	**toilette**	toilets
le	**vacanze**	holidays

IMPORTANT WORDS (feminine)

la	**biancheria del letto**	bed linen
la	**camminata**	walk
un'	**escursione**	hike; trip
la	**guida**	guidebook; guide
la	**tessera (associativa)**	membership card

USEFUL PHRASES

passare una notte in un ostello to spend a night at a youth hostel
vorrei comprare un sacco a pelo I would like to buy a sleeping bag
non c'è più posto there's no more room

The vocabulary items on pages 662 to 700 have been grouped under parts of speech rather than topics because they can apply in a wide range of circumstances. Use them just as freely as the vocabulary already given.

ARTICLES AND PRONOUNS

What is an article?
An **article** is one of the words *the*, *a* and *an* which is given in front of a noun.

What is a pronoun?
A **pronoun** is a word you use instead of a noun, when you do not need or want to name someone or something directly, for example, *it*, *you*, *none*.

alcuni/alcune some
altrettanto the same
altro/altra: un altro/un'altra
  another one
  altri/altre others
  gli altri/le altre other people
ambedue both
che what; which; that
chi who; whoever
chiunque whoever; anyone
ci us; to us; ourselves; each other
ciascuno/ciascuna each
ciò this
cui to whom; of whom; whose
egli he
entrambi both
essi/esse they
esso/a it
gli the; him; to him; it; to it
i the
il the
io I
la the; her; it; you
le the; her; to her; to you; them

lei she; her; you
li them
lo the; him; it
loro they; them; theirs
lui he; him
me me; to me
mi me; to me; myself
mio/mia/miei/mie: il mio/la mia/
  i miei/le mie mine
ne of it; of them; about it; about them
nessuno/nessuna nobody; no-one; none; anyone
niente nothing
noi we; us
nostro/nostra/nostri/nostre:
  il nostro/la nostra/i nostri/le
  nostre ours
nulla nothing; anything
ognuno each; everbody
parecchio/parecchia quite a lot
qualcosa something; anything
qualcuno somebody; someone; anybody; anyone

quale (*pl* **-i**) which; what
quanti/quante how many
quanto/quanta how much
quelli/quelle/quegli those ones
quello/quella that one
questi/queste these ones
questo/questa this one
sé himself; herself; itself;
  themselves; oneself
si oneself; himself; herself; itself;
  themselves; each other
stesso/stessa: lo stesso/la stessa
  the same one
  gli stessi/le stesse the same ones
suo/sua/suoi/sue: il suo/la sua/
  i suoi/le sue his; hers; yours
tanti/tante many; so many

tanto/tanta much, so much
te you; to you
ti you; to you; yourself
troppi/troppe too many
troppo/troppa too much
tu you
tuo/tua/tuoi/tue: il tuo/la tua/
  i tuoi/le tue yours
tutti everybody
tutto everything
uno/una a, an; one
ve to you
vi you; to you; yourselves; each other
voi you
vostro/vostra/vostri/vostre:
  il vostro/la vostra/i vostri/le
  vostre yours

CONJUNCTIONS

> **What is a conjunction?**
> A **conjunction** is a word such as *and, but, or, so, if* and *because*, that links two words or phrases of a similar type, or two parts of a sentence, for example, *Diane and I have been friends for years; I left because I was bored.*

a meno che unless
affinché so that
anche too; even
ancora still; even
anzi in fact
anziché rather than; instead of
appena as soon as
benché although
che that; than
come how; as
comunque however
così: così ... che so ... that ...
  così ... come as ... as
dopo after
dunque so; well
e(d) and; but
eppure and yet
finché until; as long as
infatti in fact
ma but; however; nevertheless
mentre while

né: né... né... neither... nor...
nonostante even though
o or
  o... o... either... or...
oppure or
perché because; so that
perciò so
però but
per quanto however
pertanto therefore
poiché since
prima di before
purché as long as
pure too; even though
quando when
  da quando since
quindi so
se if; whether
sebbene even though
sia... che... both... and...
siccome since

ADJECTIVES

> **What is an adjective?**
> An **adjective** is a 'describing' word that tells you more about a person or thing, such as their appearance, colour, size or other qualities, for example, *pretty, blue, big*.

abbondante big
abile skilful
abituato(a): abituato a used to
acceso(a) on; burning; lit
accogliente pleasant; welcoming
accurato(a) detailed
acido(a) acid; sour
acuto(a) high; sharp; acute
adatto(a) right (for); suitable
addormentato(a) sleeping; asleep
aderente tight
affascinante very attractive
affaticato(a) tired
affettuoso(a) affectionate
affidabile reliable
affilato(a) sharp
affollato(a) crowded
afoso(a) muggy
aggiornato(a) up-to-date
agitato(a) nervous
allegro(a) cheerful
allucinante awful
alternativo(a) alternative
alto(a) high; tall; loud; deep
altro(a) other
amaro(a) bitter
ambedue both
amichevole friendly
ammalato(a) ill
ammobiliato(a) furnished
ampio(a) spacious; loose

analcolico(a) soft
anonimo(a) anonymous
antipatico(a) unpleasant
antiquato(a) old-fashioned
anziano(a) old
aperto(a) open
appuntito(a) sharp
armato(a) armed
arrabbiato(a) angry
arredato(a) furnished
arrugginito(a) rusty
asciutto(a) dry
aspro(a) sour
assente absent
assetato(a) thirsty
assortito(a) assorted
assurdo(a) ridiculous
astemio(a) teetotal
astratto(a) abstract
astuto(a) cunning
attento(a) careful
attillato(a) tight
attivo(a) active
attrezzato(a) equipped
attuale present; current
avaro(a) mean; stingy
bagnato(a) wet
basso(a) low; short; shallow
beato(a) blessed; lucky
bello(a) lovely; good-looking
benvenuto(a) welcome

biondo(a) blond
bollente boiling
bravo(a) good; clever
breve short
brusco(a) abrupt
brutto(a) ugly; bad
buffo(a) funny
buio(a) dark
buono(a) good
caldo(a) hot; warm
calmo(a) calm
capace able
capriccioso(a) naughty
carino(a) nice; nice-looking
caro(a) dear; expensive
cattivo(a) bad; nasty
celebre famous
certo(a) sure; certain
  certi(e) some
chiaro(a) clear; light; fair
chiuso(a) closed; locked
cieco(a) blind
colpevole guilty
colto(a) well-educated
comodo(a) comfortable
completo(a) complete; full
comprensivo(a) understanding
compreso(a) inclusive
comune common
congelato(a) frozen
conosciuto(a) well-known
contento(a) happy; glad
continuo(a) constant; nonstop
contrario(a) opposite
conveniente cheap
coperto(a) indoor; covered;
  overcast
corto(a) short
costoso(a) expensive

cotto(a) cooked
crespo(a) frizzy
cretino(a) stupid
croccante crisp; crusty
crudele cruel
crudo(a) raw
dannoso(a) harmful
debole weak
deluso(a) disappointed
denso(a) dense; thick
deprimente depressing
destro(a) right
determinato(a) certain;
  determined
difettoso(a) faulty
difficile difficult
diffidente suspicious
diffuso(a) common
diligente hard-working
dimagrante slimming
diretto(a) direct; through
diritto(a) straight
disabitato(a) uninhabited
disastroso(a) disastrous
discreto(a) reasonable; discreet
disgustoso(a) disgusting
disinvolto(a) relaxed
disonesto(a) dishonest
disordinato(a) untidy
dispari odd
disperato(a) desperate
dispettoso(a) spiteful
disponibile available
dissetante refreshing; thirst-
  quenching
distinto(a) distinguished; distinct
distratto(a) absent-minded
disubbidiente disobedient
diversi(e) several

diverso(a) different
divertente funny
dolce sweet
doloroso(a) painful; sad
doppio(a) double
dotato(a) gifted
drammatico(a) dramatic
duro(a) hard
eccellente excellent
eccezionale really good
eccitato(a) excited; aroused
ecologico(a) ecological
economico(a) inexpensive; economic
educato(a) polite
efficace effective
efficiente efficient
egoista selfish
elasticizzato(a) stretch
elementare basic; elementary; primary
elettrico(a) electric
emotivo(a) emotional
emozionante exciting
emozionato(a) moved; emotional
enorme huge
entrambi(e) both
entusiasta enthusiastic; delighted
ereditario(a) hereditary
esatto(a) exact
esaurito(a) sold out; run down
esausto(a) exhausted
esclusivo(a) exclusive
escluso(a) except
esigente demanding
esotico(a) exotic
esplicito(a) explicit
esteriore exterior
esterno(a) outside

estero(a) foreign
estivo(a) summer
estremo(a) extreme
estroverso(a) outgoing
evidente obvious
facile easy
facoltativo(a) optional
falso(a) false; forged; fake
familiare familiar
famoso(a) famous
fantastico(a) great
fastidioso(a) annoying
faticoso(a) tiring
favoloso(a) fabulous
fedele faithful
felice happy
femminile feminine
feriale: giorno feriale week day
fermo(a) still; stopped
festivo(a): giorno festivo Sunday; holiday
fiero(a) proud
fine thin; fine; refined
finto(a) false; artificial; imitation
fisico(a) physical
fisso(a) fixed; permanent; regular
flessibile flexible
fondo(a) deep
forte strong; loud
fortunato(a) lucky
freddo(a) cold
frequentato(a) popular
frequente frequent
fresco(a) fresh; cool
fritto(a) fried
frizzante sparkling
furbo(a) clever
furibondo(a) furious
gassato(a) fizzy

gelato(a) frozen
gelido(a) icy
geloso(a) jealous
generoso(a) generous
geniale brilliant
gentile nice; kind
ghiacciato(a) frozen
gigante giant
giornaliero(a) daily
giovane young
giusto(a) right
goffo(a) clumsy
gonfio(a) swollen
grande big; great; grown-up
grasso(a) fat
gratuito(a) free
grave serious
grazioso(a) charming
grosso(a) big; large
guasto(a) not working
gustoso(a) tasty
ideale ideal
identico(a) identical
idiota stupid
idratante moisturizing
ignorante ignorant
imbarazzante awkward
imbarazzato(a) embarrassed
imbattibile unbeatable
imbottito(a) filled
imbranato(a) awkward; clumsy
immaturo(a) immature
immenso(a) huge
immobile motionless
impacciato(a) awkward
impanato(a) in breadcrumbs
impegnativo(a) demanding
impegnato(a) busy
impermeabile waterproof

impressionante terrible
imprevedibile unpredictable
imprevisto(a) unexpected
improvviso(a) sudden
inaffidabile unreliable
inaspettato(a) unexpected
incantevole lovely
incerto(a) uncertain
incinta pregnant
incluso(a) included
incollato(a) glued
incosciente unconscious; reckless
incustodito(a) unattended
indaffarato(a) busy
indimenticabile unforgettable
indipendente independent
indiretto(a) indirect
indispensabile essential
individuale personal
inesperto(a) inexperienced
infantile childish
infedele unfaithful
infelice unhappy
infinito(a) endless
infortunato(a) injured
infreddolito(a) cold
ingenuo(a) naïve
ingiusto(a) unfair
ingombrante cumbersome
innamorato(a) in love
insicuro(a) insecure
insolito(a) unusual
insopportabile unbearable
integrale wholemeal
internazionale international
interno(a) inside
intero(a) whole
intraprendente enterprising
inutile useless

invadente interfering
invalido(a) disabled
invernale winter
inverso(a) opposite
invidioso(a) jealous
istruito(a) well-educated
largo(a) wide
lavorativo(a) working
leale loyal
leggero(a) light
lento(a) slow
lesso(a) boiled
libero(a) free
limpido(a) clear
liquido(a) liquid
liscio(a) smooth; straight
logico(a) logical
logoro(a) threadbare
lontano(a) distant; far off
loro their
lucido(a) shiny; lucid
luminoso(a) bright; luminous
lunatico(a) temperamental
lungo(a) long
lussuoso(a) luxury
maggiore bigger; older
maggiorenne of age
magico(a) magic
magnetico(a) magnetic
magnifico(a) wonderful
magro(a) thin; low-fat
maiuscolo(a) capital
malato(a) ill, sick
maldestro(a) clumsy
maledetto(a) damn
maleducato(a) rude
malinconico(a) sad
malizioso(a) mischievous
malvagio(a) wicked

mancino(a) left-handed
manuale manual
marcio(a) rotten
maschile male; masculine
maschio(a) male
massimo(a) maximum
materno(a) maternal
matrimoniale matrimonial; double
matto(a) mad
maturo(a) ripe; mature
medesimo(a) same
medico(a) medical
medio(a) average
mensile monthly
meraviglioso(a) wonderful
meridionale southern
mezzo(a) half
migliore better
milionario(a) millionaire
minimo(a) minimum; minimal
minore less; younger; smaller
minorenne under age
mio(a) *(pl* **miei, mie)** my
miope short-sighted
misterioso(a) mysterious
misto(a) mixed
moderno(a) modern
modesto(a) modest
molle soft
molto(a) a lot of; much
molti(e) many
mondiale world
morbido(a) soft
mortale fatal
morto(a) dead
mosso(a) rough; wavy; blurred
muto(a) silent
nasale nasal
nascosto(a) hidden

natalizio(a) Christmas
naturale natural; still
nauseante disgusting
necessario(a) necessary
nervoso(a) irritable
nessuno(a) no
netto(a) clear
neutro(a) neutral; neuter
nobile aristocratic
nocivo(a) harmful
noioso(a) boring
nostro(a) our
noto(a) well-known
notturno(a) night
nubile unmarried
nudo(a) naked
numeroso(a) numerous
nuovo(a) new
nutriente nourishing
nuvoloso(a) cloudy
obbediente obedient
obbligatorio(a) compulsory
obiettivo(a) objective
obliquo(a) oblique
occidentale western
occupato(a) occupied
odioso(a) hateful
offeso(a) offended
ogni every
onesto(a) honest
opportuno(a) right
ordinale ordinal
ordinato(a) tidy
orgoglioso(a) proud
orientale eastern
orizzontale horizontal
orrendo(a) awful
osceno(a) obscene
oscuro(a) unclear

ostile hostile
ostinato(a) stubborn
ottimista optimistic
ottimo(a) excellent
ovvio(a) obvious
pacifico(a) peaceful
pallido(a) pale
paralizzato(a) paralyzed
parecchi(e) quite a lot of
pari even
parziale partial
passato(a) last
passivo(a) passive
pauroso(a) awful
pazzo(a) crazy
pedonale pedestrian
peggiore worse
pelato(a) bald
peloso(a) hairy
pensieroso(a) thoughtful
penultimo(a) second from last
perfetto(a) perfect
pericoloso(a) dangerous
permaloso(a) touchy
permanente permanent
perplesso(a) puzzled
perso(a) lost
personale personal
perverso(a) perverse
pesante heavy
pessimista pessimistic
pessimo(a) very bad
piacevole pleasant
piatto(a) flat
piccante hot; spicy
piccolo(a) small; little; young
pieghevole folding
pieno(a) full
pignolo(a) fastidious

pigro(a) lazy
pittoresco(a) picturesque
poco(a) little
  pochi(e) few
popolare popular
portatile portable
potente powerful
povero(a) poor; unfortunate
pratico(a) practical
precipitoso(a) rash
preciso(a) precise
preferito(a) favourite
preoccupato(a) worried
presbite long-sighted
presuntuoso(a) conceited
prezioso(a) precious
primo(a) first
principale main
privato(a) private
profondo(a) deep
profumato(a) fragrant
pronto(a) ready
prossimo(a) next
provvisorio(a) provisional; temporary
prudente careful
pubblico(a) public
pudico(a) modest; demure
pulito(a) clean
puzzolente stinking
quadrato(a) square
qualche some
quale(i) which; what
qualsiasi any
quanto(a) how much
  quante(i) how many
quello(a) that
  quelli(e) those
questo(a) this
  questi(e) these

quotidiano(a) daily
radicale radical
raffinato(a) sophisticated
ragionevole sensible; reasonable
randagio(a) stray
rapido(a) quick
raro(a) rare
rauco(a) hoarse
reale true
recente recent
redditizio(a) profitable
regionale regional
regolare regular
resistente strong
responsabile responsible
rettangolare rectangular
ricamato(a) embroidered
ricaricabile rechargeable
riccio(a) curly
ricco(a) rich
riconoscente grateful
ricoperto(a) covered
ridicolo(a) funny
ridotto(a) reduced
riflessivo(a) reflexive
rigido(a) stiff
ripido(a) steep
ripieno(a) stuffed
rischioso(a) risky
riservato(a) reserved
risolto(a) solved
robusto(a) strong
roco(a) hoarse
rotondo(a) round
rotto(a) broken
rumoroso(a) noisy
ruvido(a) rough
sacro(a) sacred
saggio(a) wise

salato(a) salty
sano(a) healthy; sane
santo(a) holy
saporito(a) tasty
sbadato(a) careless
sbagliato(a) wrong
sbiadito(a) faded
sbronzo(a) drunk
scadente poor-quality
scalzo(a) barefoot
scarico(a) not loaded; flat
scarso(a) scarce
scemo(a) stupid
schifoso(a) disgusting
schizzinoso(a) fussy
sciocco(a) silly
scivoloso(a) slippery
scolastico(a) school
scollato(a) low-cut
scolorito(a) faded
scomodo(a) uncomfortable
sconosciuto(a) unknown
scontento(a) unhappy
sconvolto(a) upset
scoperto(a) bare; uncovered
scorretto(a) incorrect
scorrevole flowing; fluent
scorso(a) last
scortese rude; impolite
scosso(a) shaken
scotto(a) overcooked
scremato(a) skimmed
scuro(a) dark
seccato(a) annoyed
secco(a) dry
secondo(a) second
segreto(a) secret
seguente following
selvaggio(a) wild

selvatico(a) wild
semplice simple
sensibile sensitive
sensuale sensual
sentimentale sentimental
separato(a) separate; separated
serale evening
sereno(a) calm
serio(a) serious
sessuale sexual
settentrionale northern
settimanale weekly
severo(a) strict; severe
sfacciato(a) cheeky
sfinito(a) exhausted
sfocato(a) out of focus
sfortunato(a) unlucky
sgarbato(a) rude
sgonfio(a) flat
sgradevole unpleasant
sgraziato(a) clumsy
sicuro(a) safe
sieronegativo(a) HIV-negative
sieropositivo(a) HIV-positive
silenzioso(a) quiet
simile similar
simpatico(a) nice
sincero(a) honest
sinistro(a) left
sintetico(a) synthetic
sleale disloyal
snello(a) slim
snervante stressful
sobrio(a) sober
sociale social
socievole sociable
soddisfatto(a) pleased
soffice soft
soffocante stifling

sofisticato(a) sophisticated
solare solar; sun
solido(a) solid
solitario(a) lonely
solito(a) usual
solo(a) alone
sonoro(a) loud
soprannaturale supernatural
sordo(a) deaf
sorprendente surprising
sorpreso(a) surprised
sorridente smiling
sospettoso(a) suspicious
sotterraneo(a) underground
sottile thin
sottinteso(a) understood
sovraccarico(a) overloaded
spaesato(a) lost
spaventoso(a) terrible
spazioso(a) spacious
speciale special
spensierato(a) carefree
spento(a) off
spesso(a) thick
spettinato(a) uncombed
spezzato(a) broken
spiacevole unpleasant
spiritoso(a) witty
spontaneo(a) spontaneous
sporco(a) dirty
sposato(a) married
squallido(a) dingy
squilibrato(a) deranged
squisito(a) delicious
stabile stable
stagionato(a) seasoned
stanco(a) tired
stonato(a) tone-deaf
stordito(a) stunned

storico(a) historical; memorable
storto(a) crooked
stradale road
straniero(a) foreign
strano(a) strange
straordinario(a) extraordinary
stravagante eccentric
stravolto(a) distraught
stressante stressful
stressato(a) stressed
stretto(a) narrow; tight
stridulo(a) shrill
studioso(a) studious
stufo(a) fed up
stupendo(a) wonderful
subacqueo(a) underwater
successivo(a) following
sudato(a) sweaty
suo(a) (pl suoi, sue) his; her; your
superbo(a) proud; haughty
superfluo(a) superfluous
superiore upper; secondary
supplementare extra
surgelato(a) frozen
svantaggiato(a) disadvantaged
sveglio(a) awake
svelto(a) quick
tagliente sharp
tale such
tanto(a) a lot of
tascabile pocket-sized
tenero(a) tender
teso(a) tense
testardo(a) stubborn
tiepido(a) lukewarm
tipico(a) typical; traditional
tirchio(a) mean
tondo(a) round
tranquillo(a) quiet

triste sad
troppi(e) too many
troppo(a) too much
tuo(a) *(pl* **tuoi, tue)** your
turbato(a) upset
tutto(a) all
ubriaco(a) drunk
ufficiale official
uguale equal
ultimo(a) last; latest
umano(a) human
umido(a) damp
umile humble
unico(a) only
unto(a) greasy
urgente urgent
usato(a) second-hand
utile useful
valido(a) valid

vario(a) varied; various
vecchio(a) old
vegetale vegetable
vegetariano(a) vegetarian
velenoso(a) poisonous
veloce fast
vergognoso(a) terrible
vero(a) true; real; genuine
vicino(a) near; close by
vietato(a) forbidden
vivace lively; bright
vivo(a) alive; live
viziato(a) spoilt
vostro(a) your
vuoto(a) empty
zitto(a) quiet
zoppo(a) lame
zuccherato(a) sweetened
zuppo(a) soaked; drenched

ADVERBS AND PREPOSITIONS

What is an adverb?
An **adverb** is a word usually used with verbs, adjectives or other adverbs that gives more information about when, how, where or in what cirumstances something happens, or to what degree something is true, for example, *quickly*, *happily*, *now*, *extremely*, *very*.

What is a preposition?
A **preposition** is a word such as *at*, *for*, *with*, *into* or *from*, which is usually followed by a noun, pronoun, or, in English, a word ending in -*ing*. Prepositions show how people or things relate to the rest of the sentence, for example, *She's at home; a tool for cutting grass; It's from David*.

a at; in; to
abbastanza quite; enough
accanto near
addirittura even
adesso now
affatto at all
allora then; so
almeno at least
altrettanto equally
altrimenti or; another way
ancora still; more; again
appena just; only just
apposta on purpose; specially
assai very; much
assieme together
attorno round
attraverso through
attualmente at the moment
avanti forward
  in avanti forward
bene well
ci there; here
cioè that is
circa about

come how; like; as
comunque anyway
con with
continuamente nonstop
contro against
correntemente fluently
così so; like this
da from; to; since
daccapo from the beginning
dappertutto everywhere
davanti at the front; in front of; opposite
davvero really
dentro in; inside
di of; by
dietro behind
diritto straight on
domani tomorrow
dopo after; later; then
dopodomani the day after tomorrow
doppio double
dove where
dovunque wherever; everywhere

durante during
eccetto except
ecco here
entro by
  entro domani by tomorrow
esattamente exactly
essenzialmente essentially
estremamente extremely
evidentemente obviously
fa ago
finalmente at last
fino a until; as far as
finora yet; so far
forse maybe
forte fast; hard; loud
fra between; among; in
  fra poco soon
fuori outside; out
già already
giù down
giusto just
gratis free
gravemente seriously
ieri yesterday
improvvisamente suddenly;
  unexpectedly
in in; to; into; by
incirca: all'incirca about
indietro back
infine finally
infuori out
innanzitutto first of all
inoltre besides
insieme together
insomma well
intanto for now; but
intorno round
inutilmente unnecessarily
invece but

invece di instead of
là (over) there
laggiù down there; over there
lassù up there
lentamente slowly
lì there
liscio smoothly
lontano far
  da lontano from a distance
lungo along
mai never
  quasi mai hardly ever
  mai più never again
malapena: a malapena hardly
male badly
malgrado in spite of
mediante by means of
meglio better
meno less; fewer; minus; except
  a meno che unless
  di meno less
  più o meno more or less
  meno ... di less... than
molto a lot; much; very
naturalmente of course
neanche not even; neither
  non ... neanche not even...
nemmeno not even; neither
  non ... nemmeno not even...
no no; not
non not
nonostante in spite of
nuovamente again
oggi today
oggigiorno nowadays
oltre over
  oltre a apart from
ora now; per ora for now
ormai by now

ovunque wherever; everywhere
peggio worse
per for; through; by; to
perché why
perfettamente perfectly
perfino even
persino even
piano slowly; quietly
  pian piano little by little
più more
  più di more than
  di più more
  in più more
  mai più never again
  più o meno more or less
piuttosto rather
po': **un po'** a little
poco not much
  tra poco soon
poi then; later
  prima o poi sooner or later
praticamente practically
precisamente precisely
pressappoco about
presto soon; early
prima before; earlier
  prima possibile as soon as
  possible
principalmente mainly
proprio just; really
purtroppo unfortunately
qua (over) here
quaggiù down here
quando when
quanto how much; how long
quasi nearly; hardly
  quasi mai hardly ever
quassù up here
qui here

quindi then
rapidamente quickly
raramente rarely
realmente really
recentemente recently
salvo except
secondo according to
sempre always; still
  per sempre forever
  sempre meno less and less
senza without
sì yes
solamente only
solo only
soltanto only
sopra over; above; on top of
  di sopra upstairs
soprattutto mainly; especially
sotto under; below
  di sotto downstairs
sottosopra upside down
sottoterra underground
sottovoce in a low voice; softly
specialmente especially
spesso often
stamattina this morning
stanotte tonight; last night
stasera this evening
stavolta this time
su on; up; about
subito immediately
talmente so much; so
tanto so; so much
tardi late
tra between; among; in
tranne except
troppo too
tuttavia but
ultimamente lately

veramente really; actually
verso towards; about *(of time)*
vi there

via away
viceversa vice versa
volentieri willingly

SOME EXTRA NOUNS

> **What is a noun?**
> A **noun** is a naming word for a living being, a thing, or an idea, for example, *woman*, *Andrew*, *desk*, *happiness*.

l'**abbazia** abbey
l'**abbigliamento** clothes
l'**abbreviazione** f abbreviation
l'**abilità** (pl inv) skill
l'**abitante** m/f inhabitant
l'**abitudine** f habit
l'**aborto** abortion; miscarriage
l'**accento** accent; stress
l'**accesso** access
l'**accordo** agreement; chord
l'**addestramento** training
l'**addizione** f sum
l'**affermazione** f statement
l'**affetto** affection
l'**aggettivo** adjective
l'**aiuto** help
l'**alfabeto** alphabet
l'**alimentazione** f diet
l'**alito** breath
l'**allarme** m alarm
l'**allenamento** training
l'**allenatore** m coach
l'**allenatrice** f coach
l'**alloggio** accommodation
l'**allusione** f hint
l'**alternativa** alternative
l'**ambiente** m environment
l'**ambizione** f ambition
l'**amicizia** friendship
l'**ammirazione** f admiration
l'**amore** m love
l'**analfabeta** m/f illiterate
l'**analgesico** painkiller

l'**anestesia** anaesthesia
l'**angelo** angel
l'**angolo** corner; angle
l'**anima** soul
l'**anticipo** advance
   essere in anticipo to be early
l'**antifurto** (pl inv) burglar alarm; car alarm
l'**apertura** opening
l'**apostrofo** apostrophe
l'**apparecchio** device; brace
l'**appoggio** support
l'**apprendimento** learning
l'**argomento** subject
l'**ascella** armpit
l'**aspetto** appearance
l'**assenza** absence
l'**assicurazione** f insurance
l'**associazione** f association
l'**astuccio** case
l'**atmosfera** atmosphere
l'**atrio** entrance; concourse
l'**attaccapanni** m (pl inv) hook
l'**atteggiamento** attitude
l'**attentato** attack
l'**attenzione** f attention
l'**attesa** wait
l'**attimo** minute
l'**attività** (pl inv) activity
l'**attualità** current affairs
l'**audizione** f audition
l'**aumento** increase
l'**autografo** autograph

l'autorità (pl inv) authority
l'avorio ivory
l'avvenimento event
l'avventura adventure; affair
l'azione f action; deed; share
la bacinella bowl
la badante care worker
la bancarella stall
la banconota note
la bandiera flag
la bara coffin
la baracca (pl -che) hut
il barattolo jar; tin; pot
il barboncino poodle
il barbone tramp
la barella stretcher
la barzelletta joke
la battuta joke
il becco (pl -chi) beak
la beneficenza charity
la bevanda drink
la biancheria sheets and towels;
  underwear
la bilancia (pl -ce) scales
il bisogno need
il bivio junction
la bolletta bill
il bollitore kettle
la bombola cylinder
il bordo edge; border
  a bordo on board
il borotalco talcum powder
la briciola crumb
il brillante diamond
il brindisi toast
la buccia (pl -ce) peel; rind
la bugia lie
la bugiarda liar
il bugiardo liar

il buonumore: essere di
  buonumore to be in a good mood
il burattino puppet
la bussola compass
la busta envelope
la bustarella bribe
la caccia hunting
il cacciatore hunter
il cadavere dead body
la caduta fall
la calamita magnet
il calcagno heel
la calligrafia handwriting
la calma calm
il calo drop
il camino chimney
il cammello camel
il campanile bell tower
il campionato championship
il cancello gate
la cannuccia (pl -ce) drinking straw
il capitolo chapter
il capriccio whim
la capriola somersault
la caratteristica (pl -che) feature
il carcere prison
la carestia famine
la cascata waterfall
la caserma barracks
il castigo (pl -ghi) punishment
il catalogo (pl -ghi) catalogue
il catrame tar
la causa cause
la cenere ash
il cerchietto hairband
il cerchio circle
il cespuglio bush
la cicatrice scar
il cimitero graveyard

la **circostanza** circumstance
il **citofono** entry phone; intercom
il **ciuccio** dummy
la **civiltà** *(pl inv)* civilization
la **classifica** *(pl -che)* results; charts;
   league table
il **codino** ponytail
il **collasso** collapse
il **collegamento** link
la **colpa** fault; blame
il/la **colpevole** culprit
il **colpo** blow; shot; raid
la **combinazione** combination;
   coincidence
la **comitiva** group
la **commozione** emotion
il/la **complice** accomplice
la **complicità** collusion
il/la **concorrente** competitor;
   contestant
la **condizione** condition
la **confezione** packet
la **consegna** delivery
la **conseguenza** consequence
il **consiglio** advice
la **consolazione** consolation
i **contanti** cash
il **contenitore** container
il **contenuto** contents
il **continente** continent; mainland
il **conto** bill; account; calculation
   per conto mio in my opinion; on
   my own
il **contrabbando** smuggling
il **contratto** contract
la **conversazione** conversation
il **coro** choir
la **correzione** correction
la **costruzione** building

il **crimine** crime
la **crisi** *(pl inv)* crisis; fit
la **croce** cross
la **crociera** cruise
il **cronometro** stopwatch
il **culturismo** body-building
la **cupola** dome
la **custodia** case
il **danno** damage
la **dattilografia** typing
il **debito** debt
la **debolezza** weakness
la **decisione** decision
il **delitto** crime
la **delusione** disappointment
la **descrizione** description
la **destinazione** destination
il **dialetto** dialect
la **dichiarazione** declaration;
   statement
la **didascalia** caption; subtitle
il **difetto** fault
la **differenza** difference
la **diga** *(pl -ghe)* dam; breakwater
il **digiuno** fasting
il/la **dipendente** employee
il **dipinto** painting
la **disapprovazione** disapproval
la **discesa** slope; descent
la **disciplina** discipline
il **discorso** speech
il **disordine** mess
il **disprezzo** contempt
la **distruzione** destruction
la **dormigliona** sleepyhead
il **dormiglione** sleepyhead
la **dozzina** dozen
l'**eccezione** *f* exception
l'**eclisse** *f* eclipse

l'entusiasmo enthusiasm
l'epoca (pl -che) era
l'equitazione f riding
l'equivoco misunderstanding
l'eredità (pl inv) inheritance
l'esclamazione f exclamation
l'esempio example
l'esercito army
l'esilio exile
l'esperimento experiment
l'espressione f expression
l'estinzione f extinction
l'etichetta label
la faccenda matter
il fallimento bankruptcy; failure
la fantascienza science fiction
la fantasia imagination; pattern
il fascino charm
la fase phase
la fata fairy
la fatica (pl -che) effort
il fatto fact
la felicità happiness
la ferita injury; wound
la fessura crack; slot
il fiato breath; stamina
il fidanzamento engagement
la fiducia trust
la filastrocca (pl -che) nursery
  rhyme
il filo thread; yarn; wire
la finanza finance
il fine end
  fine settimana weekend
la fine end
  alla fine in the end
la firma signature
il fischio whistle
la fodera lining; cover

la fogna sewer
la folla crowd
la follia madness
la fortuna luck; fortune
la fototessera passport-size photo
la frattura fracture
la freccia (pl -ce) arrow; indicator
la frusta whip
il fumetto comic strip; comic
la funivia cablecar
la funzione function
la gabbia cage
la galera prison
il gambo stem
il gancio hook
la gara competition
la gelosia jealousy
la generazione generation
il genere kind; gender
il gesso chalk; plaster
la gestione management
il gettone token
la giornata day
la giostra roundabout
  le giostre funfair
la gita trip
il giudizio opinion
la giustificazione excuse
la goccia (pl -ce) drop
il gonfiore swelling
il granello grain; speck
la gravidanza pregnancy
la gru (pl inv) crane
la gruccia (pl -ce) crutch; coat
  hanger
il guasto failure
la guerra war
il guinzaglio dog lead
l'identità (pl inv) identity

l'idolo idol
l'illusione f illusion
l'imballaggio packing
l'immaginazione f imagination
l'impegno engagement; commitment
l'impianto system
l'importo amount
l'imposta shutter; tax
l'imprenditore m entrepreneur
l'imprenditrice f entrepreneur
l'impresa business
l'incertezza uncertainty
l'incubo nightmare
l'incursione f raid
l'indagine f investigation
l'indovinello riddle
l'inesperienza inexperience
l'inferno hell
l'infezione f infection
l'ingrediente m ingredient
l'iniezione f injection
l'inizio beginning
l'insegnamento teaching
l'intimità privacy
l'inviata correspondent
l'inviato correspondent
l'invidia envy
l'iscrizione f registration
il labbro lip
la lama blade
il lampadario chandelier
il lampo flash of lightning
la larghezza width
la lastra slab; sheet; X-ray
il lato side; aspect
la letteratura literature
il lievito yeast
la lineetta hyphen; dash

la lisca (pl -che) fishbone
il livido bruise
la lotta struggle
il lucchetto padlock
la lunghezza length
il luogo (pl -ghi) place
la macchia stain
la madrelingua mother tongue
la maga (pl -ghe) sorceress
il magazzino warehouse
la maggioranza majority
il/la maggiore the older; the oldest
la magia magic
il male evil
la maledizione curse
la maleducazione bad manners
la malinconia melancholy
il malinteso misunderstanding
la mancanza lack
la manciata handful
le manette handcuffs
la manifestazione demonstration; event
la maniglia handle
la maratona marathon
la marca (pl -che) make; brand
il mazzo bunch; pack
la media average
il/la mendicante beggar
la mensola shelf
la mente mind
la menzogna lie
la merce goods
il mestiere job
la metà (pl inv) half
il miglioramento improvement
la minaccia (pl -ce) threat
la minoranza minority
il miracolo miracle

la **miseria** poverty
il **mito** myth
la **mitologia** mythology
il/la **mittente** sender
la **modifica** (*pl* -che) modification; alteration
il **modulo** form
la **morte** death
la **mostra** exhibition
il **motivo** reason
la **muffa** mould
la **multa** fine
il **mutuo** mortgage
il **nascondiglio** hiding place
il **nastro** ribbon; tape
la **nazione** nation
il **neo** mole
la **neonata** newborn baby
il **neonato** newborn baby
la **ninnananna** lullaby
il **nodo** knot; tangle
la **noia** boredom
la **norma** norm
la **nostalgia** homesickness
le **nozze** wedding
l'**obbligo** (*pl* -ghi) obligation
l'**obiettivo** lens; aim
l'**obiezione** f objection
l'**occasione** f opportunity; occasion; bargain
l'**odio** hatred
l'**odore** m smell
l'**offesa** insult
l'**omaggio** gift
l'**ombelico** (*pl* -chi) navel
l'**omicidio** murder
l'**onestà** honesty
l'**opinione** f opinion
l'**opuscolo** booklet

l'**organizzazione** f organization
l'**origine** f origin
l'**orizzonte** m horizon
l'**orlo** edge; brink; brim; hem
l'**orma** track; footprint
l'**ormone** m hormone
l'**ortografia** spelling
l'**osservazione** f observation; remark
l'**ossigeno** oxygen
l'**ostacolo** difficulty; hurdle
l'**ostaggio** hostage
l'**ottimismo** optimism
l'**otturazione** f filling
il **paesaggio** landscape
la **palestra** gym
la **palude** marsh
il **pannello** panel
il **panno** cloth
il **paracadute** (*pl inv*) parachute
il **paradiso** heaven
il **paragrafo** paragraph
il **pareggio** draw
la **parentesi** (*pl inv*) bracket
il **parere** m opinion
la **parolaccia** (*pl* -ce) swearword
il **particolare** detail
il/la **passante** passer-by
il **passatempo** pastime
il **passato** past
la **passione** passion
il **pasto** meal
il **patto** pact
la **pazza** madwoman
il **pazzo** madman
il **peccato** shame; sin
il **pedaggio** toll
il **pedone** pedestrian
il/la **pendolare** commuter

il **pennello** paintbrush
il **pensiero** thought; worry
la **pensionata** pensioner
il **pensionato** pensioner
la **percentuale** percentage
il **percorso** route
la **perdita** loss; waste
la **permanenza** stay
il **personaggio** character
il **personale** staff
la **personalità** *(pl inv)* personality
la **peste** plague; pest
la **pettinatura** hairstyle
il **pettine** comb
il **pianerottolo** landing
il **pianeta** planet
il **piatto** dish; plate
 i **piatti** the cymbals
la **piega** *(pl -ghe)* fold; pleat; crease
la **pietà** pity
la **pigrizia** laziness
la **pinacoteca** *(pl -che)* art gallery
il **pisolino** nap
la **pistola** gun
la **piuma** feather
il **pizzico** *(pl -chi)* pinch
il **podio** podium
la **polemica** *(pl -che)* controversy
il **polline** pollen
la **pomata** ointment
la **popolazione** population
il **popolo** people
il **portatelefonino** mobile phone
 case
il/la **portavoce** *(pl inv)*
 spokesperson
il **portone** main entrance
la **porzione** portion
la **posa** exposure; pose

le **posate** cutlery
la **posizione** position
la **possibilità** *(pl inv)* possibility;
 opportunity
la **potenza** power
il **potere** power
la **povertà** poverty
la **pozzanghera** puddle
la **precauzione** precaution
la **preda** prey
la **prefazione** preface
la **preferenza** preference
la **preghiera** prayer
il **pregio** good quality
il **pregiudizio** prejudice
il **prelievo** withdrawal
la **premiazione** prize-giving; award
 ceremony
la **preoccupazione** worry
i **preparativi** preparations
la **presa** grip
il **presepio** crib
il **preservativo** condom
la **pressione** pressure
il **prestito** loan
il **preventivo** estimate
il/la **principiante** beginner
il **principio** beginning; principle
la **probabilità** *(pl inv)* chance
il **problema** problem
la **profondità** depth
il **progetto** plan
il **progresso** progress
il **proiettile** bullet
la **prolunga** *(pl -ghe)* extension
il **pronome** pronoun
la **pronuncia** *(pl -ce)* pronunciation
il **proposito** intention
la **proposizione** clause

la proposta suggestion
la prospettiva prospect;
  perspective
la protezione protection
la provetta test tube
il provino screen test; trailer
la provocazione provocation
il provvedimento measure
il pubblico public; audience
la punizione punishment
la punta point; top; touch
  doppie punte split ends
la puntata episode; flying visit
la punteggiatura punctuation
il punteggio score
il punto point; stitch; full stop
la puntura injection; sting; bite
la puzza stink
il quadrifoglio four-leaf clover
la questione matter
la quota membership fee
il quotidiano daily paper
la raccolta collection
il raccolto harvest
il racconto short story
la radiazione radiation
la radice root
la ragione reason
il ramo branch; field
il rapimento kidnapping
la rapina robbery
il rapporto relationship; report
la rappresentazione
  representation; play
la rata instalment
la razza race; breed; sort
il razzismo racism
il reato crime
la reazione reaction

il rebus (pl inv) picture puzzle
la recensione review
il recipiente container
il reddito income
il regolamento rules
la reputazione reputation
il requisito requirement
la respirazione breathing
il respiro breath
la riabilitazione rehabilitation
il riassunto summary
il ricatto blackmail
il ricciolo curl
la ricerca (pl -che) search; research;
  project
la richiesta request
la ricompensa reward
la ricreazione recreation; break
il riferimento reference
il rifiuto refusal
la riflessione remark; thought
il riflesso reflection; reflex
il rimorso remorse
il rimpianto regret
il Rinascimento Renaissance
la ringhiera railing; banisters
il rinvio (pl -ii) postponement
il risparmio saving
il rispetto respect
la risposta answer
il ritornello refrain
il ritratto portrait
la rivelazione revelation
la rivincita rematch
la ruga (pl -ghe) wrinkle
la ruggine rust
la rugiada dew
il sacrificio sacrifice
la sagoma outline; shape

la **salita** climb; hill
il **salvadanaio** money box
lo **sbadiglio** yawn
lo **sbaglio** mistake
la **sbarra** bar
la **scadenza** expiry date; sell-by date; use-by date
lo **scaffale** bookcase
lo **scatto** click; spurt
la **scelta** choice
lo **sceneggiato** TV drama
lo **scheletro** skeleton
lo **schema** diagram
lo **scherzo** joke
la **schiava** slave
lo **schiavo** slave
la **schiuma** foam; lather
lo **schizzo** splash; sketch
la **sciagura** disaster
lo **scioglilingua** (pl inv) tongue-twister
la **scommessa** bet
la **sconfitta** defeat
lo **sconto** discount
lo **scontrino** receipt slip
lo **scontro** crash; clash
la **scoperta** discovery
lo **scopo** aim
lo **scoppio** explosion; bang
la **scorciatoia** short cut
la **scottatura** burn; sunburn
la **scrittura** writing
la **scrivania** desk
lo **scudo** shield
la **scusa** excuse
la **seccatura** nuisance; bother
la **semifinale** semifinal
la **sensazione** feeling
il **senso** sense; direction

il **settore** sector
la **sezione** section
la **sfida** challenge
lo **sfondo** background
la **sfortuna** bad luck
lo **sforzo** effort
lo **sfruttamento** exploitation
la **sfumatura** shade; tone
lo **sgabello** stool
lo **sgabuzzino** junk room
lo **sguardo** look
la **siccità** (pl inv) drought
la **sicurezza** safety
la **sigla** acronym
il **significato** meaning
il **silenzio** silence
la **sillaba** syllable
il **simbolo** symbol
il **sinonimo** synonym
il **sintomo** symptom
il **sistema** system; way
la **sistemazione** accommodation
la **situazione** situation
lo **smacchiatore** stain remover
la **smagliatura** ladder; stretch mark
la **soddisfazione** satisfaction
il **soffio** breath
il **solitario** game of patience
la **solitudine** loneliness
il **sollievo** relief
la **soluzione** solution
il **sommario** summary
la **sonnambula** sleepwalker
il **sonnambulo** sleepwalker
il **sonnifero** sleeping pill
il **sonno** sleep
il **soprannome** nickname
il **sorso** sip
la **sorte** fate

il/la sosia (*pl inv*) double
il sospetto suspicion
il sospiro sigh
il sostantivo noun
la sostituzione substitution
la sovvenzione subsidy
la spaccatura split
la spacciatrice drug dealer
lo spacciatore drug dealer
lo spacco (*pl* -chi) slit
lo spago (*pl* -ghi) string
la spallina shoulder strap
lo sparo shot
lo spavento fright
lo specchietto pocket mirror
la specialità (*pl inv*) speciality
la specie (*pl inv*) sort; species
la speculazione speculation
la speranza hope
lo spettatore viewer; spectator
gli spettotori the audience
le spezie spices
la spia spy; light
gli spiccioli loose change
lo spiedino kebab; skewer
la spiegazione explanation
la spinta push
lo sportello door; window
lo spuntino snack
lo starnuto sneeze
la stenografia shorthand
la stilografica (*pl* -che) fountain pen
la stima respect
la strage massacre
lo straordinario overtime
lo strappo tear; lift
lo strato layer
la strega (*pl* -ghe) witch
lo strillo scream

la striscia (*pl* -sce) strip
lo striscione banner
la struttura structure
lo stupore amazement
lo stupro rape
il suggerimento suggestion
il suicidio suicide
la suoneria alarm; ringtone
il suono sound
la superficie surface
il/la superiore superior
la superstizione superstition
lo svantaggio disadvantage
il taglio cut
la tappa stop
la targa (*pl* -ghe) number plate
la targhetta nameplate; name tag
la tastiera keyboard
il tatuaggio tattoo
la teiera teapot
la tela cloth
il temperino penknife
la tentazione temptation
la teoria theory
il terreno land; ground
il territorio territory
il/la terrorista terrorist
il teschio skull
il tessuto fabric
il testamento will
il/la testimone witness
la tifosa supporter
il tifoso supporter
il tipo sort; type
la tomba grave
il tono tone
il torcicollo stiff neck
il tornante hairpin bend
il torneo tournament

supplementary vocabulary

il **totocalcio** the pools
la **traccia** (pl -ce) trace
la **tradizione** tradition
la **traduzione** translation
la **trama** plot
il **tramonto** sunset
il **trapano** drill
il **trapianto** transplant
il **trasloco** (pl -chi) removal
la **trasmissione** programme
il **trattino** hyphen
il **tratto** stretch
il **trauma** shock
la **treccia** (pl -ce) plait
il **tribunale** court
il **triciclo** tricycle
il **trono** throne
Il **truffatore** swindler
il **tumore** tumour
il **tuorlo** yolk
il **turbante** turban
l'**udito** hearing
l'**umore** m mood
l'**unificazione** f unification
l'**urlo** scream
l'**usanza** custom
l'**uso** use; usage
l'**ustione** f burn
la **valanga** (pl -ghe) avalanche
la **valvola** valve
il **valzer** (pl inv) waltz
il **vandalismo** vandalism
il **vangelo** gospel
la **varietà** variety
il **vasetto** jar

il **vassoio** tray
la **vedova** widow
il **vedovo** widower
il **veicolo** vehicle
il **veleno** poison
la **vergogna** embarrassment
la **vernice** varnish; paint; patent
   leather
la **verità** (pl inv) truth
il **vero** truth
la **vicenda** event; story
il **vincitore** winner
la **vincitrice** winner
la **virgola** comma; point
le **virgolette** inverted commas
la **vita** life; waist
la **vittima** victim
la **vittoria** victory
il **vizio** bad habit; vice
il **vocabolario** dictionary
il **volo** flight
la **volontà** wIll
il **volume** volume
il **voto** mark; vote
il **vuoto** gap
il **wafer** (pl inv) wafer
il **water** (pl inv) toilet
il **W.C.** (pl inv) W.C.
la **zingara** gypsy
lo **zingaro** gypsy
la **zitella** spinster
lo **zoccolo** clog; hoof; skirting
   board
lo **zodiaco** zodiac

VERBS

> **What is a verb?**
> A **verb** is a 'doing' word which describes what someone or something does, what someone or something is, or what happens to them, for example, *be*, *sing*, *live*.

abbandonare to abandon; to give up
abbassare to lower
abbracciarsi to hug
abbronzarsi to get tanned
abitare to live
abituarsi: abituarsi a (fare) qc to get used to (doing) sth
accadere to happen
accamparsi to camp
accarezzare to stroke
accelerare to accelerate
accendere to light; to turn on
accettare to accept
accludere to enclose
accogliere to welcome
accomodarsi to sit down
accompagnare to take ... to
accontentare to please
  accontentarsi di to make do with
accorciare to shorten
accorgersi to notice; to realize
acquistare to buy
addormentarsi to go/fall to sleep
adottare to adopt
afferrare to grab; to catch
affettare to slice
affittare to rent
affogare to drown
affondare to sink
affrettarsi to hurry up
agganciare to hook; to hang up

aggiungere to add
aggiustare to mend; to straighten
aggredire to attack
agire to act
agitare to shake
  agitarsi to worry
aiutare to help
allacciare to fasten; to connect
allagare to flood
allargare to widen
allearsi to join forces
allegare to enclose
allenare to train
alloggiare to stay
allungare to lengthen
alzare to lift; to raise
  alzarsi to get up
amare to love
ammalarsi to get ill
ammazzare to kill
ammettere to admit
ammirare to admire
andare to go
  andarsene to leave
annaffiare to water
annegare to drown
annoiare to bore
  annoiarsi to get bored
annullare to cancel
annunciare to announce
apparire to appear
appartenere to belong

appendere to hang
appoggiare to put; to lean
approfittare: approfittare di qc to make the most of sth
aprire to open; to turn on
arrabbiarsi to get angry
arrampicarsi to climb
arrangiarsi to get by
arrestare to arrest
arrivare to arrive
arrossire to blush
asciugare to dry
ascoltare to listen to
aspettare to wait; to expect
assaggiare to taste
assicurare to insure; to assure
assistere to look after; to watch; to witness
assomigliare a to look like
assumere to take on
atterrare to land
attirare to attract; to appeal to
attraversare to cross; to go through
aumentare to go up
avanzare to be left over
avere to have
  avere fame to be hungry
  avere paura to be afraid
  avere sete to be thirsty
  avere sonno to be sleepy
avvelenare to poison
avvertire to warn
avvicinare to move closer
baciare to kiss
badare to pay attention; to mind
bagnare to get wet; to water
ballare to dance
bastare to be enough
battere to beat; to hit

bere to drink
bestemmiare to swear
bisbigliare to whisper
bisticciare to quarrel
brillare to shine
brontolare to moan
bruciare to burn
bucare to have a puncture
  bucarsi to puncture; to be on heroin
bussare to knock
buttare to throw
  buttare via to throw away
cacciare to hunt
cadere to fall
calare to decrease; to drop
calcolare to work out
cambiare to change
  cambiarsi to get changed
camminare to walk
cancellare to cancel; to delete
cantare to sing
capire to understand
  capire male to misunderstand
capitare to happen
caricare to (up)load; to charge
cavalcare to ride
cenare to have dinner
cercare to look for; to look up; to try
chiacchierare to chat
chiamare to call; to phone
chiarire to clarify
chiedere to ask; to ask for
  chiedersi to wonder
chiudere to close; to turn off
  chiudere a chiave to lock
cogliere to pick
coinvolgere to involve
collegare to connect

colpire to hit
comandare to be in charge
combattere to fight
cominciare to start
compilare to fill in
comporre to dial; to compose
comportarsi to behave
comprare to buy
condire to dress; to season
condividere to share
confermare to confirm
confondere to mix up
  confondersi to get mixed up
connettere to connect
conoscere to know
  conoscersi to meet
consegnare to deliver
conservare to keep
consigliare to recommend; to
  advise
consumare to wear out; to use
contare to count
  contare su qn to count on sb
contenere to contain
continuare to carry on
controllare to check
  controllarsi to control oneself
convenire to be cheaper
convincere to convince
  convincere qn a fare qc to
  persuade sb to do sth
copiare to copy
coprire to cover
correggere to correct; to mark
correre to run
costare to cost
credere to believe; to think
crescere to grow
cucinare to cook

cucire to sew
curare to treat
danneggiare to damage
dare to give
  dare su to look onto
decidere to decide
  decidersi to decide
decollare to take off
deludere to disappoint
denunciare to report; to expose
derubare to rob
descrivere to describe
desiderare to want
detrarre to deduct
deviare to divert
dichiarare to declare; to state
digerire to digest
dimagrire to lose weight
dimenticare to forget
dimettersi to resign
diminuire to decrease; to reduce
dimostrare to demonstrate
dipingere to paint
dire to say
dirigere to manage
discutere to discuss; to argue
disdire to cancel
disegnare to draw; to design
disfare to undo
distendere to stretch
  distendersi to lie down; to relax
distrarre to distract
  distrarsi to take one's mind off
  things
distribuire to distribute
distruggere to destroy
disubbidire: disubbidire a qn to
  disobey sb
diventare to become

divertire to amuse
  divertirsi to have a good time
divorziare to get divorced
domandare to ask
  domandarsi to wonder
dondolarsi to rock; to swing
dormire to sleep
dovere to have to
  dovere qc a qn to owe sb sth
durare to last
emozionare: emozionarsi to be moved; to be excited
entrare to enter
esagerare to exaggerate
esaurire to sell out; to run out of
eseguire to carry out; to perform
esercitare to practise; to train
esigere to demand
esporre to display; to exhibit
esportare to export
esprimere to express
essere to be
estrarre to extract
evadere to escape
evitare to avoid
fabbricare to make
fallire to go bankrupt; to fail
fare to make; to do
fasciare to bandage
ferire to injure; to wound
fermare to stop
festeggiare to celebrate
fidanzarsi to get engaged
fidarsi: fidarsi di qn to trust sb
fingere to pretend
finire to finish
firmare to sign
fischiare to whistle
fissare to fix; to stare at

fornire to supply
forzare to force
fraintendere to misunderstand
fregare to pinch; to rub
frenare to brake
frequentare to go to; to see
friggere to fry
fuggire to escape
fumare to smoke
funzionare to work
galleggiare to float
garantire to guarantee
gelare to freeze
gestire to manage
gettare to throw
giocare to play
girare to turn
giudicare to judge
giurare to swear
gocciolare to drip
gonfiare to inflate
  gonflarsi to swell
graffiare to scratch
gridare to shout
guadagnare to earn; to gain
guardare to look at; to watch
guarire to cure; to heal up
guastarsi to break down
guidare to drive; to lead
ignorare to ignore
illudersi to deceive oneself
imbiancare to whitewash; to paint
imbrogliare to cheat
imbucare to post
immaginare to imagine; to think
impallidire to go pale
imparare to learn
impazzire to go mad

impedire: impedire a qn di fare qc to stop sb doing sth

impegnarsi: impegnarsi a fare qc to try hard to do sth

impiccarsi to hang oneself

importare to matter; to import

incartare to wrap

incassare to cash

incazzarsi *(inf!)* to get pissed off *(!)*

incendiare to set fire to

inciampare to trip

incominciare to start

incontrare to meet

incoraggiare to encourage

indagare: indagare su to investigate

indebolirsi to get weak

indicare to show; to point to

indirizzare to address; to send

indossare to wear

indovinare to guess

informare: informarsi su qc to ask about sth

ingannare to deceive

ingannarsi to be mistaken

ingelosire to make jealous

ingessare to put in plaster

inghiottire to swallow

ingrandire to enlarge; to extend

ingrassare to make fat

ingrassarsi to put on weight

iniziare to start

innaffiare to water

innamorarsi to fall in love

inquinare to pollute

insegnare to teach

inserire to insert

intasarsi to be blocked

intendere to mean

interrompere to interrupt

intervistare to interview

intitolare to name

intitolarsi to be called

introdurre to introduce; to insert

invecchiare to get old

investire to run over; to invest

inviare to send

invidiare to envy

invitare to invite

iscriversi to register; to enrol; to join

lamentarsi to complain

lanciare to throw; to launch

lasciare to leave

lasciarsi to split up

laurearsi to graduate

lavare to wash

lavarsi i denti to brush one's teeth

lavorare to work

legare to tie

leggere to read

levare to take off

liberare to set free

liberarsi to get away

licenziare to sack; to make redundant

licenziarsi to give up one's job

litigare to quarrel

lottare to fight

lucidare to polish

maledire to curse

maltrattare to ill-treat

mancare to be missing; to be lacking

mandare to send

mangiare to eat

marcire to go rotten

masticare to chew

mentire to lie

meravigliarsi to be surprised
mescolare to mix
mettere to put
migliorare to improve
minacciare to threaten
misurare to measure
molestare to torment; to sexually harass
montare to assemble; to whip up
mordere to bite
morire to die
morsicare to bite
mostrare to show
muovere to move
nascere to be born
nascondere to hide
navigare to sail
  navigare in Internet to surf the Internet
negare to deny
nevicare to snow
noleggiare to hire; to hire out
notare to notice
  farsi notare to draw attention to oneself
nuotare to swim
obbedire to obey
obbligare: obbligare qn a fare qc to make sb do sth
occupare to occupy
  occuparsi di qn to look after sb
odiare to hate
offendere to insult
  offendersi to take offence
offrire to offer
ordinare to order
osare to dare
osservare to observe; to notice
ottenere to get

pagare to pay
parcheggiare to park
pareggiare to draw
parlare to speak; to talk
partecipare to take part in
partire to leave
passare to pass; to call by
passeggiare to stroll
peggiorare to get worse
pendere to hang
pensare to think
  pensare a to think about
perdere to lose; to leak
  perdersi to get lost
perdonare to forgive
permettere to allow
pesare to weigh
  pesarsi to weigh oneself
pescare to fish
pettinare to comb
piacere: mi piace I like it
piangere to cry
plantare to plant; to dump
picchiare to hit; to knock
piegare to fold; to bend
piovere to rain
piovigginare to drizzle
pisciare (inf!) to piss (!)
pitturare to paint
pizzicare to pinch; to itch
poggiare to place; to put
porre to put; to place
portare to take; to carry; to wear
posare to put
posteggiare to park
potere can
pranzare to have lunch
precipitare to fall
preferire to prefer

pregare to pray
  pregare qn di fare qc to ask sb to do sth
prelevare to withdraw
premere to press
premiare to give a prize to
prendere to take; to get
prenotare to book
preoccupare: preoccuparsi to worry
preparare to prepare
prescrivere to prescribe
prestare to lend
  prestare attenzione to pay attention
prevedere to foresee; to plan for
procedere to get on
produrre to produce
progettare to plan
proibire to forbid
promettere to promise
proporre to suggest
proteggere to protect
provare to try; to try on; to feel; to prove
pubblicare to publish
pulire to clean
pungere to sting
punire to punish
puntare su to bet on
puzzare to stink
raccogliere to collect; to pick
raccomandare to recommend
raccontare to tell
raddrizzare to straighten
radere to shave
  radersi to shave
raffreddare to cool
  raffreddarsi to get cold

raggiungere to reach
ragionare to think
rallentare to slow down
rapinare to rob
rapire to kidnap
rappresentare to represent
rasare to shave off
rassicurare to reassure
reagire to react
realizzare to come true; to realize
recitare to act
recuperare to recover; to get back
regalare to give
reggere to hold
registrare to record
regnare to reign
regolare to adjust
remare to row
rendere to give back
  rendersi conto di qc to realize sth
respirare to breathe
restare to stay; to remain
riaddormentarsi to go back to sleep
ricaricare to reload; to refill; to recharge
ricevere to receive
richiamare to call back
richiedere to ask for; to require
riciclare to recycle
ricominciare to start again
riconoscere to recognize
ricordare to remember
  ricordare a qn di fare qc to remind sb to do sth
ridare to give... back
ridere to laugh
ridurre to reduce

riempire to fill (in)
rifare to do again
  rifare il letto to make the bed
rifiutare to refuse
riguardare to concern; to consider
rilassarsi to relax
rimandare to put off
rimanere to stay; to remain
rimborsare to refund
rimettere to put back
  rimettersi to recover
rimpiangere to be sorry
rimproverare to tell off
rinchiudere to lock up
rinfrescare to freshen
  rinfrescarsi to freshen up
ringraziare to thank
rinnovare to renew
rintracciare to find
rinunciare to give up
rinviare to postpone
riparare to repair
  ripararsi da to shelter from
ripassare to come back; to revise
riposare to rest
riprendere: riprendersi to recover
riprovare to try again
riscaldare to warm up; to heat
rischiare to risk
risciacquare to rinse
riservare to book
risolvere to solve
risparmiare to save
rispettare to respect
rispondere to answer
ritirare to take out
ritornare to go back; to return
riuscire: riuscire a fare qc to succeed in doing sth

rivedere to see again
rompere to break
rotolare to roll
rovinare to ruin
rubare to steal
russare to snore
saldare to settle; to solder
salire to go up; to climb
  salire su to board
  salire in to get into
saltare to jump
salutare to say hello to; to say goodbye to
salvare to save; to rescue
sanguinare to bleed
sapere to know; to taste; to smell
sbadigliare to yawn
sbagliare to make a mistake
  sbagliarsi to be wrong
sbattere to slam
sbrigare to do
  sbrigarsi to hurry
sbucciare to peel; to shell
scadere to expire
scaldare to heat
scambiare to exchange
scappare to get away
scaricare to unload; to download
scartare to unwrap; to reject
scavare to dig
scegliere to choose
scendere to go down
  scendere da to get out of; to get off
scherzare to joke
schiacciare to squash
sciacquare to rinse
sciare to ski
scintillare to sparkle

sciogliere to dissolve; to undo
scivolare to slip; to slide
scommettere to bet
scomparire to disappear
sconfiggere to defeat
scongelare to defrost
sconsigliare to advise against
scontrarsi to clash; to run into
scopare to sweep
scoppiare to go off; to burst
scoprire to discover
scoraggiarsi to get discouraged
scottare to be hot
  scottarsi to get burnt
scrivere to write
scusare to excuse
  scusarsi to apologize
sdraiarsi to lie down
sedere to be sitting
  sedersi to sit
segnare to mark; to score
seguire to follow
selezionare to select
sembrare to look; to seem
sentire to hear; to feel
  sentirsi bene to feel well
  sentirsi male to feel ill
separare to separate
  separarsi to split up
seppellire to bury
servire to serve
  servire per qc to be for sth
sfidare to challenge
sfogliare to leaf through
sfuggire to escape
sgonfiare to deflate
sgridare: sgridare qn to tell sb off
significare to mean
singhiozzare to sob; to hiccup

sistemare to arrange; to settle
  sistemarsi to settle down; to find a job
slacciare to undo
slegare to untie
smarrire to lose
  smarrirsi to get lost
smettere to stop
smontare to take apart
soddisfare to satisfy
soffiare to blow
sognare to dream
somigliare: somigliare a to look like
sopportare to stand; to put up with
sorpassare to overtake
sorprendere to catch; to surprise
sorridere to smile
sorvegliare to watch
sospettare to suspect
sospirare to sigh
sostenere to support; to claim
sostituire to change
sottolineare to underline
sottovalutare to underestimate
sottrarre to subtract
spaccare to break
sparare to shoot
sparecchiare to clear the table
sparire to disappear
spaventare to scare
  spaventarsi to be scared
spedire to send
spegnere to put out; to turn off
spendere to spend
sperare to hope
spezzare to break
spiegare to explain
  spiegarsi to explain oneself

spingere to push; to drive
spogliare to undress
  spogliarsi to get undressed
spolverare to dust
sporcare to dirty
sposare to marry
  sposarsi to get married
spostare to move
sprecare to waste
spremere to squeeze
sputare to spit
stabilire to fix
  stabilirsi to settle
staccare to remove; to tear out
stampare to print
stancare: stancarsi to get tired
stare to be
  stare fermo to keep still
  stare zitto to be quiet
starnutire to sneeze
stendere to stretch; to hang out
  stendersi to lie down
stirare to iron
stracciare to tear up
strappare to tear up
strillare to scream
stringere to be tight; to clasp
stufarsi: stufarsi di qc to get fed up
  with sth
subire to suffer; to undergo
succedere to happen
sudare to sweat
suicidarsi to commit suicide
suonare to play; to ring
superare to exceed; to overcome;
  to pass
supporre to suppose
svegliare: svegliarsi to wake up
svenire to faint

svestirsi to get undressed
sviluppare to develop
svitare to unscrew
svolgersi to happen
tacere to be quiet
tagliare to cut
tardare to be late
telefonare to phone
  telefonare a qn to phone sb
tenere to hold; to keep
tentare to try
timbrare to stamp
tirare to pull; to throw
toccare to touch
togliere to take off; to take out
tornare to get back; to be back
tossire to cough
tradurre to translate
trascorrere to spend; to pass
trasferire to transfer
  trasferirsi to move
traslocare to move
trasmettere to broadcast
trasportare to carry
trattare to treat
  trattare di to be about
trattenere to hold back
tremare to shake
trovare to find
truccarsi to do one's make-up
tuffarsi to dive
ubriacarsi to get drunk
uccidere to kill
ungere to oil; to grease
unire to put together; to join
  unirsi a to join
urlare to shout
usare to use
uscire to go out

utilizzare to use
valere to be worth
  valere la pena to be worth it
valutare to value
vantarsi to boast
vedere to see
  farsi vedere to be seen
vendere to sell
venire to come
vergognarsi to be ashamed; to be embarrassed
verificare to check
  verificarsi to happen
verniciare to varnish; to paint
versare to pour; to spill; to pay in
vestirsi to get dressed
  vestirsi da to dress up as

viaggiare to travel
vietare to forbid
vincere to win
violentare to rape
visitare to visit
vivere to live
volare to fly
volere to want
  voler bene a qn to like sb; **voler dire** to mean
voltare to turn
votare to vote
vuotare to empty
zoppicare to limp

Notes

Notes

Notes

Notes

Notes

Notes

Notes

Collins

easy learning Italian

Easy Learning Italian Dictionary
978-0-00-753093-9 £10.99

Easy Learning Italian Conversation
[Second edition] 978-0-00-811199-1 £8.99

Easy Learning Italian Grammar
978-0-00-736780-1 £7.99

Easy Learning Italian Verbs
978-0-00-736977-5 £7.99

Easy Learning Italian Vocabulary
978-0-00-748394-5 £7.99

Easy Learning Complete Italian Grammar, Verbs and Vocabulary
(3 books in 1) 978-0-00-732495-8 £12.99

Easy Learning Italian Grammar & Practice
978-0-00-745600-0 £10.99

Available to buy from all good booksellers and online.
Many titles are also available as ebooks.
www.collins.co.uk/languagesupport

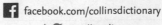 facebook.com/collinsdictionary
 @collinsdict